INTERNATIONAL CRIMINAL PROCEDURE

INTERNATIONAL CRIMINAL PROCEDURE

CHRISTOPH SAFFERLING

in cooperation with

LARS BÜNGENER
HILDE FARTHOFER
ALENA HARTWIG
YVONNE KOBERG

OXFORD
UNIVERSITY PRESS

OXFORD
UNIVERSITY PRESS

Great Clarendon Street, Oxford OX2 6DP
United Kingdom

Oxford University Press is a department of the University of Oxford.
It furthers the University's objective of excellence in research, scholarship, and education by publishing worldwide. Oxford is a registered trade mark of Oxford University Press in the UK and in certain other countries

First published 2012

Impression: 1

British Library Cataloguing in Publication Data
Data available

Library of Congress Cataloguing in Publication Data
Library of Congress Control Number: 2012931699

ISBN 978–0–19–956288–6

Printed in Great Britain by
CPI Group (UK) Ltd, Croydon, CR0 4YY

PREFACE

This book is the result of a three-year research project, which was financially supported by the Fritz-Thyssen Foundation, Germany. It is connected to my previous study *Towards an International Criminal Procedure*, which was published in 2001. The speed at which international criminal procedure develops has increased at such a rate that it seems impossible for one person alone to cover the entire procedural process. Alongside this current extensive study on international criminal procedure, several individual research projects were undertaken focusing on specific aspects of the ICC procedure by Dr Hilde Farthofer (evidence), Alena Hartwig (pre-trial detention), and Lars Büngener (disclosure of evidence). Also part of the team was Yvonne Koberg, whose special expertise on the SCSL and English criminal law was of immense value. Their contributions to this book are identified throughout; the rest of the unattributed content is mine. Nadine Peter (STL, Timor L'este), and Florian Hansen (ECCC) added their knowledge to this book. Finally, Patrick Donath was part of the team and contributed considerably to the research necessary for this book. In regular meetings, ideas on criminal procedure and international law were developed and discussed, so this is very much a cooperative work.

I am immensely grateful to Sascha Hörmann, Sebastian Kluckow, Franziska Kowalski, and Martin Luber for helping in organizing the content, and pulling together the bibliography and the table of cases. Thanks also to my assistant Daniela Ziegler, who managed to keep other obligations at bay, thus giving me the time necessary to write this book. I am also indebted to the law firm, Salleck & Partner in Erlangen, Germany, for letting me have a quiet room away from the daily grind at the University. Many thanks also to John Louth and Anthony Hilton at Oxford University Press, who believed in this project and swallowed several delays in the submission of the manuscript.

Finally, I need to thank my family who have endured a husband and father who—in particular towards the end of the drafting process—was too often absent both physically and mentally.

Marburg, 5 September 2011
Christoph Safferling

CONTENTS

TABLES OF CASES

INTERNATIONAL CRIMINAL COURT

Pre-Trial Chamber

Trial Chamber

Appeals Chamber

Others

PRESIDENCY

REGISTRY

INTERNATIONAL CRIMINAL COURT FOR THE FORMER YUGOSLAVIA

Indictment

Pre-Trial Chamber

Trial Chamber

Appeals Chamber

Others

INTERNATIONAL CRIMINAL TRIBUNAL FOR RWANDA

Appeals Chamber

Indictment

Trial Chamber

SPECIAL COURT FOR SIERRA LEONE

Pre-Trial Chamber

Trial Chamber

Appeals Chamber

EXTRAORDINARY CHAMBERS OF THE COURTS OF CAMBODIA

EUROPEAN COURT OF HUMAN RIGHTS

GERMAN COURTS

ENGLISH COURTS

AMERICAN COURTS

EUROPEAN COMMISSION ON HUMAN RIGHTS

OTHER COURTS

LIST OF ABBREVIATIONS

AC	Appeals Chamber
AfCHR	African Charter on Human and People's Rights
Ahlbrecht/Author	H Ahlbrecht, K-M Böhm, R Esser, H Hugger, S Kirsch, M Rosenthal, Internationales Strafrecht in der Praxis (CF Müller 2008)
AJIL	American Journal of International Law
AmCHR	American Convention on Human Rights
ARIEL	Austrian Review of International and European Law
Austrian JPIL	Austrian Journal of Public and International Law
BGHSt	Reports of the German Federal High Court of Justice in Criminal Matters
Boas/Bischoff/Reid/Taylor	G Boas, J Bischoff, N Reid, and B Don Taylor, International Criminal Law Practitioner Library, Vol III—International Criminal Procedure (Cambridge University Press 2011)
BVerfGE	Reports of the German Federal Constitutional Court
BYIL	British Yearbook of International Law
Cassese/Gaeta/Jones/Author	A Cassese, P Gaeta, and J Jones (eds), The Rome Statute of the International Criminal Court. A Commentary (Oxford University Press 2002)
Chi J Int' l L	Chicago Journal of International Law
Chi-Kent J Int'l & Comp L	Chicago-Kent Journal of International and Comparative Law
Chi-Kent L Rev	Chicago-Kent Law Review
CLF	Criminal Law Forum
CLJ	Cambridge Law Journal
Colum J Transnat'l L	Columbia Journal of Transnational Law
Conn J Int'l L	Connecticut Journal of International Law
DCC	Documents containing the charge
Denv J Int'l L & Pol'y	Denver Journal of International Law and Policy
ECCC	Extraordinary Chambers in the Courts of Cambodia
ECHR	European Convention on Human Rights
ECommHR	European Commission on Human Rights
ECtHR	European Court of Human Rights
eg	for example
EJIL	European Journal of International Law
et subs.	subsequent pages
fn	footnote
Fordham Int'l L J	Fordham International Law Journal

Geo J Int'l L	Georgetown Journal of International Law
GLJ	German Law Journal
Harv Int'l L J	Harvard International Law Journal
HJIL	Heidelberg Journal of International Law
HLR	Harvard Law Review
Houst J Int'l L	Houston Journal of International Law
HRC	Human Rights Committee
HRLR	Human Rights Law Review
ibid	ibidem: in the same place
ICC	International Criminal Court
ICCPR	International Covenant on Civil and Political Rights
ICCSt	Statute of the ICC
ICJ	International Court of Justice
ICJSt	Statute of the ICJ
ICL	International Criminal Law
ICLR	International Criminal Law Review
ICTR	International Criminal Tribunal for Rwanda
ICTRSt	Statute of the ICTR
ICTY	International Criminal Tribunal for the Former Yugoslavia
ICTYSt	Statute of the ICTY
id.	idem: the same
ie	that is
ILR	International Law Reports
ILSA J Int'l & Comp L	International Law Students Association Journal of International and Comparative Law
IMT	International Military Tribunal
IMTFE	International Military Tribunal for the Far East
IMTSt	Statute of the IMT
Ind Int'l & Comp L Rev	Indiana International and Comparative Law Review
Int'l Legal Prac	International Legal Practitioner
IRRC	International Review of the Red Cross
J App Prac & Process	Journal of Appellate Practice and Process
JICJ	Journal of International Criminal Justice
Jud Stud Inst J	Judicial Studies Institute Journal
JZ	Juristen Zeitung
Khan/Buisman/Gosnell	K Khan, C Buisman, and C Gosnell, Principles of Evidence in International Criminal Justice (Oxford University Press 2010)
LJIL	Leiden Journal of International Law
Max Planck UNYB	Max Planck Yearbook of United Nations Law
Melb J Int'l L	Melbourne Journal of International Law
Mich J Int'l L	Michigan Journal of International Law
MN	Margin Number
New Engl L Rev	New England Law Review
Northwestern JIHR	Northwestern Journal of International Human Rights
NStZ	Neue Zeitschrift für Strafrecht

OPCV	Office of Public Counsel for Victims
OTP	Office of the Prosecutor
PTC	Pre-Trial Chamber
RegC	Regulation of the Court
RegP	Regulation of the Prosecutor
RegR	Regulation of the Registrar
RPE ICC	Rules of Procedure and Evidence of the ICC
RPE ICTR	Rules of Procedure and Evidence of the ICTR
RPE ICTY	Rules of Procedure and Evidence of the ICTY
RPE SCSL	Rules of Procedure and Evidence of the SCSL
San Diego Int'l L J	San Diego International Law Journal
SCSL	Special Court for Sierra Leone
SCSLSt	Statute of the SCSL
SPSC	Special Panels for Serious Crime
STL	Special Tribunal for Lebanon
STLSt	Statute of the STL
StV	Strafverteidiger
TC	Trial Chamber
Triffterer/Author	O Triffterer, Commentary on the Rome Statute of the International Criminal Court (2nd edn, CH Beck 2008)
Tulsa J Comp & Int'l L	Tulsa Journal of Comparative and International Law
UC Davis J Int'l L and Pol'y	University of California, Davis Journal of International Law and Policy
UN	United Nations
U Pa L Rev	University of Pennsylvania Law Review
Va J Int'l L	Virginia Journal of International Law
Vand J Transnat'l L	Vanderbilt Journal of Transnational Law
Wash U Global Studies L Rev	Washington University Global Studies Law Review
WLR	Weekly Law Reports
VWU	Victims and Witnesses Unit
YB Int'l Hum L	Yearbook of International Humanitarian Law
ZaöRV	Zeitschrift für ausländischesöffentliches Recht und Völkerrecht
ZIS	Zeitschrift für internationale Strafrechtsdogmatik
ZStW	Zeitschrift für die gesamte Strafrechtswissenschaft

INTRODUCTION

Juris effectus in executione consistit—'the effect of the law consists in its execution'. The fact that international criminal law did not contribute a great deal to prevent mass atrocities in the second half of the twentieth century is, amongst many other reasons, due to the lack of its execution at the international level. The international community has come a long way since then in its establishment of an institution for the prosecution of international crimes. The International Military Tribunal in Nuremberg in 1945 is rightly seen as the beginning of this development. The necessity of an international normative order and of an international criminal court was described in drastic terms in the aftermath of World War II:

> As long as there is no judicial organ for the trial of international crimes, there will be neither a serious codification of international criminal law nor any serious application of an international sanction. The world will go on living in a judicial anarchy under violence and injustice with the risk of running into destruction.[1]

The horror scenario described here did not materialize, but in the sixty-five years since the end of that war, the world has been shattered by a number of armed conflicts involving millions of casualties. Some fundamental parameters changed during the 1990s. Several international criminal tribunals have been established by the United Nations. With the adoption of the Rome Statute for the International Criminal Court (ICC) in 1998 and the establishment of the ICC on 1 July 2002, the institutionalization of international criminal law reached its peak, and the world now has both a code of international crimes and an international court to execute these norms. Thereby the international community has begun a new chapter of history and demonstrated its willingness to end impunity for massive human rights violations. The ICC has today 117 members worldwide, despite many important states refusing to become signatories to its treaty, including the USA, Russia, China, India, and Israel. Still, the number of States Parties to the Rome Statute continues to rise. The normative structure is in place. Now it must prove its worth in application.

This is a book about international criminal procedure. It takes issue with the procedural order which is to be followed in executing the code of international crimes

[1] Jean Graven in 1948, cited by V Pella, 'Towards an International Criminal Court', 44 *AJIL* (1950) 37, 47.

at the international level. The ICC's legal regime stands in the foreground, as it is believed to be the future of international criminal procedure. However, the ICC's Statute and Rules of Procedure and Evidence are placed in context with other international tribunals like the UN Tribunal for former Yugoslavia (ICTY), the UN Tribunal for Rwanda (ICTR), and the Special Court for Sierra Leone (SCSL).

Since the renaissance of international prosecution in 1993 with the establishment of the ICTY, a great deal of attention has been paid to the development of substantive international criminal law. Questions about the interpretation of genocide, crimes against humanity, and war crimes have given rise to a myriad of books and articles together with the question of a general part of international criminal law, as the *imputatio* of law and facts.[2] Recently, a great deal of energy has been invested in the drafting of the crime of aggression. The definition which was finally adopted at the Review Conference in Kampala, Uganda, in 2010, completes the Nuremberg legacy.[3]

The concentration on the substantive law has worked in a sense to the disadvantage of procedural law. This is surprising because much of the substantive law has been developed *ad hoc* by judges in ongoing procedures. It is important, therefore, to reflect on the structure of the procedural law as this obviously influences the interpretation of the law in its material sense. But somehow, back then, it was felt that the completion and the acceptance of the code of crimes were more important than procedural law, which was somehow taken as read. However, it was rather obvious from the beginning that nothing could be taken for granted in this regard. As Göran Sluiter, one of the protagonists of research in the field of international procedure, has stated: 'in the international criminal justice system . . . the Achilles' heel lies in procedural law.'[4]

There are several issues at stake which warrant a new and more systematic way of thinking about procedural matters. This holds true for the integration of victims into criminal procedure. For political reasons, victim participation has been integrated into the Rome Statute, but until today no viable concept of participation has been developed. The protection of witnesses in a highly sensitive field—in particular victims of sexual abuse—influences the conduct of the trial. How can a prosecutor investigate properly if s/he is denied cooperation by national states, and what influence would such a denial have on the quest for the truth? Furthermore it is debatable how the presumption of innocence can be implemented regarding high-profile accused like Radovan Karadžić or Slobodan Milošević. Finally,

[2] A Eser, 'Procedural Structure and Feature of International Criminal Justice: Lessons from the ICTY', in: B Swart, A Zahar, and G Sluiter (eds), *The Legacy of the International Criminal Tribunals for the Former Yugoslavia* (OUP 2011) 108, 110.

[3] Resolution RC/Res. 6 (Advanced Version, 28 June 2010), adopted on the 13th Plenary session of the Review Conference in Kampala on 11 June 2010 by consensus.

[4] G Sluiter, 'Karadzic on Trial—Two Procedural Problems', 6 *JICJ* (2008) 617.

it seems that the procedural system based on the interplay of different judicial chambers, with an extremely complicated system of disclosure of evidence, oscillating between a party-driven system and inquisitorial powers of judges, can readily lose track of its final responsibility. Who, at the end of the day, is responsible for an improper and incomplete searching for the truth? This question needs to be answered. Likewise we need to be clear about the aims and purposes we intend to follow by prosecuting international crimes on an international level, and we need to address the question of how the interaction between national jurisdictions and international prosecution should work in order to establish an effective international criminal justice system.[5]

In 1950, the Romanian law professor, Vespasian Pella, who fought for the establishment of an international criminal court between the two World Wars, wrote: '[T]he new branch of law which international penal law constitutes is as yet little known even to many lawyers'.[6]

To some extent this is true today. While several thousand people work within international criminal courts and tribunals, public attention with regard to international trials seems scant, and university curricula rarely cover this area of international law. International criminal law remains a highly specialized enterprise.

In this book we address students of international criminal law as well as scholars and practitioners. We aim to provide an introduction to the working of the ICC Statute (ICCSt) and previous international tribunals. Our intention is also to put procedural law into context and address questions which reach beyond the interpretation of statutory norms.

The book comprises ten sections. Chapters 1–4 introduce the topic and its key principles and Chapters 5–9 analyse the procedural steps chronologically (as far as is possible). Chapter 10 deals with contempt of court as a specific safeguard for the fairness of the proceedings.

At the outset, an overview of the history of international criminal procedure is introduced in the context of different international tribunals which have dealt in the past with the execution of international criminal law, or still do. The history of the different courts and tribunals unfolds the difficulties in coming to terms with the different procedural ideas, which are commonly referred to as the Anglo–American, or adversarial, system on the one hand, and the Continental European system of inquisitorial investigation on the other. Notwithstanding these differences, human rights law is applicable universally and thus influences criminal

[5] *See* also Th Buergenthal and D Thürer, *Menschenrechte. Ideale, Instrumente, Institutionen* (Nomos 2010) 135.

[6] V Pella, 'Towards an International Criminal Court', 44 *AJIL* (1950) 37, 66.

procedure everywhere. This is why one has to deal with human rights law in detail, when talking about criminal procedure.

In Chapter 2, issue is taken with circumstances that are specific to international criminal procedure compared to those in national prosecution systems. For this reason, the question is raised whether the aims and purposes of international criminal procedure are different from those of national procedures. One obvious difference in international criminal procedure is its conflict with state sovereignty and its founding in a system of executing international criminal law which is cooperative. These two issues are addressed by looking at the jurisdictional questions, in particular the so-called trigger mechanisms at the ICC, and the principle of complementarity, which influences the admissibility of a case at the ICC and forms one of the basic philosophies of the ICC as a backup structure for national jurisdictions.

The history of international criminal procedure provides us with some twenty years of experience in this kind of prosecution all over the world. This is of course minimal when compared to the domestic systems, whose history runs to several hundred years or more. Under these circumstances, it is striking how self-assured international prosecutors and judges are in acting to fulfil their roles at international tribunals and courts. It seems that the only common rationale on which international criminal practitioners practise is according to the first Nuremberg principle: to end impunity for massive human rights violations. This is a starting point, but does not suffice as a solid theoretical basis for a procedural system. Lacking a long tradition and an international legal culture, such a theoretical underpinning, however, seems inevitable. Even if we cannot answer the relevant questions to the full, we attempt, in Chapter 3, to develop a functional–normative theory for international criminal procedure which will serve as a methodological framework for the further development of the ICC procedural system.

Before looking at the individual procedural steps, we consider, in Chapter 4, the different participants in criminal procedure. We analyse the structure of the ICC in detail, comprising the Presidency, the different judicial divisions, Appeals, Trial and Pre-Trial Chambers, the Registry and the Prosecutor. The incorporation of victims in the criminal trial process is a recent development, which gives rise to many questions concerning proceedings. Therefore it is necessary not only to look at the rules which concern victims, but also to analyse the role of victims in the crime and in the process of dealing with the crime. Lastly, the accused and his defence counsel participate in the prosecution process and their specific procedural roles are analysed.

The remaining sections of the book are reserved for the analysis of the individual steps of the procedure at the ICC in chronological order. The analysis will be based not only on the Rome Statute and the Rule of Procedure and Evidence of the ICC, but take into account the practice at the *ad hoc* Tribunals and the human rights requirements. At first, we take issue with the procedural questions concerning admissibility and jurisdiction, in Chapter 5. In Chapter 6, the complex topic of investigation is addressed and comprises discretion in whether or not to investigate, the decision to prosecute, and the collection of evidence. As part of the Prosecutor's task to investigate, the difficult cooperation model foreseen in Part IX of the ICCSt is analysed. Pre-trial detention and the rights of the suspect are further elements discussed.

The following stage of the proceeding is the 'confirmation' proceeding, covered in Chapter 7. The ICC entertains a rather laborious and time-consuming procedure. A hearing is necessary for the confirmation of the charges, which has until now rather unfortunately developed into some sort of 'mini-trial'. As part of this stage, the important issue of disclosure of evidence will also be discussed even if 'disclosure', at least in a material sense, takes place in all stages of the trial. Yet as it pertains mainly to the preparation of the defence, it is placed in this pre-trial phase.

The trial, covered in Chapter 8, is the core element of the prosecution process. This is the decisive stage in the sense that the verdict as to the guilt of the accused is being passed. The trial is influenced by a number of general principles, like trial fairness, publicity, orality, and others. Concerning the specific structure of the trial at the ICC, the Statute and Rules leave more questions open than answered. It is presumed, however, that in principle the trial will follow an adversarial structure, which relates the presentation of evidence to the respective parties; ie prosecutor and defence. Yet the judges have an obligation to hear all the evidence which is relevant to the case. The law of evidence—the different forms of evidence and the admissibility of evidence—is the most important topic at trial, as only admissible evidence which has been presented at trial may form the basis of the judgment.

Judgments in criminal matters must be capable of review, discussed in Chapter 9, by a court or chamber of higher instances. This is a human rights prerequisite and is well respected in modern international courts and tribunals. The ICC and the *ad hoc* tribunals go a step further and allow so-called interlocutory appeals which can be raised against many decisions in the pre-trial and trial phase. Despite this being a time-consuming enterprise, these appeals help to develop the procedural law. If new facts appear, the verdict must also be capable of review in favour of the accused at a later stage.

In the final chapter of this book, contempt of court is addressed. As the fairness of the proceedings and the adherence to the legal provisions rests mainly with the participants in the proceeding, there are special norms which address professional misconduct and sanction against misbehaviour. Even if these norms contain substantive criminal law, they are closely related to the fulfilment of procedural obligations and aim at the protection of the criminal procedure as such. Therefore it was deemed necessary to include a chapter on disclosure of evidence in this treatise on criminal procedure.

What was excluded from this book was a consideration of the principles of sentencing and the execution of the punishment. Neither question is procedural in character. Our conviction remains that the parameters for the decision on the nature and quantity of punishment is closely related to the crime in the material sense. As concerns procedural law, the only issue to raise in this regard is that the parties have been given time and opportunity to state their views on the issue and present evidence concerning aggravating and mitigating circumstances.

This view is certainly debatable,[7] and discloses one important factor: the author of this book is a German lawyer, raised and trained in the German legal system. This holds true also for the co-authors and members of the research team—although one of them is Austrian, which nevertheless has a 'Germanic' system of law. All have international experience, but they remain 'Continental' lawyers. This has effects not only on language and style—and I sincerely hope that a native speaker will turn a blind eye to the many 'Germanicisms'—but also on the understanding of the law in general and procedural law in particular. In that sense, this book does not lay claim to present the ultimate truth concerning international criminal procedure. It seeks to explain and describe the structure of international criminal procedure as it appears to an outside observer—none of the authors practises international criminal law—and it raises some critical questions. In this, it is hoped that we will contribute to the exchange between academia and practice, and add a little to the ongoing struggle to refine international criminal procedure. It is, after all, in our all interests to arrive at an international criminal justice system which is acceptable both to the affected societies and to the international community, and thus can promote a more secure life throughout the world.

[7] *See* Boas/Bischoff/Reid/Taylor, *ICL III*, 392–410, who contribute a considerable part of their book on procedure on sentencing guidelines.

1

THE DEVELOPMENT OF INTERNATIONAL CRIMINAL PROCEDURE

The history of international criminal law has been described in many books and articles.[1] In this book however, the focus is on procedural law as applied by international courts and tribunals. The history of substantive international criminal law, like the crimes themselves—the crime of aggression, genocide, crimes against humanity, war crimes, and possibly other crimes as well—and the question of imputation of facts and law, is thus irrelevant to this book. What is of interest is how international criminal law has been executed.

One general fact of international criminal law should be explained first. There are two ways of executing international criminal law as shown in Figure 1.1: it can be implemented by national courts, which is called an indirect form of execution, and it can be implemented by international courts and tribunals, which would be called a direct form of execution.

When speaking about international criminal procedure, we are talking only about the execution of international criminal law in its direct form. National courts would not apply an international procedural framework. They operate within their domestic legal parameters—they apply the *lex fori*[2]—even if prosecuting international crimes. In the history of international criminal law, national courts have conducted many more trials than international tribunals. In particular, after World War II some 20,000 trials took place in Europe and in the Pacific theatre,

---

[1] H Ahlbrecht, *Geschichte des völkerrechtlichen Strafgerichtsbarkeit* (Nomos 1999); A Cassese, *International Criminal Law* (2nd edn, OUP 2008) 317 *et subs.*; G Werle, *Völkerstrafrecht* (2nd edn, 2007) MN 1 *et subs.*

[2] As to the *lex fori* rule, which is commonly known within private international law: A Heldrich, *Internationale Zuständigkeit und anwendbares Recht* (DeGruyter 1969) 14; D Coester-Waltjen, *Internationales Beweisrecht* (CH Beck 1983) MN 102 fn 380; F Jaeckel, *Die Reichweite der lex fori im internationalen Zivilprozessrecht* (Duncker and Humblot 1995) 19 *et subs.*; as to English law, *see* J Fawcett, J Carruthers, and P North, *Private International Law* (14th edn, OUP 2008) 75: 'one of the eternal rules of every system of private international law'.

Figure 1.1 Direct and indirect execution of international criminal law

whereas only two trials were staged in international forums—in Nuremberg and Tokyo.[3]

In Chapter 1, we provide a general introduction to the history and the legal framework of international courts and tribunals (A). In a way, the IMT (International Military Tribunal), the ICTY, and the ICTR, as the 'real' international criminal tribunals in history, will be dealt with as predecessors to the ICC in the course of this book. Their procedure will be discussed in detail in Chapters 5–10.

Two other issues fundamental to the historic and current development of international criminal procedure will be addressed thereafter: the fact that different systems and traditions in domestic criminal procedure have shown to be obstacles in the development of an international procedural system (B); and the importance of human rights law for the structuring of procedural law (C).

A. Forerunners

The history of international crimes begins with the Geneva Convention of 1864.[4] In this document certain acts of warfare were prohibited and declared illegal for the first time in history. Consequently, the then President of the ICRC, Gustave Moynier, suggested establishing an international criminal court to prosecute grave breaches of the 1864 Convention in 1872.[5] This idea did not come to fruition as it did not meet the interests of a large enough number of states. It was only after World War I that the idea of prosecuting war crimes arose again on the international agenda.

[3] The number relates to the documents available at the International Research and Documentation Centre War Crimes Trials at the Philipps-University of Marburg, Germany.

[4] C Safferling, *Internationales Strafrecht* (Springer 2011) § 4 MN 19.

[5] *See* also Th Buergenthal and D Thürer, *Menschenrechte. Ideale, Instrumente, Institutionen* (Nomos 2010) 135.

I. Versailles: an international trial for the German Emperor

After the end of the World War I, the Peace Treaty of Versailles foresaw in Art. 227 the punishment of the German Emperor Wilhelm II, who was identified as the aggressor.[6] It states the following:

> ARTICLE 227.
>
> The Allied and Associated Powers publicly arraign William II of Hohenzollern, formerly German Emperor, for a supreme offence against international morality and the sanctity of treaties.
>
> A special tribunal will be constituted to try the accused, thereby assuring him the guarantees essential to the right of defence. It will be composed of five judges, one appointed by each of the following Powers: namely, the United States of America, Great Britain, France, Italy and Japan.
>
> In its decision the tribunal will be guided by the highest motives of international policy, with a view to vindicating the solemn obligations of international undertakings and the validity of international morality. It will be its duty to fix the punishment which it considers should be imposed.
>
> The Allied and Associated Powers will address a request to the Government of the Netherlands for the surrender to them of the ex-Emperor in order that he may be put on trial.

Despite the fact that the 'crimes' established in this norm were somewhat odd ('morality and sanctity of treaties'), the establishment of a special tribunal was envisaged. The composition of the tribunal of five judges, which would be appointed by the victorious powers, the USA, the UK, France, Italy, and Japan, was laid down as was the assurance that the right of defence would be guaranteed.

Such a tribunal was never established, as the Netherlands refused to surrender the 'ex-Emperor' so that he may be tried.[7] The Netherlands argued that such a trial would be contrary to the prohibition of retroactive criminality (*nullum crimen sine lege*).[8]

With regard to other war criminals, Arts. 228 and 229 gave directions:

> ARTICLE 228.
>
> The German Government recognises the right of the Allied and Associated Powers to bring before military tribunals persons accused of having committed acts in violation of the laws and customs of war. Such persons shall, if found guilty, be sentenced to punishments laid down by law. This provision will apply notwithstanding any

[6] *See* H Wiggenhorn, *Verliererjustiz. Die Leipziger Kriegsverbrecherprozesse nach dem Ersten Weltkrieg* (Nomos 2005) 21 *et subs.*

[7] M C Bassiouni, 'World War I: "The War to End all Wars" and the Birth of a Handicapped International Criminal Justice System', 30 *Denv J Int'l L & Pol'y* (2002) 244.

[8] Ibid, 283–5.

> proceedings or prosecution before a tribunal in Germany or in the territory of her allies.
>
> The German Government shall hand over to the Allied and Associated Powers, or to such one of them as shall so request, all persons accused of having committed an act in violation of the laws and customs of war, who are specified either by name or by the rank, office or employment which they held under the German authorities.
>
> ARTICLE 229.
>
> Persons guilty of criminal acts against the nationals of one of the Allied and Associated Powers will be brought before the military tribunals of that Power.
>
> Persons guilty of criminal acts against the nationals of more than one of the Allied and Associated Powers will be brought before military tribunals composed of members of the military tribunals of the Powers concerned.
>
> In every case the accused will be entitled to name his own counsel.

The onus of prosecuting war criminals below the Emperor was finally transferred to Germany—ie within the national jurisdiction. The extradition of alleged German war criminals to the Allied Powers was attempted at first, but due to immense resistance by Germany this idea was ultimately dropped.[9] Nevertheless the Allied Powers reserved their right to prosecute anew should the German efforts to do justice not satisfy their governments, on the basis of Art. 228 of the Versailles Treaty.[10]

On the basis of the Law for the Prosecution of war crimes,[11] some twelve persons out of a list of around 890 alleged criminals were finally tried before the *Reichsgericht* (Court of Justice of the 'Reich') situated in Leipzig. These trials are therefore known as the *Leipziger Prozesse* and are synonyms for a total failure of national prosecution of war crimes.[12] Allied prosecution was successively hindered by a constant refusal to extradite alleged war criminals from Germany. As to the means to execute their right to prosecution pursuant to Art. 228 of the Versailles Treaty, the Allied Powers had none. As Justice Robert H Jackson pointed out in his opening address at Nuremberg, 'An international law which operates only on states can be enforced only by war because the most practicable method of coercing a state is warfare.'[13] A new war in Europe, however, was obviously not in the interest of anyone.

---

[9] M El Zeidy, *The Principle of Complementarity in International Criminal Law* (M Nijhoff 2008) 14 *et subs*; C Safferling, *Internationales Strafrecht* (Springer 2011), § 4 MN 21.

[10] This could be seen as an early form of the complementarity principle according to Arts 17, 20 ICCSt. *See* section 2.C.

[11] Gesetz zur Verfolgung von Kriegsverbrechen und Kriegsvergehen, 18 December 1919, RGBl. 1919, 2125 *et subs*. *See* also H Wiggenhorn, *Verliererjustiz. Die Leipziger Kriegsverbrecherprozesse nach dem Ersten Weltkrieg* (Nomos 2005) 42–61.

[12] G Hankel, *Die Leipziger Prozesse* (Hamburger Edition 2003).

[13] IMT Protocols II, 177.

These *Leipziger Prozesse*, of course, took place procedurally on the basis of the *lex fori*, the German Code of Criminal Procedure of the time. These trials were thus not comparable to any run under what we know as international criminal procedure.

During the time of the League of Nations, several attempts were made to establish an international criminal court. In 1920, the Advisory Committee of Jurists suggested the establishment, along with the Permanent Court of International Justice, of a High Court of Justice with the following aim:

> The High Court of International Justice shall be competent to hear and determine cases which shall be submitted to it by the Assembly of the League of Nations or by the Council of the League, and which concern international public order, for instance: crimes against the universal law of nations.[14]

The proposal did not succeed due to several uncertainties regarding criminal responsibility of individuals or states and regarding applicable crimes; in short, the proposal was considered premature.

In 1937, the international criminal court reappeared on the international agenda. The reason for this was the contemporary need to fight and prevent acts of terrorism. Thus it was determined that the international criminal court should serve the interests of heads of states, who were frightened of assassination by terrorists. Two drafts were prepared by a Committee of Experts—the Convention for the Prevention and Punishment of Terrorism, and the Convention for the Creation of an International Criminal Court—and were discussed at the International Conference on the Repression of Terrorism, which finally took place at Geneva from 1–16 November 1937. The idea of an international criminal court was reduced to establishing an international platform for prosecution, whereas the substantive law to be applied would have been the national laws.[15] Both conventions never entered into force.[16]

II. Nuremberg: the birth of international criminal procedure

In World War II, the aggression and brutality of warfare, and systematic human rights violations reached a previously unimaginable peak. The Moscow Declaration of 1 November 1943 was the first to declare that the Allied Powers at that time— the USA, the UK, and Russia—would not be willing to tolerate

---

[14] UN Secretary-General, 'Historical Survey of the Question of International Criminal Jurisdiction', UN Doc. A/CN.4/7/Rev. 1 (1949) 9–12.

[15] For a comparison between the 1937-ICC and the Rome Statute, *see* E Chardwick, 'A Tale of Two Courts: The "Creation" of a Jurisdiction', 9 *Journal of Conflict & Security Law* (2004) 71. The author favours the 1937 approach, arguing that the Rome Statute could severely damage the international balance of power.

[16] UN Secretary-General, 'Historical Survey of the Question of International Criminal Jurisdiction', UN Doc. A/CN.4/7/Rev. 1 (1949) 16–18.

the war conducted by Germany against all of Europe, and would hold the persons responsible for the unspeakable suffering brought to the entire Continent. The heads of government agreed that German war criminals would be prosecuted by that state on the territory of which they committed their crimes. Yet in the final sentence it was held: 'The above declaration is without prejudice to the case of German criminals whose offenses have no particular geographical localization and who will be punished by joint decision of the government of the Allies.'[17]

Thereby they stated their willingness to establish an international tribunal for the most important war criminals, whose influence went beyond that of a single territorial entity. The sentence also unveils the basis of legitimacy that the Allied Powers attributed to an international tribunal: the Allies would refer their respective jurisdictional powers which would rest on the territoriality principle to an international court.

Parallel to this Declaration, the Western allies and their confederates founded the United Nations War Crimes Commission (UNWCC) on 20 October 1943 in order to document German war crimes, collect and preserve evidence to be used in the trials against German war criminals.[18] The Soviet Union, although involved in the establishment of the UNWCC, decided not to participate, but founded its own Commission.[19]

1. *The origins of the IMT Statute*

The general political will to punish war criminals as expressed in the Moscow Declaration does not contain the specific ways and means used to achieve this. The idea of a criminal trial based on the rule of law had yet to win recognition. It contrasted with Churchill's call for summary execution, made because he feared that it would be too difficult to prove the guilt of the offenders beyond reasonable doubt.[20] Stalin also had a different design in mind. Even if he favoured a trial, he was convinced that the guilt of the alleged offenders was already determined and

---

[17] The phrasing is not unlike that found in Art. 229 § 2 of the Versailles Treaty.

[18] W Form, 'Justizpolitische Aspekte west-allierter Kriegsverbrecherprozesse 1942–1950', in: L Eiber and R Sigel (eds), *Dachauer Prozesse–NS-Verbrechen vor amerikanischen Militärgerichten in Dachau 1945–1948* (Wallstein 2007).

[19] *See* S Karner, 'Zum Umgang mit der historischen Wahrheit in der Sowjetunion. Die "Außerordentliche Staatliche Kommission" 1942*bis* 1951', in: *Festschrift für A Ogris* (Verlag des Geschichtsvereines für Kärnten 2001) 509; MY Sorokina, 'On the Way to Nuremberg: The Soviet Commission for the Investigation of Nazi War Crimes', in: A B Griech-Polelle (ed.), *The Nuremberg War Crimes Trial and its Policy Consequences Today* (Nomos 2009) 21; a general overview of the Soviet Union and the IMT is given by: F Hirsch, 'The Soviets at Nuremberg: International Law, Propaganda, and the Making of the Postwar Order', 113 *American Historical Review* (2008) 701.

[20] *See* R Overy, 'The Nuremberg Trials: International Law in the Making', in: P Sands (ed), *From Nuremberg to The Hague* (CUP 2003) 1, 3 *et subs.*

the only question to be answered by the judges was the amount of punishment. For that matter, advised by the Soviet Procurator-General Andrei Vyshinsky, Stalin was prepared to stage a public 'show trial'.[21] It was mainly due to the perseverance of the later Chief Prosecutor for the USA, Supreme Court Justice Robert H Jackson, supported by Henry Stimson, US Secretary of War, that a trial in accordance with the rule of law prevailed. Jackson publicly pronounced his conviction on 14 April 1945, only hours after the death of his patron President Roosevelt, in an address to the American Society of International Law: 'That is one of the risks that are taken whenever trials are commenced. The ultimate principle is that you must put no man on trial under the forms judicial proceedings if you are not willing to see him freed if not proven guilty.'[22]

From April until August 1945, delegations from Allied governments, now including France, negotiated a Statute for the International Military Tribunal (IMT) in London, where most of the European governments-in-exile were situated. The topics which were discussed were not only those of procedure. The crimes had to be defined. The seat and venue of the Tribunal had to be fixed,[23] and the accused had to be identified. The London Conference was on the brink of failure more than once, as the difference between the Russian delegation, headed by the later IMT Judge General Rudenko, and the US delegation, led by the man who was to become the Chief Prosecutor Justice, Jackson, sometimes seemed irreconcilable.[24] The success of the negotiations was nevertheless assured because all four delegations were committed to the ultimate aim: the joint prosecution of the Nazi war criminals.[25]

Finally, on 8 August 1945, the London Agreement for the Prosecution and Punishment of the Major War Criminals of the European Axis, was signed.[26] The Charter of the International Military Tribunal was issued as an Annex to the Agreement and according to Art. 2 of the Agreement, became an integral part thereof. The Agreement was signed by the representatives of the four Allied Powers and was supported by several other states.[27] It thus has a solid international, even global, basis.

---

[21] As to the Soviet position *see* also M Bazyler, 'The Role of the Soviet Union in the International Military Tribunal at Nuremberg, in: H Reginbogin and C Safferling (eds), *The Nuremberg Trials: International Criminal Law since 1945* (Saur 2006) 42.

[22] *Robert H Jackson*, 14 April 1945, Washington DC, American Society of International Law.

[23] *See Report of Robert H Jackson United States Representative to the International Conference on Military Trials, London 1945* (Department of State 1949) 157. Henceforth: Jackson Report (1949).

[24] The meetings are meticulously recorded in the Jackson Report (1949) 71 *et subs.*

[25] *See* eg, General Nikitchenko, in: Jackson Report (1949) 414; *see* also S Aldermann, 'Negotiating on War Crimes Prosecution, 1945', in: R Dennett and J Johnson (eds), *Negotiating with the Russians* (Boston World Peace Foundation 1951) 52 *et subs.*

[26] 82 UNTS 279.

[27] These were: Greece, Denmark, Yugoslavia, the Netherlands, Czechoslovakia, Poland, Belgium, Ethiopia, Australia, Honduras, Norway, Panama, Luxemburg, Haiti, New Zealand, India, Venezuela, Uruguay, and Paraguay.

According to Art. 22 of the IMT Statute (IMTSt), the Seat of the Tribunal was Berlin, but the first of several possible trials was to take place at Nuremberg. The city of Nuremberg played a particular role in Nazi Germany. It was the place where major Nazi party rallies took place from 1933 to 1938. It was also the place where the so-called Nürnberger Rassegesetze (race laws) were finalized and passed in a special meeting of the Reichstag on 15 September 1935.[28] These symbolic reasons, although not unknown to the delegates of the London Conference, were not crucial to the decision to stage the trial in Nuremberg. Practical reasons and security issues tipped the scale in favour of the medieval city in northern Bavaria. Despite the fact that the inner city was severely damaged, the ruins of the Palace of Justice and the adjacent large prison facility, situated a few miles north of the inner city, were fully operational. Nuremberg was also part of the American Zone of Occupation, a decisive factor for the USA.

2. *The trial system*

The IMT Charter contained only a rudimentary procedural system. The Tribunal consisted of four judges, one from each of the Allied Powers, and the same number of alternate judges pursuant to Art. 2 IMTSt. Each signatory appointed one Chief Prosecutor according to Art. 14 IMTSt. The procedural rules, filling the frame given by the Charter, were to be drafted by the judges themselves pursuant to Art. 13 IMTSt. On 29 October 1945 the Rules of Procedure were passed comprising only eleven Rules.

The structure of the Tribunal and its procedure were mainly based on the adversarial trial system as can largely be found in countries which practice common law. Yet there was one major change: there was no trial by jury. The judges themselves were competent to pass the verdict and had to give reasons for the decision according to Art. 26 IMTSt. These facts made other minor changes to the Anglo-Saxon trial structure possible. According to Art. 19 IMTSt, the Tribunal was not bound by any rules of evidence, as indeed there was no need 'to insist upon jury rules for a trial where no jury would be used'.[29] Art. 17 IMTSt empowered the Tribunal to summon witnesses and put questions to them. It was also competent to interrogate the defendants and could require the production of documents or other evidentiary material. These inquisitorial powers of the judges resemble continental European criminal procedure. The IMT was happy to make use of these powers.[30]

[28] These were: Gesetz zum Schutze des deutschen Blutes und der deutschen Ehre, so-called Blutschutzgesetz (RGBl. I [1935] 1146) and Reichsbürgergesetz (RGBl. I [1935] 1146); *see* K Kastner, 'Nazi Party, the Rallies and the Racial Laws', in: H Reginbogin and C Safferling (eds), *The Nuremberg Trials: International Criminal Law since 1945* (Saur 2006) 114.

[29] Jackson Report (1949) XI.

[30] After the disappointing cross-examination of the defendant Fritzsche by Rudenko, President Lawrence intervened and continued the questioning, *see* IMT Protocols XVII, 234 *et subs.*; B Schäfers, *Freispruch in Nürnberg* (Diss. Bielefeld 2010) 186.

However, the main structure of the trial was adversarial in nature. According to Art. 24 IMTSt, the prosecution and the defence presented their respective 'case', witness testimony was presented to the Tribunal by way of examination in chief, whereas the other party had the right to cross-examination according to Art. 24 (g) IMTSt.[31] In the same instance, the judges had the right to put questions to the witnesses if they so wished according to Art. 24 (f) IMTSt. The accused were allowed to act as witnesses which would, however, put them under cross-examination by the prosecution. According to Art. 24 (j) IMTSt, the defendants were allowed the 'last word', which was seen as a major new contribution to the German system of criminal procedure and treatment of the accused persons.[32] It is interesting to note however, that with the exception of General Rudenko, none of the other Chief Prosecutors were present on 31 August 1946, when the defendants could make their short and final un-sworn statements.[33]

The IMTSt foresaw in Art. 16 IMTSt a number of fair trial requirements. These rights of the accused comprised first of all the requirement that the Tribunal must communicate with the defendant in a language he or she understands. Secondly, the defendant must be handed the indictment in order to prepare for trial. Thirdly, he or she has the right to defend him or herself or if he or she so wishes be represented by counsel. Finally he or she has the right to call witnesses on his or her behalf and cross-examine witnesses for the prosecution.

Fundamentals of procedural 'due process of law' were seen by the drafters of the Charter as essential for the acceptance of the international trial.[34]

3. *Flaws in the system*

When considering the fairness of the proceedings in Nuremberg, it has to be kept in mind that modern fair trial standards are considerably higher than those in the 1940s. Nevertheless, the Charter raises some serious doubts concerning trial fairness. All in all we raise three issues with regard to the independence of the participants, the structural inequality between prosecution and defence, and the procedural novelty:

---

[31] The discussions at the London Conference on Military Trials make clear that the drafters voted in favour of the Anglo-American trial order after considerable pressure by both the US and the British delegate, *see* Jackson Report (1949) 405–15.

[32] *See* the statement of Justice Jackson at the London Conference, in: Jackson Report (1949), 409, and his introduction Jackson Report (1949), XI; *see* also § 258 (2) German Code of Criminal Procedure.

[33] *See* T Taylor, *The Anatomy of the Nuremberg Trials* (Bloomsbury 1993) 535, who suggests that that was the case because the British and American lawyers were unfamiliar with such proceedings. This excuse would certainly not be available to the French Chief Counsel. The absence contrasts with the interest of the general public. Room 600 in Nuremberg was packed, as the audience was keen on hearing the defendants.

[34] *See* Jackson Report (1949), X–XI.

a. Independence and impartiality It is unfortunate that the judges would dominate the proceedings in such a way that they would draft the procedural rules. This is highly questionable from a point of view of the requirement of an independent court and impartial judges. Yet Art. 3 IMTSt disallowed any discussion on the impartiality of the judges.[35] Several participants in the London Conference who drafted the IMT Charter later participated in the trial as judges or prosecutors. General Nikitchenko, was later the appointed Russian Judge, Judge Falco acted as the French alternate judge, Justice Jackson was US Chief Prosecutor, and Sir Maxwell Fyfe was the UK Deputy Prosecutor.[36] One must concede that at the time there was no discussion about how to integrate judges from neutral countries, let alone from Germany.[37] That is hardly surprising, as neutrality was not seen as a reliable concept, and Germany had failed to deliver a serious war crimes prosecution after World War I.[38]

In addition, the political independence of the prosecutors was questionable, in particular with regard to the Soviet Union. The Soviet prosecutors' plan to blame the Katyn massacre on the German accused was detrimental to the acceptability of the entire prosecution by the German people, and complicated the work of the other prosecution teams.[39] After tiring discussions, the Soviet delegation finally dropped the charge. The judgment contains no mention of the Katyn incident.

The constant refusal to accept the secret protocol to the Molotov–Ribbentrop pact of 23 August 1939 as evidence demonstrated for many Germans the one-sidedness of the proceedings, in particular vis-à-vis the Soviet Union.[40]

b. Structural inequalities The structural differences between the prosecution on the one hand and the defence on the other were immense. Twenty seven defence counsels and fifty four junior counsels worked with sixty seven secretaries for the defence of twenty one accused and six indicted organizations. In contrast,

---

[35] *See* K Kastner, *Von den Siegern zur Rechenschaft gezogen* (Hoffmann 2001) 216.

[36] The German defence lawyers complained about this fact before the trial started on 19 November 1945, but without success, *see* IMT Protocols I, 186 *et subs*. *See* also O Kranzbühler, 'Nuremberg Eighteen Years Afterwards', 14 *DePaul Law Review* (1964–1965) 333, 338.

[37] *See* M Marrus, *The Nuremberg War Crimes Trial 1945–46. A Documentary History* (Bedford/St Martin's 1997) 251. Similarly defence counsel to Ernst Kaltenbrunner, K Kauffmann, 9 *Whittier Law Review* (1987–1988), 537, 538 and 550 *et subs*. Other German commentators have expressed their disappointment that no German judge was involved, *see* H H Jescheck, *Die Verantwortlichkeit der Staatsorgane nach Völkerstrafrecht* (Röhrscheid 1952) 416 *et subs*.

[38] *See* section 1.A.I, *see* also R H Jackson, 'Introduction, in: W Harris, *Tyranny on Trial* (3rd edn, Southern Methodist University Press 1999) p xxxii.

[39] *See* W Harris, *Tyranny on Trial* (Southern Methodist University Press 1999) 251–71. *See* also M Bazyler, 'The Role of the Soviet Union in the International Military Tribunal at Nuremberg, in: H Reginbogin and C Safferling (eds), *The Nuremberg Trials: International Criminal Law since 1945* (Saur 2006) 42, 47.

[40] *See* IMT Protocols X, 14–16, 56 *et subs*., 215, 354 *et subs*.

the American delegation consisted of some 2000 staff, the British had 170, there were twenty four Soviet prosecutors and a dozen French jurists.

These inequalities in human resources continued with regard to access to documents. Despite several efforts to gain access,[41] the archives of the prosecutors remained closed to the German defence counsels.[42] Later, Telford Taylor admitted that the defence should have had unlimited access to the relevant documents. Yet he justified the restrictions adopted by the prosecutors by referring to the mistrust they felt towards the defence counsels that was harboured regarding the unusual circumstances of the case.[43]

The defence was further weakened by post-war infrastructure deficits and by the slender financial resources granted to the defence lawyers by the IMT.[44] Under these circumstances, the defence lawyers were barely able to investigate and produce exculpatory material, which would be their responsibility according to the Anglo-American trial structure.

These inequalities could only be tolerated because the evidence against the defendant was overwhelming due to the fact that the Nazi bureaucracy readily documented even the most heinous crimes.

c. **Procedural novelty** A final issue to be mentioned here is the fact that the IMT followed the Anglo-American trial structure to a large extent and was thus foreign to the German defence counsels and, of course, the accused themselves. A German defence attorney is not used to present a 'defence case', nor is he or she familiar with the issue of 'cross-examination'.[45] It might be added that the Russian Chief Prosecutor (and other participants) were also unfamiliar with this way of presenting evidence. There is a good argument that Fritzsche's acquittal was due to the disastrous performance of Rudenko in the courtroom.[46] The use of 'affidavits' in order to introduce a testimony into the trial was also new to German lawyers. Yet the Nuremberg defence counsels were keen and ready to learn.[47] Kranzbühler, for example, obtained an affidavit by the US Admiral

[41] *See* C Haensel, 'The Nuremberg Trial Revisited', 13 *DePaul Law Review* (1963–1964) 248, 256; O Kranzbühler, 'Nuremberg Eighteen Years Afterwards', 14 *DePaul Law Review* (1964–1965) 333, 336; H Laternser, 'Looking Back at the Nuremberg Trials with Special Consideration of the Processes against Military Leaders', 8 *Whittier Law Review* (1986–1987) 557, 561.

[42] IMT Protocols XX, 307 *et subs.*

[43] T Taylor, *The Anatomy of the Nuremberg Trials* (Bloomsbury 1993) 627.

[44] C Safferling and P Graebke, 'Strafverteidigung im Nürnberger Hauptkriegsverbrecherprozess: Strategien und Wirkungen', 123 *ZStW* (2011) 47, 75 *et subs.*

[45] T Taylor, *The Anatomy of the Nuremberg Trials* (Bloomsbury 1993) 396 *et subs.* describes difficulties in 'cross-examination' by the defence attorneys.

[46] B Schäfers, *Freispruch in Nürnberg* (Diss. Bielefeld 2010) 168–86 (not yet published).

[47] Defence counsel for Wilhelm Frick, O Pannenbecker, opined that the accused did not suffer any disadvantage by the fact that the Charter followed an adversarial trial structure, *see* O Pannenbecker, 14 *DePaul Law Review* (1964–1965) 348, 350.

Nimitz, admitting that the submarine warfare of the allies was similar to the German military strategy, so that the German practice could no longer be termed illegal.[48]

It is interesting to note, however, that no defence counsel with a common-law background was approached in order to defend the accused German war criminals. From a professional point of view, this would have been advisable.[49] All in all, the German defence lawyers were not wholly unsuccessful despite the difficult tasks they undertook.

4. General evaluation

The Nuremberg trial was the first international criminal trial. It thus sets a precedent for all subsequent international trials from a procedural point of view. It must be said that the judges were mindful of that very fact—that any international criminal trial in the future would relate back to this first trial. The Charter of the IMT itself envisaged future trials against war criminals on the national level but also as a joint enterprise in Arts 10, 11, and 22 IMTSt.[50] Notwithstanding criticism of several aspects, the judges at Nuremberg strived for a fair and just trial. The accused were indeed presumed innocent and had a genuine chance to defend themselves. The well-balanced judgment of the IMT proves this, as of the twenty one accused present in Nuremberg, eleven were sentenced to death by hanging, seven received imprisonment, and three were acquitted altogether. As Henry Stimson rightly stated: 'But we may take pride in the restraint of a tribunal which has so clearly insisted upon certain proof of guilt. It is far better that a Schacht should go free that than a judge should compromise his conscience.'[51]

III. Tokyo: the forgotten sister tribunal?

World War II did not only take place in Europe. It had a Pacific theatre too. Many European countries were involved in this part of the war as colonial powers in the region, as well as Russia, China, and—due to geopolitical interests—the USA. Japan as the aggressor was defeated by the dropping of two atomic bombs on Hiroshima and Nagasaki in August 1945. As at Nuremberg, the allied powers established an International Military Tribunal for the Far East (IMTFE). In contrast to its European archetype, the Tokyo Tribunal was founded not by

[48] IMT Protocols XVII, 415 *et subs.*; *see* also the Judgment IMT Protocols I 189, 352 *et subs.*; see also T Taylor, *The Anatomy of the Nuremberg Trials* (Bloomsbury 1993) 399 *et subs.*, 408 *et subs.*

[49] C Safferling and P Graebke, 'Strafverteidigung im Nürnberger Hauptkriegsverbrecherprozess: Strategien und Wirkungen', 123 *ZStW* (2011) 47, 51.

[50] *See* M Marrus, *The Nuremberg War Crimes Trial 1945–46. A Documentary History* (Bedford/St Martin's 1997) 253.

[51] H Stimson, 'Nuremberg: Landmark in Law', 25 *Foreign Affairs* (1947) 187 *et subs.*

an international agreement but by 'special proclamation' of General MacArthur, Supreme Commander of the Allied Forces.[52]

The tribunal consisted of eleven judges, stemming from the Allied Powers as well as Australia, China, India, Canada, New Zealand, the Netherlands, and the Philippines. Joseph Keenan served as Chief Prosecutor, working jointly with one prosecutor from each participating state. Twenty eight defendants were charged with crimes against peace, war crimes, and crimes against humanity, amongst them leading military and political figures. The Japanese Emperor was spared the humiliation of being prosecuted as an ordinary criminal.

The Charter of the IMTFE resembles the Nuremberg IMT Charter in particular with respect to the fair trial standard according to Art. 9 of the IMTFE Statute (IMFTSt), and the course of trial proceedings as contained in Art. 15 IMTFESt. The trial started on 3 May 1946. All defendants were convicted by the judgment of 12 November 1948. Seven were sentenced to death by hanging, and the rest were sentenced to life imprisonment or long prison terms. The defence team consisted of over 100 lawyers, three-quarters of these Japanese, one quarter American, and a team of supporting junior attorneys.

The Tokyo Tribunal never attained the same prominence as the Nuremberg Tribunal. One might speculate as to why this was so. One reason is certainly that Nuremberg came first. Another reason may have been the reluctance of the Japanese to acknowledge the fact that war crimes were committed, something that remains an issue today.[53] Even if this had also been the case in Germany, events during the 1960s and the 1990s stimulated a major turn in the politics of dealing with the past there, and Germany adopted a more open approach towards its own history. It may also be argued that the crimes committed by Germany were even more brutal and systematic, and thus attracted more attention. Be all of this as it may, the strategies and efficiency of the IMFTE still need to be researched.

IV. The Nuremberg subsequent trials

The trial against the major war criminals in Nuremberg was not the only judicial reaction to the German war of aggression and the Holocaust, yet no other international trial was conducted as a joint enterprise of the Allied Powers. The so-called Nuremberg subsequent trials were thus purely national trials, staged by the US in its role as occupying power, on the basis of Control Council Law No 10

[52] *See* H Ahlbrecht, *Geschichte des völkerrechtlichen Strafgerichtsbarkeit* (Nomos 1999) 105 *et subs.*, and N Boister and R Cryer, *The Tokyo International Military Tribunal: A Reappraisal* (OUP 2008) 28 *et subs.*

[53] *See* Ph Osten, *Der Tokioter Kriegsverbrecherprozess und die japanische Rechtswissenschaft* (Berliner Wissenschaftsverlag 2003) analysing the scientific research in Japan on the Tokyo Trial.

of 20 December 1945.[54] The prominence of these twelve subsequent trials relates to the fact that they attempted to concentrate the prosecution on several groups of professionals as representatives for the whole of society. Thus trials were conducted against doctors, jurists, diplomats, Einsatzgruppen, industries, and high-ranking military leaders.[55]

Other trials were held at Dachau, and by the British and the French in their respective zones of occupation. The impact of these trials on the substantive international criminal law is undeniable. Regarding procedure, however, they did not develop new standards, as they were conducted as national trials following national criminal procedure.

V. The ILC drafts: intermediaries without future?

It is well known that during the so-called Cold War, international criminal law lay dormant. Despite the attempts by the UN to preserve the achievements of Nuremberg by adopting the 'Nuremberg Principles' on 11 December 1945[56] and their elaborated version of 29 July 1950,[57] and despite ideas to establish a judicial organ as a Criminal Chamber of the International Court of Justice (ICJ),[58] international criminal law was not administered for almost fifty five years. Nevertheless Principle V of the Nuremberg Principles stated that international criminals must have a fair trial. This is a vital legacy of Nuremberg.

However, one should not forget that the years following World War II were used to amend the normative basis of international law in many regards. The humanitarian law was codified in the 1949 Geneva Conventions and the 1977 Additional Protocols. The Genocide Convention was adopted on 9 December 1946. Human rights law was developed by the Universal Declaration of Human Rights of 8 December 1946 and the 1966 Conventions on Civil and Political Rights (ICCPR) and on Social, Economic and Cultural Rights. Several regional instruments on human rights were adopted, most prominently the European Convention on Human Rights (ECHR), which was even equipped with a judicial body to monitor the implementation of the human rights provisions by accepting individual complaints. These drafts and organs are extremely important for criminal procedure too. Art. 14 ICCPR and Art. 6 ECHR contain fair trial standards and minimum guarantees for defendants, which relate to some extent to Art. 16 IMTSt.

---

[54] Control Council Law No 10: Punishment of Persons Guilty of War Crimes, Crimes against Peace and against Humanity.

[55] An overview is given by W Harris, *Tyranny on Trial* (1999) 532 *et subs.*

[56] UNGA Res. 95 [I].

[57] Yearbook of the International Law Commission 1950 vol II, 374–8.

[58] *See* Report of the Sixth Committee of the General Assembly, UN Doc. A/760, 5 December 1948 (Rapporteur: Mr J Spiropoulos).

An institutional implementation of the Nuremberg Principles in a permanent international criminal court, however, failed. On 21 November 1947, the UN General Assembly did indeed instruct[59] the International Law Commission (ILC) to draft a code of international crimes, which was published with commentaries in 1954.[60] The Genocide Convention adopted by the UN General Assembly on 9 December 1948 envisaged a permanent criminal court in Art. VI for the prosecution of the crime of genocide.[61] At the same time, the ILC commissioned a special committee to draft a Statute for a permanent international criminal court. A draft was furnished in 1951 and revised 1953.[62] Both drafts withered in the political chill of the Cold War atmosphere.[63] The formal argument for a constant delay in discussing the draft statute was that at first, the draft code of international crimes should be heard before the issue of a permanent court was to be addressed. Voices that warned that a judicial organ was necessary before a serious codification of international criminal law could be addressed, were overheard.[64]

Yet the code of international crimes was incomplete until the 'crime of aggression' was defined. A definition of aggression was however not agreed until 1974.[65] To make the execution of international crimes by an international criminal court dependent upon an operational 'crime of aggression' was a mistake, not repeated at the Rome Conference in 1998.[66] In the meantime, the prosecution of international crimes remained within the jurisdiction of national courts as foreseen, for example, by the Geneva Conventions regarding the 'grave breaches' regime. Prosecution thus remained rather small in numbers.[67]

A draft Statute was finally set up forty years after the end of the Cold War, in 1994.[68] The original idea in the General Assembly was to establish a specialized international criminal court to deal with the problem of drug trafficking,

---

[59] UNGA Res. 177/II.

[60] Draft Code of Offences against the Peace and Security of Mankind (1954), *see* Yearbook of the International Law Commission, 1954, vol. II.

[61] S Zappalá, 'International Criminal Jurisdiction over Genocide', in: P Gaeta (ed), *The Genocide Convention* (OUP 2009) 259, 262–5.

[62] Report of the Committee on International Criminal Jurisdiction, UNGAOR, 7th Session, Supp. No. 12 at 21, UN Doc. A/26645 (1954).

[63] In more detail, M C Bassiouni, *International Criminal Law Vol 3: International Enforcement* (3rd edn, Nijhoff 2008) 117–22.

[64] Such a lone voice as V Pella, 'Towards an International Criminal Court', 44 *AJIL* (1950) 37, 42–7.

[65] Definition of Aggression, UNGA Res. 3314 (XXIX) adopted on 14 December 1974.

[66] *See* section 1.A.XII.

[67] N Combs, 'International Criminal Jurisprudence Comes of Age: the Substance and Procedure of Emerging Discipline', 42 *Harv Int'l LJ* (2001) 555, 558.

[68] Draft Statute for an International Criminal Court (1994), *see* Yearbook of the International Law Commission 1994, vol. II (Part Two).

following a suggestion by Trinidad and Tobago.[69] The draft presented by the ILC consisted of sixty Articles and established rather a rudimentary procedural order.[70] Above all, the court as described in the draft statute was limited in several regards. In particular the powers of the prosecutor were rather limited in that no *ex offico* authority to initiate an investigation was foreseen. At the same time, the powers of the UN Security Council were rather extensive, thus the ILC submitted itself to the political will of the superpowers.[71] The rudimentary character of the draft statute is particularly highlighted as regards the rights of the accused. Despite the fact that the presumption of innocence was recognized in a prominent place of the statute (Art. 40 Draft Statute ILC 1994), and despite the fair trial provision in Art. 41 Draft Statute ILC 1994, the rights of the accused seemed to take second place behind the protection of victims and witnesses on a general level, as foreseen in Arts 41 and 43 Draft Statute ILC 1994. Nevertheless in the following discussion on the statute of a permanent international criminal court, the ILC draft was an important point of reference, even if the occurrence of the ICTY, which will be discussed in the following section, marginalized the work to a certain extent.

VI. The ICTY: the re-inventor of international criminal procedure

1. The development of the ICTY

The political winds changed with the disintegration of Yugoslavia in the early 1990s. The international community, still celebrating the fall of the Berlin Wall, was buoyed with new hopes for a more peaceful, secure, and stable world, when demands for autonomy by several entities on the territory of the former Yugoslavia erupted in brutal military conflict. The civil war evolved in several phases. The first started when both Slovenia and Croatia declared independence on 26 June 1991, followed by Bosnia and Herzegovina on 15 October 1991 after the first democratic elections. Whereas an escalation of military operations was avoided in the case of Slovenia, the partly Serb-populated areas of Croatia, namely the regions of Krajina and Slovenia, were taken by the Yugoslavian People's Army (JNA), and the Croats deported from their homes. In 1992 there were already some 1.4 million displaced persons in the region.

The conflict entered its second phase when the Serbian population in Bosnia declared itself independent from the Republic of Bosnia and Herzegovina on 7 April 1992, and the JNA occupied about two-thirds of the Republic of Bosnia and Herzegovina. In the course of this conflict between at least three religious

69 A Cassese, *International Criminal Law* (2nd edn, OUP 2008) 328.

70 *See* J Crawford, 'The ILC adopts a Statute for an International Criminal Court', 89 *AJIL* (1995) 404.

71 M C Bassiouni, *International Criminal Law Vol 3: International Enforcement* (3rd edn, Nijhoff 2008) 123 *et subs.*

groups, the most appalling cruelties were reported, including systematic rapes, ethnic cleansing, and mass murders.

Unwilling or unable to intervene, both the European Union and the United Nations watched helplessly as the civilian population was murdered, deported, and tortured. All diplomatic measures by the European Union, like the Yugoslavian Conference in September 1991, failed to solve the conflict. The attempt to release pressure on the separatist entities by officially recognizing the independence of Slovenia and Croatia on 15 January 1992, and of Bosnia and Herzegovina on 17 April 1992 by the European Community and the USA turned out to be counter-productive, and further fuelled the conflict.[72] The first forcible measures under Chapter VII of the UN Charter were taken by the UN Security Council on 25 September 1991 by Resolution 713. The economic sanctions—an arms embargo— however, never operated effectively. Also, the peace-keeping force (UNPROFOR), established by SC Resolution 743 on 21 February 1992, did not prevent the most heinous atrocities on European soil since World War II.

As the rules for the protection of the civilian population and for humane warfare were totally ignored, the Security Council decided to appoint a Commission of Experts[73] in order to investigate war crimes on the territory of the former Yugoslavia by Resolution 780 of 6 October 1992. In this resolution, the Security Council requested the help of both governmental and non-governmental organizations to investigate and bring their results to the Security Council. The interim report of the—heavily underfinanced[74]—Commission of Experts of 9 February 1993 (S/25274) gave proof of war crimes and ethnic cleansing, and recommended the establishment of an *ad hoc* international tribunal in order to prosecute the crimes being committed.[75] The Security Council took up this idea and stated in Resolution 808:

> Determined to put an end to such crimes and to take effective measures to bring to justice the persons who are responsible for them,
>
> Convinced that in the particular circumstances of the former Yugoslavia the establishment of an international tribunal would enable this aim to be achieved and would contribute to the restoration and maintenance of peace,

---

[72] S Oeter, 'Völkerrechtliche Rahmenbedingungen und die Staatengemeinschaft', in: D Melcic (ed), *Der Jugoslawienkrieg* (2nd edn, VS 2007) 485–503.

[73] The Commission consisted of Mr Frits Kalshoven (Netherlands) as Chairman (later substituted by Ms Christine Cleiren, Netherlands), Mr M Cherif Bassiouni (Egypt), who chaired the Commission after Kalshoven's resignation, Mr William J Fenrick (Canada), Mr. Keba M'baye (Senegal), and Mr Torkel Opsahl (Norway), who was after his death substituted by Ms Hanne Sophie Greve (Norway).

[74] S Oeter, 'Völkerrechtliche Rahmenbedingungen und die Staatengemeinschaft', in: D Melcic (ed), *Der Jugoslawienkrieg* (2nd edn, VS 2007) 485–503.

[75] The final report was received on 27 May 1994 (S/1994/674).

Noting in this regard the recommendation by the Co-Chairmen of the Steering Committee of the International Conference on the Former Yugoslavia for the establishment of such a tribunal (S/25221).

The Secretary-General was requested to prepare a draft statute for an *ad hoc* tribunal, which the Security Council received and adopted by Resolution 827 on 25 May 1993, deciding in an as yet unprecedented step for the establishment of the International Tribunal for the Prosecution of Persons Responsible for Serious Violations of International Humanitarian Law Committed in the Territory of the Former Yugoslavia since 1991 (ICTY). The seat of the tribunal was to be The Hague, as it was impossible to set the court up in the territory of the former Yugoslavia, and because The Hague was already a traditional place for international judiciary.[76] As a legal basis, the Security Council used Chapter VII of the UN Charter, for which it was heavily criticized. Yet many states supported this step.[77] However, the power of the Security Council to establish *ad hoc* criminal tribunals is now widely accepted, at least since the establishment of a similar tribunal for Rwanda and the ground-breaking decision of the ICTY Appeals Chamber in the case against *Tadić* of 2 October 1995.[78]

Altogether, the work of the ICTY has been impressive, considering also the difficulties it was facing as the first international criminal tribunal after Nuremberg (*see results as tabulated in Table 1.1*).

Table 1.1 Overview of the work of the ICTY. December 2010

Accused Persons	161
Acquittals	12
Convictions	64
Surrender to domestic courts	13
Other terminations	36
Trials underway	36
Staff	1039 from 83 States
Cost per year	150 million US $

[76] In the years after Nuremberg, it was even suggested that one common Registry for the ICJ and the International Criminal Court be established: V Pella, 'Towards an International Criminal Court', 44 *AJIL* (1950) 37, 61. This suggestion however misunderstood the huge differences between a court which acts akin to an arbitration tribunal for states, and a criminal court, which is dealing with private individuals.

[77] Member states of the Security Council, apart from the five permanent Members comprising USA, UK, Russia, China, and France were: Austria, Belgium, Cape Verde, Ecuador, Hungary, India, Japan, Morocco, Venezuela, and Zimbabwe. Other supporting states were: Australia, Brazil, Canada, Chile, Denmark, Egypt, Germany, Iran, Ireland, Italy, Malaysia, Mexico, Netherlands, New Zealand, Pakistan, Portugal, Saudi Arabia, Senegal, Slovenia, Spain, Sweden, Turkey, Yugoslavia, and Switzerland. *See* the Report of the Secretary General pursuant to paragraph 2 of SC Res. 808 (1993), para 13.

[78] ICTY *Prosecutor v Tadić*, AC, IT-94-1, 2 October 1995, Decision on the Defence Motion for Interlocutory Appeal on Jurisdiction.

2. The trial system

The procedural law at the ICTY took heed of the Nuremberg Charter. The modern approach to criminal procedural law in the early 1990s put more emphasis on the rights of the accused and due process of law than was the case in the mid-1940s. The development of more humane treatment and a fair trial as conceptualized in Arts 9 and 14 of the ICCPR or Arts 5 and 6 of the ECHR needed to be taken into account.[79] Nevertheless, the ICTY Statute resembles the IMT at Nuremberg insofar as it is rooted mainly in the Anglo-American legal structure of a criminal trial, but it also incorporates several aspects of the European legal tradition. It might also be a lesson learned from Nuremberg that continental European states now accept an adversarial trial structure as fair and adequate and do not insist on a structure similar to their own national legal systems when it comes to creating an international level of criminal prosecution.

The ICTYSt contains a threefold structure, which became the benchmark for the other tribunals to come:

Court—Registry—Office of the Prosecutor
Appeals Chamber
Trial Chambers

The procedure was laid down in the Statute of the ICTY, consisting of merely thirty four articles, and the Rules of Procedure and Evidence (RPE). As was the case in Nuremberg, the judges drafted the RPE themselves according to Art. 15 ICTYSt. Of course this poses a certain deficit in legitimacy[80] and has led to an unmanageable number of amendments. Forty eight revisions in eighteen years means that the procedural laws have been modified 2.6 times each year.

Also, the RPE have their basis in the Anglo-American trial system which is due to the fact that the USA submitted the most advanced draft to the judges, which was well received and widely adopted.[81] However, in the course of the subsequent trials, the rules drifted further from the Anglo-American structure and more continental aspects were integrated.[82] One can identify two main reasons for this development. First, the ICTY operates with an international staff. Judges and prosecutors come from different backgrounds and influence the proceedings according to their procedural culture and understanding. Secondly, the Anglo-American system is often directed towards the jury. As the ICTY is not equipped with a jury, many procedural issues need to be reconsidered. As Justice Jackson

[79] *See* Report of the Secretary General (1993), para 106
[80] *See* G Werle, *Völkerstrafrecht* (2nd edn, Mohr Siebeck 2007) MN 52 fn 95.
[81] *See* V Morris and M Scharf, *An Insider's Guide to the International Criminal Tribunal for the Former Yugoslavia. vol. I* (Hotei Publisher 1995) 177.
[82] G Werle, *Völkerstrafrecht* (2nd edn, Mohr Siebeck 2007) MN 261.

states regarding the IMT at Nuremberg, there is no need for jury rules if there is no jury.[83]

3. Flaws in the system

Obviously, these parallels between Nuremberg and the ICTY provoked a serious amount of criticism alleging that the flaws of Nuremberg were repeated some fifty years hence.[84] This criticism pertains mainly to the extensive use of post-World War II jurisprudence and the wide interpretation of the substantive law. Difficulties concerning the prohibition of retroactive criminality were discussed as well as the unusual legal basis of the tribunal as a sub-organ of the UN Security Council according to Art. 29 UN-Charter.

At the beginning, analysis of the procedural law was not the main focus of criticism. This changed as the ICTY granted anonymity to witnesses and restricted the right of the accused to confront prosecution witnesses in order to protect both witnesses and victims.[85] The ICTY needed to come to terms with the situation of an ongoing armed conflict and a highly sensitive security situation. The RPE, which were originally drafted as analogies to a domestic prosecution system, did not foresee (and possibly could not have foreseen) the dangers and problems of a criminal prosecution at the international level. Much of what happened followed a trial-and-error approach, a constant work in progress.

The most difficult challenge the ICTY has to meet is the length of the proceedings. Due to a complicated system of interlocutory appeals, trials with multiple defendants, translation issues and, last but not least, many novelties regarding both substantive law and procedural law, trials lasting five years or longer are the general rule and not the unfortunate exception. As early as 2002 the UN adopted the so-called completion strategy, which intended to speed up the proceedings and reduce the caseload of the ICTY by restricting the tribunal to the most serious offenders. Now as Radovan Karadžić, Ratko Mladić, and Goran Hadžić, the most-wanted alleged war criminals, are all detained at the tribunal pending or awaiting trial, the Prosecutor's list of suspects is settled. Nonetheless, it will take several years to terminate the prosecution against these three most senior defendants.

VII. The ICTR: a dissimilar–similar copy

1. The establishment of the ICTR

Shortly after the establishment of the ICTY, the world community witnessed the slaughtering of some 800,000 people in Rwanda in an outbreak of long-

[83] Jackson Report (1949) XI. *See* also section 1.A.II.1

[84] *See* eg, J Alvarez, 'Nuremberg Revisited: The *Tadić* Case', 7 *EJIL* (1996) 245.

[85] *See* eg, M Leigh, 'The Yugoslav Tribunal: Use of Unnamed Witnesses against Accused', 90 *AJIL* (1996) 216 and the same, 'Witness Anonymity is Inconsistent with Due Process', 91 *AJIL* (1997) 80 on the one hand, and C Chinkin, 'Due Process and Witness Anonymity', 91 *AJIL* (1997) 74, on the other.

standing civil strife between Hutu and Tutsi. The genocide took place in April 1994. The UN created a similar tribunal following advice of a Commission of Experts.[86] By the time the tribunal was established by Security Council Res. 955 of 8 November 1994, the outbreak was over and the conflict had, for the time being, ended. The International Criminal Tribunal for Rwanda (ICTR) was largely constructed as a satellite of the ICTY. At first, they had one common Office of the Prosecutor according to Art. 15 (3) ICTRSt until they were separated from the ICTY in 2003.[87] They still share one Appeals Chamber in The Hague according to Art. 13 (4) ICTRSt. The tribunal itself was not established in Rwanda but in Arusha, in neighbouring Tanzania, for security reasons.[88]

The ICTR is competent to prosecute genocide (Art. 2 ICTR), crimes against humanity (Art. 3 ICTR), and Violations of Article 3 common to the Geneva Conventions, and of Additional Protocol II (Art. 4 ICTR). The incorporation of Additional Protocol II is surprising as its customary law status was not accepted prior to the establishment of the ICTR, but borne out of the necessity to cover the non-international armed conflict in Rwanda. The jurisdiction does not only cover crimes committed on Rwandan territory but also crimes which had been committed by Rwandan nationals on the territory of neighbouring countries pursuant to Art. 1 ICTRSt.

The importance of the ICTR lies without doubt in the developing of the law of genocide pursuant to Art. 2 ICTRSt. The ICTR was the first international criminal tribunal which applied the prohibition of genocide. Jean Paul Akayesu was the first person ever to be charged with and convicted for genocide as an international crime, on 2 September 1998, almost fifty years after the adoption of the genocide convention.[89] The ICTR was also the first international tribunal after Nuremberg to convict a former prime minister of a national state, *Jean Kambanda*.[90]

2. Procedural issues

Procedurally, the ICTR corresponds largely to its predecessor and sister tribunal, the ICTY. The Statutes are almost identical, as are the Rules of Procedure and Evidence. According to Art. 14 ICTRSt, the judges in Arusha adopted the RPE of the ICTY

[86] *See* UN SC Res. 935, 1 July 1994.
[87] UN SC Res. 1503 (2003).
[88] UN SC Res. 977, 22 February 1995.
[89] ICTR *Prosecutor v Akayesu*, TC, ICTR-96–4-T, 2 September 1998, Judgment. He was sentenced two months later: *Prosecutor v Akayesu*, TC, ICTR-96–4-T, 2 October 1998, Sentencing Judgment.
[90] ICTR *Prosecutor v Kambanda*, TC, ICTR 97–23-S, 4 September 1998, Judgment and Sentence; upheld on Appeal: *Prosecutor v Kambanda*, AC, ICTR 97–23-A, 19 October 2000, Judgment.

Table 1.2 Overview of the work of the ICTR: December 2010

Accused persons	90
Acquittals	8
Convictions	36
Surrender to national jurisdiction	2
Other terminations	4
Trials running	30
Staff	690 from 73 States
Overall cost per year	120 Million US $

and could only amend as deemed necessary. Thus far, nineteen amendments were initiated. Compared to the ICTY this seems a rather slender number, but it stems partly from the fact that often the work of the ICTY was summarily copied.

The most pressing procedural problem of the ICTR is the length of proceedings. Despite the completion strategy, which originally foresaw that the trials be concluded by 2010,[91] there seems to be no real pressure to bring the work of the Tribunal to an end. The Tribunal is understaffed and not everyone working for the UN in Arusha fulfils the high standard required to bring about a successful conclusion to this complicated and ambitious enterprise.

Another important issue is that of witness protection. In the small communities in Rwanda, cooperation with the international prosecutor or defence lawyer does not remain undetected. Witness anonymity at trial is thus often a useless tool to protect the integrity of the witness.

Finally, the genocide in Rwanda has seen far too many perpetrators and abetters to prosecute all of them. To date, several thousands of people are in Rwandan detention facilities awaiting trial. The ICTR should thus only try the top-level planners and instigators of the genocide. Minor offenders will either be prosecuted by the national Rwandan authorities or by so-called Gacaca tribunals. This traditional form of conflict resolution has been re-invented in order to deal with the mass of perpetrators in a more communal and restorative way.[92] Yet even if hopes were high that these tribunals would guarantee some kind of justice, Gacaca tribunals are not free from political pressure and ethnic struggle.[93] Even if the ICTR cooperates with the Rwandan national judicial system, it is very questionable whether the rule of law is being respected.[94]

[91] UN SC Res. 1503 (2003).

[92] S Schilling, *Gegen das Vergessen: Justiz, Wahrheitsfindung und Versöhnung nach dem Genozid in Rwanda durch Mechanismen transitionaler Justiz* (Peter Lang 2005).

[93] G Hankel, 'An der Realität vorbei. Ruanda dreizehn Jahre nach dem Völkermord', 1 *der überblick* (2007) 78–87.

[94] Germany declines to cooperate with the Rwandan government and does not extradite Rwandan citizens. According to the international rule '*aut dedere, aut judicare*', Rwandan nationals are being tried by German courts.

Social acceptance of all three levels of prosecution—international, national, and regional—suffers greatly from the influence of political circumstances. It is more than doubtful whether or not the international and national efforts will help the stabilization and healing process of Rwandan society.

VIII. Special Court for Sierra Leone

1. *Establishment of the Special Court for Sierra Leone*

The Special Court is a 'hybrid' tribunal, which came into existence in the aftermath of a decade of brutal civil war, through an agreement between the Government of Sierra Leone and the United Nations.[95] Set up in January 2002, the Court is mandated to try those bearing the greatest responsibility for the atrocities committed during the Sierra Leonean civil war.[96] Due to an amnesty contained in the Abidjan Peace Agreement of November 1996[97] the jurisdiction of the Tribunal is further restricted to include only those atrocities committed after 30 November 1996. Under this very narrow mandate, the Court has issued only thirteen indictments[98] against the alleged key contributors to the war. It follows that this significantly smaller number of cases, as opposed to the proceedings brought before the *ad hoc* Tribunals,[99] is the direct result of the deliberate restrictive mandate of the Special Court.

2. *The hybrid court—differences to the* ad hoc *Tribunals*

Like the ICC and *ad hoc* Tribunals, the SCSL is made up of three institutions; the Registry, the Chambers, and the Office of the Prosecutor. Similarly, the SCSLSt and RPE set out provisions regarding the establishment, composition, duties, functions, and regulation of these institutions. Due to the adversarial process prevailing at the Special Court, many procedures are similar to those practised in its *ad hoc* sister tribunals. However, some important fundamental and structural differences are worth noting. One essential difference is the hybrid nature of the Court, which is marked in particular by the way the SCSL was established, the appointment of its judges, as well as the applicable law.

---

95 Agreement between the United Nations and the Government of Sierra Leone on the establishment of a Special Court for Sierra Leone, 16 January 2002.

96 The war began in March 1991 and was declared as officially ended in January 2002 by the President of Sierra Leone, Ahmad Tejan Kabbah.

97 Peace Agreement between the Government of the Republic of Sierra Leone and the Revolutionary United Front of Sierra Leone (RUF/SL), 30 November 1996.

98 Indictments have been issued against: Charles Taylor, Sam Hinga Norman (Case has been, closed due to the accused's death during the proceedings), Moinina Fofana, Allieu Kondewa, Foday Saybana Sankoh (indictment withdrawn on 8 December 2003 due to accused's death), Sam Bockarie (indictment withdrawn on 8 December 2003 due to accused's death), Issa Hassan Sesay, Morris Kallon, Augustine Gbao, Alex Tamba Brima, Brima Bazzy Kamara, Santigie Borbor Kanu, and Johnny Paul Koroma.

99 The ICTY has issued 161 indictments.

a. Legal status of the SCSL An important procedural issue, raised in the case against ex-Liberian President Charles Taylor, concerned the legal status of the SCSL. Shortly after the indictment was unsealed, Mr Taylor's lawyers attempted to claim head-of-state immunity for their client, on the grounds that the Special Court did not constitute an international court.[100] As opposed to the *ad hoc* Tribunals, which came into existence through Security Council Resolutions based on the UN Chapter VII powers, the SCSL, as mentioned above, was created by way of a treaty between the UN and the Sierra Leonean state. Whereas both the ICTY and ICTR were established as subsidiary organs of the UN[101] and are therefore undoubtedly international courts, the hybrid nature of the Special Court meant that its international character was not so clear-cut. After concluding that the SCSL was established under international circumstances, that it pursues an international mandate, and that it applies instruments typical of those of international criminal tribunals (Statute and RPE), the SCSL Appeals Chamber held that the Special Court did indeed have international status[102] and thereupon denied the accused's application for immunity from prosecution.

b. Composition of chambers A ratio of 1:2 and 2:3 of UN and Sierra Leonean selected judges sit in the two Trial Chambers and one Appeals Chamber of the SCSL respectively.[103] A high percentage of local staff is also employed in the Court's other institutions—the Registry and the Office of the Prosecutor (OTP).[104] The purpose of this is to distinctively and demonstrably allow Sierra Leone to be involved in bringing those primarily responsible for the terrorization of its population for over a decade, to justice and not to simply outsource justice to an international tribunal distant from and alien to those concerned. Particularly in contrast to the ICTY, where trials were held far from where atrocities took place, the accused before the Special Court, with the exception of Charles Taylor, were tried in Freetown, Sierra Leone. Locating the proceedings in the country in which the crimes were committed was a deliberate and significant step.

c. Location and legacy The location of the court in Freetown has placed the SCSL in a better position than her sister *ad hoc* Tribunals to leave a positive legacy

---

100 SCSL *Prosecutor v Taylor*, AC, SCSL-2003–01-I, 31 May 2003, Decision on Immunity from Jurisdiction, para 14 *et subs*.

101 Report of the Secretary-General on the Establishment of a Special Court for Sierra Leone 4 October 2000, UN Doc. S/2000/915 para 9.

102 SCSL *Prosecutor v Taylor*, AC, SCSL-2003–01-I, 31 May 2003, Decision on Immunity from Jurisdiction, para 39–42.

103 Art. 12 (1) SCSLSt. See also Art. 2 of the Agreement between the United Nations and the Government of Sierra Leone on the establishment of a Special Court for Sierra Leone, 16 January 2002. Note in the proceedings against Charles Taylor an 'alternate judge' pursuant to Art. 12 (4) SCSLSt has been appointed by the UN.

104 *See* eg, Third Annual Report of the President of the Special Court of Sierra Leone, 2005–2006, p 33.

in the post-conflict region. The Office of Outreach and Public Affairs (OPA), a section within the Registry, was set up to communicate the proceedings to the general public. The Outreach Unit of the OPA is charged with informing the ordinary Sierra Leonean of the meaning of transitional justice and the work of the Special Court.[105] Despite the many challenges faced in pursuing this task, the Outreach Unit has employed many innovative methods, organizing projects, workshops, and events to reach the general public of Sierra Leone, increasing the profile of issues such as justice, accountability, humanitarian law, human rights, the rule of law, due process, and the rights of the accused.[106] Furthermore, it is hoped that through the transfer of knowledge, expertise, and professional skills the Special Court will have a lasting impact on the judicial system in Sierra Leone, leaving a legacy and contributing to securing stability and peace within the region.[107] It was feared that the relocation of the Charles Taylor trial would hinder the effectiveness of Outreach and Legacy programmes. However, most members of staff have remained in Freetown and the Outreach department has continued its work.

d. Applicable law The hybrid nature of the Special Court is further illustrated by the applicable law. Art. 5 SCSLSt provides that in addition to international law, the Tribunal may also apply national criminal law of Sierra Leone. This example, however, only exists on paper, as none of the indictments refer to Sierra Leonean law.

e. The Defence Office Another more notable and structural difference to the *ad hoc* Tribunals lies in the defence provision of the SCSL. Whereas a legal aid system is in place at the *ad hoc* Tribunals to ensure that defendants receive proper legal representation, the Special Court, supplementary to the provision of legal aid, set up as required by Rule 45 SCSL RPE, a Defence Office within the institution of the Registry. The Defence Office is responsible for 'ensuring the rights of suspects and accused before the Special Court.'[108] A more detailed description of the Defence Office can be found in Chapter 4.

f. Funding Last, but by no means least, the funding and budget of the SCSL differs from that of the *ad hoc* Tribunals. From the moment it was established,

---

105 First Annual Report of the President of the Special Court of Sierra Leone, 2002–2003, p 26.

106 *See* eg, Seventh Annual Report of the President of the Special Court of Sierra Leone, 2009–2010, pp 43–6.

107 *See* eg, First Annual Report of the President of the Special Court of Sierra Leone, 2002–2003, p 28; Seventh Annual Report of the President of the Special Court of Sierra Leone, 2009–2010, pp 47–51. For a brief description of the impact of the SCSL on the Sierra Leonean legal system, *see* J Jones, C Carlton-Hanciles, H Kah-Jallow, S Scratch, I Yillah, 'Notes and Comments—The Special Court for Sierra Leone: A Defence Perspective', 2 *JICJ* (2004) 211, 229 *et subs*. Note that not just the Outreach Unit, but all organs of the Court have been involved in legacy activities.

108 Rule 45 (A) SCSL RPE.

the SCSL has been run on a shoestring budget.[109] Art. 6 of the Agreement between the United Nations and the Government of Sierra Leone provides that the Special Court be funded by voluntary contributions from the international community. Whereas the ICTY and ICTR are funded by the United Nations and had at their disposal, for example, a budget for the financial year 2010/2011 of over $320 million USD[110] and $245 million USD[111] respectively, the SCSL, in most years, has had to survive on approximately $30 million USD.[112] Clearly one must take into account that the *ad hoc* Tribunals are much larger institutions, and have indicted and prosecuted a great many more persons than the Special Court. Nonetheless, the funding mechanism of the SCSL has been a burden and forced the Registrar of the SCSL to scrabble for funds via fundraising activities and calls on diplomatic contacts to make ends meet.[113]

3. Cases before the SCSL

a. The CDF, RUF, and AFRC cases Charged with crimes against humanity, violations of Article 3 common to the Geneva Conventions and of Additional Protocol II and other serious violations of international humanitarian law, three leaders of each of the warring factions, the Revolutionary United Front (RUF), the Armed Forces Revolutionary Council (AFRC), and the pro-government civil militia, the Civil Defence Forces (CDF),[114] have been tried, convicted and sentenced by the Tribunal, in Freetown, in three separate proceedings. On the application of the Prosecution, the Trial Chamber ordered the separate joint trials of the three warring factions,[115] upon which the relevant indictments were consolidated. Having been arrested and indicted in March 2003, most of the accused spent at least one year in pre-trial custody before the start of their trial. In the

109 In the first year of operation the SCSL was run on a budget of $19 million USD (*see* First Annual Report of the President of the Special Court of Sierra Leone, 2002–2003, p 29). For a critical discussion of the funding of the SCSL *see* A Cassese, Independent Expert Report on the Special Court of Sierra Leone (2006).

110 UNGARes. A/Res/65/253.

111 UNGA Res. A/Res/65/252.

112 The SCSL survived on an estimated $125 million USD in the first four years of existence *see* A Cassese, Independent Expert Report on the Special Court of Sierra Leone (2006), para 39: The budget for the financial year 2009/2010 was $36.1 million USD (Seventh Annual Report of the President of the Special Court of Sierra Leone, 2009–2010).

113 Seventh Annual Report of the President of the Special Court of Sierra Leone, 2009–2010, p 40; A Cassese, Independent Expert Report on the Special Court of Sierra Leone (2006), para 41.

114 Note, that in the CDF case only two of the accused were convicted, as the case against Sam Hinga Norman was closed, due to his death during the proceedings.

115 SCSL *Prosecutor v Sesay et al.*, TC I, SCSL-03–09-PT-078, 27 January 2004, Decision and Order on Prosecution Motions for Joinder (RUF and AFRC cases); SCSL *Prosecutor v Norman et al.*, TC I, SCSL-03–11-PT, 27 January 2004, Decision and Order on Prosecution Motions for Joinder (CDF case).

AFRC case, one of the defendants spent precisely two years in pre-trial custody before his trial began.[116] Of particular novelty and significance were the charges of recruiting child soldiers.[117]

All in all the three trials, including appeals, took between three and five years to complete. One of the defendants, Sam Hinga Norman, died during his three-year trial. Following his death the proceedings against Mr Norman were closed.[118] Although not found guilty of every count, the majority of charges were upheld against all the accused. In contrast to the proceedings before the ICTY and ICTR, not one of the accused before the Special Court was acquitted completely.[119]

In the CDF case, two of the accused were convicted in August 2007 and received astonishingly mild sentences. The Trial Chamber assessed each count individually and passed concurrent custodial sentences of six years for the accused Fofana and eight years for the accused Kondewa.[120] Upon the Prosecution's appeal the sentences were increased to fifteen and twenty years respectively.[121] The accused in the RUF and AFRC cases received custodial sentences of between twenty five and fifty two years.[122]

b. The Charles Taylor case The most prominent case before the SCSL is that of ex-Liberian President Charles Taylor. Following many requests to the Government of Nigeria, both from the Special Court and the international community, to hand over Mr Taylor for trial for atrocities committed during the Sierra Leonean civil war, he was finally extradited on 29 March 2006 to Freetown from Nigeria, where he had enjoyed several years of asylum.

In April 2006, the President of the Special Court sent a request to the UN Security Council for the trial of Charles Taylor to be relocated to The Hague for security reasons.[123] On 16 June, the UN Security Council issued Resolution

[116] Brima was indicted on 7 March 2007 and his trial commenced on 7 March 2005.

[117] All the accused in the AFRC case were convicted of enlisting child soldiers (see SCSL *Prosecutor v Brima et al.*, SCSL-04-16-T, TC II, 20 June 2007, Judgment, para 1244–78); In the CDF case, the accused were charged with enlisting child soldiers (see Count 8 of the consolidated indictment SCSL *Prosecutor v Norman et al.*, SCSL-03-04-I, 4 February 2004). The accused Kondewa was found guilty of enlisting child soldiers, whereas the accused Fofona was found not guilty on this count (see SCSL *Prosecutor v Fofana et al.*, SCSL-04-14-T, TC I, 2 August 2007, Judgment, para 182–99, 957–73).

[118] SCSL *Prosecutor v Norman et al.*, TC I, SCSL-04-14-T, 21 May 2007, Decision on Registrar's Submission of Evidence of Death of Accused Samuel Hinga Norman and Consequential Issues.

[119] Note, one trial, that of Charles Taylor, is ongoing.

[120] SCSL *Prosecutor v Fofana et al.*, TC I, SCSL-04-14-T, 9 October 2007, Judgment on the Sentencing of Moinina Fofana and Allieu Kondewa.

[121] SCSL *Prosecutor v Fofana et al.*, AC, SCSL- 04-14-A,28 May 2008, Judgment.

[122] SCSL *Prosecutor v Sesay et al.*, TC I, SCSL- 04-15-T, 8 April 2009, Sentencing Judgment; SCSL *Prosecutor v Brima et al.*, TC II, SCSL- 04-16-T, 19 July 2007, Sentencing Judgment. In both cases the sentences were upheld by the Appeals Chamber.

[123] SCSL OTP press release, 12 April 2006.

1688 (2006) permitting Mr Taylor to be tried on the premises of the ICC in The Hague.[124] Thereupon the President of the SCSL issued an order authorizing the change of venue in accordance with Art. 10 of the Agreement between the Government of Sierra Leone and the UN, and Rule 4 SCSL RPE.[125] The decision to relocate the proceedings was held to be non-reviewable by both the Chambers and the President of the SCSL. Deeming the order to be an administrative decision, the Appeals Chamber held that it did not have the power to review it, since the order did not constitute a judicial decision.[126] The President of the Special Court also refused to review his decision on the ground that he had acted properly within his powers and finding that 'the Rules [did] not provide the Applicant an avenue for "reconsideration" or review before the President'.[127] This meant that the defendant, who opposed the move, was not heard on the issue. In his attempts to reverse the relocation of his trial, the accused argued that it was discriminatory and unfair for him to be tried in The Hague, when all other defendants before the SCSL had been prosecuted in Freetown.[128] The proceedings are currently at the trial stage and are being heard by Trial Chamber II of the SCSL. Although located in The Netherlands, the law applicable remains that of the Special Court.

IX. East Timor

1. Background

East Timor had been a Portuguese colony since the sixteenth century. As the UN intervened in 1960, it became a non-self-governing territory and a final Portuguese governor was appointed who allowed political parties and prepared the territory for its first elections in the course of the decolonization process. There were several new parties formed, which mostly favoured either independence, integration into Indonesia, or continuing a close relationship with Portugal, as political solutions for East Timor.[129] In September 1975, the Indonesian armed forces invaded Timor and occupied the territory until 1999. During that time the East Timorese resistance sought to achieve independence for East Timor. In 1999 an agreement

---

[124] Note, that due to scheduling difficulties at the ICC courthouse in The Hague, the trial was relocated on 17 May 2010 to the premises of the Special Tribunal for Lebanon in Leidschendam, The Netherlands (*see* SCSL Outreach and Public Affairs press release, 13 May 2010).

[125] SCSL *Prosecutor v Taylor*, SCSL-2003–01-PT, 19 June 2006, Order Changing Venue of Proceedings.

[126] As cited in SCSL *Prosecutor v Taylor*, SCSL-2003–01-PT, 12 March 2007, Decision of the President on the Defence Motion for Reconsideration of Order Changing Venue of the Proceedings, p 3.

[127] Ibid.

[128] *See* J Easterday, 'The Trial of Charles Taylor Part I: Prosecuting Persons who bear the Greatest Responsibility', *UC Berkeley War Crimes Studies Center* (2010), p 7.

[129] SPSC *Prosecutor v Domingos De Deus*, 2 a/2004, 12 April 2004, C. 1–2, para 29.

was established between the UN, Portugal, and Indonesia, that the people of East Timor would be allowed to decide for themselves regarding the independence of their territory.[130]

This announcement, however, was followed by systematic attacks directed against the civilian population including the Liquiçá Church Massacre, the Manuel Carrascalão House Massacre, and the Suai Church Massacre by several pro-Indonesian militia groups.[131] Even with a later agreement, which stated that Indonesia had the responsibility to maintain 'peace and security in East Timor in order to ensure that the popular consultation is carried out in a fair and peaceful way in an atmosphere free of intimidation, violence or interference from any side',[132] nothing was done to ensure the security of the civilian population and to avert the threat posed by over two dozen militia groups. The result was increasing attacks by militia members.[133]

2. *The courts in East Timor and the Special Panels for Serious Crimes*

The United Nations Security Council designed a model for 'parallel accountability in East Timor and Indonesia'.[134] In Indonesia, an *ad hoc* Human Rights Court was established, which in the end proved to be ineffective.[135] The civilian administration in East Timor was established through the United Nations Transitional Administration in East Timor (UNTAET). Several regulations were released to stabilize the situation and to establish a judicial institution.[136]

Eight district courts, which were later reduced to four,[137] were installed to exercise jurisdiction for crimes such as looting which do not fall under the definition of serious crimes.[138] During the transitional period, the District Court in Dili

---

[130] 'Situation of Human Rights in East Timor, Note by the Secretary-General', UN Doc. A/54/660, 10 December 1999, para 5.

[131] 'Situation of Human Rights in East Timor, Note by the Secretary-General', UN Doc. A/54/660, 10 December 1999, paras 26–8.P Burgess, 'Justice and Reconciliation in East Timor. The Relationship between the Commission for Reception, Truth and Reconciliation and the Courts', 15 *CLF* (2004) 135, 179.

[132] 'Agreement between the Republic of Indonesia and the Portuguese Republic on the Question of East Timor', 5 May 1999, New York, Art. 3; full text available on <http://www.un.int/portugal/acordos.htm>

[133] Eg, the case of SPSL *Prosecutor v Domingos De Deus,* 2 a/2004, 12 April 2004.

[134] M Othman, 'East Timor: A Critique of the Model of Accountability for Serious Human Rights and International Humanitarian Law Violations', 72 *Nordic Journal of International Law* (2003) 449.

[135] Ibid.

[136] Relevant are especially UNTAET Regulation 1999/3, 2000/11, 2000/15, and 2000/30.

[137] Section 7 of the UNTAET Regulation 2000/14.

[138] Section 10.1 of the UNTAET Regulation 2000/11.

was given exclusive rights and jurisdiction over serious crimes—genocide, war crimes, crimes against humanity, murder, sexual offences, and torture committed between 1 January 1999 and 25 October 1999.[139] Thereafter, the Special Panels for Serious Crime (SPSC) for East Timor were established in the Dili District Court.[140]

The Panels were composed of three judges, two international and one East Timorese.[141] The Transitional Administrator upon recommendation by the Transitional Judicial Service Commission appointed the judges and prosecutors.[142] The foundation of a court of appeal was stipulated.[143]

The SPSC were required to apply the law as set out by UNTAET Regulations and Indonesian Law, which did not conflict with the former, UN Security Council Resolution 1272 and internationally recognized standards on human rights.[144]

3. Procedural issues discussed at the SPSC

The SPSC ruled on several procedural issues. They held that hearsay evidence was generally admissible and referred to the ICTR case against Akayesu as a relevant authority.[145] There was some discussion in the SPSC regarding the admissibility of accused pre-trial statements. It was argued that 'admitting the statement would amount to a violation of the right to silence of the accused'.[146] However, some judges held against the discretion given to the Panels to determine the relevance and reliability of the previous statement.[147]

In *Ena et al.*, the court discussed the problem to call a co-accused as a witness.[148] The defence brought up a motion to call *Umbertus Ena*, a co-accused in the same trial, as a witness for the defence of *Carlos Ena*. This of course is problematic with a view to the right of the accused not to incriminate him or herself, if being cross-examined.[149]

---

[139] Sections 7.3 and 10.1 of the UNTAET Regulation 2000/11.

[140] *See* S Bertodano, 'Current Developments in Internationalized Courts', 2 *JICJ* (2004) 910.

[141] Section 22 of the UNTAET Regulation 2000/15.

[142] Sections 1, 10, and 11.1 of the UNTEAT Regulation 1999/3.

[143] Section 7.2 of the UNTAET Regulation 2000/11.

[144] Sections 2 and 3.1 of the UNTAET Regulation 1999/1.

[145] SPSC *Prosecutor v Jose Cardoso*, 4/2001, 5 April 2003, para 296.

[146] 'Digest of the Jurisprudence of the Special Panels for Serious Crimes', Judicial System Monitoring Programme, Dili, Timor L'este, April 2007, p 51.

[147] Ibid; Section 24 of the UNTAET Regulation 2000/30 on Transitional Rules of Criminal Procedure.

[148] SPSC *Prosecutor v Umbertus Ena and Carlos Ena*, 5/2002, 4 December 2003; Final Judgment: SPSL Dili, East Timor, *Prosecutor v Umbertus Ena and Carlos Ena*, 2/2002, 23 March 2003: the former was found guilty of crimes against humanity, other inhumane acts; the latter was found not guilty.

[149] Section 35.4 of the UNTAET Regulation 2000/30.

The Dili District Court finally ruled against the defence motion based on the argument that 'one being a witness of the other would mean that the accused is asked to testify on the facts he is himself charged'.[150] Furthermore, the court states that 'there is no need for the accused to testify on the facts he himself and his co-accused are charged'.[151] The court argued that the protection of the rights of the accused outweighed the status of becoming a witness.[152] In addition, the Transitional Rules of Criminal Procedure do not contain a provision of the accused becoming a witness himself. The defendant is only entitled to address any relevant issue during the proceedings and to give an unsworn statement.[153] The accused is always permitted to make a statement on his or her own behalf during the case, which is then admitted into evidence; the same shall be possible for the co-accused on behalf of the other co-accused.[154]

4. *Critique of the East Timorese model*

One serious problem with the hybrid system in East Timor was the non-functional Court of Appeal. Unfortunately, since the end of 2001 until June 2003 'suspects have been effectively denied access to the right to appeal'.[155] The SPSL was also confronted with the unavailability of the main perpetrators.[156] Most have retained their residence in Indonesia, where they did not fear prosecution, and the lack of cooperation from Indonesia complicated the criminal prosecution even further.[157] This applies especially to high-ranking Indonesian officials such as *Wiranto*.[158] Another problem was the long pre-trial detention, with suspects detained for up to three years.[159]

---

150 SPSC *Prosecutor v Umbertus Ena and Carlos Ena*, 5/2002, 4 December 2003, para 10.

151 Ibid, para 10.

152 Ibid, para 11.

153 Sections 30.7 and 33.1 of the Regulation No. 2000/30.

154 SPSC *Prosecutor v Umbertus Ena and Carlos Ena*, 5/2002, 4 December 2003, para 11.

155 'Situation of Human Rights in Timor-Leste—Report of the United Nations High Commissioner for Human Rights', E/CN.4/2003/37, 4 March 2003, para 6; full text <http://daccess-dds-ny.un.org/doc/UNDOC/GEN/G03/114/48/PDF/G0311448.pdf?OpenElement>; M Hirst and H Varney, 'Justice Abandoned? An Assessment of the Serious Crimes Process in East Timor', *International Centre for Transitional Justice* (June 2005) 1, 9, <http://es.ictj.org/images/content/1/2/121.pdf>.

156 'Digest of the Jurisprudence of the Special Panels for Serious Crimes', Judicial System Monitoring Programme, Dili, Timor L'este, April 2007, p 14.

157 P Burgess, 'Justice and Reconciliation in East Timor. The Relationship between the Commission for Reception, Truth and Reconciliation and the Courts', 15 *CLF* (2004) 135, 140; M Hirst and H Varney, 'Justice Abandoned? An Assessment of the Serious Crimes Process in East Timor', *International Centre for Transitional Justice* (June 2005) 1, 16,

158 *See* for further information on the Wiranto case: M Hirst and H Varney, 'Justice Abandoned? An Assessment of the Serious Crimes Process in East Timor', International Centre for Transitional Justice (June 2005) 1, 9–11.

159 'Digest of the Jurisprudence of the Special Panels for Serious Crimes', Judicial System Monitoring Programme, Dili, Timor L'este, April 2007, p 23.

Another problem has been the inefficient funding. The East Timorese judges were inexperienced and had no administrative staff appointed to them,[160] the public defenders handled crimes against humanity cases and were ill-equipped to deal with these cases.[161] All in all, the SPSC in the Dili District convicted ninety four accused and acquitted three.[162] The Panels were able 'to issue indictments in respect of 572 of the approximately 1400 murders committed in 1999'.[163]

X. Extraordinary Chambers in the Court of Cambodia

Since the Khmer Rouge (KR) came to power in 1975, *Pol Pot's* mechanism to consolidate his position was simple: eliminate the middle-class and any other possible opposition. The first step in this strategy was the notorious forced eviction that came into effect soon after the KR's victory over the previous regime. The population was forced to leave the cities and was reorganized into cooperatives in the countryside.[164] This measure was undertaken based on the division of the population into two groups: the 'old people' and the 'new people'. The 'old people' were those who had lived in the KR-controlled territories prior to the forced evacuation in 1975. Most of the 'new people' had lived in the cities. Many were educated people such as teachers, doctors, police officers, or former government officials. They were considered to be the middle-class and needed to be 'reformed' by making them part of the peasant class. This 'reform' was enacted by forcing them to engage in manual labour, mainly farming and construction work at the cooperatives, in inhumane conditions.[165]

The other part of the strategy was the elimination of any possible opposition to the regime. This was undertaken through extensive efforts to locate and purge traitors. Therefore the leading clique of the Khmer Rouge, the *Angkar*, established a prison system throughout the country. In these prisons, people were tortured until they disclosed other 'traitors' to the satisfaction of the prison chiefs, composing a list that would be used as the basis for further arrests. Since providing names would be the only means to end the torture, there was always a new list provided by each new inmate. The people on this list would be arrested, and in turn they too would

[160] M Hirst and H Varney, 'Justice Abandoned? An Assessment of the Serious Crimes Process in East Timor', *International Centre for Transitional Justice* (June 2005) 1, 21, 27; 'Digest of the Jurisprudence of the Special Panels for Serious Crimes', Judicial System Monitoring Programme, Dili, Timor L'este, April 2007, p 15.

[161] M Othman, 'East Timor: A Critique of the Model of Accountability for Serious Human Rights and International Humanitarian Law Violations', 72 *Nordic Journal of International Law* (2003) 449, 464; 'Digest of the Jurisprudence of the Special Panels for Serious Crimes', Judicial System Monitoring Programme, Dili, Timor L'este, April 2007, p 15.

[162] 'Digest of the Jurisprudence of the Special Panels for Serious Crimes', Judicial System Monitoring Programme, Dili, Timor L'este, April 2007, p 14.

[163] Ibid, p 13.

[164] Human Rights Center, *So We Will Never Forget* (University of California 2009) 13.

[165] Ibid, p 14.

accuse others. The cruel cycle, combined with the forced labour in the countryside and malnutrition, resulted in the death of at least 1.7 million (which amounted to approximately one-quarter of the Cambodian population at the time).[166]

1. *Establishing the ECCC*

After several years of border wars, the Vietnamese troops ended the regime of the Khmer Rouge on 6 January 1979 by occupying the capital city, Phnom Penh. The occupying forces of Vietnam decided to seek the accountability for the crimes committed during the KR period by organizing a tribunal against the KR leaders.[167] Although this was the first attempt to bring justice to the Cambodian and the Vietnamese people, the trials lacked constitutional legality. Despite this, the most senior leaders of the KR, Pol Pot and Ieng Sary, were tried and found guilty *in absentia* after a few days of trial.[168]

These trials failed to bring about peace in Cambodia and the conflict continued for almost two more decades. As a part of the effort to end the prolonged conflict, in the 1990s the United Nations proposed an international tribunal to try the most senior leaders of the KR.[169] After years of negotiation, the talks between the UN and the Cambodian government were close to failure. The Cambodian government was willing to try the most senior leaders again, but only in the national courts, referring to the responsibility stemming from the Genocide Convention.[170] Moreover, the Cambodian government was suspicious about the UN because they were aware of the fact that the UN was supporting KR even long after Cambodia had been 'liberated' from the KR by Vietnam.[171] The United Nations, on the other side, wanted to ensure an impartial court and were concerned about the legality, impartiality, and quality of a national court.[172]

In 2003 negotiations between the government of Cambodia and the United Nations finally came to an end. An agreement was signed to establish a tribunal named the Extraordinary Chambers in the Court of Cambodia (ECCC) with

---

166 Ibid, p 14.

167 *See* F Selbmann and D Wesemann, 'Der Pol Pot-Ieng Sary-Prozess revisited—Anmerkung zum Prozess gegen führende Rote Khmer im Jahr 1979', 4 *ZIS* (2010) 116.

168 About trials *in absentia*, *see* R Skilbeck, 'Frankenstein's Monster: Creating a New International Procedure', 8 *JICJ* (2010) 459.

169 *See* C Safferling, P Graebke, F Hansen, and S Hörmann, 'Das Monitoring-Projekt des Forschungs- und Dokumentationszentrums für Kriegsverbrecherprozesse (ICWC), Marburg', 5 *ZIS* (2011) 566.

170 *See* C Etcheson, *The Extraordinary Chambers* (A publication of the Open Society Justice Initiative 2006) 10.

171 Y Chang, 'The Thief of History—Cambodia and the Special Court', 1 *International Journal of Transitional Justice* (2007) 161.

172 *See* C Etcheson, *The Extraordinary Chambers* (A publication of the Open Society Justice Initiative 2006) 10.

the mandate to try the senior leader and those most responsible for the crimes committed during the KR between 17 April 1975 and 6 January 1979.

2. *The code of procedure*

The legal basis of the ECCC is the agreement between the parties, the law on the establishment of the extraordinary Chambers in the Court of Cambodia (ECCC Law), and the Internal Rules (IRs).[173]

The agreement between the UN and Cambodia stipulates a hybrid court[174] within the court system of Cambodia,[175] which is based in Phnom Penh. Although its status is that of a national court, it is hybrid in nature because each component of the Court is comprised of national and international staff, who retain equal rights at every level. This includes the chambers, which consist of both international and national judges. Although the majority of the judges are Cambodian, the mechanism of *supermajority* ensures that at least one of the international judges has to support the chambers' decision.[176]

According to the ECCC Law the Tribunal has jurisdiction over crimes committed by the senior leaders of the KR during the KR period from 17 April 1975 to 6 January 1979.[177] The punishable crimes taken from the Cambodian Penal Code are homicide, torture, and religious persecution.[178] Also included in the jurisdiction of the Court are genocide, crimes against humanity, grave breaches of the Geneva Conventions of 12 August 1949, destruction of cultural property during armed conflict pursuant to the 1954 The Hague Convention for Protection of Cultural Property in the Event of Armed Conflict, and crimes against internationally protected persons pursuant to the Vienna Convention of 1961.[179]

---

173 About the IRs *see* G Acquaviva, 'New Paths in International Criminal Justice? The Internal Rules of the Cambodian Extraordinary Chambers', 6 *JICJ* (2008) 129 *et subs.*; S Starygin, 'Internal Rules of the Extraordinary Chambers in the Courts of Cambodia (ECCC): Setting an Example of the Rule of Law by Breaking the Law?', 3 *Journal of Law and Conflict Resolution* (2011) 21; G Sluiter, 'Due Process and Criminal Procedure in the Cambodian Extraordinary Chambers', 4 *JICJ* (2006), 314 *et subs.*

174 E Meijer, 'The Extraordinary Chambers In the Courts of Cambodia', in: C Romano, A Nollkaemper, and J Kleffner (eds), *Internationalized Criminal Courts* (OUP 2004) 204; F Mégret, 'In Defence of Hybridity: Towards a Representational Theory of International Criminal Justice', 38 *Cornell International Law Journal* (2005) 725; *see* also S Schulz, *Transitional Justice und hybride Gerichte* (Lit 2009) 99 *et subs.*

175 Art. 2 Law on the Establishment of the Extraordinary Chambers.

176 *See* M Bohlander and R Winter, 'Internationalisierte Strafgerichte auf nationaler Ebene—Kosovo, Kambodscha, Sierra Leone und Timor-Leste', in: S Kirsch (ed), *Internationale Strafgerichtshöfe* (Nomos 2005) 261; C Etcheson, *The Extraordinary Chambers* (A publication of the Open Society Justice Initiative 2006) 7; S Bertodano, 'Problems Arising from the Mixed Composition and Structure of the Cambodian Extraordinary Chambers', 4 *JICJ* (2006) 289.

177 Art. 2 Law on the Establishment of the Extraordinary Chambers.

178 Art. 3 Law on the Establishment of the Extraordinary Chambers.

179 Art. 4 *et subs.* Law on the Establishment of the Extraordinary Chambers; *See* also J Aßmann, 'The Challenges of Genocide Trials: "The Cambodian Situation", in: C Safferling and E Conze (eds), *The Genocide Convention 60 Years after its Adoption* (Asser 2010) 183.

The rules of procedure and evidence are laid down in the IRs which are divided into a part about provisions (rules 1–3), a part about the organization of the court (rules 4–20), and a part about the procedures (rules 21–114).

3. *The trial procedures*

The ECCC is the first international court which uses investigating judges and a primarily civil law-based court system.[180] The decision to launch an investigation for criminal prosecution, however, lies in the hands of the Co-Prosecutors. According to Rule 49 (1) the 'Prosecution of crimes within the jurisdiction of the ECCC may be initiated only by the Co-Prosecutors, whether at their own discretion or on the basis of a complaint.'

Should a decision be made to initiate a prosecution of crimes, the Co-Prosecutors shall file an introductory submission according to Rule 53 (1) IRs. After receiving the introductory submission, the Co-Investigating Judges shall investigate the facts mentioned in the submission (Rule 55 (2)), and based on their investigation they shall compose a closing order. The closing order serves as the indictment.

During the trial phase, the parties to the proceedings are not limited to the ones usually found in other international tribunals, namely the Prosecution and the defence,[181] but also civil parties who, in the tradition of the Cambodian Code of Criminal Procedure (Cambodian CPC), are equipped with extensive rights.

According to Rule 23*bis* IRs any person who can demonstrate that they suffered physical, material, or psychological injury caused as a direct consequence of at least one of the crimes alleged against the charged person, is considered as a victim and may participate in the proceedings as a civil party.[182] The purpose of the civil party action is on the one hand to participate in the criminal proceedings against those responsible for the crimes within the jurisdiction of the ECCC, while on the other to enable them to seek reparation, albeit in limited form, for their suffering.

Victim participation as a civil party to a case is further defined in the IRs as 'supporting the prosecution'.[183] During the first trial of the ECCC, namely of defendant

[180] About the differences between a civil law based court system and an adversarial-based court system, *see* section 1.B.

[181] About the organs, main actors, and proceedings *see* G Acquaviva, 'New Paths in International Criminal Justice? The Internal Rules of the Cambodian Extraordinary Chambers', 6 *JICJ* (2008) 129.

[182] Critical about civil party participation at the ECCC *see* M Mohan, 'The Paradox of Victim-Centrism: Victim Participation at the Khmer Rouge Tribunal', 9 *ICLR* (2009) 733. A more positive view is held by S Studzinsky, 'Nebenklage vor den Extraordinary Chambers of Cambodia (ECCC)—Herausforderung und Chance oder mission impossible?', 4 *ZIS* (2009) 43; and E Hoven, 'Opfer im Völkerstrafrecht—Probleme der Nebenklägerbeteiligung am Rote-Khmer-Tribunal, 122 *ZStW* (2010) 706.

[183] *See* Rule 23 IRs.

Kaing Guek Eav (alias Duch), questions on the extent of the civil party's participation had to be addressed in an extensive manner as there had been no prior jurisprudence in the Court that could clarify the civil party's role.[184]

The first question arose during the pre-trial stage of the case, on the matter of whether the civil parties were allowed to give submissions against the charged person's appeal against pre-trial detention. In its decision the Pre-Trial Chamber noted that according to Art. 12 of the ECCC Agreement, the Pre-Trial Chamber was obliged to refer to the Cambodian CPC for guidance when deciding matters that are not regulated in the IRs.[185] In the case the relevant Cambodian CPC rule is consistent with international standards, the pre-trial chamber has to take the said stipulation into consideration. Following this rationale, the Pre-Trial Chamber compared the Cambodian CPC with the international standards formed by the UN Victims Declaration, the ICC Statute, the Transitional Rules of Criminal Procedure of East Timor, and the Criminal Procedure Code of Kosovo, and concluded that the relevant articles of the Cambodian CPC are in accordance with the international standards.[186] Therefore the Pre-Trial Chamber read Art. 23 IRs in the light of the relevant articles of the CPC and decided that the civil party's right to participate in all stages of the proceeding also imply that they were allowed to participate in the pre-trial proceedings.[187] Furthermore, the Chamber also concluded that unlike the stipulations in the ICC statute, the civil parties in the ECCC were not obliged to prove their special interest as the requirement for their participation in the pre-trial proceedings.

A final evaluation of the ECCC is not possible to give at this time. However, according to the intensive political influence by the Cambodia government and a general mistrust of the public in court proceedings it remains doubtful whether the few trials will help the Cambodian society to come to terms with the Khmer Rouge past.[188] Several international jurists working for the ECCC have left rather frustrated. From a procedural point of view the exorbitant participatory rights of

[184] M Kelsall *et al.*, 'Lessons Learned from the "Duch" Trial, A Comprehensive Review of the First Case before the Extraordinary Chambers in the Courts of Cambodia', A report produced by the Asian International Justice Initiative's KRT Trial Monitoring Group, 2009; available at <http://www.ocf.berkeley.edu/~changmin/documents/Lessons%20Learned%20from%20the%20Duch%20Trial_MRSK_FINAL.pdf>; about the role of the civil parties *see* also K Gibson and D Rudy, 'A New Model of International Criminal Procedure? The Progress of the Duch Trial at the ECCC', 7 *JICJ* 2009, 1014.

[185] ECCC *Prosecutor v Nuon Chea et al.*, Case File/Dossier No. 002/19–09-2007/ECCC/OCIJ (PTC01), 20 March 2008, decision, para 39.

[186] Ibid, para 40.

[187] Ibid, para 49; dismissive: C Safferling, Amicus Curiae, *Prosecutor v Nuon Chea et al.*, Case File/Dossier No. 002/19–09-2007/ECCC/OCIJ(PTC01), 22 February 2008; available at <http://www.eccc.gov.kh/sites/default/files/documents/courtdoc/Amicus_Christoph_Safferling_C11_39_EN.pdf>.

[188] A more positive view is given by P Kroker, 'Auf gutem Weg: Die Verfahren vor dem Rote-Khmer-Tribunal in Kamodscha', 122 *ZStW* (2010) 685.

victims as civil parties remain one of the greatest challenges for the ECCC. In any case, the quantity of the participating civil parties alone threatens to blast the procedural framework of the ECCC.

XI. Special Tribunal for Lebanon

1. Background

Between 1975 and 1990 approximately 120,000 people died during the civil war in Lebanon. Among others, militias were involved in the fighting reflecting the various confessions in Lebanon.[189] During the civil war, France, Italy, the UK, the Syrian Arab Republic, the USA, and several other states sent forces to Lebanon at the request of its government.[190] In the 1970s further tensions started to arise between Lebanon and Israel when several Palestinians relocated as refugees from Jordan to Lebanon after the events of Black September in Jordan.[191] On 11 March 1978 Israel was attacked by the Palestinian Liberation Organization (PLO). Subsequently, Israel invaded on the night of 14 March, and took control of vast southern parts of Lebanon. The Security Council adopted several resolutions, which were designed to stop Israel from continuing its armed invasion, and put pressure on it to withdraw its forces.[192] In the 1980s the conflict warmed up and Israel invaded for a second time and kept southern parts of Lebanon under control until 2000 when it withdrew its forces. As a reaction to the Israeli invasion, a resistance group, Hezbollah, arose in the early 1980s, which declared an armed struggle to end the occupation of Lebanese territory by Israel. This group remains the most influential and powerful militia in Lebanon.[193]

The Syrian military was present in Lebanon from May 1976, with the consent of the Lebanese Government.[194] When Israel finally withdrew its forces in 2000, the opposition in Lebanon demanded a withdrawal of Syrian forces and supported the implementation of the Taif Agreement of 1989, which would result in reducing the presence of Syrian forces.

After a resolution of the UN Security Council, Syria had to withdraw its forces from Lebanon.[195] In the same resolution the Security Council expressed its concern about the lasting presence of militia in Lebanon and 'call[ed] for the

[189] Report of the Secretary-General pursuant to SC Res. 1559 (2004), S/2004/777, 1 October 2004, p 1.

[190] Ibid.

[191] UNHCR, Survey Report on the Situation of Non-ID Palestinian Refugees in Lebanon, (Beirut, September 2007) 5, available at <http://www.unhcr.org/refworld/pdfid/47fdfad80.pdf>.

[192] Res. 425 (1978) and 426 (1978).

[193] Report of the Secretary-General pursuant to SC Res. 1559 (2004), S/2004/777, 1 October 2004, p 5.

[194] Report of the International Independent Investigation Commission established pursuant to SC Res. 1595 (2005), p 5; available at <http://www.un.org/News/dh/docs/mehlisreport/>.

[195] UN SC Res. 1559 of 2 September 2004.

disbanding and disarmament of all Lebanese and non-Lebanese militias'.[196] The former Lebanese Prime Minister Rafiq Hariri played a key role in the adoption of this resolution.[197] On 14 February 2005, his motorcade passed a hotel in Beirut. Explosives were activated which killed the former Prime Minister and twenty two other people.[198] After the assassination, Lebanon was in need of a judicial authority, which would conduct the investigation and the following criminal proceedings.

2. The Special Tribunal for Lebanon

The Government of Lebanon tried to craft an agreement with the UN Secretary-General regarding the establishment of the Special Tribunal for Lebanon (STL),[199] which was similar to the agreement with Sierra Leone.[200] However, the Lebanese Parliament refused to ratify the agreement as required under Art. 52 of the Lebanese Constitution. Therefore the Security Council adopted Resolution 1757 (2007) under Chapter VII of the UN Charter and thereby set the Statute into force as of 10 June 2007.[201] The UN Resolution remains the primary legal basis of the Tribunal.[202]

The STL 'is unique in that it is the first international tribunal with subject-matter jurisdiction extending only to criminal offences defined by reference to domestic law'.[203] It has jurisdiction only over the terrorist attack that killed Rafiq Hariri; surprising, since there have been several other terrorist attacks and political assassinations in Lebanon.[204] The definition of terrorism in international criminal law was the first startling decision which gave rise to serious criticism.[205] According to Art. 1 STLSt, the jurisdiction can be extended with consent of the Security Council insofar as the parties of the Statute determine that other attacks between 1

196 Res. 1559 (2004).

197 N Shehadi and E Wilmshurst, 'The Special Tribunal for Lebanon: The UN on Trial?' Middle East/International Law Briefing Paper (Chatham House July 2007) 3–4.

198 C Aptel, 'Some Innovations in the Statute of the Special Tribunal for Lebanon', 5 *JICJ* (2007) 1107.

199 Pursuant to UN SC Res. 1664 (2006) of 29 March 2006.

200 N Shehadi and E Wilmshurst, 'The Special Tribunal for Lebanon: The UN on Trial?' Middle East/International Law Briefing Paper (Chatham House July 2007) 6.

201 UN SC Res. 1757 of 30 May 2007.

202 B Fassbender, 'Reflections on the International Legality of the Special Tribunal for Lebanon', 5 *JICJ* (2007) 1091, 1092.

203 International Law Middle East and North Africa Programmes, 'The Special Tribunal for Lebanon and the Quest for Truth Justice and Stability' (London, Meeting Report December 2010) 6.

204 C Aptel, 'Some Innovations in the Statute of the Special Tribunal for Lebanon', 5 *JICJ* (2007) 1107, 1109.

205 *See* M Gillett and M Schuster, 'Fast Track Justice. The Special Tribunal for Lebanon Defines Terrorism', 9 *JICJ* (2011) forthcoming; and S Kirsch and A Oehmichen, 'Judges Gone Astray: The Fabrication of Terrorism as an International Crime by the Special Tribunal for Lebanon', 1 *Durham Law Review* (2011) 32.

October 2002 and 12 December 2005 or later of similar gravity, such as the attack of 14 February 2005 which killed the former Prime Minister, should be investigated and prosecuted by the Special Tribunal.

In contrast to the ICC, the Tribunal has primacy over the domestic jurisdiction, pursuant to Art. 4 STLSt.[206] Notably, the Tribunal is not part of the regular court system of Lebanon as the ECCC in Cambodia is, and does not even reside on Lebanese territory but in Leidschendam, The Netherlands, with a field office in Beirut.[207]

The STL is composed mainly of international judges. At the pre-trial stage, the appointment[208] of an international judge is mandatory, according to Art. 8 (1) (a) STLSt. The Trial Chamber is assembled of two international and one national judges while the Appeals Chamber consists of two national and three international judges. This implies that the international judges dominate the Chambers of the Tribunal, even if they have to apply Lebanese law, pursuant to Art. 2 STLSt. Considering this composition, it is doubtful whether the STL is a hybrid court, as the international components clearly overshadow the national influence.[209]

3. *The Rules of Procedure and Evidence*

One important task for the judges of the Special Tribunal was the adoption of Rules of Procedure and Evidence, according to Art. 22 (1) STLSt. Its content was ideally thought to be a mixture of the Lebanese Code of Criminal Procedure and the Rules of Procedure and Evidence of other international criminal institutions reflecting 'the highest standards of international criminal procedure'.[210] In 2009, the developed Rules were adopted, and they have been amended subsequently several times.[211]

Learning from the experience of the UN *ad hoc* Tribunals, the STL is equipped with a Pre-Trial Judge, who is not part of a Chamber, Art. 8 (1) (a) STLSt. It is his or her duty to manage the case in the pre-trial phase, decide on jurisdictional issues,

---

[206] *See* section 2.C.

[207] N Shehadi and E Wilmshurst, 'The Special Tribunal for Lebanon: The UN on Trial?' Middle East/International Law Briefing Paper (Chatham House July 2007) 7.

[208] The judges are appointed by the UN Secretary General and not elected, Art. 9 (3) STLSt.

[209] *See* also M Gillett and M Schuster, 'The Special Tribunal for Lebanon Swiftly Adopts its Rule for Procedure and Evidence', 7 *JICJ* (2009) 885, 887. In favour of the national character, *see* W Schabas, 'The Special Tribunal for Lebanon: Is a "Tribunal of an International Character" Equivalent to an "International Criminal Court"?', 21 *LJIL* (2008) 513, 523

[210] Rules of Procedure and Evidence, Explanatory Memorandum by the Tribunal's President, p 1.

[211] For a general overview *see* M Gillett and M Schuster, 'The Special Tribunal for Lebanon Swiftly Adopts its Rule for Procedure and Evidence', 7 *JICJ* (2009) 885.

review the indictment, and rule on pre-trial disclosure. He or she is thus a central figure of the proceedings.[212]

Of course, provisions on the protection of witnesses pose an important factor which had been left to the judges to determine according to Art. 28 (1) STLSt. The Statute requires the judges to uphold the 'highest standards' by adopting the Rules which must be comparable to international standards. However it might seem unsatisfactory to leave the witness protection to the judges.[213] One ought to be reassured by the fact that most judges are international judges, and thus familiar with the standards of international procedural law, and who will fulfil their duty by upholding them.

One characteristic of the Special Tribunal is the opportunity to hold a trial in the absence of the accused, pursuant to Art. 22 STLSt. This includes scenarios in which the accused has expressly and in writing waived his or her rights to be present at court, but it also applies in cases in which the accused has not been handed over to the tribunal by the state authorities concerned with the arrest, or is untraceable, according to Art. 22 (1) STLSt. These trials *in absentia* could be criticized as 'show trials'[214] since a fair trial can only be upheld in the presence of the accused, according to Art. 14 ICCPR or Art. 6 ECHR. However, since this is an exceptional rule, the accused has the right to be retried if no defence counsel chosen by the accused had been representing him or her at trial pursuant to Art. 22 (3) STLSt. One has to bear in mind that according to the Lebanese Criminal Procedure Law, trials *in absentia* are possible.[215] Thus as mentioned above, the Special Tribunal is required to apply Lebanese law and this implies the rule on proceedings *in absentia*.[216] Bearing in mind that until now, the accused are at-large, the Special Tribunal would be blocked without this procedural rule. There might be no trial at all if the Court would be denied the trial *in absentia*. In this way, at least 'partial' justice might be achieved through sentencing the accused *in absentia*.[217]

---

[212] *See* also M Gillett and M Schuster, 'The Special Tribunal for Lebanon Swiftly Adopts its Rule for Procedure and Evidence', 7 *JICJ* (2009) 885, 889.

[213] *See* C Aptel, 'Some Innovations in the Statute of the Special Tribunal for Lebanon', 5 *JICJ* (2007) 1107, 1121.

[214] N Shehadi and E Wilmshurst, 'The Special Tribunal for Lebanon: The UN on Trial?', Middle East/International Law Briefing Paper, (Chatham House July 2007) 12.

[215] *See* Lebanese Republic Judicial Council *Plaintiffs v Dr Samir Geagea et al.*, Judicial Council, 2/1999, Judgment in the case of Karami Attack, 25 June 1999, pp 140–2; available at <http:www.stl-tsl.org/x/file/TheRegistry/Library/BackgroundDocuments/RelevantLebanese-CaseLaw/250699_Omar_Karami_Decision_EN.pdf>.

[216] *See* M Gardner, 'Reconsidering Trials in Absentia at the Special Tribunal for Lebanon: An Application of the Tribunals Early Jurisprudence', *George Washington International Law Review* (forthcoming) 13; available at <http://ssrn.com/abstract=1904840>.

[217] Ibid, 33; available at <http://ssrn.com/abstract=1904840>.

The RPE STL allow for a Defence Office, similar to the SCSL, Rules 57–59 RPE STL. It is within the responsibility of the Head of Defence Office to appoint defence counsel and if the interests of justice so require, to assign defence counsel to a case.[218] The Head of Defence Office is granted similar status to the Prosecutor.[219]

In the beginning, some criticism has arisen *inter alia* regarding the detention practice of the Special Tribunal. Since 2005, four generals were detained but never charged. In 2009, the pre-trial judge finally decided to release the four detainees since there was no incriminating evidence against them which would have satisfied further detention.[220] After the detained generals were released, Syria issued thirty three arrest warrants for Lebanese and international officials including the German prosecutor who requested the arrest warrants against the generals in 2005. The officials were accused of 'allegedly misleading the UN-backed investigation into the assassination of Lebanon's former Prime Minister Rafik Hariri'.[221]

In 2011, the Special Tribunal made public the identities of four accused.[222] They are all Lebanese citizens with a clear link to Hezbollah. The accused have been charged with conspiracy, committing an act of terrorism, intentional homicide, and attempted homicide, as either main perpetrators or accomplices.[223] One of the accused has already been convicted for terrorist acts in Kuwait in 1983, where he escaped from prison in 1990.[224] All accused remain at large.

XII. The ICC: the ultimate benchmark

The establishment of the two *ad hoc* Tribunals in 1993 and 1994 respectively motivated those who had always been in favour of a permanent criminal court, and it somehow defused the general political resistance against such an institution demonstrated by many, albeit not all, states. The topic was on the agenda of the highest international organs. The time seemed ripe to undertake a new attempt to create an international criminal court.[225]

---

218 M Gillett and M Schuster, 'The Special Tribunal for Lebanon Swiftly Adopts its Rule for Procedure and Evidence', 7 *JICJ* (2009) 885, 890 *et subs.*

219 Report of the Secretary-General on the Establishment of a Special Tribunal for Lebanon, UN Doc. S/2006/893, 15 November 2006, para 30.

220 STL *Prosecutor v Messrs Jamil Mohamad Amin El Sayed et al.,* PTJ, CH/PTJ/2009/06, 29 April 2009, pp 8–15.

221 J Muir, 'Rafik Hariri Inquiry: Syria Issues 33 Arrest Warrants', *BBC*, 4 October 2010, available at <http://www.bbc.co.uk/news/world-middle-east-11470051>.

222 *See* <http:www.stl-tsl.org/action/home>; <http://edition.cnn.com/2011/WORLD/meast/08/17/lebanon.hariri/index.html?iref=allsearch>.

223 *See* <http:www.stl-tsl.org/action/home>.

224 STL *Prosecutor v Mustafa Amine Badreddine*, PTJ, Arrest warrant, STL-11-01/I, 28 June 2011, p 3.

225 As to the drafting of the Rome Statute, *see* also P Kirsch and V Oosterveld, 'Negotiating an Institution for the Twenty-First Century: Multilateral Diplomacy and the International Criminal Court', 46 *McGill Law Journal* (2001) 1141.

1. The road to Rome

Joining the draft statute of the ILC, the General Assembly of the UN established a Preparatory Committee on the Establishment of an International Criminal Court (PrepComm) in 1996.[226] After only two years, the PrepComm furnished a comprehensive draft statute to be discussed at the Diplomatic Conference at Rome from 15 June to 17 July 1998.

The stakes were high. The procedural law of the court to be created was not at the centre of discussion. The primary issues were the jurisdictional scope of the court, the crimes, and the prosecutorial powers of the prosecutor. Some states, the group of so-called 'like-minded' states, favoured a rather narrow solution, focusing on the 'Nuremberg experience' and limiting the jurisdiction *ratione materiae* to genocide, crimes against humanity, war crimes, and the crime of aggression. Others, like the USA, Russia, and China, were heavily opposed to the inclusion of the crimes of aggression. Some states wanted to include drug trafficking and terrorism within the definition of international crimes.

Regarding the powers of the prosecutor, the like-minded states opted for an independent prosecutor, who would have *ex officio* powers to investigate, whereas others, again mainly the permanent members of the Security Council, USA, Russia, and China, preferred a prosecutor whose authority derived from the UN Security Council.

One important factor in the drafting history of the Rome Statute was the inclusion of civil society actors in the PrepComm and the Rome Conference.[227] Their influence, backed by the moral authority of some former Nuremberg prosecutors including Whitney R Harris, Ben Ferencz, and Henry T King, is not to be underestimated.[228] The presence of different NGOs also prompted an attempt to embrace a holistic approach, which would do justice to victims, as well as consider gender-related issues.[229]

Germany, one of the like-minded states and presenting itself with a large delegation full of deeply experienced people, was expected to act as mediator in several instances. Not least because of its Nuremberg history, a great amount of reliability and sincerity was attributed to Germany by other states. For many

---

226 A Cassese, *International Criminal Law* (2nd edn, OUP 2008) 329.

227 In general: Z Pearson, 'Non-Governmental Organizations and the International Criminal Court: Changing Landscapes of International Law', 39 *Cornell International Law Journal* (2006) 243. Critical as to this 'new form of diplomacy': A Paulus, 'Legalist Groundwork for the International Criminal Court: Commentaries on the Statute of the International Criminal Court', 14 *EJIL* (2003) 843, 848 *et subs.*

228 *See* the personal remarks of the later ICC Judge H-P Kaul, 'Begegnungen mit Whitney Harris', in: W Harris, Tyrannen vor Gericht (BWV 2009) V *et subs.*

229 P Kirsch and V Oosterveld, 'Negotiating an Institution for the Twenty-First Century: Multilateral Diplomacy and the International Criminal Court', 46 *McGill Law Journal* (2001) 1141, 1150.

decades Germany did not accept the Nuremberg trial and would not incorporate the Nuremberg principles into its own law. It was only after German unification and a change in generation that German politics and society started to appreciate the 'Nuremberg process' and adopted a positive view on international criminal law.[230]

On 17 July 1998 the Rome Statute was adopted by 120 votes to seven (USA, Libya, Israel, Iraq, China, Syria, Sudan) with twenty abstentions. The Rome Statute entered into force on 1 July 2002 after the 60th instrument of ratification was deposited with the UN Secretary-General according to Art. 126 (1) ICCSt. To date, the Rome Statute has 114 member states,[231] an extremely high number, even if some of the most powerful and influential states, like the USA, Russia, China, Israel, and most North African States, are still outside the ICC's jurisdiction.

From 4 to 7 February 2003, the Assembly of States Parties (ASP) elected eighteen judges, so that the ICC could start working on 11 March 2003. On 21 April 2003 the Argentinean lawyer the ASP elected Luis Moreno Ocampo as Prosecutor. In the spring of 2003, the ICC was fully operational.

2. *The Rome Statute and the completion of the procedural framework*

The Rome Statute consists of 128 articles and is thus considerably more detailed compared to any previous statute or charter. But as the Statute comprises also the definition of the international crimes (Part II), general principles of criminal law (Part III), penalties (Part VII), and the financing (Part XII), criminal procedure is only regulated in a rudimentary way. This statutory framework had to be filled in by Rules of Procedure and Evidence (RPE). In contrast to the *ad hoc* Tribunals, these RPE are to be adopted by a two-thirds majority of the members of the Assembly of States Parties pursuant to Art. 51 ICCSt. This provision addresses the qualms regarding the principle of separation of powers, which were raised against the *ad hoc* Tribunals, but at the same time it diminishes the flexibility of the law-making process. As a compromise the judges may adopt provisional Rules in cases of urgency until the Assembly of States Parties adopts or rejects the provisional Rule according to Art. 51 (3) ICCSt.

Together with the Final Act of the Rome Conference[232] a Preparatory Commission (PrepComm) was established to submit proposals for practical arrangements for the establishment of the Court, including draft texts of *inter alia* Rules of Procedure

---

[230] *See* C Safferling, 'German Participation in the Nuremberg Trials and its Implications for Today', in: B Griech-Polelle (ed), *The Nuremberg War Crimes Trial and Its Policy Consequences for Today* (Nomos 2009) 33.

[231] As of August 2011.

[232] Final Act Resolution F, UN Doc. A/CONF.183/10 (1998).

and Evidence. The draft, which was submitted to the ASP on 2 November 2000,[233] was adopted by the ASP in its first session, which took place from 3 to 10 September 2002 in New York. The RPE ICC comprise 225 Rules, which aim to fill the gaps of the Statute.

The practical operational questions of the routine functioning of the Court are to be solved by so-called Regulations according to Art. 52 ICCSt. The judges adopt these Regulations (RegC) after consultation with the Prosecutor and the Registry. The States Parties exercise a certain control; they can outvote the Regulations as adopted by the judges by a majority vote according to Art. 52 (3) ICCSt. The Regulations were adopted by the judges of the Court on 26 May 2004 at their Fifth Plenary Session in The Hague.[234] Despite their lower-ranking nature, the Regulations have at some points developed into rather fundamental rules stretching far beyond the 'routine functioning' of the Court, as will be seen in the course of this study.[235]

Similarly, the Office of the Prosecutor (OTP) has adopted Regulations (RegP) pursuant to Art. 42 (2) ICCSt and Rule 9 RPE ICC, which entered into force on 23 April 2009,[236] and the Registry adopted its Regulations (RegR) pursuant to Art. 43 (2) ICCSt and Rule 14 RPE ICC, which entered into force on 6 March 2006.[237]

This completes the basic procedural texts of the ICC. Art. 21 ICCSt contains these, in hierarchy, as follows:

- the Statute of the Court;
- the Rules of Procedure and Evidence;
- the Regulations of the Court;
- the Regulations of the Office of the Prosecutor;
- the Regulations of the Registry.

Despite these extensive legal texts, and their 'unprecedented complexity',[238] they present a rather rough sketch of the procedural order of the ICC. In many regards these texts need to be completed. The term 'constructive ambiguity' has been used for describing the procedural texts of the ICC.[239] This means three things:

---

233 PCNICC/2000/1/Add.1.

234 Official documents of the ICC, ICC-BD/01–01-04.

235 *See* also Boas/Bischoff/Reid/Taylor, *ICL III*, 7

236 Regulations of the Office of the Prosecutor, ICC-BD/05–01-09.

237 The Regulation of the Registry was revised on 25 September 2006 and is available in its consolidated form as Official document of the ICC, ICC-BD/01–03-06/Rev. 1.

238 C Kreß, 'The Procedural Texts of the International Criminal Court', 5 *JICJ* (2007) 537. This term says more about the simple structure of the ICC predecessors than about the sufficiency of the ICC rules.

239 *See* C Kreß, 'The Procedural Law of the International Criminal Court in Outline: Anatomy of a Unique Compromise', 1 *JICJ* (2003), 603, 605 *et subs.*; *see* also D Hunt, 'The International Criminal Court', 2 *JICJ* (2004) 56, 58 who speaks of 'creative ambiguity'.

(1) The legal texts are the result of multilateral negotiations and thus are the result of some extensive compromises.[240]
(2) The terms used do not have the same meaning as they might have in a domestic system. The texts need to be interpreted 'autonomously'.
(3) Sometimes the drafters knowingly avoided establishing a clear structure, thus referring the question of how to solve procedural issues more often than not to the Court, ie the judges.

Several consequences follow for the interpretation and implementation of these procedural texts.

(1) The necessity to deploy a dynamic and sometimes creative interpretation.
(2) The necessity to reach clarity in the basic parameters of criminal procedure.
(3) The system depends heavily on the authority, and thus also the quality, of the judges.

The methodological idiosyncrasies of international criminal procedure will be dealt with in a separate part of this study.[241] For now, suffice it to say that the drafters of the Rome Statute, the Rules of Procedure and Evidence, and the different Regulations crafted a rudimentary framework, which needs to be developed to gain a complete and concise international criminal procedural order. Much will depend on the work of the judges.[242]

3. *The structure of the ICC according to the Rome Statute*

a. The institutional background The ICC is an international organization in its own right, vested with legal subjectivity under international law according to Art. 4 (1) ICCSt. Other than the ICJ or the *ad hoc* Tribunals, the ICC is a treaty-based organization and as such, institutionally independent from the UN. Despite this, the ICC has a special relationship to the UN as envisaged by Art. 2 ICCSt. The Rome Statute envisages several specific rights and duties by the UN. The general relationship between the UN and the Court, however, is laid down in the 'Relationship Agreement between the International Criminal Court and the United Nations'.[243]

As a treaty body, the ICC depends upon the consensus of states according to general public international law.[244] The competences of the ICC thus depend on the membership of states. The ICC therefore is not a 'world court' (yet). One hundred

[240] P Kirsch and V Oosterveld, 'Negotiating an Institution for the Twenty-First Century: Multilateral Diplomacy and the International Criminal Court', 46 *McGill Law Journal* (2001) 1141, 1153.

[241] *See* section 3.C.III.

[242] D Hunt, 'The International Criminal Court', 2 *JICJ* (2004) 56, 58.

[243] ICC-ASP/3/Res.1.

[244] *See* generally A Verdross and B Simma, *Universelles Völkerrecht* (4th edn, Duncker and Humblot 1984) para 77.

and fourteen Member States is an impressive number, but global consent has not yet been attained. As a consequence, the jurisdiction and powers of the Court are complex. We will look at this in the next chapter.[245]

The international organization 'ICC' is directed and controlled by the Assembly of States Parties (ASP) pursuant to Art. 112 ICCSt, which is coordinated by a special secretariat, the 'Bureau', consisting of a President, two Vice-Presidents, and eighteen members elected by ASP according to Art. 112 (3) ICCSt. The President of the ICC, the Prosecutor, and the Registrar may participate in the meetings of both the ASP and the Bureau as appropriate. The ASP decides on budgetary issues and on amendments to the Statute and the Rules, and elects the judges.

b. Structure of the Court The ICC is crafted along the lines of predecessors like the ICTY or ICTR, but its main structure results also from rule of law requirements. One of these is the accusatory principle, which itself is a consequence of the separation of powers. This means that there need to be two separate institutions: the judges and the prosecutor. The judge as part of the judiciary must be institutionally independent from the office of the prosecutor, which is part of the executive branch of government. It is not quite so simple to fulfil these parameters in one single institution, the ICC.[246]

The Rome Statute anticipates a threefold structure, similar to that of the *ad hoc* Tribunals.[247] The judicial branch, the office of the Prosecutor, and the Registry are to be seen as institutionally separate organs according to Art. 34 ICCSt. The head of the court, however, will be the Presidency as a distinct organ.[248] The different organs will be looked at in detail in Chapter 4.

B. The Different Systems and Traditions

We have seen above that discussions about international courts and tribunals have always suffered from dramatically different approaches to criminal procedure in domestic systems. This conflict is mostly described by 'common law versus civil law', the 'adversarial against the inquisitorial approach', or 'the hierarchical against the coordinate model',[249] referring to the Anglo-American tradition of criminal procedure on the one hand and the European Continental system on the other.

[245] *See* section 2.B.
[246] *See* Triffterer/*Khan*, Art. 34 MN 1.
[247] For a comparison *see* W Schabas, *ICC* (OUP 2010) 518.
[248] *See* Triffterer/*Khan*, Art. 34 MN 4.
[249] M Damaska, 'Structures of Authority and Comparative Criminal Procedure', 84 *Yale Law Journal* (1975) 480.

From the London Conference onwards it has always been difficult to find a way to prosecute jointly in the form of an international criminal procedure.

I. Misunderstandings

Before we look at the general differences in greater detail, I want to offer an illustration of how drastic misunderstandings between lawyers can be. The telling example stems from the London Conference on Military Trials, and pertains to the question of 'cross-examination', discussing the draft of Art. 16 (d) IMTSt.[250]

The Russian delegate General Nikitchenko asks

> What is meant in English by 'cross-examination'?

The English Lord Chancellor comes up with the following explanation:

> In an English or American trial, after a witness has given testimony for the prosecution, he can be questioned by the defense in order that the defense may test his evidence—verify his evidence, to see whether it is really worthy of credit. In our trials the defendant or his counsel is always entitled to put questions in cross-examination. And I think the same situation prevails in the courts of France.

The French delegate Judge Falco hurries to agree:

> Yes, the same.

Of course it is not the same. Everyone knows this who has ever witnessed criminal trials under either system. 'Cross-examination' does not simply mean to have the right to put questions to the witness, as the Lord Chancellor insinuates. 'Cross-examination' follows the 'examination-in-chief' and thus refers to a specific technical procedure which is based mainly on the fact that the 'parties' of the trial, the prosecutor and defence counsel, present evidence in support of their respective cases to a jury.

Shortly afterwards Nikitchenko makes clear that he has a different concept in mind, when he says:

> If we say 'put question to any witness', would it be the same? 'Cross-examine' does not translate well.

The answer of the Lord Chancellor reveals that it is not merely a linguistic, but rather than a structural problem:

> It would be better to say 'to cross-examine', if you can translate that, because we understand it.

The delegates finally agree on this point of issue, and have thus accepted the Anglo-American way of taking witness testimony in court.

---

[250] *See* Jackson Report (1949) 403.

As said earlier, the Russian Chief Prosecutor was not able to perform at cross-examination as required.[251] President Lawrence intervened after the re-examination of the defendant Fritzsche by his Defence Counsel Fritz and continued the examination.[252] Jackson is even reported to have advised against letting French and Russian prosecutors cross-examine witnesses due to their inexperience in this matter.[253] This shows that despite all these platitudes about integrating five different criminal procedures into one international procedure,[254] Jackson wanted a trial primarily in the American style and did not in the end dare to become too experimental.[255]

As is shown by the above example, 'States have traditionally been rather chauvinistic about their own criminal justice systems and suspicious of foreign systems.'[256] This is not only true for the criminal justice system, but for any system of law. However, criminal prosecution is the main and most repressive form of executive power, hence its importance in any given state, and the reason states are defensive about their own system.

One ought to keep in mind, however, that criminal law in particular is not merely a series of technical legal issues. It is most closely related to the society as a whole and depends to a great extent upon the acceptance of the people. It is part of the legal culture and the expression of what people are used to and what they expect.[257]

II. Structural differences

It is not the aim of this chapter to go into detail about the particularities, the pros and cons of different criminal procedural systems. Even with the 'groups' of common and civil law, the differences between domestic systems would be so extensive that several books would be needed to analyse their underlying concepts.

Instead I want to point to the general differences between Anglo-American and continental criminal procedure as specific types of procedure in an idealistic form, in order to make this dichotomy understandable for the following discussions on the ICC. Simplifications are sometimes necessary as they 'liberate us from the

---

251 *See* section 1.A.II.3.C.

252 IMT Protocols XVII, 234 *et subs.*

253 B Smith, *Reaching Judgment at Nuremberg* (Basic Books 1977) 124.

254 IMT Protocols III, 608. *See* also his foreword in W Harris, *Tyranny on Trial* (Southern Methodist University Press 1999), p xxxvii.

255 *See* also B Schäfers, *Freispruch in Nürnberg* (Diss. Bielefeld 2010) 54, who argues that Jackson was convinced that the criminal procedure of the USA was much superior to the continental approach.

256 N Amoury Combs, 'Copping a Plea to Genocide: The Plea Bargaining of International Crimes', 151 *U Pa L Rev* (2002) 1, 152 ; with regard to the drafting of the Rome Statute *see* also P Kirsch and V Oosterveld, 'Negotiating an Institution for the Twenty-First Century: Multilateral Diplomacy and the International Criminal Court', 46 *McGill Law Journal* (2001) 1141, 1154.

257 *See* 113 BVerfGE 273 pertaining to the European Arrest Warrant.

tyranny of details, so that we can discern the overall distinguishing attributes of complex phenomena'.[258]

In order to do this, I want to differentiate between three elements of criminal procedural law and analyse how they are dealt with in the different systems: (1) the investigative element, (2) the procedural element, and (3) the judging element.

(1) By the investigative element, I mean the question of what is the aim of the inquiry throughout the prosecuting process and the trial in particular. It has often been said that establishing the truth is the main aim of the trial.[259] Even if this is the case, it is unclear what is meant by 'truth'. One aspect might be that the truth is external to the trial, ie it exists outside the trial and needs to be detected by the judges. This could be called the 'material truth' or truth according to the 'correspondence theory'. An opposite view might be that truth is always relative to the trial; ie it is made up only of these facts which are being admitted into the courtroom. One could call this 'procedural truth' or truth according to the 'consensus theory'.[260]

(2) The procedural element pertains to the basic procedural parameters during the trial process. If one sees the trial as a competition between to antagonistic parties, it would be mandatory to treat these parties equally and fairly. The defendant must be given a proper chance to falsify the hypothesis of the prosecutor as to his or her guilt. Another way of looking at criminal procedure would be to see the judge as the inquiring body, who by all available means has to respect the dignity of the accused and treat the defendant as a subject of the trial and not as a mere object. The quest for the truth in any way is limited by the respect for the dignity of the person concerned.[261]

(3) The judging element takes up the question of who is passing the verdict. The decisive point in this regard is whether one would leave the decision on the question of guilt to a group of laypersons, jurors, or whether one prefers professional lawyers to judge on the guilt of the defendant. In the jury system the number of jurors, who represent the society as a whole, legitimizes the judgment. Systems without juries rely on the authority of the judges in a democratic society in order to legitimize the verdict.

---

[258] M Damaska, 'Structures of Authority and Comparative Criminal Procedure', 84 *Yale Law Journal* (1975) 480, 482.

[259] *See* most recently: T Weigend, 'Should We Search for the Truth, and Who Should Do it?' 36 *North Carolina Journal of International Law and Commercial Regulation* (2011) 389 with further references.

[260] T Weigend, 'Should We Search for the Truth, and Who Should Do it?', 36 *North Carolina Journal of International Law and Commercial Regulation* (2011) 389, 395.

[261] *See* eg, K Peter, *Strafprozeß* (CF Müller 1985) 82.

Table 1.3 Anglo-American and continental system of criminal procedure

	Continental	Anglo-American
(1) Investigative element	Material truth	Procedural truth
(2) Procedural element	Protection of basic rights	Fairness
(3) Judging element	Professional judges	Jury

In all three elements, Continental and Anglo-American procedure adopt different solutions, which can be demonstrated by Table 1.3.

Following these conceptual differences is the question of who is responsible for the implementation of these respective elements.

(1) The Continental system entrusts the investigative element to the judge alone. Notwithstanding the fact that the prosecutor and defence counsel and even civil party representative are allowed to submit evidence and are allowed to raise questions to witnesses, the responsibility for the proper investigation remains solely with the judge. In German criminal procedure, this duty is laid down in Sec. 244 (2) of the German Code of Criminal Procedure. A violation of this obligation—incomplete investigation—is a ground for an appeal (so-called *Aufklärungsrüge*).[262] This system is buttressed by the fact that the prosecutor is obliged to collect both incriminating and exonerating evidence proactively.

In Anglo-American criminal procedure, the investigative element rests with the parties. Whereas the prosecutor collects incriminating evidence, the defence team is under the obligation to inquire the case in order to find exonerating evidence. If the defence counsel refuses to work properly, the accused can claim 'ineffective assistance of counsel' either on appeal or for revision of the judgment.[263]

(2) In both systems the procedural element is attributed to the judge. Either way s/he is responsible for the protection of the basic and human rights of the defendant or s/he must ensure that the accused has a fair chance to defend her/himself against the allegations by the prosecutor. Should s/he fail to do so, s/he runs the danger of the case being quashed on appeal because of a procedural miscarriage.

(3) The responsibility for the judgment rests on the judge alone in Continental practice. S/he has to give a reasoned opinion and is controlled by an appellate court, which can review the decision and the reasoning in its entirety. The judge has to take into account all the evidence, which s/he has heard, but is not bound by any 'rules of evidence'.[264]

---

[262] *See* eg, L Meyer-Goßner, *StPO* § 244 MN 80.

[263] *See* M P Henderson, 'Truly Ineffective Assistance: A Comparison of Ineffective Assistance of Counsel in the United States of America and the United Kingdom', 13 *Ind Int'l & Comp L Rev* (2002–2003) 317, 323; E Primus 'Structural Reform in Criminal Defense: Relocating ineffective assistance of counsel claims', 92 *Cornell L Rev* (2006–2007) 679, 686 *et subs.*

[264] *See* eg, Sec. 261 German Code of Criminal Procedure.

In the Anglo-American system the judging element is passed to the jury. Yet the instruction of the jury is the responsibility of the judge. The judge has therefore, (1) to explain the substantive law to the jury, and (2)—more importantly—to rule on the admissibility of evidence according to the 'rules of evidence'. The judge thus acts as the watchdog who only permits such evidence to be presented to the jury which has an unequivocal relevance to the facts of the case. For example, hearsay evidence is not admissible as evidence in an American courtroom as this form of indirect evidence is difficult for jurors to evaluate. Erroneous procedural decisions as to the admissibility of evidence or for false instructions as to the substantive law are grounds for appeal and can be a reason for a retrial or for an acquittal.

III. Consequences for international criminal procedure

The archetypes of criminal procedure, briefly analysed above, do not exist in their pure forms any longer and maybe they never have. In many regards continental and Anglo-American criminal procedure have been brought closer together.[265] As one commentator has rightly stated: '[T]he venerable frontier between Anglo-American and Continental European criminal procedures has become increasingly ill-marked, open and transgressed.'[266]

This development is, at least in Europe, strongly influenced by Art. 6 (1) ECHR and the jurisprudence of the ECtHR. The concept of 'fairness' has thus entered the jurisprudence of the German Federal Court of Justice (*Bundesgerichtshof*), when it comes to procedural issues.[267] At the same time respect for the human dignity and for human rights has become an argument in Britain since the adoption of the Human Rights Act 1998.[268]

Still, differences remain even within the European Union and there are no reasons why the domestic systems should not remain truthful to their own traditions and laws. After all, criminal procedure is an important body of law which is attributed to the most severe and restrictive form of executive power a state can impose. Yet these conditions should not prevent cooperation in criminal matters or—as is the case with international criminal procedure—prevent the development of an international legal order which is acceptable by all or at least by many. 'Chauvinism' is certainly the wrong approach in this regard and mistrust, which is still to be

[265] A sort of natural inclination to develop towards an Anglo-Saxon structure can be made out at the Scottish procedural system, which has civil law roots, *see* I Bonomy, 'The Reality of Conducting a War Crimes Trial', 5 *JICJ* (2007) 348.

[266] M Damaska, 'Negotiated Justice in International Criminal Courts', 2 *JICJ* (2007) 1018, 1019.

[267] *See* eg, 46 BGHSt 159, 171 (concerning the requirement of a speedy trial).

[268] *See* J Sprack, *Criminal Procedure* (OUP 2008) 28.05–28.07.

observed,[269] should be abolished step by step in the attempt to understand other nations more deeply.

After almost twenty years of experience in international criminal procedure through the *ad hoc* tribunals, and after ten years of making the Rome Statute operational, the willingness of the participants and the commentators to develop a new and unique international procedural order is obvious.[270] It is not helpful to discuss whether the ICC is based on a common law structure with civil law elements or vice versa.[271] If international criminal procedure is to be developed successfully, however, the three fundamental questions raised above need to be answered. This has not been yet been achieved satisfactorily, as we will see in the course of this study.

C. The Importance of Human Rights

Human rights are to be seen as the normative basis of any legal system and executive activity by states and governments. Their relevance for criminal prosecution has been discussed many times. Yet the concept of human rights and our perception of unalienable normative values have changed, in particular during more recent times, as we no longer consider the perpetrator alone, but now include the victim as an important actor within the criminal law system. Furthermore, human rights are not only individual rights but also form the basis of state responsibility to protect these values, and this has different consequences for criminal procedure. In the following we want to address these issues in that we look at the history of 'fair trial' (I) and try to give an idea of the multidimensional structure of a human rights regime as the normative basis for criminal trials (II).

I. History of the fair trial

As a human right, 'fair trial' was born alongside the other rights of the 'first generation'. Absolutist monarchs used criminal justice as a tool to suppress non-conformist individuals. Ultimately, accused persons were dependent on the grace and favour of the monarch or the colonial power. For subjects there was no protection whatsoever against the arbitrariness of their sovereign. During the Enlightenment, the ontological understanding of 'citizen' changed fundamentally. From being

[269] *See* eg, W Schomburg, 'Wahrheitsfindung im Internationalen Gerichtssaal', *Vereinte Nationen* (2009) 3; G Gordon, 'Toward an International Criminal Procedure: Due Process Aspirations and Limitations', 45 *Colum J Transnat'l L* (2007) 635.

[270] *See* R Cryer, H Friman, D Robinson, and E Wilmshurst, *An Introduction to International Criminal Law and Procedure* (2nd edn, CUP 2010) 349; J Jackson, 'Finding the Best Epistemic Fit for International Criminal Tribunals: Beyond the Adversarial-Inquisitorial Dichotomy', 7 *JICJ* (2009) 17, 19–24; K Ambos and D Miller, 'Structure and Function of the Confirmation Procedure Before the ICC from a Comparative Perspective', 7 *ICLR* (2007) 335, 349.

[271] This is done by Boas/Bischoff/Reid/Taylor, *ICL III*, 15.

regarded as mere objects of state authority, human beings moved to being the reason for statehood and its focus, and they needed to be treated accordingly; that is, as subjects of governmental powers. Consequently, no power of the executive branch of government over the liberty and security of the person was to be without limits. Only in cases that had previously been established by law, like a strong suspicion of having committed a criminal offence or a conviction by a competent criminal tribunal, could a person be legally detained.[272] Similarly, a number of inalienable rights stemming from the duty to respect the dignity of the human person were formulated, like the right to silence,[273] the right to be informed of the accusations and have time to prepare one's defence,[274] and to be presumed innocent until state authorities can convincingly establish guilt.[275] Furthermore, liberty against arbitrary criminal conviction by state authorities was to be guaranteed by participation of the public, through the jury, and the publicity of the proceedings.[276] Punishment was only feasible where and as much as strictly necessary, and where previously established by law.[277] Both the American as well as the French Bill of Rights were of great influence on other European criminal justice systems. Sooner or later, most states adopted the 'fair trial' principles that were laid out in these instruments.

As these rights permeated the different systems, they were soon regarded as essential in a democratic society. However, it took two world wars to establish a document that would enshrine human rights at the international level.

On 8 December 1948 the General Assembly of the young United Nations agreed on a Resolution that is known as the Universal Declaration of Human Rights (UDHR).

The UDHR enshrines in Arts 10 and 11 the principle of a 'fair trial'. This document has never gained binding effect on the Member States of the UN. Although Cassese likes to attribute to the provisions encapsulated in this document moral and political weight that would bind all states in the world, he admits that legal norms they are not.[278]

It was therefore with the establishment of the UN that human rights endeavoured to obtain an international character. From this moment on, the verification of basic rights attributed to all human beings was no longer conceived of as a purely national matter, important only for domestic legal and constitutional

[272] Compare Art. 7 Déclaration des Droits de L'Homme et du Citoyen, 26 August 1789.
[273] As found in Art. 5 Virginia Bill of Rights, 25 September 1788.
[274] Art. 6 Virginia Bill of Rights, 25 September 1788.
[275] Compare Art. 9 Déclaration des Droits de L'Homme et du Citoyen, 26 August 1789.
[276] Art. 6 Virginia Bill of Rights, 25 September 1788.
[277] The *nullum crimen, nulla poena sine lege* sentence is embodied alongside the necessity principle in Art. 8 Déclaration des Droits de L'Homme et du Citoyen, 26 August 1789.
[278] A Cassese, *Human Rights in a Changing World* (CUP 1990) 48.

orders. The UN as an international body was made responsible for the promotion of and respect for fundamental human rights.[279] It was under the auspices of the UN that the international community, soon after the UDHR, started to draft two covenants on human rights that would serve as truly legally binding instruments for their signatories. Two documents, one on economic, social, and cultural rights, and another on civil and political rights, were open for signature in 1966 and entered into force in 1976. The right to 'fair trial' was enshrined in the second of these treaties, the International Covenant on Civil and Political Rights (ICCPR), largely in Arts 14 and 15. Alongside these global developments, four main regional instruments evolved. Most prominent amongst these is probably that of the Council of Europe with its European Convention on Human Rights (ECHR), which entered into force in 1950. This, because of its functioning supervisory machinery comprising the European Court of Human Rights (ECtHR), has the power to issue legally binding decisions. It is mainly in Arts 6 and 7 ECHR that the 'fair trial' principle is addressed. In the American context, we find Art. 26 of the American Declaration of Rights and Duties of Man (1948) and the Inter-American Convention on Human Rights (IACHR 1969), which enshrines 'fair trial' in Art. 8. The most recent embodiment of human rights on a regional basis is the African Charter on Human and Peoples' Rights (AfCHPR, 1981) containing the right to a 'fair trial' in Art. 7 AfCHPR. On the states party to these agreements, the provision certainly has binding impact to the extent that a 'fair' procedure could even be enforced through the equivalent supervising body.

II. The relevance of human rights from a normative perspective

The historic importance of the fair trial and right of the accused has been shown. The question now is, what impetus can human rights have on criminal procedure from a normative point of view? The answer is twofold: (1) criminal procedure is the most repressive form of state intervention into the private sphere of citizens. The rights of the individual are thus crucial for the legitimacy of the trial. (2) At the same time, human rights foresee a duty to prosecute in some instances and the duty for the state to implement an efficient criminal justice system. The dilemma of fairness and efficiency is thus inherent in the modern understanding of human rights (3).

1. Criminal procedure

It is soon clear from reading the texts of the human rights treaties, Art. 14 ICCPR in particular, that 'fair trial' does not just comprise one peculiar right. It consists of a whole range of different rights and obligations. Nevertheless it encompasses a single concept: how to make a trial 'fair'. Several positions are meant to be

[279] Preamble of UN Charter and Art. 1 UN Charter.

indispensable to achieve this aim as they are outlined in the human rights treaties. We can differentiate between three components that are inherent in what we call 'fair trial'.

Amongst these are first, institutional guarantees, such as the independence and impartiality of the tribunal or court. These address, first of all, the legislator, who is called upon to establish the institutions needed in a way compatible with human rights.

Secondly, there are moral principles that should preside over each step of the procedure, like the presumption of innocence or the principle of equality of arms. These principles are to be closely followed by the legislator when forming procedural systems, but perhaps their main impact lies within the interpretation and application of the law to the individual case. In particular, in difficult cases with conflicting interests, the solution has to be found according to these legal principles. It is this second component that Dworkin would conceive of as 'principles of law'.[280] According to the terminology of the German BVerfG one could call this 'objektive Menschenrechtsordnung' which stems from the individual 'rights' and penetrates all areas of criminal procedure.[281]

Finally, there are rights, conceived of in a classically narrow manner, as legal claims to be free of something or to be given something, like the right not to be arbitrarily detained or the right to counsel. Some of these rights are of overall validity and are precise enough to be called 'self-executing'. They are not a merely accidental reflex, but grant the individual a legal claim that can be realized. All three concepts, institutional guarantees, moral principles, and individual rights, are compiled in one 'right': the right to procedural 'fairness'. The individual is entitled to have all three components verified in his or her confrontation with the penal system. In that sense the individual has a 'right' to a 'fair trial'.[282] What this means in the different stages and situations the individual finds him or herself in during the course of prosecution and trial is the subject of later chapters.

Yet it would be a fallacy to believe that an entire criminal procedural system can be derived from human rights for two reasons:[283] First, the structure of human rights norms as principles and minimum guarantees gives them a general character. A criminal procedural system in many regards needs to be much more precise. Take, for example, the guarantee of an independent and impartial judiciary as contained in Art. 14 (1) ICCPR and Art. 6 (1) ECHR. This guarantee says nothing about

[280] R Dworkin, *Taking Rights Seriously* (Duckworth 1996).

[281] 7 BVerfGE 198; 21 BVerfGE 362 at 372.

[282] Boas/Bischoff/Reid/Taylor, *ICL III*, 12 seem to agree when they call human rights the legal principles behind criminal procedure.

[283] The human rights relevance was stressed too much in the previous book; C Safferling, *Towards an International Criminal Procedure* (OUP 2003), as rightly criticized by C Kreß, 150 *Goltdammer's Archiv für Strafrecht* (2003) 61 (book review).

the length of judiciary's term in office. One could foresee a life term or eight year term. Both options would fulfil the requirement that the judge be independent. If on the other hand, the judge would have to be re-elected after, say, two years in office, some doubt would justifiably arise as to the political independence of such a judge, who naturally wants to stay in office and would thus not decide against government interests for fear that government might vote him or her out of office. Human rights thus offer an underlying rationale for the office term, but do not give a prescriptive answer.

Secondly, there are other parameters which are relevant in criminal procedure. There are several other human rights involved. The rights of the accused contrast with the rights of victims and witnesses to privacy or physical integrity.

Furthermore, there are functional underpinnings to criminal procedure. We will look at the aim and purpose of criminal procedure in the next chapter, but what can be said already now is that one of the predominant aims of a criminal trial is the quest for the truth.

2. Duty to prosecute

Connected with what has been said about the human rights of others is a more recent development in human rights law. The right to life cited in Art. 2 ECHR and in Art. 4 IACHR, has been attributed a positive duty to protect the right to life on the side of the state. Both the ECtHR[284] and the Inter-American Court of Human Rights (IACtHR)[285] have developed such a responsibility in several cases. One of the consequences of this is a positive obligation by the state to investigate and prosecute in homicide cases. As the death of a person could not be prevented, repressive mechanisms must be implemented after such a violation occurred.[286] This obligation comes into play only after the fact. Similarly, the ECtHR has developed the duty to establish an efficient system of prosecuting torture and degrading and inhumane treatment as violations of Art. 3 ECHR.[287]

Obviously the obligation to investigate and prosecute goes beyond the individual case. The duty to establish an effective criminal justice system aims at protecting human rights in that it deters others from violating the basic rights of others and punishes those who have deviated, thereby deterring others from committing the same offence. Human rights are thus protected through criminal prosecution.

[284] ECtHR, *Streletz, Kessler, und Krenz v Germany*, Judgment 22 March 2001 (Grand Chamber), Rep. 2001-II, para 86; *Mastromatteo v Italy*, Judgment 24 October 2002 (Grand Chamber), Rep. 2002-VIII, para 89; *see* also C Grabenwarter, *Europäische Menschenrechtskonvention* (4th edn, CH Beck 2011), § 20 MN 16–19.

[285] IACtHR *Malary* (Haití), Case 11.335, 27 December 2002, Rep. 78/02 (Merits Report), *see* also S Bourgon, 'Judgments, Decisions and Other Relevant Materials Issued by International Courts and Other International Bodies on Human Rights', 1 *JICJ* (2003) 555, 562.

[286] ECtHR, *Calvelli and Ciglio v Italy*, Judgment 17 January 2002, Rep. 2002-I, para 51.

[287] ECtHR, *Labita v Italy*, Judgment 6 April 2000, Rep. 2000-IV, para 130–6.

3. Fairness versus efficiency

In summarizing the impact of human rights on criminal procedure, we discover the following dichotomy: on the one hand the state must have an efficient criminal justice system; on the other the accused must have a fair trial. The prosecution must thus be both, fair and efficient.

This is not necessarily a contradiction. The evaluation depends on the definition of 'efficiency'. It would be erroneous to understand 'efficiency' of the criminal justice system as simply having a quick and easy trial; rather, efficiency pertains to the ability to solve the conflict in a sustainable way. The procedure as such and the result must be acceptable to all parties involved, ie in criminal matters to the victim, the perpetrator, and the society.[288]

This has several consequences. The criminal justice systems must be supported adequately, with regard to personnel and infrastructure. An under-financed system will not be able to work properly and will not be taken seriously by the public. Prosecution can only be efficient if it is applied in an equal and non-arbitrary manner, or the accused and society will not accept such a criminal justice system as genuinely just. It means also that the proceedings must be directed toward establishing the truth. Neither the accused nor the victim or the society would accept a judgment—acquittal or conviction—based solely on suspicion or rumour. Finally, the entire process needs to be 'fair' towards the accused. That means the defendant must be granted a fair chance to defend her/himself and s/he must be respected as a human being who is a subject of the proceedings and not a mere object.

It is thus true that legitimacy is gained through human rights adherence.[289] Yet the concept of how human rights influence proceedings is complex and multidimensional.

---

288 *See* H Landau, 'Die Pflicht des Staates am Erhalt einer funktionstüchtigen Strafrechtspflege', 27 *NStZ* (2007) 121.

289 *See* Boas/Bischoff/Reid/Taylor, *ICL III*, 14.

2

THE SPECIAL CIRCUMSTANCES OF INTERNATIONAL CRIMINAL PROCEDURE

As we have seen, international criminal procedure provides the means to execute substantive international criminal law in a direct way compared to the indirect execution by national courts. One could presume that procedural law would be the same, independent of the level it is being applied be it national or international. In reality, this is not the case. International criminal procedure finds itself in a rather different environment. This is demonstrable in the following three aspects: (A) the purposes and aims of procedure, (B) questions of competence, and (C) the principle of complementarity, which is strongly linked to the jurisdiction.

A. Purposes and Aims

Procedural law serves the execution of substantive law. Indeed, the meaning of substantive law comes into effect only by its execution. Thus the purposes of substantive law and procedural law respectively are closely intertwined. It would be wrong to presume that procedural law is detached from the goals of substantive law and that its only meaning lies in the mere execution of the substantive law. Procedural law is a highly complex issue and in many ways autonomous vis-à-vis the substantive law. It is thus in need of a genuine justification, and the question of legitimacy must be addressed in all stages of the proceedings.[1] This is most obvious when it comes to the question of pre-trial detention, as this deprivation of personal liberty establishes a serious infringement of one of the most important human rights. In a less obvious way, the question of legitimacy arises also with a view to the admissibility of evidence, as the evidence will be the basis of the conviction, and any suspicion of slanted evidence will be decisive in the acceptability of the

[1] C Safferling, 'The Justification of Punishment in International Criminal Law', 4 *ARIEL* (1999) 126, 130 *et subs.* with further references.

procedure. For these reasons, it is necessary to have 'at least a rough understanding of its purpose'.[2]

Before we look at procedural law it is necessary to summarize the purposes of international criminal law in the material sense (I). After this, we will take issue with the specific aspects of international criminal procedure (II).

I. Purpose of international criminal law

When asked what the purpose of criminal law is, we are often referred to two specific aims: (1) retribution, and (2) deterrence. In principle, these aims also apply to international criminal law as has been held by the ICTY in several cases,[3] but with certain new dimensions. The question may also be posed as to whether there are also other relevant criteria including more positive aspects of prevention (3), and the integration of the victim (4).

1. Retribution

Vengeance is, it seems, a natural human emotion.[4] A legal system attempts to contain this irrational emotion within a rational process. Criminal law aims at rendering acts of retaliation superfluous by establishing a catalogue of wrongs and expressing the injustice and the unacceptability of deviant behaviour in publicly pronounced judgment and the infliction of punishment. 'A pain can be inflicted upon the wrong-doer, of a sort which does not restore the injured party to his former situation, or to another equally good, but which is inflicted for the very purpose of causing pain.'[5]

This rather abstract functioning of a criminal justice system is—at least in theory—also applicable to the international level. Nowhere else has this better been expressed than by Robert H Jackson in his opening address at the Nuremberg Trial:

> That four great nations, flushed with victory and stung with injury, stay the hand of vengeance and voluntarily submit their captive enemies to the judgment of the law is one of the most significant tributes that Power ever has paid to Reason.[6]

Channeling the feeling of vengeance in a public procedure and substituting retaliation with the imposition of a sentence serves to establish the rule of law and prevent individuals to take the law into their own hands.

What is needed, however, is a certain amount of trust in such a public system in order for it to function properly. If the party who has suffered injustice does not see

[2] M Damaska, 'Problematic Features of International Criminal Procedure', in: A Cassese (ed), *The Oxford Companion to International Criminal Justice* (OUP 2009) 175.

[3] ICTY *Prosecutor v Kupreškić et al.*, TC, IT-95–16-T, 14 January 2000, Judgment, para 848 *et sub. Prosecutor v Naletilić and Martinović*, TC, IT-98–34-T, 31 March 2003, Judgment, para 739.

[4] *See* F von Liszt, 'Der Zweckgedanke im Strafrecht', 3 *ZStW* (1883) 1, 45; also O Höffe, *Gibt es ein interkulturelles Strafrecht* (Suhrkamp 1999) 68.

[5] O W Holmes, *The Common Law* (Belknap Press of Harvard University Press 2009) 39.

[6] IMT Protocols II, 99.

justice to be administered in a reasonable way, it will probably not be persuaded to refrain from reprisals.

What we have described above is a rather 'relative' aspect of retribution. Punishment is being imposed in order to achieve certain goals in society. There is also a more 'absolute' aspect to the retributive theory. According to this theory, the offender needs to be punished only because he has offended. Punishment thus is an end in itself. The guilt with which the criminal has burdened himself needs to be assuaged. The negation of the law that was accomplished by the culprit is itself negated by the punishment, as Hegel has put it in his idealistic view of the authority of the law.[7]

2. Deterrence

Criminal law is meant to deter others from offending. The Preamble of the Rome Statute as well as UN Security Council Res. 827 and 955, the founding documents of the *ad hoc* Tribunals, attribute such an effect to the decision to establish international criminal courts and tribunals. However we must acknowledge that the massacre of Srebrenica and the humanitarian crisis in Kosovo took place after the establishment of the ICTY. An immediate deterrent effect can thus not be observed. Again, Robert H Jackson in his opening address in Nuremberg:

> We are able to do away with domestic tyranny and violence and aggression by those in power against the rights of their own people only when we make all men answerable to the law. This trial represents mankind's desperate effort to apply the discipline of the law to statesmen who have used their powers of state to attack the foundations of the world's peace and to commit aggressions against the rights of their neighbors.[8]

Jackson expresses his hope that international criminal law—in particular, as regards the crime of aggression—can work on the international level similarly to the workings of national criminal law in domestic society. Statesmen will desist from offending against the world's legal order if they submit to the 'discipline of the law'. When Jackson appeals to the discipline of the law he implies two things: first, such a system works only with intelligent people who are willing to accept reasonable arguments; and second, the disciplinary effect of the law presupposes its execution, ie an offence must be followed by a penal sanction.

The ICTY accepts general deterrence as one of the aims of criminal law but gives it a slightly different twist. The Appeals Chamber has upheld in the case of Kordić and Čerkez:

> In the context of combating international crimes, deterrence refers to the attempt to integrate or to reintegrate those persons who believe themselves to be beyond the

[7] 'Strafe als Negation der Negation des Rechts', G W F Hegel, *Grundlinien einer Philosophie des Rechts*, Zusatz zu § 97.

[8] IMT Protocols II, 154.

> reach of international criminal law. Such persons must be warned that they have to respect the fundamental global norms of substantive criminal law or face not only prosecution but also sanctions imposed by international tribunals.[9]

To date, there is no reliable system of international criminal justice. A deterrent effect, however, can only materialize when the law is executed, ie when there is a real threat that the offender will be caught and punished. This circularity is proven by all research available as regards the deterrent effects of criminal law.[10] Nowadays punishment for international crimes is imminent only after a military defeat.[11] Even if the UN Security Council has developed a Chapter VII-intervention regime comprising criminal prosecution by establishing the ICTY and ICTR, this highly political organ has thus far not proven to have a reliable human rights agenda.[12] Its competence to refer cases to the ICC pursuant to Art. 13 (b) ICCSt has to-date also been applied somewhat randomly.[13] The result is a highly selective and thus arbitrary application of international criminal law, whereas only a uniform execution would add to the deterrent effect which criminal law can have in general.[14]

A deterrent effect furthermore presupposes a set of shared values in the form of a commonly accepted catalogue of international crimes. In a domestic society, basic values are mostly accepted as the foundation of the constitutional order. In the international setting, such a common denominator is still developing. More often statesmen and military commanders consider themselves fighting for a 'good and just cause', and do not consider their actions as criminal.[15] Furthermore, what reason would they have to stop the fighting if they might face prosecution afterwards?[16] Lower-level participants too do not see themselves as criminals as they may consider that they live in a repressive social atmosphere and find themselves under immense pressure. Under these circumstances the criminal is the conformist rather than the deviant.[17]

---

[9] ICTY *Prosecutor v Kordić and Čerkez*, AC, IT-95–14/2-A, 17 December 2003, Judgment, para 1078.

[10] D Dölling, 'Generalprävention durch Strafrecht: Realität oder Illusion', 102 *ZStW* (1990) 1; F Streng, 'Schuld ohne Freiheit', 101 *ZStW* (1989) 273, 286 m.w.N.

[11] H H Jescheck, *Die Verantwortlichkeit der Staatsorgane nach Völkerstrafrecht* (Röhrscheid 1952) 194 *et subs.*; K Ambos and C Steiner, 'Vom Sinn des Strafens auf innerstaatlicher und supranationaler Ebene', 41 *Juristische Schulung* (2001) 9, 13; Th Buergenthal and D Thürer, *Menschenrechte. Ideale, Instrumente, Institutionen* (Nomos 2010) 129.

[12] *See* M Aznar-Gómez, 'A Decade of Human Rights Protection by the UN Security Council: A Sketch of Deregulation?', 13 *EJIL* (2002) 223.

[13] *See* section 2.B.II.2.

[14] R Cryer, H Friman, D Robinson, and E Wilmshurst, *An Introduction to International Criminal Law and Procedure* (2nd edn, CUP 2010) 38.

[15] D Golash, 'The Justification of Punishment in the International Context', in: L May and Z Hoskins (eds), *International Criminal Law and Philosophy* (CUP 2010) 201, 211–16.

[16] *See* M Damaska, 'What is the Point of International Criminal Justice?', 83 *Chi-Kent L Rev* (2008) 329, 332.

[17] M Drumbl, *Atrocity, Punishment and International Law* (CUP 2007) 32.

3. Positive–preventive aspects

Apart from deterrence, other, more positive aspects of 'prevention' can also be described. Establishing and fostering an international normative conscience can achieve the prevention of further crimes. The drafting of a catalogue of crimes can serve as a basis of such an international conscience. In order to promote and stabilize these principles, those who break them must be prosecuted and punished. This concept has been developed mostly by German scholars under the heading of 'positive Generalprävention'.[18] In recent years however, it has arisen in the international discussion about the justification of punishment.[19] The jurisprudence of international tribunals has taken up these positive aspects, as did the ICTY in the case against *Rajić,* under the heading of 'affirmative prevention':

> In the context of the Tribunal, the punishment aims at reinforcing the validity and the effectiveness of the breached rules of international humanitarian law vis-à-vis the perpetrator, the victims and the public.[20]

> Thus, both stigmatising the offender's conduct and ending impunity serve the same goal pursued by affirmative general prevention: to reassure the public that the legal system has been upheld and to influence the public not to violate this legal system.[21]

Even if in the context of this ICTY judgment, the sentencing was in the foreground, the parameters, which were applied here to the question of the right and just amount of punishment to be imposed, can also be adopted to justify the entire criminal justice system.

Next to these aspects, which pertain to the public, a more individual view can be applied directed towards the person of the offender. By detaining the offender, the offender can no longer offend. The punishment should also 'dishearten him from re-offending once he has served his sentence and has been released.'[22]

Whereas these aspects are important notions in the national context in particular as regards the execution of the sentences, in international criminal law their influence is minimal. The aspect of a social incapacitation fails because rarely will the offender be caught while committing his or her criminal acts; regularly the capture of a suspect will only take place after the circumstances have changed and the situation has been pacified. A return to the society after release from prison will also bring the criminal into a different society than the one s/he left, and into different social circumstances, where the culture of mass atrocities has been defused.

---

[18] *See* eg, C Roxin, *Strafrecht. Allgemeiner Teil Vol I* (4th edn, CH Beck 2006) § 3 MN 24.

[19] *See* M Drumbl, *Atrocity, Punishment and International Law* (CUP 2007) 61, 173 *et subs.*

[20] ICTY *Prosecutor v Rajić*, TC I, IT-95–12-S, 8 May 2006, Sentencing Judgment, para 69.

[21] Ibid, para 1081.

[22] ICTY *Prosecutor v Kordić and Čerkez* , AC, IT-95–14/2-A, 17 December 2003, Judgment, para 1077.

However, the importance of individual prevention could rise in the course of the further developing of the international criminal justice system. In the Democratic Republic of Congo, for example, atrocities are still being committed while Thomas Lubanga is being tried in The Hague and the leaders of the *Forces démocratiques de libération du Rwanda* are being prosecuted both in Germany and in The Hague.

4. *Justice for the victims*

Greater importance is being attributed to the aspect of 'justice for the victims'.[23] In traditional criminal law the victim does not play a primary role. Quite the contrary was true: 'criminal law is established through the neutralisation of the victim'.[24] The conflict between the offender and the victim is mediated by the state and turned into a conflict between the offender and the legal order. The shift towards the victim-orientated debate over crime has been accompanied by a change in social awareness of the criminal process. Whereas the aim of the criminal process up to the 1970s can be said to have been the social rehabilitation and reintegration of the offender, which itself was seen to be in the public interest,[25] now reference is made to 'justice for the victims'.[26] This is not a mere change in terminology, but represents a clear shift of focus away from the public interest and towards the individual conflict between an offender and the victim.[27] Previously the criminal process was governed by the principle that this conflict must be dealt with by way of the conventional public trial, which conforms to constitutional standards. The violation of the criminal law was the focal point of the proceedings, not the collateral injury inflicted on the victim. During the impersonalized procedure, the prosecutor represents the interests of the public, which include the interests of the victim. In fact, personal interests have no place here.

There can be no question that the state has the responsibility to prevent the social marginalization of crime victims and to protect them, where necessary offering material or immaterial assistance.[28] Criminal proceedings in which victims

[23] In greater detail: C Safferling, 'The Role of the Victim in the Criminal Process—A Paradigm Shift in National German and International Law?', 11 *ICLR* (2011) 183, 185, *see* also K Ambos, 'The Legal Framework of Transitional Justice: A Systematic Study with a Special Focus on the Role of the ICC', in K Ambos, J Large, and M Wierda (eds), *Building a Future on Peace and Justice* (Springer 2009) 19, 33 stating that 'justice' in transitional justice is mostly 'justice for the victims'.

[24] W Hassemer, *Einführung in die Grundlagen des Strafrechts* (CH Beck 1990), 72 (author's translation).

[25] B Schünemann, 'Der Ausbau der Opferstellung im Strafprozess—Fluch oder Segen?', in: R Michalke *et al.* (eds), *Festschrift für Rainer Hamm* (DeGruyter 2008) 687, 688.

[26] Cf. Human Rights Watch, who describe the arrest warrant for Al Bashir as a 'major step towards justice for the victims in Dafur', *see* <http://www.hrw.org/en/news/2009/03/04/icc-bashir-warrant-major-step-toward-justice-victims-darfur>.

[27] *See* also S Garkawe, 'Victims and the ICC: Three Major Issues', 3 *ICLR* (2003) 345, 347.

[28] Collected decisions of the German Federal Constitutional Court (Entscheidungssammlung des Bundesverfassungsgerichts; hereinafter cited as 'BVerfGE') 57 BVerfGE 250, at 284. Collected decisions of the German Federal Court, Chamber for Criminal Law; hereinafter cited as 'BGHSt' 33 BGHSt 83, 91.

are exploited as useful witnesses, after which they are abandoned and left to fend for themselves, is contrary to the respect for human dignity.[29] No-one should be reduced to the status of a mere object of the state.[30] Victim protection is a social necessity and equally, a victim's right.

Yet it is still unclear what 'justice for victims' actually means. There are several aspects attached to this concept, some bringing only slight changes in the perception of criminal law, others turning a criminal trial upside down. We will discuss the role of the victim in greater detail below.[31] In respect of the general aims of international criminal law, it is primarily important to note that victims' considerations need to be analysed, and they need to be protected from being reduced to the role of a witness. It is certainly true that support by victims 'will strengthen the legitimacy of the court proceedings in such area and increase the effectiveness of the Court's function to disseminate a culture of accountability for human rights violations.'[32] Yet the ICC needs to be accepted not only by victims but also by the perpetrator in order to have a positive effect on the corroboration of a reliable human rights protection scheme. The victim's view is only one part of the whole picture. Furthermore, the more the positive effects of a prosecution of the offender on the victim are emphasized, the greater the restorative effect for the victim, which is induced by participating at the trial, is stressed, and thus the higher the expectations. With expectations rising, the danger of disillusionment increases as well.[33]

5. *International legal order*

Whether international criminal law establishes a genuine legal order or whether it is nothing more than an extension of national criminal law and mainly a question of jurisdiction, is debatable. We have seen above that international criminal law in many respects shares the aims and purposes of a national criminal system. What we have not yet looked at is the question of what international criminal law is actually protecting. Is it the life and personal integrity of individuals? Are collective interests in focus? Is it a mixture of both?

These questions are not easy to answer. It reveals the ambiguity and tension international criminal law has to endure by being both criminal and public international law.[34] Both sets of laws have a different background and history. Their means of execution

[29] 38 BVerfGE 105, at 114.

[30] Cf. 27 BVerfGE 1, at 6.

[31] *See* section 4.D.

[32] *ICC Prosecutor v Katanga and Chui*, PTC I, ICC-01/04–01/07–474, 13 May 2008, Decision on the Set of Procedural Rights Attached to Procedural Status of Victim at the Pre-Trial Stage of the Case, para 163.

[33] N Bhuta, 'How Shall We Punish the Perpetrators? Human Rights, Alien Wrongs and the March of International Criminal Law', 27 *Melbourne University Law Review* (2003) 255, stating that disillusionment with international criminal justice amongst victims is not difficult to find in Rwanda and East Timor.

[34] A Cassese, *International Criminal Law* (2nd edn, OUP 2008) 8 *et subs.*

vary dramatically and lawyers are trained differently in each field. To understand this tension more fully, I want to juxtapose a few antagonistic terms, as follows.

Whereas criminal law pertains to the individual, public international law is concerned with the state. Criminal law is at the forefront a repressive means of executing governmental power; public international law in contrast is based on the principle of consent. Criminal law is executed by an independent branch of government, the judiciary, which in a sense controls the executive power. Public international law is a highly politicized field of law based on compromise and not on execution.

Criminal law has an immediate influence on the individual life in a domestic society. In Western democracies, the protection of the basic and fundamental values of the human co-existence relies heavily on criminal law. Public international law relies on voluntary cooperation of independent states. There is no controlling instance; political influence, economic and military power are decisive factors in international relations. Even if there are certain mechanisms available to avoid or solve conflicts, their functioning depends to a great extent on the willingness of states. Means to execute public international law by force against the will of a state are rare.[35] Public international law has a normative and not a repressive character;[36] it is thus always relative to the power equilibrium and therefore selective.

In this context it is questionable whether a criminal law on the international level aims at executing fundamental values of the international community and thereby introduces executive means into a consent-oriented legal order, or whether it aims at protecting the basic values of the domestic society on an international level if it is necessary, under circumstances to be discussed.

One argument in favour of the latter approach might be the parallel with human rights law. International criminal law, one could argue, is nothing other than a special protection scheme for a set of core human rights. Humanitarian law is in essence *lex specialis* with regard to human rights law in case of an armed conflict.[37] Without doubt, human rights aim at the protection of the individual. Human rights law, however, is part of public international law, but its implementation and execution lies within the responsibility of the national state. International criminal law comes into play only if the human rights violation has reached such a scale that several states are concerned or the state responsible is unwilling or unable to fulfil its duty to protect.[38] International criminal law is thus closely related to the

[35] *See* B Kempen and C Hillgruber, *Völkerrecht* (CH Beck 2007) Chapter 7 MN 21–63.

[36] A Cassese, *International Criminal Law* (2nd edn, OUP 2008) 9.

[37] ICJ *Legality of the Threat or Use of Nuclear Weapons*, Advisory Opinion, 6 July 1996, ICJ Rep 1996, 226, 240 para 25; ICJ *Legal Consequences of the Construction of a Wall in the Occupied Palestinian Territory*, Advisory Opinion, 9 July 2004, ICJ Rep 2004, 136, 178.

[38] *See* Th Buergenthal and D Thürer, *Menschenrechte. Ideale, Instrumente, Institutionen* (Nomos 2010) 119 *et subs.*, who argue that states are reluctant to prosecute their own military personnel and desist from prosecuting members of the opposing party for fear of reprisals.

implementation of individual human rights and shares the same basis as national criminal law.[39]

One argument in favour of the former approach—the theory of a criminal legal order at the international level—might be that the set of crimes (that is, genocide, crimes against humanity, war crimes, and the crime of aggression according to Art. 5 ICCSt) bears a unique and individual character, and does not comprise only ordinary crimes which take place at a different level and on a different scale. With the crime of aggression, this is particularly obvious. The criminal offence is connected to a gross violation of the UN Charter and the prohibition of the use of force therein. On the national level there would be no equivalent.

This is also true for the concept of war crimes. The law of armed conflict has a special set of norms, which is applicable only in case of an armed conflict and only to the addressees—that is, combatants— or those in a non-international armed conflict, for that matter. Thus the circumstances of these rules depend on public international law, ie the existence of an armed conflict. Therefore there are not only human rights violations on a gradually greater scale. The law of armed conflict and human rights law have a common end, but are formally separated.[40] The separation is visible in particular when one looks at the methods of warfare. Employing weapons, projectiles, and material, and methods of warfare, which are of a nature to cause superfluous injury or unnecessary suffering, which is a war crime in an international armed conflict according to Art. 8 (2) (b) (xx) ICCSt, lacks an equivalent in domestic law. As the killing or wounding of a combatant is allowed in armed conflict, personal integrity, and the right to life of the individual soldier cannot be the underlying aim of the norm.

Similarly the crime of genocide does not relate to a sum of individuals but to specific groups. In particular, the core element of the crime of genocide, the special intent requirement, reveals that in the focus of the protection scheme is not the individual but the existence of the minority, be it national, ethnic, racial, or religious. A purely individual approach could also not explain the criminalization of the birth-prevention measure (Art. 6 (d) ICCSt), or the forcible transfer of children (Art. 6 (e) ICCSt). The survival of the group, ie the minority or the people, is at stake and this is the reason for the criminal norm and not the protection of the individual's human rights.

The only norm, which indeed seems to fit into the core human rights scheme, is the crimes against humanity concept. These crimes pertain to a widespread

---

[39] *See* S Kirsch, *Der Begehungszusammenhang der Verbrechen gegen die Menschlichkeit* (Peter Lang 2009).

[40] *See* eg, Th Buergenthal and D Thürer, *Menschenrechte. Ideale, Instrumente, Institutionen* (Nomos 2010) 116 *et subs*.

or systematic attack according to Art. 7 (1) ICCSt and thus embrace large-scale human rights violations of individuals.

Another indicator as to why international criminal law and domestic criminal law have to be understood as two separate entities with different protection schemes can be derived from the sentencing practice. National laws attribute the most stringent punishment for the taking of an individual life, as the right to life is the highest value in a domestic system. In international criminal law there have to be different parameters, otherwise every person responsible for an intentional killing punishable as a crime against humanity must be punished with life-long imprisonment. This is not how international sentencing works and rightly so, because the parameters are different.

As we have seen that international criminal law does not aim at protecting individual values, but that there are specific international values, we have to explain what these values are. We have to look at the international context and the basic rules of the international community. The fundamental norms of the international community are contained in the UN Charter in particular. From this document we can derive a triangle of basic values on which the international community is based:[41]

- The principle of peaceful co-existence of peoples and the prohibition of the use of force.
- The human rights law as the normative backbone of the international community.
- The protection of minorities as a specific moulding of human rights law.

The international values which international criminal law aims to protect are to be established from these three parameters, which are interrelated and enjoy a certain reciprocity. Therefore respect for human rights and the protection of minorities are to be seen with reference to the goal to ensure a peaceful co-existence of peoples and nations. It is thus not the human right of an individual but rather the responsibility to protect human rights on the side of governments, and the danger for international peace and security in the case of a failure to do so. These are the interests which pertain to the 'international community as a whole',[42] and only through the infringement of these can interference into state sovereignty can be justified.[43]

---

[41] Similarly, F Melloh, *Einheitliche Strafzumessung in den Rechtsquellen des ICC-Statuts* (Duncker and Humblot 2010) 84 *et subs.*, who however does not differentiate between the protection of human rights and minorities.

[42] *See* Preamble of the Rome Statute.

[43] *See* Judge Kaul in his dissenting opinion in the decision of the IStGH, *Situation in the Republic of Kenya*, PTC II, ICC-01/09–19, 31 March 2010, Decision Pursuant to Article 15 of the Rome Statute on the Authorization of an Investigation into the Situation in the Republic of Kenya, para 10.

Most writers favour a combined approach and argue that international criminal law aims at protecting both individual and collective rights.[44] But there is no reason and no current drive for such a mixture. Both concepts, international and national criminal law, may be applied alongside one another. But as national law pertains to the social cohesion of the domestic society, international criminal law regulates the coexistence of nations and peoples.[45]

II. Purpose of international criminal procedure

On the basis of what we have identified as the aims and purposes in the context of substantive international criminal law, we must now address the purpose of international criminal procedure.[46] The procedural aims are often discussed with a view to plea bargaining, as it is questionable whether 'justice can be negotiated'.[47] Similarly the length of proceedings gives rise to a discussion about the purposes of a criminal trial. In particular, the enormous time pressure, which was established by the so-called completion strategies for the *ad hoc* Tribunals, leaves doubts as to whether swift justice equates to justice incomplete.[48]

We can differentiate between primary procedural aims and indirect aims parallel to the preventive purposes we have described above.

1. Direct procedural aims

The procedural aims are, in a way, a precondition to the fulfilment of the purposes connected to substantive criminal law. Retribution as well as prevention can only take place and can only be acceptable if the conviction is addressed to the right person.

Therefore the primary aim of the prosecution is to identify the perpetrator and prove the allegations, which were brought against the accused.[49] In other words, the criminal procedure has to reveal the 'truth', and at the end of the trial a decision

[44] *See* eg, K Ambos, *Internationales Strafrecht* (3rd edn, CH Beck 2011) § 5 MN 3; § 7 MN 130; H Satzger, *Internationales und Europäisches Strafrecht* (4th edn, Nomos 2010) § 16 MN 7 (concerning genocide).

[45] C Safferling, *Internationales Strafrecht* (Springer 2011) § 4 MN 65.

[46] A summary is also given by A Eser, 'Procedural Structure and Feature of International Criminal Justice: Lessons from the ICTY', in: B Swart, A Zahar, and G Sluiter (eds), *The Legacy of the International Criminal Tribunals for the Former Yugoslavia* (OUP 2011) 108–17.

[47] Eg, A Petrig, 'Negotiated Justice and the Goals of International Criminal Tribunals', 8 *Chi-Kent J Int'l & Comp L* (2008) 1.

[48] A Whiting, 'In International Criminal Prosecutions, Justice Delayed can be Justice Delivered', 50 *Harv Int'l LJ* (2009), 323.

[49] *See* also: ICC *Prosecutor v Lubanga*, AC, ICC-01/04–01/06–1432, 11 July 2008, Judgment on the Appeals of The Prosecutor and The Defence against Trial Chamber I's Decision on Victims' Participation of 18 January 2008, para 62.

must state whether or not the accused has indeed committed the crime with which he or she was charged.[50]

As a second aim, the guilt of the offender needs to be 'translated' into a just sentence in the case of a conviction. The trial does not end with a statement about the guilt of the offender, but with the imposition of a definite sentence.

The perpetrator is thus at the centre of the prosecution. The investigation is about his or her acts and whether or not they constitute international crimes, and about how serious the individual wrongdoing was. The conviction communicates a clear moral blame and a public censure to the accused, which s/he is willing to understand. If so, the trial can have a rehabilitative effect on the perpetrator himself and should open the door for re-entry into society.

2. Indirect aims (prevention)

There are several preventative aspects which are being aimed at by staging a trial at the international level.

First, the prosecution should assist in healing the social conflict between the perpetrator on the one side, and society together with the victim, on the other. At the international level, however, the proceedings do not only pertain to the society or societies in which the conflict originally took place. Because the crimes which are at issue shock the conscience of mankind as a whole and because the values to be protected by international criminal law are primarily those of an international character, the process affects the international community as a whole.

Secondly, it is hoped that an international trial will achieve a stabilizing effect between the parties of the conflict. Prosecution leads to an individualization of the conflict.[51] The responsibility for the humanitarian catastrophe is taken away from the collective as such and transferred to one or several individuals. 'Of course, the idea that a state, any more than a corporation, commits crimes, is a fiction. Crimes always are committed only by persons.'[52] By putting individual faces to the crimes, mutual respect between former belligerents can be reinforced. Otherwise the image of collective responsibility will prevail, inducing resentment, hatred, and frustration which may lead to further violence and new crimes.[53]

---

50 ICC *Prosecutor v Lubanga Dyilo*, TC I, ICC Case No. 01/04–01/06–1295-US-Exp-Anxl, 28 April 2008, Separate and Dissenting Opinion of Judge Blattmann attached to Decision on Disclosure Issues, Responsibilities for Protective Measures and other Procedural Matters, para 17 *et subs*.

51 C Safferling, 'The Justification of Punishment in International Criminal Law', 4 *ARIEL* (1999) 126, 159.

52 Robert H Jackson, Opening Statement Nuremberg, IMT Nuremberg, Vol 2, 150.

53 ICTY Annual Report 1994, UN Doc A/49/159, para 15.

Thirdly, it is hoped that international prosecution deters future deviance. The sole existence of norms does not have a deterrent effect. This is an empirical fact.[54] The prohibition needs to be connected to a threat of punishment and a reasonable chance that this sentence will be executed.[55]

Fourthly, the public nature of the proceeding aims at establishing the rule of law amongst the people. The message, which is to be canvassed by the trial, is that impunity is ending[56] and human rights are being effectively protected.[57] Putting an end to impunity is not only Principle I of the Nuremberg Principles. It is also one of the main goals of the so-called transitional justice process.[58] '[International trials] reflect a growing shift in the international community, away from a tolerance for impunity and amnesty and towards the creation of an international rule of law.'[59]

This effect is not limited to the post-conflict society but to the international community. 'The era of impunity is ending'.[60]

A fifth purpose of the trial is to give victims a voice.[61] The trial is the stage on which the victims get to 'tell their story'.[62] Thereby the victims leave their passive victimhood and attain an active role. This should allow them respect for their suffering and support for their needs.[63]

A sixth and final purpose of international criminal prosecution can be seen in the establishment of an official record. This might help in the further transitional justice process in order to fulfil the 'right to the truth', which is often related to victims' rights in transitional justice processes.[64] Thus a documentary purpose is being attributed to the international trial.

---

54 *See* A von Hirsch and A Ashworth, *Principled Sentencing* (Northeastern University Press 1992) 57.

55 C Safferling, 'The Justification of Punishment in International Criminal Law', 4 *ARIEL* (1999) 126, 157.

56 ICTY *Prosecutor v Kordić and Čerkez* , AC, IT-95–14/2-A, 17 December 2003, Judgment, para 1081.

57 M Damaska, 'Problematic Features of International Criminal Procedure', in: A Cassese (ed), *The Oxford Companion to International Criminal Justice* (OUP 2009) 175, 181 *et subs.*

58 *See* eg, Nuremberg Declaration on Peace and Justice, UN Doc A/62/885 Principle 2.

59 *See* Report of the UN Secretary-General, *The Rule of Law and Transitional Justice in Conflict and Post-conflict Societies*, 23 August 2004, UN Doc. S/2004/616, para 40.

60 The ICC Chief-Prosecutor Moreno Ocampo in his opening address of the first trial before the ICC ever, 26 January 2009, Transcripts, ICC-01/04–01/06-T-107-ENG, p 36.

61 In further detail, C Safferling, 'The Role of the Victim in the Criminal Process: A Paradigm Shift in National German and International Law?', 11 *ICLR* (2011) 183, 200 *et subs.*

62 E Kiza, C Rathgeber, and H-C. Rohne, *Victims of War: An Empirical Study on Victimization and Victims' Attitudes towards Addressing Atrocities* (Hamburger Edition HIS-Verlags GmbH 2006) 128.

63 *See* F Neubacher, *Kriminologische Grundlagen einer internationalen Strafgerichtsbarkeit* (Mohr Siebeck 2005) 209.

64 K Ambos, 'The Legal Framework of Transitional Justice: A Systematic Study with a Special Focus on the Role of the ICC', in: K Ambos, J Large, and M Wierda (eds), *Building a Future on Peace and Justice* (Springer 2009) 19, 34.

We can conclude by stating that we can measure several positive effects an international trial is intended to have. These affirmative effects can be attributed to the international community as such, to the parties to the conflict, to the victim, and to the perpetrator.

3. *The caveats concerning the positive effects of an international trial*

The positive effects attributed to international criminal prosecution are mostly stressed by literature on transitional justice. They match several of the goals, which are related to transitional justice processes as such. These are:[65]

- Unfolding the truth about the crimes.
- Identifying and punishing the persons responsible for these crimes.
- Preventing future crimes.
- Reinstating the dignity of the victims.
- Rehabilitating and compensating the victims.
- Promoting reconciliation

No doubt criminal prosecution can add to these aims, but one must guard against overestimating the role of criminal law and criminal procedure.

The (secondary) preventive aims, which can in general be ascribed to international criminal procedure, have to take into account the (primary) procedural aims. In the course of considering this, we discover the somewhat limited scheme of a criminal trial.

(1) The general aim attributed to criminal prosecution is that it might add to stabilizing the society in which the crimes took place. This is doubtful for several reasons. First, it is presumed that to know the truth about events which took place in the past might help the society to deal with them and build a common future. It is unclear whether this is indeed the case or whether silence is sometimes more helpful.[66] Furthermore, as will be discussed later (below the next point), the concept of truth that can be achieved by a criminal trial is too limited as to fulfil this aspect. Secondly, despite criminal prosecution of several individuals, the question of peace or conflict is still a political question which needs to be negotiated. A judicial proceeding cannot replace this political process.[67] The situation in Uganda

[65] *See* S Buckley-Zistel, *Transitional Justice als Weg zu Frieden und Sicherheit* (SFB-Governance Working Paper Series, No 15, July 2008) 6.

[66] A strong argument in favour of such a positive influence of international criminal trials on peace and stability is made by C Murphy, 'Political Reconciliation and International Criminal Trials', in: L May and Z Hoskins (eds), *International Criminal Law and Philosophy* (CUP 2010) 224.

[67] *See* L Francis and J Francis, 'International Criminal Courts, the Rule of Law, and Prevention of Harm', in: L May and Z Hoskins (eds), *International Criminal Law and Philosophy* (CUP 2010) 58, 70 *et subs*.

and the deadlock in the peace negotiations there offers a vivid example of this dilemma.[68] Thirdly, the economic development of a society is highly relevant for the peace process. The relationship between the normative and economic aspect of transitional justice seems to be underestimated and is certainly not in the scope of research in this field.

(2) A criminal trial has a limited scope as regards the truth. First, it is limited in a personal way, in that it pertains only to the accused. The activities of persons other than the accused will not be discussed. Secondly, the theme of the trial is limited in a material sense as it concerns itself only with criminal behaviour. Thematically, the trial is thus tied to the substantive and mental elements of the crime.[69] Both boundaries result in a somewhat restricted aspect of the truth, which is ascertained by a criminal trial. The truth that a trial can reveal is thus not a comprehensive truth in the material sense but a 'forensic truth', limited by the procedural aims and purposes of a trial.[70]

(3) A criminal trial follows a black and white scheme in that it foresees only two possible results: guilty or not guilty. *Tertium non datur*. There is no third alternative. There is only some differentiation possible as regards individual charges or counts, and as regards the amount of punishment. But to the basic question of identifying the true offender, a criminal trial offers only these two options: conviction or acquittal. Needless to say, a conflict in which crimes on a large scale occur is never a black and white issue. It is full of different shades of grey.

(4) Damaska takes the limited trial structure even further and emphasizes its bipolar structure.[71] He argues that as regards the promotion of human rights, a criminal trial can have a detrimental effect because the trial gives a platform for the accused to articulate his or her version of human values. Pedagogical aspirations, which might be connected to international criminal courts, would thus be badly frustrated. Even if Damaska has the two-case structure of the Anglo-American trial system in mind, his reservations apply at least to a certain extent also to the Continental criminal trial system. In any system of criminal prosecution, the accused must have a chance to defend him/herself by advancing grounds which

[68] K Apuuli, 'The ICC Arrest Warrants for the Lord's Resistance Army Leaders and Peace Prospects for Northern Uganda', 4 *JICJ* (2006) 179; K Hanlon, 'Peace or Justice: Now that Peace is Being Negotiated in Uganda, will the ICC Still Pursue Justice?', 14 *Tulsa J Comp & Int'l L* (2007) 295, and L Keller, 'Achieving Peace with Justice: The International Criminal Court and Ugandan Alternative Justice Mechanisms', 23 *Conn J Int'l L* (2008) 209.

[69] Damaska describes by saying that a conventional criminal court puts a 'magnifying glass on criminal conduct', M Damaska, 'What is the Point of International Criminal Justice?' 83 *Chi-Kent L Rev* (2008) 329, 337.

[70] As to the concept of 'truth' in a criminal trial, *see* also T Weigend, 'Should We Search for the Truth, and Who Should Do it?' 36 *North Carolina Journal of International Law and Commercial Regulation* (2011) 389, 394 *et subs.*

[71] M Damaska, 'Problematic Features of International Criminal Procedure', in: A Cassese (ed), *The Oxford Companion to International Criminal Justice* (OUP 2009) 175, 181.

exclude criminal liability.[72] The prosecuting authorities react to this problem by going 'underground'; ie by avoiding a public trial and negotiating instead. A negotiated outcome of a trial, reached behind the scenes and outside of the control by the public,[73] will be perceived as biased, and cannot achieve the positive and affirmative effects of an adjudicated outcome.[74]

(5) The documentary purpose attributed to a criminal trial is not without difficulties. The selection of evidence according to selected technical requirements would be detrimental to this aim.[75] Yet the truth, which is being pursued in a criminal trial, is different from the historical truth in the sense of an accurate record of the conflict. Any social purpose attributed to the trial must be seen through the lens of the procedural purposes, which have been specified above. This tells us that the scope of the trial is limited as the presentation of the evidence mirrors the charges and the individual guilt of the accused and is not directed towards establishing historic facts. Also, the accused has a right to a speedy trial. Delays, which would be necessary in order to clarify the entire etiology of the conflict, would have to be considered as undue, if they are not relevant for the individual responsibility, and would thus render the trial unfair towards the accused.[76]

Having said that, it is obvious that a criminal investigation and trial produces a huge amount of historic evidence. It is fair to raise the question of how much longer it would have taken to collect all the evidence about the Nazi crimes and the Holocaust if we had not had the Nuremberg trials. A public prosecutor is, after all, in a much better position to collect evidence than a historian as—in general—he or she can proceed by implementing forcible means. The collected data can be seen as relatively reliable as the prosecutor must be objective and investigate in favour too of the accused according to Art. 54 (1) (a) ICCSt. Further, the evidence is tested not only by a defence strategy but also by a bench of judges.

As to this final aim attributed to the international trial, we can summarize that indeed the documentary purpose of a trial ought to be taken into account, yet it should be noted that the trial does not aim at making a proper historical record. But criminal prosecution can add to that purpose, as the evidence presented at trial can be presumed as reliable.

---

[72] *See* as to the rights of the accused, section 6.D

[73] As to the requirement of a public trial *see* section 8.A.III.

[74] M Damaska, 'Problematic Features of International Criminal Procedure', in: A Cassese (ed), *The Oxford Companion to International Criminal Justice* (OUP 2009) 175, 182.

[75] *See* Jackson Report (1949) XI.

[76] Critical in this regard also M Damaska, 'What is the Point of International Criminal Justice?', 83 *Chi-Kent L Rev* (2008) 329, 336 *et subs.*

4. Conclusion

Developed from the background of the aims and purposes of international criminal law, we have attempted to establish a number of aims which would be central to the international criminal trial. The considerations were based on the assumption that what we called procedural aspects establish a structural framework of a criminal trial. The social aspects, which have been raised in different contexts, in particular with a view to the transitional justice as a whole, need to be tested regarding the general procedural structure of a criminal trial.

Our answer to the question 'what are the goals of international criminal justice', is thus structurally different from the approach adopted by Damaska, but the outcome is similar. Damaska asks whether there is a paramount goal of international criminal trials and identifies the pedagogical effect, the 'expressive function',[77] or in the words of Drumbl, the 'affirmative aspect',[78] as the fragile but nevertheless commonly accepted primary basis.[79] I would accept this, but for different reasons.

B. Questions of Competencies

In a legal system, every institution needs to be given a 'framework' in which it can exercise its powers. The field of competence of a court is usually called its 'jurisdiction'. We could define 'jurisdiction' in this sense as the 'official power to make legal decisions and judgments'.[80]

The rule of law requires that the parameters for this jurisdiction are laid down beforehand in order to exclude arbitrary activity of the organ. In a national system of law, jurisdictional questions are sometimes difficult in detail, but they are structurally quite straightforward. This is due to the fact that in national legal systems one would only have to differentiate according to the area of law—civil or criminal matters, and so forth. Furthermore, courts and tribunals are usually established for a specific region, so one needs to have rules for the regional competence.

The issue of jurisdiction is much more intricate at international courts and tribunals. In civil law matters, international corporations often anticipate arbitration agreements in their contractual relations. In case of conflict, an arbitration tribunal will be established *ad hoc*, operating on the basis of pre-existing Statutes and

[77] D Golash, 'The Justification of Punishment in the International Context', in: L May and Z Hoskins (eds), *International Criminal Law and Philosophy* (CUP 2010) 201, 217–20.

[78] M Drumbl, *Atrocity, Punishment and International law* (CUP 2007) 173 *et subs.*

[79] M Damaska, 'Problematic Features of International Criminal Procedure', in: A Cassese (ed), *The Oxford Companion to International Criminal Justice* (OUP 2009) 175, 184–6.

[80] The term 'jurisdiction' has two other meanings: (1) it is also used to describe the system of law courts, a judiciary, and (2) it is used as name the territory or sphere of activity over which the legal authority of a court or other institution extends.

Rules of the International Chamber of Commerce or other institutions offering services in this regard. The arbitration tribunal can decide on the issue of jurisdiction itself, determining whether the conflict at hand is one covered by the arbitration agreement. This is the so-called '*competence de la competence*'.[81] Therefore at the end, it is the parties themselves which determine the jurisdiction of the tribunal in the arbitration agreement.

When it comes to public international law, the international courts operate on a similar jurisdictional basis. State sovereignty is a concept which is similar to the private autonomy of natural persons or corporations in contract law. Courts like the ICJ in The Hague or the International Tribunal for the Law of the Sea in Hamburg derive their jurisdiction from an agreement reached by the states on a bilateral or multilateral level. As is largely the case in public international law, consent on the side of the affected states is necessary.

In the case of international criminal law, a different solution needed to be developed. As international criminal law concerns itself with large-scale crimes, which are often state-supported, a purely consent-driven legal system would be detrimental to this end. However, criminal law and criminal procedure are traditionally attributed to state sovereignty. Solving this dilemma has been a major issue in the history of international criminal law. A fully satisfactory resolution has not yet been reached. The legal rules which are applicable today are thus the result of a complex political compromise. We have to differentiate between two different forms of institutions: the *ad hoc* Tribunals (I) and the permanent International Criminal Court (II).

I. *Ad hoc* Tribunals

As we have seen earlier, until the establishment of the ICC, only *ad hoc* Tribunals executed international criminal law on the international level. These tribunals are limited in their jurisdictional scope as laid down in the respective founding document. One limit, which is common to all *ad hoc* Tribunals, is to be observed regarding the substantive law. Despite variations in one or the other regard, the jurisdiction was limited to international crimes as war crimes, crimes against humanity, genocide, and aggression. Second, according to their *ad hoc* character, the temporal and geographical scope is restricted to the specific 'situation', which was the cause for their establishment in the first place. Therefore the jurisdiction of the IMT was limited to the crimes committed by Germans during the Nazi regime or—even more restricted—during World War II. The ICTY's competence is contained in Art. 1 ICTYSt: 'The International Tribunal shall have the power to prosecute persons responsible for serious violations of international humanitarian

[81] C Wolf, *Die Institutionelle Handelsschiedsgerichtsbarkeit* (CH Beck 1992).

law committed in the territory of the former Yugoslavia since 1991 in accordance with the provisions of the present Statute.'

However, at the ICTY the question arose whether the tribunal had the power to develop its own jurisdictional scope. As we have seen above, the international character and its nature as an *ad hoc* institution warrant a broader view and relates jurisdictional questions to substantive law and the interpretation of the underlying international agreement. The Appeals Chamber of the ICTY has ruled accordingly:

> A narrow concept of jurisdiction may, perhaps, be warranted in a national context but not in international law. International law, because it lacks a centralized structure, does not provide for an integrated judicial system operating an orderly division of labour among a number of tribunals, where certain aspects or components of jurisdiction as a power could be centralized or vested in one of them but not the others. In international law, every tribunal is a self-contained system (unless otherwise provided). This is incompatible with a narrow concept of jurisdiction, which presupposes a certain division of labour.[82]

The Appeals Chamber thus felt competent to rule not only on the scope of the substantive law of war crimes,[83] but also on the question of whether its founding document, ie UN Security Council Res. 827, conformed with the UN Charter; ie the constitutionality of a Security Council Resolution was questioned.[84]

II. The ICC jurisdiction

With regard to the Rome Statute, the issue of jurisdiction is different compared to the *ad hoc* Tribunals. A permanent institution such as the ICC operates as an ordinary court. The Court has thus to find its proper place in the structure consisting of national and international criminal jurisdiction. Other than the ICTY, the ICC should thus restrict itself to a narrower interpretation of 'jurisdiction' and do exactly what the Appeals Chamber in Tadić did not do: analyse the 'integrated judicial system operating an orderly division of labour among a number of tribunals' both at the national and international level.

The Rome Statute uses the term 'jurisdiction' on several occasions. It defines 'jurisdiction' in the material sense (Art. 5 ICCSt), in the temporal sense (Art. 11 ICCSt), and in a personal sense (Arts 25 (1) and 26 ICCSt). Art. 12 ICCSt lists preconditions

---

[82] ICTY *Prosecutor v Tadić*, AC, IT-94-1, 2 October 1995, Decision on the Defence Motion for Interlocutory Appeal on Jurisdiction, para 11.

[83] Ibid, para 71 *et subs*. As regards the concept of war crimes in non-international armed conflicts the AC's decision of 2 October 1995 has established new paradigms. *See* A Cassese, *International Criminal Law* (2nd edn, OUP 2008) 86; G Werle, *Völkerstrafrecht* (2nd edn, Mohr Siebeck 2007) MN 806 *et subs*.

[84] ICTY *Prosecutor v Tadić*, AC, IT-94-1, 2 October 1995, Decision on the Defence Motion for Interlocutory Appeal on Jurisdiction, para 26 *et subs*.

to the exercise of jurisdiction, but contains nothing other than the jurisdictional issue in the formal sense. Furthermore, Art. 13 ICCSt states how the Court may exercise its jurisdiction—what is commonly referred to as 'trigger mechanisms'. The whole issue is further complicated by the inclusion of the word 'admissibility' in Art. 17 ICCSt. The question therefore arises how these different criteria interact.

Three different issues have to be separated: (1) 'jurisdiction' in the material, temporal, personal, and formal sense, (2) 'trigger mechanisms', and (3) 'complementarity'.

1. Jurisdiction

Jurisdictional questions can be separated into four different issues: jurisdiction in the material sense (a), the temporal (b), the personal (c), and the formal sense (d).

a. Jurisdiction *ratione materiae* The jurisdiction *ratione materiae* is addressed by Art. 5 ICCSt. Accordingly the ICC only has jurisdiction over genocide, crimes against humanity, war crimes, and the crime of aggression. These so-called 'core crimes'[85] are further defined in Arts 6–8 ICCSt.

Concerning the crime of aggression, a compromise was found at the Rome Conference. Whereas the ICC received jurisdiction over the crime of aggression, this jurisdiction was declared dormant by Art. 5 (2) ICCSt until agreement could be reached on the definition of this crime.[86] In the meantime the Review Conference, held in Kampala in June 2010, established the definition as stipulated in Art. 5 ICCSt.[87] The exercise of jurisdiction over the crime of aggression, however, is still resting, as the states have consented to allow 'breathing room' until 1 January 2017 according to Art. 15*bis* (3) and Art. 15*ter* (3) ICCSt. After that date, the Member States of the ICC will have to 'activate' the definition by a two-thirds majority before the crime of aggression will truly be within the jurisdiction of the ICC. Other conditions for the prosecution of the crime of aggression have been agreed and will be discussed amongst the 'trigger mechanisms'.[88]

b. Jurisdiction *ratione temporis* Regarding the temporal scope of ICC jurisdiction, Art. 11 ICCSt rules that the ICC can only prosecute crimes which were committed after 1 July 2002 (see Art. 126 ICCSt), ie after the establishment of the Court. Retroactive jurisdiction is thus ruled out.[89] Art. 22 ICCSt buttresses

---

[85] As to the debate on the subject matter jurisdiction, *see* section 1.A.XII and W Schabas, *ICC* (OUP 2010) 101 *et subs.*

[86] *See* A Seibert-Fohr, 'Das Verbrechen der Aggression im Rom-Statut: Fragen der Vertragsänderung und Jurisdiktion', 3 *Zeitschrift für Internationale Strafrechtsdogmatik* (2008) 361.

[87] Resolution RC/Res. 6 (Advanced Version, 28.06.2010), adopted on the 13th Plenary Session at the Review Conference in Kampala on 11 June 2010 by consensus. *See* C Kreß and L von Holtzendorff, 'The Kampala Compromise on the Crime of Aggression', 8 *JICJ* (2010) 1179. Further references are given at 1187 fn 30.

[88] *See* section 2.A.II.2.

[89] Triffterer/*Williams*, Art. 11 MN 1.

this. In this the ICC differs from the *ad hoc* Tribunals, which were enacted by the Security Council after the crime occurred.

Art. 5 (2) ICCSt stretches this principle further and combines it with the consent principle. For a state which becomes a member to the Rome Statute after 1 July 2002, the temporal jurisdiction begins only after the entry into force for that state, ie after the ratification process in this state has been concluded successfully. A state may accept the jurisdiction of the ICC even if it is not party to the Rome Statute according to Art. 12 (3) ICCSt. Art. 5 (2) ICCSt is inapplicable in the case of a referral of the situation by the UN Security Council according to Art. 13 (b) ICCSt.[90] However the Security Council cannot alter Art. 5 (1) ICCSt and refer a situation to the ICC where crimes have been committed prior to 1 July 2002.[91]

c. Jurisdiction *ratione personae* The ICC only has jurisdiction over natural persons pursuant to Art. 25 (1) ICCSt. States cannot be prosecuted by the ICC, yet 'state responsibility' will not be affected by the criminal responsibility of individuals according to the Rome Statute, Art. 25 (4) ICCSt. State responsibility must be claimed before other courts, like the ICJ.

According to Art. 26 ICCSt, the ICC can only prosecute persons who were over the age of eighteen at the time of the alleged commission of the crime. The Rome Statute brings the issue of the age of the offender to a procedural level and does not treat age as a question of culpability.[92] Juvenile offenders could thus be prosecuted by national courts according to the national laws.[93]

d. Jurisdiction in the formal sense The broadest restriction of the jurisdiction of the ICC however is contained in Art. 12, which is headed 'preconditions of the exercise of jurisdiction', and refers to issues of territoriality and personality.[94]

(1) Universality When contemplating an International Criminal Court whose responsibility it is to try a set of 'core crimes', one would presume that such a court would be equipped with similar jurisdictional powers over these crimes as the national courts. On a national level these core crimes, ie genocide, crimes against humanity, and war crimes, are attributable to 'universal jurisdiction'.[95] According to this principle, a national state has jurisdiction over international

90 *See* section 2.A.II.2; and W Schabas, *ICC* (OUP 2010) 275.

91 K Ambos, *Internationales Strafrecht* (3rd edn, CH Beck 2011) § 8 MN 6.

92 C Safferling, *Internationales Strafrecht* (Springer 2011) § 7 MN 16.

93 Triffterer/*Clark*/*Triffterer*, Art. 26 MN 23 *et subs.*

94 W Schabas, *ICC* (OUP 2010) 283.

95 The 'universality' of the core crimes, namely genocide, crimes against humanity, and war crimes, is disputable. With a view to genocide, the universal jurisdiction is clear, not least because Art. VI of the Genocide Convention foresees an international tribunal. Regarding the other crimes, the customary law status is more ambiguous. See A Zimmermann, 'Die Schaffung eines ständigen Internationalen Strafgerichtshofes. Perspektiven und Probleme vor der Staatenkonferenz in Rom', 58 *ZaöRV* (1998) 45, 84; H-P Kaul, 'Der Internationale Strafgerichtshof: Das Ringen um seine Zuständigkeit und Reichweite', 11 *Humanitäres Völkerrecht* (1998) 138, 140f.

crimes independent both of the place the offence was committed and of the person of perpetrator and victim.[96] An international court based on the principle of universality would thus have jurisdiction over the core crimes committed anywhere in the world, regardless also of ratification or accession. Such a structure of the ICC was envisaged by a clear majority of states at the Rome Conference.[97] After all, states could combine forces and undertake jointly what each could have done individually.[98] Yet were this to be the case, the drafters would have genuinely deviated from the consent principle in public international law and would have submitted individuals under the authority of a 'foreign' power.

The Rome Statute in the end avoids such a conflict and relies on a concept of developing the universality of the Court step by step by consent, and thus—hopefully—gains a more sustainable basis for prosecution and cooperation with the States Parties.[99]

(2) Jurisdictional basis of Art. 12 ICCSt In rejecting universal jurisdiction, the ICCSt relies on the classical principles of jurisdiction: territoriality and personality. Art. 12 ICCSt foresees a threefold system:

(a) States submit to 'automatic jurisdiction' of the ICC the crimes mentioned in Art. 5 ICCSt by accession to the Rome Statute.[100] Regarding war crimes, Art. 124 ICCSt foresees an opt-out mechanism for a period of seven years. Other reservations are not permitted.[101]
(b) The exercise of this jurisdiction by the ICC is possible, if either the crime occurred on the territory of a State Party according to Art. 12 (2) (a) ICCSt—principle of territoriality, or the crime was committed by a national of a State Party according to Art. 12 (2) (b) ICCSt—principle of personality in the active sense.
(c) The ICC may furthermore exercise jurisdiction, if the state where the crime occurred or of which the perpetrator is a national has submitted to the jurisdiction of the ICC on an *ad hoc* basis without being party to the Rome Statute according to Art. 13 (3) ICCSt—declaration on temporal

96 C Safferling, *Internationales Strafrecht* (Springer 2011) § 3 MN 46; as to the political difficulties with operating on the basis of universal jurisdiction in the European context *see*: J Geneuss, 'Fostering a Better Understanding of Universal Jurisdiction', 7 *JICJ* (2009) 945.

97 *See* A Abass, 'The International Criminal Court and Universal Jurisdiction', 6 *ICLR* (2006) 349; W Schabas, *ICC* (OUP 2010) 283.

98 This of course was the reasoning given by the drafters of the IMTSt. *See* A Zimmermann, 'Das juristische Erbe von Nürnberg', in: H Reginbogin and C Safferling (eds), *The Nuremberg Trials: International Criminal Law since 1945* (Saur 2006) 247, 248

99 O Bekou and R Cryer, 'The International Criminal Court and Universal Jurisdiction—A Close Encounter?', 56 *International & Comparative Law Quarterly* (2007) 48.

100 K Ambos, *Internationales Strafrecht* (3rd edn, CH Beck 2011) § 8 MN 6.

101 W Schabas, *ICC* (OUP 2010) 284.

jurisdiction.[102] The formal requirements for this declaration are laid down in Rule 44 RPE ICC.[103]

By establishing this complex system of formal jurisdiction, the drafters of the Rome Statute made an innovative attempt to widen the reach of the ICC. The scope of the consent principle has been reduced considerably by relying on territoriality and personality as alternatives. Because of this, the ICC can indeed prosecute individuals from non-signatory states when they have committed a crime in the territory of a Member State. Likewise the ICC can proceed against a national of a States Party, even if the crimes where not committed in the territory of a Member State.[104] The ICC has thus come as close to universal jurisdiction as possible.

Yet despite this wide jurisdictional scope, the ICC is further limited by Art. 13 ICCSt in exercising its jurisdiction. The so-called 'trigger mechanisms' contained therein will be discussed in the following.

2. Trigger mechanisms

The ICC may not exercise its jurisdiction automatically even if the conditions which were discussed above are fulfilled. Its jurisdiction must be invoked, it must be triggered. Art. 13 ICCSt offers three scenarios, with different consequences as to the procedure to be adopted, which clear the way for prosecution:

(a) A State Party refers a 'situation' to the ICC—Art. 13 a) and Art. 14 ICCSt.

(b) The UN Security Council refers a 'situation' to the ICC—Art. 13 b) ICCSt.

(c) The Prosecutor initiates an investigation *proprio motu*—Art. 13 c) and Art. 15 ICCSt.

In general, the Rome Statute thus foresees a twofold system: either a situation is referred to the Court, or the Prosecutor proceeds on his own initiative, ie *proprio motu*.[105]

---

[102] C Stahn, 'Why Some Doors May be Closed Already: Second Thoughts on a 'Case-by-Case' Treatment of Article 12 (3) Declarations', 75 *Nordic Journal of International Law* (2006) 243.

[103] In the short history of the ICC three states have made use of Art. 12 (3) ICCSt and Rule 44 RPE ICC. These were Côte d'Ivoire, Uganda, and Palestine. Concerning the Côte d'Ivoire, the ICC Prosecutor has declared to be willing to submit to PTC II for authorizing an investigation. Uganda has become a State Party on 1 September 2002. The Palestinian declaration is difficult in several regards but has not been brought before the ICC yet, *see* W Schabas, *ICC* (OUP 2010) 289 *et subs.*

[104] *See* D Akande, 'The Jurisdiction of the International Criminal Court over Nationals of Non-Parties: Legal Basis and Limits', 1 *JICJ* (2003) 618.

[105] F Hoffmeister and S Knoke, 'Das Vorermittlungsverfahren vor dem Internationalen Strafgerichtshof—Prüfstein für die Effektivität der neuen Gerichtsbarkeit im Völkerstrafrecht', 59 *ZaöRV* (1999) 785, at 806 *et subs.*

This system has been described as 'dormant jurisdiction' or latent jurisdiction, because jurisdiction must be 'activated' before it can be exercised.[106] As a consequence, the work of the ICC becomes more difficult and time consuming. For these reasons, voices are raised in favour of abolishing this complex system in order to have an effective ICC. However it must be understood that Art. 13 ICCSt is the result of the political compromise which was reached at the Rome Conference.[107] Considering the state interest in protecting sovereignty, it must be considered a great achievement to have an ICC Prosecutor who is empowered to initiate an investigation *proprio motu* at all. We will now describe the three different 'triggers' and discuss their difficulties.

a. State referral On the basis of Arts 13 (a) and 14 ICCSt, a State Party is empowered to refer a situation to the ICC in which international crimes according to Art. 5 ICCSt appear to have been committed and thereby may ask the ICC Prosecutor to determine whether one or more specific person could be charged with the commission of such crimes. At the Rome Conference, this trigger mechanism was relatively undisputed.[108] Experience with 'state complaints' in other circumstances, for example within the system of the council of Europe, shows that states tend to be reluctant to discredit other states.[109] The fear of diplomatic reprisals or other counter-measures is far too great. After all, most states have some skeletons in the closet.

However, surprisingly, a different routine developed at the ICC: self-referrals.[110] States refer a case extant in their own territory to the ICC to investigate. Such a self-referral is compatible with the wording of Arts 13 (a) and 14 ICCSt, and is thus admissible.[111] To date, the Democratic Republic of Congo, Uganda, and the Central African Republic have transferred cases to the Court by way of self-referrals.

The practice of self-referral is not entirely without problems.[112] States do not invite the international prosecutor to conduct investigations in their territory without reason. It is suspected that states may be happy to submit rebel groups to the ICC, but not crimes allegedly committed by official troops. The ICC Prosecutor is under the duty to investigate all aspects of a crime objectively pursuant to Art. 54 (1) (a)

---

[106] H Olásolo, 'Reflections on the ICC's Jurisdictional Reach', 16 *CLF* (2005) 279 at 281.

[107] As to the drafting history *see* Triffterer/ *Williams/Schabas*, Art. 13 MN 11–13.

[108] *See* W Schabas, *ICC* (OUP 2010) 295.

[109] *See* Art. 33 ECHR, *see* also C Safferling, *Internationales Strafrecht* (Springer 2011) § 13 MN 113.

[110] Critical in this regard, P Gaeta, 'Is the Practice of "Self-Referrals" a Sound Start for the ICC?', 2 *JICJ* (2004) 949.

[111] Whether this concurs with the drafting history is not relevant, *see* for methodological questions, section 1.A.XIII; also W Schabas, *ICC* (OUP 2010) 311.

[112] *See* also R Cryer, H Friman, D Robinson, and E Wilmshurst, *An Introduction to International Criminal Law and Procedure* (2nd edn, CUP 2010) 166.

ICCSt. Nevertheless, the state is in a position to influence the ongoing investigation of the international body by applying a selective cooperation scheme. Such a development is highly dangerous for the credibility and independence of the ICC and the Prosecutor in particular. The ICC should be wary of being accused of taking governments' sides and should accept only 'symmetric self-referrals'.[113]

In formal terms, the state referral must be in writing (Rule 45 RPE ICC), be directed to the ICC Prosecutor, and must be accompanied by such supporting documentation as is available to the referring state according to Art. 14 (2) ICCSt. The Prosecutor will inform the Presidency of this referral in writing according to Regulation 45 RegC. The Presidency will in accordance with Regulation 46 RegC assign the situation to a Pre-Trial Chamber.[114] The Prosecutor will then analyse the material and decide whether or not to initiate investigation according to Art. 53 (1) ICCSt.[115]

Even if Art. 17 ICCSt were applicable to state referrals only, it would be a misuse of power if, in the case of a self-referral, the state later insists on its own primacy in jurisdiction.[116] The ICCSt is also silent on the question of whether the state can withdraw a referral.[117] If the state has second thoughts and regrets the referral, it remains unclear what the correct way out of this dilemma might be. It is suggested that we proceed as per Art. 18 ICCSt. The prosecutor could thus refer the case back to the national state and at the same time keep supervisory power over further activity by that state.

b. Referral of UN Security Council A second option for bringing a situation before the ICC is a referral by the UN Security Council. The role of the UN Security Council was heavily disputed amongst the representatives to the Rome Conference. Whereas some favoured the Security Council's control over the work of the Prosecutor, others aimed at abolishing any political influence altogether. Art. 13 (b) ICCSt anticipates as a compromise a power for the Security Council

---

[113] *See* C Kreß, '"Self-Referrals" and "Waivers of Complementarity". Some Considerations in Law and Policy', 2 *JICJ* (2004) 944, 946 *et subs*.

[114] *See* eg, ICC *Situation in the Central African Republic*, Presidency, ICC-01/05–1, 19 January 2005, Decision Assigning Situation in the Central African Republic to PTC III.

[115] *See* section 5.B.I.1.

[116] K Ambos, *Internationales Strafrecht* (3rd edn, CH Beck 2011) § 8 MN 7, *see* also M El Zeidy, 'Critical Thoughts on Art. 59 (2) of the ICC Statute', 4 *JICJ* (2006) 448, 463, who argues that self-referral implies a waiver of complementarity.

[117] *See* in detail: A Maged, 'Withdrawal of Referrals—A Serious Challenge to the Function of the ICC', 6 *ICLR* (2006) 419, who is more in favour of a right to withdraw for reason of state sovereignty. The opposite view is taken by M El Zeidy, 'The Legitimacy of Withdrawing State Party Referrals and ad hoc Declarations under the Statute of the International Criminal Court', in: C Stahn and G Sluiter, *The Emerging Practice of the International Criminal Court* (Brill 2009) 55–78. He concludes that the Statute does not allow for a withdrawal. *See* also M Scharf and P Dowd, 'No Way Out? The Question of Unilateral Withdrawals or Referrals to the ICC and Other Human Rights Courts', 9 *Chi J Int'l L* (2009) 573, who argue that a withdrawal is only legitimate before the Prosecutor has started to investigate. However a political solution must be found to deal with situations like this.

to refer situations to the ICC where international crimes have allegedly occurred. In other words, the Security Council can use the ICC for its own purposes and thereby avoid establishing an *ad hoc* tribunal.

The Rome Statute thereby adds another competence to the UN Security Council even if in principle its powers are laid down in the UN Charter. The Security Council proceeds by adopting a Chapter VII Resolution. In general it must respect the prerequisites of Art. 39 *et subs.* of the UN Charter in order to do this.[118] The legitimacy of the competence to establish a 'judicial intervention' is generally accepted from the time of the creation of the ICTY and the ICTR.[119] The ICC in this regard assumes the character of a 'permanent and institutionalized *ad hoc* tribunal' from the perspective of the UN Security Council.[120]

The Security Council has acted accordingly on different occasions. By Resolution 1593 (2005), the Council referred the situation in the Dafur region to the ICC Prosecutor.[121] On 26 February 2011 the Security Council decided to also refer the Situation in the Libyan Arab Jamahiriya to the ICC.[122]

This option of referral has several advantages for the UN Security Council. It does not need to establish an *ad hoc* tribunal, which would put an enormous burden on the UN budget as has been the case at the ICTY and ICTR. Indeed, the UN does not even carry the costs of the ICC proceedings, as these will be borne by the States Party supported only by voluntary donations.[123] However, together with the referral, the Security Council accepts the ICCSt and the RPE ICC as relevant and submits to the procedural practice of the ICC.[124]

One might posit that a Security Council referral has advantages for the ICC. First, jurisdiction is not limited by territoriality or personality because Art. 12 ICCSt is not applicable. Secondly, the ICC Prosecutor can rely on the cooperation of all states, not only on the cooperation regime provided for in Part IX of the ICCSt, as the Chapter VII Resolution has mandatory effect on the UN Member states, when it states:

> *Decides* that the Libyan authorities shall cooperate fully with and provide any necessary assistance to the Court and the Prosecutor pursuant to this resolution and, while recognizing that States not party to the Rome Statute have no obligation under the Statute, urges all States and concerned regional and other international organizations to cooperate fully with the Court and the Prosecutor.[125]

---

118 W Schabas, *ICC* (OUP 2010) 301.

119 *See* section 2.B.I

120 C Safferling, *Internationales Strafrecht* (Springer 2011) § 7 MN 21.

121 UN SC Res. 1593 of 31 March 2005.

122 UN SC Res. 1970 of 26 February 2011.

123 *See* UN SC Res. 1593 of 31 March 2005, para 7; and UN SC Res. 1970 of 26 February 2011, para 8.

124 *See* W Schabas, *ICC* (OUP 2010) 301, who gives the example that the ICC would not be in a position to add other crimes to the jurisdiction *ratione materiae*.

125 *See* UN SC Res. 1970 of 26 February 2011, para 5.

The ICC Prosecutor has in the case of a referral from the Security Council, the strongest mandate in comparison to the other two trigger mechanisms.[126]

Nevertheless the relation between the ICC and the Security Council remains troubled. There are some doubts as to the applicability of Art. 17 ICCSt to a Security Council referral.[127] The ICC Prosecutor thus far seems to take for granted that the admissibility provision applies.[128] As the UN Security Council also has the power to defer the Prosecutor's investigation for twelve months according to Art. 16 ICCSt, the political influences can operate both ways and thus have a negative impact on the ICC's independence.[129] Furthermore it is unclear, if at all and to what extent the Prosecutor is limited by the wording of the Resolution by which the situation is referred to the ICC. For example, the text of Res. 1970 mentions 'crimes against humanity'.[130] Does this mean that the Prosecutor is not allowed to bring charges for war crimes?

It is submitted, that a broad approach should be applied: a 'situation' as such is referred to the ICC Prosecutor and not just some aspects of it.[131] The ICC would after all lose its stature as a judicial body if it were bound by legal determination established by a political organ.

As with state referrals, the UN Security Council must address the ICC Prosecutor in writing. The Prosecutor will inform the Presidency, who will then refer the case to a Pre-Trial Chamber.[132]

c. ***Proprio motu*** Finally, the ICC Prosecutor can also act without referral upon his or her own initiative according to Arts 13 (c) and 15 ICCSt. This option is of immense importance for the political independence of the international criminal justice system and was included amongst the trigger mechanisms, despite profound and powerful opposition.[133] However, as a courtesy to these critics, the powers of the ICC Prosecutor were restrained. By virtue of Art. 15 (3) and (4) ICCSt, the Prosecutor requires authorization by the Pre-Trial Chamber before he or she can initiate an investigation. He or she must establish a 'reasonable basis'

---

[126] C Gallavin, 'Prosecutorial Discretion within the ICC: Under Pressure of Justice', 17 *CLF* (2006), 43, who wants to build an entire hierarchy on this fact.

[127] This was left open at the Rome Conference, *see* R Philips, 'The International Criminal Court Statute: Jurisdiction and Admissibility', 10 *CLF* (1999) 61, 73, 81. *See* section 2.C.

[128] Bi-annual Reports of the Prosecutor to the Security Council, UN Doc.S/PV.5216, 2; UN Doc. S/PV.5321, 3; UN Doc. S/PV.5459, 4; UN Doc. S/PV.5589, 2.

[129] K Ambos, *Internationales Strafrecht* (3rd edn, CH Beck 2011) § 8 MN 8.

[130] UN SC Res. 1970 of 26 February 2011, Preamble: '*Considering* that the widespread and systematic attacks currently taking place in the Libyan Arab Jamahiriya against the civilian population may amount to crimes against humanity.'

[131] *See* also C Gallavin, 'Prosecutorial Discretion within the ICC: Under Pressure of Justice', 17 *CLF* (2006) 43, 57.

[132] *See* section 2.B.II.2.a.

[133] *See* eg, D Scheffer, 'The United States and the International Criminal Court', 93 *AJIL* (1993) 12 presenting the view of the USA.

in order to start an official proceeding. The details of this authorization process will be discussed at a later stage.[134]

The power of *proprio motu* is the embodiment of prosecutorial independence. This offers the Prosecutor the original meaning of the term in that s/he exercises control over governments. Hopes and expectations for justice in particular on the side of victims of mass crimes are high. Since the establishment of the ICC, the Prosecutor has received 8,792 complaints.[135] Whereas many of these communications refer to alleged crimes where the ICC does not have jurisdiction, the OTP (the Office of the Prosecutor) would be helplessly overburdened if it were called on to investigate in all these circumstances.

To-date, the Prosecutor has requested authorization in only one situation pertaining to unrest in the context of general elections in Kenya. Pre-Trial Chamber II has granted authorization even if Judge Kaul had doubts whether the ICC did indeed have jurisdiction *ratione materiae* in this case.[136]

The ICC Prosecutor is undertaking further preliminary examinations in Afghanistan, Colombia, Côte d'Ivoire, Georgia, and Palestine. On 14 October 2009, the Office made public its preliminary examination in Guinea. In none of these situations however has the Prosecutor requested authorization for the initiation of investigations thus far.

This trigger mechanism is decisive in the further development of the ICC. Only by establishing a firm policy of moving ahead without referrals by states or by the UN Security Council can the Prosecutor develop as a politically independent body, which represents humanity and works towards putting an end to impunity.

d. Triggering aggression Regarding the prosecution of the crime of aggression, the Kampala compromise has brought about several modifications of the trigger mechanisms, which are contained in Arts 15*bis* and 15*ter* ICCSt.[137]

(1) State referrals and proprio motu investigations As regards state referrals and *proprio motu* investigations, Art. 15*bis* (4)–(8) ICCSt states the following:

- Every State Party can issue a declaration, withdrawing jurisdiction regarding the crime of aggression according to Art. 15*bis* (4) ICCSt (opt-out mechanism).

---

[134] *See* section 6.C.I.

[135] *See* Report of the International Criminal Court to the UN General Assembly for 2009/2010, 19 August 2010, UN Doc. A/65/313, 16.

[136] *See* ICC, *Situation in the Republic of Kenya*, PTC II, ICC-01/09–19, 31 March 2010, Decision Pursuant to Article 15 of the Rome Statute on the Authorization of an Investigation into the Situation in the Republic of Kenya; *see* also Dissenting Opinion of Judge Kaul.

[137] C Kreß and L von Holtzendorff, 'The Kampala Compromise on the Crime of Aggression', 8 *JICJ* (2010) 1179, 1211 *et subs.*

- Acts, which have been committed by nationals of a non-state party or in the territory of a non-state party, cannot be made an issue of investigation by the ICC Prosecutor according to Art. 15*bis* (5) ICCSt.
- Otherwise the Prosecutor may proceed but needs to confer with the UN Security Council as foreseen by Art. 15*bis* (6) ICCSt. If the Security Council has already made a determination of an act of aggression committed by the state concerned, the Prosecutor may proceed with his investigation. Lacking such a Security Council determination the Prosecutor may after six months ask the Pre-Trial Chamber for authorizing the investigation with a view to the crime of aggression in accordance with Art. 15 ICCSt.

(2) Security Council referrals As regards Security Council referrals, Art. 15*ter* ICCSt provides a less complicated procedure.[138] First, the state will not profit from the opt-out mechanism pursuant to Art. 15*bis* (4) ICCSt. Secondly, no further consultation with the Security Council is needed as the referral substitutes the extra determination of an act of aggression. Finally, as is always the case with Security Council referrals, no further authorization from the Pre-Trial Chamber is necessary.

3. Differentiation between 'situation' and 'case'

After these descriptions of the different trigger mechanisms we need to consider some specific terms which appear in the Rome Statute. Art. 13 ICCSt relates the referrals to 'situations'. Whereas this term is defined nowhere in the procedural texts of the ICC, there appears a corresponding term in the Rome Statute: the 'case'. In the following we will attempt to differentiate properly between these two technical terms and propose definitions.

In Regulation 20 of the RegR we are told the following:

Regulation 20

Opening of a situation or case record

1. The Registry shall open a situation record once the Presidency has assigned the situation to a Pre-Trial Chamber pursuant to regulation 46, subregulation 2, of the Regulations of the Court, or as ordered by a Chamber or the President of a Devision.
2. Subject to an order of a Chamber, the Registry shall open a case record upon receipt on an application requesting the issuance of a warrant of arrest or a summons to appear pursuant to article 58.

Thus 'situation' is the more general, and 'case' is the more specific term. Whereas a 'situation' exists from the beginning of the procedure, and will be formally

[138] *See* K Schmalenbach, 'Das Verbrechen der Aggression vor dem Internationalen Strafgerichtshof: Ein politischer Erfolg mit rechtlichen Untiefen', 65 *JZ* (2010) 745, 751.

established in a record, a 'case' comes into play at a much later stage of the prosecution. A 'case' presupposes the identification of an individual who is the suspect of an international crime. It is unclear why the drafters of the Rome Statute decided to use the term 'situation'. As an alternative, the word 'matter' was suggested.[139] A dictionary offers a definition of 'situation' as 'a set of circumstances in which one finds oneself', or 'a state of affairs', or 'the location and surroundings of a place'.[140] But these definitions are ambiguous and not comprehensive enough for a legal term. It has to be kept in mind that the interpretation of technical terms of the Statute must be done autonomously and functionally, ie according to the specific role in the procedural setting of the ICC.

The procedural aspect of the term 'situation' defines a specific part for which the jurisdiction of the ICC is being triggered. A 'situation' describes an extract from the jurisdiction of the Court; it must sketch this 'jurisdictional island' regarding territory and time.[141] On the other side, a 'situation' must not have a direct or indirect relation to an individual person, as this would jeopardize the independence of the Prosecutor, otherwise a state or the Security Council could, according to Art. 13 (a) and (b) ICCSt, order the ICC to prosecute a specific individual. If this were the case, it would be the end of the rule of law, which relies on the separation of powers as a general structural requirement.

Under these conditions, the Pre-Trial Chamber's opinion that situations 'are generally defined in terms of temporal, territorial and in some cases personal parameters' is debatable.[142] We would agree with the first two parameters, but not with the third. A situation must by all means remain distinct from being attributed to specific individuals. For this reason it would be improper to delimit a 'situation' by referring to a specific group of individuals, like the 'situation concerning the Lord's Resistance Army'.[143] The scope of the situation has to be defined by geographic and political regions.

As regards the referrals by the Security Council, Resolution 1970 on Libya is straightforward because reference is made to 'the Libyan Arab Jamahiriya' and the starting point is determined as 15 February 2011.[144] In the context of Sudan the issue is more complex. Whereas the Security Council determines the 'the situation in Sudan continues to constitute a threat to international peace and security',[145] it

139 *See* with regard to the drafting history: W Schabas, *ICC* (OUP 2010) 297 *et subs.*
140 *See* Concise Oxford English Dictionary (11th edn, OUP 2008): 'situation'.
141 *See* also Boas/Bischoff/Reid/Taylor, *ICL III*, 68.
142 ICC *Situation in the Democratic Republic of the Congo*, PTC I, ICC-01/04–101-tEN-Corr, 17 January 2006, Decision on Application for Participation in the Proceedings of VPRS-1, VPRS-2, VPRS-3, VPRS-4, VPRS-5 and VPRS-6, para 65.
143 Similarly W Schabas, *ICC* (OUP 2010) 299.
144 UN SC Res. 1970 of 26 February 2011, para 4.
145 UN SC Res. 1593 of 31 March 2005, Preamble.

refers to the ICC Prosecutor 'the situation in Darfur since 1 July 2002'.[146] In Libya the 'situation' pertains to the entire state, in Sudan only to one specific province of one country.[147] In the case of Uganda, a purely territorial determination of the situation was adopted by referring to 'Northern Uganda', which might not be so easy to define.

Another difficulty is the end date of a situation. Whereas the Security Council defines the specific date for the investigation to begin, it cannot limit the temporal scope of the situation in advance. At the end of the day, the determination of the final date of investigation must be left to the Prosecutor. The only further way of influencing the ICC prosecution on the side of the Security Council is through Art. 16 ICCSt.[148]

We can summarize as follows: a situation is defined as a state of conflict, in which international crimes allegedly occurred, and which is limited to a certain geographical region and has a specific starting point.

As regards the definition of a 'case', Pre-Trial Chamber I has adopted a rather formal approach: 'Cases, which comprise specific incidents during which one or more crimes within the jurisdiction of the Court seem to have been committed by one or more identified suspects, entail proceedings that take place after the issuance of a warrant of arrest or a summons to appear.'[149]

It correlates with Regulation 20 RegR quoted above in that the issuance of an arrest warrant is the point in time during the prosecution process when a case is defined as coming into existence. From a normative point of view this definition seems both too narrow and too formal. In the course of the investigation of a 'situation', the ICC Prosecutor will start to identify one or several individual suspects. According to Art. 53 (2) ICCSt s/he will at one point decide whether or not and whom to prosecute. Somewhere between the identification of the individuals and the decision to prosecute the Prosecutor has a 'case'. 'Cases' are developed out of 'situations'. Certainly there can be several 'cases' pertaining to one 'situation'. A case could thus be described as 'the specific incidents in which the crimes were committed by identified perpetrators' even before they were interviewed.[150]

This differentiation between 'situation' and 'case' is mirrored in the registration numbers. Two numbers, one for the situation and one for the individual case identify every case. The *Lubanga* case number is 'ICC-01/04–01/06'. This means that

[146] UN SC Res. 1593 of 31 March 2005, para 1.

[147] *See* also W Schabas, *ICC* (OUP 2010) 299.

[148] Similarly, W Schabas, *ICC* (OUP 2010) 299.

[149] ICC *Situation in the Democratic Republic of the Congo*, PTC I, ICC-01/04–101-tEN-Corr, 17 January 2006, Decision on Application for Participation in the Proceedings of VPRS-1, VPRS-2, VPRS-3, VPRS-4, VPRS-5 and VPRS-6, para 65. Similarly: Boas/Bischoff/Reid/Taylor, *ICL III*, 69.

[150] *See* Triffterer/*Hall*, Art. 19 MN 3 referring to the OTP Report on Sudan.

case is part of the situation 01 referred the court in 2004; this is the situation in the Democratic Republic of Congo. Further the case against *Lubanga* was the first (01) to be opened in 2006. For the time being, the situation 01/04 has two other cases: *Ntagana* is 02/06 as it was filed in 2006 after *Lubanga*, and *Katanga* and *Chui* is 01/04–01/07 because it was filed 2007.

C. Complementarity (*Hilde Farthofer*)

The issue of complementarity[151] was one of the most controversial points discussed during the preparatory work for the establishment of the ICC.[152] In this regard, the content of Art. 17 ICCSt restricts the inherent competence of states to decide whether they wish to apply its national criminal jurisdiction. In the Report of the ILC 1993,[153] it was proposed that in every case any state, without limitation to interference with the state's interests, as well as those of the accused, should have the right to challenge the jurisdiction and admissibility of the Court.

Only one year later, the ILC suggested in Art. 35 Draft Statute 1994[154] that the Court may not have jurisdiction if the state which is primarily responsible for the investigation and prosecution of the crime is investigating or has duly investigated the case or if the crime in question fails to reach the gravity threshold. The wording of Art. 35 Draft Statute 1994 was ambiguous, ie the majority of legal measures taken by the state concerned with regard to the alleged crime would have blocked the jurisdiction of the Court.[155] This is particularly evident in the synopsis of Art. 35 and Art. 42 Draft Statute 1994, where the guiding principle of '*ne bis in idem*' is stipulated. According to the latter, the Court may only exercise its jurisdiction if the crime in question is 'characterized by that [national] court as an ordinary crime', or the proceedings before the national court were not carried out in an impartial or independent manner.

Finally, at the Rome Conference, the issue of complementarity was enshrined in the Preamble, in Art. 1 ICCSt and in Art. 17 ICCSt.[156] The current solution is, of course, a compromise based on a wide range of proposals and, hence, it is not perfect but is the best possible option.

---

151 On 2 August 2011, the Secretariat of the ICC established an extranet dedicated to providing information on the issue of complementarity.

152 As to the drafting history, *see* also Triffterer/*Williams*/*Schabas*, Art. 17, MN 1 *et subs.*

153 ILC, Report of the Working Group on the Draft Statute for an International Criminal Court, 3 May–23 July 1993, A/CN.4/L.488/Add.2, 12 July 1993, p 4 *et subs.*

154 ILC, Draft Statute for an International Criminal Court with commentaries, 1994, p 52.

155 L Lafleur, *Der Grundsatz der Komplementarität, Der Internationale Strafgerichtshof im Spannungsfeld zwischen Effektivität und Staatensouveränität* (Nomos 2011) 87 *et subs.*

156 For a comprehensive overview of the evolution of the concept of complementarity *see* O Solera, 'Complementary Jurisdiction and International Criminal Justice', 84 *International Review of the Red Cross* (2002) 145–71.

I. Purpose of Art. 17 ICCSt

Art. 17 ICCSt includes different scenarios which can lead to a specific 'case' being *ultra vires* the jurisdiction of the Court.[157] As in the first version of the draft, the legal text is formulated in a negative manner, ie it states the four prerequisites on which the Court has to determine whether a particular case is inadmissible. The list is mandatory and exhaustive and thus it permits the reverse conclusion that, if no mentioned exception exists, there is no reason for the Court not to have jurisdiction.[158] The final decision regarding the admissibility of a case brought before the Court by the Prosecutor is initially the responsibility of the Pre-Trial Chamber.

In the following, the key points regarding the prerequisites required by the Pre-Trial Chamber to render a case admissible will be discussed in detail. The ICC is based on (1) concurrent jurisdiction, distinguished from the system of precedence at the *ad hoc* Tribunals. To avoid intervention by the Prosecutor of the ICC, the state has to carry out (2) genuine investigation and prosecution.

1. Concurrent jurisdiction

It is without doubt that the jurisdiction of the ICC is complementary to the jurisdiction of domestic courts and is not the primary jurisdiction. Complementarity is central to the philosophy of the Court.[159] During the Review Conference in Kampala 2010, one reason for this strategy was highlighted; namely 'that the best forum for dealing with crimes was the location where they were committed, closer to affected communities and in the local language'.[160] As has been indicated, the decision to give up part of its sovereignty is not an easy one for a state, particularly when the population is opposed to power sharing with international institutions.[161]

In contrast, each statute of the *ad hoc* Tribunals encompasses a regulation concerning the relationship between the tribunal and the national jurisdiction. Art. 9

---

[157] As to the differences between a 'case' and a 'situation' *see* section 2.B.II.3.

[158] M Benzing, 'The Complementarity Regime of the ICC', 7 *Max Planck UNYB* (2003) 591, 601.

[159] W Schabas, *ICC* (OUP 2010) 336.

[160] Review Conference on the Rome Statute, ICC RC/ST/CM/1, 'Stocktaking of international criminal justice, Tacking stock of the principle of complementarity: bridging the impunity gap', 22 June 2010, Statement of S Brammertz, Prosecutor of the International Criminal Tribunal for the former Yugoslavia, para 16; J Kleffner, 'The Impact of Complementarity on National Implementation of Substantive International Criminal Law', 1 *JICJ* (2003) 86, 88 *et subs.*, the author rightly pointed out that complementarity acts as an incentive to the development of domestic criminal law codes regarding international humanitarian law with the purpose of preventing the intervention of the ICC.

[161] D Scheffer, 'The United States and the International Criminal Court', 93 *AJIL* (1999) 12, 15 *et subs.*; the author mentioned three grounds on which the USA refused to implement the Rome Statute, *inter alia,* because the ICC 'should leave to national jurisdictions the job of disciplining the isolated war crimes committed by errant soldiers'. This view is out of step with reality, at least according to the example of Abu Ghraib, where the world became aware that violations of human rights by soldiers are not isolated acts of war.

ICTYSt, Art. 8 (2) ICTRSt/SCSLSt, and Art. 4 (1) SCLSt clearly stipulate the primacy of the tribunals over the national courts which will also be exercised by issuing binding orders to states.[162]

In view of the complementary structure of the ICC, the question arises of which 'states' have primacy with regard to Art. 17 ICCSt. These could be (1) national states, (2) truth and reconciliation commissions, and (3) other international(ized) tribunals.

(1) There are several internationally recognized principles for determining which state has the right and, above all, the duty to exercise its national criminal jurisdiction over a person who has committed atrocities on its territory (territorial principle), or against its population (passive personality principle), or is a national of the state in question (active personality principle). Moreover, a state may establish offences in its criminal laws which allow it to prosecute serious international crimes regardless of the existence of one of the above-mentioned principles (universality principle),[163] eg if an alleged perpetrator received asylum status in a state, that state will probably bring the suspect before its own national court. Most recently, Germany started prosecuting two suspects who allegedly committed crimes on the territory of the DRC.[164]

(2) In addition to the difficulties caused by the relationship between national criminal jurisdiction and the jurisdiction of the ICC, the controversial issue of a truth and reconciliation commission as an institution carrying out both investigations and prosecutions is also at issue. Legal scholars are undecided and either favour or oppose the idea that a truth and reconciliation commission could satisfy the requirements of a judicial process and, hence, any investigation carried out would block the investigation of the Prosecutor.[165] In the present author's view, both the commission and the ICC co-exist because of their different addressees and, of course, they should cooperate when carrying out their duties.[166] The former should

[162] ICTY *Prosecutor v Blaškić*, AC, IT-95-14-A, 29 October 1997, Judgment on the Request of the Republic of Croatia for review of the decision of Trial Chamber II of 18 July 1997, para 29.

[163] The application of the universality principle is disputed because of the impossibility of carrying out effectively the evidence-gathering process; M Benzing, 'The Complementarity Regime of the ICC', 7 *Max Planck UNYB* (2003) 591, 623.

[164] At 4 May 2011, the trial against two alleged leaders of the *Forces Démocratiques de Libération du Rwanda* (FDLR) has commenced due to charges of crimes against humanity and war crimes committed in the DRC, according to the German universal jurisdiction statute (*Völkerstrafgesetzbuch*).

[165] In favour, C Stahn, 'Complementarity, Amnesties and Alternative Forms of Justice: Some Interpretative Guidelines for the International Criminal Court', 3 *JICJ* (2005) 695, 697; against L Lafleur, *Der Grundsatz der Komplementarität. Der Internationale Strafgerichtshof im Spannungsfeld zwischen Effektivität und Staatensouveränität* (Nomos 2011) 169.

[166] A Bisset, 'Rethinking the Powers of Truth Commissions in Light of the ICC Statute', 7 *JICJ* (2009) 963, 966 *et subs.*, the author mentioned the problems which could be caused by obliging truth and reconciliation commissions to cooperate with the ICC. However, the main purpose of the ICC is to fill the gap of immunity and this should not be undermined by considerations of whether the commission can be compelled to disclose information.

investigate and make public the crimes committed by subordinates, while the latter should investigate and prosecute the crimes committed by leaders and head of states. The Prosecutor, and subsequently the Court, face the same problems when dealing with national amnesty laws.[167] The solution should be found in the cooperation between these two judicial systems to deal with atrocities. The amnesty or pardon should only be for direct perpetrators, as for example for child soldiers,[168] and not for high level leaders who, for example, have directed the commission of genocide.

(3) The hierarchy between the jurisdiction of other international courts and the ICC must be considered as well. The temporal jurisdiction of the ICC, starting on 1 July 2002, and the jurisdiction of the ICTY and SCSL respectively overlap. According to Art. 8 ICTYSt, for the ICTY the starting point is 1 January 1991 and according to Art. 1 SCSLSt, for the SCSL it is 30 November 1996 but no deadline is mentioned for either. After commencement of investigation, both tribunals have precedence over the jurisdiction of the ICC.

Generally, the jurisdiction of the STL is limited to the attack on the former Lebanese Prime Minister Rafiq Hariri on 14 February 2005. Art. 1 STLSt further provides for the opportunity to extend the temporal jurisdiction but only if the parties, ie the Government of Lebanon and the UN, decide to do so and the Security Council does not object. If this occurs, there will be an overlap of jurisdiction between the ICC and the STL. In this instance, the STL would have primacy after initiating investigations. Concerning other hybrid courts, no problems regarding temporal jurisdiction will arise. The jurisdictions of the ECCC and the Special Panels for Serious Crimes in the District Court of Dili, East Timor, date before 1 July 2002 due to their fixed time frames.

This demonstrates that the term 'state' used in Art. 17 ICCSt comprises more than its literal meaning. However, a broader interpretation is to be preferred because of the multitude of institutions, state actors, and non-state actors involved in the peace process in a country after an armed conflict. In the present author's opinion, the Court should only step in as an instrument of last resort where crimes falling under the definition of Art. 5 ICCSt are committed and the responsible state fails to investigate and prosecute.[169]

2. *Genuine investigation and prosecution*

To prevent the intervention of the Prosecutor of the ICC, it is not sufficient for a state to carry out investigations genuinely but afterwards fail to properly conduct

[167] C Stahn, 'Complementarity, Amnesties and Alternative Forms of Justice: Some Interpretative Guidelines for the International Criminal Court', 3 *JICJ* (2005) 695, 709 *et subs.*

[168] L Moreno-Ocampo, 'Keynote Address: Integration the Work of the ICC into Local Justice Initiatives', 21 *American University International Law Review* (2005) 497, 500.

[169] This is key principle of OTP, Prosecutorial Strategy 2009–2012, 1 February 2010, para 16 *et subs.*

prosecution, according to Art. 17 (1) (a) ICCSt. The threshold for a proper investigation is laid down in Part 5 of the Statute. Art. 54 (1) (a) ICCSt determines that the investigation must 'cover all [relevant] facts and evidence' in order to establish the truth. Moreover, the state authority must take all appropriate measures and, by doing so, must respect the rights of the accused as well as the interests of victims and witnesses. Investigation should not only be understood as criminal investigation but also as 'procedures which are designed to establish the evidence and facts'.[170]

It is not necessary that the investigation is subsequently followed by the prosecution of the alleged perpetrator. The wording of Art. 17 (1) (b) ICCSt allows the state to decide to refrain from prosecuting on reasonable grounds and, therefore, the work of truth and reconciliation commissions as well as the implication of an amnesty or pardon can cause the inadmissibility of a specific case.

II. Inadmissibility as the rule

If one of the criteria mentioned in Art. 17 (a)–(c) ICCSt is fulfilled, the Pre-Trial Chamber must rule the case inadmissible. The rationale for this consideration is that the sovereignty of a state may not be infringed if it conducts its duties properly, ie investigating and prosecuting large-scale crime. In the situation of the Congo, the Pre-Trial Chamber drew attention to the exception of the above mentioned principle by stating that 'when a State with jurisdiction over a case is investigating, prosecuting or trying it, or has done so, it is not sufficient to declare such a case inadmissible'.[171]

According to Art. 17 (1) (b) ICCSt, the domestic prosecutor also has the opportunity to decide not to prosecute but only if the case in question is fully investigated and the reasons for refraining from prosecuting are not in opposition to the interests of justice. If there is *prima facie* evidence that the decision was taken simply because the state was unwilling, the Court will determine the case admissible.

If the requirements of the principle of *ne bis in idem* are fulfilled, the case is inadmissible. But if the proceedings were only carried out, for example, to shield the perpetrator from being prosecuted in other courts, the jurisdiction of the ICC will fill the gap. A genuinely investigated and prosecuted case, especially when resulting in an acquittal, should not be tried unless the Court is satisfied that the proceedings were carried out for the above-mentioned reason, ie to shield the alleged perpetrator.

---

[170] C Stahn, 'Complementarity, Amnesty and Alternative Forms of Justice: Some Interpretative Guidelines for the International Criminal Court', 3 *JICJ* (2005) 695, 711.

[171] ICC *Situation in the Democratic Republic of Congo*, PTC, ICC-01/04–02/06–20-Anx2, 10 February 2006, Decision on Prosecutor's Application for Warrants of Arrest, Article 58, para 32.

The last criterion which has to be taken into consideration is the 'gravity of the crime', where the standard given in Art. 5 ICCSt, ie 'the most serious crimes of concern', is to be applied. If the crime does not meet this threshold, the case should not be investigated by the Prosecutor. The legal text clearly points to the primacy of domestic criminal jurisdiction and, again, the Court may only step in to prevent impunity. One has to bear in mind that the final decision on this issue falls within the discretionary power of the Court and the state concerned will not be able to prevent the investigations by the Prosecutor if an appeal is not successful.

In *Katanga and Chui*, the Appeals Chamber ruled that 'inaction on the part of a State having jurisdiction (that is, the fact that a State is not investigating or prosecuting, or has not done so) renders a case admissible before the Court'[172] and, hence, the unwillingness and inability criteria have not yet been examined.[173]

III. Challenges

The Court has the discretion to decide 'on any challenge or question of admissibility', according to Rule 58 (4) RPE ICC. A challenge might be brought by the accused or suspect or the state which has jurisdiction.[174] If the state is not a Member State, it must have accepted the jurisdiction of the Court, pursuant to Art. 19 (2) (a)–(c) ICCSt, or the Prosecutor must have started to examine the situation based on a Security Council referral.

Remarkably, each party can only challenge the admissibility once, while the Chamber can decide on this issue as often as necessary.[175] In *Katanga and Chui*, the Pre-Trial Chamber determined three stages for challenging admissibility within the period stipulated. In the first phase ending with the decision on the confirmation of charges, the challenge of admissibility is permitted on all four grounds included in Art. 17 (1) ICCSt. Then, up until the establishment of the Trial Chamber, the parties can bring challenges based on the principle of *ne bis in idem*. And, finally, after this stage, challenges of admissibility are allowed 'on the *ne bis in idem* principle only under exceptional circumstances and with the authorization of the Trial Chamber'.[176]

---

[172] ICC *Prosecutor v Katanga and Chui*, AC, ICC-01/04–01/07–1497, 25 September 2009, Judgment on the Appeal of Mr Germain Katanga against the Oral Decision of Trial Chamber II of 12 June 2009 on the Admissibility of the Case, para 78.

[173] Ibid, para 97.

[174] Arts 18 and 19 ICCSt are discussed in detail, *see* section 5.B.

[175] ICC *Prosecutor v Kony et al.*, PT II, ICC-02/04–01/05–377, 10 March 2009, Decision on the Admissibility of the Case under Article 19 (1) of the Statute, para 25; M Newton, 'Comparative Complementarity: Domestic Jurisdiction Consistent with the Rome Statute of the International Criminal Court', 167 *Military Law Review* (2010) 20, 58.

[176] ICC *Prosecutor v Katanga and Chui*, TC II, ICC-01/04–01/07-T-67-ENG, 12 June 2009, Transcript of the oral decision on the admissibility of the case, p 3 *et subs.*

Notably, no challenge has yet been brought. Nevertheless, the Court shall determine the admissibility of the case or situation on its own initiative as stipulated in Art. 19 (1) ICCSt.[177] In the situation of Libya, Pre-Trial Chamber I noted that it would not rule on admissibility at that stage[178] because as long as the armed conflict persists, it would not make sense to decide *ex ante* without knowing if the potentially new government of Libya will investigate and prosecute.

In the case of a Security Council referral and when the Prosecutor starts investigation *proprio motu*, the proceedings operate as follows. According to Art. 18 (1) ICCSt, the Prosecutor has to inform the state concerned. Subsequently, the state has one month to offer a written submission stating that it is investigating and prosecuting the alleged perpetrators based on domestic jurisdiction. In *Garda*, the Sudan did not reply to the notification by the Prosecutor and therefore the Chamber rendered the case admissible.[179] Art. 18 (2) ICCSt is mandatory in regard to the duty of the Prosecutor to defer the case to the national courts if requested by the affected state. However, the Pre-Trial Chamber has the discretion to overturn the request and to determine the case admissible.

A particular case, not mentioned in the Statute, emerges from self-referrals by the state which gives jurisdiction to the Court.[180] In such cases, the referring state is obviously willing to bring the alleged perpetrators to justice.[181] However, the Chamber ruled in *Katanga and Chui* that 'a State which chooses not to investigate or prosecute a person before its own courts, but has nevertheless every intention to seeing that justice is done, must be considered as lacking the will'.[182] Meanwhile in *Kony et al.*, the Court determined that Uganda was able as well as willing to investigate and prosecute the crimes in question but decided that the ICC would be the better forum to do so *inter alia* because the accused were acting from the territory of Southern Sudan and therefore it would be very difficult to arrest them.[183] The same problem

177 ICC *Prosecutor v Kony et al.*, PTC II, ICC-02/04–01/05–377, 10 March 2009, Decision on the Admissibility of the Case under Article 19 (1) of the Statute, para 45 *et subs*.

178 ICC *Situation of Libya Arab Jamahiriya*, PTC I, ICC-01/11–01/11–2, 27 June 2011, Warrant of Arrest of Muammar Mohammad Abu Minyar Gaddafi, p 3 *et subs*.

179 ICC *Prosecutor v Garda*, PTC I, ICC-02/05–02/09–243-Red., Decision on the Confirmation of Charges, 8 February 2010, para 29.

180 *See* section 2.B.II.2.a. In favour of self-referrals being waived for complementarity, C Kreß, "Self Referrals' and 'Waiver of Complementarity", 2 *JICJ* (2004) 944, 946; against this approach A Müller and I Stegmiller, 'Self-Referrals on Trial, From Panacea to Patient', 8 *JICJ* (2010) 1267, 1290.

181 M Zeidy, 'The Ugandan Government Triggers the Complimentary Principle', 5 *ICLR* (2005) 83, 101, the author argues that it would be illogical to reject a request by a state which waives its right to investigate and prosecute in favour of the Court.

182 ICC *Prosecutor v Katanga and Chui*, TC, ICC-01/04–01/07–1213-tENG, 16 June 2009, Reasons for the Oral Decision on the Motion Challenging the Admissibility of the Case (Article 19 of the Statute), para 77.

183 ICC *Prosecutor v Kony et al.*, PTC I, ICC-02/04–01/05–377, 10 March 2009, Decision on the Admissibility of the Case under Article 19 (1) of the Statute, para 37.

arose in *Bemba* where the defence argued that the self-referral of a particular case would absolve the state which was under the duty to investigate and prosecute from its obligations.[184] The Chamber argued in its findings that '[b]y this referral, the CAR indicated its "unwillingness" to prosecute the accused domestically'.[185] The self-referral problem might be better resolved by the implementation of *aut dedere aut judicare* than by declaring the unwillingness or inability of a state to fulfil either of the two options.[186] The duty of a self-referring state to investigate and prosecute is modified into the duty to cooperate with the ICC.

IV. Exceptions to the inadmissibility principle

As mentioned above, the case is admissible if none of the provided scenarios in Art. 17 (1) ICCSt can be established. But even if a state is in the process of investigating, the Court can determine the admissibility of the case; namely, if the state is unwilling or unable to carry out the investigation properly. Indicia for this could be modest progress or the omission of obvious facts.

1. Unwillingness genuinely to investigate or prosecute

First and foremost according to Art. 17 (2) ICCSt, the Pre-Trial Chamber must determine if the principles of due process[187] recognized in international law have been complied with, ie if the rights stipulated in Art. 14 ICCPR and Art. 6 ECHR are implemented; for example the principle of presumption of innocence as well as the right to be assisted by counsel. Notably, the fair trial standard test according to the wording of Art. 17 (2) ICCSt is a prerequisite and has to be taken into consideration before ruling on the options mentioned in (a)–(c) of Art. 17 ICCSt. By implication, the shielding of a person, unjustified delay, and lack of impartiality and independence will be in inviolation of fair trial standards.

Notably 'a State's failure to guarantee a defendant due process is not currently a ground for admissibility'.[188] The individual has no right to refer his or her case to the ICC arguing that his or her right to due process is being violated. The case is

---

[184] ICC *Prosecutor v Bemba*, OTP, ICC-01/05–01/08–739, 29 March 2010, Prosecution's Response to Motion Challenging the Admissibility of the Case by the Defence for Jean-Pierre Bemba Gombo pursuant to Article 17 and 19 (2) (a) of the Rome Statute, para 47.

[185] ICC *Prosecutor v Bemba*, TC III, ICC-01/05–01/08–802, 24 June 2010, Decision on the Admissibility and Abuse of Process Challenges, para 243.

[186] M Cross and S Williams, 'Recent Developments at the ICC: *Prosecutor v Germain Katanga and Mathieu Ngudjolo Chui*—A Boost for "Co-operative Complementarity"?', 10 *HRLR* (2010) 336, 344.

[187] Regarding the European Convention on Human Rights a comprehensive overview can be found in N Mole and C Harby, *The Right to a Fair Trial, A Guide to the Implementation of Article 6 of the European Convention on Human Rights* (2nd edn, Council of Europe 2006).

[188] K Heller, 'The Shadow Side of Complementarity: The Effect of Article 17 of the Rome Statute on National Due Process', 10 *CLF* (2006) 255, 260.

only admissible because the proceedings are carried out to the advantage of the alleged perpetrator and not because they are contrary to recognized international human rights law.

If the state which has jurisdiction has begun to investigate this 'must encompass both the person and the conduct',[189] the so-called 'conduct test'. Challenging the admissibility of the case of three accused, the Government of Kenya argued that it had started the investigation of groups of individuals at the same hierarchical level as the accused before the Court. The Chamber clearly pointed out that this declaration did not satisfy the Court, that according to Art. 19 (1) ICCSt, genuine investigations are to be initiated.[190]

If the proceedings were intentionally conducted to shield a perpetrator in order to prevent the intervention of the Prosecutor, the case would be admissible.[191] The specialized courts established in Sudan to deal with large-scale crimes committed in the Darfur region have only one practical purpose, namely to hinder investigations by the ICC Prosecutor.[192]

The second option regarding the unwillingness of a state, enshrined in Art. 17 (2) (b) ICCSt, mentions unjustified delay 'which in the circumstances is inconsistent with an intent to bring the person concerned to justice'. The criterion to determine the time span which has to be exceeded depends on the normal length of national proceedings.[193]

Art. 17 (2) (c) ICCSt stipulates the last criterion to be examined by the Court to determine admissibility of a specific case: a lack of independence and impartiality of the domestic court as well as of the investigative authorities may result in the decision that the case is admissible. Rule 51 RPE ICC explicitly refers to the

---

[189] ICC *Situation in the Democratic Republic of the Congo*, PTC I, ICC-01/04–02/06–20-Anx2, 10 February 2006, Decision on the Prosecutor's Application for Warrants of Arrest, Article 58, para 38.

[190] ICC *Prosecutor v Ruto et al.*, PTC II, ICC-01/09–01/11–101, 30 May 2011, Decision on the Application by the Government of Kenya Challenging the Admissibility of the Case Pursuant to Article 19 (2)(b) of the Statute, para 53 *et subs.*, *see* also M Delmas-Marty, 'Interactions between National and International Criminal Law in the Preliminary Phase of Trial at the ICC', 4 *JICJ* (2006) 2, 4.

[191] Eg, an 'undue delay' combined with disrespect for the procedural law clearly indicates the shielding of a person, M Zeidy, *The Principle of Complementarity in International Criminal Law: Origin, Development and Practice* (Martinus Nijhoff Publishers 2008) 170 *et subs.* and M Benzing, 'The Complementarity Regime of the International Criminal Court: International Criminal Justice between State Sovereignty and the Fight against Impunity', 7 *Max Planck UNYB* (2003) 591, 610.

[192] K Heller, 'The Shadow Side of Complementarity: The Effect of Article 17 of the Rome Statute on National Due Process', 10 *CLF* (2006) 255, 256.

[193] M Benzing, 'The Complementarity Regime of the International Criminal Court: International Criminal Justice between State Sovereignty and the Fight against Impunity', 7 *Max Planck UNYB* (2003) 591, 611; the author suggests that the Court should determine a time frame common to all domestic legal systems. This approach is not feasible, because of the different stages of development of judicial systems throughout the world.

requirement that the domestic court must 'meet internationally recognized norms and standards' regarding impartiality and independence.[194]

Examining the jurisdiction of the ECtHR, there are four considerations to be taken into account concerning the independence of the Court. Thus 'the Court has had regard to the manner of appointment of its members and the duration of their term in office, the existence of guarantees against outside pressures and the question whether the body presents an appearance of independence.'[195]

Regarding the determination of whether a court is impartial, the ECtHR decided that:

> impartiality normally denotes absence of prejudice or bias, its existence or otherwise can, notably under Article 6 § 1 (art. 6–1) of the Convention, be tested in various ways. A distinction can be drawn in this context between a subjective approach, that is endeavouring to ascertain the personal conviction of a given judge in a given case, and an objective approach, that is determining whether he offered guarantees sufficient to exclude any legitimate doubt in this respect.[196]

Regarding the ICC, the term 'impartiality' has been defined by the Prosecutor. In his statement, he clearly pointed out that 'impartiality does not mean that we must necessarily prosecute all groups in a given situation. Impartiality means that we will objectively apply the same criteria for all'.[197]

Proceedings which lack impartiality and independence are called sham proceedings and are clearly not in the interests of justice, and thus the explicit reference to them is an important step in removing impunity, in particular regarding persons in high-level government positions. The crucial point is not the 'goodwill' of the state in carrying out proper proceedings but rather the *de facto* situation in a country. According to the state of affairs on the ground the ICC will decide whether the domestic jurisdiction has met the fair trial standards. To render a case admissible a *prima facie* presumption would be sufficient for the Pre-Trial Chamber.

2. *Inability to investigate or prosecute*

The second basis for the Court to determine the admissibility of a particular case, albeit when criminal proceedings have been carried out, is the inability of the state authorities to conduct an investigation and prosecution properly. Firstly, inability can be caused by *de facto* circumstances, for example the absence of trained judges

[194] For a comprehensive overview on this topic *see* M Zeidy, *The Principle of Complementarity in International Criminal Law: Origin, Development and Practice* (Martinus Nijhoff Publishers 2008) 195 *et subs.*

[195] ECtHR *Campbell and Fell v the United Kingdom*, Judgment (Merits and just satisfaction), Series A No 80, 28 June 1984, para 78.

[196] ECtHR *Piersack v Belgium*, Judgment (Merits), Series A No 53, 1 October 1992, para 30.

[197] L Moreno-Ocampo, Statement at the Informal Meeting of Legal Advisors of Ministers of Foreign Affairs, (24 October 2005), 6.

owing to the effect of an ongoing armed conflict, as in Colombia.[198] Undeniably, in many states there will not be sufficient technical or other resources to carry out investigations as may exist in wealthier countries. This is particularly the case with regard to large-scale crimes. This should not be a reason, however, for the Court to automatically deny the exercise of national criminal jurisdiction.[199]

Secondly, there may be legal reasons for the inability, as for example the absence of any specific provision for the charges in the domestic criminal laws; the case of *Lubanga* is one in point because the DRC does not provide for criminal offences regarding the enlistment and recruitment of child soldiers.[200]

In deciding whether a state is unable to carry out its duties regarding criminal jurisdiction 'due to a total or substantial collapse or unavailability of its national judicial system', the Court has to determine if the state authorities are able (1) to apprehend the suspect, or (2) to gather evidence including testimonies, and, as a catch-all element, (3) 'to carry out its proceedings' (Art. 17 (3) ICCSt).

In the case of *Bemba*, the Central African Republic (CAR) started investigations and charged the accused with broadly the same offences now being brought by the Prosecutor at the ICC. The Chamber rightly noted 'that the CAR does not have the capacity to conduct a trial of this kind, given the human resources required, the number of cases pending before the national courts and the shortage of judges'.[201] Furthermore, the senior investigating judge of Bangui ruled that the accused could not be prosecuted due to his diplomatic immunity as Vice-President of the DRC. This decision was appealed and subsequently reversed. Trial Chamber III pointed out that the first finding had the sole purpose of shielding the accused and was thus not justified on a legal basis.[202] The Trial Chamber's decision was affirmed by the Appeals Chamber and hence, the case was deemed admissible.[203]

---

[198] J Easterday, 'Deciding the Fate of Complementarity: A Columbian Case Study', 26 *Arizona Journal of International & Comparative Law* (2009) 50, 88.

[199] The author has a different view, arguing that every country 'possesses the juridical ability to proscribe and prosecute the crimes detailed in the Rome Statute', M Newton, 'Comparative Complementarity: Domestic Jurisdiction consistent with the Rome Statue of the International Criminal Court', 167 *Military Law Review* (2001) 20, 35.

[200] Review Conference on the Rome Statute, ICC RC/ST/CM/1, Stocktaking of international criminal justice, Tacking stock of the principle of complementarity: bridging the impunity gap, 22 June 2010, Statement of Colonel Toussaint Muntazini Mukimapa, Deputy Auditor General of the DRC, para 34.

[201] ICC *Prosecutor v Bemba*, TC III, ICC-01/05–01/08–802, 24 June 2010, Decision on the Admissibility and Abuse of Process Challenges, para 245.

[202] Ibid, para 221.

[203] ICC *Prosecutor v Bemba*, AC, ICC-01/05–01/08–962, 19 October 2010, Judgment on the appeal of Mr Jean-Pierre Bemba Gombo against the decision of Trial Chamber III of 24 June 2010 entitled 'Decision on the Admissibility and Abuse of Process Challenges'.

V. *Ne bis in idem*

In examining the admissibility of a particular case, the Court has to determine if the rule of double jeopardy, enshrined in Art. 17 (1) (c) ICCSt and Art. 20 ICCSt, prevails.[204] No one should be tried by the Court if he or she has already been prosecuted by another court[205] and vice versa.[206] The charges must pertain to the same conduct as proscribed in Arts 6, 7, and 8 ICCSt. Notably, Art. 20 (3) (a) and (b) ICCSt refers to Art. 17 (2) (a) and (c) ICCSt, by stipulating exceptions to the principle of *ne bis in idem*. Firstly, the proceedings were carried out for the main purpose of shielding the person concerned, and secondly, the trial did not meet the internationally recognized standard of impartiality and independence. If the Court finds one of these criteria *prima facie*, it has to rule the case admissible.

In *Bemba*, the CAR had commenced investigations and subsequently brought charges against the accused. The domestic judge determined that 'the accused could not be prosecuted for the charges... because he was the Vice-President of the DRC, and accordingly enjoyed immunity'.[207] The national prosecutor appealed against the decision and proximately, the Cour de Cassation of the CAR referred the case to the ICC. In its challenge, the defence argued that the double jeopardy rule, according to Art. 17 (1) (c) ICCSt, would be fulfilled and therefore the Court must rule the case inadmissible. The Chamber determined that '[t]he decision at first instance in the CAR was not in any sense a decision on the merits of the case... and it did not result in a final decision or acquittal of the accused'.[208] Hence, the case was ruled admissible. This was also possible because immunity from criminal prosecution due to the official capacity of a suspect is irrelevant at the ICC, pursuant to Art. 27 ICCSt, in contrast to the domestic criminal jurisdiction.[209]

The *ne bis in idem* principle is also stipulated in Art. 10 RPE ICTY[210] and Art. 9 RPE ICTR/SCSL but it is focused on the primacy of the *ad hoc* Tribunals over the jurisdiction of the national courts and hence is not a concept relating to complementarity.[211] In *Haradinaj et al.*, the Appeals Chamber ordered the partial retrial

204 The *ne bis in idem* concept is also stipulated in Rule 168 RPE regarding offences against the administration of the Court, pursuant to Art. 70.

205 W Schabas, *ICC* (OUP 2010) 379.

206 As to the *ne bis in idem* principle in general, *see* C Safferling, *Towards an International Criminal Procedure* (OUP 2003) 319–31.

207 Ibid, para 221.

208 Ibid, para 248.

209 D Akande, 'The Legal Nature of Security Council Referrals to the ICC and its Impact on Al Bashir's Immunities', 7 *JICJ* (2009) 333.

210 G Conway, '*Ne bis in idem* and the International Criminal Tribunals', 14 *CLF* (2003) 351, 361 *et subs*.

211 For an overview of main tribunal case law *see* ibid.

of the accused because 'the Trial Chamber I failed to take sufficient steps to counter the witness intimidation that permeated the trial'.[212] In a later decision the Appeals Chamber clearly pointed out that a retrial, also when following an acquittal, does not place the accused in alleged double jeopardy.[213]

VI. Gravity threshold

The last criterion to be analysed by the Court in order to determine admissibility is the gravity threshold enshrined in Art. 17 (1) (d) ICCSt.[214] This should restrict the intervention by the prosecutor to situations where mass crimes were or are being committed. Regarding individual responsibility, the Court should focus on the leader and head of state, and not on the single direct perpetrator acting under the direction of the former.

The criteria for establishing the gravity threshold were first defined by the prosecutor regarding the selection of situations. The gravity of a crime depends on 'the number of persons killed, the number of victims, particularly in the case of crimes against "physical integrity", such as wilful killing and rape, the severity of the crimes, the scale of the crimes, the systematicity of the crimes, the nature of the crimes, the manner in which those crimes were committed and the impact of the crimes'.[215]

Schabas claims that the criteria are unduly orientated towards quantity and hence should be amended by several features. Crimes committed by direct perpetrators who are acting on behalf of a state fulfil the gravity threshold because of the higher probability that their conduct will remain unpunished.[216] In the situation in the DRC, the Court comprehensively examined the wording of Art. 17 (1) (d) ICCSt and pointed out the two main features for determining the gravity threshold: 'First, the conduct which is the subject of a case must be either systematic (patterns of incidents) or large scale' or '[s]econd, [...] due consideration must be given to the social alarm such conduct may have caused in the international community.'[217]

---

[212] ICTY *Prosecutor v Haradinaj et al.*, AC, IT-04–84-A, 19 July 2010, Judgment, para 49. In contrast, Schabas, Art. 20, 376 *et subs.*; the author mentioned that 'the whole idea of retrial before the Court is so remote probably explains why the corresponding provisions of the *ad hoc* Tribunals do not even consider this possibility', a now disproven assumption.

[213] ICTY *Prosecutor v Haradinaj et al.*, AC, IT-04–84*bis*-A73.1, 31 May 2011, Decision on Haradinaj's Appeal on the Scope of Partial Retrial, para 32.

[214] A gravity-requirement appears also in Art. 53 ICCSt and will be discussed in detail there, *see* section 5.B.

[215] S SáCouto and K Clearly, 'The Gravity Threshold of the International Criminal Court', 23 *American University International Law Review* (2008) 807, 824 *et subs.*

[216] W Schabas, 'Complementarity in Practice: Some Uncomplimentary Thoughts', printed in ICC *Prosecutor v Bemba*, ICC-01/05–01/08–721-Anx11, p 25.

[217] ICC *Situation in the Democratic Republic of the Congo*, PT I, ICC-01/04–02/06–20-Anx2, 10 February 2006, Decision on the Prosecutor's Application for Warrants of Arrest, Article 58, para 47.

Even if the case were admissible on the grounds, for example, that the national proceedings were only carried out to shield a person from the jurisdiction of the ICC, the crime cannot be brought before the ICC if the gravity threshold is not met.

VII. Conclusion

The system of the ICC provides many safeguards for states to avoid intervention into their domestic affairs by the Prosecutor. However, if the state fails to act properly, the ICC will step in to fill the gap of impunity. Within the above-mentioned requirements, the gravity threshold will be the main obstacle to achieving the admissibility of a particular case.

The Prosecutor already interprets the gravity threshold in a restrictive manner when selecting the situation. In the situation of Iraq, the Prosecutor received over 240 communications. However, he decided that the gravity threshold was not met. The specific gravity threshold for war crimes, ie that the crime committed is part of a plan or policy or part of a large-scale commission, was not evident thus there was no reasonable basis to proceed with investigations.[218] One has to bear in mind that the Pre-Trial Chamber has only to render a decision on admissibility if the Prosecutor decides that there is a reasonable basis to proceed with investigation and subsequently requests the authorization of the Court. This approach aims to achieve the main goal of the ICC, namely to prosecute exclusively those persons most responsible for the crimes committed, the leaders and heads of state.

The remaining prerequisites of admissibility enshrined in Art. 17 ICCSt are interpreted in a broad manner whereby the Prosecutor has to balance the information provided. As history has shown, national courts dealing with mass-scale crimes, in particular war crimes, always face considerable problems and can lose credibility. The main complaints against national proceedings in such cases are based on the alleged lack of impartiality and independence of the courts concerned as, for example, in the *Leipziger Prozesse*.[219]

---

[218] The Office of the Prosecutor, Situation in Iraq, 9 February 2006, p 8.

[219] For further information on the history of international criminal proceedings *see* section 1.A.II.

3

A METHODOLOGY FOR INTERNATIONAL CRIMINAL PROCEDURE

International criminal procedure consists of a challenging mixture of criminal law and public international law and is placed in the interstices between different national traditions, experiences, and philosophical ideas about criminal law and criminal procedure. The previous part of this book sought to demonstrate the set of frictions this causes. In this chapter, I set out some thoughts about how to come to terms with this dilemma. We must find a set of methodological parameters which will help to identify the problematic issues and to deal with them in a flexible manner. In the first section of this chapter, I emphasize the need for such a procedural theory in international criminal procedure (A). Secondly, the positivistic basis for such a theory must be clarified (B). Thirdly some general methodological remarks are warranted (C), before finally, a framework for an international criminal procedural methodology is developed (D).

A. The Necessity of a Procedural Theory

Why is it necessary to develop a procedural theory for international criminal courts and tribunals at all? Several other options have been identified, like those propounded by Delmas-Marty, who opines that the search for the common denominator would be a sufficient solution for tackling procedural problems at international courts:

> Like the ICT Statutes but in clearer terms, the Rome Statute encourages the Court to take domestic law into account and Article 21 requires it to apply not only the principles and rules of international law, but, 'failing that' (i.e. in the event of imprecision or a gap in international law), 'general principles of law derived by the Court from national laws of legal systems of the world....' This ambitious formula refers to the search through comparative law studies for a 'common denominator', which could be a true interpretive tool provided it does not lead, under cover of comparative law, to the domination of one system by another.[1]

[1] M Delmas-Marty, 'Interactions between National and International Criminal Law in the Preliminary Phase of Trial at the ICC', 4 *JICJ* (2006) 2, 3 (references omitted).

As plausible as this approach might be at first sight, the practice of the ICC and the *ad hoc* Tribunals has shown that it is critical to identify whether such a common denominator exists and whether it could help solve procedural questions. Refer to the question of protective measures in the *Tadić* case at the ICTY.[2] There, even the ICTY 'uncovers a deep uncertainty about the sources of international procedural law and the relevance of international standards in making procedural decisions'.[3] The solution which in the end was offered by the judges caused some argument amongst legal scholars, to put it mildly.[4]

At the ICTY, judges largely relied on identifying 'customary international law' as the methodological tool to deal with debated issues. I will come back to this point a little later as 'international custom' and procedural law do not, in the present author's opinion, go well together.[5] Indeed the problems discussed at the ICTY were mostly pertaining to substantive criminal law regarding the concept of war crimes,[6] or the question of duress as a defence.[7] Methodologically, this is a rather attractive and clever approach, as it is likely to silence critics. After all, the contention that a norm is of an *international* customary nature insinuates that is does not derive from one or another domestic legal order. In truth, however, such an approach is likely to blur the differences, and what is even worse, does not allow for discussion of normative arguments.

One could also seek refuge in a specific approach; that is, one bases the interpretation of the law on the requirements of the individual case only. The ICC Prosecutor allegedly favours such a case-by-case approach. In his policy paper of September 2007 on the interests of justice, he states that the paper's scope would only 'offer limited clarification in the abstract' as 'the particular approach then will necessarily have to depend on the facts and circumstances of the case or situation'.[8] Even if every decision is about an individual case and must take the circumstances of each individual case into account, total freedom of

---

[2] The details of witness protection are discussed in section 8.E.

[3] N Affolder, 'Tadić, the Anonymous Witness and the Sources of International Procedural Law', 19 *Mich J Int'l L* (1998) 448.

[4] *See* the notorious controversy between Monroe Leigh and Christine Chinkin documented in the AJIL: M Leigh, 'The Yugoslav Tribunal: Use of Unnamed Witnesses against Accused', 90 *AJIL* (1996) 216; C Chinkin, 'Due Process and Witness Anonymity', 91 *AJIL* (1997) 74; M Leigh, 'Witness Anonymity is Inconsistent with Due Process', 91 *AJIL* (1997) 80.

[5] *See* pp 114–16.

[6] *See* ICTY *Prosecutor v Tadić*, AC, IT-94-1, 2 October 1995, Decision on the Defence Motion for Interlocutory Appeal on Jurisdiction; critical in this regard A Zahar and G Sluiter, *International Criminal Law* (OUP 2007) 81.

[7] *See* ICTY *Prosecutor v Erdemović*, AC, IT-96-22-A, 7 October 1997, Appeals Judgment, and the attached dissenting opinion by Judge Cassese; *see*, in general, A Cassese, *International Criminal Law* (2nd edn, OUP 2008) 284 *et subs.*, and K Ambos, *Der Allgemeine Teil des Völkerstrafrechts* (Duncker and Humblot 2002) 266 *et subs.*

[8] This has been rightly criticized by M Delmas-Marty, 'Interactions between National and International Criminal Law in the Preliminary Phase of Trial at the ICC', 4 *JICJ* (2006) 2, 10.

interpretation as allegedly envisaged here would result in arbitrariness and be contrary to the rule of law.

Furthermore, different courts and tribunals adopt different legal standards as regards procedure. This approach is present in the practice of international criminal procedure today and most prominently shown by the various ways of handling the concept of 'witness proofing'.[9] Whereas witness proofing is an accepted practice under *ad hoc* Tribunals jurisprudence, it is prohibited by the ICC. Such diverging standards might not be desirable, but might well be unavoidable. It is consistent with the *lex fori* principle, according to which every court applies and interprets its own procedural legal regime.[10] In this regard, procedural law is very different from substantive law. Diverging regimes of substantive international criminal law are not only undesirable but must be avoided under all circumstances.[11] In contrast, procedural law is relative to the organ which applies it, and could thus vary to a certain extent. It is thus perfectly imaginable and in a sense harmless that 'proofing [is] "acceptable" at the *ad hoc* Tribunals but *per se* inappropriate at the ICC'.[12]

These examples show that today the approach to international criminal procedure is somewhat erratic, depending heavily on the persons involved. The problem with this situation is that it poses a serious threat to the requirement of reliability and foreseeability of official acts. As much as law is a dictate of reason, it can quickly turn into a pure execution of power if it is not applied in a uniform way. International criminal law has been developed as a tool to control power by reason.[13] It would be naïve to assume that staging an international trial would not in itself also be a statement of power, yet this power is the power of the rule of law, the power of persuasion of uniform and general abstract normative values.

We have come a long way to establish a core set of normative values, which are now embodied in the international crimes referred to in Art. 5 ICCSt. Even if we assume that these norms are universally acceptable and accepted, it is now time to develop a concise framework of how these norms should be implemented and executed. Therefore we need to discuss procedural theories and develop reliable parameters which would be applicable to all international trials. A purely positivist approach as often relied on by the ICC and by the *ad hoc* Tribunals will not help

---

9 This will be looked at in detail, *see* section 8.C.II.4.

10 *See*, section 1.A.I.

11 This is why the differentiation between the unlawful enemy combatant and the lawful enemy combatant which was introduced into US law and is blatantly in breach with international humanitarian law is so unfortunate and should be corrected sooner rather than later.

12 A different view is taken by R Karemaker, B Don Taylor, and T W Pittman, 'Witness Proofing in International Criminal Tribunals: Response to Ambos', 21 *LJIL* (2008) 917.

13 As stated by Justice Robert H Jackson in his opening address in Nuremberg, *see* IMT Protocols II, 99; *see* also section 2.A.I.

in this regard.[14] A procedural system, which is so complex that the rules could be interpreted in a purely positivistic way, does not exist at the international level. Quite the contrary is true, as the Rome drafters more often than not relied on the 'constructive ambiguity' of the legal texts, burdening the judges with the task to fill in the positivistic frame. Before going further, we thus need to analyse the legal sources and the legal framework applicable at the ICC.

B. The Legal Sources

I. The applicable law according to Art. 21 ICCSt

The starting point of any methodology is the legal source. When looking at the ICC, Art. 21 ICCSt gives a list of the applicable law. The list is rather odd, as despite the fact that a partial parallel to Art. 38 ICJSt exists which names as sources of international law, treaties, customary international law, and general principles of international law,[15] at some point the wording of the ICCSt deviates from this basic norm.[16]

Nevertheless Art. 21 ICCSt is the authority on which the methodology of international criminal procedure must be focused. It establishes three different levels of norms:

1. Art. 21 (1) (a) ICCSt

On the first level, the Statute is placed as the crucial legal source in the form of an international treaty. The Rules of Procedure and Evidence and the Elements of Crimes complement the Statute, according to Art. 21 (1) (a) ICCSt.

These are the primary sources for the ICC. The following Art. 21 (1) (b) and (c) can—according to the ICC in the case against Al Bashir—only be applied if:

(i) there is a *lacuna* in the written law contained in the Statute, the Elements of Crimes and the Rules; and

(ii) such *lacuna* cannot be filled by the application of the criteria provided for in articles 31 and 32 of the Vienna Convention of the Law of the Treaties and article 21 (3) of the Statute.[17]

[14] *See* eg, ICC *Prosecutor v Lubanga*, AC, ICC-01/04–01/06–1432, 11 July 2008, Judgment on the Appeals of The Prosecutor and The Defence against Trial Chamber I's Decision on Victims' Participation of 18 January 2008, para 29–39, where the definition of the 'victim' is done purely by literal and systematic interpretation of the ICCSt and the RPE ICC.

[15] *See* eg, A Verdross and B Simma, *Universelles Völkerrecht* (4th edn, Duncker and Humblot 1984) para 516 *et subs*.

[16] For the drafting history of Art. 21 ICCSt *see* Triffterer/*McAuliffe deGuzmann*, Art. 21 MN 14.

[17] ICC *Prosecutor v Al Bashir*, PTC I, ICC-02/05–01/09–1, 4 March 2009, Decision on the Prosecutor's Application for a Warrant of Arrest against Omar Hassan Ahmad Al Bashir, para 126.

The Pre-Trial Chamber is indeed very strict on this point, as the wording of Art. 21 (1) (b) ICCSt allows for a more open approach ('where appropriate').[18] Furthermore, this decision raises the question whether there can be a *lacuna* in the law at all.[19] One could argue that in a codified system, there can be no gap in the law which cannot be filled by interpretation. Even if this were true, we have to consider that the procedural system established at the ICC is not a systematic codification in that sense. It is based on 'constructive ambiguity', as we have already seen.[20] It would thus be advisable to adopt a more open methodology and allow all of the sources listed in Art. 21 ICCSt to be reflected in interpreting the Statute.[21]

There is also a hierarchy within Art. 21 (1) ICCSt. The primary source is the Rome Statute. The Rules of Procedure and Evidence or Regulations[22] cannot modify the Statute. If necessary the Rules or Regulations have to be brought into conformity with the Statute by interpretation.[23] It has to be kept in mind that the legal status and enforceability of the Regulations of the Court are not entirely clear. According to Regulation 1 (1) RegC, they must be read 'subject to the Statute and the Rules'; in fact, they are not mentioned in the applicable law of the ICC according to Art. 21 ICCSt. Art. 52 (1) ICCSt also shows that the Regulations are lower in rank than both the Statute and the Rules, underlined by the relatively low threshold set for their adoption.[24]

2. Art. 21 (1) (b) ICCSt

On the second tier, Art. 21 (1) (b) ICCSt mentions applicable treaties, and the principles and rules of international law.[25] This terminology is new insofar as it does not match the wording used by Art. 38 ICJSt. Its actual meaning is disputable. I suggest the following:

(a) Treaties are agreements between two or more States or other subjects of international law.[26]

---

[18] Critical in this regard: B Burghardt and J Geneuss, 'Der Präsident und sein Gericht: Die Entscheidung des Internationalen Strafgerichthofs über den Erlass eines Haftbefehls gegen Al Bashir', 4 *ZIS* (2009) 126.

[19] *See* U Fastenrath, *Lücken im Völkerrecht* (Duncker and Humblot 1991). See also Dissenting Opinion of Judge Shahabuddeen in ICJ *Legality of the Threat or Use of Nuclear Weapons*, Advisory Opinion, 6 July 1996, ICJ Rep. 1996, 375, 389, arguing that—due to the Lotus-Formula—there is no 'gap' in international law.

[20] *See* section 1.A.XII.2.

[21] Similarly W Schabas, *ICC* (OUP 2010) 385.

[22] *See* section 1.A.XII.2.

[23] *See* ICC *Prosecutor v Lubanga*, TC I, ICC-01/04–01/06–1048, 13 December 2007, Decision on the Status Before the Trial Chamber of the Evidence Heard by the Pre-Trial Chamber and the Decision of the Pre-Trial Chamber in Trial Proceedings, and the Manner in which Evidence shall be Submitted, para 47; *see* also W Schabas, *ICC* (OUP 2010) 651.

[24] Absolute majority of the Judges v two-thirds majority of the members of the ASP, *see* Art. 51 (1) and 52 (1) ICCSt, respectively.

[25] The reference to humanitarian law in particular in Art. 21 (b) ICCSt is of no relevance to procedural law.

[26] B Kempen and C Hillgruber, *Völkerrecht* (CH Beck 2007) Chapter 3 MN 8.

(b) Rule of international law correlates to customary international law in the meaning of Art. 38 (b) ICJSt.[27]

(c) The principles of international correspond to the general principles of international law as foreseen in Art. 38 (c) IJCSt.[28]

3. Art. 21 (1) (c) ICCSt

The third—subsidiary—level is contained in Art. 21 (1) (c) ICCSt: general principles of law derived from national laws of legal systems of the world. These principles are ontologically different from those mentioned in Art. 21 (1) (b) ICCSt as they do not appear to be placed on the international level. Instead, the principles of national laws can be applied in cases where the international legal order is insufficient or fragmentary. That the Rome Statute differentiates between general principles of international law and general principles of national law is made obvious by the fact that Art. 21 (1) (c) ICCSt refers to the domestic legal systems of those states who would normally exercise jurisdiction over the crime. In this regard, the Statute expresses the complementary nature of the ICC.[29] Furthermore these principles of national law are to be tested with a view to international law and internationally recognized norms and standards as Art. 21 (1) (c) ICCSt states. Such a test is only sensible in the case where the norm which is to be tested stems from a national background. Otherwise the Statute would presuppose a schizophrenic international legal order where general principles of international can contradict internationally recognized norms.

This completes the list of the applicable law. Strictly speaking, the following paragraphs (2) and (3) of Art. 21 ICCSt contain no provision as to the applicability of norms but instead name two methodological parameters for the interpretation of the law, which are applicable according to paragraph (1). Art. 21 (2) ICCSt states that the Court is not bound by precedents and Art. 21 (3) ICCSt contains the principle of interpretation in conformity with internationally recognized human rights.[30] These parameters will be discussed amongst others in the following chapter.

II. The problem of customary law and criminal procedure

In international criminal law, the role of customary law has always been debatable. This is largely due to the fact that civil law countries rely primarily on codified law

[27] *See* also G Werle, *Völkerstrafrecht* (2nd edn, Duncker and Humblot 2007) MN 168 and Triffterer/*McAuliffe deGuzmann*, Art. 21 MN 13.

[28] *See* also A Cassese, *International Criminal Law* (2nd edn, OUP 2008) 22; K Ambos, *Internationales Strafrecht* (3rd edn, CH Beck 2011) § 5 MN 5.

[29] As to the principle of complementarity, *see* section 2.C.

[30] A different view is taken by A Zahar and G Sluiter, *International Criminal Law* (OUP 2007) 18, who opine that Art. 21 (3) ICCSt pertains to the question of applicable law and gives human rights the highest place in the hierarchy of norms.

and are thus hesitant to accept customary law as the basis of criminal responsibility. The prohibition of retroactive criminality (*nullum crimen sine lege*) contains this aspect that the law, which must be extant before the offence is committed, and must be a written law (*nullum crimen sine lege scripta*).[31] This might have been the reason why Art. 21 ICCSt avoids the phrase 'customary law' altogether.[32] Further, the ICTY has from its beginning always relied on custom as a ground for criminal responsibility.[33]

This is not our concern, however, as we deal exclusively with procedural law. There, the question arises whether there is such a thing as customary international criminal procedural law. Such an idea might arise if one looks at the *ad hoc* Tribunals and other internationalized criminal courts and tribunals, and attributes to these entities the power to act as an international (customary) rule maker.[34] Let us take an example: the ICTY, with the ICTR closely following, has developed a practice to combine conviction and sentencing in one judgment.[35] Rule 87 C RPE ICTY was amended in this regard in 1998 in order to speed up proceedings and thereby be in a position to meet the requirements of the completion strategy. It has passed its judgments in that way for almost fourteen years of constant practice. The Rome Statute is unclear in this regard (see Arts 65, 74, and 76 ICCSt). However, do we indeed have a customary rule, stemming from ICTY and ICTR practice, saying that the trial chambers of international criminal tribunals and courts pass only one judgment containing both the conviction and the sentencing?[36] It seems not, for the following reasons.

In general terms, the view of the ICJ expressed in the *North Sea Continental Shelf* case and others prevails; that customary law arises out of state practice and *opinio juris*.[37] I would submit that the routine functioning of an *ad hoc* Tribunal is not 'state practice' in this sense. Operational questions of an international organ are

---

[31] *See* C Roxin, *Strafrecht Allgemeiner Teil Vol 1* (4th edn, CH Beck 2006) § 5 MN 7.

[32] *See* Triffterer/*McAuliffe deGuzman*, Art. 21 MN 13.

[33] Critical in this regard, A Zahar and G Sluiter, *International Criminal Law* (OUP 2007) 92–105.

[34] *See* Boas/Bischoff/Reid/Taylor, *ICL III*, 8, being skeptical about customary law but stating that the 'widespread agreement... is evidence of the development and crystallisation of a body of rules of international criminal procedure'. Whether this would be customary norms remains open.

[35] *See* section 5.A.

[36] A different view is taken by B Burghardt and J Geneuss, 'Der Präsident und sein Gericht: Die Entscheidung des Internationalen Strafgerichthofs über den Erlass eines Haftbefehls gegen Al Bashir', 4 *ZIS* (2009) 126, 132. The authors are of the opinion that the *ad hoc* Tribunals' jurisprudence is relevant for the ICC under Art. 21 (1) (b) ICCSt. Their reasoning however pertains to substantive law, the crime of genocide in particular, and not to procedural law.

[37] *See* ICJ *North Sea Continental Shelf* case (*Germany v Denmark, Germany v The Netherlands*) Rep. 1969, 44; and the prevailing view amongst scholars, eg A Verdross and B Simma, *Universelles Völkerrecht* (3rd edn, Duncker and Humblot 1984) para 560–6, or I Brownlie, *Principles of Public International Law* (5th edn, OUP 1998) 10.

a matter for this body alone. There is only a somewhat indirect connection between decisions of the judges of a tribunal and the State. Furthermore, procedural issues are relevant only for the ICJ. Circumstances might be different at a different institution. This is the case with the ICTY and the ICC. Whereas the former was intended as an *ad hoc* instrument to solve one conflict, to do with the former Yugoslavia, the ICC is established on a permanent basis. Even if these situations might be similar, the contrast between them becomes visible if one looks at the ECCC. The practice there in a very specific procedural situation mixing national and international criteria cannot serve as a basis of customary international law. Finally, the *opinio juris* of the states involved pertains only to the one institution and not to all similar institutions. Again it might be stated that what is sensible in one situation could be useless or unnecessary in a different situation.[38]

C. General Methodological Remarks

Before we go into the detail of the idiosyncrasies of procedural law, some general remarks on legal methodology are necessary. In discussing these, we have to come back to the division between common law and civil law. Whereas the former is based on organic case law, developing by the interpretation of precedents, the latter is related to fixed codified norms.[39]

I. Legal methodology in civil law

Interpretation of legal texts follows a list of specific methods. The classical list going back to *Friedrich-Carl von Savigny*[40] is: (1) language, (2) systematic, (3) historic, and (4) teleological interpretation. Recently, this list has been amended by the inclusion of: (5) interpretation with regard to the degree of conformity with constitutional law, (6) with European law, and (7) with human rights law, in particular with the ECHR.[41]

The relevance of precedents shows only amongst the systematic interpretation of a norm when the meaning other courts have given to the text of a norm in its systematic context is being analysed.[42] The impact of the historic interpretation—the question which meaning the drafters imagined the norm should have—is disputable. The problem is that a strict adherence to the intention of the drafters would lead to a rather static application of the law and hinder the development of the legal

[38] *See* also M Damaska, 'Problematic Features of International Criminal Procedure', in: A Cassese (ed), *The Oxford Companion to International Criminal Justice* (OUP 2009) 175.

[39] *See* R Zimmermann, 'Statuta Sunt Stricte Interpretanda?', 56 *CLJ* (1997) 315, 318.

[40] *See* F C von Savigny, *System des heutigen Römischen Rechts*, vol 1 (1840) 212 *et subs.*

[41] *See* C Safferling, *Internationales Strafrecht* (Springer 2011), § 4 MN 90.

[42] *See* G Hager, *Rechtsmethoden in Europa* (Mohr Siebeck 2009) Chapter 3 MN 87.

system. Therefore the view in favour of a primarily objective and more dynamic interpretation of legal norms prevails.

These methods of interpretation can be applied to any legal text, not only to codified law in the strict sense.[43] However they presuppose an abstract rule and are not suitable for interpreting judgments.

The amended canon of methodological steps reveals the necessity to interpret historic rules with a view to the reality of the present circumstances and the normative circumstances of the European, constitutional, and human rights context. It would be erroneous to suppose that a codified system turns a blind eye to reality in order to be truthful to the purity of the system. The system has to adapt, and must develop, balancing the letter of the law with the normative requirements of the modern society. This development of the law in weighing the different interests rests in the lap of the judge.[44]

II. Legal methodology in common law

In common law, which is based on precedents, the methodological approach is dramatically different. There the analysis of a judgment—the decision pertaining to an individual case and not an abstract norm—is in the foreground. Precedents are binding to later cases, but not in their entirety but only as regards the substance of the case, the *ratio decidendi*.[45] Thus the first methodological step would be to separate the *ratio decidendi* of a relevant case from the *obiter dicta*. In a second step, the facts of the new case must be compared with the facts of the precedent and evaluated as to whether the law which was applied in the precedent is fitting for the new case or whether the new case can be 'distinguished' from the precedent so that the legal consequence should be different. Under certain circumstances a precedent can be overruled and a new norm can be established. For reasons of security under the law, however, this option is to be applied with caution.[46]

In English law, the extent to which laws conform to human rights legislation has gained importance with the implementation of the Human Rights Act 1998. As with German law, the judges have to apply a further test to a given result which was achieved by applying the classical methods of interpretation.[47] Even if the jurisprudence of the ECtHR is not binding in the sense of the *stare decidis* rule, it is to be respected as offering 'persuasive precedents'. English courts thus have to apply the judgments of the Strasbourg court as authoritative.[48]

---

[43] R Zimmermann, 'Statuta Sunt Stricte Interpretanda?,' 56 *CLJ* (1997) 315, 322.
[44] See G Hager, *Rechtsmethoden in Europa* (Mohr Siebeck 2009) Chapter 7 MN 128–32.
[45] K Langenbucher, 'Argument by Analogy in European Law', 57 *CLJ* (1998) 481, 490 *et subs.*
[46] *See* W Fikentscher, *Methoden des Rechts*, vol 2 (Mohr Siebeck 1975) 95 *et subs.*
[47] *See Wilson v Secretary of State for Trade and Industry* [2003] HRLR 33.
[48] *See* Smith and Hogan, *Criminal Law* (Buttworth 2008) 23 *et subs.*

The importance of the judge is even more obvious in the Anglo-American system than in the civil law system. S/he has to decide whether to apply the precedent or to overrule it and is called upon to analyse the historic case law with a view to the modern circumstances and the normative needs of today. S/he has to weigh the authority of the precedent in the light of present needs in order to arrive at a good decision.[49] In that sense O W Holmes said, 'The life of the law has not been logic: it has been experience'.[50]

III. Legal methodology in international law

1. General remarks

In international law, the methodology contains some aspects of both traditions. As far as treaty law is concerned, international law is quite similar to the civil law in that an abstract text is interpreted in order to make it operational for the legal question at hand. The methodological framework is established by Arts 31 and 32 of the Vienna Convention on the Law of Treaties.[51] There we find four methods. The interpretation has to be (1) the ordinary meaning, (2) the contextual meaning, (3) in the light of its object and purpose, and, as a subsidiary tool, (4) must take into account the preparatory work. This methodological approach is widely accepted as a customary rule.[52]

In international law, the subjective interpretation—the interpretation according to the intention of the drafters—thus has a supplementary nature only. The interpretation of treaties has to be exercised in an objective way; that is, according to the aim and purposes of the treaty.[53] This objective character has led to a further approach that is adopted in particular regarding multinational treaties and international agreements that establish an institution—the dynamic interpretation. Documents like the UN Charter or the ECHR are to be seen as 'living instruments', which 'must be interpreted in the light of present-day conditions'[54] and 'of the ideas prevailing in democratic States today'.[55]

Yet despite the fact that the drafters of the Statute and the Rules were quite ambitious—for some, too ambitious[56]—in creating a concise and complete set

[49] *See* L Fuller, 'Reason and Fiat in Case Law', 59 *HLR* (1946) 376.

[50] O W Holmes, *The Common Law* (Belknap Press of Harvard University Press 2009) 3.

[51] Adopted on 23 May 1969. Entered into force on 27 January 1980. United Nations, *Treaty Series*, vol. 1155, p 331.

[52] *See* ICJ *Iran v USA (Case concerning Oil Platforms)*, 12 December 1996, Rep. 1996, 803 para 23.

[53] This might surprise as regards treaty law in general because not all treaties consist of abstract and general rules. One thinks, for example, of bilateral treaties.

[54] *See* eg, ECtHR *Tyrer v UK*, 25 April 1978, Series A No 26 para 31.

[55] *See* most recently ECtHR *Bayatyan v Armenia*, 7 July 2011, Appl No 23459/03, para 102.

[56] D Hunt, 'The International Criminal Court', 2 *JICJ* (2004) 56, 58.

of rules, the 'constructive ambiguity' which has been mentioned[57] sets limits on the civil law methodology of textual exegesis. The answer to this structural reality must be found in developing a set of principles which would help to fill the gaps.

2. The Rome Statute

The Rome Statute—as we have seen—contains two explicit methodological remarks in Art. 21 ICCSt:

(1) Art. 21 (2) ICCSt clarifies that the *stare decisis* rule does not apply to the ICC, this means that the ICC is not bound by its previous judgments.[58] This of course does not generally prohibit the ICC judges to refer to previous decisions. Quite the contrary is true for two reasons: (a) the requirement of a standard of security under the law warrants a high degree of consistency and reliability. The decision of a court should thus always relate to its previous decision. (b) From an empirical point of view, judges tend to refer to their own jurisprudence not only because it is psychologically difficult to change one's mind, but also in order to shorten the reasoning. Certain issues, which have been argued in previous decisions, need not be discussed anew.[59] The further the jurisprudence of a court develops, the more it becomes self-referential. This is true for the ICJ,[60] the ECtHR,[61] the *ad hoc* Tribunals,[62] and other national and international courts.[63] The ICC is developing in this direction as well. This is not necessarily a bad thing. As has been said before, the jurisprudence thereby becomes more predictable and thus in a sense more reliable. However, judges should always be ready to remain open-minded about new ideas and new situations, and keep both themselves and the court flexible. This is what Art. 21 (2) ICCSt wants to ensure.

(2) As with the domestic methodology, which we have already considered, Art. 21 (3) ICCSt establishes the rule that every decision has to be tested with regard to its conformity with human rights. This provision might have been necessary as the ICTY was, at its start, hesitant to apply international law beyond its own Statute and Rules.[64] Likewise it was difficult to argue that the ICTY was formally bound by human rights law, despite the UN Secretary General's view that the compliance

---

57 *See* section 1.A.XII.2.

58 G Werle, *Völkerstrafrecht* (2nd edn, Mohr Siebeck 2007) MN 169; Triffterer/*McAuliffe deGuzman*, Art. 21 MN.

59 *See* G Hager, *Rechtsmethoden in Europa* (Mohr Siebeck 2009) Chapter 5 MN 9.

60 *See* Triffterer/*McAuliffe deGuzman*, Art. 21 MN 21.

61 *See* C Safferling, *Internationales Strafrecht* (Springer 2011) § 13 MN 33: the ECtHR has developed a genuine legal system substantially limited to human rights.

62 A Zahar and G Sluiter, *International Criminal Law* (OUP 2007) Preface viii: 'This bootstrapping tendency is another reason to maintain a critical watch'.

63 In one of the earlier decisions of 1958 of the German Federal Constitutional Court, the famous Lüth-case, *see* 7 BVerfGE 198 at 208, the Court refers to the writings of US Supreme Court Judges Benjamin N Cardozo in a question concerning the interpretation of basic rights. In later years such an influence from the outside can only rarely be observed.

64 *See* A Zahar and G Sluiter, *International Criminal Law* (OUP 2007) 16.

with the 'fair trial' requirement was 'axiomatic' for the tribunal.[65] As neither the tribunal itself nor the UN are signatories to the ICCPR as the relevant human rights treaty regarding civil and political rights, and as it was always difficult to argue that these relevant rights were binding due to their customary law status, the adherence to this human rights standard could only be derived from a general, moral obligation to respect the basic fair trial standard.[66]

It has been said that this provision would not only limit the judges' discretion in interpreting the law, but has also the potential to broaden the Court's power significantly.[67] This could indeed be the case. As we will see, the need to implement a normative view on the legal sources can lead to the consequence that judges develop the law further in order to make it compatible with human rights and thereby go beyond the language of the applicable law. This, however, is only true of procedural law. Substantive law can never be expanded to the detriment of the defendant due to the *nullum crimen* principle contained in Art. 22 (2) ICCSt.[68]

Apart from these provisions, the Statute itself does not lay down any methodological parameters. But as the Rome Statute is an international treaty, it should come as no surprise that the ICC judges refer to the Vienna Convention for the interpretation of the Statute:

> The Chamber, in determining the contours of the statutory framework provided for in the Statute, the Rules and the Regulations, must, in addition to applying the general principle of interpretation set out in article 21(3) of the Statute, look at the general principles of interpretation as set out in article 31(1) of the Vienna Convention on the Law of Treaties, according to which 'a treaty shall be interpreted in good faith in accordance with the ordinary meaning to be given to the terms of the treaty in their context and in light of its object and purpose'.[69]

The Appeals Chamber of the ICC has made the Vienna Convention's methodological tools also applicable to the Rules of Procedure and Evidence.[70]

---

[65] Report of the UN Secretary General pursuant to para 2 of Security Council Resolution 808 (1993), UN Doc. S/25704, of 3 May 1993, para 101, 106

[66] An in depth analysis of the ICTY's respect for human rights is given by A Reinisch, 'Das Jugoslawientribunal der Vereinten Nationen und die Verfahrensgarantien des II. VN-Menschenrechtspaktes: Ein Beitrag zur Frage der Bindung der Vereinten Nationen an nicht ratifiziertes Vertragsrecht', 47 *Austrian JPIL* (1995) 173, 183, and 184–5.

[67] *See* Triffterer/*McAuliffe deGuzman*, Art. 21 MN 24; and M H Arsanjani, 'The Rome Statute of the International Criminal Court', 93 *AJIL* (1999) 22, 29.

[68] *See* W Schabas, *ICC* (OUP 2010) 410, who argues that this provision is the only norm establishing rules of interpretation. As we have seen before, this is not the case as Art. 21 ICCSt contains rules of interpretation as well.

[69] ICC *Prosecutor v Katanga and Chui*, PTC I, 10 March 2008, ICC-01/04–01/07–257, Decision on the Joinder of the Cases against Germain Katanga and Mathieu Ngudjolo Chui, p 7.

[70] ICC *Prosecutor v Lubanga*, AC, ICC-01/04–01/06–1432, 11 July 2008, Judgment on the Appeals of The Prosecutor and The Defence against Trial Chamber I's Decision on Victims' Participation of 18 January 2008, para 55. The wording used is rather axiomatic. No reasons are given.

3. Summary

We learn from Art. 21 ICCSt and the jurisprudence of the Court that the applicable law is to be interpreted along the lines of the Vienna Convention on the Law of Treaties. The interpretation is thus of an objective nature, and the object and purpose of the Statute has to be duly considered. There are no binding precedents; the interpretation has to be brought into conformity with the international standard of human rights.

The ICCSt is thus superior to the *ad hoc* Tribunals' statutes in that it contains a norm which addresses methodological questions. Yet Art. 21 ICCSt offers only a skeleton framework for this, and we need to add some flesh to the bones. In the following we will thus attempt to tie the 'aims and purposes' of international criminal procedure together with the methodological question as to how to interpret the procedural texts of the ICC, and indeed other international criminal tribunals as well.

D. Basic Parameters of a Procedural Methodology

I have stated the legal sources relevant to the ICC. I have also developed the general methodological framework of the ICC according to Art. 21 ICCSt and the Vienna Convention on Treaty Law. On this basis, I will identify four methodological pillars on which a common theory of international criminal procedure could be based. These are:

(1) Autonomous interpretation

(2) Functional interpretation

(3) Normative interpretation

(4) Comparative interpretation

The intention is to establish a commonly accepted methodological frame for the development of procedural law and the interpretation of procedural texts. The adherence to these tools of interpretation should put the participants of an international criminal trial in a position to identify critical questions and discuss the issues in an open and honest way. It should also avoid the possibility of participants turning a blind eye to teleological questions. Rather, they should be forced to address the aims and purposes of different procedural steps and of the prosecution process in its entirety.

I. Autonomous interpretation

We have seen above that criminal procedure is based on one of two different approaches, the adversarial and the inquisitorial system.[71] Any international criminal tribunal and the ICC in particular should avoid being absorbed by one or other

[71] *See* section 1.B.III.

system. The benchmark in any case is the international law that is applicable to the court or tribunal. National law or domestic traditions and systems cannot simply be applied to the international institution. Rather, each international body is in need of establishing its own legitimacy and legal regime.

This has consequences for the interpretation of the law. As mentioned above, the first methodological step in interpreting a certain norm would be to look at the wording and the ordinary meaning. Concerning substantive law, this might well be a formidable undertaking. With regard to procedural law, extreme caution is to be applied. The meaning of a term in the context of procedural law depends on the legal system in which it is imbedded.

As an example, let us look at the term 'cross-examination'.[72] One could attribute to this term the ordinary meaning of simply questioning a witness. In the context of procedural law, however 'cross-examination' is a precise term used for describing of what comes after the 'examination-in-chief' and it insinuates a specific technique of testing the reliability of the witness for 'the other side'.

Another example would be the term 'charge', as it is used in Art. 61 ICCSt.[73] To attribute to this term the same meaning as in English law would be fallacious. It also provides little value to contemplate whether the drafters misused the word 'charge' and intended rather to use the phrase 'count'. Be that as it may, the right solution to these oddities is to adopt an autonomous interpretation, detached from national heritage. The interpretation instead has to be developed out of the Statute and Rules themselves.

The most important institution adopting such an approach is the ECtHR.[74] Starting with the judgment in *Deweer,* it has developed the concept of 'autonomous interpretation' according to which the ECHR and the terms used by it need to be understood 'within the meaning of the Convention'.

The criterion of an autonomous interpretation is much more a negative parameter than a positive expression of what has to be done. It says what not to do, which is to give to a term the same meaning as in national law.[75] It then refers to the statute itself, when it says that the term is to be understood within the meaning of the statute. The question remains as to exactly what the meaning of the statute actually

[72] *See* section 1.B.I.

[73] This issue will be discussed in Chapter 6.

[74] ECtHR *Deweer v Belgium*, 27 February 1980, Series A No 35, para 43 *et subs.*, and *König v Germany*, 28 June 1978, Series A No 27, para 88, these cases referred to the scope of application of Art. 6 (1) ECHR and the meaning of the English term 'charge' or the French 'accusation'; *see* also D J Harris *et al.*, *Law of the European Convention on Human Rights* (London 1995) 16, and K Gaede, *Fairness als Teilhabe—Das Recht auf konkrete und wirksame Teilhabe durch Verteidigung gemäß Art. 6 EMRK* (Duncker and Humblot 2006) 79–81.

[75] Similarly, ICTY *Prosecutor v Jelisić*, AC, 5 July 2001, IT-95–10-A, Judgment, para 34.

is. In order to find answers to this question, we must turn to the next interpretative tool: the functional analysis.[76]

II. The functional approach

A functional perspective is part of the teleological interpretation. It puts the norm into the context of the reality that surrounds it. What do we mean by that? Functionality in this regard is twofold: when we speak about a 'functional approach', we need, first, to relate the methodology to the purposes of criminal procedure, of international criminal procedure, to be precise (social functionality). In addition we need to take into account the divide between the different participants in the proceedings and their respective interests (institutional functionality). Whereas the 'social functionality' of criminal procedure pertains to the communicative aspects between court and society—to external factors—the 'institutional functionality' refers to the internal structuring of the different institutions.

1. Social functionality

The aims and purposes of criminal procedure have already been discussed above.[77] We can summarize these as follows:

(1) The execution of criminal law helps to end impunity for state-sponsored crimes.

(2) The primary aim of the prosecution is to identify the perpetrator and prove the allegations brought against him/her.

(3) The guilt of the offender is to be 'translated' into a just sentence.

(4) As a secondary effect, the prosecution should assist in healing the social conflict between the perpetrator on the one side and society as well as the victim on the other.

(5) Future deviance is hoped to be deterred by prosecuting the offenders.

(6) The public proceeding aims at stabilizing the rule of law amongst the people and peoples.

(7) An official record of the crimes is established which may help in the further transitional justice process to develop a commonly accepted narrative of the incident.

(8) Victims are given a voice by presenting them with a forum where they can 'tell their story'.

[76] Similarly, K Ambos and D Miller, 'Structure and Function of the Confirmation Procedure before the ICC from a Comparative Perspective', 7 *ICLR* (2007) 335, 349: 'modern international criminal procedure is of a mixed *sui generis* nature and as such its problems must be tackled from a *functional* perspective' (footnote omitted).

[77] *See* section 2.A.I.

This socio-psychological value of a criminal trial is hard to prove empirically. Yet a purely non-utilitarian view of the criminal justice system runs the risk of making revenge and retaliation into absolutes. The notion of deterrence and, in particular, the positive aspects of confirming the reliability of international criminal law must be put into context here as elements of the functions of an international criminal trial.

The social functionality of a criminal trial exacts high demands. What needs to be taken into account is that there is no consensus yet on the aims and purposes of international prosecution. The combined or mixed approach which is being adopted by the ICC and the tribunals resembles a self-service store, where one theory or the other is picked out as deemed appropriate. In any case, the discourse on the purposes and aims of international criminal law is mostly reduced to the question of sentencing; procedural issues as matters of fact are not discussed by the use of these terms. The functional approach would thus be called on to address these questions and enter into a discourse about the requirements of an international criminal trial. This normative form of evaluation must be buttressed by empirical facts; indeed, we must continuously ask ourselves whether our vision of these aims is in that sense realistic, that is, achievable.

2. Institutional functionality

Institutional functionality refers to the internal layout of the interaction and communication at the court or tribunal. There are several participants in the criminal process, each of which has its own role according to which powers and competences are crafted. The interests of the participants are in a sense antagonistic, as the prosecutor, and the victim, want to convict the accused, whereas the accused and the defence counsel want to disprove the allegations. This arena of conflict must be solved by a criminal procedural order in a fair and effective way.

The procedural texts form a basis for this interplay. The important question for the interpretation is whether it is possible to discern a precise role for each of the participants. Again, some of the points are normative in the sense that we need to clarify which role we want the party to play. However, an empirical test must be adopted and the question be posed whether the normative view was realistic.

3. Interrelated functionality

A functional view on a criminal trial must take heed of the overall goal and the role and interests of the participants in order to develop a structure which can be acceptable to all parties to the process.

An example will make the interplay between the social and the institutional functionality clear. The Rome Statute has a unique system of victim participation. According to Art. 68 (3) ICCSt, the views and concerns of the victims should be heard where their personal interests are affected. A decisive question in this regard is the definition of the word 'victim' according to Rule 85 RPE ICC. The Appeals Chamber of the ICC adopted a rather sober approach and interpreted the relevant Rule 85 according to the Vienna Convention.[78] The judges applied the literal and systematic interpretation and in particular draw a parallel to the UN Declaration of Basic Principles of Justice for Victims of Crime and Abuse of Power.[79] The judges however, did not explain why under the auspices of Art. 21 ICCSt they were empowered to use this UN Declaration as quasi-binding authority. The judges thus treated the definition of 'victim' according to the ICC procedure as an ontological question, which can be answered in absolute terms. Instead they should have adopted the functional approach, admitting the relative and autonomous character of every legal term, and should have addressed the following two questions: (1) what realistic impact can an international criminal trial have on the victims of the international crime (social functionality), and (2) how would the interplay between the victim and the other participants turn out (institutional functionality)? Even if the result had been identical, which I very much doubt, this approach would have opened the door for a serious and open discourse on victim participation at the ICC.[80]

III. The normative approach

By normative approach, we mean the relevance of basic and human rights for criminal procedure. A criminal trial is governed by a whole set of human rights as has already been mentioned. Any trial structure must take into account that the accused has a right to a fair trial. Equality before the court is a general requirement stemming from the rule of law, which is even more important in international criminal law, where selective application emerges as a real threat to the social acceptance of the trials.

The normative approach, however, is not a one-way enterprise. As we have seen[81] there are several human rights norms relevant to both the victim and the witness in a criminal trial. Trial fairness is necessary for the general acceptability and legitimacy of international criminal procedure. Beyond the individual human rights perspective, the normative approach also embraced the principle of an efficient trial system. As discussed above, the trial is also for the benefit of the general public. Above all the trial in and of itself, as well as its outcome, must be accepted by all participating parties and the general public as fair and just.

[78] ICC *Prosecutor v Lubanga*, AC, ICC-01/04–01/06–1432, 11 July 2008, Judgment on the Appeals of The Prosecutor and The Defence against Trial Chamber I's Decision on Victims' Participation of 18 January 2008, paras 29–39

[79] UN Doc. A/RES/40/34 of 29 November 1985, *see* also section 4.D.

[80] As to the question of victim participation, *see* section 4.D.

[81] *See* section 2.A.I.4.

IV. The comparative approach

Criminal procedure is a matter of different historic traditions and legal developments, as has been shown above.[82] The diverging ideas of a criminal trial, which have been described above, need to be considered in order to understand the different expectations. Whereas the Continental European idea of the 'material truth' in a criminal trial is little more than a myth, the Anglo-American adversarial approach is often viewed as biased. 'Truth' in international criminal procedure has another aspect to it: an international criminal trial is also a tool used to collect and present evidence in order to document the historic facts.[83] It is also necessary to take into account the fact that international criminal law is international law and thus often dependent on non-judicial actors or policy developments. The willingness to cooperate on the side of the national states influences the efficiency of the trial, as does the UN Security Council, which can intervene in ICC proceedings by virtue of Art. 16 ICCSt, or by referring a situation to the ICC by virtue of Art. 13 (b) ICCSt or adopt other more indirect measures. Any international criminal procedural theory must take this circumstance into account.

Thus, the 'comparative interpretation' asks two questions: (1) how does international criminal procedure relate to the national procedural systems, and (2) how does international criminal procedure fit into the wider context of public international law?

As to the first question, the ICTY has held that a comparative perspective is important, but is not decisive: in the end it adopts 'an interpretation aided by reference to particular municipal concepts but not controlled by them.'[84] A comparative view is thus auxiliary in character. It helps to clarify semantic or systematic misunderstandings, which arise on a frequent basis when lawyers using different languages and from cultural backgrounds work together.[85] As stated once by the ICTY Appeals Chamber: 'The Trial Chamber in this case consisted wholly of non-common law judges; account must be taken of that fact in interpreting the language in which their judgement was cast. To require strict conformity with a common law verbal formula would not be appropriate; it is the substance which is important.'[86]

It might also be helpful to compare different systems of law to discover what might work at the international level as well. However, this approach must be applied with due respect for the differences of the systems. Comparative law must thus also follow a functional approach.[87]

---

[82] *See* section 1.B.

[83] *See* section 1.B.II.

[84] ICTY *Prosecutor v Jelisić*, AC, 5 July 2001, IT-95–10-A, Judgment, para 35.

[85] *See* also, the 'cross-examination' example, section 1.B.I.

[86] Ibid, para 34.

[87] *See* the different views on comparative law articulated in: S Beck, C Burchard, and B Fateh-Moghadam (eds), *Strafrechtsvergleichung als Problem und Lösung* (Nomos 2011).

V. Summary: a functional–normative theory of international criminal procedure

Beyond traditional approaches and specific views, a theory of international criminal procedure must be based on the apparent generally accepted basic functions of a criminal trial; that is, the 'distribution of guilt' in a process which balances the interests of the participating institutions and persons in a fair and efficient way. Such an approach must also take into account the aims and purposes attributed to international criminal procedure in the social sphere. This functional basis is influenced by a number of categorical impacts; that is, rights of the accused and rights of victims and witnesses. International criminal procedure must incorporate both approaches and at the same time be acceptable for the different legal traditions. A purely functional approach, which is dominated by logic and efficiency,[88] would be too laborious and would dominate the normative aspects which have to be respected in order to make the procedure acceptable.

As has been said, this idea is based on a methodological approach. In several respects, the answer to procedural questions depends on the general concept of international criminal law and procedure. The proposed methodology leaves the door ajar to social and political influences. Indeed it would force international judges and other participants to address these external factors and combine efforts in an open and fair discussion on the aims and purposes of international criminal procedure.

[88] In this direction, A Cassese, *International Criminal Law* (2nd edn, OUP 2008) 74.

4

THE PARTICIPANTS

In this part of the book we want to take a closer look at the different participants in criminal procedure. Understanding the role of the participants and the interplay between these entities is an important prerequisite for understanding criminal procedure. In modern criminal procedure, which follows an accusatorial principle, one needs to differentiate between first, the Prosecutor—that is, the entity which brings the charges—and secondly, the Court—that is, the body which will hear the evidence and decide the matter. Thirdly, the accused aided by defence counsel, if s/he so wishes, is a subject of the proceeding and not merely a mute object. Fourthly, there is the victim of the crime, who serves as an important witness for the prosecution but also has an interest in the outcome of the trial. Any criminal procedure, domestic or international, takes place between these four 'parties'. Their interaction however differs broadly in the varying systems of criminal prosecution. It is the aim of this chapter to analyse international criminal procedure according to the different roles attributable to these four parties. We will thus start out with the Court and its different organs (A), continue with looking at the Prosecutor's Office (B), and then explain the many tasks of the Registry (C). We will then consider the victims (D), before we finally take a look at the defence (E).

A. The Court (*Hilde Farthofer*)

According to Art. 34 ICCSt, the Court comprises four organs as shown in Figure 4.1, namely: (1) the Presidency, (2) the three divisions of the Court, that is, the Appeals, Trials, and Pre-Trial divisions, (3) the Registry, and (4) the Office of the Prosecutor (OTP). In spite of the fact that the latter is formally part of the Court, it is independent in its decision-making process.[1] The Registry works for all the other organs, ie, for the Chambers, for the Presidency, as well as for the Office of the Prosecutor and, moreover, in support of the defence.

[1] *See* also section 2.B.II.c.

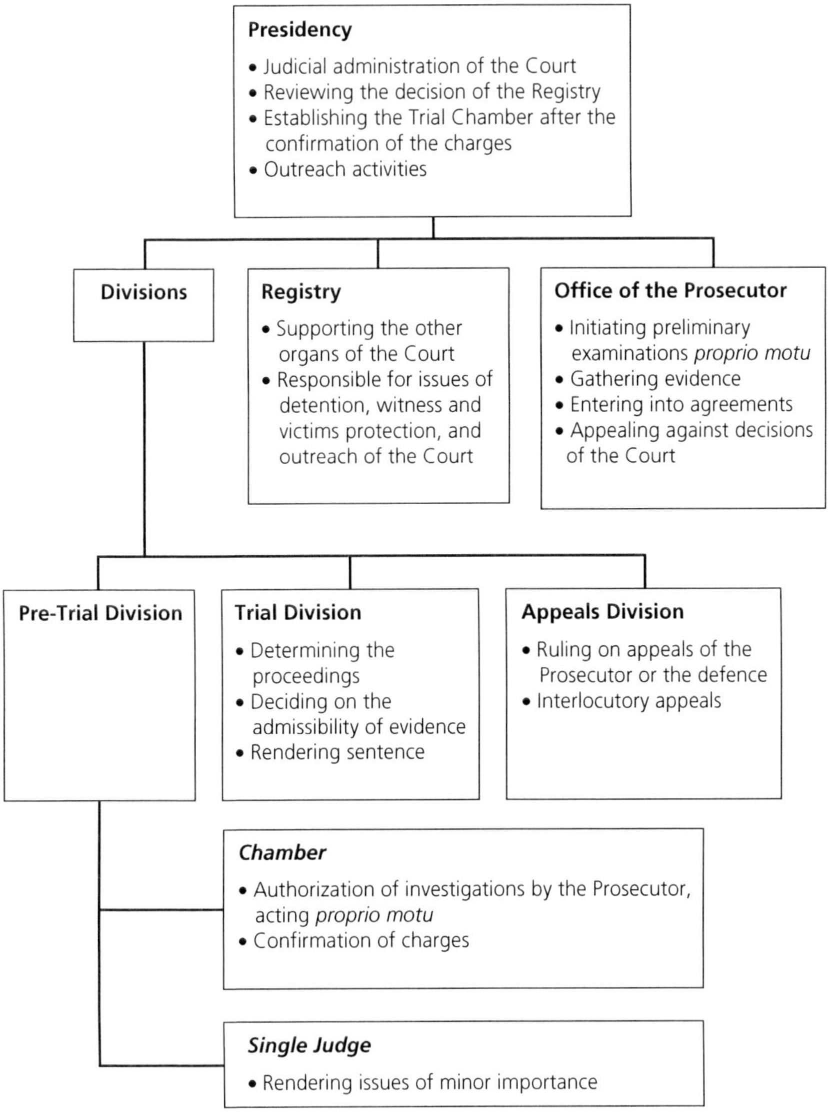

Figure 4.1 Composition of the Court

Each division has separate functions in order to carry out different stages of proceedings, headed by the Presidency.

Collectively, the Court is made up of eighteen judges but this number can be increased if necessary, pursuant to Art. 36 (2) ICCSt. The required qualifications in the field of criminal law and procedure as well as in international human rights and humanitarian law and a stringent competence in at least English or French, the working languages of the Court, are established in Art. 36 (3) (b) and (c) ICCSt.

Regarding the ICTY, there are major concerns based on the alleged lack of qualification of judges appointed by the UN. '[T]he judges elected by the UN General Assembly reflects the non-legal culture of those who elect them' and 'have no idea of the need for a judge to approach a task of determining guilt impartially and without pre-existing conclusions in relation to that guilt.'[2]

The absence of trial experience can amount to a grave risk for the fair trial standard, stipulated *inter alia* in Art. 21 ICTYSt. However, the required qualification is not clearly defined by Art. 13 ICTYSt. Similar criticism was levelled regarding the insufficient qualification of judges at the ICTR.[3]

The ICTY is composed of three Trial Chambers and one Appeals Chamber, pursuant to Art. 11 ICTYSt, as is the ICTR, pursuant to Art. 10 ICTRSt. For the Special Court for Sierra Leone, the numbers of Trial Chambers are not defined in Art. 11 SCSLSt. However, there are currently two Trial Chambers and one Appeals Chamber.

I. Electoral procedure

Each Member State has the right to nominate a candidate whose above-mentioned qualifications must be substantiated. The proposed person has to be national of a State Party, according to Art. 36 (4) (b) ICCSt. They need to be of high moral character, impartial, and have integrity, and must possess the qualification required in their national states for appointment to the highest judicial offices according to Art. 36 (3) (a) ICCSt.[4] The candidates are divided according to their qualifications in lists A and B. Art. 36 (5) ICCSt stipulates that nine persons from list A and five from list B shall be elected, and the proportion shall remain equal after each election. Members of the Assembly of the State Parties vote in secret but not entirely freely because they must observe several statutory provisions. Art. 36 (8) ICCSt lists certain points which may be taken into account, that is, equal representation of female and male judges, representation of the principal legal systems, different geographical origin, and the specialization of a single judge.

The Statute provided different terms of office for judges at the first elections in 2003, thus staggering the terms of all the judges so that turnover would be evenly spaced over time. One-third of judges were elected for a term of three years, one-third for a term of six years, and the last third for a term of nine years. The judges elected at this

[2] D Hunt, Address at the Conference of the Australian and New Zealand Society International Law, Canberra, 19 June 2004, *cit.* in: Boas/Bischoff/Reid/Don Taylor, *ICL III*, Part 9, fn. 6.

[3] *See* in general M Bohlander, 'The International Criminal Judiciary: Problems of Judicial Selection, Independence and Ethics', in: M Bohlander (ed), *International Criminal Justice: A Critical Analysis of Institutions and Procedures* (Cameron May 2008) 325.

[4] Critical as to the uniformity of this standard, M Bohlander, 'Pride and Prejudice or Sense and Sensibility? A Pragmatic Proposal for the Recruitment of Judges at the ICC and other International Criminal Courts', 12 *New Criminal Law Review* (2009) 529.

initial ballot for nine years were not eligible for re-election. In the subsequent elections, the term of office was limited to a period of three years; however, re-election is possible.[5] Nevertheless according to Art. 36 (10) ICCSt, a judge appointed to the Trial Chamber or to the Appeals Chamber remains in office as long as the case he or she is involved with continues. The last election of six judges took place at the tenth session of the Assembly of States Parties in December 2011.

At the *ad hoc* Tribunals, the judiciary is separated into permanent and *ad litem* judges. The former should not exceed a maximum of sixteen and the latter a maximum of nine judges. The Security Council submits a list of candidates to the General Assembly after examining the qualifications of the proposed permanent or *ad litem* judge who is to be nominated by a Member State of the United Nations. A judge needs the absolute majority of votes to be elected. The term of office of a permanent judge is limited to four years, although he or she is eligible for re-election, while an *ad litem* judge is appointed for a particular case, but his or her term in office should not exceed three years.

The composition of the chambers of the Special Court for Sierra Leone is different. The Government of Sierra Leone has the power to appoint one judge to the Trial Chamber and two judges to the Appeals Chamber. The remainder will be elected by the Secretary-General of the United Nations, according to Art. 12 SCSLSt. The appointed judges should serve a term of office of three years and are eligible for re-election.

II. Guiding principles for judges

Contrary to the function of the judges in common law systems, the judges at the ICC play a much more active role in establishing the truth.[6] Bear in mind, however, that 'notwithstanding the fact that the ICC judges can be quite active in determining the scope of the taking of evidence during trial, they don't need to be—and there is no guarantee at all that they will be.'[7]

This approach derives from the inquisitorial system of civil law and, therefore, judges are imbued 'with a specific and broad investigative mandate to find all information that could lead to the truth.'[8] Nevertheless, there is no guarantee that a more active judge would carry out his or her duty better than one who is more passive in conducting proceedings. The judges have to decide if their intervention is *de facto* needed to assist the truth-finding process or if it would be an interruption and therefore would

[5] For more information *see* W Schabas, *ICC* (OUP 2010) 524.

[6] S De Smet, 'A Structural Analysis of the Role of the Pre-Trial Chamber in the Fact-finding Process of the ICC', in: C Stahn and G Sluiter (eds), *The Emerging Practice of the International Criminal Court* (Martinus Nijhoff Publishers 2009) 405, 419 *et subs.*

[7] S Kirsch, 'The Trial Proceedings before the ICC', 6 *ICLR* (2006) 275, 279.

[8] S De Smet, 'A Structural Analysis of the Role of the Pre-Trial Chamber in the Fact-finding Process of the ICC', in: C Stahn and G Sluiter (eds), *The Emerging Practice of the International Criminal Court* (Martinus Nijhoff Publishers 2009) 405, 411.

be counterproductive to the establishment of the truth.[9] In the present author's view, there is no right or wrong approach on this issue because the conduct of a judge during proceedings must be analysed on a case-by-case basis. However, the judge must have the power to play an active role in establishing the truth. Of course, judges should always take into consideration their main responsibility to establish the truth and do not have discretionary power to delegate this duty.

In contrast to the *ad hoc* Tribunals, at the Special Court for Lebanon the judges should take an active role. For example, according to Art. 20 (2) STLSt, the presiding judge has the right to question a witness before both parties can ask their questions.[10]

Regarding criminal proceedings, Art. 14 (1) ICCPR stipulates that 'everyone shall be entitled to a fair and public hearing by a competent, independent and impartial tribunal'. The same wording can be found in the Basic Principles on the Independence of the Judiciary (hereinafter, Basic Principles).[11]

First, a 'competent' court has to be pre-established by law; ie the commission of the crimes to be tried occurs after the establishment of the court concerned.[12] This issue is not problematic for the ICC because it was established by the Rome Statute in 1998, and has jurisdiction only over crimes committed after 1 July 2002, the date when the treaty entered into force.

More debatable are the guiding principles for the judges about how the terms should be interpreted. Art. 40 ICCSt determines the independence of judges but does not conclusively define the issue by stating only that judges should not be engaged in any activity which could cause bias. However, the Basic Principles clearly define in Art. 6[13] that 'The principle of the independence of the judiciary entitles and requires the judiciary to ensure that judicial proceedings are conducted fairly and that the rights of the parties are respected.'[14]

The Iraqi High Tribunal pointed out that the accused 'was an executive employee for the regime, carrying out the duties of his job ... without being an independent judge of the court deciding the fate of innocent people.'[15] This example shows that a judge who is acting under the instructions of other authorities, like the head of state, does

---

[9] Regarding the 'responsibility gap' *see* section 1.B.2.

[10] G Higgins, 'Fair and Expeditious Pre-trial Proceedings: The Future of International Criminal Trials', 5 *JICJ* (2007) 394, 397.

[11] Basic Principles on the Independence of the Judiciary, GA Res. 40/32 (29 November 1985) and GA Res. 40/146 (13 December 1985).

[12] C Safferling, *Towards an International Criminal Procedure* (OUP 2003) 86 *et subs.*

[13] Basic Principles on the Independence of the Judiciary, GA Res. 40/32 (29 November 1985) and GA Res. 40/146 (13 December 1985), Art. 6.

[14] Ibid.

[15] Iraqi High Tribunal *Prosecutor v Saddam Hussein Al Majeed et al.*, AC, 29/c/2006, 26 December 2006, p 16.

not fulfil the internationally recognized requirements of the independence of the judiciary and, therefore, renders sentences acting as a criminal and not as a judge.

According to the jurisdiction of the ECtHR, to assume the independence of a court, one must take into account 'the manner of appointment of its members and the duration of their term of office ... the existence of guarantees against outside pressures ... and the question whether the body presents an appearance of independence'.[16]

Any pressure applied on the judges from outside should be avoided and appropriate measures to safeguard their independence should be taken, for example to grant them certain privileges and immunities pursuant to Art. 48 ICCSt. Another safeguard is the need for a vote by the absolute majority of judges for disqualifying a judge from a particular case, according to Art. 41 ICCSt. Further, removal from office is only possible by a vote of a two-thirds majority of the judges who afterwards recommend the disqualification to the Assembly of States Parties. Pursuant to Art. 46 (2) (a) ICCSt, once the Assembly of States Parties receives the recommendation, a two-thirds majority of the States Parties is needed to remove the judge from office.

In the Statutes of the ICTY, ICTR, and SCSL the word 'independent' is only used regarding the composition of the Court; that is, the permanent as well as the *ad litem* judges should be independent. In *Delalić et al.*, the Bureau on Motion on Judicial Independence comprised the President of the ICTY, the Vice-President, and both Presiding Judges of the Trial Chambers, determined that the independence of a judge, who holds the position of a Vice-President of a state concurrently with her position at the Court, is not infringed if the judge in question does not take up the duties of her post as long as her term of office at the ICTY continues.[17]

The concept of independence is to be strictly separated from the second important requirement, the impartiality of judges.[18] On taking up his or her term in office, a judge has to undertake a solemn declaration 'in open court to exercise his or her respective functions impartially and consciously', according to Art. 45 ICCSt. Details concerning the code of conduct for a judge are summarized in the Code of Judicial Ethics.[19]

Art. 4 of that Code determines that a judge 'should avoid any conflict of interest' but does not clearly define the circumstances which could lead to a presumption of reliance. Therefore, one should refer to the jurisdiction of the ECtHR which held that, 'As to the condition of "impartiality" within the meaning of that provision, there are two tests to be applied: the first consists in trying to determine the personal conviction

[16] ECtHR *Campbell and Fell v The United Kingdom*, Judgment 28 June 1984, Series A No. 80, para 78.

[17] ICTY *Prosecutor v Delalić et al.*, Bureau on motion on judicial independence, IT-96-21, 4 September 1998, Decision of the bureau on motion on judicial independence, Chapter II.2.

[18] C Safferling, *Towards an International Criminal Procedure* (OUP 2003) 92.

[19] Code of Judicial Ethics, ICC-BD/02-01-05, Art. 4.

of a particular judge in a given case and the second in ascertaining whether the judge offered guarantees sufficient to exclude any legitimate doubt in this respect.'[20]

Impartiality is thus split into two parts. The first part concerns the personal link of a judge to the specific case; for example, family links to a victim or to the accused or the judge having made a prior statement on the possible outcome of the trial. Secondly, the judge should not be engaged in any proceedings at a prior stage, for example first as prosecutor at the national level and later, as judge acting at the Pre-Trial Chamber in the same case.

In *Furundžija*, the ICTY Appeals Chamber developed a standard to be applied regarding the impartiality of a judge. Therefore, a presumption exists if:

A. A Judge is not impartial if it is shown that actual bias exists.
B. There is an unacceptable appearance of bias if:

i) a Judge is a party of the case, or has a financial or proprietary interest in the outcome of a case, or if the Judge's decision will lead to the promotion of a cause in which he or she is involved, together with one of the parties. Under these circumstances, a Judge's disqualification from the case is automatic; or

ii) the circumstances would lead a reasonable observer, properly informed, to reasonably apprehend bias.[21]

Applying the above-mentioned standard, the ECCC drew the conclusion that 'it is unavoidable that one of the parties may not be satisfied with a judicial decision. Dissatisfaction does not, by itself, raise grounds for disqualification but rather for appeal.'[22]

The conscience of a judge ruling on criminal matters mainly depends on his or her trial experience which is one of the requirements for an individual on the election list B, and therefore, to be eligible as judge for the ICC Trial and Pre-Trial Divisions pursuant to Art. 39 (1) ICCSt.

The next criterion set out by the Code of Judicial Ethics refers to the integrity of a judge. He or she may not accept any bribes, gifts, or other advantages which may be offered in order to influence the outcome of proceedings.[23] Furthermore, the judge shall not make public any information he or she received in confidence in the course of the proceedings, according to Art. 6 Code of Judicial Ethics.

The last prerequisite enshrined in the Code of Judicial Ethics concerns the diligence of the judges. They should carry out their duty by respecting the right of the

[20] ECtHR *Incal v Turkey*, Judgment 9 June 1998, Rep. 1998-IV, para 65.
[21] ICTY *Prosecutor v Furundžija*, AC, IT-95-17/1-A, 21 July 2008, Judgment, para 189.
[22] ECCC *Prosecutor v Nuon Chea*, PTC, 002/17-06-2010-ECCC-PTC (09), 10 September 2010, Decision on the Application for Disqualification of Judge You Bunleng, para 38.
[23] Code of Judicial Ethics, ICC-BD/02-01-05, Art. 5.

accused to an expeditious trial[24] and should avoid any undue delay of the findings. Of course, the judges also have to safeguard adherence to other internationally recognized rights of the accused, such as, for example, the right to a public hearing or the general principle of oral testimony.[25]

III. Presidency

The Presidency is one of the four organs of the Court. Its members are judges who are elected by the judges themselves from amongst those of the Court on the occasion of a plenary session, according to Rule 4 RPE ICC. During the session two-thirds of the judges have to be present and, importantly, a majority is needed for the President and the two Vice-Presidents to be elected. Their term of office is restricted to three years, or at least until the end of their regular term as appointed judge, but re-election is possible.[26] Pursuant to Regulation 10 (2) RegC, the members of the Presidency have precedence over the other judges.

The functions of the Presidency are stipulated in Art. 38 (3) ICCSt. Performing its duty concerning the proper administration of the Court, the Presidency has *inter alia* to assign cases to the Chambers and to organize them as well as to increase the numbers of judges if necessary. For example, immediately after the confirmation of charges by the Pre-Trial Chamber, a case will be transmitted from the Registry to the Presidency, which has to appoint a Trial Chamber, pursuant to Art. 61 (11) ICCSt and Rule 130 RPE ICC.

Remarkably, the Office of the Prosecutor is explicitly excluded by the wording of Art. 38 (3) (a) ICCSt from being under the instructions of the Presidency and thereby affirms once more the independence of the OTP. However, the Presidency is responsible for working to align the issues which fall within the interest of the Chambers as well as of the Prosecutor. As mentioned, the Presidency does not have the authority to issue binding orders to the Prosecutor.

Regarding its legal function, the Presidency may review the decisions of the Registry, pursuant to Regulation 216 RegR. In *Katanga and Chui*, one of the accused appealed against a decision of the Registry to fund either two visits a year by three family members or three visits a year by two family members. In fact, the Registry allowed visits by his wife and his six children but refused to fund more than two of the visitors, taking the view that the permission to visit has to be strictly separated from the funding of such visits. The Presidency overruled the decision on the ground that Regulation 179 (1) RegC was violated. Restricting the

---

24 *See* section 8.B.
25 *See* section 8.A.V.
26 W Schabas, *ICC* (OUP 2010) 541.

number of funded family visits would put the social contact between the suspect and his family in jeopardy.[27]

Furthermore, pursuant to Art. 48 (5) (b) ICCSt, the Presidency can waive the privileges and immunities granted by the Registrar on the basis of serious reasons. Equally, if there are reasonable grounds to believe that a judge or the Prosecutor is not carrying out his or her duties in an impartial or independent manner, the Presidency can, on the request of the judge concerned or the Prosecutor, disqualify him or her from the specific case, in particular if he or she was engaged in the same case, for example at the national level, according to Art. 41 ICCSt.

Under Rule 171 (3) RPE ICC, the Presidency rules on offences of misconduct before the Court[28] committed by the Registrar, a judge, the Prosecutor, defence counsel, or counsel of a victim if the Presiding Judge of the affected Chamber is of the opinion that exclusion from the proceedings for longer than thirty days is warranted.

Moreover, the Presidency has to maintain a relationship with states and is responsible for the outreach work of the Court. Therefore, it is the President's responsibility to visit different countries and convince their governments to ratify the Rome Statute.[29] Hence, 'the Presidency acts as the "external face" of the Court as a whole'.[30]

The Presidency is not listed as an organ of the Court in Art. 11 ICTYSt/ICTRSt/SCSLSt. However, each of the *ad hoc* Tribunals is headed by a President. The President of the ICTY and of the SCSL concurrently is the Presiding Judge of the Appeals Chamber (Art. 14 (2) ICTYSt, Rule 18 (2) RPE SCSL) while at the ICTR, the President is the Presiding Judge of one of the Trial Chambers (Art. 13 (2) ICTRSt).

The Presidency coordinates the judicial administration of the tribunals; that is, the respective President oversees the procedure of the Chambers. Regarding the ICTY and ICTR, the President and Vice-President are members of the Bureau which decides *inter alia* on a motion regarding the independence and impartiality of a judge. Furthermore, the Plenary Meetings are chaired by the President, who also acts as member of the tribunal's Coordination Council. The

---

[27] ICC *Prosecutor v Katanga and Chui*, Presidency, ICC-RoR-217-02/08-8, 10 March 2009, Decision on 'Mr. Mathieu Ngudjolo Chui Complain under the Regulation 221(1) of the Regulation of the Registry against the Registrar's Decision of 18 November 2008'.

[28] *See* section 10.II.

[29] In August 2011, the President visited Mozambique, a state which has signed the Statute but has not yet ratified it, ICC-CPI-20110808-PR709, 8 August 2011.

[30] The Registry's Public Information and Documentation Section, Integrated Strategy for External Relations, Public Information and Outreach available at <http://www.icc-cpi.int/NR/rdonlyres/425E80BA-1EBC-4423-85C6-D4F2B93C7506/185049/ICCPIDSWBOR0307070402_IS_En.pdf>.

provisions in the Statute of the SCSL regarding the functions of the President of the Court are similar to those of the Rome Statute. The President is responsible for proper administration; ie, has to coordinate the Chambers and review the activities of the Registry. Notably, one of his or her functions is 'furthering the conduct of fair, impartial and expeditious trials and appeals', pursuant to Rule 19 RPE SCSL.

The Presidency heads the Court externally, that is, through its function as the 'face of the Court', and internally by administering the other organs of the Court. Its power is limited regarding influence over ongoing proceedings. However, the acceptance of the Court and its interference in domestic affairs depends to a certain degree on the diplomatic capacity of the President and on any developed outreach programme.

IV. Pre-Trial Chamber

Currently, there are two Pre-Trial Chambers established at the ICC, comprising six judges, pursuant to Art. 39 (1) ICCSt. Currently, one of the pre-trial judges is the second Vice-President of the Presidency. Each of the two Chambers has appointed a Presiding Judge who conducts proceedings. The functions of the Pre-Trial Chamber are enshrined in Art. 57 ICCSt.

As soon as a situation is referred by the Security Council or by a state to the Prosecutor, or the Prosecutor decides to commence investigation *proprio motu*, pursuant to Art. 13 ICCSt, the Presidency may assume responsibility for this situation via a determined Pre-Trial Chamber regarding all associated issues. One has to bear in mind that in spite of the power given to the Pre-Trial Chamber, it does not have either the function or the power of an 'investigating judge'; that is, it does not supervise the Prosecutor regarding the investigation in an objective manner in order to establish the truth.[31] It should be taken into consideration whether the implementation of an investigating judge would be better for the purpose of speeding up the trial and as a result, to protect the rights of the accused to an expeditious trial in a more adequate manner than the now established Pre-Trial Chambers at the ICC. The power to assist the defence on request would no longer be required.[32] Another approach could be the establishment of an independent investigative commission, which would support the investigation of the Prosecutor as well as of the defence and therefore, would reduce the cost of the trial and would expedite proceedings.[33]

[31] S De Smet, 'A Structural Analysis of the Role of the Pre-Trial Chamber in the Fact-finding Process of the ICC' in: C Stahn and G Sluiter (eds), *The Emerging Practice of the International Criminal Court* (Martinus Nijhoff Publishers 2009) 405, 422 *et subs*.

[32] *See* also J de Hemptinne, 'The Creation of Investigation Chambers at the International Criminal Court: An Option Worth Pursuing?', 5 *JICJ* (2007) 402.

[33] G Higgins, 'Fair and Expeditious Pre-trial Proceedings: The Future of International Criminal Court', 5 *JICJ* (2007) 394, 396 *et subs*.

The judicial system of the ECCC, modelled along the lines of the French system of criminal procedure, is the only one of the international and internationalized tribunals which provides for investigating judges to supervise the prosecutor.[34] According to Art. 23 ECCCSt, the judges have *inter alia* the right to question witnesses and suspects and to collect evidence.

The Pre-Trial Chamber *inter alia* may rule on the issuance of a warrant of arrest or a summons to appear, pursuant to Art. 58 ICCSt. It is also called upon to confirm the charges, according to Art. 61 ICCSt. While rendering its decision on the requested warrant of arrest as well as on the confirmation of charges, the Court has to take into account, regarding the former, the 'reasonable basis to believe' test, and regarding the latter, the 'substantial grounds to believe' test. This constitutes a considerably lower threshold than the basis on which a Trial Chamber renders its decision; that is, proof without reasonable doubt. The double standard on which both Chambers base their findings can be a risk to the rights of the accused. First, if the Pre-Trial Chamber addresses each issue with the rigour and in such depth as it currently does,[35] it will be hard for the Trial Chamber to rule differently on the same issue and, therefore, it could be accused of prejudice. Remarkably in *Lubanga*, the Trial Chamber clearly determined its relationship to the Pre-Trial Chamber and the finding of the latter in stating that 'the Trial Chamber has not been given a power to review the only decision of the Pre-Trial Chamber that is definitely binding for the Trial Chamber: the Decision on the confirmation of the charges'.[36]

Secondly, the right of the accused to expeditious proceeding will be in jeopardy because of repeated requests by the Pre-Trial Chambers to hear further evidence. On this issue Pre-Trial Chambers I and II are currently following different approaches.

None of the *ad hoc* Tribunals operates with a Pre-Trial Chamber as an organ of the Court. According to Rule 65*ter* (A) RPE ICTY, the President of the Trial Chamber shall appoint a judge who is responsible for the pre-trial stage of a particular case; that is, to reach an agreement between the parties regarding uncontested facts or to review the indictment. Confirming the indictment, the Pre-Trial Judge should satisfy him or herself 'that a *prima facie* case has been established by the Prosecutor', pursuant to Art. 19 ICTYSt and Art. 18 ICTRSt. Remarkably, the threshold is lower than the one provided for the confirmation

---

34 *See* section 2.B.

35 *See* section 7. B.

36 ICC *Prosecutor v Lubanga*, TC I, ICC-01/04-01/06-1084, 13 December 2007, Decision on the status before the Trial Chamber of the evidence heard by the Pre-Trial Chamber and the decisions of the Pre-Trial Chamber in trial proceedings, and the manner in which evidence shall be submitted, para 43.

of the charges at the ICC.[37] This also becomes clear through the volume of documentation at the ICC; for example, the *Bemba* decision on the confirmation of charges[38] runs to 186 pages while review of the indictment at the ICTY regularly consists of only one or two pages.[39] From a human rights perspective this implies two things. On the one hand, the trial will be expedited, but on the other, the threshold to commence a trial is considerably lower, therefore the risk that a case is to be taken to court is significantly higher at the *ad hoc* Tribunals than at the ICC.

At the ICTY, the Pre-Trial judge will be assisted by a Senior Legal Officer who presides the *inter partes* meetings between the Prosecutor and the defence, pursuant to Rule 65*ter* (D) (v) RPE ICTY. Bearing in mind that the lack of judicial authority will not help to bridge the different interests of both parties, this provision should be abolished and the Pre-Trial Judge should carry out his or her tasks personally.[40]

1. Chamber

At the pre-trial stage, the decisions are made either by a Chamber, composed of three Judges, or by a single judge, according to Art. 39 (2) (b) (iii) ICCSt. The judges of each Chamber elect from amongst themselves a Presiding Judge. The Chamber is responsible for rendering decisions *inter alia* regarding requests for authorization of investigations by the Prosecutor acting on his or her own motion, according to Art. 15 ICCSt. In the situation in Kenya, such proceedings were necessary for the first time in ICC history. The Pre-Trial Chamber reviewed the conclusion of the Prosecutor that the 'reasonable basis to proceed' threshold was met to start investigations on the post-election violence in Kenya between 1 June 2005 and 26 November 2009. It noted before rendering its decision on the initiation of investigations that the Chamber had to rule over the 'reasonable basis to believe' test stipulated in Art. 53 (1) (a) ICCSt. The Pre-Trial Chamber ruled by majority, Judge Kaul dissenting, that there was a reasonable basis to believe that the alleged crimes were committed and that therefore the Prosecutor had passed the 'reasonable basis to proceed' threshold.[41]

---

[37] This will be discussed in greater detail later, *see* section 7.A.II.

[38] ICC *Prosecutor v Bemba*, PTC II, ICC-01/05-01/08-424, 15 June 2009, Decision Pursuant to Article 61 (7) (a) and (b) of the Rome Statute on the Charges of the Prosecutor Against Jean-Pierre Bemba Gombo, and *see* also section 7.B.II.

[39] Eg, ICTY *Prosecutor v Milošević*, PTC, 22 November 2001, Decision on Review of Indictment, and ICTR *Prosecutor v Akayesu*, PTC, ICTR-96-4-I, 16 February 1996, Decision on the Review of Indictment, and SCSL *Prosecutor v Taylor*, PTC, SCSL-2003-01-I, 7 March 2003, Decision Approving the Indictment and Order of Non-disclosure, each consists of three or four pages only.

[40] M Harmon, 'The Pre-Trial Process at the ICTY as a Means of Ensuring Expeditious Trials', 5 *JICJ* (2007) 377, 387.

[41] ICC *Situation in the Republic of Kenya*, PTC II, ICC-01/09-19, 31 March 2010, Decision Pursuant to Article 15 of the Rome Statute on the Authorization of an Investigation into the Situation in the Republic of Kenya.

The same method is used for a disagreement between a state which has jurisdiction over a case and the Prosecutor over deferral of a situation to the national authorities, pursuant to Art. 18 (2) ICCSt.[42] In the case of Kenya, the government appealed against the decision of the Pre-Trial Chamber to commence investigation and not to defer the situation to the national courts.[43] It should be borne in mind that the Pre-Trial Chamber has to rule over 'any' challenges against admissibility, according to Art. 19 ICCSt.[44]

Ruling over the confirmation of charges[45] constitutes the main function of the Pre-Trial Chamber, pursuant to Art. 61 ICCSt. The finding can only be rendered by the Chamber as a whole, not by a single judge, due to the crucial influence of this decision to the entire course of the proceedings. In *Garda*, the Pre-Trial Chamber declined the confirmation of charges reasoning that the 'substantial grounds to believe' threshold was not met.[46] It is unfortunate that the Pre-Trial Chamber felt compelled to analyse each fact of the case in such detail that it referred to the decision denying confirmation in the following proceedings againsts *Banda and Jerbo*. Such an approach could infringe the rights of the accused because it prejudices the decision.

2. Single judge

Only at the pre-trial stage, has a single judge the power to render certain decisions, according to Art. 57 (2) (b) ICCSt and Art. 39 (2) (b) (iii) ICCSt. Each pre-trial division has to designate a judge from their division to carry out the duties of a single judge. If it is necessary for the efficiency of the trial, they can also appoint more single judges, pursuant to Regulation 47 RegC. The exact duties and powers of the single judge are not determined either in the Statute or in its Rules of Procedure and Evidence and, therefore, only issues of minor importance fall within the responsibility of the single judge.

In *Bemba*, Judge Trendafilova acted as a single judge regarding the defence request of interim release of the accused. She rightly noted that the 'deprivation

[42] In greater detail in section 5.B.

[43] ICC *Situation in the Republic of Kenya*, AC, ICC-01/09-78, 10 August 2011, Decision in the Admissibility of the 'Appeal of the Government of Kenya against the "Decision on the Request for Assistance Submitted on Behalf of the Government of the Republic of Kenya Pursuant to Article 93(3) of the Statute and Rule 194 of the Rules of Procedure and Evidence";' the impugned decision ICC *Situation in the Republic of Kenya*, PTC II, ICC-01/09-63, 29 June 2011, Decision on the Request for Assistance Submitted on Behalf of the Government of the Republic of Kenya Pursuant to Article 93(3) of the Statute and Rule 194 of the Rules of Procedure and Evidence.

[44] *See* section 5.B.II.

[45] *See* section 7.A.

[46] ICC *Prosecutor v Garda*, PTC I, ICC-02/05-02/09-243-Red, 8 February 2010, Decision on the Confirmation of Charges, para 236.

of liberty should be an exception and not a rule'[47] but rejected the release of the accused, reasoning that 'the risk of him absconding becomes a real possibility'.[48] Nevertheless, as pre-trial detention constitutes a major infringement of the personal liberty of the suspect,[49] it seems inappropriate that a single judge should render the decision. The high level of importance afforded to the rights of the suspect should require the Chamber to take on this responsibility.

Moreover, the single judge has to rule on requests of pre-confirmation disclosure of materials, as was the case in *Lubanga*. In particular, the repeated rejection of disclosure[50] of *inter alia* the names of intermediaries by the Prosecutor jeopardized the interests of justice because of his refusal to comply with several court orders.[51] Judge Steiner rightly pointed out that:

> the Chamber is the ultimate guarantor of the Defence's timely access to the said evidence and materials because it is the ultimate guarantor of the respect for all other aspects of Thomas Lubanga Dyilo's right to a fair trial; and that, for this reason, redactions in the said evidence and materials are the exception and not the general rule, are permissible only on a case-by-case basis and are subject to the approval of the Chamber.[52]

3. Conclusion

The core task of the Pre-Trial Chamber is to safeguard the rights of the accused in the investigation phase carried out by the Prosecutor. This constitutes the most sensitive and important stage for inference with human rights.[53] The Court has to protect the suspects *inter alia* against illegal seizures and unsubstantiated warrants of arrest. However, the main goal of the Pre-Trial Chamber is confirmation of the charges.

The Chamber has faced many criticisms in this regard in the last few years, in particular, regarding the practice of performing a 'mini-trial', or a 'trial before trial'. In its decisions, the Pre-Trial Chamber has denied this, but the fact is that the decision on the confirmation of charges probably consists of more pages than the first judgment that will eventually be handed down by the Trial Chamber. One must consider alternatives to the existing Pre-Trial Chambers, such as the

---

[47] ICC *Prosecutor v Bemba*, PTC III, ICC-01/05-01/08-321, 16 December 2008, Decision on Application for Interim Release, para 31.

[48] Ibid, para 36.

[49] *See* section 6.E.

[50] *See* section 7.D.

[51] ICC *Prosecutor v Lubanga*, TC I, ICC-01/04-01/06-T-314-ENG, Hearing, 15 July 2010, p 22, line 9 *et subs.*, and to the issue of contempt of court *see* section 10.I.

[52] ICC *Prosecutor v Lubanga*, PTC I, ICC-01/04-01/06-355, 25 August 2006, Decision on the Prosecution's Practice to Provide to the Defence Redacted Versions of Evidence and Material without Authorization by the Chamber, p 4.

[53] These measures will be called 'qualified investigative measures', comprising search and seizure and arrest warrants among others, *see* section 6.D.

implementation of an 'investigating judge'. In any event, the power of the Pre-Trial Chamber should not be underestimated.

V. Trial Chamber

The Trial Chamber is composed of three judges. Currently, there are eight judges appointed to the Trial Chamber division, forming four Trial Chambers. According to Art. 39 ICCSt, the number should never be less than six but can be increased depending on the workload of the Court. At the moment, one judge of the Pre-Trial Chamber division is working for both the Pre-Trial and the Trial Chambers. This situation is provided for in Art. 39 (4) ICCSt, whereby the power to decide the issue falls within the responsibility of the Presidency.

As mentioned above, the *ad hoc* Tribunals have used the opportunity to appoint *ad litem* judges for a particular case in order to deal with the workload. Notably, the rotation of permanent judges between Trial and Appeals Chambers is not only permitted in the absence of a judge but must be carried out on a regular basis, according to Rule 27 RPE ICTY/ICTR.

Contrary to the Pre-Trial Chamber, the Trial Chamber adopts all findings by majority in chamber. However, the Presiding Judge of the Trial Chamber has additional functions and therefore may deal with different legal matters. He or she has the power to give directions on the conduct of proceedings, pursuant to Art. 64 (8) ICCSt, and to issue the declaration of the closure of evidence submissions, according to Rule 141 (1) RPE ICC. Nevertheless, the appointment of a single judge to determine decisions of minor relevance is provided neither in the Statute nor in the Rules of Procedure and Evidence. Art. 74 (1) ICCSt clearly determines that '[a]ll judges of the Trial Chamber shall be present at each stage of the trial and throughout their deliberations'. It is at the discretion of the Trial Chamber to refer preliminary issues to a Pre-Trial Chamber or to a single judge of a Pre-Trial Chamber, pursuant to Art. 64 (4) ICCSt. In *Lubanga*, the Trial Chamber ruled that due to the lack of time 'to familiarize itself with the record', it was requesting the Pre-Trial Chamber to render a decision on the merits concerning questions of detention.[54]

However, the Statutes of the *ad hoc* Tribunals do not provide for the eventuality that the Pre-Trial Judge will be involved in the Trial Chamber after handing over the record of a case. Such an approach could speed up the trial, and would also be feasible for the ICC.[55] Nevertheless, such provision may

---

[54] ICC *Prosecutor v Lubanga*, TC I, ICC-01/04-01/06-921, 6 June 2007, Request of Review of Detention, p 2.

[55] M Harmon, 'The Pre-Trial Process at the ICTY as a Means of Ensuring Expeditious Trials', 5 *JICJ* (2007) 377, 390.

violate the rights of the accused, namely the right to be tried by an impartial tribunal.[56]

Immediately after the appointment of the Trial Chamber by the Presidency, it must convene a status conference in order to fix the date of trial, pursuant to Rule 132 RPE ICC. Between the status conference and setting up the Trial Chamber, challenges to admissibility concerning *ne bis in idem* can be brought. In *Katanga*, the defence challenged the admissibility of the Court for the first time at the trial stage arguing that, 'it is only after the confirmation hearing... in a position to know the charges with the required level in detail and is in a position to assess fully whether one of the grounds in Article 17 (1) is applicable.'[57]

The Trial Chamber ruled that the defence motion was out of time according to the three-phase test;[58] that is: (1) prior to the issuance of the decision on the confirmation of charges a challenge based on all four grounds stipulated in Art. 17 (1) ICCSt is possible, (2) up to the convening of the Trial Chamber a challenge grounded on *ne bis in idem* is possible, (3) henceforth, a challenge based on *ne bis in idem* requires the permission of the Trial Chamber. In *Katanga,* arguing that the wording of the finding of the Pre-Trial Chamber could have led to the misunderstanding which caused the delay, the Trial Chamber examined the reasons advanced by the defence.[59]

According to Rule 72 (A) (i) RPE ICTY/ICTR and Rule 72 (B) (i) RPE SCSL, the Trial Chamber should decide on challenges of jurisdiction. Notably, the Chamber will render its finding 'based solely on the briefs of the parties'; ie, without a public hearing.

In fulfilling its functions, the Trial Chamber possesses a broad discretionary power. At the status conference, the Chamber determines the course of proceedings by deciding on matters of pre-trial disclosure,[60] the length of legal arguments, the time permitted for presenting evidence, and the way in which evidence should be presented, according to Rule 140 RPE ICC. Notably, the course of proceedings is not strictly divided into prosecution and defence as in

---

[56] *See* section 4.E.

[57] ICC *Prosecutor v Katanga and Chui,* Defence of Mr Germain Katanga, ICC-01/04-01/07-949, 11 March 2009, Motion Challenging the Admissibility of the Case by the Defence of Germain Katanga, pursuant to Article 19 (2) (a) of the Statute, para 2.

[58] *See* section 2.C.III.

[59] ICC *Prosecutor v Katanga and Chui,* TC II, ICC-01/04-01/07-T-67-ENG, 12 June 2009, Transcript, p 3 *et subs.*

[60] R Gallmetzer, 'The Trial Chamber's Discretionary Power to Devise the Proceedings before it and its Exercise in the Trial of *Thomas Lubanga Dyilo*', in: C Stahn and G Sluiter (eds), *The Emerging Practice of the International Criminal Court* (Martinus Nijhoff Publishers 2009) 501 and V Röben, 'The Procedure of the ICC: Status and Function of the Prosecutor', 7 *Max Planck UNYB* (2003) 513, 513; the latter rightly noted that this power should be used to speed up the trial.

common law.[61] *Inter alia* pursuant to Art. 64 ICCSt, the Trial Chamber may require additional evidence that the witness is present at Court, it may rule over protection measures for witnesses and victims if the Pre-Trial Chamber has not done so previously, and it has the power to determine the admissibility of evidence, according to Art. 69 ICCSt.

Moreover, the Trial Chamber may rule on information provided by confidential sources. In *Katanga and Chui*, the Prosecutor requested the redaction of the name of an organization working in the conflict area which provided information, by arguing that the neutrality of the entity would be seriously jeopardized and hence its staff would be endangered. The Trial Chamber rightly pointed out that neither the Statute nor the Rules of Procedure comprise a provision which 'protect[s] the neutral image of information providers'.[62] However, it concluded that the outward appearance of active collaboration with the Court would pose an unquantifiable risk on the fulfilment of the mandate of the organization and, thus, the Chamber must 'exceptionally use its discretion under article 64 (6) (c) and (f) of the Statute and regulation 54 (1) of the Regulations to issue an order in the interest of justice, in order to prevent that the image of impartiality of [the entity concerned] suffers unduly.'[63]

The most drastic measure within the power of the Trial Chamber is to stay proceedings in cases of abuse of power by the Prosecutor; that is, if the fair trial standard is gravely breached. In *Lubanga*, the Prosecutor refused to comply with several orders by the Trial Chamber to disclose potential exculpatory material and, therefore, the Trial Chamber determined that 'the trial process has been ruptured to such a degree that it is now impossible to piece together the constituent elements of fair trial. In consequence a stay is imposed on these proceedings.'[64]

After both parties have made their closing statements, the Trial Chamber retires to reach a verdict. One has to bear in mind that the Chamber has to render its decision regarding each charge separately, pursuant to Rule 142 RPE ICC. When subsequently determining the penalty in the case of a conviction, the Chamber has to take into account all mitigating as well as aggravating circumstances concerning the accused, according to Rule 145 (2) RPE ICC.

Pursuant to Rule 87 (B) RPE ICTY/ICTR/SCSL, the judges of the Trial Chamber 'shall vote separately on each charge contained in the indictment'. Subsequently, it

---

61 S Kirsch, 'The Trial Proceedings before the ICC', 6 *ICLR* (2006) 275, 279.

62 ICC *Prosecutor v Katanga and Chui*, TC II, ICC-01/04-01/07-2055-Red, 5 May 2010, Decision on the protection of the neutral and impartial status of information providers, para 17.

63 Ibid, para 23.

64 ICC *Prosecutor v Lubanga*, TC I, ICC-01/04-01/06-1401, 13 June 2008, Decision on the consequences of non-disclosure of exculpatory materials covered by Article 54 (3) (e) agreements and the application to stay the prosecution of the accused, together with certain other issues raised at the Status Conference on 10 June 2008, para 93 *et subs*.

shall impose a penalty regarding the charges if the Court has established the guilt of the accused.

Untill now, the Trial Chamber has not yet rendered a judgment: nevertheless, it remains the core organ of the ICC which finally decides on the guilt or innocence of an accused. The Chamber has the power to rule on any evidence admitted by the parties and is therefore the main body in conducting the trial. It has discretionary powers to order the protection of witnesses or victims as well as to halt the proceedings. This makes it obvious that the crucial functions of criminal proceedings belong to the Trial Chambers.

VI. Appeals Chamber

The third and final organ, the Appeals Chamber, is composed of six judges including the President. A judge appointed to the Appeals Chamber cannot substitute a judge of lower rank but a judge of the Trial Chamber or Pre-Trial Chamber may temporarily replace an absent Appeals Chamber judge, pursuant to Art. 39 (4) ICCSt.

The Appeals Chamber has equal powers to those of the Trial Chamber, pursuant to Art. 83 (1) ICCSt. After the Trial Chamber renders its final decision, the outcome can be appealed. Art. 81 (1) (a) ICCSt comprises a list of grounds on which the Prosecutor can appeal, for example an error of fact or an error of law.[65] Importantly, the Prosecutor is also obliged to appeal on behalf of the accused if he or she acquires knowledge about, for example, a procedural error or a violation of the rights of the accused.[66] According to Art. 83 (2) ICCSt, the Appeals Chamber can reverse or amend the decision or sentence, and has the power to order a new trial before a different Trial Chamber.

Not only can a judgment be appealed but so too can 'other decisions', pursuant to Art. 82 ICCSt, the so-called interlocutory appeals. Findings of the Pre-Trial Chamber as well as of the Trial Chamber concerning the interim release of the accused can be reviewed by the Appeals Chamber. In *Mbarushimana*, the Appeals Chamber pointed out that '[t]he Appeals Chamber will not interfere with a Pre-Trial or Trial Chamber's evaluation of the evidence just because the Appeals Chamber might have come to a different conclusion. It will interfere only in the case of a clear error.'[67]

In *Brđanin*, the Appeals Chamber of the ICTY denied a request for provisional release of the offender, arguing that 'where a convicted person simply wishes to spend

[65] *See* in greater detail, section 9.A.

[66] *See* section 9.A.III.

[67] ICC *Prosecutor v Mbarushimana*, AC, ICC-01/04-01/10–283, 14 July 2011, Judgment on the appeal of Mr Callixte Mbarushimana against the decision of Pre-Trial Chamber I of 19 May 2011 entitled 'Decision on the "Defence Request for Interim Release"', para 17.

time with his family or seeks to visit a close relative in poor health, the Appeals Chamber has not found special circumstances.'[68]

Furthermore, the Appeals Chamber has to decide over motions concerning jurisdiction and admissibility. In *Bemba*, the Appeals Chamber affirmed the finding of the Trial Chamber that an impugned decision does not constitute a final judgment and therefore does not fulfil the prerequisites enshrined in Art. 17 (1) (b) ICCSt. The state had investigated the crimes but decided to refer the case to the ICC, in particular because the accused possessed, at the moment in question, immunity due to his position as Vice-President of the DRC.[69]

The last category of interlocutory appeals enshrined in Art. 82 (1) (d) ICCSt can only be used in exceptional circumstances; that is, if the court of first instance comes to the conclusion that an Appeals Chamber decision is needed to clarify an issue, which has been decided by different Chambers in a different way.[70] Importantly, the issue must affect the expeditious and fair trial standard or the outcome of proceedings. However, as a first step, the court at first instance has leave to appeal its own decision, which is clearly an exception to the rule.[71] 'This system helps to maintain the possibility of interlocutory appeals only for those issues which are truly important and rids the court of the burden of slowing the process with countless interlocutory appeals on irrelevant issues.'[72]

Another remarkable decision by the Appeals Chamber concerned the disagreement between the Trial Chamber and the Prosecutor regarding the disclosure of the identity of intermediaries. The Appeals Chamber determined that, '[o]rders of the Trial Chamber are binding orders, to be implemented unless and until they are suspended, reversed or amended by the Appeals Chamber' and furthermore that '[t]his is a fundamental criterion for any trial to be fair'.[73]

---

[68] ICTY *Prosecutor v Brđanin*, AC, IT-99-36-A, 23 February 2007, Decision on Radoslav Brđanin's Motion for Provisional Release, para 6.

[69] ICC *Prosecutor v Bemba*, AC, ICC-01/05-01/08-962, 19 October 2010, Judgment on the appeal of Mr Jean-Pierre Bemba Gombo against the Decision of Trial Chamber III of 24 June 2010 entitled 'Decision on the Admissibility and Abuse of Process Challenges', para 65 *et subs.*

[70] ICC *Prosecutor v Katanga and Chui*, PTC I, ICC-01/04-01/07-149, 18 January 2008, Decision on the Defence Application for Leave to Appeal the Decision on the Defence Request Concerning Languages, p 6, the single Judge ruled that she 'agrees with the Defence and the Prosecution that an immediate resolution of the issue raised by the Defence may materially advance the proceedings' and therefore, granted leave to appeal against the decision on a request for the assistance of an interpreter during hearings for the accused.

[71] For further information *see* section 9.A.III and H Friman, 'Interlocutory Appeal in the Early Practice of the International Criminal Court', in: C Stahn and G Sluiter (eds), *The Emerging Practice of the International Criminal Court* (Martinus Nijhoff Publishers 2009) 553.

[72] ICC *Prosecutor v Lubanga*, TC I, ICC-01/04-01/06-1191, 26 February 2008, Decision on the Defence and Prosecution Requests for Leave to Appeal the Decision on Victims' Participation of 18 January 2008, Dissenting opinion of Judge Blattmann, para 5.

[73] ICC *Prosecutor v Lubanga*, AC, ICC-01/04-01/06-2582, 8 October 2010, Judgment on the Appeal of the Prosecutor against the Decision of Trial Chamber I of 8 July 2010 entitled 'Decision

In *Nzirorera*, the Appeals Chamber of the ICTR decided that the defence had to 'specify' the required material which it wanted the Prosecutor to disclose and for which the threshold should not be so high; that is, that the specification of the category of the material should be sufficient.[74]

The Appeals Chamber, as the highest judicial authority of the Court, has the power to dismiss, revise, reject, and confirm any decision or judgment on the motion of the Prosecutor or the defence. Bearing in mind that interlocutory appeals can interfere at any stage of the proceedings, this procedural option is highly criticized. However, it can prevent the necessity of a retrial after a judgment is rendered by the Trial Chamber due to an early intervention by the Appeals Chamber. The Appeals Chamber also fulfils human rights requirements as every offender has the right to a review of the judgment by a higher authority.[75]

B. The Prosecutor (*Hilde Farthofer*)

As has already been stated, according to Art. 34 (b) ICCSt, the Office of the Prosecutor forms part of the organs of the Court, while simultaneously being a 'separate organ' pursuant to Art. 42 (1) ICCSt. This reflects the difficulties that arose during the drafting process; there was a wide range of proposals concerning the extent to which the Prosecutor should be subject to directives. One such proposal suggested a non-permanent Prosecutor who would be appointed by the claiming state[76] notably, *inter alia*, the USA which favoured a non-independent working Prosecutor.[77] Eventually, the Assembly of States Parties established the Office of the Prosecutor which is headed by an independent Prosecutor and which should act independently and impartially, pursuant to Regulation 13 RegP.[78] Apart from this independent Prosecutor, there is a Deputy Prosecutor, a head of the Prosecutions Divisions, a head of the

on the Prosecution's Urgent Request for Variation of the Time-Limit to Disclose the Identity of Intermediary 143 or Alternatively to Stay Proceedings Pending Further Consultations with the VWU', para 48.

[74] ICTR *Prosecutor v Karemera et al.*, AC, ICTR-98-44-AR73.18, 17 May 2010, Decision on Joseph Nzirorera' Appeal from Decision on Alleged Rule 66 Violation, para 32.

[75] In greater detail, *see* section 9.A.I.

[76] W Schabas, *ICC* (OUP 2010) 577, and M Newton, 'Comparative Complementarity: Domestic Jurisdiction consistent with the Rome Statute of the International Criminal Court', 167 *Military Law Review* (2001) 20, 46, and A Danner, 'Enhancing the Legitimacy and Accountability of Prosecutorial Discretion at the International Criminal Court', 97 *AJIL* (2003) 510, 512 *et subs.*

[77] D Scheffer, 'The United States and the International Criminal Court', 93 *AJIL* (1999) 12, 15.

[78] M Delmas-Marty, 'Interactions between National and International Criminal Law in the Preliminary Phase of Trial at the ICC', 4 *JICJ* (2006) 2, 10.

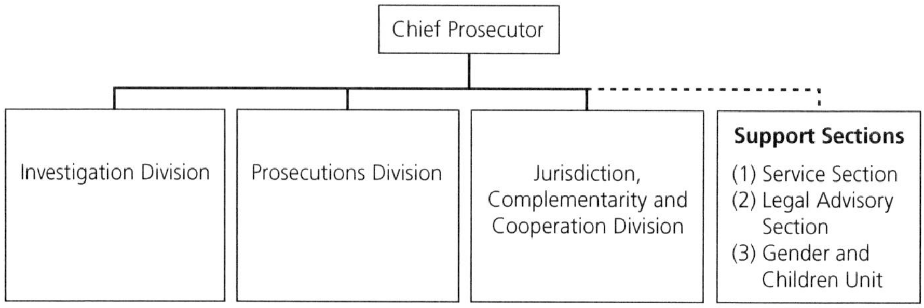

Figure 4.2 Office of the Prosecutor

Jurisdiction, Complementarity and Cooperation Division, and a head of the Investigation Division (see Figure 4.2).

In addition, there is the Service Section, *inter alia* responsible for the budget of the Office, pursuant to Regulation 10 RegP, the Legal Advisory Section, *inter alia* responsible for the maintenance of legal research tools, according to Regulation 11 RegP, and the Gender and Children Unit which should support the Prosecutor in all cases of sexual violence, pursuant to Regulation 12 RegP. According to Regulation 4 RegP, the 'Executive Committee' (ExCom) is composed of the Chief Prosecutor and the heads of the three divisions of the Office of the Prosecutor. The ExCom is responsible for the development and adoption of prosecutorial strategies and policies as well as for the budget.

The Pre-Trial Chamber currently authorizes the initiation of investigations and the joint team to be established, according to Regulation 32 (1) RegP. The joint team is composed of members of all three divisions and is responsible for the investigation and, later, for the prosecution. Based on all information and gathered evidence, it is responsible for identifying the persons most responsible for the crime in question, pursuant to Regulation 34 (1) RegP. The composition of the joint team varies according to the stage of proceedings; that is, during the first stage a greater number of investigation experts are needed, while during trial the shift is towards a greater number of experts in the area of criminal proceedings.

Remarkably, since 2008 the Office of the Prosecutor of the ICTY has established an investigation division which is composed of academics as well as military experts, which has been necessitated by the nature of the conflict in the former Yugoslavia. Various academics are needed to provide background information regarding, for example, the ethnical and linguistic diversity in the former Yugoslavia. This composition of the investigation team will enhance the outcome of investigations, as prior to this the Prosecutor had used external military advisers.

I. Electoral procedure

The Prosecutor is elected by secret ballot. The majority of the Assembly of States Parties is required, according to Art. 42 (4) ICCSt. This indicates the importance of the position of the Prosecutor. His or her term in office is limited to nine years and no re-election is possible. The first Prosecutor of the ICC took office on 16 June 2003. His term ends in June 2012. The electoral procedure to appoint his successor has already begun. In February 2011, a search commission was established to prepare a list of at least three candidates. The nomination period ran from 13 June to 2 September 2011. In December 2011, the secret ballot took place at the tenth session of the Assembly of States Parties.[79]

At the ICTY and ICTR, the Prosecutor is appointed for a term of office of four years, thereafter it is open for reappointment. The term of office of the Prosecutor for the STSL is limited to three years, after which the post-holder can be re-elected.

Deputy Prosecutors are also elected by secret ballot but the list of the three candidates is presented by the Prosecutor and, hence, this voting procedure shows the independence of the Office of the Prosecutor. It is not in the power of the Assembly of States Parties to decide on the staff of the Office of the Prosecutor. The Member States can only choose between the persons nominated by the Prosecutor and do not have the right to propose a candidate of their own choosing. Art. 42 (4) ICCSt provides for a nine-year term of office and re-election is not possible.

II. Guiding principles for the Prosecutor

The Office of the Prosecutor is the first organ of the Court which has to react when atrocities are committed. Therefore, it is the leading organ fulfilling the function of the Court; that is, to fill the gap of impunity. Starting with a preliminary examination of a given situation, the Prosecutor must be aware of the two main principles which should guide him/her while conducting his/her duties: first, the principle of the 'presumption of innocence' enshrined in Art. 66 ICCSt and, secondly, the principle of objectivity stipulated in Art. 54 (1) (a) ICCSt. These principles are to be respected if the investigation and all following trial phases are to meet the internationally recognized fair trial standards.

Art. 14 (2) ICCPR stipulates that '[e]veryone charged with a criminal offence shall have the right to be presumed innocent until proved guilty according to law'. The provision determines the end of the right of the presumption of innocence, or more precisely, after conviction the accused can no longer be assumed to be innocent,

[79] ICC-ASP/10/S/06, 7 February 2011, a document containing detailed information on the electoral procedure of the Prosecutor, its Deputy Prosecutors as well as of the Judges is annexed.

but it does not specify the starting point. From the time when a particular individual is identified as an alleged perpetrator, that person must be granted the right to be presumed innocent.[80] The Prosecutor should not proceed on the basis of that person's guilt until guilt is proven beyond reasonable doubt and thus declared by the competent Trial Chamber.[81]

The principle of objectivity is closely linked with the presumption of innocence.[82] Regulation 24 RegP clearly implies that the staff of the Office of the Prosecutor shall examine the evidence by applying 'a consistent and objective method for the evaluation of sources, information and evidence'. Bearing in mind that if the Prosecutor does not carry out the investigation in an impartial and independent manner, the right to be presumed innocent will be violated and it is up to the Court to intervene.

In *Kupreškić*, the Trial Chamber of the ICTY noted that even if the Statute and the Rules of Procedure and Evidence are silent on the duty of the Prosecutor to collect incriminatory as well as exculpatory evidence, and merely obliged the Office of the Prosecutor to disclose evidence helpful to the defence,[83]

> it should be noted that the Prosecutor of the Tribunal is not, or not only, a Party to adversarial proceedings but is an organ of the Tribunal and an organ of international criminal justice whose object is not simply to secure a conviction but to present the case for the Prosecution, which includes not only inculpatory, but also exculpatory evidence, in order to assist the Chamber to discover the truth in a judicial setting.[84]

The Office of the Prosecutor is an organ of the Court but it concurrently possesses the power to act entirely independently. Consequently, the head of this independent institution, the Prosecutor as well as the Deputy Prosecutors, are not bound by any order of other organs of the Court, governments, or institutions

---

[80] C Safferling, *Towards an International Criminal Procedure* (OUP 2003) 69 *et subs.*; the author rightly noted that the burden of defence would be on the suspect if he or she had to wait to go to trial to prove his or her innocence is clearly against the interest of justice.

[81] The Prosecutor published in *The Guardian* an article about the situation in Darfur, in which he clearly blamed the President of the Sudan Omar Al'Bashir and the minister for humanitarian affairs, Ahmad Harun, for the genocide in Darfur. On the request of the Office of Public Counsel for the Defence (OPCD), Pre-Trial Chamber I determined that the 'behaviour addressed in the Request neither occurred in the context of proceedings, nor was in violation of any direction given by the Court and that, accordingly, falls outside the scope of the power vested by the Chamber', ICC *Prosecutor v Omar Hassan Ahmad Al Bashir*, PTC I, ICC-02/05-01/09-112, 13 September 2010, Decision on the 'OPCD Request for Authorization to Submit Observations Concerning Guardian Article dated 15 July 2010', para 9; this conclusion is unacceptable, the Prosecutor has infringed his duty to be objective and violated the principle of presumption of innocence, although he made the statement concerned in his personal capacity.

[82] C Safferling, *Towards an International Criminal Procedure* (OUP 2003) 75.

[83] G Higgins, 'Fair and Expeditious Pre-trial Proceedings: The Future of International Criminal Trials', 5 *JICJ* (2007) 394, 395.

[84] ICTY *Prosecutor v Kupreškić et al.*, TC, IT-95-16-T, 21 September 1998, Decision on Communications between the Parties and their Witnesses, p 3.

related to the Court, such as the United Nations or Amnesty International. The authority to act independently of instructions is enshrined in Art. 42 (1) ICCSt and reaffirmed by Regulation 13 RegP. It applies not only to the Prosecutor but to the entire staff of the Office of the Prosecutor regarding external interference. This duty can cause difficulties and is therefore not without its critics. It is also disputed in national legal systems.[85]

Furthermore, the Prosecutor is responsible for the staff working at the headquarters of the Office of the Prosecutor as well as for supervising external investigators working in the field in order to ensure that they will carry out their duties respecting the law and internationally recognized human rights, pursuant to Art. 8 (2) Draft Code of Professional Conduct for Prosecutors of the ICC (Draft Code).[86] Moreover, any activity of the Prosecutor or of the Deputy Prosecutor which could infringe their independence or impartiality is not permitted and could lead to their disqualification. They may also be disqualified if they were previously engaged in a case which is now under preliminary examination or investigation by the Office of the Prosecutor, or if such a case is related to the state of their nationality.

Serving the interest of justice, he or she must, pursuant to Art. 8 (4) Draft Code, '[c]onduct his or her investigations with the goal of establishing truth, ensuring confidentiality, fully respecting the rights of all persons under the Statute'. This indicates that the Prosecutor has the duty to gather incriminatory as well as exculpatory evidence with the purpose of establishing the truth, pursuant to Art. 54 (1) (a) ICCSt. Thus, the principles are safeguarded by the high demands placed on the persons who are appointed as Prosecutor or Deputy Prosecutor under Art. 42 (3) ICCSt; that is, they 'shall be... of high moral character, be highly competent in and have extensive practical experience in the prosecution or trial of criminal cases.' Furthermore, he or she shall act with 'due competence and diligence', according to Art. 8 (2) Draft Code.

Regarding the duty of the Prosecutor for due diligence, based on his or her position as the initiator of the entire proceedings, the Appeals Chamber of the ICTR noted that the Prosecutor has the obligation to request the initial appearance of an accused within a reasonable time, even if this falls within the primary responsibility of the Registry and the Chambers. If he or she has failed to do so, it is a clear

[85] S De Smet, 'A Structural Analysis of the Role of the Pre-Trial Chamber in the Fact-finding Process of the ICC', in: C Stahn and G Sluiter (eds), *The Emerging Practice of the International Criminal Court* (Martinus Nijhoff Publishers 2009) 405, 422 *et subs*.

[86] Secretariats of the International Association of Prosecutors and The Coalition for the International Criminal Code, Draft Code of Professional Conduct for Prosecutors of the International Criminal Court, available at: <http://www.amicc.org/docs/prosecutor.pdf>.

violation of his or her duty to respect the rights of the accused during the entire proceedings.[87]

III. Preliminary examination

Before starting an investigation, a situation has to be referred to the Prosecutor by a state or by the UN Security Council, or he or she might act of his or her own motion, for example due to complaints against a state, institutions, or individual persons, according to Regulation 25 (1) RegP.[88] If the latter, after preliminary examination of the situation, the Prosecutor needs the authorization of the Pre-Trial Chamber to proceed with the investigation.[89] This is a safeguard limiting the power of the Prosecutor to intervene in domestic affairs. In this regard, '[r]eview proceedings help to check the Prosecutors' exercise of their discretionary powers, protect members of the public from frivolous, mischievous, and oppressive prosecutions, and save the Tribunals' time and resources.'[90]

That notwithstanding, the Prosecutor has no obligation to start investigation *proprio motu* and, therefore, is under no obligation to request authorization for a particular situation.[91] In the case of a referral by the Security Council, the Prosecutor has the duty to initiate investigations but has discretionary power to conclude, after preliminary examination, that there is no reasonable basis on which to proceed.[92]

While selecting the situations where preliminary examination should be carried out due to information available to the Prosecutor, the considerations listed in Art. 53 (1) ICCSt should be taken into account. First, the 'sufficient basis to proceed' threshold has to be met; ie, that it is highly probable that a crime listed in Art. 5 ICCSt was or is being committed.[93] The Prosecutor must further determine whether the situation is admissible according to Art. 17 ICCSt.[94] Lastly, the

[87] ICTR *Prosecutor v Barayagwiza*, AC, ICTR-97-19-A, 3 November 1999, Decision, para 91 *et subs*.

[88] *See* section 3.C.III.

[89] *See* section 5.B.I and V Röben, 'The Procedure of the ICC: Status and Function of the Prosecutor', 7 *Max Planck UNYB* (2003) 513, 520.

[90] D Natanda Nsereko, 'Prosecutorial Discretion before National Courts and International Tribunals', *Guest Lectures series of the Office of the Prosecutor* (2004) 12, available at <http://www.old.icc-cpi.int/library/organs/otp/Nsereko.pdf>.

[91] V Röben, 'The Procedure of the ICC: Status and Function of the Prosecutor', 7 *Max Planck UNYB* (2003) 513, 522, and for the difference between situation and case *see* section 2.B.II.2.

[92] W Schabas, *ICC* (OUP 2010) 659 and J Ohlin, 'Peace, Security, and Prosecutorial Discretion', in: C Stahn and G Sluiter (eds), *The Emerging Practice of the International Criminal Court* (Martinus Nijhoff Publishers 2009) 185, the author argued that the Rome Statute in regard to prosecutorial discretion is inconsistent with the functions and powers of the Security Council. The Prosecutor shall not have the right to refuse to carry out a preliminary examination determining that he believes that there is no reasonable basis on which to proceed.

[93] M Delmas-Marty, 'Interactions between National and International Criminal Law in the Preliminary Phase of Trial at the ICC', 4 *JICJ* (2006) 2, 8.

[94] *See* section 2.C.

gravity of the crime must be taken into consideration, as well as the interests of the victims, and whether or not the investigation would be in the interests of justice. Currently, preliminary examinations are to be carried out in eleven countries, *inter alia* in Afghanistan, Iraq, Colombia, Georgia, and Guinea. Only if the Prosecutor decides not to investigate based on the consideration that the 'reasonable grounds to believe' threshold is not fulfilled, he or she has to inform the Pre-Trial Chamber, and therefore, the situation is open to review. The selection proceedings fall under the exclusive discretionary power of the Prosecutor and he or she has to ensure that the Court will not be overloaded with cases.[95] Therefore, it becomes clear that the selection process regarding these situations will always be a problematic issue[96] and '[t]he Office of the Prosecutor will be forced to make difficult, probably unpopular but also unavoidable decisions.'[97]

In cases of a state referral or a referral by the Security Council, the decision not to proceed with investigation can be reviewed on a request by the referring state or the Security Council or by the Pre-Trial Chamber on its own motion, pursuant to Art. 53 (3) ICCSt.

IV. Investigation phase

As mentioned above, one of the guiding principles for the Prosecutor is to establish the truth; ie, to investigate objectively, according to Art. 54 (1) ICCSt.[98] The rights of the accused have to be respected at all times as, for example, the right not to be subjected to cruel treatment, according to Art. 55 (1) (b) ICCSt.[99] Moreover, the interests and personal circumstances of the persons affected by the crime, as victims but also as witnesses, have to be taken into consideration.[100]

The investigation proceedings are similar to those in the national sphere, that is, the investigative officer shall collect and evaluate evidence as well as question victims, witnesses, and, of course, the suspected perpetrator. Furthermore, the Prosecutor of the ICC can enter into agreements to facilitate cooperation with states as well as organizations, for example the United Nations. This arrangement can include the

---

[95] In the first year of its existence, the OTP received 499 communications from 66 states; *see* M Brubacher, 'Prosecutorial Discretion within the International Criminal Court', 2 *JICJ* (2004) 71, 76; and V Röben, 'The Procedure of the ICC: Status and Function of the Prosecutor', 7 *Max Planck UNYB* (2003) 513, 524.

[96] A Danner, 'Enhancing the Legitimacy and Accountability of Prosecutorial Discretion at the International Criminal Court', 97 *AJIL* (2003) 510, 520 *et subs.*

[97] F Guariglia, 'The Selection of Cases by the Office of the Prosecutor of the International Criminal Court', in: C Stahn and G Sluiter (eds), *The Emerging Practice of the International Criminal Court* (Martinus Nijhoff Publishers 2009) 209, 216.

[98] *See* section 4.B.II.

[99] *See* section 6.D.

[100] *See* section 4.D.

proviso not to disclose the information made available by the supplier but, rather, to use the information only for further investigation.[101]

Of course, the Prosecutor has to take all measures necessary to protect victims and witnesses, according to Regulation 36 (1) RegP. Not only ought these two groups to be protected, but also the staff working for the ICC in the field and, in particular, if they originate from the region where the crime was committed, for example intermediaries. The refusal of the Prosecutor to disclose the name of one intermediary nearly caused the termination of the proceedings in *Lubanga*.[102]

V. Pre-trial phase

Once investigations have led to the identification of a person as the alleged perpetrator of the crime in question, the Prosecutor may request a warrant of arrest or summons[103] issued by the Pre-Trial Chamber. The application has to be based on evidence which satisfies the Court that there is a reasonable basis to believe that the person concerned has committed the crime.[104] The warrant of arrest remains in force until the Court orders its reversal, according to Art. 58 (4) ICCSt.[105]

In addition, the Prosecutor may inform the Pre-Trial Chamber about a unique opportunity to obtain evidence; for example, the existence of a witness who is in poor health and may die before proceedings commence. According to Art. 56 (1) (b) ICCSt, in this instance the Pre-Trial Chamber should take measures to protect the rights of the persons affected by the trial; in particular, the suspect.

For the purpose of confirmation of the charges, the Prosecutor has to submit 'sufficient, relevant and credible evidence' supporting each charge, pursuant to Regulation 59 (1) RegP. The Court has to be satisfied that there are 'substantial' grounds to believe that the suspect is the perpetrator, pursuant to Art. 61 (5) ICCSt.[106] Unfortunately, the Pre-Trial Chamber seems to apply a higher standard by requesting additional evidence and by examining each charge with a higher degree of precision than provided for by the Rome Statute regarding undisputed facts.[107]

---

[101] *See* section 7.D.

[102] *See* section 4.A.IV.2.

[103] ICC *Prosecutor v Banda and Jerbo*, PTC I, ICC-02/05-03/09-01, 27 August 2010, Second Decision on the Prosecutor's Application under Article 58, para 32 *et subs.*; both suspects have expressed 'their willingness to pursue the route', according to the Prosecutor.

[104] V Röben, 'The Procedure of the ICC: Status and Function of the Prosecutor', 7 *Max Planck UNYB* (2003) 513, 533.

[105] ICC *Prosecutor v Kony et al.*, PTC II, ICC-02/04-01/05-248, 11 July 2007, Decision to Terminate the Proceedings Against Raska Lukwiya. The Chamber terminated the proceedings against Lukwiya based on forensic evidence that the human remains found were those of the suspect. This clearly requires the termination of proceedings.

[106] *See* section 7.A.II.

[107] *See* section 7.B.

Remarkably, the hearing of the confirmation of charges can be held in the absence of the suspect. Firstly, if he or she has waived the right to be present[108] and, secondly, if the person is at large and, for example, the state which should arrest the suspect is not able to do so. Until now, this procedure has not been used, although requests to Sudan to arrest and surrender four suspects in the case of Uganda has remained unacknowledged since 27 September 2005.[109]

The Prosecutor does not have an obligation to stop the investigation after a decision on the confirmation of charges is issued. He or she can carry out any investigative step after the end of the confirmation phase. This assumption is based on the ruling by the Appeals Chamber that '[t]he duty to establish the truth is not limited to the time before confirmation hearing'.[110] Bear in mind that if the confirmation of charges is rejected, the Prosecutor may appeal the decision.

VI. Trial phase

In the trial phase, the functions and duties of the Prosecutor change. Whereas previously, he or she investigated a situation and subsequently a particular case, he or she now presents the case before the Trial Chamber. In other words, this is the stage at which the case becomes the main responsibility of the prosecution division. The core task is to prove the guilt of the accused without reasonable doubt by presenting sufficient reliable evidence. By carrying out his or her duty, the Prosecutor must always take into account the rights of the accused and the principle of objectivity.

In this context, it falls to the discretion of the Prosecutor to enter into an agreement with the defence, as long as it is not against the purpose of the Statute. This includes an announcement of a partial or entire guilty plea as part of such an arrangement. However, in this situation, the Trial Chamber must satisfy itself that the evidence provided fits with the guilty plea and that it was voluntarily made by the accused.[111] Notably, agreements between the Prosecutor and the defence concerning guilt, the charges, and the penalty are not binding on the Court and therefore, it can, for example, impose a higher penalty than requested by the Prosecutor even if this would breach the earlier arrangement, pursuant to Art. 65 (5) ICCSt.[112]

[108] ICC *Prosecutor v Banda and Jerbo*, PTC I, ICC-02/05-03/09-87, 27 October 2010, Second Decision Setting a Deadline for the Submission of the Suspects' Written Request to Waive their Right to Attend the Confirmation Hearing, para 6; the Chamber noted that the request has to be filed personally by the suspect and this issue cannot be delegated to the counsel.

[109] ICC *Situation in Uganda*, PTC II, ICC-02/04-01/05-35, 27 September 2005, Request to the Republic of Sudan for Arrest and Surrender of Joseph Kony.

[110] ICC *Prosecutor v Lubanga*, AC, ICC-01/04-01/06-568, 13 October 2006, Judgment on the Prosecutor's Appeal against the Decision of Pre-Trial Chamber I entitled 'Decision Establishing General Principles Governing Applications to Restrict Disclosure Pursuant to 81 (2) and (4) of the Rules of Procedure and Evidence', para 52.

[111] For more information *see* section 8.C.I.2.

[112] V Röben, 'The Procedure of the ICC: Status and Function of the Prosecutor', 7 *Max Planck UNYB* (2003) 513, 527.

In any event, before starting trial, both parties may agree on uncontested facts; for example, the content of a document or the suitability of an expert witness, pursuant to Rule 69 RPE ICC and Regulation 51 RegP.[113] Another task to fulfil at this stage of the proceedings is the obligation to disclose potentially exculpatory evidence or mitigating facts. This should be done as soon as possible by the Prosecutor.[114] The Office of the Prosecutor should also maintain relations with the legal representatives of the victims, pursuant to Regulation 52 RegP.

According to Rule 68 (i) RPE ICTY and Rule 68 (A) RPE ICTR, the Prosecutor is obliged to disclose any exculpatory or mitigating evidence to the defence 'as soon as practicable' and if he or she does not fulfil this duty, the Pre-Trial Judge or the Trial Chamber can order disclosure.

In the course of the proceedings, the Prosecutor must provide sufficient evidence, including, for example, the statements of witnesses, to prove the guilt of the accused without reasonable doubt. The Prosecutor is obliged to present aggravating as well as mitigating circumstances, pursuant to Regulation 64 RegP. This is an essential part of the implementation of the principle of objectivity. Moreover, he or she has the right to question defence witnesses and to rebut evidence submitted by the defence. It must be noted that the Prosecutor has to take into consideration the above mentioned guidelines; that is, the presumption of innocence and the principle of objectivity, at all times. Therefore, he or she may withdraw part or all of the charges at any stage of proceedings, according to Regulation 60 RegP. At trial stage, the permission of the Chamber is needed;[115] this may be the case if the Prosecutor realizes, for example, that he or she has based his or her assumptions on faked evidence.

In the course of proceedings, the Prosecutor can appeal decisions of the Trial Chamber, for example not to admit into evidence a particular item. Such interlocutory appeal has to be based on Art. 82 ICCSt.[116]

VII. Appeals phase

According to Art. 81 (1) (a) ICCSt, the Prosecutor has the right to appeal due to (1) a procedural error, (2) an error of fact, and (3) an error of law. An appeal against sentence is to be based on considerations that the sentence and the crime committed are disproportionate, according to Art. 81 (2) (a) ICCSt. The Office of the Prosecutor has to ensure that its appeal is supported by sufficient evidence, and if

---

[113] *See* section 8.D.I.3.

[114] *See* section 7.D and V Röben, 'The Procedure of the ICC: Status and Function of the Prosecutor', 7 *Max Planck UNYB* (2003) 513, 544.

[115] ICC *Prosecutor v Lubanga*, TC I, ICC-01/04-01/06-1084, 13 December 2007, Decision on the Status before the Trial Chamber of the Evidence Heard by the Pre-Trial Chamber and the Decisions of the Pre-Trial Chamber in Trial Proceedings, and the Manner in which the Evidence shall be Submitted, para 42.

[116] *See* section 9.A.IV.

necessary, must attach new evidence. As mentioned above, the Appeals Chamber has the same powers as the Trial Chamber and therefore it can also request additional evidence from the Prosecutor.

To fulfil the function of an objective Prosecutor, he or she is also obliged to appeal on behalf of the convicted person or make an application regarding revision of the judgment, according to Regulation 70 RegP.

VIII. Conclusion

The Office of the Prosecutor has broad discretionary power owing to its function as a trigger for the situation and cases which will be investigated and prosecuted by the ICC. A situation which is not selected by the Prosecutor, will neither be investigated nor prosecuted before the ICC.

In carrying out his or her function, the Prosecutor must take into account the rights of the accused as well as the witnesses and victims at all stages of proceedings. The investigations must be carried out in an objective manner without prejudice to a particular person. This includes careful use of the possibility of Art. 54 (3) (e) ICCSt agreements and a fairly conducted disclosure regime.

The Prosecutor has a double function; as investigator and as courtroom specialist. In the latter function, he or she represents the community as a whole and therefore also represents the general interest in re-establishing peace and security by filling the gap of impunity. The Prosecutor must always have in mind the guiding principles of: (1) the presumption of innocent until the Trial Chamber has declared the guilt of the person concerned, and (2) the principle of objectivity which could also lead to the decision to drop charges.

C. The Registry (*Hilde Farthofer*)

The Registry is one of the organs of the Court and its main function is to support the Divisions, the Prosecutor, and the defence. Judicial administration is within the remit of the Presidency, whereas non-judicial administration lies in the hands of the Registry, pursuant to Art. 43 (1) ICCSt.

The Registry is headed by the Registrar who may be supported by a Deputy Registrar, if necessary. The Presidency shall establish a list of candidates which will be transmitted to the Assembly of States Parties which recommends the Registrar as well as the Deputy Registrar who needs a majority of votes of the judges to be elected by secret ballot. The term of office is limited to five years after which re-election is possible for one further term, pursuant to Art. 43 (5) ICCSt. The required qualification set out in Art. 43 (3) ICCSt is similar to the requirements for the Prosecutor and the judges, with the exception that no experience in criminal proceedings is needed.

The office has to fulfil various functions and should 'serve as the channel of communication of the Court', pursuant to Rule 13 RPE ICC. One of the functions of the Registry is to develop and implement a strategic plan for the outreach of the ICC; that is, 'ensuring the quality of justice and being well-recognized and adequately-supported institution'.[117] In addition to this task, the Registry is responsible for all services needed by witnesses and victims throughout their stay at the seat of the Court.

I. Preliminary phase

Pursuant to Rule 44 (1) RPE ICC, the Registry has to communicate with non-Member States where crimes falling under Art. 5 ICCSt were or are being committed on their territory and to try to assure that state's acceptance of the jurisdiction of the Court by issuing a declaration under Art. 12 (1) ICCSt. The Registry never acts on its own motion but, rather, by request of the Prosecutor or defence or on an order of the Court.

As soon as the Presidency assigns a Pre-Trial Chamber to a particular situation, the Registry 'shall open a situation record', according to Regulation 20 RegR. This record should contain *inter alia* a list of victims, orders, and decisions of the Presidency and the Chambers.

From the outset, the Prosecutor should engage the Victims and Witness Unit, a subsection of the Registry, to prevent secondary victimization when questioning witnesses and victims. The Registry has to create a support programme in the field for the victims and witnesses. This includes, for example, social assistance for victims; ie, to provide medical care for victims of rape, or offer psychological help for affected families, pursuant to Regulation 83 RegR.

The Registry should develop a strategic plan for any particular situation. This generally involves recruitment of local staff and a media campaign concerning the functions and role of the Court.[118] It is extremely important for the victims to know that the perpetrators will be brought to justice and that victims can participate in the proceedings. It also has the purpose of preventing further commission of crimes in an ongoing armed conflict.

II. Investigation phase

After identification of an individual who seems to be the person most responsible for the commission of the crimes in question, the Registry opens a case record. As

[117] ASP, Strategic Plan for Outreach of the International Criminal Court, ICC-ASP/5/12, 29 September 2006, para 12.

[118] *See* eg, the media campaign proposed for the DRC, ASP, Strategic Plan for Outreach of the International Criminal Court, ICC-ASP/5/12, 29 September 2006, p 28.

mentioned above, the Registry not only supports the organs of the Court but also supports the defence in carrying out their duties. This involves measures to safeguard the requirement of defence counsel or the staff of defence counsel to travel unhampered in the state concerned, for example by negotiating certain privileges and immunities.

Under Regulation 122 RegR, the Registry has to maintain a list of counsels. If the Court so decides, appointed counsel will be funded and the Registry must arrange for payment. It has also to minimize defence expenses and fees by making available investigators and other staff. In *Bemba*, the defence team received 42,701 Euros a month but refused to cooperate with the Registry. Thus, the Registrar stated in her report, 'that, from an accounting point of view, the recovery of funds advanced to the Defence team for the payment of legal fees was now considered doubtful'.[119]

Another institution supported by the Registry is the Office of Public Counsel for the Defence. This body is independent and may request backing from the Registry *inter alia* by providing a list of professional investigators, pursuant to Regulation 137 RegR. The Office of Public Counsel for the Defence does not have to follow any instructions of the Registry or other institutions and is therefore entirely free in making its decisions.

A suspect has the right to choose a legal representative who is not on the list of the Registry. If the appointment of counsel could cause a conflict of interest, as might be the case, for example, in the appointment of a former member of the Office of the Prosecutor, the Registry must merely inform the parties. In *Bemba*, the Registrar stated in her observations that

> [t]he Registry of the Court in its neutral role can only act within the limits set by the legal framework … Beyond this facilitation role, the Registry cannot *proprio motu* bar or act as an impediment to the appointment of counsel or a team member if counsel with carriage over the matter, and who has the sole authority to make such appointments, insists on the appointment. It bears repeating that the onus to refuse and to properly manage a conflict of interest issue is a requirement that rests with counsel in accordance with his or her Code obligations, with the Chamber acting as the ultimate arbiter.'[120]

[119] ICC *Prosecutor v Bemba*, Registry, ICC-01/05-01/08-1596, 13 July 2011, Fourth report of the Registrar pursuant to the '*Decision on the Defence Application for Review of the Registrar's Decision of 15 October 2010 on the Application for Adjustment of the Expenses and Fees of the Defence*' (ICC-01/05-01/08-1007-Red) dated 7 December 2010, p 5.

[120] ICC *Prosecutor v Bemba*, Registry, ICC-01/05-01/08-674, 27 January 2010, Observations of the Registrar on invitation by the Chamber dated 19 January 2010, concerning the request of the 'Prosecution's Request to Invalidate the Appointment of Legal Consultant to the Defence Team' dated 18 January 2010, paras 5 and 6.

The Registrar of the ICTY has a greater possibility to influence the appointment of counsel by refusing a legal representative chosen by the accused because he or she would not meet the standards required for the ICTY, enshrined in Art. 14 Directive on assignment of defence counsel.[121]

The mixed nature of the law of the Statute and the Rules of Procedure and Evidence, that is partly inquisitorial and partly adversarial, requires the familiarization of counsel for the defence as well as for the victims with the procedure at the Court. Hence, the Registry has to provide training programmes, according to Regulation 141 RegR.

Another function of the Registry is to establish protection measures for witnesses and victims in the field to guarantee their 'safety, physical and psychological well-being, dignity and privacy'.[122] Furthermore, it must inform the victims of their right to be represented or assisted by counsel. For this purpose, the independent Office of Public Counsel for Victims shall be assisted by the Registry in providing all information necessary with the exception of confidential issues. *Inter alia* the Registry should inform the Office of Public Counsel for Victims on the concerns of unrepresenton victims who will subsequently receive legal representation from the Office of Public Counsel for Victims.[123] One has to bear in mind that the right of the victims to participate in proceedings and subsequently to be represention can cause massive problems for the resources of the Registry. In *Mbarushimana*, the Registry had to examine 783 applications several weeks before the hearing of the confirmation of charges was scheduled, and, therefore, it proposed an alternative approach to victim participation. Due to exceptional circumstances, the Office of Public Counsel for Victims should be granted permission to make an opening statement on behalf of all potential participating victims. This approach would reduce the burden imposed on all parties to the trial.[124]

In supporting all parties of the trial, the guiding principle for the Registry and its staff must be to safeguard confidentiality under all circumstances. The Presidency has to decide on complaints and has the power to disqualify the Registrar from a particular case.[125]

---

[121] Directive of the Assignment of Defence Counsel, IT/73/REV.11, last amended 29 July 2006.

[122] S Arbia, 'The International Criminal Court: Witness and Victim Protection and Support, Legal Aid and Family Visits', 36 *Commonwealth Law Bulletin* (2010) 519, 520.

[123] ICC *Prosecutor v Bemba*, Registry, ICC-01/05-01/08-1615, 27 July 2011, Notification of Designation of the Office of Public Counsel for Victims as Legal Representative of Unrepresented Applicants.

[124] ICC *Prosecutor v Mbarushimana*, Registry, ICC-01/04-01/10–213, Proposal on Victim Participation in the Confirmation Hearing, 6 June 2011, para 7 *et subs*.

[125] *See* p 136.

III. Pre-trial phase

If the Pre-Trial Chamber has issued a warrant of arrest requested by the Prosecutor, the Registry has to inform the states concerned to effect immediate implementation; ie, arrest and surrender of the suspect to the Court, pursuant to Art. 59 ICCSt and Regulation 76 RegR. This requires presentation of the warrant of arrest at the embassy of the state in question as was the case in Sudan. The Sudanese ambassador did not accept the notification and 'voiced his disapproval of the Court' and subsequently, the Registry requested the redaction of the names of the staff members engaged in the consultation.[126]

In order to protect witnesses and victims who are to testify at Court, the Registry has to establish a protection programme. Both the Prosecutor and the defence can apply for the inclusion of their witnesses in the programme and the decision will be rendered by the Registrar, pursuant to Regulation 96 (4) RegR. This decision can be reviewed by the Presidency.

Another function of the Registry is to provide a language service. Notably, the training of interpreters will not start before the issuing of an order of the Court.[127] This may cause difficulties and, in particular, can violate the right of the suspect or accused to an expeditious trial.[128] In *Banda and Jerbo*, the Registry could not provide interpreters in the language required by the suspects. Therefore both waived their right to be present at the confirmation hearing in order to avoid further delay to the proceedings. Several months later, the Registry made a proposal for translation in the courtroom during trial. The language in question, Zaghawa, is not a written language and, in addition, it lacks legal terminology. For this reason it seemed a better approach to take the developed Court-related legal terminology from Arabic. Notably, the procedure of consecutive translation[129] extends the time frame of a hearing by 30–35 per cent.[130] It should be taken into consideration whether training court interpreters in advance; that is, at the moment of a state referral, would better serve the interests of justice. Any delay in beginning proceedings due to a lack of trained interpreters cannot serve the interests of justice, and it is a right of the accused enshrined in Art. 67 (1) (a) ICCSt to be informed in a language fully understandable to them.

126 ICC *Prosecutor v Harun and Aliabd-al-Rahman*, Registry, ICC-02/05-01/07-62, 26 July 2010, Report of the Registrar on the notification of the *'Decision Informing the United Nations Security Council about the Lack of Cooperation by the Republic of Sudan'* to the Sudanese authorities, para 2.

127 ICC *Prosecutor v Banda and Jerbo*, TC IV, ICC-02/05-03/09-172, 1 July 2011, Order to the Registry to Commence Training of Zaghawa Interpreters.

128 *See* Chapter 8, p 383.

129 According to Regulation 61 (1) (c) RegR, consecutive interpretation means 'where the interpreter interprets aloud, usually taking notes as the speaker speaks and then concisely interpreting several sentences at a time for an unlimited number of listeners'.

130 ICC *Prosecutor v Banda and Jerbo*, Registry, ICC-02/05-03/09-150, 24 May 2011, Report of the Registrar Pursuant to Regulation 24*bis* of the Regulations of the Court Concerning on the Issue of Languages to be used in the Proceedings.

Finally, the Registry is responsible for the transmission of the decision of confirmation of charges and the record of proceedings to the Presidency.[131] As mentioned, the Registry will become active only following an order of a Chamber.[132]

IV. Trial phase

During the trial phase, the Registry is responsible for court management. That involves *inter alia* assistance for witnesses and expert witnesses to travel to the seat of the Court as well as, for example, care for dependants of victims and witnesses appearing before the Court; that is, the Registry will take care of children of the witness, for example during his or her presence at Court, pursuant to Regulation 90 RegR.

The Registry is also involved in maintaining a list of forensic and other experts in different fields necessary for the Court.[133] The parties may choose one of the registered experts or propose a different one, in which case they must prove his or her qualifications as an expert in a particular field.

Within the courtroom, the Registry, via the court officer, must arrange all measures necessary for technical equipment, such as enabling testimony via video-link and presentation of evidence via technical means.

On several occasions, the Trial Chamber of the ICTR has ordered the transfer of detained witnesses from Rwanda to the seat of the Court in Arusha, Tanzania, arranged by the Registry. Furthermore, the Registry *inter alia* had to inform the government of Rwanda that the time of transfer and testimony at the ICTR could not extend the time of imprisonment of the detained witnesses.[134]

The Chamber can request legal clarification from the Victims and Witnesses Unit regarding victim- and witness-related matters. In *Lubanga*, the Trial Chamber requested from the Victims and Witnesses Unit a submission on the issue as to '[w]hether there are circumstances when a Chamber can order the communication of a medical report of any kind without the consent/informed consent of the individual concerned'.[135] As mentioned, the guiding principle for the Registry is

[131] ICC *Prosecutor v Banda and Jerbo*, Registry, ICC-02/05-03/09-123, 15 March 2011, Transmission to the Presidency of the Decision on the Confirmation of Charges and of the Record of the Proceedings.

[132] ICC *Prosecutor v Banda and Jerbo*, PTC I, ICC-02/05-03/09-122, 15 March 2011, Order to the Registrar to Transmit the Decision on Confirmation of Charges and the Record of the Proceedings to the Presidency.

[133] *See* Chapter 8, p 482.

[134] ICTR *Prosecutor v Rukundo*, TC II, ICTR-2001-70-T, 27 June 2007, *Proprio motu* order for the transfer of detained witness, Rules 54 and 90*bis* of the Rules of Procedure and Evidence, p 2.

[135] Cit. in ICC *Prosecutor v Lubanga*, Registry, ICC-01/04-01/06-2166, 15 October 2009, Victims and Witnesses Unit Report on Confidentiality of Medical Records and Consent to Disclose Medical Records, p 3.

confidentiality which constitutes an important issue, in particular for the victims. Hence, the Registrar clearly pointed out that 'medical information must only be disclosed to the extent which the person it concerns has consented' and only in 'exceptional circumstances, where emergency situations so require and where it is assessed to be in the interest of the witness, the VWU will disclose medical records without the informed consent of the witness.'[136]

V. Detention

The Registrar supervises the Chief Custody Officer regarding detention matters. The accused, or later, the convicted person has the right for decisions rendered by the Chief Custody Officer to be reviewed by the Registrar, pursuant to Regulation 215 RegR. If the detainee is subject to any disciplinary measures listed in Regulation 215 (2)–(8) RegR or he or she is held in an isolation cell, the opportunity to refer the issue to the Presidency is enshrined in Regulation 216 RegR.

During detention, the person shall be provided with medical service or he or she can consult an external medical practitioner at his or her own expense. Notably, the medical records of the detainee 'shall be kept strictly confidential', according to Regulation 156 RegR, and can only be disclosed with the written consent of the person concerned.

In *Karadžić*, the Trial Chamber of the ICTY ordered a medical report on the health of the accused regarding his ability to participate in the trial. The medical officer concluded that the 'general health state is satisfactory with exception of his overweight and lack of physical exercise and fresh air'.[137] The accused had filed a motion against a five-day sitting schedule reasoning that this would put his health in jeopardy. To make public the entire wording of the statement of the medical service does not seem to have been the right approach to determine the health of the accused. It is submitted that publication of medical reports clearly violates the right of an individual to privacy, as in the instant case it violated the rights of the accused.

During detention, email communication as well as telephone communication will be monitored, pursuant to Regulation 169 RegR. The Registry has to take into account when imposing such measures that the lawyer–client relationship is privileged and, therefore, such means cannot be applied to interactions between those parties.

---

136 ICC *Prosecutor v Lubanga*, Registry, ICC-01/04-01/06-2166, 15 October 2009, Victims and Witnesses Unit Report on Confidentiality of Medical Records and Consent to Disclose Medical Records, paras 4 and 20.

137 ICTY *Prosecutor v Karadžić*, TC, IT-95-5/18-T, 23 September 2010, Decision on Accused's Second Submission on Trial Schedule, para 2.

In *Taylor*, the defence filed an urgent motion regarding video surveillance during consultation by a lawyer with his client, reasoning that the lawyer–client privilege might be violated. Unfortunately, the motion was dismissed because review of decisions by the Registrar fell within the power of the President and not within the competence of the Trial Chamber of the Special Court of Sierra Leone. However, the Chamber issued an order to the Chief of Detention and the Registrar to 'deal with the matter promptly'.[138]

VI. Conclusion

The Registry has more functions than powers because it can only act when prompted by a Court order. It operates as the communication channel between all participants in the trial. In the preliminary phase, the field of duties of the Registry commences with support of the Prosecutor in all witness- and victim-related matters. This includes *inter alia* the permanent or provisional relocation of endangered persons.

After the alleged perpetrator is identified, the Registry provides legal aid by way of help and advice for the suspect in choosing counsel whose funding will be arranged by the Registry. Furthermore, it has to deal with all matters relating to pre-trial detention, comprising, for example, arranging family visits.

Concurrently, the Registry supports the legal representatives of the victims by handing over all information needed which does not fall under the confidentiality requirement.

During court procedure, the Registry is responsible for the technical as well electronic equipment to facilitate the presentation of evidence as well as carrying out witness protection measures, such as closed-circuit television.

The Registry is the only neutral organ of the Court which means that it has to interact without prejudice with all parties and participants in a trial. Therefore, the guiding principle for the Registry is confidentiality. In all matters, the Registrar can only give recommendations to the Court in written observations. He or she does not have the power to request, for example, specific witness protection measures. The Registry is the administrative body of the ICC and cannot bind any other organs of the Court.

D. Victims and Witnesses

Victims are natural participants in criminal procedure as their testimony on the criminal offence is often decisive for establishing the truth as to the factual basis of

[138] SCSL *Prosecutor v Taylor*, TC II, SCSL-03-1-PT, 30 November 2006, Decision on Urgent and Public Defence Motion Requesting Removal of Camera from Conference Room, p 4.

a conviction. The victim takes the role of a witness in the criminal trial. Yet this is not the only role attributed to the victim at the beginning of the twenty first century. As has been seen above,[139] the interests of victims have turned into a central argument for fighting impunity on the international level in the first place. 'Justice for the victims' is not only achieved by prosecuting alleged international criminals; according to the Rome Statute, victims have a right to participate in the criminal process as laid down in Art. 68 (3) ICCSt. Similarly the ECCC have—based on the Continental European system inspired by the French procedural laws—a wide concept of 'civil party participation' in the criminal trials. At the *ad hoc* Tribunals, however, victim participation does not play an important role.[140]

Before we look at the different aspects of the role of the victim in an international criminal trial (III), we first must take issue with the situation of the victims of international crimes and their specific interests (I). We then need to address the question of defining 'victim' on the international stage (II).

I. Victims of international crimes

The phenomenon of macro-criminality is discussed largely with regard to the perpetrator. Criminological research on victims of state-sponsored crimes is rare. The questions of how and why someone becomes a victim of an international crime and what are the consequences crime might have on the victim and his or her environment are largely unanswered. However, these questions have an impact on the role of the victim in criminal proceedings. Therefore it is necessary to develop at least a rough idea of what the situation of the victims might be.

1. The background to the concept of 'the victim'

Victimization by international crimes is always a collective experience. Genocide, crimes against humanity, and war crimes never have just one victim but pertain to a whole group of persons, maybe even a specific part of the society. The idiosyncrasies of this combining of individual and collective aspects will be described in the following nine points:[141]

(1) The victim conceives of him or herself not only as violated in his or her own personality but also in relation to his or her social network. The attack was directed not only against this one person but against the family, the village, and the ethnic or religious group to which the victim belongs.[142] This notion of 'group attack' might

[139] *See* Chapter 2, p 69.

[140] *See* Boas/Bischoff/Reid/Taylor, *ICL III*, 309 *et subs*.

[141] This catalogue is oriented at national victimology parameters named by H Richter, *Opfer krimineller Gewalttaten* (Weisser Ring 1997) 10–12. *See* in greater detail: C Safferling, 'Das Opfer völkerrechtlicher Verbrechen', 115 *ZStW* (2003) 352, 355–60.

[142] As concerns crimes against humanity, *see* G Manske, *Verbrechen gegen die Menschlichkeit als Verbrechen an der Menschheit* (Duncker and Humblot 2003) 201.

even be rather vague when considering a civil society which is being attacked despite being not involved in the conflict.[143]

(2) The victim experiences the breakdown of all social security. Public and social protection schemes prove incapable of preventing the victimization. This is particular important in case of an international armed conflict, where a foreign power enters into the societal home by force and destroys all trust in public safety.

(3) This loss of trust is even more dramatic in cases of an internal conflict when the victimization is organized or tolerated by the government. If police and military forces turn against parts of their own population, persecuting and humiliating members of minorities, this group is deprived of the basis of social life.[144] The sentiment of helplessness and disintegration can intensify if international aid is unavailable or ineffective.[145]

(4) The sentiment of shame arising out of the victimization is higher compared to ordinary crimes as the disgrace and disrespect for the victim pertains to the entire environment of the victim. The category of 'hate crimes' which is used in victimological writing referring to the national context to describe persecution of juveniles against foreigners[146] has a parallel in international criminal law. The prejudice is directed not only against the personal existence but also against the cultural existence of the victim.[147]

(5) The disrespect goes even further. It pertains to human existence as such.[148] The offender acts in negation of the personality of his victim. The person of the victim is of no importance to the perpetrator, which means that any victim is interchangeable. Only the membership of a certain group is the decisive factor.[149] The offender treats the victim as a mere object, an object for his hatred and for elimination.

(6) Violence against women and children is a central issue in international research into victims. The circumstances of an armed conflict are prone for abuse of women and children. Sexual abuse of women is not only a by-product of war. Sexual violence is often used as a specific form of warfare, destruction, and humiliation.[150]

---

[143] *See* C Möller, *Völkerstrafrecht und Internationaler Strafgerichtshof—kriminologische, straftheoretische und rechtspolitische Aspekte* (LIT 2003) 353 *et subs.*

[144] As an historic example one might think of the persecution of Jews in Nazi Germany, *see* A-E Brauneck, *Allgemeine Kriminologie* (Rowolth 1974) 166–9.

[145] The incidents in Srebrenica or Sarajevo during the war in Bosnia are an historic example, where despite the determination as UN safe areas mass-crimes took place.

[146] *See* K Krupna, *Das Konzept der 'Hate Crimes' in Deutschland* (Peter Lang 2010).

[147] From the perspective of the perpetrator: H Jäger, *Makrokriminalität* (Suhrkamp 1989) 194 *et subs.*

[148] C Möller, *Völkerstrafrecht und Internationaler Strafgerichtshof—kriminologische, straftheoretische und rechtspolitische Aspekte* (LIT 2003) 353.

[149] J Schneider, *Kriminologie der Gewalt* (Hirzel 1994) 43.

[150] C Möller, *Völkerstrafrecht und Internationaler Strafgerichtshof—kriminologische, straftheoretische und rechtspolitische Aspekte* (LiT 2003) 356–69.

Children are particularly vulnerable persons. They are directly abused; for example, being made to watch the murder or torture of their parents and being forced to serve in the armed forces.[151]

(7) The experiences of a victim of international crimes result in long-term psychological damage. No doubt the trauma felt by victims caused by the sheer brutality and inescapability of international criminal offences is far greater than it is in the national context.[152] The intensity of their trauma will increase with the duration of the conflict if one thinks of children who then spend their entire childhood under ongoing armed conflict. Persistent trauma will inevitably lead to the internalization of the social stigma.[153] Under these circumstances chances for rehabilitation after the conflict are frail.

(8) This list of possible consequences of victimization in an international context on the individual must be complemented by a set of consequences on the collective. However, these effects are rarely discussed. Whereas it is common to speak about 'collective guilt' on the side of the perpetrators, 'collective victimization' is seldom invoked.

(9) Finally, the question regarding the responsibility of the victim for his or her victimization will generally not pertain to the individual but to the collective. An individual member of a group will not ask, 'what have I done wrong to be made the victim of an attack', but instead will ask, 'what have we done wrong, why are we being treated this way?'

These specific circumstances of victimhood in international crimes will need to be taken into account when discussing the role of the victim in criminal procedure.

2. Victims' interests

In a unique study, the Max Planck Institute for Foreign and International Criminal Law in Freiburg has examined the needs of victims of international conflicts.[154] The study covers eleven areas of conflict.[155] To ensure that the study was representative, participants were chosen according to age, sex, and religious affiliation. The

---

[151] *See* M Wessells, *Child Soldiers: From Violence to Protection* (Harvard University Press 2007).

[152] F Neubacher, *Kriminologische Grundlagen einer internationalen Strafgerichtsbarkeit* (Mohr Siebeck 2005) 209.

[153] C Möller, *Völkerstrafrecht und Internationaler Strafgerichtshof—kriminologische, straftheoretische und rechtspolitische Aspekte* (LiT 2003) 399.

[154] E Kiza, C Rathgeber, and H-C Rohne, *Victims of War: An Empirical Study on Victimization and Victims' Attitudes towards Addressing Atrocities* (Hamburger Edition HIS Verlag 2006), available online at <http://www.his-online.de>.

[155] Afghanistan (5 per cent), Bosnia und Herzegovina (11 per cent), Cambodia (5 per cent), Croatia (10 per cent), Democratic Republic Congo (5 per cent), Israel (12 per cent), Kosovo (7 per cent), Macedonian Republic (10 per cent), Palestinian Territories (22 per cent), Philippines (5 per cent), Sudan (8 per cent); cf. p 71, Table 1, earlier in this book.

study shows that most victims are in favour of prosecuting those responsible for their suffering; that is, military commanders and, more particularly, political leaders.[156] On various occasions, criminal prosecution has been proven to contribute to the social healing process as well as to individual reconciliation.[157] Almost three-quarters of those questioned asked to take part in the criminal proceedings.[158] The satisfaction that was gained from taking part in the prosecution process was not analysed.[159] Some wished to simply appear as witnesses and others wanted the opportunity 'to tell their story'.[160] The need to tell one's story is the leading factor in motivating victims to participate.[161] When asked how they wished to participate, the respondents replied as follows: 56 per cent wished to testify as witnesses, 46 per cent said that their main concern was to tell their story, and 29 per cent wanted to become actively involved in the prosecution.[162] Scholars presume that such an active participation in a formal procedure will help the victim to regain his or her dignity, to feel reintegrated into society, and to resume control.[163] While this hypothesis has some intrinsic plausibility, it is yet empirically unproven.[164] Furthermore it has not been challenged as to whether participation must necessarily take place in a criminal trial.

The distinction between the formal role of testifying as a witness and the opportunity to tell one's story stems from the fact that victims of international criminal offences have usually had no personal contact with the accused. Quite often they have only encountered the subordinates of the accused or were part of a large group that was collectively victimized during an attack. Although connected with the crimes charged, the story the victim wishes to tell may, therefore, not directly relate to the actions of the accused, but instead merely set the context for his criminal responsibility.

The victims expressed much less support for using a truth commission as a means of telling their story and coming to terms with the past. Admittedly, this may have

---

156 Ibid, p 97, at 108 and 115. What is interesting is that the great majority of those questioned favoured a prosecution at an international court/tribunal and the application of international criminal law.

157 Ibid, p 127 *et subs.*

158 Ibid, p 104.

159 As regards victims needs in Bosnia Prijedor in this regard, see R Hodžić, 'Living the Legacy of Mass Atrocities: Victims' Perspectives on War Crimes Trials', 8 *JICJ* (2010) 113.

160 E Kiza, C Rathgeber, and H-C Rohne, *Victims of War* (Hamburger Edition HIS Verlag 2006) 105.

161 Ibid, p 128.

162 Ibid, p 105; note that more than one answer was possible and that the study also showed substantial regional differences.

163 N Roht-Arriaza, 'Impunity and Human Rights', in N Roht-Arriaza (ed), *Impunity and Human Rights in International Law and Practice* (OUP 1995) 21; R Aldana-Pindell, 'An Emerging Universality of Justiciable Victims' Rights in the Criminal Process to Curtail Impunity for State-Sponsored Crimes', 26 *Human Rights Quarterly* (2004) 607, 675.

164 *See* M Mohan, 'The Paradox of Victim-Centrism: Victim Participation at the Khmer Rouge Tribunal', 9 *ICLR* (2009) 733, 736 *et subs.*

been due to the fact that many of those questioned had no real conception of what a truth commission is.[165] On the issue of reparations, 42 per cent of those questioned required monetary compensation, 40 per cent demanded an apology, and almost 30 per cent sought some type of public monument commemorating the victims. A mere 3 per cent were driven by revenge and 24 per cent simply wished to come to terms with their traumatic experiences.[166]

II. Definition of victims

'Victim' is a technical term which requires definition. In the procedural texts of the ICC a definition can be found amongst the Rules of Procedure and Evidence:

> Rule 85 Definition of victims
>
> For the purposes of the Statute and the Rules of Procedure and Evidence:
>
> (a) 'Victims' means natural persons who have suffered harm as a result of the commission of any crime within the jurisdiction of the Court;
>
> (b) Victims may include organizations or institutions that have sustained direct harm to any of their property which is dedicated to religion, education, art or science or charitable purposes, and to their historic monuments, hospitals and other places and objects for humanitarian purposes.

This definition which, in its first part, is modeled after the definition of the 1985 UN Declaration of Basic Principles of Justice for Victims of Crime and Abuse of Power,[167] leaves open many questions:

(a) The definition is restricted to natural persons.[168] Collective victims are covered only by para (b). These are related to the specific scope of protection offered by several crimes. For example, Art. 8 (2) (b) (ix) ICCSt prohibits the attack on buildings dedicated to religion, education, art, etc. Under these circumstances, churches could be seen as organizations that have suffered direct harm.[169] However, recognition as a victimized organization is not automatic but depends on the decision of the Court.[170]

---

165 Ibid, p 110 *et subs.*

166 Ibid, p 118.

167 UN Doc. A/RES/40/34 of 29 November 1985; *see* also: ICC *Prosecutor v Bemba*, PTC III, ICC-01/05-01/08-320, 12 December 2009, Fourth Decision on Victims' Participation, para 16.

168 Under certain circumstances 'deceased persons' can be represented at the proceedings by their successor, *see* ICC *Prosecutor v Bemba*, PTC III, Single Judge Kaul, ICC-01/05-01/08-320, 12 December 2009, Fourth Decision on Victims' Participation, paras 39–52.

169 *See* eg, ICC *Prosecutor v Bemba*, PTC III, Single Judge Kaul, ICC-01/05-01/08-320, 12 December 2009, Fourth Decision on Victims' Participation, paras 53–6, where the application of a church has been dismissed because of lack of information.

170 *See* S de Gurmendi and H Friman, 'The Rules of Procedure and Evidence of the ICC', 3 *YB Int'l Hum L* (2000) 157, 182.

(b) The definition does not differentiate between physical, psychological, and emotional harm. In this regard the ICC definition is less specific than the UN declaration, which includes 'physical or mental injury, emotional suffering, economic loss or substantial impairment of fundamental rights'.[171] For immediate relatives of a deceased person such emotional suffering has been accepted as 'harm' in the meaning of Rule 85 RPE ICC.[172] The Appeals Chamber has adopted a broad approach and declared material, physical, and psychological harm as relevant.[173]

(c) The definition does not refer to a single explicit act, nor does it refer to a specific offender. The harm to the victim must merely have been caused by the perpetration of an international criminal offence, which falls within the jurisdiction of the ICC.[174] The link to the crime charged is construed by the Appeals Chamber by the 'personal interest' requirement of Art. 68 (3) ICCSt.[175]

(d) Finally, the definition does not differentiate between direct and indirect victim. Apparently the question whether relatives of the direct victim could be seen as victims before the ICC has been left open deliberately.[176]

This question has been made central in the *Lubanga* case: the charge was conscripting, enlisting, or using child soldiers punishable as a war crime according to Art. 8 (2) (b) (xxvi) for the international conflict, and Art. 8 (2) (e) (vii) ICCSt respectively, in a non-international armed conflict. Therefore 'child soldiers' were the direct victims of the crime charged. But what about persons who suffered harm from the crimes these child soldiers had committed? Trial Chamber I referred to Rule 85 RPE ICC and found that indirect victims would not qualify for participation under the legal regime of the ICC.[177] This decision has been criticized,[178] but nevertheless it seems correct. Even if in this particular case the integration of

---

[171] *See* § 1 of the Declaration of Basic Principles of Justice for Victims of Crime and Abuse of Power.

[172] ICC *Prosecutor v Bemba*, PTC III, Single Judge Kaul, ICC-01/05-01/08-320, 12 December 2009, Fourth Decision on Victims' Participation, para 51.

[173] ICC *Prosecutor v Lubanga*, AC, ICC-01/04-01/06-1432, 11 July 2008, Judgment on the appeals of The Prosecutor and The Defence against Trial Chamber I's Decision on Victims' Participation of 18 January 2008, para 32.

[174] Cf. ICC *Prosecutor v Lubanga*, PTC I, ICC-01/04-01/06, 18 January 2008, Decision on Victims' Participation, para 93; *See* also A Guhr, 'Aktuelle Entwicklungen zur Beteiligung von Opfern im Strafverfahren vor dem ICC, 3 *ZIS* (2008) 367, 368 *et subs.*

[175] ICC *Prosecutor v Lubanga*, AC, ICC-01/04-01/06-1432, 11 July 2008, Judgment on the appeals of The Prosecutor and The Defence against Trial Chamber I's Decision on Victims' Participation of 18 January 2008, para 58.

[176] *See* B Timm, 'The Legal Position of Victims in the Rules of Procedure and Evidence' in Fischer/Kreß/Lüder (eds), *International and National Prosecution of Crimes Under International Law: Current Developments* (Spitz 2001) 289, 290.

[177] ICC *Prosecutor v Lubanga*, TC I, ICC-01/04-01/06-1813, 8 April 2009, Decision on 'Indirect Victims'.

[178] See V Spiga, 'Indirect Victims' Participation in the *Lubanga* Trial', 8 *JICJ* (2010), 183 arguing that indirect witnesses should be admitted.

the indirect victims would seem just and fair, it would open the door to abolishing the link between the participation rights of the victim and the criminal charge. Furthermore it would in this case deny the victimhood of the child soldiers in that it would stress the fact the child soldiers are a means to an end; that is, to commit crimes as direct perpetrators within the meaning of Art. 25 (3) (a) ICCSt.[179] However, the Appeals Chamber has held that close relatives of the child soldier could be admissible as indirect victims.[180]

These points are in need of interpretation. It is submitted that the definition can vary according to the different procedural situation. The different functionality may well lead to specified applications of the definition of the victim.

III. The role of the victim in criminal procedure

The role of the victim in criminal procedure can be described as threefold: Protection—Participation—Compensation. As a witness, the victim, in particular the traumatized victim, is in need of protection. Any court is under the obligation to prevent secondary victimization and any possible harm to the witness (1). The most difficult part is the question of participation of the victim in the trial procedure, as foreseen by Art. 68 (3) ICCSt (2). Finally the victim has a right to compensation (3).

1. Victim protection

The issue of victim protection is of much greater significance on the international level than it is in national systems. Witnesses testifying in international prosecutions in The Hague and Arusha have repeatedly been threatened and some even murdered.[181] The procedure set up to protect victims at the ICC is very similar to the procedures adopted in national systems and those adopted at the *ad hoc* Tribunals: exclusion of the public during the victim's testimony or the use of electronic technology for hearing evidence (*see* Art. 68 (2) ICC).[182] The Rules of Procedure and Evidence lay down the specific procedure.[183] According to Rule 87 RPE the victim's identity may be kept secret from the public and s/he may be given a pseudonym for this purpose. Rule 88 RPE makes further provision for

---

179 V Spiga, 'Indirect Victims' Participation in the *Lubanga* Trial', 8 *JICJ* (2010), 183 would probably be willing to accept this consequence.

180 ICC *Prosecutor v Lubanga*, AC, ICC-01/04-01/06-1432, 11 July 2008, Judgment on the appeals of The Prosecutor and The Defence against Trial Chamber I's Decision on Victims' Participation of 18 January 2008, para 32.

181 O Abo Youssef, *Die Stellung des Opfers im Völkerstrafrecht* (Schulthess 2008) 125; S Bock 'Das Opfer vor dem internationalen Strafgerichtshof', 119 *ZStW* (2007) 664, 676 *et subs*.

182 For more detail *see* C Safferling, *Towards an International Criminal Procedure* (OUP 2003) 226–39.

183 For a detailed description *see* O Abo Youssef, *Die Stellung des Opfers im Völkerstrafrecht* (Schulthess 2008) 129–40.

particularly vulnerable witnesses and victims such as traumatized persons, children, the elderly, and victims of sexual violence. In practice, after consulting those concerned, the court will generally allow a legal representative, a psychologist, or a family member to accompany a vulnerable victim or witness during his or her testimony.

All organs of the ICC are under a duty to ensure the protection of victims throughout the proceedings. A special Victims and Witness Unit is responsible for the coordination of victim protection measures.[184] Victims testifying at trial find themselves in a uniquely vulnerable situation. To prevent secondary victimization[185] and to ensure the safety of witnesses, the Rules of Procedure and Evidence place all chambers under an obligation to protect a witness as follows:

> Rule 88 (5) RPE: Taking into consideration that violations of the privacy of a witness or victim may create risk to his or her security, a Chamber shall be vigilant in controlling the manner of questioning a witness or victim so as to avoid any harassment or intimidation, paying particular attention to attacks on victims of crimes of sexual violence.

The adversarial procedure, in which the parties, not the court, are chiefly responsible for questioning witnesses, necessitates the above safeguard. The ICC judges are given the function of supervising the manner in which the prosecution and defence examine a witness. This type of control of witness examination, although not foreign to Anglo-American proceedings, is exercised sparingly by national judges for fear that the trial may be appealed on grounds of procedural irregularity.[186] In contrast, the ICC judge is placed under a duty to control the questioning of witnesses. In the first case to be prosecuted at the ICC, the trial of Thomas Lubanga Dyilo, the presiding judge, Judge Fulford, was repeatedly forced to intervene in the examination of the first prosecution witness to protect the testifying Congolese child soldier.[187] No doubt the ICC Rules of Procedure and Evidence still need to be refined by practice.[188]

---

[184] For more detail *see* O Abo Youssef, *Die Stellung des Opfers im Völkerstrafrecht* (Schulthess 2008) 150–8; and Ahlbrecht/*Kirsch* MN 1454.

[185] We use the phrase 'secondary victimization' instead of 're-traumatization'. In our view the term victimization is more general in the sense that it covers not only trauma but also humiliation or degrading treatment which might be experienced during the prosecution process but might not lead to a trauma. Furthermore we consider 'secondary victimization' the correct technical term as used in criminology; *see* H Göppinger, *Kriminologie* (6th edn, CH Beck 2008), § 29 MN 9 *et subs.*; H-L Kröber, D Dölling, N Leygraf, and H Sass, *Handbuch der forensischen Psychiatrie*, Vol 4 (Springer 2009) 678.

[186] *See* C Safferling, *Towards an International Criminal Procedure* (OUP 2003) 217 *et seq.*

[187] ICC *Prosecutor Lubanga*, ICC-01/04-01/06, *see* Transcript of Trial Chamber I Sessions on 27 and 28 January 2009 (these can be found at: <http://www2.icc-cpi.int/Menus/ICC/Situations+and+Cases/Cases/>). The main issue here was the protection of the witness against self incrimination in accordance with Rule 74 RPE. The independent NGO Open Justice Initiative provides a constantly up-to-date description of the case; *see* <http://www.lubangatrial.org/>.

[188] As to the trial structure *see* p 436.

2. Victim participation

Victim participation is the real novelty of the Rome Statute.[189] Yet often enough the provisions contained in the Statute and the Rules are rudimentary in character and leave the decision as to the requirements and of the proceedings up to the competent chamber. 'Each case', one commentator has written, 'is a blank page upon which victim's participatory rights have yet to be written'.[190] In this part of the book we want to analyse the specific functionality of the different participants in a criminal procedure. Rather than consider the generic participatory right of the victims, we look instead at the general role which is attributable to the victim with a view to the proceeding in its entirety. To this end we will first summarize how the ICC sees the role of the victim (a), and then discuss critical voices (b), before we present our own views on the matter (c).

a. State of the art The ICC Chambers must decide on victims' issues in all cases and situations before it. It appears that victims readily make use of the participatory rights contained in the Rome Statute. Yet as regards the role of the victim in the overall procedure, the Chambers have not added much to clarify the Statute's vagueness. However one can observe a rather positive attitude towards victim participation.

For example, in one decision Single Judge Steiner has warned that victims must not 'become "second-class" participants, who have a sort of "in-courtroom observer status" and must request the leave of the Court at any time if they would like to perform any kind of procedural activity'.[191]

> Quite the contrary, the Single Judge considers that the object and purpose of article 68(3) of the Statute and rules 91 and 92 of the Rules is to provide victims with a meaningful role in criminal proceedings before the Court (including at the pre-trial stage of a case) so that they can have a substantial impact in the proceedings.[192]

Judge Steiner sees in the victim's participation more than just an abstract chance to enhance the acceptance of the work of the ICC in the region affected by the proceedings. Victims who participate in a criminal trial have the important task to, for example, 'ensure that certain cultural features and perceptions that are specific to the DRC in general, and to the Ituri region in particular, be taken into consideration by the Chamber when assessing the evidence.'[193]

---

[189] *See* W Schabas, *An Introduction to the ICC* (3rd edn, CUP 2007) 327.

[190] Boas/Bischoff/Reid/Taylor, *ICL III*, 323.

[191] ICC *Prosecutor v Katanga and Chui*, PTC I, ICC-01/04-01/07-474, 13 May 2008, Decision on the Set of Procedural Rights Attached to Procedural Status of Victim at the Pre-Trial Stage of the Case, para 156.

[192] Ibid, para 157.

[193] Ibid, para 162.

More generally it could be said that 'victims clearly have the capacity to provide the Court with relevant and important information regarding the crimes.'[194]

In a decision of the entire Pre-Trial Chamber I the purpose of victim participation has been summarized as follows: '[T]he victims may participate (. . .) by presenting their view and concerns in order to help contribute to the prosecution of the crimes from which they allegedly have suffered and to, where relevant, subsequently be able to obtain reparations for the harm suffered.'[195]

In the *Bemba* proceedings before Pre-Trial Chamber III, Single Judge Kaul placed considerable weight on the compensation claim of the victim. With a view to the admission of the successor of a deceased victim, he held that the purpose of victim participation was 'to be found *inter alia* in the right to receive reparations'.[196] In any case, victims are not a party to the proceedings; this position is reserved for the Prosecutor and the Defence. But they are allowed to lead and challenge evidence as to the guilt of the accused.[197]

In other words, by participating in the criminal process, victims support the criminal prosecution of the accused, while at the same time preparing their own claim to financial compensation. Thus their participation is not just a matter of protecting their own interests. A further purpose of victim participation at the ICC is to offer support to the Office of the Prosecutor and help the Chamber to determine the truth.[198] One might even venture that victims adopt the role of a kind of 'private prosecutor'. This explains the right of victims to participate in the confirmation hearing. By their involvement at this early stage, victims ensure that their goal, the prosecution of the accused, may be achieved.

b. Criticism The ICC has by no means yet made participation of the victims 'meaningful'.[199] Denying party status and at the same time allowing them to present their own evidence as to the guilt of the offender and to challenge

---

[194] *See* C Stahn, H Olásolo, and K Gibson, 'Participation of Victims in Pre-Trial Proceedings of the ICC', 4 *JICJ* (2006) 217, 238.

[195] ICC *Prosecutor v Lubanga*, TC I, ICC-01/04-01/06-462-tEN, 22 September 2006, Decision on the Arrangements for Participation of Victims a/0001/06, a/0002/06 and a/0003/06 at the Confirmation Hearing, para 5.

[196] ICC *Prosecutor v Bemba*, PTC III, ICC-01/05-01/08-320, 12 December 2009, Fourth Decision on Victims' Participation, para 46.

[197] ICC *Prosecutor v Lubanga*, AC, ICC-01/04-01/06-1432, 11 July 2008, Judgment on the appeals of The Prosecutor and The Defence against Trial Chamber I's Decision on Victims' Participation of 18 January 2008, para 93.

[198] *See* eg, ICC *Prosecutor v Lubanga*, AC, ICC-01/04-01/06-1432, 11 July 2008, Judgment on the appeals of The Prosecutor and The Defence against Trial Chamber I's Decision on Victims' Participation of 18 January 2008, para 98.

[199] Although the Appeals Chamber said it would do so: ICC *Prosecutor v Lubanga*, AC, ICC-01/04-01/06-1432, 11 July 2008, Judgment on the appeals of The Prosecutor and The Defence against Trial Chamber I's Decision on Victims' Participation of 18 January 2008, para 97.

the admissibility of evidence presented by the parties,[200] raises the question whether the Appeals Chamber sees the difference between a party and a participant.

By adopting such an extensive approach towards the integration of the victim into the trial procedure, the ICC runs the danger of distorting the structure of the proceedings. Judging by the decisions presented above, the traditional party structure of the trial before the ICC has become highly questionable. Furthermore, the law of evidence is tilted if the Chambers use the victims as sources of information *ad libidum*, by giving Rule 93 RPE ICC an extremely wide scope.[201] Any formality of the criminal trial proceeding would thus be abolished,[202] and a blind eye would be turned to the fact that the victim is not a neutral observer but—naturally—has an interest in the outcome of the trial.[203]

Critics of the expansion of victim participation are easy to find, particularly among Anglo-American commentators:

> Melding this 'ICC victims' bill of rights' into critical procedural stages of its criminal litigation schema, the Rome Statute may adulterate, and ultimately dilute, basic structural due process protections of ICC defendants.[204]

On the other hand, some attribute this disequilibrium to the European Continental legal system.[205]

> [T]he victim-oriented, civil law model of human rights 'leads to inordinate 'concern for symbolic vindication of violations of victims' human rights' and 'has proven a more potent influence than worries over potential violations of defendants' rights'.[206]

In return, German-speaking participants in international criminal cases identify the Anglo-American procedural structure as the basic problem, since 'both parties

[200] As has been done, ICC *Prosecutor v Lubanga*, AC, ICC-01/04-01/06-1432, 11 July 2008, Judgment on the Appeals of The Prosecutor and The Defence against Trial Chamber I's Decision on Victims' Participation of 18 January 2008, para 93 *et subs*.

[201] *See* C Stahn, H Olásolo, and K Gibson, 'Participation of Victims in Pre-Trial Proceedings of the ICC', 4 *JICJ* (2006) 217, 237.

[202] *See* Boas/Bischoff/Reid/Taylor, *ICL III*, 320.

[203] R Cryer, H Friman, D Robinson, and E Wilmshurst, *An Introduction to International Criminal Law and Procedure* (2nd edn, CUP 2010) 478; *see* also M Damaska, 'What is the point of International Criminal Justice?', 83 *Chi-Kent L Rev* (2008) 329, 334 describing the dangers of relying on victims accounts. Some examples are given by M Mohan, 'The Paradox of Victim-Centrism: Victim Participation at the Khmer Rouge Tribunal', 9 *ICLR* (2009) 733, 738 *et subs*.

[204] G Gordon, 'Toward an International Criminal Procedure: Due Process Aspirations and Limitations' 45 *Colum J Transnat'l L* (2007) 635, 699.

[205] As to the different domestic systems and victim participation *see* also Boas/Bischoff/Reid/Taylor, *ICL III*, 306 *et subs*.

[206] A Danner and J Martinez, 'Guilty Associations: Joint Criminal Enterprise, Command Responsibility, and the Development of International Criminal Law', 93 *California Law Review* (2005) 75, 146.

are determined to win the case at all costs.'[207] The obstinate adherence to differing legal traditions must finally come to an end. The issue here is not to determine which legal system is superior, but rather to develop a functional international criminal justice process based on international human rights, which serves as an example for national criminal systems.[208] The Rome Statute and the ICC RPE explicitly provide the legal framework for the participation of victims in proceedings before the court. However, the extent of victim participation has yet to be clearly defined. The subtle difference between the procedure for reparation payments and the criminal trial itself proves that there is no intention to award the victim party status in proceedings in order to determine the guilt or innocence of the accused. This corresponds to the jurisprudence of the ECHR on the participation of victims in criminal process, which has held: 'that a civil party cannot be regarded as either the opponent—or for that matter necessarily the ally—of the prosecution, their roles and objectives being clearly different.'[209]

It follows that the role of victim is essentially restricted to reparations for the harm suffered, which is to a certain extent related to the question of the accused's guilt. Victims are not a party to the proceedings against the accused—only with regards to the compensation claim in Art. 75 ICCSt is a party status adequate.[210] Thus, providing victims with the status of private prosecutors is completely out of the question.

c. Solutions One could read the Statute and Rules in many ways. The jurisprudence of the ICC to-date has done much to enhance the influence of the victim.[211] Whether this was intended by the drafters or not is doubtful.[212] However, what is missing is a clear definition of the role of the victim. Without a general idea of the purpose of victim participation, it will not be possible to develop a concise procedural structure at the ICC. Consequently the individual Chambers would have to decide to what extent victims are permitted to participate. Such a

[207] Author's Translation; cf. W Schomburg, 'Wahrheitsfindung im internationalen Gerichtssaal', in *Vereinte Nationen* (2009) 3; for a detailed and critical analysis *see* Ahlbrecht/*Kirsch*, MN 1333–45.

[208] O Lagodny, 'Legitimation und Bedeutung des ständigen Internationalen Strafgerichtshofes', 113 *ZStW* (2001) 800, 815.

[209] EtCHR *Berger v France*, Rep. 2002-X, para 38; confirmed in *Perez v France*, Rep. 2004-I, para 68.

[210] S Zappalá, 'The Rights of Victims *v.* the Rights of the Accused', 8 *JICJ* (2010) 137, 149.

[211] S Johnson, 'Neither Victims nor Executioners: The Dilemma of Victim Participation and the Defendant's Right to a Fair Trial at the International Criminal Court', 16 *ILSA J Int'l & Comp L* (2010) 489, 490.

[212] *See* Ph Kirsch: 'My reading of the various provisions of the Statute and the Rules…leads me to the conclusion that it was not the intention of the drafters that victims should lead evidence on guilt or innocence. In addition, determining that it is the parties that lead evidence on guilt or innocence, and not the victims, is consistent with the overall desire to ensure that proceedings at the ICC are both fair and expeditious.' ICC *Prosecutor v Lubanga*, AC, 23 July 2008, ICC-01/04-01/06-OA9OA10, Judgment on the appeals of The Prosecutor and The Defence against Trial Chamber I's Decision on Victims' Participation of 18 January 2008, Partially Dissenting Opinion of Judge Philippe Kirsch, para 23.

particularized approach would prove detrimental also for the acceptance of the ICC proceedings.

When thinking about the role of the victim in criminal proceedings, two parameters seem now to be settled: (1) the victim is an important witness, and (2) the victim needs to be compensated. The witness status has immediate impact on the proceedings. The right to compensation does not necessarily relate to the criminal trial directly, as it consists of a civil law claim. However, the question of whether a crime took place or not does influence the outcome of a civil action, so criminal and tort law are substantially intertwined in this regard.

As regards victim participation there are three options available. (1) Focus the participatory rights at the criminal trial with the aim of being awarded compensation afterwards. (2) Rethink the entire criminal trial structure and build the prosecution system not on a two-party but on a three-party regime. (3) Rethink the definition of 'the victim' in international criminal law.

This is not the place to develop these ideas in detail. However, one should keep in mind that as long as the focus lies on the participation of individual victims at the criminal procedure, many victims will be excluded from participating. It must not be forgotten that by inviting some victims to participate, others are rejected, as they cannot prove to be affected in their personal interests pursuant to Art. 68 (3) ICCSt. Maybe they are victims of a person who cannot be prosecuted for whatever reason, or who is being prosecuted by a national court which does not allow victims to participate. Therefore victim participation as it is practised at the ICC at present is highly selective, produces inequalities amongst the victims, and is prone to frustrate high expectations.

De lege ferrenda I would thus suggest to differentiate between the individual 'victim' who has a right to be compensated and the 'victim' of an international crime who might participate in the criminal proceeding. The former must only show that he or she has suffered harm from the situation and not from an individual perpetrator in order to receive compensation. The latter is to be identified as the collective in parallel to the protected values in international criminal law.[213] Some representative of the collective is invited to participate in the proceedings, but not as an individual victim.[214] In order to pursue the restorative purposes for the individual victim other 'fora' should be found beyond the judicial process.[215]

213 *See* Chapter 2, p 70.

214 I have elaborated this idea further in: C Safferling, 'Das Opfer völkerrechtlicher Verbrechen', 115 *ZStW* (2003) 352, 369–71.

215 *See* M Mohan, 'The Paradox of Victim-Centrism: Victim Participation at the Khmer Rouge Tribunal', 9 *ICLR* (2009) 733, 740.

3. Compensation for victims

Art. 75 of the ICC Statute gives victims the right to reparations; that is, restitution, compensation, and rehabilitation. The relevant procedures are set down in Rules 94–99 RPE.[216] According to these provisions, the court may require the accused, by way of restoration, to place the victim in the position in which he or she would have been had the crime not been committed. Generally speaking, the Trust Fund established under Art. 79 of the ICC Statute will be responsible for implementing and coordinating compensation payments or other rehabilitative measures.[217] The correlation between collective victims and individual victims remains unclear.[218] The nature of the reparation claims referred to in Art. 75 are equally vague. Do such claims represent a civil law claim, or are they part of the criminal sanction?[219] Aside from the practical problems of implementing the measures, further difficulties arise when determining actions concerning individual compensation claims brought simultaneously before civil courts. It therefore seems appropriate to restrict compensation payments made out of the fund to collective or symbolic payments, with the exception of the very few cases of direct personal confrontation between the victim and the perpetrator.[220]

An interesting procedural difference between the trial procedure and that of the reparations hearing can be observed. Where the Court decides issues that do not relate to the guilt of the accused, but purely concern civil compensation claims, the Court no longer exercises stringent control over the questioning of witnesses and/or the accused (Rule 91 (4) RPE). Furthermore, in connection to the civil claim, the victim's representative may be seen to attain the status of a party.[221]

Regarding compensation, a different line has been taken by the ECCC. Civil parties may seek reparation for injuries caused by the accused. However, the form of reparations is limited to collective and moral reparation.

---

[216] For more detail regarding the various forms of reparation *see* O Abo Youssef, *Die Stellung des Opfers im Völkerstrafrecht* (Schulthess 2008) 162 *et subs.*, 165–71; also C Safferling, *Towards an International Criminal Procedure* (OUP 2003) 378–81.

[217] S Bock 'Das Opfer vor dem Internationalen Strafgerichtshof', 119 *ZStW* (2007) 664, 679.

[218] O Abo Youssef, *Die Stellung des Opfers im Völkerstrafrecht* (Schulthess 2008) 176–9.

[219] Under Regulation 88 (1) the Registrar is required to develop a standard form for the application for reparations by victims.

[220] For more detail, *see* C Safferling, *Towards an International Criminal Procedure* (OUP 2003) 381.

[221] On this point regarding German procedural law *see* D Dölling, 'Zur Stellung des Verletzten im Strafverfahren', in H Müller-Dietz *et al.* (eds), *Festschrift für Jung* (Nomos 2007) 77, 82, who describes the 'dual function' of the victim to be, first, in his role as a witness to tell the truth and second, as participant to the proceedings, to secure his claim for reparations; *see* also ICC *The Prosecutor v Lubanga*, TC I, ICC-01/04-01/06-1119, 18 January 2008, Decision on Victims' Participation, para 119–22, where the Court held that it determines which reparations related evidence is presented at trial and ensures that the rights of the defendant are not infringed.

The meaning of 'collective' and 'moral' is debatable. The Civil Parties in the first case against the S-21 chairman *Kaing guek Eav* alias *Duch* filed a joint submission and requested that reparations awarded against the Accused should include as a minimum:[222]

- the compilation and dissemination of statements of apology made by KAING Guek Eav throughout the trial acknowledging the suffering of victims, including comments by the Civil Parties;
- access to free medical care (both physical and psychological), including free transportation to and from medical facilities;
- funding of educational programmes which inform Cambodians of the crimes committed under the Khmer Rouge regime and at S-21 in particular;
- erection of memorials and pagoda fences at S-21 (Choeung Ek and Prey Sar) as well as in the local communities of the Civil Parties; and
- inclusion of the names of the Civil Parties in Case 001 in the final judgment, along with a description of their connection to S-21.[223]

These requested reparations were also partly mentioned in the result of a survey where Cambodians were asked about what kind of reparations they wanted.[224] In the Judgment, however, the Trial Chamber denied most of the requests. According to the Chamber, not only the ECCC has no means to substitute or supplement awards requested with funds provided by national authorities or other third parties, but also the perpetrator did not have the financial resources necessary to pay for the reparations.[225]

E. The Accused and the Defence Counsel (*Alena Hartwig*)

The defence is of crucial importance.[226] Not only does the concept of defence relate to a number of fundamental safeguards that need to be protected, but it also acts as the counterpart to the prosecution.

When speaking of the 'defence' as a participant in the proceedings, we mean the defence counsel as well as the suspect or accused, who together constitute the defence.[227]

[222] ECCC *Prosecutor v Kaing Guek Eav alias Duch*, TC, Judgment, Case File/Dossier No. 001/18-07-2007/ECCC/TC, 26 July 2010, para 652.

[223] Ibid, para 652.

[224] Human Rights Center, *So We Will Never Forget* (University of California 2009) 44.

[225] ECCC *Prosecutor v Kaing Guek Eav alias Duch*, Case File/Dossier No. 001/18-07-2007/ECCC/TC, 26 July 2010, Judgment, para 663.

[226] The ICC introduces the remarks as to the Defence on its website with the following words: 'The defence is a fundamental pillar of the scales of justice at the International Criminal Court, and a key component of a fair trial.'

[227] A Zahar and G Sluiter, *International Criminal Law* (OUP 2007) 64.

I. The defence within the structure of the Court

Unlike the Office of the Prosecutor, the defence is not a part of, but situated outside, the organizational structure of the Court. It is questionable whether such lack of institutional status generally affects the quality and effectiveness of the defence in a negative way. Considering the organizational and financial deficiencies, compared to the Office of the Prosecutor as an organ of the Court, an affirmative response seems natural.[228] However, when incorporated within the structure of the Court, doubts as to the independence of the institution might arise. Furthermore, the defence cannot be said to be completely excluded from the structure of the Court, but is somewhat 'institutionalized' in close vicinity to it. Pursuant to Regulation 77 RegC, the Office of the Public Counsel for the Defence (OPCD) has been established by the Registry.

The OPCD is designed as a semi-independent office, falling within the remit of the Registry for administrative purposes, Regulation 77 (2) RegC. This intended independence is further specified in Regulation 144 (1) RegR which states that the members of the OPCD shall not receive any instructions relating to the execution of their tasks.

The SCSL was the first international criminal tribunal to establish a Defence Office. The creation of this Office has been a novel and innovative step in the establishment of the first institutionally based defence provision at an international criminal tribunal. The aim and objective of establishing the Defence Office was to provide a better coordinated defence at the Special Court and to facilitate a more efficient, effective, and cost-saving system than those in place at the ICTR and ICTY.

The Defence Office was set up by the Registry pursuant to Rule 45 RPE SCSL. Structurally, the Defence Office is part of the Registry and its head, the Principle Defender, is answerable to the Registrar.[229] Though technically part of the Registry, in practice the Defence Office at the SCSL nonetheless fulfils its duties and tasks independently of the Registry and may fairly be described as a quasi-autonomous entity.

The Defence Office provides direct legal advice, assistance, and representation to the defendant until defence counsel takes over responsibility for the management of the case. From this point in time, the Defence Office takes on the new role of

---

228 Compare R Wilson, 'Assigned Defence Counsel in Domestic and International War Crimes Tribunals: The Need for a Structural Approach', 2 *ICLR* (2002) 145, 176 *et subs.*, A Zahar and G Sluiter, *International Criminal Law* (OUP 2007) 62.

229 This is not quite the construction originally envisaged. It was initially intended that the Defence Office should be an independent organ of the court alongside the Chambers, Registry and OTP—a so-called fourth pillar—charged with its own functions and duties and enjoying the autonomy of a court organ. For a chronological summary of the creation of the Defence Office *see* R Skilbeck, 'Building the Fourth Pillar: Defence Rights at the Special Court for Sierra Leone', 1 *Essex Human Rights Review* (2004) 66, 79 *et subs.*

supporting the defence team when required, as well as supervising and authorizing payment of defence counsel.

Regulation 77 (4), (5) RegC assigns specific tasks to the OPCD. These include the representation and protection of the rights of the defence during the preliminary and the investigation stage, as well as providing support and assistance, including legal research and advice. The support and assistance referred to shall be provided 'to defence counsel and to the person entitled to legal assistance'. Members of the Office may also act as duty counsel or as an *ad hoc* counsel for the person entitled to legal assistance before a Chamber in respect of specific issues. For this purpose, Regulation 145 RegR imposes the duty on the Registrar to provide the members with all information and documents as are necessary for the fulfilment of those functions. Furthermore, the OPCD may act as a mediator in case of a dispute occurring between the person entitled to legal assistance, and his or her counsel; see Regulation 119 (3) RegR. When discharging its functions, the Registry is obliged to ensure confidentiality, Regulation 144 (5) RegR.

According to Regulation 143 RegR, the provisions governing the recruitment of staff of the Court shall apply to the appointment of the members of the OPCD. The Office may include a counsel meeting the criteria set out for defence counsel in general,[230] and shall include assistants as referred to in Regulation 68 RegC, Regulation 77 (3) RegC. The members of the Office are bound by the Code of Professional Conduct for Counsel when representing a person or assisting defence counsel, Regulation 144 (2) RegR. For all other issues, they are bound by the same provisions applicable to all staff members of the Court, Regulation 144 (3) RegR.[231] Being administratively incorporated into the Registry, the Office shall file reports on administrative issues and submit an annual report of its work, Regulation 146 RegR.

At the ICTY and the ICTR, the Registry is responsible for issues relating to defence counsel. These are basically limited to the assignment of counsel. According to Rule 45 RPE ICTY/ICTR, the assignment of counsel is undertaken by the Registry. For the purpose of further clarification, the Registrar shall set out a Directive on the Assignment of Defence Counsel.[232] If the suspect or accused has sufficient means to remunerate defence counsel, s/he shall file a power of attorney with the Registrar, Rule 44 RPE ICTY/ICTR.

The lack of an autonomous (or quasi-autonomous) defence unit situated within the Registry was considered to be disadvantageous.[233] Thus, the establishment

---

230 *See* p 183.

231 'Staff Rules of the International Criminal Court' (ICC-ASP/4/3) as of 25 August 2005.

232 ICTY Directive on the Assignment of Defence Counsel as of 11 July 2006; ICTR Directive on the Assignment of Defence Counsel as of 14 March 2008.

233 Compare M Ellis, 'The Evolution of Defence Counsel Appearing before the International Criminal Tribunal for the Former Yugoslavia', 37 *New Engl L Rev* (2003) 949, 971 *et subs.*

of the 'Association of Defence Counsel practising before the ICTY' was welcomed as a major breakthrough in focusing on the interests of the defence, and as 'indispensable for a professional administration of justice'.[234] This Association was recognized by the ICTY as the official representative of defence counsel appearing before the Tribunal, Rule 44 (A) (iii) RPE ICTY.[235] Within the context of the ICTR, the 'Association des Avocats de la Defense auprès du Tribunal International pour Rwanda' was established as a counterpart, though no formal recognition on part of the Tribunal has taken place.[236]

II. Defence counsel at the ICC

According to Rule 20 (1) (c) ICCSt, the Registrar is responsible for the assignment of counsel. He or she shall assist arrested persons, persons to whom Art. 55 (2) ICCSt applies, and the accused in obtaining the proper legal assistance. Hence, Rule 20 (1) (c) ICCSt refers to all stages of the proceedings at which a person believed to have committed a crime within the jurisdiction of the Court depends essentially on legal advice.

Basically, the person entitled to legal assistance has two options to be represented by defence counsel. The person may either choose defence counsel in accordance with Rule 21 (2) RPE ICC, or a Chamber may appoint counsel in accordance with the statutory framework, Regulation 74 (1) RegC.

For the purpose of choosing counsel, the Registrar shall create and maintain a list of counsel meeting certain required criteria, Rule 21 (2) RPE ICC. The person shall freely choose a counsel from that list. If the person chooses a counsel not on the list, a possibility anticipated by Rule 21 (2) RPE ICC, the Registrar shall decide on the eligibility of that counsel, Regulation 75 (2) RegC. After having chosen a counsel included in the list, the Registrar shall contact that counsel, Regulation 75 (1) RegC. Prior to the assignment, it must be established that the counsel is willing and ready to represent the person, Regulation 75 RegC, and in the case of Regulation 75 (2) RegC, that s/he is willing to be included into the list. Once a counsel is chosen, that counsel shall file a power of attorney with the Registrar as soon as possible, Rule 22 (2) RPE ICC.

Pursuant to Regulation 76 RegC, a Chamber may also appoint counsel in specific cases, specified in the Statute and the Rules of Procedure and Evidence, or where

[234] H Holthuis, 'Operational Aspects of Setting up the International Criminal Court: Building on the Experience of the ICTY', 27 *Int'l Legal Prac* (2002) 41, 43.

[235] S de Bertodano, 'What Price Defence? Resourcing the Defence at the ICTY', 2 *JICJ* (2004) 503, 506 speaks of the membership to the ADC as being 'effectively compulsory for defence counsel practising before the ICTY'.

[236] A Zahar and G Sluiter, *International Criminal Law* (OUP 2007), 61, criticize this 'endeavour' as lacking 'a structural, integrated and well-thought-through approach'.

the interests of justice so require.[237] This procedure applies to the initial phase of the proceedings before the Court. Here, a person is subject to investigations but has not been arrested and, hence, has not had the opportunity to choose defence counsel.

The 'required criteria' to be met by counsel referred to above are further specified in Rule 22 (1) RPE ICC. First, a counsel is required to have competence and practical experience in the field of international *or* criminal law and procedure. The necessary experience in criminal proceedings shall be at least ten years, Regulation 67 RegC. In addition, he or she shall have an excellent knowledge of at least one of the working languages of the Court.[238] Furthermore, Rule 22 (2) RPE ICC stipulates that counsel for the defence may be assisted by other persons, who in turn must also fulfil certain requirements. Here, Regulation 68 RegC stipulates that these criteria shall be determined by the Regulations of the Registry. Regulation 124 RegR requires assistants to have either five years of relevant experience in criminal proceedings or specific competence in international or criminal law and procedure. The Registrar shall also create and maintain a list of persons qualified to assist counsel pursuant to Regulation 125 RegR. The assistants are then appointed by counsel and selected from that list, Regulation 127 RegR.

The details of a formal application by a person wanting his or her name to be added to the list of counsel are provided for by Regulation 69 (1), (2) RegC. Thereafter, the Registrar establishes whether the person has provided the required information and hence has met the relevant selection criteria. In case of a refusal to include the person on the list as a counsel, that person may apply for review to the Presidency by virtue of Regulations 70 (2), 72 RegC. The conduct of defence counsel in the performance of their duties is mainly governed by the Code of Professional Conduct for counsel,[239] containing a disciplinary regime and established pursuant to Rule 8 RPE ICC.[240]

Once included on the list, the Registrar shall remove or suspend a counsel from that list under the circumstances of Regulation 71 RegC. While the suspension is temporarily, the removal is of a final nature.

[237] For instance, Pre-Trial Chamber II has appointed counsel for the defence when it decided to initiate proceedings under Art. 19 ICCSt in the case of *Kony et al.* The Chamber found that it was within the interests of justice to have the suspects represented by counsel 'within the context and for the purposes of the present proceedings'. *See* ICC *Prosecutor v Kony et al.*, PTC, ICC-02/04-01/05-320, 21 October 2008, Decision Initiating Proceedings under Article 19, Requesting Observations and Appointing Counsel for the Defence, p 8.

[238] Art. 50 (2) ICCSt stipulates that the working languages of the Court are English and French.

[239] Resolution ICC/ASP/4/Res.1, adopted on 2 December 2005.

[240] For the discussion of the different proposals as to the Code of Professional Conduct *see* M Walsh, 'The International Bar Association Proposal for a Code of Professional Conduct for Counsel Before the ICC', 1 *JICJ* (2003) 490.

At the *ad hoc* Tribunals, the assignment of counsel follows the procedure set out in the respective Directive on the Assignment of Defence Counsel set out by the Registrar. The person entitled to legal assistance may choose a counsel from a list retained by the Registrar. The Directives also provide guidance on the qualifications of counsel before the tribunals.[241] With respect to the performance of their duties, the Registrar issued a Code of Professional Conduct for the Defence Counsel.[242] From all this it follows that the *ad hoc* Tribunals' procedure is similar to the one adopted at the ICC.[243]

According to Regulation 73 RegC, the Registrar shall establish a roster of duty counsel who are available at any time. These duty counsel are intended to represent any person requiring urgent legal assistance. This applies to cases where the person has not yet secured legal assistance or where the person's counsel is unavailable. Thus, Regulation 73 RegC is aimed at securing a proper defence through legal assistance at any time. For this purpose, the Registrar is responsible for contacting duty counsel and providing him or her with all the information available, Regulation 129 (2) RegR.

As soon as the Registrar contacts the person entitled to legal assistance in order to assist him or her with respect to legal representation, that person may apply for legal assistance paid by the Court. The scope of 'legal aid' in this sense by the Court is such that it covers all costs determined to be necessary for an effective and efficient defence, Regulation 83 (1) RegC.[244] On an application for legal assistance paid by the Court, the Registrar determines the means of that person and whether he or she shall receive full or partial payment of the legal assistance, Regulation 84 (1) RegC and Regulation 132 RegR. Here, Regulation 84 (2) RegC gives further guidance on the means of the applicant that shall be included in the determination of the Registrar. The Registrar shall decide within one month of the submission of the application as to whether the legal assistance should be paid by the Court, Regulation 85 (1) RegC. During that period, legal assistance is paid by the Court on a provisional basis, Regulation 132 (3) RegR. In case that 'legal aid' is granted by the Court, the procedure of payment is further specified in Regulations 133 RegR *et subs.* If legal assistance paid by the Court is refused, the Registrar may seek an order from the Presidency for recovery of the costs of providing counsel, Regulation 85 (4) RegC.

---

[241] Art. 14 ICTY-Directive; Art. 13 ICTR-Directive. *See* also C Safferling, 'International Criminal Procedure and its Participants: An Examination of Judges, Prosecutor and Defence at the Yugoslav Tribunal', 5 *YB Int'l Hum L* (2002) 219, 226.

[242] Compare C Safferling, *Towards an International Criminal Procedure* (OUP 2003) 225.

[243] For further analysis *see* R Wilson, 'Assigned Defence Counsel in Domestic and International War Crimes Tribunals: The Need for a Structural Approach', 2 *ICLR* (2002) 145, 164 *et subs.*

[244] This provision provides for an overall assumption of costs. This includes the remuneration of counsel, the assistants and staff, expenditure for the gathering of evidence, as well as administrative costs, translation, and interpretation costs, etc.

Both Art. 6 ICTY-Directive and Art. 3 ICTR-Directive provide for a right to legal assistance paid by the court under certain circumstances.[245] At the SCSL, Rule 45 (C) RPE SCSL requires the Defence Office to compile and maintain a list of suitably qualified international criminal defence lawyers available to represent indigent defendants.[246] Once an indigent defendant has chosen his or her defence counsel from the list, the Defence Office enters into a Legal Services Contract with the selected lawyer and is responsible for the assessment of his or her fees throughout the contract.[247]

III. Basic functions of the Defence

1. The defendant

As mentioned above, it is the defendant together with defence counsel who constitute the 'defence'. However, they have different roles and positions.[248]

The 'defendant' is used here as a broader term for the person entitled to legal assistance; that is, the suspect or the accused. With the confirmation of charges according to Art. 61 (7) ICCSt, the status of the person charged with crimes within the jurisdiction of the Court becomes that of an 'accused'. Prior to the confirmation of charges, it seems rather obvious to speak of the person as a 'suspect'. However, neither the Rome Statute nor the Rules of Procedure and Evidence use the word 'suspect'.[249] Instead, the drafters of the Rome Statute established the expression of 'persons during an investigation', as can be seen from Art. 55 ICCSt. Both the accused and the 'person during an investigation' are entitled to legal assistance by virtue of Arts 55 (2), 67 ICCSt.

The Rules of Procedure and Evidence of the *ad hoc* Tribunals provide guidance on the terms expressing the status of the defendant. Rule 2 (A) RPE ICTY/ICTR expressly defines both 'suspect' and 'accused'. According to this provision, the 'accused' is 'a person against whom one or more counts in an indictment have been confirmed in accordance with Rule 47'. A 'suspect', on the other hand, is 'a person concerning whom the Prosecutor possesses reliable information which tends to show that the person may have committed a crime over which the Tribunal has jurisdiction'.

[245] The concept of indigence and legal assistance paid by the tribunal is criticized in R Wilson, 'Assigned Defence Counsel in Domestic and International War Crimes Tribunals: The Need for a Structural Approach', 2 *ICLR* (2002) 145, 169 *et subs.* As to the financial aspects and the lack of proper management at the ICTY *see* S de Bertodano, 'What Price Defence? Resourcing the Defence at the ICTY', 2 *JICJ* (2004) 503.

[246] The exact procedure is set out in Part II of the Directive on the Assignment of Counsel 2003.

[247] For a description of the 'contract system' *see* J Jones *et al.*, 'Notes and Comments—The Special Court for Sierra Leone: A Defence Perspective', 2 *JICJ* (2004) 211, 215 *et subs.* Regarding selection and payment of defence counsel *see* also R Skilbeck, 'Building the Fourth Pillar: Defence Rights at the Special Court for Sierra Leone', 1 *Essex Human Rights Review* (2004) 66, 81.

[248] *See* A Zahar and G Sluiter, *International Criminal Law* (OUP 2007) 64 *et subs.*

[249] *See* S Zappalá, *Human Rights in International Criminal Proceedings* (OUP 2003) 49 on that intention.

2. Functions of defence counsel

The basic function of the defence counsel is to safeguard the rights of the defendant throughout the course of the proceedings and to assume the role of a 'defender'. Depending on the individual case, the defence counsel might have to conduct investigations on its own in order to be in a position to counter the allegations brought forward by the prosecution. In a sense he or she has to fulfil similar tasks as the OTP, which—as we have seen before—has a special division on investigation and one on prosecution. Defence counsel must do both in one person. Overarching principles, such as fair trial guarantees or, more specifically, the principle of equality of arms,[250] constitute the cornerstones of the concept of defence in criminal trials. Therefore, the primary function is to ensure that the defendant is properly legally represented throughout the proceedings, thereby promoting a fair trial and endorsing the principle of equality of arms.

The defence counsel holds a somewhat ambiguous position.[251] On the one hand, s/he provides legal assistance to the defendant and hence serves the interests of and has duties towards his or her client.[252] On the other hand, the defence counsel serves the proper administration of justice.[253]

The principle of equality of arms has been subject to broad discussions. What matters here is the question of equality with respect to procedural matters. As already mentioned, the defence counsel does not constitute a fourth pillar to the structure of the Court. Whilst the Prosecutor is an organ of the Court and hence vested with tremendous resources, this does not hold true for the defence. At least theoretically, the statutory framework of the ICC provides for sufficient mechanisms to safeguard the equality of arms. However, it remains doubtful whether a defence as constituted according to the above is truly in the same position as the Prosecutor.

The system at the *ad hoc* Tribunals is of an adversarial nature. The Prosecutor is not obliged to investigate incriminating and exonerating circumstances equally. What prevails is the 'dynamic of winning' as the 'driving engine for the prosecution'.[254] this is even more of a disadvantage than is the case here. At the

---

[250] *See* Chapter 8, p 410.

[251] Compare A Eser, 'Verteidigung in der internationalen Strafgerichtsbarkeit—Eine rechtsvergleichende Analyse', in H Schöch *et al.*, *Strafverteidigung, Revision und die gesamten Strafrechtswissenschaften* (Carl Heymanns Verlag 2008) 147, 165.

[252] Generally M Wladimiroff, 'The Assignment of Defence Counsel before the International Criminal Tribunal for Rwanda', 12 *LJIL* (1999) 957, 958 *et subs.*

[253] This is illustrated by the Code of Professional Conduct for Counsel. Especially Art. 7 (3) ICC-Code of Conduct stipulates that counsel shall comply all times with the Statute, the Rules of Procedure and Evidence and the Regulations of the Court.

[254] M Karnavas, 'Gathering Evidence in International Criminal Trials—The View of the Defence Lawyer', in M Bohlander (ed), *International Criminal Justice: A Critical Analysis of Institutions and Procedures* (Cameron May 2007) 75, 88.

ICC, the defence constitutes the counterpart to the Prosecutor in a 'competitive process'.[255]

The Defence Office at the SCSL carries out different functions with respect to safeguarding a proper legal representation. Besides promoting the concepts of fair trial and equality of arms, providing legal advice, and assistance to unrepresented defendants, the Defence Office is also responsible for the attainment and distribution of funds and resources for the defence.[256] The Defence Office also represents the interests of the accused generally, for example, at plenary sessions organized by the judges of the Special Court, and in the preparation, drafting, or amendment of key documents affecting the accused.[257] The concept of establishing an institutional counterbalance to the Prosecutor in the form of a defence office is commendable and brings with it many benefits. The main lesson to be learnt from the Defence Office at the SCSL is that the successful operation of such an institution depends upon its status and mandate. Despite its many accomplishments, the Defence Office has been rendered a somewhat toothless tiger, struggling to find its place within the SCSL, and trying to carry out an unclear mandate. To optimize the potential benefits and to enable a defence unit to operate freely, competently, and effectively, it must be established by Statute as an independent organ of the tribunal, and its role and function must be clearly defined.

IV. The defence throughout the course of the proceedings

As a general rule, the person entitled to legal assistance shall act before the Court through his or her counsel when represented by defence counsel, Regulation 74 (2) RegC. In order to secure a proper defence, the defence counsel is under an obligation to give his or her client all explanations needed to make informed decisions regarding his or her representation, Art. 15 (1) Code of Professional Conduct for Counsel.

1. Initial phase of the proceedings

The development of a 'case' in the course of the Prosecutor's investigations and, thus the identification of a suspect, triggers the appearance of the defence. Here, with respect to the investigation and the pre-trial stage, the provision of Art. 55 ICCSt becomes relevant.

Art. 55 (2) ICCSt provides for fundamental human rights guarantees of the suspect when being questioned by the Prosecutor or national authorities. As soon as a

[255] Ibid. For instance, more than often, the accessibility of evidentiary material is simply limited, *see* M Ellis, 'The Evolution of Defence Counsel Appearing before the International Criminal Tribunal for the Former Yugoslavia', 37 *New Engl L Rev* (2003) 949, 964.

[256] The Defence Office is involved in the planning of the Special Court's budget. It prepares a formal request for funds required for the Defence as a whole and attends budget meetings.

[257] R Skilbeck, 'Building the Fourth Pillar: Defence Rights at the Special Court for Sierra Leone', 1 *Essex Human Rights Review* (2004) 66, 82.

person questioned is suspected of having committed crimes within the jurisdiction of the Court, Art. 55 (2) (c), (d) ICCSt give the suspect the right to legal assistance and to be questioned only in the presence of counsel. Hence, these provisions are aimed at securing an effective defence from the beginning, attributing the defence counsel with a vital role.

More often than not, issues related to pre-trial detention after the issuance and execution of a warrant of arrest also illustrate the importance of legal representation. Rule 117 (2) RPE ICC illustrates that the assignment of counsel at the early stage of the proceedings is not limited to the questioning of a suspect.

The defence counsel is responsible for developing a defence strategy, for giving legal advice to his or her client at this initial stage of the proceedings, and securing the protection of his rights.[258] With respect to detention, the defence counsel should check whether the arrest and detention was proceeded with in accordance with the respective provisions and whether the custody of the defendant can be challenged. Furthermore, it is believed to be essential at this early stage of the proceedings for the defence to conduct own investigations and to probe the factual allegations raised by the Prosecutor.[259]

Similar to Art. 55 (2) ICCSt, Rule 42 RPE ICTY/ICTR provides for a right to legal assistance for a suspect who is to be questioned by the Prosecutor. From this it follows that defence counsel may be involved at a stage of the proceedings prior to the indictment. However, in many cases the indictment and, subsequently, a warrant of arrest have already been issued.[260] Under these circumstances, the defence counsel comes into play when the defendant is already an accused in the technical sense; that is, after the indictment has been confirmed. From this point on, the defence in the Tribunals' proceedings which is of an adversarial nature, must try to reduce the advantage of the Prosecution which has been involved in the case for a long time. Hence, it is one main task of the defence team to conduct its own investigations in order to probe and challenge the allegations raised by the Prosecutor.[261] Apart from the specialties arising out of the purely adversarial

[258] J Tuinstra, 'Defending the Defenders—The Role of Defence Counsel in International Criminal Trials', 8 *JICJ* (2010) 463, 478.

[259] J Turner, 'Defense Perspectives on Law and Politics in International Criminal Trials', 48 *Va J Int'l L* (2008) 529, 554.

[260] This is also due to the course of the proceedings adopted at the Tribunals, since there does not exist such an extensive pre-trial phase as is anticipated by the Rome Statute. The indictment is confirmed even before a warrant of arrest is issued, since the issuance of a warrant of arrest is conditioned by the confirmation of the indictment.

[261] M Karnavas, 'Gathering Evidence in International Criminal Trials—The View of the Defence Lawyer', in M Bohlander (ed), *International Criminal Justice: A Critical Analysis of Institutions and Procedures* (Cameron May 2007) 75, 105 holds that 'the defence lawyer should be preparing both an attack and defence: preparing to attack, discredit, and impeach every possible prosecution witness, while also identifying evidence from the disclosure material and gathering evidence in the field to be introduced through prosecution witnesses'.

nature of the proceedings,[262] the functions of the defence at the initial stage of the proceedings remain the same as they were pointed out before the ICC.

During the initial phase of proceedings at the SCSL and prior to the appointment of defence counsel, the Defence Office provides direct preliminary legal advice, assistance, and representation to unrepresented suspects and accused. In effect, Defence Office duty counsel filled the shoes of a defence lawyer until he or she was appointed. This involved advising suspects whilst they were being questioned, explaining the indictment, and appearing in court at the initial hearing as well as dealing with bail applications.[263]

Apart from possible infringements of the rights of a suspect according to Art. 55 (2) ICCSt, other investigative measures might also jeopardize the rights of the defendant at this stage of the proceedings, concerning scenarios which are not related to the questioning of the suspect. The Rome Statute does not entail provisions preserving the right to physical and mental integrity of a person or the right to privacy or data protection.[264] Lacking protective provisions which safeguard the defendant's rights, it is submitted that these investigatory measures need authorization by the Pre-Trial Chamber according to Art. 57 (3) (a) ICCSt.[265]

Defence counsel may also be involved at an earlier stage of the proceedings, prior to the identification of a suspect referred to in Art. 55 (2) ICCSt. This situation is governed by Art. 56 ICCSt. While the purpose of this provision is to ensure that evidence obtained during the investigation will be admissible at the later trial stage,[266] the protection of defence rights is considered a 'necessary and logical reflex' of the intention to preserve evidence.[267] Art. 56 (1) (b) explicitly states that the Pre-Trial Chamber shall ensure that specific investigative acts are carried out in a way that, *inter alia*, protects the rights of the defence.[268] This applies irrespective of the actual existence of a defendant.[269] Here, Art. 56 (2) (d) ICCSt identifies three possible scenarios.[270] (1) If the suspect is present before the Court and counsel has been

262 Ibid, p 88 *et subs.*

263 J Jones *et al.*, 'Notes and Comments—The Special Court for Sierra Leone: A Defence Perspective', 2 *JICJ* (2004) 211, 214 *et subs.*

264 On these issues *see* C Safferling, 'The Rights and Interests of the Defence in the Pre-Trial Phase', 9 *JICJ* (2011) 651, 656 *et subs.*

265 Ibid, p 658.

266 C Kreß, 'The Procedural Law of the International Criminal Court in Outline: Anatomy of a Unique Compromise', 1 *JICJ* (2003) 603, 607.

267 C Safferling, 'The Rights and Interests of the Defence in the Pre-Trial Phase', 9 *JICJ* (2011) 651, 660.

268 Triffterer/*Guariglia and Hochmayr*, Art. 56 MN 8.

269 For the appointment of so called *ad hoc* counsel *see* J Dieckmann and C Kerll, 'Representing the "General Interests of the Defence": Boon or Bane?—A Stocktaking of the System of *ad hoc* Counsel at the ICC', 11 *ICLR* (2011) 105, 109 *et subs.*

270 C Safferling, 'The Rights and Interests of the Defence in the Pre-Trial Phase', 9 *JICJ* (2011) 651, 662.

assigned, the counsel may be authorized to participate. (2) If the suspect is present but counsel has not been designated yet, the Pre-Trial Chamber may, by virtue of Regulation 76 RegC, assign counsel who takes part in the proceedings under Art. 56 ICCSt. (3) If a suspect has not been identified yet, the Pre-Trial Chamber may appoint counsel to attend and represent the interests of the defence. While the functions of defence counsel in the first two scenarios seem obvious—that is, to secure the rights of the defendant—the third scenario seems striking. However, referring to the 'interests of the defence', Art. 56 (2) (d) ICCSt provides for the possibility of an *ad hoc* counsel participating in the proceedings under Art. 56 ICCSt in order to ensure that these proceedings are conducted in accordance with the 'rule of law'.[271] Thus, the rights of possible later suspects shall be safeguarded by placing a counsel in the position of attempting to protect the interests of potential suspects.

2. *Trial stage*

In preparation for the trial, disclosure of evidence is one of the main duties of the defence counsel. S/he must also carefully screen the record of the proceedings according to Rule 131 RPE ICC in order to prepare properly for trial. During the trial stage of the proceedings, the defence counsel has broad responsibilities with respect to issues relating to evidence and, thus, safeguarding the rights of the accused provided for in Art. 67 (1) (e) ICCSt. This applies particularly to the examination of witnesses, the presentation of exonerating evidence, and the building of the defence. Furthermore, defence counsel should hold the Prosecutor to their burden of proof, as any reversal would contradict Art. 67 (1) (i) ICCSt.

The specific tasks will vary according to the structure of the trial which the Trial Chamber opts for.[272] In an adversarial system, in which the presentation of evidence rests primarily with the parties, the defence counsel, being only one party of the trial, needs to present his or her case; that is, the exonerating evidence. If cross-examination is being done, which is not necessarily the case,[273] obviously defence counsel must scrutinize the reliability and test the credibility of the witnesses for the prosecution. This requires both special skills in cross-examination and knowledge on the background of the witnesses.

3. *Appeals stage*

The defence counsel represents the defendant on appeal. The counsel files the appeal as well as other motions and observations for the purposes of the appeal.

---

[271] Ibid. Here, four possible issues are identified constituting the 'interests of the defence' at this stage of the proceedings.

[272] We will discuss later the fact that the Trial Chamber has a rather broad discretion as to the structure of the trial, *see* Chapter 8, p 436.

[273] *See* Chapter 8, p 448.

The assistance of counsel is of vital importance even at the post-trial stage, considering the complex issues of substantive and procedural international criminal law.

V. Self-representation

From a comparative law perspective, one detects that there is no agreement between the major procedural systems of the world as to the question of whether an accused should be allowed to represent him- or herself at trial. Looking at the major human rights conventions and reading, for example, Art. 14 (3) (d) ICCPR or Art. 6 (3) (c) ECHR one could get the impression that the accused has a right to conduct his or her defence without the help of a lawyer. However, many legal systems do not recognize such a right for reason of trial efficiency.

At the IMT in Nuremberg, self-representation was indeed allowed following the US American procedural tradition. In contrast, the German Code of Criminal Procedure has always anticipated duty counsel, at least in capital cases. At the Nuremberg trial, all the accused were represented by counsel, and apparently even the US prosecution team imposed pressure on the accused to choose legal representation.[274]

At the *ad hoc* Tribunals, one did not learn from that experience but rather adhered to the principle of self-representation.[275] As a consequence, several defendants took the defence in their own hands, which caused quite some chaos at trial. Vojislav Šešelj managed to prolong his trial almost indefinitely; Slobodan Milošević died pending trial; Radovan Karadžić has started with a massive team of advisors, yet represents himself in the courtroom. It seems that the ICTY has not found a proper way to deal with situations of high-profile accused who represent themselves.[276] In particular with regard to accused, who are skilled demagogues and clever seducers, self-representation offers them a floor for political agitation which has been described as a 'perverse right of spectacle'.[277]

The ICC has taken a slightly different line even if the right to self-representation could not be entirely abolished. Art. 67 (1) (d) ICCSt provides for the right of the accused 'to conduct the defence in person'. In fact, sub-paragraph (d) mirrors the same guarantees as stipulated in Art. 14 (3) (d) ICCPR, and Art. 21 (4) (d) ICTYSt, Art. 20 (4) (d) ICTRSt and is thereby clear about the right to self-representation. However, the provision also refers to the possibility of having legal assistance assigned by the Court 'in any case where the interests of justice so require'. This is a valuable option worth pursuing should the issue of self-representation

---

274 C Safferling and P Graebke, 'Strafverteidigung im Nürnberger Hauptkriegsverbrecherprozess: Strategien und Wirkungen', 123 *ZStW* (2011) 47

275 *See* G Boas, 'Self-Representation Before the ICTY. A Case for Reform', 9 *JICJ* (2011) 53.

276 G Sluiter, 'Karadžić on Trial—Two Procedural Problems', 6 *JICJ* (2008) 617, 618 *et subs*.

277 E Cerruti, 'Self-Representation in the International Arena: Removing a False Right of Spectacle', 40 *Geo J Int'l L* (2009) 919.

arise in future cases. Regulation 76 (1) RegC, concerned with the matter of the appointment of counsel by a Chamber, provides for the necessary discretion to appoint counsel 'where the interests of justice so require'. This provision may be considered as somewhat imperfect as it does not specify on the relevant criteria.[278] Nonetheless, as self-representation may jeopardize the fair and expeditious conduct of the proceedings, the Court, by virtue of this provision, has a powerful tool at hand. Since the 'interests of justice' certainly include the interest to conduct fair and expeditious proceedings, Art. 64 (2) ICCSt, the Chamber may appoint legal assistance to the accused in these cases.[279]

Self-representations should be avoided in order to abolish any disruptive behaviour of the accused.[280]

Maybe one should even think the other way round: the fair trial requirement necessitates the best defence possible for the accused. In particular in cases as complex as international criminal law cases and those in which so much is at stake for the defendant, the best defence will not be achieved by self-representation.[281] The principle of 'fair trial' in other words warrants representation by defence counsel.

VI. Conclusion

The defence consisting of the accused and his or her defence counsel constitute the counterpart to the Prosecutor. The defence counsel's primary task is to ensure respect for the human rights of the defendant throughout the proceedings. At trial, the counsel takes on the representation of the accused in that s/he questions the witnesses of the prosecution in order to test their credibility and presents the evidence for the defence case. As a professional lawyer, defence counsel is called upon to add to the overall aim of the proceeding; that is, establishing of the truth. This means that defence counsel has to act with due diligence regarding the truthfulness of his or her own strategies and statements. At the same time s/he has to work towards achieving the 'best' result possible for his client. These antagonistic tasks are not easy to bridge. Thus the defence counsel's job might be counted as the most challenging amongst all the participants in a criminal trial.

---

[278] N Croquet, 'The International Criminal Court and the Treatment of Defence Rights: A Mirror of the European Court of Human Rights' Jurisprudence?', 11 *HRLR* (2011) 91, 108.

[279] Compare with R Heinsch, 'How to Achieve Fair and Expeditious Trial Proceedings before the ICC: Is it Time for a more Judge-Dominated Approach?', in C Stahn and G Sluiter (eds), *The Emerging Practice of the International Criminal Court* (Martinus Nijhoff Publishers 2009) 479, 493.

[280] M Scharf, 'Self-Representation versus Assignment of Defence Counsel before International Criminal Tribunals', 4 *JICJ* (2006) 31, 38 *et subs.*

[281] E Cerruti, 'Self-Representation in the International Arena: Removing a False Right of Spectacle', 40 *Geo J Int'l L* (2009) 919.

5

THE PROCEDURAL STRUCTURE AND PRELIMINARY ISSUES

A. The Procedural Structure

In the following chapters of the book the individual procedural steps before the ICC will be described in detail. The procedural structure can be divided into the following phases as identified in Figure 5.1, which are attributed to specific Chambers.[1]

This differentiation in general is common to most democratic legal systems and is the outcome of both logic and normative considerations. Clearly before public proceedings can be started, evidence must be collected and evaluated. Secondly, in order to protect the persons involved from arbitrary allegations, the judge supervises the investigation process as an independent authority. This supervision takes place during and after the investigation, as the prosecutor needs authorization for many investigatory measures and is required to present the result of his or her investigation in a confirmation procedure before the actual trial starts. Finally, it is a prerequisite of human rights that a higher authority level in an appeals procedure reviews the outcome of the trial itself. Art. 14 (5) ICCPR and the ECHR recognize a right to appeal in Art. 2 of the 7th Additional Protocol.[2] The trial itself is the key, and the focus of the entire prosecution. After all, it is where judges determine the guilt of the accused and thereby invalidate, so to speak, the presumption of innocence. The verdict on the guilt or innocence of the accused is the goal towards which all other stages are oriented. This does not mean that the other stages are of lesser importance. Quite the contrary is true. Since the pre-trial phase largely

---

[1] This basic division into different stages is also described by H Olásolo, 'Reflections on the ICC's Jurisdictional Reach', 16 *CLF* (2005) 279, 284 *et subs*. A slightly different approach is taken by K Ambos and D Miller, 'Structure and Function of the Confirmation Procedure before the ICC from a Comparative Perspective', 7 *ICLR* (2007) 335, 338.

[2] *See* 7th Additional Protocol of 22 November 1984. Art. 2: 'Everyone convicted of a criminal offence by a tribunal shall have the right to have his conviction or sentence reviewed by a higher tribunal. The exercise of this right, including the grounds on which it may be exercised, shall be governed by law.'

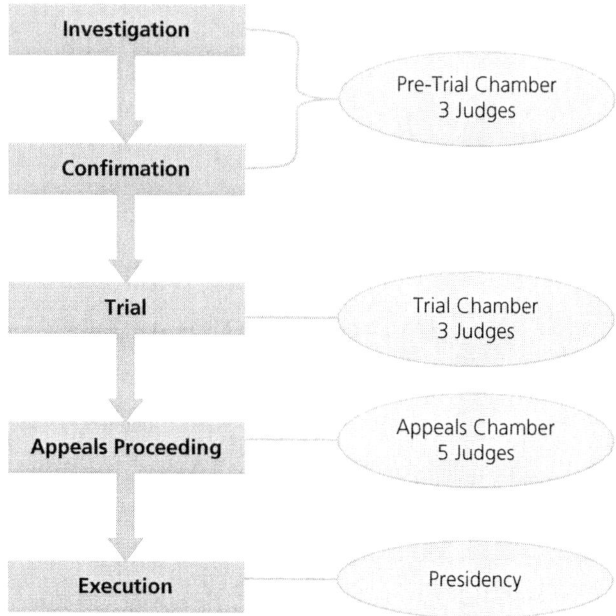

Figure 5.1 The procedural structure

serves the preparation of the trial, the methods and means employed during the investigation have a direct impact upon the evidence presented at trial.[3] Erroneous results produced at this stage might be irreversible at trial.[4] This means that in particular with a view to modern technical devises of investigation, the pre-trial phase requires just as much attention as the trial phase.

Thus all five stages have their unique theme and are governed by different rules and principles, which will be explored in the following chapters. Before doing so however, we need to look at a special procedure which the ICCSt anticipates regarding questions of jurisdiction and admissibility. Despite the fact that these questions can become relevant at different stages of the procedure, they are preliminary questions. This is why I will discuss them in advance.

B. Preliminary Questions of Jurisdiction and Admissibility

It has already been emphasized that the independence of the Prosecutor is one of the most contentious and critical issues in the ICC structure.[5] Since a truly

[3] *See* K Ambos, 'Der EGMR und die Verfahrensrechte', 115 *ZStW* (2003) 583.

[4] C Nestler, 'European Defence in Trans-National Criminal Proceedings', in: B Schünemann (ed), *A Programme for European Criminal Justice* (Carl Heymanns 2006) 415, 423.

[5] *See* Chapter 4.

independent Prosecutor poses a threat to the principle of state sovereignty, the Member States have set up several hurdles and review procedures for the Prosecutor at the ICCSt.[6] In addition to the authorization needed for a *proprio motu* investigation from the Pre-Trial Chamber pursuant to Art. 15 ICCSt, questions concerning both admissibility and jurisdiction can be subjected to a preliminary ruling by the Pre-Trial Chamber, by virtue of Arts 18 and 19 ICCSt. Thus it might be said that the Prosecutor is under constant surveillance by Chambers and may be put under scrutiny by Member States. The need for such a procedure is part of the compromise that was agreed upon during the Rome Conference. Whereas the majority of States favoured a relatively independent Office of the Prosecutor, particularly regarding the power of the Office of the Prosecutor to investigate of its own accord, this political independence was counterbalanced by a constant judicial review.[7]

At this point a brief mention of terminology must be made. The Rome Statute refers to four different issues: jurisdiction (*see* Arts 5 (1) and 11 ICCSt), preconditions to the exercise of jurisdiction (Art. 12 ICCSt), exercise of jurisdiction (Art. 13 ICCSt), and admissibility (Art. 17 ICCSt). These elements compose a unique system, virtually unknown to national legal systems or any of the previous international criminal tribunals. Bringing a case to the ICC is thus more complex and multidimensional. Chronologically speaking, the test to be applied involves the following steps:

(1) Art. 13 ICCSt: at the very outset there must be a referral of the case to the ICC or a *proprio motu* situation; the following steps are triggered by this.
(2) Arts 5 (1), 11 ICCSt: does the case or situation involve a crime which falls within the jurisdiction of the ICC *ratione materiae* and *ratione temporis*?
(3) Art. 12 (2) ICCSt: was the alleged crime committed on the territory of a State Party, or is the alleged perpetrator a national of a State Party?
(4) Art. 17 ICCSt: admissibility issues.

Yet this chronology is not sustained in the structure of the Statute. Nevertheless, steps (1) to (3) concern jurisdictional issues, and only step (4) refers to admissibility.

Arts 18 and 19 ICCSt must be read in the light of the statute's ambivalence concerning the role of the Prosecutor, especially in relation to the pre-trial phase. Art. 18 ICCSt pertains to the issues of admissibility under Art. 17 ICCSt; that is, the principle of complementarity. In a sense it provides for a specific procedure for the safeguarding of the sovereignty aspects encompassed in and limited by the complementarity principle. Art. 19 ICCSt in contrast grants the participants in the proceedings, namely the accused or the suspect, the State,—if it is affected by the

[6] *See* eg, W Schabas, *An Introduction to the International Criminal Court* (4th edn, CUP 2011) 294.
[7] Triffterer/*Nsereko*, Art. 18 MN 1 and 2.

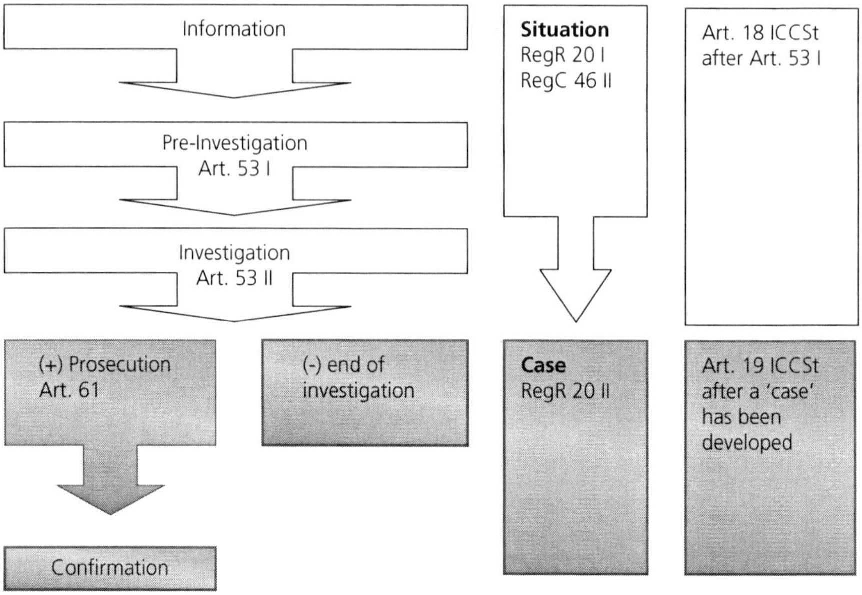

Figure 5.2 From information to confirmation

proceedings before the ICC—and the Prosecutor, the opportunity to raise issues of admissibility or jurisdictional before a Pre-Trial Chamber. Whereas Art. 18 ICCSt pertains solely to the question of admissibility of a situation with regard to the thresholds of Art. 17 ICCSt, Art. 19 ICCSt contains a general right of judicial review relating to both admissibility and jurisdiction in a case.[8] Although there is a certain overlap in the scope of their application, the two provisions will be looked at separately in the following.[9]

It should be noted also that the exact relationship between Arts 15, 18, and 19 ICCSt was not resolved at the Rome Conference due to time constraints; however it was agreed to keep these three different provisions separate.[10] Unfortunately, the RPE failed to solve the difficulties.[11] This must be kept in mind, when in the following we refer to the underlying rationale in order to explain the different procedural 'institutions' and try to solve structural deficiencies. In order to make sense of the chronology of the proceedings in the phase before the commencement of the trial, the following is an expansion of the chart presented at the beginning of this

[8] As to the differences of a 'situation' and a 'case', *see* Chapter 2, p 92.

[9] For a short comparison of Arts 18 and 19 ICCSt, *see* Triffterer/*Hall*, Art. 19 MN 6.

[10] J Lindenmann, 'The Rules of Procedure and Evidence on Jurisdiction and Admissibility', in: H Fischer, C Kreß, and S R Lüder (eds), *International and National Prosecution of Crimes under International Law* (Berlin Verlag 2001) 173, 178 *et subs.*

[11] *See* Triffterer/*Hall*, Art. 19 MN 4.

Part, which includes a 'third dimension' in order to integrate Arts 18 and 19 ICCSt in a 'linear' structure as attempted in Figure 5.2.[12]

I. Admissibility rulings pursuant to Art. 18 ICCSt

The provision of Art 18 ICCSt is concerned only with the relation between the ICC and States affected by the investigatory activities of the Prosecutor. Substantially the relationship between the ICC and the Member States is governed by Art. 17 ICCSt. The principle of complementarity contained in Art. 17 ICCSt grants the state priority regarding investigation and prosecution.[13] The safeguarding of this 'superior jurisdiction' at an early stage of the investigation process is one of the main aims of Art. 18 ICCSt.[14] On the other hand, the admissibility ruling can also have an effect of approving the investigation of the Prosecutor. This is because an independent judicial ruling will silence allegations of political manipulation and bias on the part of the Prosecutor.[15] At the same time Art. 18 ICCSt should also guarantee the efficiency of the complementarity principle. The superior jurisdiction of the Member States does not present an excuse for doing nothing. Indeed the procedure of Art. 18 ICCSt also gives the Prosecutor the right to supervise the national investigation and scrutinize the effectiveness of the Member State's organs.[16]

The judicial institutions ICTY and ICTR are of a special nature. As sub-organs of the Security Council they have been given the power to issue binding decisions on UN Member States.[17] Equally, the states are obliged to grant the Tribunals any assistance they need. The duty to cooperate is laid down in the Statutes, which provide for particular forms of cooperation. However, this list is not exhaustive and implies that the Tribunals have the power to decide the scope of the duty to cooperate in each particular case. Nevertheless, in practice, the Tribunals are often faced with great difficulties regarding the lack of a functioning system of cooperation, and have encountered many problems.[18]

[12] J Lindenmann, 'The Rules of Procedure and Evidence on Jurisdiction and Admissibility', in: H Fischer, C Kreß, S R Lüder (eds), *International and National Prosecution of Crimes under International Law* (Berlin Verlag 2001) 173, 177–80.

[13] M Benzing, 'The Complementarity Regime of the International Criminal Court: International Criminal Justice between State Sovereignty and the Fight against Impunity', 7 *Max Planck UNYB* (2003) 591, 594.

[14] Triffterer/*Nsereko*, Art. 18 MN 3.

[15] Ibid.

[16] Similarly Triffterer/*Nsereko*, Art. 18 MN 19.

[17] *See* Triffterer/*Nsereko*, Art. 18 MN 4; Boas/Bischoff/Reid/Taylor, *ICL III*, 107.

[18] *See* eg, R Bank, 'Cooperation with the International Criminal Tribunal for the Former Yugoslavia in the Production of Evidence', 4 *Max Planck UNYB* (2000) 233; D Stroh, 'State Cooperation with the International Criminal Tribunals for the Former Yugoslavia and for Rwanda', 5 *Max Planck UNYB* (2001) 249 and M Harmon and F Gaynor, 'Prosecuting Massive Crimes with Primitive Tools: Three Difficulties Encountered by Prosecutors in International Criminal Proceedings', 2 *JICJ* (2004) 403, 408 *et subs.*

As already stated, Art. 18 ICCSt is a procedural safeguard of the principle of complementary jurisdiction, which characterizes the relationship between the ICC and the Member States, and is laid down in Art. 17 ICCSt. Yet Art. 18 ICCSt does not cross-refer to Art. 17 ICCSt. The only connection to Art. 17 ICCSt can be found in the headings of Arts 17 and 18 ICCSt, which both use the word 'admissibility'. However, it is odd that Art. 18 ICCSt refers only to 'situations', whereas Art. 17 ICCSt refers to 'cases'. The provisions do not seem to match in this regard. In order to solve this anomaly it is suggested to interpret Art. 17 ICCSt as including 'situations' too. With regard to Art. 17 (1) (c) ICCSt, which refers to the double jeopardy provision in Art. 20 (3) ICCSt, such a wide interpretation would, however, be meaningless, as the *ne bis in idem* principle requires an individual person; that is, a 'case'.

1. *Scope and structure*

The Art. 18 ICCSt process is applicable only after the Prosecutor has decided to initiate an investigation according to Arts 13 (a), 53 (1) ICCSt or after the Pre-Trial Chamber has authorized the initiation of an investigation pursuant to Arts 13 (c), 15 (4) ICCSt.[19] It is thus, temporarily speaking, part of the investigation phase of the ICC procedure.[20] Yet it is impossible to name an exact chronology.[21] Whether or not the Prosecutor has already started a 'case' against an individual person is irrelevant. However, Art. 18 ICCSt is—according to its wording—only concerned with a 'situation' as such.[22] Following the decision to investigate, Art. 18 ICCSt sets down three stages, which may have to be undergone before the investigation can continue:[23] (1) notification, (2) request for deferral, and (3) decision to defer.

2. *Notification*

The Prosecutor must inform all State Parties and States which would normally exercise jurisdiction according to Art. 18 (1) ICCSt.[24] There are therefore three groups of States to be notified: State Parties, States which have jurisdiction and are State Parties, States which have jurisdiction and are not Parties to the Rome

[19] Security Council referrals according to Art. 13 (b) ICCSt do not trigger the Art. 18 mechanisms; *see* L Sadat, *The International Criminal Court and the Transformation of International Law: Justice for the New Millennium* (Transnational Publishers 2002) 123 *et subs.*

[20] The requirement that there needs to be a 'reasonable basis' is therefore only a determination of the temporal scope of application of Art. 18 ICCSt, and refers to the test in Art. 53 (1) ICCSt or Art. 15 (4) ICCSt. The Prosecutor must not decide again on the necessary 'basis' to prosecute. A different view is taken by Triffterer/*Nsereko*, Art. 18 MN 7, who attribute substantial value to the 'reasonable basis' requirement in Art. 18 (1) ICCSt. This seems detrimental to the efficiency of the proceedings and adds nothing to their normative framework.

[21] W Schabas, *An Introduction to the International Criminal Court* (4th edn, CUP 2011) 294, misinterprets the non-linear structure of the pre-trial phase in this regard, when he states, that the Prosecutor must fulfil the Arts 18 and 19 procedure before investigation can proceed.

[22] As to the differentiation between 'situation' and 'case', *see* Chapter 2, p 92.

[23] *See* also Boas/Bischoff/Reid/Taylor, *ICL III*, 89 *et subs.*

[24] W Schabas, *ICC* (OUP 2010) 356.

Statute.[25] The notification requirement thus fulfils three needs: (1) all Member States are informed as a matter of courtesy and in order to prepare for cooperation, if so required, (2) all State Parties which would normally exercise jurisdiction are given the opportunity to reflect on their interests to prosecute and exercise their superior jurisdiction,[26] and (3) all other states are informed as a matter of good faith, even if they cannot exercise any rights under the Rome Statute and cannot claim superior jurisdiction. In the cold light of day, however, the differentiation is unnecessary in most cases. As all states, member of the Rome Statute or not, can exercise jurisdiction under the principle of universality, the OTP should in principle simply inform them all.[27]

It is not quite clear, why such notification in general is or should be dispensable in the case of Art. 13 (b) ICCSt, (referral by the Security Council). Whereas one might take for granted that a Security Council referral is made public, the decision of the Prosecutor according to Art. 53 (1) ICCSt is not *per se* communicated to the public. Regulation 30 RegP foresees that the Office of the Prosecutor notifies the Security Council through the Secretary-General of the United Nations. Moreover, the Office of the Prosecutor should notify the State Parties and other States, which are affected by the investigation.[28] However, as has been made clear by looking at the aims of Art. 18 ICCSt, the notification of the Security Council is not required for the purpose of the Art. 18 ICCSt process, since a SC referral gives the ICC superior jurisdiction and overrides the complementarity requirements of Art. 17 ICCSt.

Notification is limited to information which is relevant for the question of complementary jurisdiction. Therefore the notification must state that the acts concerned constitute crimes according to Art. 5 ICCSt, and are thus relevant to an Art. 18 (2) ICCSt decision of the State (Rule 52 (1) RPE ICC). The information can be communicated to States on a confidential basis. According to Art. 18 (1) ICCSt, the Prosecutor may even limit the scope of information provided, if s/he considers this to be necessary for the protection of persons or evidence, or to prevent persons absconding. One can foresee that the option to limit the scope of information disclosed to states, which lies within the discretion of the Prosecutor, gives room for distrust and misunderstandings between the Office of the Prosecutor and the states concerned.

---

[25] This is controversial, as Art. 18 (1) ICCSt can also be read as being limited to State Parties 'and [particularly] those States…'; *see* Triffterer/*Nsereko*, Art. 18 MN 9, who is undecided on the issue. *See* also M Benzing, 'The Complementarity Regime of the International Criminal Court: International Criminal Justice between State Sovereignty and the Fight against Impunity', in 7 *Max Planck UNYB* (2003) 591, 622–4, arguing that states which are not party to the ICCSt need also be informed.

[26] *See* Triffterer/*Nsereko*, Art. 18 MN 8.

[27] Similarly W Schabas, *An Introduction to the International Criminal Court* (4th edn, CUP 2011) 295.

[28] Similarly A Cassese, *International Criminal Law* (2nd edn, OUP 2008) 399.

This conflict becomes even more apparent when considering the state's right to request more information under Rule 52 (2) RPE ICC. The lines of conflict form a triangle of interests: (1) adherence to the notion of state sovereignty, (2) ensuring the efficiency of the prosecution, and (3) the right of liberty and security of individual persons. As much as the ICC and the states concerned need to find an 'amicable understanding',[29] their interests, and the Prosecutor's interest to investigate must stand back, and the human rights of victims and witnesses must be given priority.

3. The request for deferral

Upon the receipt of notification pursuant to Art. 18 (1) ICCSt, a Member State which would have jurisdiction has several options and must react within a time period of one month. According to Art. 18 (2) ICCSt it can: (1) do nothing, which would allow the Prosecutor to investigate further; (2) inform the Prosecutor about national investigations which are ongoing or which will be initiated in due course,[30] yet desist from requesting deferral; or (3) inform the Prosecutor about ongoing or future investigations and request deferral of the ICC prosecution, in which case the state's request must be in writing and supported by substantial information concerning its investigatory efforts (Rule 53 RPE ICC). The Office of the Prosecutor may ask for further information.[31]

The State Party is free in its decision whether or not to request deferral. The complementarity principle according to Art. 17 ICCSt does not mean that the state must insist on its national jurisdiction. The State Party need not only refer a 'situation' to the ICC by virtue of Art. 13 (a) ICCSt; it can also—in the case of a referral by a different State Party or an *ex officio* investigation—desist from claiming superiority over the ICC. At this stage, the State Party does not waive the right to maintain its sovereignty, since at a later stage in the proceedings it may challenge the jurisdiction of the ICC or the admissibility of a 'case' by virtue of Art. 19 (2) (b) ICCSt.

4. Decision to defer

Should the State Party request the deferral of investigation, the Prosecutor has two options.

(1) The Prosecutor can comply with the request and defer to a state's investigation according to Art. 18 (2) ICCSt. In that case the Prosecutor may and indeed shall

[29] Triffterer/*Nsereko*, Art. 18 MN 11.

[30] The ICCSt does not say explicitly whether the investigation must be ongoing at present or whether future investigations would satisfy this requirement. Given the overall prevalence of the complementarity principle it is to be held that investigations which are to begin in the immediate future are comprised in Art. 18 (2) ICCSt; *see* also Triffterer/*Nsereko*, Art. 18 MN 14.

[31] J Lindenmann, 'The Rules of Procedure and Evidence on Jurisdiction and Admissibility', in: H Fischer, C Kreß, and S R Lüder (eds), *International and National Prosecution of Crimes under International Law* (Berlin Verlag 2001) 173, 185 (alleging reciprocity between OTP and the State according to Rules 52 and 53 RPE ICC, respectively).

request periodical information on the progress of the investigation from the State Party pursuant to Art. 18 (5) ICCSt. The deferral remains under the constant review of the Prosecutor and is re-evaluated every six months. In the case of a significant change in circumstances regarding the parameters of Art. 17 ICCSt, that is, unwillingness or inability to prosecute on the part of the State Party, the Prosecutor may rethink his decision to defer at any time and refer the question of admissibility to the Pre-Trial Chamber as described in option (2) below (*see* Rule 56 RPE ICC).

(2) The Prosecutor might also request a ruling from the Pre-Trial Chamber on the question of admissibility and ask the Chamber to authorize the investigation pursuant to Art. 18 (2) ICCSt.[32] The request must be in writing, supported by the necessary information regarding the reasons why the Prosecutor wishes to continue to investigate despite the State Party's submission to defer further investigations (Rule 54 RPE ICC). Once again, as a matter of courtesy, the State concerned must be notified of the request and of the main grounds supporting it (Rule 54 (2) RPE ICC). The Pre-Trial Chamber has the power to override the State's right to primacy. The parameters for this decision are not clearly spelt out in the Statute.[33] Yet the grounds for granting authority to further investigate must be connected to Art. 17 ICCSt, because, as stated above, Art. 18 ICCSt implements a procedure especially set down to give effect to the complementarity principle. Rule 55 (2) RPE ICC rightly draws this connection. Therefore the basic parameters are 'unwillingness' and 'inability' on the part of the State Party to properly investigate the 'situation'.

The procedure to be applied is a matter left to the Pre-Trial Chamber (Rule 55 (1) RPE ICC).[34] It may, for example, hold a hearing. If so, some standard rules apply. It is of the utmost importance that the State concerned is given the opportunity to present its views on the matter.[35] It would be a moot point to ask whether or not the procedure to be adopted needs to be contentious or whether an *ex parte* procedure would satisfy the requirements. In any case the Pre-Trial Chamber may hold a hearing (Rule 55 (1) RPE ICC). What must be borne in mind is the fact that the question of maintaining state sovereignty is a recurring theme within the Rome Statute and that the acceptability of the ICC procedure on the part of the Member States is essential for the success of this Court. Thus, the denial of a request for deferral and the authorization of an investigation against

---

[32] M Benzing, 'The Complementarity Regime of the International Criminal Court: International Criminal Justice between State Sovereignty and the Fight against Impunity', 7 *Max Planck UNYB* (2003) 591, 625.

[33] *See* Triffterer/*Nsereko*, Art. 18 MN 15 *et subs.*, who submits that the grounds must be 'substantial and cogent' without further elaborating.

[34] J Lindenmann, 'The Rules of Procedure and Evidence on Jurisdiction and Admissibility', in: H Fischer, C Kreß, and S R Lüder (eds), *International and National Prosecution of Crimes under International Law* (Berlin Verlag 2001) 173, 185 *et subs.*

[35] Rightly stated by Triffterer/*Nsereko*, Art. 18 MN 18.

the declared intention of a state carries with it a stigma for the state of being unwilling or, for that matter, unable to carry out a proper investigation. The state concerned is thereby publicly reprimanded for not cooperating, either because it no longer supports the aims of the Rome Statute and is therefore unwilling to investigate, or because its organs are powerless and it is close to being classified a 'failed state'.

In any event, the state that requested the deferral as well as the Prosecutor must be informed of the decision. If the Prosecutor's request is granted, s/he may continue investigating the 'situation'. Should the Pre-Trial Chamber deny authorization, the 'situation' is deferred to the state and the investigation of the ICC Prosecutor is terminated. Both State and Prosecutor have the right to appeal against the decision of the Pre-Trial Chamber to the Appeals Chamber by virtue of Art. 18 (4) ICCSt and Art. 82 (1) (a) ICCSt. An appeal must be filed within five days after notification of the decision (Rule 154 (1) RPE ICC). This right to appeal on the side of a State Party emphasizes the importance of the decision, as described above. It seems unnecessary to give the Prosecutor the same right to appeal, as he or she cannot claim to be aggrieved by the Pre-Trial Chamber's decision. This right to appeal is part of a number of interlocutory appeals which fall within the scope of Art. 82 ICCSt. These will be looked at in detail later (*see* Chapter 9 following).

5. *Investigative powers*

The procedure regarding preliminary rulings on admissibility issues can have a detrimental effect on the Prosecutor's investigation. Even where, once the investigation has begun in accordance with Art. 53 (1) or Art. 15 (4) ICCSt, the Prosecutor has been able to utilize all the powers available (discussed below),[36] these powers are partially suspended the moment the Pre-Trial Chamber is asked to authorize the investigation pursuant to Art. 18 (2) ICCSt or the Prosecutor has deferred the investigation to a state. This is a logical consequence flowing from the importance of the notion of state sovereignty. Art. 18 (6) ICCSt nevertheless gives special investigatory means to the Prosecutor during this period. Exceptionally, the Pre-Trial Chamber may authorize the Prosecutor to pursue necessary investigative steps in two alternative circumstances concerning the preservation of important evidence: (1) where there is a unique opportunity to obtain such evidence, or (2) where there is a significant risk that the evidence may not be subsequently available. Both cases display an aspect of gravity—the evidence must be important for the investigation— and an aspect of urgency—the evidence is available for a short period of time and might later be obtainable only under difficult circumstances or indeed might be destroyed altogether. Given the urgency of the measure, it is necessary for

[36] *See* Chapter 6, p 251.

the Pre-Trial Chamber to adopt an *ex parte* and *in camera* procedure and rule on an expedited basis (Rule 57 RPE ICC).[37]

II. Preliminary rulings on jurisdiction

Art. 19 ICCSt contains a number of different issues and procedures. Its aim is to guarantee the adherence to both admissibility and jurisdictional prerequisites by the ICC. In substance, the provision's scope is much wider than that of Art. 18 ICCSt which serves, as discussed above, as a procedural safeguard for the principle of complementarity immediately after an investigation has been opened by the Prosecutor.[38] Principally Art. 19 ICCSt governs two separate issues: (a) Art. 19 (1) ICCSt lays down the general rule that the Court has the right and the obligation to analyse jurisdictional questions and admissibility issues at all time, and (b) Art. 19 (2) and (3) ICCSt gives a right to individuals, states, and the Prosecutor to complain to the Court alleging a lack of jurisdiction or inadmissibility of a 'case'.[39]

On a general basis, it is necessary to clarify the standing of the UN Security Council vis-à-vis questions of jurisdiction and admissibility. It has already been stated that the trigger mechanism of Art. 13 (b) ICCSt overrides the territoriality principle and personality principle in Art. 12 ICCSt. The Security Council can exercise its right to intervene judicially, on the basis of Chapter VII of the UN Charter, on a global level and derogate state sovereignty in this regard. But does this also mean that the principle of complementarity no longer applies? That could very well be the case. Art. 18 ICCSt also suggests that admissibility issues are only relevant to State referrals or *proprio motu* initiatives.[40] Nonetheless, the ICC has acted differently. Not only has the Prosecutor stated at several points in the Darfur case, which was referred to the ICC by the UN Security Council, that he would apply Art. 17 ICCSt,[41] indeed Pre-Trial Chamber I has in the arrest-warrant decision concerning the situation in Darfur repeatedly ruled on admissibility issues.[42] So far the Security Council has not objected to this practice.[43]

---

[37] *See* also J Lindenmann, 'The Rules of Procedure and Evidence on Jurisdiction and Admissibility', in: H Fischer, C Kreß, and S R Lüder (eds), *International and National Prosecution of Crimes under International Law* (Berlin Verlag 2001) 173, 186.

[38] *See* Boas/Bischoff/Reid/Taylor, *ICL III*, 91.

[39] J Lindenmann, 'The Rules of Procedure and Evidence on Jurisdiction and Admissibility', in: H Fischer, C Kreß and S R Lüder (eds), *International and National Prosecution of Crimes under International Law* (Berlin Verlag 2001) 173, 186 *et subs.*

[40] *See* Triffterer/*Williams/Schabas*, Art. 13 MN 16.

[41] *See* the Report of the ICC Prosecutor to the UN SC, UN Doc. S/PV.5216, p 2; UN Doc. S/PV.5321, p 3; UN Doc. S/PV.5459, p 4; UN Doc. S/PV.5589, p 2.

[42] *See* ICC *Prosecutur v Harun et al.*, PTC I, ICC-02/05-01/07-2, 27 April 2007, Warrant of Arrest for Ahmad Harun, p 2.

[43] Triffterer/*Williams/Schabas*, Art. 13 MN 16.

1. The right and duty to determine its own competence

Determining *ex officio* its own competence is an inherent right of every tribunal. Any court will look into jurisdictional matters before concerning itself with the merits of the case. It will do so simply because it is the easiest way to reduce its workload. The operative equation is rather simple: if I can deny jurisdiction, the case is off my desk and the burden rests on someone else's shoulders. It is therefore not surprising that Art. 19 (1) ICCSt declares that the ICC may rule on jurisdiction and determine admissibility.

It is, however, important to note that the Nuremberg IMT did not allow challenges on jurisdictional issues. 'The jurisdiction of the Tribunal is defined in the Agreement and Charter, and the crimes coming within the jurisdiction of the Tribunal, for which there shall be individual responsibility, are set out in Article 6. The law of the Charter is decisive, and binding upon the Tribunal.'[44]

Such a ruling is understandable considering the situation at hand, where the Allied powers had decided to try the most prominent Nazi war criminals in a joint effort.[45] Each individual state would otherwise have had the power to prosecute those war criminals in its hands by itself.[46] The question of jurisdiction is from this viewpoint relatively straightforward. That, however, did not prevent the defence lawyers from objecting to the jurisdiction of the IMT.[47]

The ICTY adopted a different view. The Appeals Chamber recognized the necessity to determine the Tribunal's jurisdiction and even went a step further by scrutinizing the legitimacy of its own legal basis. It felt the necessity to do so in the tradition of international (arbitration) tribunals, which as a matter of fact are attributed with the so-called *compétence de la compétence*.[48] The Appeals Chamber thus moved onto slippery grounds, as it had to question the legitimacy of a Security Council resolution, which prior to the decision was considered sacrosanct.[49]

The ICC jurisdictional regime is complex. This is partly due to the fact that it is a permanent institution, which needs to be well equipped for dealing with different situations. The drafter of the Rome Statute inserted a rather abstract regulation in order to cover future cases. Furthermore, the ICC's authority stems from

---

44 IMT Nuremberg Vol 1, 218.

45 C Safferling, *Internationales Strafrecht* (Springer 2011), § 4 MN 26 *et subs*. The agreement to conduct war crimes trials by common effort was reached in the Moscow Declaration of 1 November 1943 between the USA, the UK, and the Soviet Union.

46 IMT Protocol I, 218; *see* also A Zimmermann, 'Das juristische Erbe von Nürnberg', in: H Reginbogin and C Safferling (eds), *The Nuremberg Trials: International Criminal Law since 1945* (Saur 2006) 247, 248.

47 *See* C Safferling and P Graebke, 'Strafverteidigung im Nürnberger Hauptkriegsverbrecherprozess: Strategien und Wirkungen', 123 *ZStW* (2011) 47.

48 ICTY *Prosecutor v Tadić*, AC, IT-94-1-A, 2 October 1995, Decision on the Defence Motion for Interlocutory Appeal on Jurisdiction, para 18, 19.

49 ICJ *Certain Expenses of the United Nations*, advisory opinion of 20 July 1962, Rep. 62, p 151.

the Rome Statute; that is, an international convention. It is thus built on horizontal cooperation and not on a vertical hierarchy. It follows that the Court itself must determine whether it has jurisdiction, as the State Parties have agreed upon in drafting the Statute. It has become clear that jurisdictional issues at the ICC are always related to state sovereignty and must thus be treated with caution.

The terminological differentiation between jurisdiction and admissibility is reproduced in Art. 19 (1) ICCSt. The Statute establishes a split system: whereas the Court is obliged to scrutinize the question of jurisdiction, there is no mandatory ruling on admissibility.[50] This structure mirrors sovereignty issues in a rather subtle way. If the Court takes on a case where it does not have jurisdiction or cannot exercise jurisdiction, it not only violates the Statute, but also acts *ultra vires*, usurping power to the detriment of States, both Member and non-Member.

Should the Court in contrast proceed with an investigation or prosecution in disregard of Art. 17 ICCSt, it does not exceed its powers as such. Moreover, Art. 17 ICCSt is formulated in a negative way, that is, the case must be declared 'inadmissible', which means *e contrario* that the case in principle is admissible as soon as jurisdictional questions have been answered in the positive. The complementarity principle can be understood as a special legal position of the State Party at the ICC, which must be invoked in order for the ICC to rest, or for that matter, defer further proceedings.[51] Should the State not intervene by exercising its rights according to Art. 18 or 19 ICCSt, it is at the Court's discretion whether or not to proceed with the case.

The question remains, when does the Court have to rule on jurisdiction and admissibility issues pursuant to Art. 19 (1) ICCSt? The provision does not shed much light on this question. The general structure of the Court, however, supposes that the Chambers are not activated without being specifically asked to become active. The Chambers are not equipped with an overall supervisory power which would enable them to step into any ongoing proceeding at any time. A ruling under Art. 19 (1) ICCSt must therefore be attached to a procedure which is anticipated by the Statute. There are two possibilities of how the 'case' can be 'brought before the Court': 'If the Prosecutor requests an arrest warrant by virtue of Art. 58 ICCSt or indeed any other investigatory measure from the Pre-Trial Chamber, this body will in its decision on the authorization of the measure express its satisfaction regarding jurisdiction and—at its discretion—determine the admissibility of the case.'

This is how the arrest warrants concerning Uganda were handled. The Prosecutor applied for the issuance of arrest warrants against Joseph Kony and others without

[50] Triffterer/*Hall*, Art. 19 MN 4.

[51] This is also the outcome of the Appeals Chamber's decision in the case against Katanga and Chui, *see* ICC *Prosecutor v Katanga and Chui*, AC, ICC-01/04-01/07-1497 (OA 8), 25 September 2009, Judgment on the Appeal of Mr. Germain Katanga against the Oral Decision of Trial Chamber II of 12 June 2009 on the Admissibility of the Case, para 82.

claiming the case to be admissible. The Prosecutor may by virtue of Art. 19 (3) ICCSt request a ruling on jurisdiction or admissibility. If, however, the Prosecutor does not desire a ruling on the matter s/he does not need to elaborate on the issue. The Pre-Trial Chamber II stated in its arrest warrant, issued on 8 July 2005 as amended on 27 September 2005, that it was satisfied that the jurisdictional requirements were met and that the case was admissible.[52] In doing so it referred to the application, the evidence, and other information presented by the Prosecutor, without going into further detail.[53]

The text reads as follows: 'BEING SATISFIED that, on the basis of the application, the evidence and other information submitted by the Prosecutor, and without prejudice to subsequent determination, the case against NAME falls within the jurisdiction of the Court and appears to be admissible.'

Interestingly, Pre-Trial Chamber I in the situation in Darfur does not use the same phrasing. It did not state that it was 'satisfied', but that 'it considered the case to fall within the jurisdiction of the Court and to be admissible'.[54] Pre-Trial Chamber III uses almost identical wording in the warrant of arrest against Bemba.[55]

Most notably Pre-Trial Chamber I in the case against Ntaganda made explicit reference to Art. 19 (1) and did not mention admissibility expressly.[56] This, with all due respect, seems to be the correct approach. A ruling on the admissibility is unnecessary. In any case the Chamber does not need to be 'satisfied' that the case would be admissible. 'The question of jurisdiction and admissibility of a case can be singled out by approaching the Court directly by challenging the jurisdiction of the Court or the admissibility of the case pursuant to Art. 19 (2) ICCSt.'

This brings us to the next issue:

2. Challenges before the Court

Art. 19 (2) and (3) ICCSt make provision for challenging admissibility and jurisdiction[57] and specify the possible claimants. In general, individual persons and states concerned have the right to challenge these issues. States are also not precluded

[52] The initial indictment against Kony *et al.*, of 8 July 2005 (Warrant of Arrest for Joseph Kony) was amended by ICC *Situation in Uganda*, PTC II, ICC-02/04-01/05-53, 27 September 2005, Warrant of Arrest for Joseph Kony Issued on 8 July 2005 as Amended on 27 September 2005, para 38.

[53] *See* Triffterer/*Hall*, Art. 19 MN 4.

[54] *See* ICC *Prosecutor v Harun et al.*, PTC I, ICC-02/05-01/07-2, 27 April 2007, Warrant of Arrest for Ahmad Harun, p 2.

[55] ICC *Prosecutor v Bemba*, PTC III, ICC-01/05-01/08-1-tENG, 23 May 2003, Warrant of Arrest for Jean-Pierre Bemba Gombo, para 8.

[56] ICC *Prosecutor v Ntaganda*, PTC I, ICC-01/04-02/06-2-US-tEN, 22 August 2006, Warrant of Arrest, p 2.

[57] It is unclear why the order in Art. 19 (2) ICCSt is backwards as compared to Art. 19 (1) ICCSt. As has been argued above, the chronological order would put jurisdictional questions at the outset and admissibility, according to Art. 17 ICCSt, at the end of the overall test.

from challenging jurisdiction and/or admissibility, even if they have already complained against a ruling by the Pre-Trial Chamber under Art. 18 ICCSt, as is noted by Art. 18 (7) ICCSt.[58] The Prosecutor may also address the Court and ask for a ruling, although strictly speaking, s/he is not 'challenging' jurisdiction or admissibility, since s/he is the one who desires a prosecution and naturally would not attack the process started before the ICC. Whereas the individual and the State desire a negative ruling, the Prosecutor seeks support in the Chamber's decision, to enable him or her to continue with the investigation or prosecution. The Statute takes note of these differences and uses different terminology: whereas the individual and the state have the 'right to challenge' according to Art. 19 (2) ICCSt, the Prosecutor may 'seek a ruling' according to Art. 19 (3) ICCSt. Despite these differences the same procedure applies to both Art. 19 (2) and (3) ICCSt. It is thus logical and consistent that the RPE treat both triggers alike (*see* Rule 58 RPE ICC).

a. The claimants Art. 19 (2) ICCSt specifies three different claimants and Art. 19 (3) ICCSt adds one more:

(a) the accused or a person for whom an arrest warrant or a summons to appear has been issued under Art. 58 ICCSt;

(b) a State which has jurisdiction over the case;

(c) a State in the sense of Art. 12 ICCSt; and

(d) the Prosecutor.

(a) An individual can only complain to the ICC if s/he is personally affected by the proceedings before the ICC in a specific way. The Statute uses the term 'accused', which is defined in the Statute and Rules as the person against whom charges have been confirmed.[59] The trial against such a person will be opened soon, and s/he is put into a position to question jurisdiction and admissibility of the case against her or him. However, the right to complain arises at an even earlier stage: The person against whom a warrant or a summons has been issued under Art. 58 ICCSt can from this point on request a ruling on jurisdiction and admissibility concerning his or her case. In the spirit of the Statute, the arrest warrant or the summons to appear represent the moment at which the person concerned, in a sense, loses his or her procedural innocence. From this moment on s/he is publicly identified as an alleged perpetrator and is made both the object and subject of the proceedings. S/he is an object because s/he can be arrested, transferred to the Court, and

[58] This provision can only be declaratory in nature. As has been seen above, Arts 18 and 19 ICCSt refer to different circumstances despite some similarities. The questions arising under Art. 19 ICCSt referring to a specific case will not equal questions regarding admissibility of a situation under Art. 18 ICCSt. Therefore facts submitted under an Art. 19 proceeding will always be 'additional' and 'significant', as the point of reference is different compared to the Art. 18 proceeding. Also the 'circumstances' have changed significantly as an individual person ('case') is now in issue.

[59] As to the terminology, *see* Chapter 4, p 185 and Chapter 7, p 317.

questioned by the investigators. S/he is a subject because s/he is given certain rights to influence the outcome of the proceedings. One of the rights granted to him or her is the right to request a ruling on the jurisdiction and the admissibility of the case against him or her before the ICC.

No other individual can ask for a jurisdiction ruling. Complaints of persons who are affected by other investigatory measures are not permissible at the ICC. Such persons can only submit information to the Court on the basis that the Chamber will take this information into account when considering jurisdiction and admissibility issues under Art. 19 (1) ICCSt.[60]

(b) A State, which has jurisdiction over the 'case' can complain to the Court, but only on one ground, namely that Art. 17 ICCSt would be violated, because the State itself is investigating or prosecuting this very case or has already investigated or prosecuted.[61] The State is thus restricted to a complaint concerning admissibility issues.[62] According to the wording of Art. 19 (2) ICCSt this right is not merely reserved for State Parties. Since allegedly all crimes under Art. 5 ICCSt can be prosecuted on the basis of universal jurisdiction under international law,[63] virtually any State can exercise the right under Art. 19 (2) ICCSt.[64] It must be noted that admissibility issues do not arise if the Security Council has referred the situation to the ICC under Art. 13 (b) ICCSt.

The relationship between a State referral pursuant to Art. 13 (a) ICCSt and the right to complain under Art. 19 (2) (b) ICCSt is questionable. Can a State, which has referred a situation, complain on the grounds of Art. 19 (2) ICCSt? The answer is 'yes, it can', for at least two reasons. First, the State refers a 'situation', whereas the admissibility challenge relates to a 'case'. Second, the State does not waive its original right to investigate and prosecute international crimes just because the ICC's jurisdiction is triggered by virtue of Art. 13 (a) ICCSt. It would be absurd to halt all national proceedings, not knowing whether, to what extent, and against whom the Prosecutor at the ICC will develop a 'case'. In that sense the complaining State does not have to prove that circumstances have changed since the referral under Art. 13 (a) ICCSt.[65] It is sufficient to show that the national authorities are fit to proceed in the particular 'case', notwithstanding the general situation referral.

(c) Art. 12 States can complain to the ICC without the restrictions regarding admissibility contained in (2) (b) above. Yet, as Art. 12 ICCSt does not apply to

---

[60] Triffterer/*Hall*, Art. 19 MN 12.

[61] Oddly, the 'gravity' requirement under Art. 17 (1) (d) ICCSt is excluded; *see* J Holmes, 'The Principle of Complementarity', in: R Lee, *The International Criminal Court: The Making of the Rome Statute* (Kluwer Law International 1999) 41, 67.

[62] W Schabas, *ICC* (OUP 2010) 368 considers this to be 'illogical'.

[63] As to the principle of universality, *see* Chapter 2, p 84.

[64] This has been disputed on the Rome Conference, W Schabas, *ICC* (OUP 2010) 363 *et subs.*

[65] This is alleged by Triffterer/*Hall*, Art. 19 MN 14.

Security Council referrals of 'situations' to the ICC, the right to complain under this provision only arises in cases of State referrals or *proprio motu* intitiatives.[66]

The following States have the right to complain. (1) A State Party on the territory or on board a vessel or aircraft of which the conduct in question occurred. (2) A State Party of which the accused is a national. (3) A non-State Party on the territory or on board a vessel or aircraft of which the conduct in question occurred, that has accepted jurisdiction under Art. 12 (3) ICCSt. (4) A non-State Party of which the accused is a national that has accepted jurisdiction under Art. 12 (3) ICCSt.

Since Art. 12 (2) (b) ICCSt only refers to the 'person accused', it can be said that a State complaint can only be brought forward on the grounds of the active personality principle. Thus the earliest point at which the complaint may be brought would be the moment the charges have been confirmed.[67] Prior to this, a State would be restricted to bringing a claim under Art. 19 (2) (b) ICCSt on the grounds that it is investigating or prosecuting the suspect itself. To avoid this anomaly, a broader interpretation of Art. 12 (2) (b) ICCSt is suggested. Regarding the issue of jurisdiction, it is necessary to encompass not only the accused person *strictu sensu*, but any person who is suspected to have committed a crime. In the spirit of the Statute, this would be the person described by Art. 19 (2) (a) ICCSt; that is, a person against who an arrest warrant or a summons to appear has been issued under Art. 58 (1) ICCSt.

(d) Lastly, the Prosecutor can call for a ruling on admissibility and jurisdiction by virtue of Art. 19 (3) ICCSt. As said above, in contrast to an individual's or a State's complaint, the application of the Prosecutor seeks a ruling of the Court supporting his or her work. Even if Art. 19 (3) ICCSt does not explicitly refer to a 'case', it would be erroneous to widen the scope to include 'situations'.[68] There are two reasons for this: first the heading of Art. 19 ICCSt clearly refers to 'cases' only; second, there is no need for clarification regarding 'situations', as the procedure of Art. 18 ICCSt gives sufficient clarity concerning the admissibility of 'situations' as such.

A ruling under Art. 19 (3) ICCSt, however, does not give the Prosecutor security regarding questions of jurisdiction and admissibility. Subsequent challenges under Art. 19 (2) ICCSt are still admissible and are only limited in quantity through Art. 19 (4) ICCSt, which states that each individual or State can apply for a ruling only once. In practice, however, a positive ruling on the application of the Prosecutor will have an effect on future challenges. Should an individual or a State not be in a position to support his or her challenge by way of new information, which sheds a different light upon the case, the Chamber is unlikely to change its view.[69]

---

[66] Triffterer/*Hall*, Art. 19 MN 15.

[67] Ibid, Art. 19 MN 15.

[68] Ibid, Art. 19 MN 19 expresses a different view on this issue. In any case, the Prosecutor has until now not made use of this claim.

[69] Rightly observed by Triffterer/*Hall* Ibid.

The second sentence of Art. 19 (3) ICCSt includes another interesting provision, under which the Prosecutor might be assisted by helpful allies, who can submit their observations in order to support his or her case. These allies consist of those persons or organizations which have passed on information to the Prosecutor in accordance with Art. 13 (c) ICCSt, and of victims. Art. 19 (3) ICCSt does not provide 'informants' or victims a right to apply for a ruling on jurisdiction or admissibility, yet it gives them a standing before the Court in a more indirect way.

b. The time frame It has already been stated that Art. 19 ICCSt only comes into play after the Prosecutor has developed a 'case' out of a 'situation'. Yet questions remain: how long can a lack of jurisdiction or admissibility be claimed, and is there a point in time after which a challenge is precluded?

The latest possible opportunity to bring a challenge under Art. 19 ICCSt is specified in Art. 19 (4) ICCSt: the start of trial. *De facto* this means the complaint must be brought before or at the confirmation hearing, as the trial commences with the referral of the case to the Trial Chamber pursuant to Rule 130 RPE ICC.[70] After that, the accused needs to request leave from the Trial Chamber to file the challenge.[71] At the confirmation hearing, the Trial Chamber collects all challenges and reviews all information that has been brought before it concerning jurisdiction and admissibility (*see* Art. 19 (6) ICCSt). The Chamber then reaches a decision on these issues before looking into the merits of the case (*see* Rule 58 RPE ICC). Any other approach would lead to an unjustified delay of the proceedings.

It seems that there is a different time requirement for States. According to Art. 19 (5) ICCSt State claimants must challenge at the earliest opportunity. This is an expression of the general notion of 'good faith' in international law. Failure to follow this rule has no effect on the claim itself, unless it is brought forward with the obvious intention to discredit the ICC proceedings. Only then could the Court reject a challenge as an 'abuse of power'.[72] The untimely submission of the challenge does

[70] The Trial Chamber in the case against *Katanga and Chui* found in an *obiter dictum*, that the time in Art. 19 (4) ICCSt referred to Rule 130 RPE ICC and considered the moment the case is referred to the Trial Chamber as decisive; *see* ICC *Prosecutor v Katanga and Chui*, TC II, ICC-01/04-01/07-1213-tENG, 16 June 2009, Reasons for the Oral Decision on the Motion Challenging the Admissibility of the Case (Article 19 of the Statute), para 56; the question was left open on appeal: ICC *Prosecutor v Katanga and Chui*, AC, ICC-01/04-01/07-1497 (OA 8), 25 September 2009, Judgment on the Appeal of Mr Germain Katanga against the Oral Decision of Trial Chamber II of 12 June 2009 on the Admissibility of the Case, para 36–8.

[71] Boas/Bischoff/Reid/Taylor, *ICL III*, 92. In the *Katanga and Chui* case the Trial Chamber nevertheless examined the challenged on the merits as the time limit had been unclear to the applicant, *see* ICC *Prosecutor v Katanga and Chui*, TC II, ICC-01/04-01/07-1213-tENG, 16 June 2009, Reasons for the Oral Decision on the Motion Challenging the Admissibility of the Case (Article 19 of the Statute), para 56–8.

[72] The general principle of 'good faith' also applies to procedural issues, in particular to those who are involved in the proceedings on a professional basis. However, it does not apply to the detriment of the accused. *See* in general H Kudlich, *Strafprozess und allgemeines Missbrauchsverbot* (Duncker & Humblot 1998) 21.

not constitute a ground as such for rejecting the claim as some authors assert,[73] since such a rejection would be unfeasible for several reasons: Firstly, it is extremely difficult to set a timeline and to pinpoint a date after which State challenges may no longer be brought. This is due to the tremendously complex pre-trial structure of the Rome Statute as well as the fact that admissibility issues might arise at a later point. Secondly, the State can—to a certain extent—rely on the competence of the Court in fulfilling its obligation under Art. 19 (1) ICCSt.

The right to bring a claim under Art. 19 ICCSt is further limited by quantity. According to Art. 19 (4) ICCSt both individuals and States may each bring a challenge only once.

Both the time and quantity restrictions on the right to challenge aim at speeding up the process and promoting the efficiency of the procedure. Yet the principle of efficiency must to be balanced against the rights of the suspect or accused. Thus Art. 19 (4) ICCSt provides for exceptions regarding both the time limit and the quantity restriction. Under exceptional circumstances the Court may grant leave for a second challenge or a challenge brought after the commencement of the trial. Neither Statute nor RPE elaborate on the exceptional circumstances which would justify a further or belated claim. The claimant will have to prove that the claim is based on new information or evidence which was not available before.[74] In any case, the Court will have to take heed of not only the failures, but also the interests, in particular those of the accused, who has a right to defend him or herself with all legitimate means and has a right to a trial without undue delay.

Notwithstanding the formalities regarding a possible second or belated claim challenging jurisdiction and admissibility, it must be borne in mind that according to Art. 19 (1) ICCSt, the Court is under a general obligation to satisfy itself, that it has jurisdiction at all times.[75] Thus, even if the Court receives information negating jurisdiction or admissibility after the commencement of the trial, and even if the Court has already granted leave to a second challenge, it would still have to reconsider the questions of jurisdiction and admissibility for a third or fourth time. The same is true, even where the proceedings are nearing an end. This is because the ICC, as indeed any court in the world, lacks the power to consider a case over which it has no jurisdiction.

c. Procedure Art. 19 (6) ICCSt and Rule 60 RPE ICC specify which Chamber has the competence to deal with the challenge. Prior to the confirmation of the charges the Pre-Trial Chamber is responsible for deciding the matter. Thereafter the Trial Chamber is competent to hear jurisdiction issues.[76] In between the confirmation of charges and the constitution of a Trial Chamber, the application

[73] This is the view of Triffterer/*Hall*, Art. 19 MN 24.
[74] Ibid, Art. 19 MN 22.
[75] *See* ibid, Art. 19 MN 23.
[76] Boas/Bischoff/Reid/Taylor, *ICL III*, 92.

must be addressed to the Presidency, which will refer the case to the relevant Chamber as soon as it is constituted.

As regards the procedure to be adopted, the competent Chamber is free to act as it deems appropriate (Rule 58 RPE ICC).[77] Notwithstanding this discretion, as a minimum standard for a judicial procedure, all persons and institutions which are affected by the decision on jurisdiction and admissibility, namely the suspect or accused person, the State(s) concerned, and the Prosecutor, must be informed and must be given the opportunity to express their views (Rule 58 RPE ICC). A hearing may be held and the challenges might be joined, which seems sensible in respect of promoting the efficiency of the procedure.

The Statute, in Art. 19 (3) sentence 2 ICCSt, grants a special right to those who have referred the situation pursuant to Art. 13 ICCSt and victims who have already communicated with the Court regarding the case, or their legal representatives to submit observations. Rule 59 RPE ICC places the Registrar under a duty to inform these people. Their submissions may only be in writing. This means that if a hearing is held, neither a victim nor any 'informant' is permitted to participate in that hearing. Further, the Chamber might set a time limit for these submissions, as it sees appropriate.

The decision of the competent Chamber can be appealed, by virtue of Art. 19 (6) and Art. 82 ICCSt. The process of the interlocutory appeal will be explained below in the chapter on the procedure before the Appeals Chamber.[78]

In addition the Prosecutor can file a re-application pursuant to Art. 19 (10) ICCSt and Rule 62 RPE ICC regarding the admissibility of the 'case'.[79] The request goes to the judge *a quo*, that is, the Chamber that made the latest ruling on admissibility (Rule 62 (1) RPE ICC). The hurdle to be passed by the Prosecutor in order to reapply is rather high. He must be 'fully satisfied' that the finding of the Chamber in the previous decision is no longer valid, as new facts have arisen and bring the 'case' into new light.[80]

3. Powers of the Prosecutor

As the ICC Statute provides a separate procedure regarding jurisdiction and admissibility after the investigation of a 'case' has begun, it produces a rather serious

---

[77] J Lindenmann, 'The Rules of Procedure and Evidence on Jurisdiction and Admissibility', in: H Fischer, C Kreß, and S R Lüder (eds), *International and National Prosecution of Crimes under International Law* (Berlin Verlag 2001) 173, 187.

[78] *See* Chapter 9, p 542.

[79] Jurisdictional question are not included here. Triffterer/*Hall*, Art. 19 MN 37 alleges that this was an oversight in the drafting process. However, there is no expansion in the RPE either, and it seems hard to believe that the same mistake was made twice.

[80] ICC *Prosecutor v Katanga and Chui*, AC, ICC-01/04-01/07-1497 (OA 8), 25 September 2009, Judgment on the Appeal of Mr Germain Katanga against the Oral Decision of Trial Chamber II of 12 June 2009 on the Admissibility of the Case, para 56.

conflict with the powers of the Prosecutor. Looking at the possible outcome of such proceedings, the question arises, whether the status of the Prosecutor is affected and if so, to what extent.

A most common effect attributed to a legal remedy in general is its suspensive effect, that is, the case rests until the court has ruled upon the preliminary issue. Whereas the case as such is halted, preliminary proceedings do not render all measures taken prior to the submission of the claim, invalid.[81] On the contrary, the measures imposed and the results thereby archived will be of relevance and need to be considered when deciding the preliminary question.

As long as the case is suspended, however, no new measure can be implemented, unless special authorization has been granted. When deciding on such special authorization the procedural situation needs to be taken into consideration. Since at this point it is unclear whether the case can be continued at all, only those measures which do not produce irreversible results are legitimate.

The Rome Statute softens the suspensive effect as follows: as a general guideline, it states that the validity of the measures taken by the Prosecutor prior to the challenge is not touched upon (Art. 19 (9) ICCSt). This is of tremendous importance, as otherwise an arrested suspect might have to be released, which would endanger the entire prosecution. Equally, the warrant of arrest or a summons to appear remains valid. Otherwise an uncooperative State could undermine the execution of a warrant by simply challenging jurisdiction and admissibility.[82]

Yet according to Art. 19 (7) ICCSt the further investigation of the 'case' is suspended during the review procedure. It must be noted that this is only the case where a State complains under Art. 19 (2) (b) and (c). It is questionable why Art. 19 (7) refers explicitly to a determination according to Art. 17 ICCSt. This, however, does not mean that the case is not suspended if the State challenges only the jurisdiction of the Court and does not challenge admissibility at the same time, as suggested by *Hall*.[83] The case is halted in both cases; yet it can only be continued, if the Court declares the case admissible under Art. 17 ICCSt.

[81] For the effect on the pre-trial detention of the accused *see* ICC *Prosecutor v Lubanga*, TC I, ICC-01/04–01/06-1418, 2 July 2008, Decision on the Release of Thomas Lubanga Dyilo; as well as ICC *Prosecutor v Lubanga*, AC, ICC-01/04–01/06-1444, 22 July 2008, Reasons for the Decision on the Request of the Prosecutor for Suspensive Effect of his Appeal against the 'Decision on the Release of Thomas Lubanga Dyilo' and ICC *Prosecutor v Lubanga*, AC, ICC-01/04-01/06-1487, 21 October 2008, Judgment on the Appeal of the Prosecutor against the Decision of Trial Chamber I entitled 'Decision on the Release of Thomas Lubanga Dyilo'. Also *see* M Cross and S Williams, 'Recent Developments at the International Criminal Court', 9 *HRLR* (2009) 267, and H Olásolo, 'The Triggering Procedure of the International Criminal Court, Procedural Treatment of the Principle of Complementarity and the Role of Office of the Prosecutor', 5 *ICLR* (2005) 78 *et subs.*

[82] *See* Triffterer/*Hall*, Art. 19 MN 35.

[83] Ibid, Art. 19 MN 29.

Should the Court deny jurisdiction in the case, the investigation is discontinued at once.

However Art. 19 (8) ICCSt gives three exceptions to the general suspensive effect of a State challenge of jurisdiction or admissibility: (a) in cases of necessity, (b) for the purpose of rounding off prior investigatory steps, and (c) in order to prevent the absconding of persons. Whereas (a) and (c) can be legitimized by referring to the need to prevent irreversible situations arise during the suspension of the case, exception (b) is a concession to the Prosecutor not to be forced to interrupt his investigation or prosecution at an unfavorable moment. It is interesting to note that the corresponding provision in Art. 18 (6) ICCSt only refers to cases of necessity.[84]

It is disputable whether or not the provision of Art. 19 (8) ICCSt is exhaustive or whether the Prosecutor has an 'inherent right to seek authority... to take additional measures not expressly listed'.[85] With due respect, it is suggest that the list is indeed exhaustive. It does not suffice to refer to the rather general remark that 'delays in investigations and prosecutions are almost always detrimental to justice'[86] and thereby justify additional measures. By requiring the Prosecutor to seek special authorization, the Rome Statute has, so to speak, fabricated the balance between justice, efficiency, and fairness. There is no indication whatsoever in the wording of Art. 19 ICCSt that the list was not meant to be an exclusive catalogue of the rights of the Prosecutor under the specific circumstances set out. In any event the Chamber is obliged to decide the issue without undue delay and thereby speed up the wheels of international justice.

Another problematic issue arises from Art. 19 (11) ICCSt, a provision which was made as a compromise on the last conference day in Rome.[87] Without going into detail as regards to the exact wording and the difficulties it raises, it is suggested that the provision be read with reference to Art. 18 (5) ICCSt and in accordance with the overall position of the Prosecutor vis-à-vis the complementarity principle. The Prosecutor takes responsibility to supervise national proceedings in the sense that he or she may re-apply to continue his or her investigation pursuant to Art. 19 (10) ICCSt. In order to fulfil his or her duty, the Prosecutor needs to be informed of investigations and prosecutions which take place in national states. This is the principle enshrined in Art. 19 (11) ICCSt. It applies, therefore, to cases of voluntary deferral to national authorities as well as mandatory deferrals determined by the competent Chamber under Art. 19 (7) ICCSt. It also applies to the interim

[84] As in Art. 18 ICCSt, there is no 'case' yet and there is also no 'person' that can abscond, it is logical that there is no corresponding provision here to Art. 19 (8) (c) ICCSt. However, one can only speculate why there is no provision equal to Art. 19 (8) (b) ICCSt in Art. 18 ICCSt.

[85] This is the view taken by Triffterer/*Hall*, Art. 19 MN 30.

[86] Ibid.

[87] Ibid, Art. 19 MN 39.

situation, when the investigation process is suspended and a ruling by the Court is awaited. In that case the Prosecutor depends upon such information in order to evaluate the need for interim measures pursuant to Art. 19 (8) ICCSt.

4. Summary

Because the questions of jurisdiction and admissibility deal with the relationship between the Court and the State, they are politically sensitive and gave rise to a great amount of discussion during the drafting process.[88] Consequently the Rome Statute contains a set of compromise-ridden rules, including Arts 15, 17, 18, and 19 ICCSt, which are sometimes too lax and sometimes too narrow, and certainly not always in harmony with each other.

Art. 18 ICCSt reflects the concept of the Rome Statute to allow the Prosecutor to be controlled by a Pre-Trial Chamber. Thus, where a State claims primacy over the ICC Prosecutor by virtue of the complementarity principle, pursuant to Art. 17 ICCSt, the Pre-Trial Chamber (and not the Prosecutor) will determine whether or not the case is inadmissible.

Art. 19 ICCSt contains challenges to jurisdiction and admissibility, which may be submitted by: (1) the accused or a person sought on the basis of an arrest warrant or a summons to appear according to Art. 58 ICCSt, (2) a State that is claiming jurisdiction over the case, (3) a State that is involved according to Art. 12 ICCSt, and (4) of course, the Prosecutor. All have a specific interest to receive a final ruling prior to the commencement of trial. Under all circumstances, however, the Court and its respective chambers must be satisfied that the preconditions of jurisdiction and admissibility are met and that international prosecution may indeed proceed.

[88] J Lindenmann, 'The Rules of Procedure and Evidence on Jurisdiction and Admissibility', in: H Fischer, C Kreß, and S R Lüder (eds), *International and National Prosecution of Crimes under International Law* (Berlin Verlag 2001) 173.

6

THE INVESTIGATION STAGE

The 'investigation' (or 'pre-trial inquiry') is the period between the discovery of the crime and the final formulation of the 'charges' or of an 'indictment' which is handed over to a court for trial. Whereas in national criminal proceedings the exact end of this stage might be difficult to define due to special proceedings and different forms of trials,[1] in international criminal procedure the investigation terminates when the 'charges' or the 'indictment' are handed over to the court.[2]

At the ICTY and ICTR, according to Arts 18 (4) and 17 (4) of the respective statutes, the Prosecutor shall, as soon as he or she determines that a *prima facie* case against the accused exists, submit the indictment to the judge of the Trial Chamber. The procedure is governed by Rule 47 of the respective Rules of Procedure and Evidence. This can be seen as the formal end of the investigation stage.[3] At the SCSL, the indictment procedure is regulated by its Rules of Procedure and Evidence (namely Rule 47) only, as the SCSL Statute makes no reference to the indictment.

At the ICC there is no provision, either in the Statute or in the Rules, which determines the end of the investigation stage. Art. 61 (1) ICCSt uses the word 'charges' in contrast to the term 'indictment' at the ICTY/ICTR, which need to be confirmed before trial on the basis of the evidence, which is presented to the Pre-Trial Chamber by the Prosecutor (Art. 61 (5) ICCSt). Thus the drafting of the charges and the collection of supporting evidence for the confirmation hearing marks the end of the investigation stage.[4] Hence, there is indeed no formal end of the investigation phase and no clear separation between the

---

[1] C Safferling, *Towards an International Criminal Procedure* (OUP 2003) 54 *et subs.*

[2] K Ambos, *Internationales Strafrecht* (3rd edn, CH Beck 2011) § 8 MN 23.

[3] K Ambos, ibid, denies that there is a formal separation between investigation and confirmation. I would interpret these ICTY/ICTR provisions differently.

[4] For details *see* p 229.

investigation and the confirmation stage.[5] In some regards these two stages may overlap chronologically at the ICC.[6] Nevertheless it is necessary to differentiate between these two stages, as they fulfil different functions in the ICC process as a whole and the participants play different roles therein (*see* Chapter 7 for the confirmation procedure).

The investigation is conducted by the Prosecutor and is essentially inquisitorial in nature.[7] It is the aim of the investigation stage to collect evidence in order to be in a position to decide whether there is enough proof against an individual person that he or she has indeed committed a crime within the jurisdiction of the ICC, which will support a conviction later at trial. The Prosecutor must therefore execute two duties during investigation:

(1) Legal obligation: Identification of possible charges; that is, analysing the situation legally, and determining whether the elements of a crime within the jurisdiction of the ICC are fulfilled; and
(2) Forensic obligation: Collection of evidence supporting these charges.

These two duties are obviously intertwined and relate to one another. Clearly the Prosecutor needs to collect information and evidence before he or she can identify a specific charge. Likewise the Prosecutor will operate on a specific hypothesis that a certain crime has occurred and let this hypothesis direct his or her search for evidence. The Prosecutor needs to identify his or her case as clearly as possible.[8]

The investigation stage itself consists of different steps, which will be looked at in detail below (B). In order to fulfil its task, the OTP has the authority to impose certain coercive measures, which may jeopardize the rights of the individual persons involved. A critical issue concerning the rights of the suspect is that of pre-trial detention. We therefore need to look not only at the different powers of the Prosecutor (below at C) but also at the rights of the suspect and other persons involved in the inquiry (below at D) and specifically at pre-trial detention (below at E). As the Rome Statute urges the integration of victims into the entire ICC procedure, we shall also deal with victims' participatory rights during the investigation stage (below at F). Before doing so, it is essential to consider two general guiding principles which relate to the investigation (at A): the principle of objectivity, and the discretionary power of the Prosecutor.

---

[5] *See* K Ambos, *Internationales Strafrecht* (3rd edn, CH Beck 2011) § 8 MN 23.

[6] A Zahar and G Sluiter, *International Criminal Law* (OUP 2007) 57: 'Although investigations may continue, with the confirmation of the indictment a new phase in criminal proceedings commences'.

[7] *See* J Hatchard, B Huber, and R Vogler, *Comparative Criminal Procedure* (BIICL 1996) 224.

[8] I Bonomy, 'The Reality of Conducting a War Crimes Trial', 5 *JICJ* (2007) 348, 352.

A. Two Normative Guidelines

Before looking at the structure of the investigation and the powers of the Prosecutor to investigate the crime, there are two basic questions which need to be addressed. All prosecution systems must choose whether they require the Prosecutor to conduct his or her investigation in a purely objective manner (below I). Furthermore a criminal justice system must make clear whether or not the prosecutor has discretionary powers (below II).

I. Principle of objectivity: searching for the truth

At the *ad hoc* Tribunals, the role of the Prosecutor is somewhat unclear. Art. 18 ICTYSt, Art. 17 ICTRSt, and Art. 15 SCSLSt respectively define the Prosecutor's powers but do not define the relevant duties. In particular the Statutes do not oblige him or her to search for the truth. He or she may thus search for incriminating evidence only. Notwithstanding this, any exculpatory evidence which the Prosecutor actually finds must be disclosed to the defence (Rule 68 RPE ICTY/ICTR). On the other hand, the ICTY has on occasion also stated that

> it should be noted that the Prosecutor of the Tribunal is not, or not only, a Party to adversarial proceedings but is an organ of the Tribunal and an organ of international criminal justice whose object is not simply to secure a conviction but to present the case for the Prosecution, which includes not only inculpatory, but also exculpatory evidence, in order to assist the Chamber to discover the truth in a judicial setting…,[9]

and that it

> takes note, with appreciation, of the position of the Prosecution which, in its view, conforms with the mandate of the Tribunal to dispense justice on behalf of the international community and with the status of the Prosecutor and her staff being, as it were, 'ministers of justice assisting in the administration of justice.'[10]

In doing this, the Prosecutor at the ICC is bound by an ideal specified in Art. 54 (1) (a) ICCSt: the finding of the truth. Therefore the Prosecutor needs to

> extend the investigation to cover all facts and evidence relevant to an assessment of whether there is criminal responsibility under this Statute, and, in doing so, investigate incriminating and exonerating circumstances equally.

---

[9] ICTY *Prosecutor v Kupreškić et al.*, TC, 21 September 1998, Decision on Communication between the Parties and their Witnesses.

[10] ICTY *Prosecutor v Blaškić*, AC, 26 September 2000, Decision on the Appellant's Motions for the Prosecution of Material, Suspension or Extension of the Briefing Schedule and Additional Filings, para 32. As regards the terminology used the AC refers to *R v Banks* [1916] 2 KB 621 at 623 (per Avory J). Also *see R v Brown (Winston)* [1998] AC 367 at 374, HL.

The fact that the OTP must apply an objective approach during the investigation has already been analysed.[11]

II. Discretionary powers of the Prosecutor

There are different ways of how an investigation is initiated. A prosecutor might be obliged to investigate every case brought to his or her attention. This approach can be called principle of legality.[12] Alternatively, it may be left to the prosecutor's discretion whether or not to prosecute.

At the ICTY and ICTR, Arts 17 (1) and 18 (1) respectively state that the Prosecutor 'shall' initiate an investigation *ex officio* or on the basis of information from any source, and he or she 'shall decide whether there is sufficient basis to proceed'. Even though the word 'shall' appears to limit the discretionary power of the Prosecutor to some extent, the words 'sufficient basis' make clear that the discretion of the Prosecutor is, at this stage, very wide. The determination of whether there is a 'sufficient basis to proceed' is to a large extent up to the Prosecutor, since neither the Statute nor the Rules provide any guidance on this point. Even if they did, the decision of the Prosecutor not to initiate an investigation is not subject to review, and his or her decisions and considerations regarding a declination to investigate are generally not published.

Two incidents at the ICTY gave rise to concerns regarding the legitimacy of the tribunal's work. First the Prosecutor of the ICTY had to decide whether or not to investigate the NATO air strikes in 1999.[13] Independent of the question of whether these air strikes were in conformity with the rules of *ius ad bellum*,[14] several NGOs had collected evidence that the bombardments violated *ius in bello* and were tantamount to war crimes. The then ICTY Prosecutor, Carla del Ponte, referred the matter to a 'Committee Established to Review the NATO Bombing Campaign Against the Federal Republic of Yugoslavia', which advised against the initiation of investigations against NATO.[15] No investigation was opened, as the Prosecutor was not satisfied that there had been deliberate targeting of non-military objects on the part of NATO.[16] Certainly it also seemed politically unwise to investigate against NATO, who at the time was the ICTY's primary supplier of suspects.[17] Not

[11] *See* Chapter 4, p 149

[12] eg, German criminal procedure operates in this maxim, *see* Sec. 152 (2) StPO.

[13] L Côté, 'Reflections on the Exercise of Prosecutorial Discretion in International Criminal Law', 3 *JICJ* (2005) 162–86.

[14] *See* eg, B Simma, 'Nato, the UN, and the Use of Force: Legal Aspects', 10 *EJIL* (1999) 1.

[15] *See* Report of the Committee Established to Review the NATO Bombing Campaign Against the Federal Republic of Yugoslavia, available at: <http://www.icty.org/x/file/Press/nato061300.pdf> (27 May 2011).

[16] *See* press release of 13 June 2000, available at: <http://www.icty.org/sid/7846> (27 May 2011).

[17] M Delmas-Marty, 'Interactions between National and International Criminal Law in the Preliminary Phase of Trial at the ICC', 4 *JICJ* (2006) 2, 8.

surprisingly the ICTY Prosecutor was criticized for adopting double standards—quite similar to the IMT—which did not prosecute war crimes committed by the allies.[18]

Secondly, as the Tribunals developed, the Prosecutor was gradually forced to concentrate on the 'most responsible' persons; this has become even more urgent with the completion strategy adopted by all of the *ad hoc* Tribunals. On the other hand, the Prosecutor decides to open an investigation, but he or she is bound by the principles underlying the Statute and internationally recognized human rights, such as the principle of equality (Arts 20 and 21, ICTR/ICTYSt, respectively), which means that a prosecution against a certain individual may not be conducted based on discriminatory motives.

As to the question whether *upon* investigation, the Prosecutor is obliged to issue an indictment, the Rules of Procedure and Evidence of the Tribunals, namely Rule 47, state that if the Prosecutor is satisfied from the available evidence that there are reasonable grounds to believe that a certain person has committed a certain crime within the jurisdiction of the Tribunal, and the Prosecutor is furthermore satisfied that this can be proven— that is, a *prima facie* case in the sense of Art. 17 (4) ICTYSt or 18 (4) ICTRSt, exists—he or she 'shall' prepare an indictment. The same holds true for the SCSL, though the term '*prima facie* case' is not used in the relevant provisions. This wording appears to limit the Prosecutor's margin of discretion considerably. However, in practice the Tribunals have recognized a broad discretion of the Prosecutor regarding the decision whether or not to indict a suspect:

In the present context, indeed in many criminal justice systems, the entity responsible for prosecutions has limited financial and human resources and cannot realistically be expected to prosecute every offender who falls within the strict terms of the court's jurisdiction. Hence, the OTP must necessarily make decisions as to the nature of the crimes and the offenders to be prosecuted. It is beyond question that the Prosecutor has broad discretion in relation to the initiation of investigations and in the preparation of indictments.

At the ICC this issue is governed by Art. 53 ICCSt. The wording in Art. 53 (1) and (2) ICCSt specifies a 'negative test'. The Prosecutor is obliged to proceed to investigate unless s/he is of the opinion that there is no 'reasonable basis' to do so (Art. 53 (1) ICCSt). Furthermore, he or she is obliged to prosecute unless s/he, *mutatis mutandis,* deems there to be no 'sufficient basis' (Art. 53 (2) ICCSt) to do so.[19] Yet the test to be applied, at any one time, grants rather wide discretion to the Prosecutor—see Art. 53 (1) (c) and (2) (c) ICCSt)—the differences between these provisions will be discussed below. Both require the Prosecutor to take the 'interests of justice' into

[18] L Côté, 'Reflections on the Exercise of Prosecutorial Discretion in International Criminal Law', 3 *JICJ* (2005) 162–86.

[19] M Brubacher, 'Prosecutorial Discretion within the International Criminal Court', 2 *JICJ* (2004) 71, 79.

consideration.[20] Thus the Prosecutor may discontinue the investigation if s/he is of the opinion that a prosecution would not be in the 'interests of justice'. This discretionary power is granted to the Prosecutor regardless of the trigger mechanism which has been invoked. Art. 53 (1) (c) and (2) (c) ICCSt are not only applicable in the case of a *proprio motu* investigation of the Prosecutor.[21] The Statute further specifies that the 'interests of justice' comprise the gravity of the crime, the interest of the victims, age and infirmity of the alleged perpetrator, and his or her role in the alleged crime.

Yet the discretion granted to the Prosecutor with one hand is taken away with the other in that the Statute foresees a review procedure for the discretionary power of the Prosecutor regarding the 'interests of justice'. Where the Prosecutor has decided not to investigate on the grounds that it is not in the 'interests of justice' to do so, the Pre-Trial Chamber, under Art. 53 (3) (b) ICCSt, may *proprio motu* re-evaluate the Prosecutor's decision.

The wording of Art. 53 (1) (c) and (2) (c) ICCSt, which creates a negative test ('would not be in the interests of justice'), reveals that in principle the prosecution of a crime within the jurisdiction of the ICC does indeed serve the 'interests of justice' and only in exceptional circumstances should the Prosecutor decline to investigate further.[22] As the decision is reviewable it needs to be reasoned.[23] Additionally the Pre-Trial Chamber may request specific or further information or documents to properly scrutinize the decision taken by the Prosecutor, as foreseen in Regulation 48 (1) RegC.

In substance, the question of what exactly serves the 'interests of justice' is to be considered in light of the overall aims and purposes of an international criminal trial. Should the Prosecutor decline to proceed on this ground, the national judiciary will have to take on the situation and possible cases by virtue of the complementary system of the ICC.[24] The 'interests of justice' is a legal term, which requires no further definition.[25] It does not give the Prosecutor an 'open door' to 'escape investigation

---

[20] *See* M Brubacher, 'Prosecutorial Discretion within the International Criminal Court', 2 *JICJ* (2004) 71, putting the discretionary powers of the Prosecutor into the wider context of the drafting history.

[21] This seems to be suggested by F Hoffmeister and S Knoke, 'Das Vorermittlungsverfahren vor dem Internationalen Strafgerichtshof—Prüfstein für die Effektivität der neuen Gerichtsbarkeit im Völkerstrafrecht', 59 *ZaöRV* (1999) 785, at 800.

[22] This is the view of the Prosecutor himself as expressed in: ICC, OTP, Policy Paper on the Interests of Justice, September 2007, available at: <http://www.icc-cpi.int/NR/rdonlyres/772C95C9-F54D-4321-BF09-73422BB23528/143640/ICCOTPInterestsOfJustice.pdf> (27 May 2011); *see* also M Delmas-Marty, 'Interactions between National and International Criminal Law in the Preliminary Phase of Trial at the ICC', 4 *JICJ* (2006) 2, 8; M Brubacher, 'Prosecutorial Discretion within the International Criminal Court', 2 *JICJ* (2004) 71, 80 seems to be of the opinion that the Prosecutor is absolutely free in his evaluation of the concurring interests. This view, in the present author's opinion, disregards the wording of Art. 53 ICCSt as stated above.

[23] Unclear Triffterer/*Bergsmo/Kruger*, Art. 53 MN 22.

[24] *See* also F Hoffmeister and S Knoke, 'Das Vorermittlungsverfahren vor dem Internationalen Strafgerichtshof—Prüfstein für die Effektivität der neuen Gerichtsbarkeit im Völkerstrafrecht', 59 *ZaöRV* (1999) 785, 799 *et subs.*

[25] The suggestion of C Kreß, 'The Procedural Law of the International Criminal Court in Out-

by invoking arbitrary grounds'.[26] Art. 53 ICCSt thus requires a systematic interpretation, as the important question of whether or not to investigate or prosecute cannot merely be left to a case-by-case analysis.[27] The Statute explicitly refers to several non-exclusive criteria. These can be identified as: (a) the gravity of the crime, (b) the interests of the victims, (c) the attributes of the perpetrator, and (d) other factors.

The gravity of the crime is a rather straightforward criterion, which is known to many jurisdictions.[28]

1. *Gravity of the crime*

The German criminal law differentiates between two categories of criminal offences. Section 12 of the German Criminal Code distinguishes between 'Verbrechen' (Serious Criminal Offences or felonies) and 'Vergehen' (Less Serious Criminal Offences or misdemeanors). This formal differentiation is made by reference to the abstract threat of punishment. According to Section 12 para 1 of the German Criminal Code, felonies are unlawful acts punishable by a minimum sentence of one year imprisonment. In contrast, misdemeanours according to Section 12 para 2 are unlawful acts punishable by a lesser minimum term of imprisonment or by the imposition of a fine.

This distinction not only bears relevance to the substantive law, but is also of importance to procedural law.[29] It is of practical relevance concerning the question of a discontinuation of the prosecution under Sections 153 *et subs.* of the German Code of Criminal Procedure. Section 153 para 1 of the German Code of Criminal Procedure allows the Prosecutor to dispense with a case if the perpetrator's guilt is considered to be of a minor nature and there is in general no public interest in the prosecution.[30]

The law in the USA adopts a similar approach. The most significant distinction in the categorization of crimes is drawn between felonies and misdemeanors. A crime is generally considered a felony when it is punishable by more than one year imprisonment. Misdemeanors are less serious crimes which are punishable by up to one

---

line: Anatomy of a Unique Compromise', 1 *JICJ* (2003) 603 at 607 to define a general framework for an interpretation of the 'interests of justice' as an cooperative enterprise of both the Chambers and the Prosecutor has not been taken up by the ICC authorities.

[26] Explicitly stated by Triffterer/*Bergsmo/Kruger*, Art. 53 MN 21 and 22.

[27] An allegedly different view is adopted by the ICC Prosecutor: ICC, OTP, Policy Paper on the Interests of Justice, September 2007, p 1, where it is stated that the paper will only 'offer limited clarification in the abstract' as 'the particular approach then will necessarily have to depend on the facts and circumstances of the case of situation'. This has been rightly criticized by: M Delmas-Marty, 'Interactions between National and International Criminal Law in the Preliminary Phase of Trial at the ICC', 4 *JICJ* (2006) 2, 10.

[28] *See* in general W Schabas, 'Prosecutorial Discretion v. Judicial Activism at the International Criminal Court', 6 *JICJ* (2008) 731, 736–41.

[29] L Meyer-Goßner, *StPO* (54th edn, CH Beck 2011) § 153 MN 1.

[30] *See* L Meyer-Goßner, *StPO* § 153 MN 7: Despite the minor guilt of the suspect a public prosecution might still be advisable according to Sec. 153 of the German Criminal Procedural Code. Reasons for this might be the public interest in detecting the criminal background, in hindering further damage, or the social situation of the suspect might necessitate prosecution.

year imprisonment. However, reference must also be made to the so-called 'petty offences', a third category. In the USA, petty offences are misdemeanors for which the penalty does not exceed imprisonment for a period of six months or a fine of no more than $500 USD, or both. As such they are defined as minor or insignificant crimes.[31] They are not worth the public expense of empanelling a jury, and in some jurisdictions they are not even deemed criminal offences.

However, the standards found in national law will not be of much assistance in interpreting the 'gravity principle' in the ICCSt. This is because the crimes which fall within the jurisdiction of the ICC, in accordance with Art. 5 ICCSt, are in any case classed as the most serious of offences in every national legal system. Therefore the prosecution of these 'core crimes' in general is not dependent on any further 'gravity requirement'.[32]

It is thus necessary to develop a novel approach for the ICC. As we have seen with regard to national legal systems, the gravity requirement is a substantive test. It was included in the Statute in addition to the selection of 'core crimes' in Arts 5 to 8 ICCSt, which *per se* are to be seen as 'grave'. These *eo ipso* 'grave' crimes must have been committed in such a way that renders them particularly grave.[33]

The RegP anticipate a set of requirements which may be applied. Regulation 29 (2) RegP states: 'In order to assess the gravity of the crimes allegedly committed in the situation the Office shall consider various factors including their scale, nature, manner of commission, and impact.'

As indicated by the word 'including', this list is not exhaustive and does not clarify the criteria, which determine the 'gravity' of a (possible) case. When looking at elements that constitute gravity in international criminal law, three different tests might be applied:

(1) One could apply an objective quantitative crime-related test and consider the result of the crime, that is, the number of victims and the seriousness of the conduct, that is, the level of systematic organization in the planning of the crime.
(2) One could also differentiate by applying a subjective test, making the culpability of the offender the decisive element.[34]
(3) Finally, one could adopt an objective qualitative community-related test. According to this approach, which was established by Pre-Trial Chamber I in the *Lubanga* case, one would have to look at the 'social alarm' such conduct may have caused in the international community.[35]

---

[31] *See* Title 18 of the United States Code Annotated § 19 (18 USCA § 19).

[32] *See* eg, MünchKommVStGB/*Ambos* § 1 MN 1.

[33] ICC *Prosecutor v Lubanga*, PTC, ICC-01/04-01/06-2, 10 February 2006, Warrant of Arrest, para 45.

[34] Ibid, para 50 *et subs.*

[35] *See* ICC *Prosecutor v Lubanga*, PTC, ICC-01/04-01/06-2, 10 February 2006, Warrant of Arrest, para 46.

Considerations of *ius ad bellum* should not be included in the gravity test applied here. To do so, as proposed by *Williams/Schabas*,[36] would mix up questions which should generally be kept separate. A war crime as such does not amount to a more serious offence, just because it has been committed in the aftermath of an aggression.[37] Such an approach would violate the culpability principle, because a soldier who is part of the occupying troops following an unlawful aggression who then commits war crimes is not *per se* connected to the prior aggression.

What is required is a triple-standard test, taking into account the elements of the crime itself.[38]

- The crime of genocide puts a strong emphasis on the mental elements. In essence the genocidal intent; that is, the intent to destroy a protected group in whole or in parts, is the core of the crime. Even though the question as to what actually constitutes the *mens rea* of the crime of genocide is heavily disputed,[39] the very essence of the crime of genocide lays in the *dolus specialis* as a means of distinguishing genocide from crimes against humanity. Yet the 'centre of the gravity requirement' so to speak is made up of objective criteria; that is, the level of organization, the system implemented for pursuing the destructive plan, and the number of people already killed. The conduct of a 'lone genocidal maniac'[40] whose plan to destroy a protected group as such remains utterly unrealistic due to a lack of supporting infrastructure,[41] would therefore generally speaking not be of sufficient gravity.
- In contrast, crimes against humanity do not require *dolus specialis*. The main focus lies on the level of systematic organization or the vastness of the human rights violations. 'Gravity' is thus related to these objective criteria. In addition it is suggested that a subjective test must be taken into account cumulatively of these objective criteria. Particularly in cases which fall short of genocide due to the lack of a protected group, the intent to destroy a group not covered

---

36 *See* Triffterer/*Williams/Schabas*, Art. 17 MN 28.

37 Thus argued by Triffterer/*Williams/Schabas*, Art. 17 MN 28 with reference to 'war crimes' committed by British soldiers in Iraq, alleging that the invasion into Iraq by US and UK troops was indeed an 'aggression'.

38 A purely quantitative evaluation of gravity is highly questionable; *see* Triffterer/*Williams/Schabas*, Art. 17 MN 28.

39 *See* C Safferling, 'The Special Intent Requirement in the Crime of Genocide' in C Safferling and E Conze (eds), *The Genocide Convention Sixty Years After Its Adoption* (TCM Asser 2010) 163 for further references.

40 Rather polemic W Schabas, 'The Jelisic Case and the Mens Rea of the Crime of Genocide' 14 *LJIL* (2001) 125, 138.

41 ICTY *Prosecutor v Jelisić*, TC, IT-95-10-T, 5 July 1999, para 100 with reference to P N Drost, *The Crime of State, Vol II: Genocide* (AW Sythoff 1959) 85, has contemplated such a setting. Whether it is possible to fulfil the crime of genocide under these circumstances is questionable.

by Art. 6 ICCSt, that is, political and social groups, is relevant for the determination of the gravity requirement.

- With regard to evaluating the gravity of the offence, war crimes are similar to crimes against humanity. Leaving aside the wording of Art. 8 (1) ICCSt for one moment, war crimes as such do not necessarily require a level of systematic organization or vastness.[42] In principle any isolated act can amount to a war crime. In establishing the level of gravity, objective criteria such as the systematic course of action, the number of victims, the organizational structure behind the operations, and the criminal policy supporting the acts must be taken into account. In addition subjective criteria need to be considered. The level of intent will affect the graveness of the crime.

A common definition of gravity is thus barred, yet it is important to note that in order to determine the gravity of the crime, both objective and subjective criteria must be taken into account. 'Gravity' has to be established according to the specific elements of the alleged crime taking into account the level of culpability and intent that can be apportioned to the alleged perpetrator.

There is one further systematic problem regarding the gravity test. As Art. 17 (1) (d) ICCSt also refers to the gravity of the crime and because the Prosecutor is required to address issues of admissibility under Art. 53 (1) (b) and (2) (b) ICCSt, the gravity test is applicable twice.[43] This obviously makes no sense unless there is a specific difference between their separate implementations.[44] However, this does not appear to be the case. Art. 17 (1) (d) ICCSt links the gravity of the case to the level of the international court and compares it to prosecutions on a national level. Similarly, the gravity test under Art. 53 ICCSt links the need to prosecute on the international level with the dimension of the crime. This corresponds with the discussion on the relevance of Art. 17 (1) (d) ICCSt in the context of the principle of complementarity, where we concluded that the gravity of the crime is not an element of complementarity.[45]

2. *Interests of victims*

The 'interests of the victims' concept has set up a rather vague parameter. Often these interests will not be easily detectable and might even conflict with each other. At the very least it is difficult to say that victims have a general interest in the

[42] K Ambos, *Internationales Strafrecht* (3rd edn, CH Beck 2011) § 7 MN 228.

[43] Regulation 29 (1) RegP stresses that 'gravity' is a matter of admissibility, and does not mention 'gravity' in relation to the 'interests of justice'. The consequences are unclear. In the present author's view the RegP is erroneous in this regard and should be amended in order to be compatible with Art. 53 ICCSt.

[44] More cautious: Triffterer/*Bergsmo/Kruger*, Art. 53 MN 19: 'the need for a repetition may be questioned'.

[45] *See* Chapter 2, p 107.

prosecution.[46] This might vary according to the circumstances of the case. Thus it may well be that victims would prefer an alternative conflict resolution as opposed to a criminal prosecution.[47]

The 'interests of victims' as a parameter for deciding whether or not to investigate and prosecute is thus not a reliable criterion and can be outweighed by other criteria.[48] Hence, the Prosecutor has to evaluate the victims' interests as a basis for his decision according to Art. 53 (1) or (2) ICCSt.

3. Alleged perpetrator

Art. 53 (2) (c) ICCSt specifies the 'age or infirmity' of the alleged perpetrator, and 'his or her role in the alleged crime' as parameters for deciding whether or not to further investigate against a person. These criteria can also be relevant to Art. 53 (1) (c) ICCSt, should such information concerning the suspect be available at that early stage of the investigation of a 'situation'.

The basis for considering the age of the perpetrator under the Rome Statute is Art. 26 ICCSt, which excludes jurisdiction *ratione personae* for suspects who are under the age of eighteen. The age of the suspect can be relevant in two ways. (1) The alleged perpetrator being above the age of eighteen is still not mature enough to be regarded as fully culpable. The question of age thus turns out in substance to be a question of maturity. It will regularly be connected to the question of infirmity and the role of the alleged perpetrator in the alleged crime. (2) The alleged perpetrator is too old; that is, his or her life expectancy makes it unlikely that he or she will survive the outcome of the prosecution.[49] This criterion is also related to the question of infirmity. If the alleged perpetrator is too frail because of his or her age and prosecution would endanger his fragile health further, the Prosecutor may discontinue the proceedings.[50]

'Infirmity' as an individual parameter relates to the physical and mental fitness of the alleged perpetrator independently of his or her 'age'. As concerns the physical fitness, the question is similar to the question of age; that is, whether the suspect will survive the outcome of the trial. The provision is also related to Art. 31 (1) (a) ICCSt, which excludes criminal responsibility of persons who suffer from a

[46] *See* the research study of E Kiza, C Rathgeber, and H-C Rohne, *Victims of War—War-Victimization and Victims' Attitudes Towards Addressing Atrocities* (HIS edition online 2006) 97, 108, and 115. The Policy Paper of ICC-OTP insinuates that in general the victims' interests will coincide with the prosecutor's; *see* ICC, OTP, Policy Paper on the Interests of Justice, September 2007, p. 5 *et subs.*

[47] M Delmas-Marty, 'Interactions between National and International Criminal Law in the Preliminary Phase of Trial at the ICC', 4 *JICJ* (2006) 2, 9.

[48] This is the position taken by Triffterer/*Bergsmo/Kruger*, Art. 53 MN 20.

[49] Constitutional Court (VerfGH) Berlin, *Honecker Prosecution Case*, Judgment 12 January 1993, 100 *ILR* 393.

[50] *See* BVerfG in the case against *Heinrich Boere*, 2 BvR 1724/09, decision of 9 October 2009.

mental disease or defect. In both situations, a prosecution is no longer in the interests of justice, for humanitarian reasons.[51] But it is not only empathy and compassion with the alleged offender which speak against prosecuting an old and ill person. Should the suspect's condition be such that it renders him or her incapable of understanding that s/he is being prosecuted at the ICC or unable to comprehend the allegations brought against him or her, a prosecution and trial would be meaningless. One of the preconditions for the legitimacy of a criminal prosecution is that the alleged offender is treated as the subject of the proceedings, and not as its object.[52] Therefore, a public prosecution is legitimate only if the suspect is in a position to understand the censure and moral blame entailed in a criminal conviction.

Finally, the role of the alleged perpetrator is relevant for the decision as to whether or not to prosecute. As it is only in the interest of the ICC and the international community to prosecute the most serious international criminals, the role of the alleged perpetrator in the alleged crime is of great importance. This criterion in a sense mirrors the gravity of the crime within the person of the alleged criminal. Thus even if the crime alleged is that of genocide and concerns many victims, it might still be advisable not to prosecute an opportunist who merely aided the overall crime. Such proceedings could endanger the prosecution of the top criminals[53] and might be detrimental to the overall healing process.

4. *Other criteria*

In addition to the criteria discussed above, other issues may be taken into consideration when determining whether a further investigation or prosecution is in the 'interests of justice'. The Prosecutor is thus given the opportunity to include (further) public policy considerations in the decision-making process regarding the discontinuation of the investigation and prosecution respectively.[54]

The Prosecutor might have to take into account the political implications of his or her investigation and their consequences on the transitional process in the societies which are affected by his or her work. S/he might even assume responsibility for international peace and security, and weigh the dangers of an investigation against the chances of peace and reconciliation in the region.[55]

---

[51] *See* M Brubacher, 'Prosecutorial Discretion within the International Criminal Court', 2 *JICJ* (2004)71, 81.

[52] S Beck, 'Does Age Prevent Punishment? The Struggles of the German Juridical System with Alleged Nazi Criminals: Commentary on the Criminal Proceedings Against John Demjanjuk and Heinrich Boere', 11 *GLJ* (2010) 347.

[53] Rightly observed by Triffterer/*Bergsmo/Kruger*, Art. 53 MN 30.

[54] These considerations are missing in the twofold test, which was developed by Delmas-Marty and is based on solely two criteria: (1) legitimacy, and (2) relativism; *see* M Delmas-Marty, 'Interactions between National and International Criminal Law in the Preliminary Phase of Trial at the ICC', 4 *JICJ* (2006) 2, 10.

[55] M Brubacher, 'Prosecutorial Discretion within the International Criminal Court', 2 *JICJ* (2004) 71, 80 *et subs.* is strongly in favour of a political discretion.

However, it is argued that the primary responsibility of the Prosecutor is the prosecution of the main international criminals. The establishment and maintenance of international peace and security comes within the ambit of the UN SC. It is therefore hard to imagine a Prosecutor who would discontinue investigating a major crime against humanity of international concern on the grounds that potential settlement negotiations may be endangered by his or her work. In doing so s/he would *de facto* grant amnesty to a person, who *de jure* is responsible for an international crime. The Prosecutor can therefore only postpone investigations, and even this decision should be referred to the UN SC by virtue of Art. 16 ICCSt.[56]

Another consideration that might be relevant at this point is the question of whether 'justice' can be achieved by means other than a criminal prosecution. A lot has been said and written about truth and reconciliation commissions and their potentials in the 'transitional justice' process.[57] The same is true of 'traditional justice' mechanisms.[58] The Prosecutor may take these experiences into consideration and give prevalence to 'alternative dispute resolution' or attempts to follow a restorative justice approach. However, when it comes to the prosecution of the most senior figures in a situation where mass crimes have occurred, the Prosecutor at the ICC cannot refer the case to regional, traditional, or alternative mechanisms. This is so for two reasons: (1) international criminal law pertains to the global international community and thus takes on a much broader responsibility than that of the national judiciary,[59] and (2) 'transitional justice' considerations require the prosecution of the top leaders.[60]

---

[56] A different and well-reasoned view is taken by M Brubacher, 'Prosecutorial Discretion within the International Criminal Court', 2 *JICJ* (2004), 71 at 83 *et subs.*, who in the present author's opinion underestimates the general duty of the Prosecutor to bring major international criminals to justice. As a consequence of this view, Brubacher needs to develop a sort of vague dependency on determinations made by the UN SC on the side of the Prosecutor. This in fact would jeopardize the ICC structure altogether, as the UN SC is not a legal organ and is thus not in a position to establish legally binding determinations. The ICC in fact is a legal organ and in that regard has the last word, for example, as regards the character of an armed conflict and the like.

[57] *See* Chapter 2, p 97.

[58] *See* Chapter 1 as concerns Rwanda, p 28.

[59] *See* as to the aims and purposes of international criminal procedure, Chapter 2, p 64.

[60] *See* 'The Nuremberg Declaration on Peace and Justice', III. Principles, 2. Ending impunity § 2. Annex to UN Doc. A/62/885 of 26 June 2008.

B. The Structure and Aim of the Investigation Stage

When looking at the ICCSt the investigation stage consists of three phases, which focus upon the two decisions the Prosecutor has to make under Art. 53 ICCSt:[61]

(1) *Pre-Investigative Phase*, Art. 53 (1) ICCSt: the Prosecutor evaluates the information immediately after it has been made available to him or her and determines whether or not there is a 'reasonable basis' to proceed and starts investigating or ends the investigation as the case may be.[62]

(2) *Investigation Phase*, Art. 53 (2) ICCSt: after investigation, in particular after the questioning of the suspect, the Prosecutor evaluates the information and determines whether or not there is a 'sufficient basis' to proceed and starts prosecution, or as the case may be, ends the investigation.[63]

(3) *Prosecution Phase*, Art. 61 ICCSt: the Prosecutor investigates further and prepares the case for the confirmation of the charges.

The Prosecutor begins by looking at a 'situation' and only in the course of the investigation does s/he develop a specific 'case' (or several 'cases') out of the 'situation', which is then the object of the further investigation and prosecution phases.

The Registrar will, in accordance with Regulation 20 (1) RegR, file a situation record as soon as a Pre-Trial Chamber has been assigned the matter according to Regulation 46 (2) RegC. Pursuant to Regulation 20 (2) RegR, the Registry will open a case record as soon as ordered to do so by the Chamber, upon the issuance of an arrest warrant or a summons to appear. As a matter of fact, this registration process is not fixed to a specific point within the three different investigation stages. This means that in substance a 'case' will evolve in the course of the investigation phase, but it will only be formally registered as such if the Prosecutor applies for an arrest warrant or a summons to appear according to Art. 58 ICCSt. This might take place during the investigation phase or prosecution phase.

The first two steps, the pre-investigation and investigation phase, are in substance concerned with three different issues:

[61] A chart explaining the different stages of the pre-trial phase can be found in Chapter 5, p 196, Figure 5.2.

[62] Ahlbrecht/*Kirsch* (2008), MN 1375, 1385 calls this 'Vorprüfungsverfahren'. K Ambos, *Internationales Strafrecht* (3rd edn, CH Beck 2011) § 8 MN 20a speaks of 'Vorermittlungsverfahren'. A Cassese, *International Criminal Law* (2nd edn, OUP 2008) 396 uses the term 'preliminary probing'. The RegP applies the terminology 'preliminary examination and evaluation of the information'; *see* heading of Section 3 RegP. The term 'pre-investigative phase' used here comprises both issues, examination, and evaluation.

[63] According to Ahlbrecht/*Kirsch* (2008), MN 1387, this is the 'Ermittlungsverfahren'.

(1) Legal and factual evaluation as to whether a crime within the jurisdiction of the ICC has occurred;
(2) Legal evaluation as concerns admissibility according to complementarity; and
(3) Policy considerations regarding the 'interests of justice'.

During the investigation phase, jurisdictional and admissibility issues must be solved in an extra procedure under Art. 18 and 19 ICCSt (see following, A. VII). The prosecution phase is solely concerned with the compilation of the charges and the supporting evidence.

I. Pre-investigation

The pre-investigation phase has two main aims:

(1) Maintaining the efficiency of the proceedings. This is done in two ways. First, the pre-investigation phase serves as a safeguard, preventing resources being spent on an investigation which does not have the prospect of succeeding at the later stages.[64] Secondly, the decision of the Prosecutor whether or not to start an investigation is supervised. This task is fulfilled by the Pre-Trial Chamber in accordance with Art. 53 (3) and Art. 15 (4) ICCSt and also endorses the efficiency of the proceedings.

(2) Protection of the rights of individuals. The process ensures that the Prosecutor may only start a formal investigation which as such has a stigmatizing effect and gives the Prosecutor authority to implement several coercive measures against the suspect and other individuals, if the information is strong enough to provide for a 'reasonable basis' to believe that a crime has indeed occurred. This means that the Prosecutor is not authorized to embark on 'fishing expeditions' to the detriment of individual rights or state sovereignty.

In order to start an investigation, the Prosecutor must have knowledge of an incident which might amount to a crime. In a national context this information is usually brought by an individual complaint or by the police who have attended the scene of the crime.

In national systems this phase of the investigation is usually not regulated. For example, under German law § 152 (II) German Code of Criminal Procedure states that if there are sufficient factual indications that an offence has occurred, the Prosecutor must initiate a formal investigation ('Ermittlungsverfahren'). In order to be in a position to decide whether there are 'sufficient factual indications', the Prosecutor must carry out a pre-investigation. The Criminal Procedure Code

[64] *See* Triffterer/*Bergsmo/Kruger*, Art. 53 MN 6.

does not anticipate any other rules for this phase.[65] This is why the Prosecutor's investigative powers are minimal during this phase, as he or she may not touch upon individual rights without legal authorization.[66]

In international criminal law the situation is more complicated.

At the *ad hoc* tribunals, the pre-investigation phase is not explicitly regulated, and it is questionable whether it is sensible to separate it from the investigation phase. As seen above, the Prosecutor enjoys ample discretion under Art. 18 (1) ICTYSt/Art. 17 (1) ICTRSt; and the pre-investigation actually takes place before that. From the wording of Art. 18 (1) ICTYSt/Art. 17 (1) ICTRSt, one must assume that the pre-investigation phase, if one were required to define it, only comprises the assessment of the information the Prosecutor has received according to the same provision. Once the Prosecutor 'proceeds' and investigates beyond that information, the actual investigation phase begins.

At the ICC a complex system of so-called trigger mechanisms (Art. 13 ICCSt) prevails.[67] Information about a possible crime that has occurred can either be supplied by a Member State, by the Security Council of the UN, or by an individual communication. In each of these cases, the issue of sovereignty of national states is relevant in different ways. The ICCSt takes heed of this and imposes a system that is highly unusual in the criminal justice process. This illustrates the difficult compromises that had to be reached during the Rome Conference. As discussed previously, the position and powers of the Prosecutor at the ICC were most controversial at the time of the drafting of the ICCSt and are at times still heavily disputed.[68]

The position of the Prosecutor bears great significance in several regards. In national legal systems, prosecutors are either 'civil servants' answerable to the minister of justice—for example, in Germany—or they are elected into office by the community—as is the case in the USA. In any event the prosecutor holds a powerful office. At the international level the powers of the prosecutor are even greater, because s/he is in a position to prosecute even government officials and heads of states. The ICCSt thus establishes a special control system for the Prosecutor, aimed at preventing the bringing of 'frivolous or politically motivated charges'.[69] A state referral or a referral by the UN SC guarantees political control and ensures respect for state sovereignty.[70] As regards to the *proprio motu* powers of the Prosecutor, the drafters of

[65] L Meyer-Goßner, *StPO* (54 edn, CH Beck 2011) § 152 Rn. 4a; G Pfeiffer, *StPO* (5th edn, CH Beck 2005) § 152 Rn. 1c.

[66] Löwe/Rosenberg/*Rieß*, *StPO*, Vor § 158 Rn 12b f.

[67] *See* Chapter 2, p 86 for a detailed discussion of the trigger mechanisms at the ICC.

[68] *See* Chapter 4, p 147.

[69] Triffterer/*Bergsmo/Pejic* Art. 15 MN 20.

[70] A Cassese, *International Criminal Law* (2nd edn, OUP 2008) 399 *et subs.*

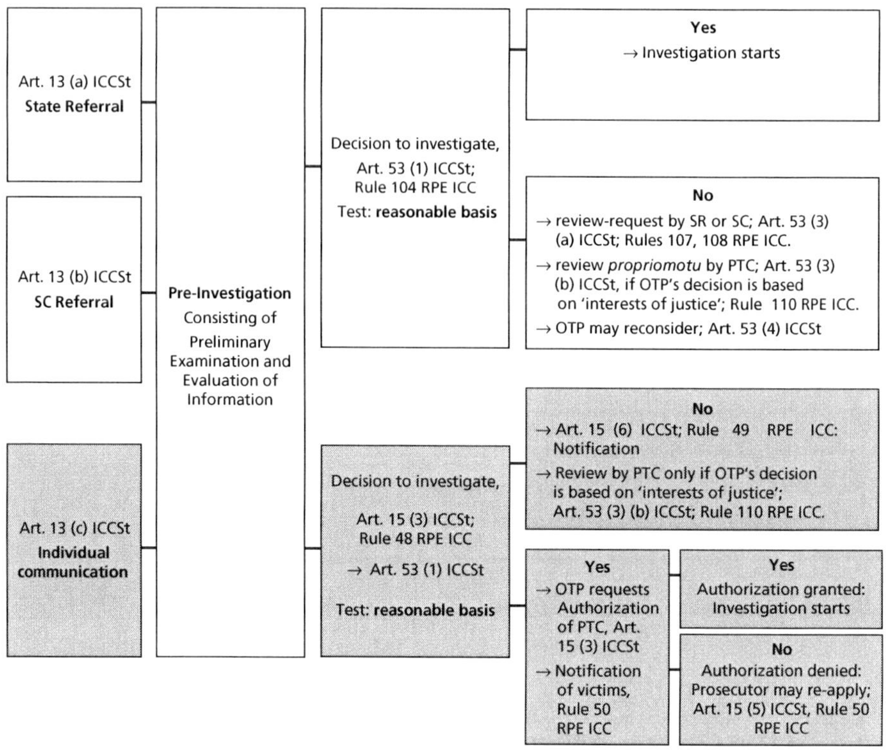

Figure 6.1 The pre-trial phase

the ICCSt found a compromise[71] and established the special authorization requirement.[72] Even if this does not equal a political control as by the veto powers in the UN SC, the judicial control through the Pre-Trial Chamber at least guarantees supervision by an independent authority.

At the ICC we must differentiate accordingly.

As is shown by Figure 6.1, the different trigger mechanisms all lead to a pre-investigation, which consists of the 'preliminary examination and evaluation of the information'. The substance of the test to be applied by the Prosecutor—whether or not to proceed—is specified in Art. 53 (1) ICCSt. Thus the Prosecutor must decide whether there is a 'reasonable basis' to believe that a crime within the jurisdiction of the Court has been or is being committed. He or she also needs to look into the issue of admissibility under Art. 17 ICCSt. Lastly, the Prosecutor must decide

[71] F Hoffmeister and S Knoke, 'Das Vorermittlungsverfahren vor dem Internationalen Strafgerichtshof—Prüfstein für die Effektivität der neuen Gerichtsbarkeit im Völkerstrafrecht', 59 *ZaöRV* (1999) 785, 806 *et subs* speak of a 'respectable compromise'.

[72] As to the different positions and proposals during the drafting of the ICCSt *see* K Ambos, *Internationales Strafrecht* (3rd edn, CH Beck 2011) § 8 MN 21a.

whether or not the investigation would be in the 'interests of justice'. This test is the same regardless of how the investigation was triggered.[73]

It is unclear whether the OTP has to undertake an in-depth analysis of the issues under Arts 11 and 12 ICCSt or whether he is merely required to look at jurisdiction and admissibility in light of Art. 5 and Art. 17 ICCSt. The wording of Art. 53 (1) suggests the latter. This view is also supported by Art. 15 (4) ICCSt, where the question of jurisdiction is referred to as an additional requirement to the 'reasonable basis' test. However, it would be completely detrimental to the efficiency of the proceedings if the Prosecutor were to investigate a situation which according to Art. 12 ICCSt clearly lies outside the ICC's jurisdiction. In fact, the question of jurisdiction pursuant to Arts 11 and 12 ICCSt is one of the first to be answered and it would be wholly 'unreasonable' to 'proceed under this Statute' and start an investigation in a situation which falls outside the temporal, territorial, or personal jurisdiction of the ICC. Regulation 27 RegP mirrors exactly this when stating that the OTP '... shall make a preliminary distinction between: (a) information relating to matters which manifestly fall outside the jurisdiction of the Court; (...).'

The systematic question of whether this evaluation is contained in the 'chapeau' of Art. 53 (1) ICCSt or in the test according to Art. 53 (1) (a) ICCSt is of secondary importance. It is suggested that Art. 53 (1) (a) ICCSt be read in a broad sense and the words 'crime within the jurisdiction of the Court' be interpreted as including jurisdiction in accordance with Arts 11 and 12 ICCSt.[74] This view is supported by Regulation 49 (1) (b) RegC, which states that the Prosecutor is required to give reasons why he or she believes the alleged crimes fall within the jurisdiction of the Court.

1. State and Security Council referral

If a situation is referred to the ICC Prosecutor by a Member State according to Art. 13 (a) 14 ICCSt, or by the Security Council in accordance with Art. 13 (b) ICCSt, the OTP will receive the necessary information together with the referral. This is specified by Art. 14 ICCSt as regards state referrals. It is, however, not expressly mentioned in relation to a Security Council referral. Nevertheless, it seems a matter of courtesy that the SC transfers to the ICC the relevant documents upon which it has based its decision. In fact, the referring state or the SC will have base their decision to address the ICC on an examination of the situation. Thus the

[73] K Ambos, *Internationales Strafrecht* (3rd edn, CH Beck 2011) § 8 MN 20b is of the opinion that under the *proprio motu* procedure the pre-investigation needs to be more comprehensive than under a State or SC referral and that the tests to be applied overlap only partially.

[74] Similarly F Hoffmeister and S Knoke, 'Das Vorermittlungsverfahren vor dem Internationalen Strafgerichtshof—Prüfstein für die Effektivität der neuen Gerichtsbarkeit im Völkerstrafrecht', 59 *ZaöRV* (1999) 785, 794.

information submitted would—in general—be more comprehensive than that submitted to the Court by an individual person.

In the first situation which was referred to the ICC by the UN SC, the Situation in Dafur (Sudan), on the basis of SC Res. 1593 of 31 May 2005, the SC had engaged a commission of international experts to conduct an international inquiry into the situation. The Commission's Report was made available to the ICC Prosecutor. Such a Report, however, might cause other difficulties for the ICC Prosecutor. It might be very detailed and suggest the culpability of individuals to such an extent that the independence of the ICC investigation might be endangered.[75] The Prosecutor must insist on his or her allegiance to the ICCSt and his or her political independence.

As soon as the Prosecutor receives a referral, s/he informs the Presidency of the Court immediately in writing (Regulation 45 RegC). The Presidency will upon receipt of this information assign the 'situation' to a Pre-Trial Chamber (Regulation 46 (2) RegC), which will be responsible for any matter, request or information arising out of the situation. As soon as the Pre-Trial Chamber has been constituted, the Registrar will open a 'situation' record (Regulation 20 (1) RegR).

In order to prepare for the decision whether or not to initiate an investigation (Art. 53 (1) ICCSt), the Prosecutor may by virtue of Rule 104 RPE ICC seek additional information from states, organs of the UN, including the SC, GOs, and NGOs, or any other source which might generate reliable information. The Prosecutor may also receive written or oral testimony, in which case, according to Rule 47 RPE ICC, Rules 111 and 112 RPE ICC apply. The OTP then prepares an internal report, which is accompanied by a recommendation whether or not to proceed (Regulation 29 (1) RegP). In this report the Prosecutor analyses the seriousness of the information received (Rule 104 RPE ICC) and evaluates whether there is a reasonable basis to initiate an investigation (Regulation 29 (3) RegP). In reaching his or her decision s/he takes advice from the Executive Committee (ExCom) within the OTP, (see Regulation 31 RegP). Should the Prosecutor decide not to proceed s/he must inform those who have referred the situation; that is, the State or UN SC, in accordance with Rule 105 RPE ICC. In the notification the Prosecutor must give reasons for the decision not to proceed, whilst at the same time taking regard of the general obligation contained in Art. 68 (1) ICCSt to ensure the protection of victims and witnesses. The referring State and the UN SC each have the right to request the Pre-Trial Chamber to review the Prosecutor's decision (see following).

[75] *See* C Gallavin, 'Prosecutorial Discretion within the ICC: Under Pressure of Justice', 17 *CLF* (2006) 43, 56 *et subs*.

2. *Individual communication*

In the case of an 'individual complaint' according to Art. 13 (c) ICCSt the procedure is even more formal[76] in that the Prosecutor is required to seek the authorization of the Pre-Trial Chamber in order to proceed with the investigation. The Prosecutor may enter into the pre-investigative phase on the basis of any information on crimes. The information might be provided by individual persons, by groups, by States, GOs or NGOs (Regulation 25 (1) RegP), or be brought to the attention of the Prosecutor in any other way.[77]

In 2009, the first *proprio motu* investigation was initiated by the Prosecutor. In the situation concerning Kenya, the Prosecutor requested authorization from the Pre-Trial Chamber. The Presidency assigned the situation to Pre-Trial Chamber II on 6 November 2009.[78] The authorization to initiate an investigation was requested by the Prosecutor on 26 November 2009.[79]

In substance the test is the same as the one to be applied after a state or SC referral. However, the normative frame is different: the 'entrance' to the *proprio motu* investigation lies with Art. 15 (3) ICCSt which is complemented by Rule 48 RPE ICC. These provisions refer the Prosecutor to the test contained in Art. 53 (1) (a)–(c) ICCSt ('reasonable basis'). This shows that the test is not only meant to be an evidentiary test, but also one of appropriateness, as the Prosecutor has to take the 'interests of justice' into account.[80] In order to properly evaluate the information made available, the Prosecutor may seek additional information on the basis of Art. 15 (2) ICCSt and needs to analyse the seriousness of the information received. The OTP thus has the power to lead a pre-investigation just as in the case of a State or SC referral.

If at the end of the pre-investigative phase the Prosecutor decides not to pursue the matter further, the OTP must by virtue of Art. 15 (6) ICCSt inform those who have complained to the ICC Prosecutor. In the notification, the Prosecutor must state the reasons for the decision, whilst again taking heed to ensure the safety of the persons affected by the decision (Rule 49 RPE ICC). The notification must be accompanied by the advice that the decision does not preclude the submission of further information regarding the same situation. However, the Prosecutor's decision cannot be appealed by those who supplied the information. Notwithstanding this, where the Prosecutor has based his or her decision not to proceed solely on the

[76] K Ambos, *Internationales Strafrecht* (3rd edn, CH Beck 2011) § 8 MN 21.

[77] Triffterer/*Bergsmo/Pejic*, Art. 15 MN 12. The list of Regulation 25 RegP is not exhaustive and in any way could not modify Art. 15 (1) ICCSt.

[78] ICC *Situation in the Republic of Kenya*, Presidency, ICC-01/09-1, 6 November 2009, Decision Assigning the Situation in the Republic of Kenya to Pre-Trial Chamber II.

[79] ICC *Situation in the Republic of Kenya*, PTC II, ICC-01/09-3, 26 November 2009, Request for Authorization of an Investigation Pursuant to Article 15.

[80] The opposite view is taken by Triffterer/*Bergsmo/Pejic*, Art. 15 MN 19.

ground that the investigation would not be in the 'interests of justice' according to Art. 53 (1) c ICCSt, Rule 48 RPE ICC, the Pre-Trial Chamber may review the decision by virtue of Art. 53 (3) b ICCSt.[81]

If, however, the Prosecutor concludes that there is a reasonable basis for an investigation, s/he must proceed as follows:

a. Step One: request for authorization A request for authorization to investigate must, according to Art. 15 (3) ICCSt, be filed in writing with the Pre-Trial Chamber and any supporting material must be transferred to the Chamber. In order to be able to do this, the Prosecutor must communicate his or her intention to submit a request for authorization to the Presidency (Regulation 45 RegC). The Presidency will then assign the situation to a Pre-Trial Chamber (Regulation 46 (2) RegC). As soon as the Pre-Trial Chamber is selected, the Registry will open a 'situation' record (Regulation 20 (1) RegR).

Details concerning the request for authorization are laid down in Rule 50 RPE ICC and are further specified by Regulation 49 RegC. The request must be in writing. The Prosecutor must state the crimes, which s/he considers to have been committed, give factual details regarding the place, time, and person(s) involved in the crime, and declare why these crimes fall within the jurisdiction of the ICC.

Not mentioned in Regulation 49 RegC are parameters for the question as to whether the prosecution is in the 'interests of justice'. This omission makes clear that the Pre-Trial Chamber does not merely review the decision of the Prosecutor; the Pre-Trial Chamber itself determines whether or not the prerequisites of Art. 53 (1) (a)–(c) ICCSt are met.

b. Step Two: authorization by the Pre-Trial Chamber Pursuant to Art. 15 (4) ICCSt the Pre-Trial Chamber decides whether to authorize an investigation. The Chamber is thus called upon to examine the information supplied and to consider whether there is a 'reasonable basis' to proceed with an investigation. It is unclear whether or not the Pre-Trial Chamber adopts the same test as the Prosecutor in the first step cited above.[82] There is no equivalent to Rule 48 RPE ICCfor the Pre-Trial Chamber concerning the parameters of Art. 53 (1) (a)–(c) ICCSt. It is indeed doubtful whether the provision applies, as Art. 15 (4) ICCSt explicitly mentions a *prima facie* assessment of the jurisdiction of the Court in the case (or rather a potential 'case' within the 'situation'). This would not have been necessary if the Pre-Trial Chamber were to apply Art. 53 (1) (a) and (b) ICCSt. Taking into account the aim of the pre-investigation and the authorization procedure, it

[81] K Ambos, *Internationales Srafrecht* (3rd edn, CH Beck 2011) § 8 MN 21, even though Art. 15 (3) ICCSt, Rule 48 does not refer to Art. 53 (3) ICCSt explicitly.

[82] Claimed by Triffterer/*Bergsmo/Pejić*, Art. 15 MN 19 without giving reasons.

is unlikely that the Statute intended to establish a new twofold test,[83] other than the requirements of Art. 53 (1) and 15 (3) ICCSt. Rather, the Statute stresses the necessity for the Pre-Trial Chamber to scrutinize jurisdictional issues.[84]After all, the rationale behind the authorization requirement is the upholding of the ICC principle of complementarity, and thus the safeguarding of state sovereignty, in relation to the investigatory powers of the Prosecutor. Hence states are protected against unjustified infringements of the principle of state sovereignty.

The procedure adopted by the Pre-Trial Chamber with regard to the authorization of the investigation is laid down in Rule 50 RPE ICC. In practice, its main concern is the questioning of victims, which will be discussed in the context of victim participation below. In order to speed up the process, Rule 50 (3) RPE ICC and Regulation 50 (1) RegC set down a time limit. Victims can make representations only within thirty days following their notification of the process. The Pre-Trial Chamber may request further information both from the OTP and from victims who have made representations, and if it considers it appropriate, may hold a hearing on the issue (Rule 50 (4) RPE ICC).

According to Art. 57 (2) (a) ICCSt, the Pre-Trial Chamber decides by a majority of its judges. The decision of the Pre-Trial Chamber must be in writing and must be reasoned (Rule 50 (5) RPE ICC). The Chamber has three options: it may (1) authorize the initiation of an investigation with respect to the entire request of the Prosecutor, (2) authorize only parts of the request to be forwarded to the formal investigation and at the same time reject the request in other parts, or (3) reject the request in its entirety and deny authorization. The Pre-Trial Chamber's decision is final, as neither the victims nor the Prosecutor have a right to appeal.[85]

The decision to authorize an investigation is a provisional decision. This provisional character is due to the fact that the factual basis for the evaluation is rather slim. The judges must operate on a hypothetical level when addressing issues of admissibility and jurisdiction. Most probably there is not even a 'case' in the sense of the ICCSt (although there could be); as in Art. 53 (1) ICCSt, we are dealing here with a 'situation' with the general suspicion that relevant crimes have been committed, perhaps by several alleged perpetrators. Only when conducting an investigation will the Prosecutor develop a proper 'case'. Hence, before the beginning of

[83] Triffterer/*Bergsmo/Pejíc*, Art. 15 MN 25.

[84] A different view altogether is taken by F Hoffmeister and S Knoke, 'Das Vorermittlungsverfahren vor dem Internationalen Strafgerichtshof—Prüfstein für die Effektivität der neuen Gerichtsbarkeit im Völkerstrafrecht', 59 *ZaöRV* (1999) 785, 792, who argue that the Pre-Trial Chamber will only evaluate the facts and the evidence presented and will not concern itself with jurisdiction and admissibility issues. This view contradicts the efficiency of the proceedings and the wording of Art. 15 (4) ICCSt.

[85] F Hoffmeister and S Knoke, 'Das Vorermittlungsverfahren vor dem Internationalen Strafgerichtshof—Prüfstein für die Effektivität der neuen Gerichtsbarkeit im Völkerstrafrecht', 59 *ZaöRV* (1999) 785, 800.

the investigation, the Pre-Trial Chamber's decision is of a provisional nature. Art. 15 (4) ICCSt takes heed of this when stating that the determination with regard to the jurisdiction and the admissibility of the case at this stage of the proceedings is without prejudice to subsequent rulings.

c. **Step Three: reapplication to the Pre-Trial Chamber** If the Pre-Trial Chamber has declined to authorize the investigation, the Prosecutor may reapply for authorization, providing s/he is in a position to present further information containing new facts or evidence which shed a new light upon the situation (Art. 15 (5) ICCSt). The Prosecutor must subject the new information to a pre-investigation test once more and evaluate the situation anew as prescribed by Art. 15 (3) ICCSt.[86] Should s/he consider the 'reasonable basis' test to be fulfilled, s/he may then submit a new request for authorization to the Pre-Trial Chamber. When deciding whether there is a 'reasonable basis' to investigate, the Prosecutor should take into consideration the decision of the Pre-Trial Chamber rejecting the prior request, In the case of a new request, the procedure set out in Rule 50 RPE ICC is simply repeated (Rule 50 (6) RPE ICC).

3. General review by the Pre-Trial Chamber

Setting aside for one moment the trigger mechanism and the follow-up authorization procedure which might be necessary, the Pre-Trial Chamber supervises the Prosecutor's decision not to prosecute pursuant to Art. 53 (1) and (2) ICCSt in two ways:

(1) It may request the Prosecutor to reconsider the negative decision at the request of the State that made the referral, or the UN SC that referred the situation, as the case may be.
(2) The Pre-Trial Chamber also has the power to make an *ex officio* request to the Prosecutor to reconsider his decision, if the latter based his or her decision to discontinue the investigation on public policy considerations pursuant to Art. 53 (1) (c) and (2) (c) ICCSt.

Upon notification of the Prosecutor's decision not to investigate, the referring State and SC have ninety days to file a request for review with the Pre-Trial Chamber (Rule 107 (1) RPE ICC). The Pre-Trial Chamber may request the Prosecutor to transmit information or documents in his or her possession in order to be in a position to review the decision properly (Rule 107 (2) RPE ICC) and ask for further observations from the applicant State or UN SC (Rule 107 (4) RPE ICC). Heed must be taken of the need to protect victims and witnesses (Rule 107 (3) RPE ICC).

The Pre-Trial Chamber passes a majority ruling on the issue. The decision must be reasoned and all participants must be duly notified (Rule 108 (1) RPE ICC).

[86] Triffterer/*Bergsmo/Pejic*, Art. 15 MN 29.

Should the Prosecutor be ordered to re-evaluate his or her prior decision, s/he is required to do so as soon as possible (Rule 108 (2) RPE ICC). If the Prosecutor declines to proceed with an investigation for a second time, the Chamber must be notified accordingly.

The powers of the Pre-Trial Chamber are even greater when it comes to the re-evaluation of a decision of the Prosecutor based on 'the interests of justice' pursuant to Art. 53 (1) (c) and (2) (c) ICCSt. Formally, the decision to terminate the investigation only enters into force upon the confirmation of the Pre-Trial Chamber (Art. 53 (3) (b) ICCSt). Thus the discretionary powers of the Prosecutor are held in check by a judicial body.[87] Within 180 days after having been notified by the Prosecutor, the Pre-Trial Chamber will reconsider its position (Rule 109 (1) RPE). The Prosecutor may add further observations and other material, as can the referring State and UN SC, (Rule 109 (1) and (2) RPE ICC). According to Rule 110 RPE ICC the decision as to whether or not to confirm the Prosecutor's decision, must be reached by a majority of the judges and shall be reasoned. It must be communicated to all participants. If the Pre-Trial Chamber does not confirm the Prosecutor's decision to discontinue the proceedings, the Prosecutor must indeed proceed with the investigation or prosecution. This means that the Pre-Trial Chamber in fact has the power to oblige the Prosecutor to investigate or prosecute.[88]

The provisions show the fundamental distrust of the original subjects of international law; that is, the states, towards the ICC Prosecutor. There is virtually no decision that the ICC Prosecutor can reach, which is not reviewable by an ICC Chamber.

II. The investigation phase

After the pre-investigation phase has been concluded with the decision that there is indeed a 'reasonable basis' to proceed with an investigation,[89] the 'investigation phase' commences.[90] It is during this phase that the Prosecutor gathers information and collects evidence. Several special investigative measures are attributed to the Prosecutor in this phase. Accordingly, the investigation phase is the heart of the entire pre-trial procedure. The powers of the Prosecutor will be discussed in detail at a later stage (*see* following, section A.III).

---

87 M Brubacher, 'Prosecutorial Discretion within the International Criminal Court', 2 *JICJ* (2004) 71, 81.

88 Rightly observed and criticized by M Brubacher, 'Prosecutorial Discretion within the International Criminal Court', 2 *JICJ* (2004) 71, 87.

89 The term 'in-depth investigation' used by M Brubacher, 'Prosecutorial Discretion within the International Criminal Court', 2 *JICJ* (2004) 71, 77 is, in the present author's view, legally incorrect. The decision according to Art. 53 (1) ICCSt triggers what is legally called the 'investigation'; therefore the phase before the Art. 53 (1) ICCSt decision is taken is something else. I called it 'pre-investigation'.

90 K Ambos, *Internationales Strafrecht* (3rd edn, CH Beck 2011) § 8 MN 20d.

1. Beginning and end of the investigation phase

At the ICC one can differentiate between two steps, which are taken in chronological order: (1) the Prosecutor develops one or several 'cases' out of a 'situation', and (2) the Prosecutor collects both incriminating and exonerating material with regard to an individual suspect (Art. 54 (1) (a) ICCSt).

At one point during the investigation phase, the Prosecutor must review the material that has been collected and decide on the future prospects of the case in accordance with Art. 53 (2) ICCSt. S/he needs to evaluate the evidence and information at his or her disposal and decide whether s/he believes there to be a 'sufficient basis' to prosecute, which seems to be a slightly different threshold from that of Art. 53 (1) ICCSt, which requires a 'reasonable basis' to investigate. As in Art. 53 (1) ICCSt, the wording in Art. 53 (2) ICCSt expresses the threshold in a negative manner. It follows, that a general assumption prevails within the Rome Statute that the Prosecutor will indeed proceed with the investigation and start a prosecution. The threshold for the decision to end the investigation is in substance similar to that for the decision to open an investigation under Art. 53 (1) ICCSt, albeit that the Prosecutor will now have more information and material at hand upon which s/he can base the decision. It is therefore not surprising that Regulation 29 RegP is applicable both to Art. 53 (1) and (2) ICCSt.[91] As discussed above (*see* II) the Prosecutor has to address three different issues: (1) the legal and factual evaluation of the conduct, (2) admissibility, and (3) policy considerations.

As regards the issue of the legal and factual evaluation of the conduct, Art. 53 (2) (a) ICCSt refers to the conditions which must be met for the application of an arrest warrant or a summons to appear according to Art. 58 (1) ICCSt. This means that there must be 'reasonable grounds to believe that the person has committed a crime within the jurisdiction of the Court'.

This test must not be confused with the 'reasonable basis'-test of Art. 53 (1) ICCSt, which is the general term for the threefold test applicable at the outset of an investigation.

It is not quite clear why the Statute refers to the prerequisites of an arrest warrant or a summons to appear. The drafters seem to have assumed that the questioning of a suspect following an arrest or summons to appear to be the crucial, and maybe final step of the investigation, and the initial step in the prosecution process.[92] However, there is no logical reason for the application of the arrest warrant test. Even Art. 58 (1) ICCSt states that an arrest warrant can be applied for at any time after the Art. 53 (1) ICCSt decision. Given the fact that the arrest of a person is the

---

[91] As laid down in Regulation 29 (5) RegP.

[92] *See* Triffterer/*Bergsmo/Kruger*, Art. 53 MN 27. Similarly Ahlbrecht/*Kirsch* MN 1391 and Cassese/Gaeta/Jones/*Turone*, Vol. II, 1177.

most drastic measure that can be imposed during the investigation stage and that pre-trial detention serves a variety of purposes, a high level of suspicion is only one pre-condition next to several others (see following, IV). The question at what point in time, if at all, the Prosecutor requests the issuance of an arrest warrant depends upon a whole set of considerations, which are not necessarily connected to the question of whether or not to prosecute. As a matter of fact, there is no obligation to question the suspect before applying for the confirmation of the charges.[93]

According to Art. 53 (2) (a) ICCSt, the Prosecutor must make a hypothetical assertion and predict whether on the basis of the information available to him or her at this stage, a Chamber would convict the suspect. If the Prosecutor's answer to this question is 'no', and if s/he is of the opinion that it is unlikely that further investigation will change this, s/he must conclude that there is no sufficient basis for a prosecution and inform the Pre-Trial Chamber and referring State, or the UN SC, as the case may be, in accordance with Art. 13 (a) and (b) ICCSt. Similarly the Prosecutor may be of the opinion that the admissibility criteria has not been met (Art. 53 (2) (b) ICCSt) or declare a prosecution to conflict with the 'interests of justice' (Art. 53 (2) (c) ICCSt). The notification that s/he has terminated the investigation must be supported by the reasons and grounds for his decision. In light of the subsequent review procedure before the Pre-Trial Chamber, as set out in Art. 53 (3) ICCSt, a differentiated approach is required in relation to the various grounds for the Prosecutor's decision not to prosecute. What has been said before regarding Art. 53 (1) ICCSt applies *mutatis mutandis* here. If the decision of the Prosecutor to end the investigation is based entirely on considerations of 'interests of justice' pursuant to Art. 53 (3) (b) ICCSt, the Pre-Trial Chamber must confirm the decision. According to Art. 53 (3) (b) ICCSt the Pre-Trial Chamber, if requested to do so by the referring State or UN SC, may review all other grounds for the Prosecutor's declination to proceed.

It must be kept in mind that the investigation can and will continue until the beginning of the trial. The 'end' of the (formal) investigation phase does not coincide with the authority of the Prosecutor to investigate the case. Even after the issuance of the document containing the charges (DCC) the Prosecutor may continue investigating. This is merely a 'waystation', a snapshot of the case, so to speak. In substance, the Prosecutor will carry on collecting evidence even after the confirmation of the charges. This certainly does not make the preparation of the trial any easier, in particular as regards to disclosure of evidence to the defence, which will be discussed later.[94]

---

[93] Ahlbrecht/*Kirsch* MN 1390.

[94] The problem has become obvious in the preparation of the trial against Katanga and Chui, *see* ICC *Prosecutor v Katanga and Chui*, TC II, ICC-01/04-01/07-747-tENG, 13 November 2008, Order Instructing the Participants and the Registry to Respond to Questions of Trial Chamber II for the Purpose of the Status Conference (Art. 64 (3) (a) of the Statute), para 9.

2. *Structure of the investigation*

The structure of the investigation is largely informal. The Prosecutor, who is responsible for the conduct and the outcome of this phase, is free to shape the investigation process as s/he finds reasonable and convenient.[95] Having said this, it must be borne in mind that s/he is free to pick and choose only those measures available to him/her within the framework of the Statute and the RPE.

Within the internal structure of the OTP, the Prosecutor will set up a 'joint team' in order to conduct the investigation (Regulation 32 RegP). As has been explained in detail in Chapter 4 section B, the OTP consists of three Divisions: the Jurisdiction, Complementarity, and Cooperation Division, the Investigation Division, and the Prosecution Division. A 'joint team' consists of staff from each of the three Divisions. The composition of the team will vary according to the requirements during the development of the investigation. The joint team will report on its activities and progress to the ExCom on a regular basis and receive strategic guidance.

In order to enhance transparency within the team and guarantee supervision and guidance through the ExCom, the joint team will compile a provisional case hypothesis on the basis of the information and evidence available. Such a case hypothesis will be composed of incidents to be investigated and persons who appear to be (most) responsible (see Regulation 34 RegP). During the course of the investigation this case hypothesis will be reviewed over and over again (see Regulation 35 (4) RegP). The investigative activities will be specified in an evidence collection plan and a cooperation plan, both of which need to be approved by the ExCom (Regulation 35 RegP). At this stage of the proceedings, the case hypothesis and all plans are classified as internal documents according to Rule 81 (1) RPE ICC and are thus not subject to disclosure.

III. The prosecution phase

At the end of the investigation the Prosecutor will have to decide whether or not to prosecute, that is, whether or not to bring 'charges' against an individual suspect, and request the Pre-Trial Chamber to confirm these. As the decision according to Art. 53 (2) ICCSt is a purely negative one, that is, a decision not to discontinue the proceedings, there is no official document stating that the OTP is 'opening' the prosecution phase. This function is assumed by the arrest warrant and the summons to appear respectively. Such an order will frequently be the first point in time at which the suspected person becomes aware that he or she is under suspicion.[96] However, the Prosecutor is under no legal obligation to question the suspect before applying to the Pre-Trial Chamber for the charges to be confirmed.

[95] *See* L Meyer-Goßner, *StPO* (54th edn, CH Beck 2011) Einl. MN 60.
[96] Ahlbrecht/*Kirsch* MN 1390.

1. *Decision to charge in substance*

We have seen that the Prosecutor has to meet different thresholds during the entire investigation process in order to either terminate or continue the investigation. S/he must find a 'reasonable basis' to proceed in order to enter into the 'investigation phase', and s/he can discontinue the investigation if s/he concludes that there is not a 'sufficient basis' for a prosecution. As a prerequisite for the termination of the investigation, the Prosecutor must be satisfied that there currently are and will be no 'reasonable grounds' to believe that the suspect has committed an international crime.

During the final phase of the investigation, that is, the prosecution phase, the Prosecutor must decide whether s/he is going to 'charge' the suspect and if so, with what crimes s/he intends to charge the suspect. Accordingly, the Prosecutor must then refer the matter to the Pre-Trial Chamber for confirmation. This means that the Prosecutor must forward precise allegations against the suspect. The Rome Statute uses the word 'charge' in order to circumscribe the allegations the Prosecutor brings against the suspect and we will address this terminology in detail in due course. The actual test to be applied is whether there are 'substantial grounds to believe that the person committed' the crimes alleged. This is the test applied by the Pre-Trial Chamber when confirming the charges according to Art. 61 (5) ICCSt. The same test is to be applied by the Prosecutor when compiling the allegations against the suspect in the so called 'charges'.

2. *Formulation of the 'charges'*

a. The use of the word 'charge' in legal texts The ICCSt uses the word 'charges' and thus deviates from the terminology used by the *ad hoc* Tribunals.

In contrast to the ICC, the general term for the document containing the charges at the *ad hoc* Tribunals is 'indictment'.[97] However, the term 'charge' also appears in the Statutes and Rules of the *ad hoc* Tribunals. It can be derived from the relevant provisions that the indictment *contains* the charges and that the 'subject' of a charge is a crime under the ICTY/ICTR Statute, in that it relates to the 'acts and conduct of the accused'. A 'provisional charge' is a prerequisite for the request and issuance of an arrest warrant. Furthermore, the charges are those of which the accused must be informed. Finally, the charges appear to be the very subject of the trial, in that the accused is 'found guilty on one or more charges'. However, the Rules of the ICTY occasionally use other seemingly related terms in this context, namely 'count' and 'crime'. Rule 2 ICTY RPE defines an accused as '[a] person against whom one or more counts in an indictment have been confirmed in accordance with Rule 47'. The plea of guilty or not guilty also refers to 'counts'; the Prosecutor's Pre-Trial brief must set out the evidence for each 'count'. Rule 73*bis* (D) RPE ICTY

[97] *See* A Cassese, *International Criminal Law* (2nd edn, OUP 2008) 404.

is of particular interest in this regard, since it appears to use the three terms quite randomly. It provides:

> After having heard the Prosecutor, the Trial Chamber, in the interest of a fair and expeditious trial, may invite the Prosecutor to reduce the number of *counts charged* in the indictment and may fix a number of crime sites or incidents comprised in *one or more of the charges* in respect of which evidence may be presented by the Prosecutor which, having regard to all the relevant circumstances, including the *crimes charged* in the indictment, their classification and nature, the places where they are alleged to have been committed, their scale and the victims of the crimes, are reasonably representative of the *crimes charged.*[98]

The 'charge' is not defined anywhere in the applicable law at the ICC. The ICCSt uses the term in Art. 61, characterizing the 'charges' as the topics 'on which the Prosecutor intends to seek trial'. According to Art. 64 (8) (a) ICCSt, the 'charges' which have been confirmed by the Pre-Trial Chamber must be read out to the accused at the commencement of the trial. The 'facts and circumstances described in the charges' serve as the basis of the Trial Chamber's decision and may not be exceeded according to Art. 74 (2) ICCSt. In addition, the term 'charge' is used in Art. 65 (1) (c) (i) ICCSt in relation to an admission of guilt on the part of the accused. The wording makes clear that the 'charges' comprise 'facts'. The same conclusion can be drawn from Rule 69 RPE ICC. The term is further used in Art. 65 (5) ICCSt, which states that the Court (in that case the Trial Chamber) is not bound by any modification of the charges discussed between the Prosecutor and the defence. Furthermore, pursuant to Art. 67 (1) (a) ICCSt, the accused must be informed of the 'nature, cause and content' of the 'charge'. This provision mirrors the wording of Art. 14 (3) (a) ICCPR[99] and at the same time exceeds the wording of the human rights provisions by adding 'content' to 'nature and cause'.[100] Despite the use of the singular here, there might indeed be several 'charges'. This is made clear by Rule 142 RPE ICC. Further, Rule 162 (2) (c) and Rule 165 (4) RPE ICC provide that offences against the administration of justice as contained in Art. 70 ICCSt can constitute a separate charge and can be combined with 'charges' under Arts 5 to 9 ICCSt.

Rule 121 (3) RPE ICC speaks of a 'detailed description of the charges' and a 'list of the evidence'. The content of the 'document containing the charges' is further specified in Regulation 52 RegC.

> **Regulation 52 RegC:** Document containing the charges
>
> 1. The document containing the charges referred to in article 61 shall include:

---

[98] Emphasis added.

[99] Interestingly Art. 6 (3) (a) ECHR avoids the word 'charge' and uses the term 'accusation' instead.

[100] *See* Triffterer/*Schabas,* Art. 67 MN 20.

(a) The full name of the person and any other relevant identifying information.

(b) A statement of the facts, including the time and place of the alleged crimes, which provides a sufficient legal and factual basis to bring the person or persons to trial, including relevant facts for the exercise of jurisdiction by the Court.

(c) A legal characterization of the facts to accord both with the crimes under articles 6, 7, or 8 and the precise form of participation under articles 25 and 28.

This is mirrored by the Regulations of the Prosecutor:

Regulation 58 RegP: Document containing the charges

1. The document containing the charges to be presented pursuant to article 61, paragraph 3 (a) shall be based on the Office's application under article 58, taking into consideration the decision on that application and any subsequent amendments thereto.

2. Pursuant to regulation 52 of the Regulations of the Court, the Office shall ensure that the document containing the charges clearly states the mode or modes of liability, pursuant to articles 25 and/or 28, which the Prosecutor alleges renders the person individually responsible and liable for punishment for each crime charged.

The picture gained, by looking at the Statute, Rules, and Regulations, of a 'charge' is somewhat unclear. There seem to be several elements comprising a 'charge'. One is the setting out of the facts.[101] Beyond the facts a 'charge' must also contain the 'crime'; that is, a legal characterization of the facts. But how much of each is necessary?

The exact definition of 'charge' is by no means a purely academic question. It is highly important for the structure of the trial and the functions and powers of the Prosecutor, the Pre-Trial Chamber, and the Trial Chamber. The question arouse in the *Lubanga* case when the victims' representatives asked the Trial Chamber to re-qualify the facts of the case, because these would not only fulfil the prohibition concerning child soldiers but could also amount to sexual slavery under Art. 7 (1) (g) ICCSt or Art. 8 (2) (b) (xxii) ICCSt. A new characterization of facts is possible under Regulation 55 RegC, but the question is, whether the proposed re-characterization would in fact alter the 'charge'.[102] A new 'charge', however, would call for a decision of the Pre-Trial Chamber, which must confirm the 'charge'.

The answer to this question depends on the respective roles of the participating institutions in the entire trial. In order to properly understand the different possibilities, we need to take a look at national systems and how they operate.

101 A Cassese, *International Criminal Law* (2nd edn, OUP 2008) 404.

102 *See* ICC *Prosecutor v Lubanga*, TC, ICC-01/04-01/06-2049, 14 July 2009, Decision Giving Notice to the Parties and Participants that the Legal Characterization of the Facts may be Subject to Change in Accordance with Regulation 55(2) of the Regulations of the Court.

b. The structural differences The question we are looking at is which of the participating institutions sets the law and is responsible for the legal characterization of a certain incident in criminal procedure?

As is so often the case, we can identify two different approaches. One system places the responsibility of the legal characterization of the facts solely with the court. This means that the prosecutor presents the facts of the case only and refrains from giving a binding legal qualification. One of the principles of Roman Law is that the court knows the law: *iura novit curia*. A further principle is *da mihi factum, dabo tibi ius*: 'if you present the facts to me, I will give you the law'.[103]

A different approach would be to leave the interpretation of the law to the prosecutor and let the court decide whether the prosecutor as regards to both the facts and the law has proved the allegations beyond reasonable doubt.

Both models are extremes and are therefore not applied in national systems. Under the Roman Law system in particular, the accused may be in danger of being taken by surprise if s/he does not expect the Court's legal interpretation of the facts. In criminal proceedings it is particularly important to know the legal provision, as the sentence regularly depends on it.

German criminal procedure counters this problem by obliging the judge to alert the accused of the amendment and the legal reference as well as affording the accused the opportunity to defend himself (§ 265 German Criminal Procedure Code). The trial may be adjourned upon the defendant's application if there has been insufficient time for the preparation of the defence.[104] This is a matter of fairness.[105] However, this caution is only feasible in situations which do not imply a completely new allegation. In cases where the accused is alleged to have committed a different crime altogether, the prosecutor must issue a new indictment ('Nachtragsanklage') according to § 266 German Criminal Procedure Code. This is due to the fact that the court cannot exceed the time frame defined by the prosecutor in his or her indictment. The prosecutor sets the topic of the trial; he or she establishes and brings forward the 'accusation' ('Anklageprinzip').[106] The court's inquiry may only pertain to the pre-defined issues, even though the exact legal interpretation of the prosecutor does not bind the judges (see § 155 German Criminal Procedure Code). This frame is known as the 'act in the procedural sense' ('prozessuale Tat') and circumscribes a uniform course of events ('einheitlicher Lebensvorgang'). The time and place of the act, the object of the

[103] K Ambos and D Miller, 'Structure and Function of the Confirmation Procedure before the ICC from a Comparative Perspective', 7 *ICLR* (2007) 335, 358 *et subs.*

[104] BGH 23 NStZ 2003, 444.

[105] K Volk, *Grundkurs StPO* (7th edn, CH Beck 2011) § 13 MN 6 *et subs.*; L Meyer-Goßner, *StPO* (54th edn, CH Beck 2011) § 265 MN 2-5; 31 BGHSt 151 speaks of 'Vertrauensschutz'.

[106] K Volk, ibid, § 13 MN 5.

act as well as the entire 'image' of the act, compose this course of events.[107] Even if the exact definition of these criteria is difficult, it is clear that the 'act in the procedural sense' is not a mere description of 'objective' facts, so to speak; it bears a normative aspect in that it refers to the 'image' of the deed and thus encompasses the harm or, for that matter, the legal interests ('Rechtsgut') protected by the criminal norm.[108]

The other system, mostly found in common law jurisdictions, may prove to be inefficient. If a prosecutor fails to convince a jury that the accused has committed a murder, the trial is over and there can be no retrial for manslaughter, due to the maxim of *ne bis in idem*. Amendments to the indictment are therefore accepted under English law, if such an amendment does not cause injustice.[109] However, after the start of the presentation of evidence an amendment will be rejected, if it contains a 'genuinely fresh charge' which alters the 'nature of the prosecution case'.[110] An amendment should also be 'foreshadowed' in the committal evidence. In any case the defence must be allowed an adjournment in order to be able to address the new allegations.[111]

From this comparative excursion we have learnt that there are three main principles relevant to the question of what constitutes a 'charge':

(1) The national criminal justice systems in general rely on a separation between an institution which represents the accusation (prosecutor) and an institution which passes the verdict (court). These two entities have precise and unique functions, which are to be kept separate.[112] Thus the court has the power and the obligation to decide the case according to the law. The court may not choose the 'topic' of the case. Setting the theme for the trial is the duty of the prosecutor.

(2) There is also a normative aspect of this issue: The accused needs to be informed of the content of the trial and have adequate time to prepare his or her defence. This requirement has often been emphasized by human rights bodies.[113] It is thus prohibited to take the defendant by surprise in the course of the trial.

(3) Yet national law also takes into account the need to make the proceedings flexible. The systems therefore allow amendments to the 'charges' and a change of legal reference, as long as the 'nature' of the allegations is not modified.

---

107 *See* 36 BGHSt 151, 154 *et subs.*; 35 BGHSt 60, 64: 'Tatzeit, Tatort, Tatobjekt, Tatbild'.

108 K Volk, *Grundkurs StPO* (7th edn, CH Beck 2011) § 13 MN 17.

109 J Sprack, *Criminal Procedure* (OUP 2008) 15, 47.

110 Ibid, 15, 48.

111 Schiemann in R Osieh [1996] 1 WLR 1260.

112 In further detail C Safferling, *Towards an International Criminal Procedure* (OUP 2003) 56 *et subs.*

113 *See* eg, ECtHR *Pelissier and Sassi v France*, Judgment 25 March 1999, Rep. 1999-II, para 52; *Abramyan v Russia*, Judgment 9 October 2008, Appl. No. 10709/02, para 34.

c. The definition of the 'charge' The 'charge', as it appears from the legal framework of the ICC, according to Art. 21 (1) ICCSt is a formal concept. The 'charges' set off the court proceedings, firstly the confirmation hearing before a Pre-Trial Chamber and then in their 'confirmed' form, the trial itself. The Prosecutor is responsible for the drafting of the 'charge', and the Pre-Trial Chamber supervises him or her in this very important task. Hence, the Prosecutor may amend the 'charges' only with the permission of the Pre-Trial Chamber (Art. 61 (9) 1 ICCSt). If this amendment contains an additional charge or an original charge is substituted with a more serious one, the confirmation hearing must be repeated (Art. 61 (9) 2 ICCSt). A functional divide runs between the Prosecutor and the Trial Chamber. Whereas the former is responsible for the accusation, the latter has no accusatory powers. The Court passes the verdict; that is, it decides whether and to what extend the 'charges' have been proven.[114] Responsibility for the 'charges' remains with the Prosecutor, which is illustrated by Art. 61 (9) 3 ICCSt. According to this provision, the Prosecutor may withdraw charges even after the commencement of s/he trial, albeit with the permission of the Trial Chamber. This must be regarded as the functional baseline of the solution to the problem discussed here.

The normative aspect identified above is of utmost importance to the practical procedure of the ICC. For the question of what is a 'charge', Art. 67 (1) (a) and (b) ICCSt contain the human rights principle, that the accused must be informed of the allegations against him in full, because this information is essential for the preparation of a proper defence. It cannot be emphasized enough that every single procedural step must conform with human rights provisions (Art. 21 (3) ICCSt). 'Fairness' towards the accused in the context of the Rome Statute is not a minimum guarantee, but one of the principal grounds for the legitimacy of the entire institution of the ICC.

Turning to Art. 67 (1) (a) ICCSt, we once again find three components of a 'charge': 'nature, cause, and content'. Taking into account the jurisprudence of the EComHR these can be defined as follows.[115] The 'nature' of a charge is the specific offence, the crime which is alleged to have been committed by the accused; that is, the legal characterization. The 'cause' of the charge consists of the relevant material facts. The 'content' requirement is not mentioned in human rights treaties. This element is a reference to evidentiary material and thus relates to disclosure issues.[116] The

[114] As to the 'judging element' *see* Chapter 1, p 55; as to the role of the judges *see*, Chapter 4, p 128.

[115] EComHR *Ofner v Austria*, 19 December 1960, Appl. No. 524/59, 3 YB (1960) 322, 344; C Safferling, *Towards an International Criminal Procedure* (OUP 2003) 117 *et subs.* as regards the ICCPR with further references.

[116] *See* Triffterer/*Schabas*, Art. 67 MN 20; arguing that the European institutions have not been very detailed on the scope of the information and whether or not it comprises evidentiary material; *see* also Safferling, *Towards an International Criminal Procedure* (2003) 118 with further references.

content of a 'charge' therefore does not seem to be part of the 'charge' itself but consists of supporting material, the notification of which follows a special procedure. In contrast, the 'nature' and the 'cause' seem to be essential parts of a 'charge'. The charge therefore consists of a description of the objective act, stipulating the time, place, and object involved, and of its legal qualification as one or several crimes.[117] These legal qualifications can be separated into several 'counts'.

When combining the functional analysis and the normative requirements, we arrive at the following definition : a 'charge' is the formal allegation that the person concerned has at a specific time and place committed a certain act directed against a certain object (factual aspect) which fulfils a specific crime or several crimes under the ICCSt (legal aspect).

This definition concurs with the opinion of the Appeals Chamber, which in the *Lubanga* decision regarding the recharacterization of facts, noted:[118]

> In the view of the Appeals Chamber, the term 'facts' refers to the factual allegations which support each of the legal elements of the crime charged. These factual allegations must be distinguished from the evidence put forward by the Prosecutor at the confirmation hearing to support a charge (article 61 (5) of the Statute), as well as from background or other information that, although contained in the document containing the charges or the confirmation decision, does not support the legal elements of the crime charged. The Appeals Chamber emphasizes that in the confirmation process, the facts, as defined above, must be identified with sufficient clarity and detail, meeting the standard in article 67 (I) (a) of the Statute.

This quote—although made in a different context—can be interpreted in such a way that the 'charge' comprises a specific crime and the factual allegations which support the legal elements of that crime. Evidence, background information, and other information do not form part of the 'charge'. A 'charge' is composed of the interplay between the criminal norm and the facts, which support the separate elements required by the norm.

3. *Form of presentation*

The OTP must prepare a document containing the 'charges'—the abbreviation 'DCC' seems to be well established[119]—as provided by Art. 61 (3) (a) ICCSt. Neither the Statute nor the RPE explicitly specifies how these 'charges' are to be

---

117 Similarly Boas/Bischoff/Reid/Taylor, *ICL III*, 198, who understand charge 'as the minimum combination of factual and legal allegations sufficient to justify the imposition of criminal liability'.

118 ICC *Prosecutor v Lubanga*, AC, ICC-01/04-01/06-2205 (OA 15 OA 16), 8 December 2009, Judgment, in fn 163.

119 *See* ICC *Prosecutor v Bemba*, PTC, ICC-01/05-01/08-424,15 June 2009, Decision Pursuant to Article 61(7)(a) and (b) of the Rome Statute on the Charges of the Prosecutor Against Jean-Pierre Bemba Gombo, para 17 speaks of 'Amended DCC'. It is unclear, why Pre-Trial Chamber II in the *Katanga and Chui*-case speaks of 'Amended charging document', ICC-01/04-01/07-717, 30 September 2008, Decision on the Confirmation of Charges, para 11. The term is used nowhere in the legal texts of the ICC.

presented. However Regulation 52 RegC, mirrored by Regulation 58 RegP,[120] both headed 'document containing the charges', state that the document must contain:

i. the suspect's full name and other identifying information;
ii. a statement of facts, such as time and place of the alleged crimes;
iii. the relevant facts for the exercise of jurisdiction by the ICC;
iv. a legal characterization of the facts with regard to Art. 6, 7, and 8 ICCSt;
v. the precise form of participation under Art. 25 and 28 ICCSt.

The list given in the Regulations is somewhat misleading as it does not clearly separate the two elements required by the definition of the 'charge'. The components of a 'charge' are thus hidden in several different numbers of this list. The document also contains additional information; background facts and facts pertaining to the exercise of jurisdiction must be given.

The evidence upon which the Prosecutor intends to rely does not form part of the 'document containing the charges'. The evidence must be listed in a separate document as envisaged by Art. 61 (3) (b) ICCSt and Rule 121 (3) RPE ICC. For some national lawyers this separation might be unusual—as, for example, the indictment under German law also includes reference to the evidence[121]—yet this distinction is necessary because of the specific disclosure rules which apply to evidence at the ICC. The need to disclose the evidence to the suspect at an early stage in order to give him or her adequate time to prepare for the confirmation hearing will be discussed later (see below C.) At this point it is important to note that the OTP must prepare two documents: (1) the document containing the charges, and (2) the list of evidence.

The few cases which have reached the confirmation stage and beyond at the ICC thus far unfold the many practical difficulties concerning the DCC. In the case of *Thomas Lubanga,* the Pre-Trial Chamber has criticized the Prosecutor for being too imprecise regarding the context and the circumstances of the alleged crimes.[122] In the *Bemba* case, the OTP prepared the DCC and submitted it to the Pre-Trial Chamber on 9 November 2008. The OTP had to amend the DCC after the Pre-Trial Chamber found at the confirmation hearing, which took place from 12–15 January 2009, that the evidence presented seemed to establish a different crime.[123] On 30 March 2009 the Prosecutor filed an amended document containing the

[120] The precise wording of Regulations 52 RegC and 58 RegP is quoted above.
[121] *See* Sec. 200 (1) German Criminal Procedure Code.
[122] ICC *Prosecutor v Lubanga*, TC, ICC-01/04-01/06-803, 29 January 2007, Decision on the Confirmation of the Charges, para 153.
[123] ICC *Prosecutor v Bemba*, PTC, ICC-01/05-01/08-388, Decision Adjourning the Hearing Pursuant to Article 61 (7)(c) (ii) of the Rome Statute, 3 March 2009.

charges and an amended list of evidence. The charges contained therein were finally confirmed on 15 June 2009.

C. Investigatory Powers of the Prosecutor

We have explored how the complex procedure of how to 'begin' an investigation is in place in order to control the investigatory authority of the Prosecutor, protect state sovereignty, and safeguard the rights of the individual persons involved. In this part we shall take a look at the various powers of the Prosecutor in the different phases of the investigation. This issue is rather complex due to the international setting and the complementary structure of the ICC.

Whereas in a national context the powers of the prosecutor are a one-dimensional issue, the Prosecutor at the ICC must take heed of the transnational dimension of his or her work.[124] The investigation thus 'depends on the receptivity of the domestic legal system to initiatives from the Prosecutor's office.'[125] This will be especially difficult in the case of sates that are not a party to the Rome Statute or states that find themselves threatened by such an investigation.

In the following we will differentiate between the two different phases of the pre-trial procedure and address (I) the pre-investigation phase, and (II) the investigation phase. The issues of the arrest warrant and summons to appear will be discussed separately at (E) Following, as they require particular attention due to their repressive nature and their importance in relation to the further procedure.

I. Pre-investigative phase

1. General powers

The Prosecutor evaluates the information. In order to do this s/he has no explicit investigatory powers.[126] S/he is not allowed to infringe the rights of individual persons. S/he can however, request further information from states, the UN, GOs, and NGOs or any other reliable source (Art. 15 (2) ICCSt and Rule 104 RPE ICC).

2. Unique investigative opportunity

Art. 56 ICCSt contains a specific power of the Prosecutor that is applicable at all stages of the pre-trial phase. It is therefore also a legitimate tool at the pre-investigative stage according to Rule 47 RPE ICC.[127] It is thus appropriate to discuss the 'unique investigative opportunity' at this point.

---

124 W Schabas, *An Introduction to the International Criminal Court* (1st edn, CUP 2001) 104.

125 Ibid.

126 K Ambos, *Internationales Strafrecht* (3rd edn, CH Beck 2011) § 8 MN 20c.

127 However, there is no cross-reference to Art. 56 ICCSt in Rule 47 (2) RPE, but the wording is equal in substance.

a. General considerations The main concern here is the preservation of testimony or other evidence for trial. It should be noted that the matter not only concerns the Prosecutor, but also the defendant, who under Art. 57 (3) (b) ICCSt has the right to request measures under Art. 56 ICCSt to be taken in order to assist the preparation of his or her defence. Preservation is necessary in cases where there is a real danger that the evidence might not be presentable at the trial stage. A reason for this might be that the witness is old or ill.[128] It could also be the case that the evidence would be destroyed if not preserved, as is the case with exhumation (transitory nature of evidence).[129] Finally the evidence might only be temporarily accessible to the Prosecutor, as is the case if in a national state a new regime threatens to decline further cooperation. In such a case, Art. 56 ICCSt foresees the involvement of the Pre-Trial Chamber in the investigation process. The involvement of a judicial body in this context is not warranted because the collection of the evidence interferes with state sovereignty or individuals' human rights. The judges' authority is required in order to ensure that the level of judicial control usually applicable at the trial stage is brought forward to the investigation phase. The safeguards that guarantee reliability of the evidence and the fairness of the proceedings at the trial stage are imported to this early phase. At trial, the results of such an investigation are merely reproduced, as the evidence is not heard by the Trial Chamber. Obviously this has a detrimental effect on the 'rights' of the accused at trial.

b. The procedure and measures A unique system has been created in Art. 56 ICCSt, and it is not surprising that the outcome is a compromise carrying the signature of both Continental European and Anglo-American criminal trial systems.[130]Once again it is of little help to trace the different strands; rather the uniqueness of the system at the ICC should be accepted and further developed. As regards Art. 56 ICCSt, there is already some case law available, because the Pre-Trial Chamber was rather willing to use the door which Art. 56 ICCSt opens to influence the investigation process.

Art. 56 ICCSt basically establishes a twofold system: (1) information must be provided to the Pre-Trial Chamber regarding 'unique investigative opportunities', and (2) certain measures can be implemented, if authorized by the Pre-Trial Chamber, to ensure the efficiency and integrity of the proceedings.

The actual measures that may be implemented are specified in a non-exhaustive list found in Art. 56 (2).[131] According to this list, the Pre-Trial Chamber

---

[128] *See* eg, Cassese/Gaeta/Jones/*Fourmy*, 1218.

[129] This was the case in ICC *Prosecutor v Lubanga*, PTC, ICC-01/04-01/06-803, 26 April 2005, Decision on the Prosecutor's Request for Measures under Art. 56; *see* also Triffterer/*Guariglia/Hochmayr*, Art. 56 MN 6.

[130] *See* eg, Triffterer/*Guariglia/Hochmayr*, Art. 56 MN 1-4 as to the drafting history.

[131] M Miraglia, 'The First Decision of the ICC Pre-Trial Chamber', 4 *JICJ* (2006) 188, 194; Triffterer/*Guariglia/Hochmayr*, Art. 56 MN 11; Cassese/Gaeta/Jones/*Fourmy*, 1219.

may: (a) make recommendations or orders regarding the procedure to be followed when ascertaining the evidence, (b) direct that a record be made of the proceedings which can later be presented at the trial stage as evidence, (c) initiate the appointment of an expert in order to assist in the investigation. The Pre-Trial Chamber made use of the latter option in the *Lubanga* investigation, where the Netherlands Forensic Institute (NFI) was authorized to perform the 'examination' as an independent body with no institutional connection to the Prosecutor.[132]

Due respect is also given to the defence counsel, who will be put in a position to participate in the taking of the evidence according Art. 56 (2) (d) ICCSt. If there is no defence counsel as yet, another counsel can be appointed in order to 'represent the interests of the defence'. The Pre-Trial Chamber can also order one of its members or another judge of the Pre-Trial or Trial division to participate and supervise the taking of evidence Art. 56 (2) (e) ICCSt.

Finally, Art. 56 (2) (f) ICCSt contains a catch-all provision, which authorizes the Pre-Trial Chamber to take any other action which it deems necessary to collect or preserve evidence. Despite the open phrasing of this provision, it must be borne in mind that the applicablility of Art. 56 (2) ICCSt depends on Art. 56 (1) ICCSt. Therefore the norm does not apply to the entire pre-trial phase, but only if there is a unique investigative opportunity.

c. **Pre-conditions** The scope of Art. 56 ICCSt is determined by (1) (a) which sets out that there must be a 'unique opportunity to take testimony... from a witness or to examine, collect or test evidence, which may not be available subsequently for the purposes of a trial'.[133] The long-winded phrasing 'for the purposes of a trial' instead of 'at trial' was arguably chosen because at an early stage of an investigation or even at the pre-investigative stage it is unclear whether a trial will take place at all or against whom or when.[134] In substance it must be shown that the collection of evidence or the hearing of testimony cannot be carried out at a later stage.[135] This presupposes that the evidence is physically existent and the person who intends to testify has already been identified. Art. 56 ICCSt does not allow fishing expeditions in order to find evidence or potential witnesses.

Apart from the situations mentioned above, it is questionable whether Art. 56 ICCSt can also be used in order to protect vulnerable witnesses from having to

[132] ICC *Prosecutor v Lubanga*, PTC, ICC-01/04-21, 26 April 2005, Decision on the Prosecutor's Request for Measures under Art. 56.

[133] The wording is misleading in so far as the provision names three powers of the Prosecutor: to examine, collect and test evidence. Art. 54 (3) (a) ICCSt mentions only 'collect and examine'. It is argued here that 'testing' evidence in the sense of Art. 56 (1) ICCSt does have no other meaning than 'examining'.

[134] *See* also Cassese/Gaeta/Jones/*Fourmy*, 1218.

[135] Triffterer/*Guariglia/Hochmayr*, Art. 56 MN 5.

appear and experience cross-examination at trial. This suggestion should be denied for two reasons: (1) a direct application of Art. 56 ICCSt is not possible, as a vulnerable witness is still physically available for trial and Art. 56 ICCSt is to be interpreted in a literal way,[136] and (2) an application of Art. 56 ICCSt by analogy is not permitted, as this would presuppose a lacuna in the ICCSt and the RPE regarding the vulnerable witness. This is not the case as the protection of the vulnerable witness is regulated in Art. 68 (2) ICCSt.

d. Responsibilities In general the Prosecutor is free to request the measures to be implemented according to Art. 56 (1) (b) ICCSt. It also seems to be up to the Prosecutor to determine whether or not there is a 'unique opportunity'. The wording of Art. 56 (1) (a) ICCSt is clear on this point ('the Prosecutor considers...'. Yet the Pre-Trial Chamber has control over the appropriateness of the measure adopted by virtue of Art. 56 (3) (a) ICCSt.

What follows is a threefold procedure: (1) the Pre-Trial Chamber consults with the Prosecutor without delay (*see* Rule 114 (1) RPE ICC) on the appropriateness of the measures to be implemented even if the Prosecutor has not requested any measures to be authorized by the Pre-Trial Chamber. (2) If upon consultation the Pre-Trial Chamber and the Prosecutor cannot agree on the investigative steps to be taken, the Pre-Trial Chamber may implement such measures on its own initiative, if agreed upon by a majority of its judges (Rule 114 (2) RPE ICC) and only where the Chamber is of the opinion that the evidence in question would be essential for the defence at trial.[137] The Pre-Trial Chamber thus appears not so much to assume the role of a subsidiary investigative body;[138] rather it supervises the adherence of the OTP to the principle of objectivity contained in Art. 54 (1) (a) ICCSt and helps to ensure a fair trial to the suspect or accused person.[139] (3) The Prosecutor may advise the Pre-Trial Chamber that the intended measure could jeopardize the proper conduct of the investigation (Rule 114 (2) RPE ICC) and may ultimately appeal against the decision by the Pre-Trial Chamber (Art. 56 (3) (b) ICCSt).

As regards the consultation according to Art. 56 (3) (a) ICCSt, Pre-Trial Chamber I has opted for a 'status conference' in the *Lubanga* case.[140] Other than the Prosecutor, the Pre-Trial Chamber saw '... [t]he need for Pre-Trial Chamber I to provide inter

[136] Similarly Triffterer/*Guariglia/Hochmayr*, Art. 56 MN 12, who also question the adequateness of such a measure to protect the witness from suffering harm through cross-examination.

[137] Rule 114 (2) RPE invokes Art. 57 (2) (b) ICCSt in that a single judge's decision is ruled out in this regard; *see* also Triffterer/*Guariglia/Harris/Hochmayr*, Art. 57 MN 8.

[138] *See* C Kreß, 'The Procedural Law of the International Criminal Court in Outline: Anatomy of a Unique Compromise', 1 *JICJ* (2003) 603, 608.

[139] Cassese/Gaeta/Jones/*Fourmy*, 1218.

[140] ICC *Prosecutor v Lubanga*, PTC, ICC-01/04-9, 17 February 2005, Decision to Convene a Status Conference.

alia for the protection of victims and witnesses and the preservation of evidence through the holding of a status conference'.

It based its decision on Art. 57 (3) (c) ICCSt and chose the 'status conference' as a procedural tool which is not foreseen in this regard by the legal texts of the ICC.[141] Status conferences are envisaged in Rules 121 and 132 RPE ICC to serve the purpose of preparing a 'hearing', namely the confirmation hearing according to Art. 61 ICCSt and the trial according to Art. 64 ICCSt.[142] Moreover, a status conference is generally an *inter partes* meeting, whereas the consultation with the Prosecutor by virtue of Art. 56 (3) (a) ICCSt is an *ex parte* hearing.[143] Nevertheless, the Pre-Trial Chamber did in fact select one of the procedural tools available under the Statute and Rules and might thus have given the 'status conference' a new focus. Miraglia commented upon the application of the status conference in this way, as follows:

> Pre-Trial Chamber I decided to intervene using the general powers provided for in Article 57(3)(c) ICCSt and the status conference procedural device after seven months of investigations during which the Prosecutor had not let the Chamber know anything about their progress and results. Thus, it could be assumed that this decision was made both to speed up the investigations and also to take care of the rights of the 'prospective suspects' a special aspect of the 'interest of justice' to whom the delay could, obviously, be prejudicial.[144]

The proactive approach of the Pre-Trial Chamber, in which it demands an account from the Prosecutor, is a pithy sign from the Judges to the OTP that it is not solely responsible for the investigation. Rather the Rome Statute assigns to the Pre-Trial Chamber a strong role regarding the beginning (Art. 15 and Art. 53 ICCSt), the end (Art. 61 ICCSt) of the investigation, and the investigative measures to be employed by the OTP in the course of the process. In this regard, the Pre-Trial Chamber has strong supervisory powers, and is obviously willing to take this obligation very serious.

e. The role of the defence The defence is referred to at several points within Art. 56 ICCSt. As has already been seen[145] the Rome Statute has come up with some novelties concerning the position of the defence. For example, Art. 55 ICCSt, with regard to the pre-trial phase, lists the rights of persons during an investiga-

---

141 *See* C Kreß, 'Grundlagen des Völkerstrafprozessrechts' in H Radtke, D Rössner, T Schiller, and W Form (eds), *Historische Dimensionen von Kriegsverbrecherprozessen nach dem Zweiten Weltkrieg* (Nomos 2007) 37, 47.

142 M Miraglia, 'The First Decision of the ICC Pre-Trial Chamber', 4 *JICJ* (2006) 188, 191 *et subs.*, referring also to the position of the Prosecutor in this regard who argued against holding a status conference.

143 M Miraglia, ibid, 188, 192 points at the fact that the 'status conference' is an Anglo-American feature.

144 Ibid, 188, 193.

145 Chapter 4, p 179.

tion and for the first time codifies these special rights which have been developed by human rights bodies, the ECtHR in particular.[146] Whereas Art. 55 ICCSt pertains to a situation of direct confrontation of the person concerned—suspect or not—with the ICC authorities, the incorporation of defence rights into Art. 56 ICCSt comprises a much broader picture. By adopting the Art. 56 ICCSt proceedings the Prosecutor intends to preserve the evidence for use at the later trial stage. Although the main aim of Art. 56 ICCSt does not lie in the protection of defence rights,[147] compliance with these rights is logical and indeed essential if the evidence is to be admissible later at trial. The result of the evidence-taking is 'transported' to the trial so that the evidence does not need to be heard again at trial.[148] This effect however can only be achieved if the taking of the evidence in the first place; that is, the 'anticipated' hearing of the evidence, was conducted in full compliance with the defendant's rights.

Applying this human rights standard to the criminal proceedings at the ICC means two things: (1) the suspect and his or her legal assistant must be informed of the investigative measure, as is foreseen in Art. 56 (1) (c) ICCSt,[149] and (2) counsel must be involved in the hearing of the evidence, because it is unlikely that the result of the evidence gathering will otherwise be admitted at trial as foreseen in Art. 56 (2) (d) ICCSt. Indeed, it is the presence of defence counsel that legitimizes its use at trial.[150]

However, as we have seen, the pre-trial phase differentiates between a 'situation' and a 'case'. During the 'situation' phase, no individual person has been identified as a suspect so there is no defendant and no defence counsel. Art. 56 (2) (d) ICCSt takes heed of the following three different scenarios. (1) If the suspect is present before the ICC and counsel has already been assigned to him or her under Art. 55 (2) (c) ICCSt, counsel is authorized to participate in the Art. 56 procedure. (2) If the suspect is present but has not chosen counsel yet, the Pre-Trial Chamber will appoint an *ad hoc* counsel to take part in the Art.56 process. (3) If there is no 'suspect' yet, the Pre-Trial Chamber will designate an *ad hoc* counsel to attend and represent the defence at the Art. 56 procedure. This last scenario is the only reason why Art. 56 (2) (d) ICCSt rightly refers to the 'interests' of the 'defence' rather than the 'rights'

[146] *See* C Safferling 'Die EMRK und das Völkerstrafprozessrecht', in: J Renzikowski (ed), *Die EMRK im Zivil-, Straf- und Öffentlichen Recht—Grundlagen einer Europäischen Rechtskultur* (Schulthess 2004) 137–68.

[147] This view is taken by Triffterer/*Guariglia/Hochmayr*, Art. 56 MN 10.

[148] C Kreß, 'The Procedural Law of the International Criminal Court in Outline: Anatomy of a Unique Compromise', 1 *JICJ* (2003) 603, 607.

[149] Such notification should be conducted on a general basis; should the Pre-Trial Chamber order otherwise, as is possible under Art. 56 (1) (c) ICCSt the result of the taking of evidence will not be 'transportable' to the trial; similarly Triffterer/*Guariglia/Hochmayr*, Art. 56 MN 10 on the basic assumption that Art. 56 ICCSt aims mainly at protecting defence rights.

[150] C Kreß, 'The Procedural Law of the International Criminal Court in Outline: Anatomy of a Unique Compromise', 1 *JICJ* (2003) 603, 608.

of the defendant.[151] Pre-Trial Chamber I had acted accordingly, having appointed *ad hoc* counsel for the defence in the situation concerning the Democratic Republic of Congo in order to 'protect the general interests of the defence' during the performance of forensic examinations.[152] In general the Office of Public Counsel for the defence, which has been established pursuant to Regulation 77 RegC, fulfils the role of representing the interests of the defence generally.

The role of the defence counsel has been discussed before.[153] This role is defined according to the needs and rights of the suspect or accused person. But what is the function of defence counsel in the absence of a client? Principally there can be said to be a genuine interest on the part of the defence that the process is conducted in accordance with the 'rule of law'. In any case, a suspect or accused person has only to endure such hardship inflicted upon him or her by an official authority; that is, coercive investigatory measures, a trial, a conviction, a sentence, and so forth, that has come about in a legally correct way. More specifically four issues, which concern the 'interests of the defence' at this stage of the prosecution can be identified:

a. Adherence to procedural provisions.
b. The legitimacy of investigatory measures.
c. The examination of a witness or an expert witness.
d. Coordination of several national legal orders and the ICC.

These issues need to be addressed by counsel for the defence even if there is no identifiable suspect as yet.

II. Investigative phase

The investigation phase is the core of the entire pre-trial phase. It is at this stage that the Prosecutor's inquiry into the 'situation' is narrowed down and one or several 'cases' are carved out. For fulfilling this task, the Prosecutor is equipped with specific powers, which are summarized in Table 6.1. S/he can collect evidence and can question the suspect, victims, and witnesses without touching upon individual's rights. I would call these 'simple investigative measures'. The Prosecutor may also be authorized to intrude into rights of individuals and impose coercive measures for fact-finding purposes. S/he can thus summon a person to appear, request the arrest of a suspect person, order specific forensic tests, search premises, and seize evidentiary material against the owner's will, implement electronic surveillance and tap the telephone without the person concerned knowing, collect and

[151] Regulation 77 RegC does not mirror this differentiation and speaks only of 'rights of the defence during the initial stages of the investigation'.

[152] ICC *Prosecutor v Lubanga*, PTC, ICC-01/04-21, 26 April 2005, Decision on the Prosecutor's Request for Measures under Art. 56.

[153] Chapter 4, p 186.

Table 6.1 Investigative measures

Simple investigative measures	= no relevance to individuals' rights	No specific authority needed
Qualified investigative measures	= intruding into individual's rights	Special legitimacy required

keep records of sensitive personal data, such as bank account information and the like. I would call these 'qualified investigative measures'.

It is therefore a special phase of both empowering the Prosecutor and at the same time endangering individuals' rights. Because of the authority to use force in order to investigate, this phase is particularly effective and most important for the entire prosecution process. This is what differentiates the investigation of a prosecutor from any other form of truth-seeking. The Prosecutor can execute his or her interests by force even against the will of a person concerned; whereas the historian depends on voluntary cooperation.

The measures at the hand of the Prosecutor might be directed both towards a suspect or a person who is not a suspect. In the investigation phase it might still be unclear whether the person is a suspect or a witness. The methods of investigation might relate to the home, privacy, or the liberty and security of the person. However, before the Prosecutor can infringe on individual rights there must be a specific authority to doing so. 'Qualified investigatory measures' require a legitimate legal basis and need to be necessary and proportionate in a democratic society. In international criminal procedure there is no regulation at all on this matter.[154]

1. Human rights law and national jurisdictions

a. Human rights The system of legal authorization stems from the jurisprudence of human rights. The prerequisite is the understanding of free and equal human beings, who enjoy specific rights which are, generally speaking, immune from intrusion by government authority.

The best example might be Art. 8 ECHR, the right to privacy and family life. It is stated in Art. 8 (2) ECHR that interference by a public authority with the exercise of this right is only legitimate if it is in accordance with the law and is necessary in a democratic society. In the reading of the ECtHR, any investigative measure adopted by the prosecution service or the police thus needs to be based on a specific legal prescription and must be implemented according to the conditions described therein. In several cases concerning secret surveillance measures, the ECtHR has held that the authorizing law must clearly state the conditions and the procedure to

[154] A Zahar and G Sluiter, *International Criminal Law* (OUP 2007) 56.

be adopted before deploying such measure.[155] In addition the law must be publicly accessible and predictable.[156]

There is no straightforward answer to the question of what the 'procedure' prescribed by law must look like in order to legitimize the interference with the human right of the individual. Is it perhaps preferable to establish an independent control before the implementation of the specific measure, or is an *ex post* adjudication sufficient for the protection of human rights? In *Funke v France* this problem came before the ECtHR with respect to Art. 8 ECHR.[157] The French Government argued that the pertinent law, concerning the powers of the customs officers to search premises, was strictly supervised by the court *ex post facto* in a very efficient manner. It furthermore argued that Art. 8 ECHR does not require judicial authority in advance of search and seizure.[158] As the French pleading suggests, *ex post* and *ex ante* control are interchangeable and rest in the discretion of the national state, as they are equally efficient and both eliminate arbitrariness. It is remarkable that the French Parliament amended the law to *ex ante* authorization after the case was filed with the ECtHR.[159] Indeed the ECtHR held that the original French law did not provide for sufficient restrictions and limitations on the capacity of the public authority.[160] We can conclude from this decision that even if the ECHR does not foresee an *ex ante* control explicitly, it is nevertheless believed to be a more effective and thus a better guarantee of human rights.[161]

b. National systems National legal systems mirror the principle of judicial control for authorizing human rights interferences.

According to German criminal procedure, any potential infringement of the right to liberty and security of person, and his or her right to privacy, cannot be permitted without a court order (§ 162 StPO). The institutionally competent authority at court is the *Ermittlungsrichter* (§ 21e GVG). The system generally operates on two levels: (1) in principle, a judge must authorize the interfering action; (2) in urgent cases (*Gefahr im Verzug*), an order issued by a prosecutor or a senior police officer is sufficient.[162] The legality of the action is subject to scrutiny by the judge.[163] The test s/he applies is twofold: first, s/he examines whether the legal

[155] ECtHR *Malone v UK*, Judgment 2 August 1984, Series A No. 82 para 64 *et subs.*; *Amann v Switzerland*, Judgment 16 February 2000, Rep. 2000-II, para 58.

[156] ECtHR *Rekvenyi v Hungary*, Judgment 20 May 1999, Rep. 1999-III, para 59.

[157] ECtHR *Funke v France*, Judgment 25 February 1993, Series A No. 256-A.

[158] Ibid, para 50.

[159] Budget Acts from 30 December 1986 and 29 December 1989.

[160] ECtHR *Funke v France*, Judgment 25 February 1993, Series A No. 256-A, para 57.

[161] Similarly A Zahar and G Sluiter, *International Criminal Law* (OUP 2007) 56, who derive from the ECtHR case law that 'judicial intervention is mandatory'.

[162] *See* eg, searching of the suspect's house (Hausdurchsuchung beim Verdächtigen) §§ 102, 105 StPO.

[163] Compare BVerfG Decision 27 April 1971, in 31 BVerfGE 43.

requirements exist and, second, s/he asks whether or not the demanded action is excessive (*unverhältnismäßig*).

In the US legal system, a warrant is theoretically necessary for police search and seizure, as set out in the Fourth Amendment of the Constitution. The Supreme Court has often stressed the necessity of a warrant for the respect of civil liberties and that searches and seizure without a warrant should only be conducted in exceptional circumstances.[164] Yet over the last forty years or so, the scope of the Fourth Amendment has been considerably reduced and exceptions to the general rule have increased considerably.[165] This is mainly due to the fact that common law recognizes searches and seizure in connection with an arrest.[166] Nevertheless constitutional law recognizes the need of an *ex ante* control over human rights and civil liberties by judges.

Similarly, in English law, arrest triggers several other rights like search and seizure, powers for which the police would otherwise need a warrant.[167] The 'proper' avenue according to common law is still the warrant for search and seizure, issued by a magistrate and based on positive law, although both alternatives are foreseen in PACE (1984) ss. 17, 18, and 32. In the English legal system, too, we find the attitude that important human rights are reliably safeguarded if their observance is reviewed by an independent, judicial authority.

2. *The* ad hoc *Tribunals and the ICC*

a. The *ad hoc* Tribunals The power of the Prosecutor to conduct investigations and to undertake investigatory measures without authorization from a judge is provided for in Art. 18 (2) ICTYSt, Art. 17 (2) ICTRSt. Also, Rules 39 and 40 of the Rules of Procedure and Evidence address the conduct of investigations. The Statutes of the *ad hoc* Tribunals do not, however, assign any function to the judge during an investigation.[168] The judge comes into play for the confirmation of an indictment according to Arts 18 (4), 19 (1) ICTYSt, Arts 17 (4), 18 (1) ICTRSt.

---

164 US Supreme Court, *Johnson v United States*, 333 US 10, 14 (1948); *McDonald v United States*, 335 US 451, 453 (1948); *Camara v Municipal Court*, 387 US 523, 528–9 (1967); *GM Leasing Corp v United States*, 429 US 338, 352–3, 355 (1977).

165 Eg, property that had not been described in the warrant was still allowed to be seized (C Osakwe, 'The Bill of Rights for the Criminal Defendant in American Law', in: J Andrews, *Human Rights in Criminal Procedure—A Comparative Study* (Martinus Nijhoff Publishers 1982) 259, 277 with references), although the exclusionary rule, which is often criticized as too strict, declares evidence obtained illegally as inadmissible in trial; *see* US Supreme Court *Silverthrone Lumber Co v US*, 251 US 385 (1920).

166 US Supreme Court, *Weeks v United States*, 232 US 383, 392 (1914); *Carroll v United States*, 267 US 132, 158 (1925); *Agnello v United States*, 269 US 20, 30 (1925).

167 L Leigh, 'The Protection of the Rights of the Accused in Pre-Trial Procedure: England and Wales', in: J Andrews, *Human Rights in Criminal Procedure—A Comparative Study* (Martinus Nijhoff Publishers 1982) 37, 44.

168 A Zahar and G Sluiter, *International Criminal Law* (OUP 2007) 56.

Based on this indictment the judge may issue a warrant of arrest, Art. 19 (1) ICTYSt, Art. 18 (1) ICTRSt.

Pursuant to Rule 39 (ii) of the Rules of Procedure and Evidence, the Prosecutor may 'undertake such... matters as may appear necessary for completing the investigation'. The Prosecutor is empowered to carry out any kind of investigatory measures in a broad sense by way of this Rule. In the absence of an actual requirement of judicial authorization, it is submitted here that this paragraph should be read in conjunction with Rule 39 (iv) of the Rules of Procedure and Evidence. The latter provision empowers the Prosecutor to 'request such orders as may be necessary from a Trial Chamber or a Judge'. Any measure that endangers human rights needs authorization from a judge.[169] Rule 40 of the Rules of Procedure and Evidence authorizes the Prosecutor to request that a state take certain measures in case of urgency.[170] The requested state must comply with this order in accordance with its own law.

Rule 54 of the Rules of Procedure and Evidence addresses the issuance of orders and warrants by a judge or a Trial Chamber with regard to pre-trial proceedings. Even though this Rule is directed at the preparation of the trial after the indictment has been confirmed, specific orders or warrants may be issued if 'necessary for the purposes of an investigation'. Put together, Rules 39 (iv) and 54 can be dealt with as a joint concept relating to judicial authorization. President Cassese elaborated on this issue in the *Celibici* case,[171] stating that this concept was subject to a twofold test: (1) an order of the International Tribunal must be necessary for the Prosecutor to obtain such material, and (2) the material being sought must be relevant to an investigation or prosecution being conducted by the Prosecutor. The Prosecutor's request will only be granted if s/he provides material that establishes a sufficient degree of probability that these criteria are met.[172]

b. The legal context at the ICC At the ICC the Prosecutor's authority is contained in the Rome Statute. The duties and powers of the Prosecutor during investigation are contained in Art. 54 ICCSt.[173] The norm is structured as follows:

- Art. 54 (1) ICCSt states the general obligations to be respected by the Prosecutor in conducting an investigation;
- Art. 54 (3) ICCSt gives a list of possible measures to be adopted by the Prosecutor for investigation;

[169] *See* C Safferling, *Towards an International Criminal Procedure* (OUP 2003) 102.

[170] Rule 40 (A) RPE ICTR.

[171] ICTY *Prosecutor v Delalić et al.*, TC, IT-96-21, 11 November 1996, Decision of the President of the Prosecutor's Motion for the Production of Notes Exchanged Between Zejnil Delalić and Zdravko Mucić, at paras 38–9.

[172] V Morris and M Scharf, *An Insider's Guide to the International Criminal Tribunal for the Former Yugoslavia* (Hotei Publishing 1995) 195.

[173] Triffterer/*Bergsmo/Kruger*, Art. 54 MN 1.

- Art. 54 (2) ICCSt foresees circumstances under which the Prosecutor may conduct investigations on the territory of a state.

This provision is an expression of the specific structure of the ICC as a complementary organ, which is not equipped with direct power to overthrow state sovereignty by deploying its own police force and investigators on the territory of a national state on its own initiative. In general the ICC and its Prosecutor depend on the cooperation of states. The effectiveness of the Prosecutor's investigation is thus severely challenged compared to the national context. It furthermore risks being biased as the national state will be willing to cooperate in instances where the interests of the state concerned and the interests of the Prosecutor coincide.[174]

3. General principles

The investigation at the ICC is governed by three general principles as they are laid down in Art. 54 (1) ICCSt.

(1) Objectivity
(2) Free design of investigation
(3) Respect for human rights

At first, the Prosecutor is committed to the principle of objectivity, as has been discussed before. This means that s/he is obliged to investigate both incriminating and exonerating circumstances equally (Art. 54 (1) (a) ICCSt). Secondly, the Prosecutor is the 'Master' of the investigating phase, that is, s/he is solely responsible for the effectiveness and appropriateness of the investigation, and can design the process and choose from the possible investigatory measures *ad libidum*. 'It is the sole duty of the Prosecutor to devise the prosecution strategy.'[175] S/he does not have to answer to any specific Chamber or any other organ of the ICC as regards the appropriateness of the investigatory measures applied.[176] One important exception is contained in Art. 56 (3) ICCSt, where the Prosecutor has to answer to the Pre-Trial Chamber regarding the requesting of measures for preserving evidence.[177] This principle of 'free design' of the investigation phase on the side of the Prosecutor is contained in Art. 54 (1) (b) ICCSt. This freedom is not 'absolute' but 'relative', as it were, to the framework of the ICCSt, in particular the duties and powers of the Prosecutor contained therein. Therefore a third principle can be established, which is that of the respect for the rights of persons arising under the

[174] M Brubacher, 'Prosecutorial Discretion within the International Criminal Court', 2 *JICJ* (2004), 71, 88 *et subs.*

[175] ICTR *Prosecutor v Ntuyahaga*, TC, ICTR-98-40-T, 18 March 1999, Decision on the Prosecutor's Motion to Withdraw the Indictment.

[176] Boas/Bischoff/Reid/Taylor, *ICL III*, 105; Triffterer/*Bergsmo/Kruger*, Art. 54 MN 12 *et subs.*, *see* also A Zahar and G Sluiter, *International Criminal Law* (OUP 2007) 57, who are of the opinion that the ICC will exercise a greater degree of supervision compared to the ICTY/ICTR.

[177] *See* p 254.

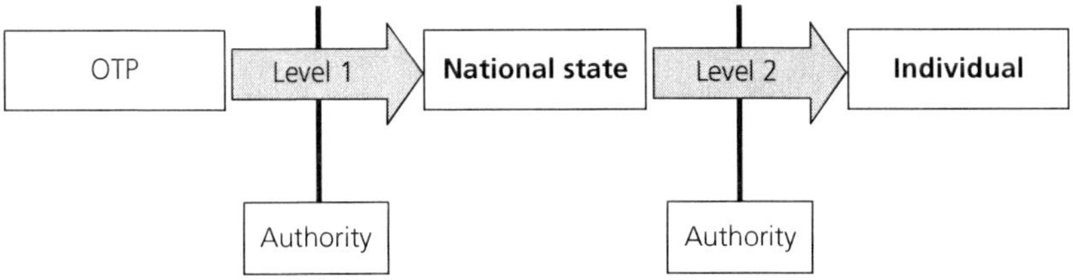

Figure 6.2 Investigative measures of the ICC Prosecutor

Rome Statute (Art. 54 (1) (c) ICCSt and more specifically regarding victims and witnesses in Art. 54 (1) (b) ICCSt).[178]

4. Different measures—general overview

The Rome Statute contains two express investigatory measures of the Prosecutor. One is to collect and examine evidence (Art. 54 (3) (a) ICCSt), the other is to request the presence of and question the suspect, victims, and witnesses (Art. 54 (3) (b) ICCSt). As a matter of fact these measures are rather broad. The power to collect evidence in particular is not specified further as to how the Prosecutor should proceed in investigating.[179] The answer to this question is essential as the collection might be in conflict with state sovereignty or individuals' rights.

In order to understand the complex nature of the investigation measures at the hand of the ICC Prosecutor, we must differentiate two levels. (1) Any mandatory measure deployed in the territory of a sovereign state touches upon the very sovereignty of that state. (2) An investigative measure against an individual person infringes the basic and human rights of that individual. Both levels require a special authority. On the first level, the Prosecutor as an agent of a foreign power would by his/her very presence in the territory of a state infringe the territorial integrity of that state. The territorial integrity is a part of the principle of state sovereignty.[180] No other subject of international law may exercise force like police powers on the territory of a state.[181] On the second level, any mandatory investigative measure imposed on an individual infringes the private sphere as protected by human rights.

The Prosecutor needs authority to intervene on both levels as is shown by Figure 6.2: (1) the violation of the territorial integrity of the state, and (2) the infringement of the individual human rights. 'Authority' might come from the state or the individual if they consent to the intrusion into their rights. In case of consent there is no violation of the legal position which is touched upon by the adoption of the

[178] Boas/Bischoff/Reid/Taylor, *ICL III*, 106.

[179] A Zahar and G Sluiter, *International Criminal Law* (OUP 2007) 56.

[180] B Kempen and C Hillgruber, *Völkerrecht* (CH Beck 2007) Chapter 4 MN 20 and 25.

[181] 'Palmas-Fall', RIAA 2, 838. *See* also US Supreme Court *United States v Alvarez-Machain*, 95 *ILR* (1994), 355 concerning CIA abduction of terror suspects; *see* also BVerfG, Decision 19 October 1994, 48 *NJW* 1995, 651 concerning the capturing of a alleged drug dealer by German police on the soil of the Netherlands.

Table 6.2 Authority for investigative measures

Consent	State	Individual
Scenario 1	yes	yes
Scenario 2	yes	no
Scenario 3	no	no
Scenario 4	no	yes

investigative measure. If there is no consent, the intrusion must be legitimized by other means provided by law.[182]

If we look at the two levels and at the possible answers, we can identify four different situations as they are summarized in Table 6.2.

In all of these four scenarios, the ICCSt offers different solutions to the Prosecutor in order to adopt and implement his/her investigative powers. The ICC model is based on cooperation as a general maxim. The structure of solutions for the different levels is therefore intertwined with the general provisions regarding cooperation between the ICC and State Parties according to Part IX ICCSt. The ICCSt gives three different options to deal with these scenarios and for the Prosecutor to implement the measures for investigation.[183]

(1) These measures can be conducted in cooperation with the State, the person, or the organization concerned on a voluntary basis. In doing this the Prosecutor can conclude agreements and under certain circumstances guarantee confidentiality in the course of such an agreement.

(2) The measure can be performed by means of Part IX ICCSt as a cooperative measure. Art. 93 ICCSt in particular gives a list of measures which can be exercised in a cooperative way, through the authorities and according to the laws and rules of the State. The ICC Prosecutor is therefore no longer in charge of the measure imposed and acts as a mere observer, if s/he is involved at all.[184] The Prosecutor can under certain circumstances also operate on the territory of a state without its explicit consent according to Art. 99 (4) ICCSt.[185]

(3) The Prosecutor can upon authorization of the Pre-Trial Chamber investigate on the territory of a State without the consent of a State, which is clearly unable to fulfil the cooperation requirements according to Part IX ICCSt. Unwillingness on the side of the State is generally speaking a ground for impeaching state sovereignty to conduct an investigation on the territory of a State. In this case the

[182] *See* eg, Art. 8 ECHR.

[183] Boas/Bischoff/Reid/Taylor, *ICL III*, 107 do not differentiate properly and misinterpret Art. 57 (3) (d) ICCSt.

[184] *See* Triffterer/*Bergsmo*/*Kruger*, Art. 54 MN 20.

[185] R Rastan, 'Testing Co-Operation: The International Criminal Court and National Authorities', 21 *LJIL* (2008) 431 at 437.

Table 6.3 Different investigative measures

	Mode 1 Consensual	Mode 2 Cooperative	Mode 3 Non-consensual
Collection of evidence	Agreement with State, IGO or individual (Art. 54 (3) (d) ICCSt) Confidentiality Agreement (Art. 54 (3) (e) ICCSt)	Art. 54 (2) (a) ICCSt and Part IX ICCSt Art. 99 (4) ICCSt	Art. 54 (2) (b) and Art. 57 (3) (d) ICCSt
Request presence and question of witness and victim	Agreement with State, IGO or individual (Art. 54 (3) (d) ICCSt) Confidentiality Agreement (Art. 54 (3) (e) ICCSt)	Art. 54 (2) (a) ICCSt and Part IX ICCSt Art. 99 (4) ICCSt	Art. 54 (2) (b) and Art. 57 (3) (d) ICCSt
Request presence and question of suspect	Summons (Art. 58 (7) ICCSt) Art. 60 ICCSt	Art. 58 (5), 59, Part IX ICCSt Art. 60 ICCSt Art. 99 (4) ICCSt	Art. 58 (1)-(4) ICCSt Art. 60 ICCSt

Prosecutor remains in charge and must carry out the measure with his/her own personnel.[186]

This differentiation is shown in Table 6.3.

When looking at this table and comparing the three different modes which we took from the ICCSt with the four scenarios we have identified in Table 6.2 above, one does not need to pause to see that they do not match entirely. Obviously there remain gaps; that is, situations in which the Prosecutor cannot force the collection of evidence or ensure the presence of a person. Yet we would allocate the different scenarios to the different modes as shown in Table 6.4.

Whereas the consent scenario 1 can be solved on the basis of the powers given to the Prosecutor under mode 1 on the condition of consent, and whereas scenario 2 depends heavily on the legal system in the nation state, scenario 3 poses the biggest loopholes. The power to investigate against the will of both the relevant State and the individual concerned are minimal and do indeed only exist in circumstances where there is a 'failed state'.[187] This is highly regrettable in particular with a view to requesting the presence of witnesses. The ICC has no means to enforce a witness to testify in The Hague.[188] An operation against the will of the state but with

[186] Triffterer/*Bergsmo/Kruger*, Art. 54 MN 25.

[187] C Kreß, 'The Procedural Law of the International Criminal Court in Outline: Anatomy of a Unique Compromise', 1 *JICJ* (2003) 603 at 615.

[188] *See* G Sluiter, '"I Beg You, Please Come Testify"—The Problematic Absence of Subpoena Powers at the ICC', 12 *New Criminal Law Review* (2009) 590.

Table 6.4 The powers of the Prosecutor

Scenario 1	Mode 1
Scenario 2	Mode 2
Scenario 3	Mode 3
Scenario 4	Mode 1

the consent of an individual (scenario 4) could be possible according to mode 1 on the basis of voluntariness, if the individual is ready to come to the Prosecutor.

In order to understand the complex structure, the following examples will be applied to the different settings.

Example A: Prosecutor needs protocol of meeting of national security council of Equatoriana prior to the invasion of neighbouring state. To be found in the archives of Equatoriana.

Prosecutor can ask the State for voluntary submission of the document. If Equatoriana denies the request, Part IX of the Statute can be invoked and the state could be asked to let the document be seized by the national prosecutor. The likelihood for a successful cooperation is low regarding the denial of a voluntary submission. The only remaining option would be to request the PTC to order the seizure according to Art. 57 (3) (d) ICCSt. A pre-condition would then be that Equatoriana is unable to produce the document. In the case presented here it seems that Equatoriana is perfectly able but unwilling to provide the document. Other than Art. 17 ICCSt 'unwillingness' is not included in the wording.[189]

Example B: After the end of the war and the inauguration of a new, democratic government, the documents containing the protocol of the meetings of the national security council have been collected by General X, who was the main military advisor in this council. All other copies of the protocols have been destroyed. The documents are at his private premises.

The Prosecutor will address General X and ask to submit the documents, which is declined, despite the offer according to Art. 54 (3) (d) ICCSt not to prosecute the General himself. The Prosecutor can than ask Equatoriana to cooperate. As the new government is willing to assist the ICC, the General Prosecutor of Equatoriana produces a warrant of seizure. The execution of the warrant fails as General X has employed a private military company to protect his premises. The police force of Equatoriana is unable to gain access to General X's home. The Prosecutor can ask the Pre-Trial Chamber to authorize the seizure according to Art. 57 (3) (d) ICCSt.

5. Collect and examine evidence: general framework

The power to collect and examine evidence pertains to every item of evidence which does not derive from the testimony of a person; it thus encompasses all materialized evidence. This might consist of documents, including electronic

[189] Triffterer/*Bergsmo/Kruger*, Art. 54 MN 26.

data, photographs, or films. In fact it might be any movable object. Likewise immoveable items, such as an estate, might serve as evidence, and can be examined— for example, a place where a mass execution took place, or a piece of land where a mass grave is suspected. Finally a person can be the object of an examination. Blood samples, fingerprints, or genetic data might be of interest for forensic purposes.

These objects can be both 'collected' and 'examined'. 'Collection' means to gain physical power over the object and comprises also covert investigative measures; 'examination' means the forensic analysis of the object and presupposes a certain level of scientific interpretation. The Prosecutor could thus 'collect' a blood sample from a certain person but only through a specific forensic test, that is, an 'examination', can the blood alcohol concentration be determined.

As we have seen, collection and examination can be achieved in three different ways, which will be described now in greater detail.

a. Mode 1: consensual The Prosecutor may seek the cooperation of any state or intergovernmental organization at any stage of the investigation as mentioned explicitly in Art. 54 (3) (c) ICCSt. Such power is not at all self-evident,[190] as usually the Presidency or indeed the President represents the Court vis-à-vis states or intergovernmental organizations (*see* Art. 2 ICCSt, Regulation 107 and 114 RegC). Yet Rule 176 (2) RPE ICC foresees that the Prosecutor as an independent organ with his or her own Office can communicate with states (under Part IX ICCSt) by him or herself. It is important to note that this power requires that the cooperation matter falls exclusively within the competences of OTP. If it goes beyond this ambit, the President will have to negotiate the agreement (Regulation 107 RegC).[191] Regarding Art. 54 (3) (c), (d), and (e) ICCSt, the Prosecutor has the sole authority to act, as these refer to investigations only. Therefore Regulation 107 (1) second sentence RegC states that Art. 54 (3) (d) ICCSt has priority. According to Regulation 107 (2) RegC, the Prosecutor needs to inform to President of any arrangement or agreement on cooperation. However, reasons of confidentiality prevail and discharge the Prosecutor from his or her general duty to inform the President of the Court.

In order to arrive at a consensual setting for collecting evidence, Art. 54 (3) ICCSt foresees two specific measures: (a) the Prosecutor may enter into 'arrangements or agreements' with a state, intergovernmental organization, or person as may be necessary to facilitate the cooperation according to Art. 54 (3) (d) ICCSt, and (b) the Prosecutor may under certain circumstance enter into confidentiality agreements according to Art. 54 (3) (e) ICCSt.

190 Ibid, Art. 54 MN 31.
191 Ibid, Art. 54 MN 33.

(1) General agreements The provision of Art. 54 (3) (d) ICCSt allows for any arrangement or agreement that is necessary to facilitate the cooperation of a State, intergovernmental organization, or person as long as it is not inconsistent with this Statute. This gives a rather wide field of activity in two regards: first, the partnership may be established with any State, whether Member to the ICCSt or not, any intergovernmental organization, or, indeed, any private person. The agreement can thus be concluded with an individual but also with any legal person; for example, a non-governmental organization (NGO).

Secondly, the object of the agreement is by no means limited, as long as it aims at facilitating the 'cooperation'. In this provision, however, cooperation does not pertain to Part IX ICCSt, as it would have been mentioned were this the case, and the term cooperation in Art. 54 is much wider than the one used in Part IX. The cooperation regime there refers only to Member States. The provision does allow for any activity that will support the ICC Prosecutor in any way, as long as the activity is not inconsistent with the ICCSt. What is consistent with the ICCSt must be judged with a view to Art. 21 ICCSt and the applicable law mentioned there.

If we look at the above example B, the Prosecutor might, in order to secure the documents from General X himself, enter into an agreement with X directly. But could the Prosecutor offer an amnesty to General X in return for his willingness to deliver the documents? Such an agreement according to Art. 54 (3) (d) ICCSt could be in conflict with the irrelevance of immunities as contained in Art. 27 (2) ICCSt. Should these documents prove that X was indeed the main instigator of the crimes, it would be detrimental to the interest of justice not to prosecute X.

(2) Confidentiality agreements Confidentiality agreements according to Art. 54 (3) (e) ICCSt connect to Art. 54 (3) (d) ICCSt and add a special obligation not to disclose at any stage of the proceedings, documents or information, unless the provider consents. The need for such a provision stems from the fact that governments often protect information on the basis of national security interests.[192] This duty to non-disclosure pertains to any stage of the proceedings and is binding upon any organ of the ICC as is laid down in Rule 81 (4) and 82 RPE and even upon the Assembly of State Parties.[193] Even if the confidential information is—with consent of the provider—presented in court, the Chamber may not request information relating to the material or information of its origins. Therefore one might speak of an absolute protec-

[192] Ibid, Art. 54 MN 36.
[193] Ibid, Art. 54 MN 37.

tion that is generated by this special agreement between the provider and the Prosecutor.

The provision foresees one important limit. Solely for the purpose of generating new evidence, the Prosecutor must obtain the material, which may remain confidential. Art. 54 (3) (e) ICCSt-material is thus only preparatory material in the sense that the Prosecutor hopes to find more (direct) evidence by evaluating the information presented to him/her on the basis of the confidentiality agreement (so-called lead evidence or springboard material).[194] It might be difficult to foresee whether the information generates more evidence or not; therefore it is important to note that this condition is not an objective one but depends on the intention of the Prosecutor, that is it needs to withstand a subjective test.

This provision might pose a direct danger to the defence case. We will deal with disclosure of evidence in Chapter X; however, the defence depends on knowledge of the evidence gathered by the Prosecutor. Otherwise the accused will not be able to comment on the charges properly and cannot follow up information which might operate in his or her favour. Therefore Art. 67 (2) ICCSt provides that the Prosecutor must disclose exculpatory evidence as soon as practical. If the Prosecutor makes use of Art. 54 (3) (e) ICCSt in a rather liberal way, the defence is seriously jeopardized. The *Lubanga* case has shown exactly this.

In the case against *Thomas Lubanga*, the Prosecutor gained access to information through the UN only by consenting to a non-disclosure agreement. It turned out that many of the 200 documents contained exculpatory evidence relating to the mental health of the defendant, the actual control he had as a superior when the alleged crimes were committed, and on necessity or duress. Trial Chamber I issued a decision on 13 June 2008 calling the prosecution to a halt as the practice of the Prosecutor that had come to light and posed a danger to the fairness of the trial. Even if the Prosecutor claimed to have acted without intention and was willing to seek permission for using the material as evidence,[195] Trial Chamber I determined that the Prosecutor must desist from concluding confidentiality agreements on a regular basis. These are reserved for extraordinary cases.[196] It would turn the ICCSt structure upside down if these agreements were used to gather as much evidentiary material as quickly as possible and only afterwards evaluate the material according to its 'springboard' character. The decision was

---

[194] ICC *Prosecutor v Lubanga*, TC, ICC-01/04-01-06, 13 June 2008, Decision on the Consequences of Non-Disclosure of Exculpatory Materials Covered by Article 54(3)(e) Agreements and the Application to Stay the Prosecution of the Accused, Together with Certain Other Issues Raised at the Status Conference on 10 June 2008, para 72.

[195] ICC *Prosecutor v Lubanga*, TC, ICC-01/04-01/06, 6 May 2008, Transcript, p 23, para 8.

[196] ICC *Prosecutor v Lubanga*, TC, ICC-01/04-01-06, 13 June 2008, Decision on the Consequences of Non-Disclosure of Exculpatory Materials Covered by Article 54(3)(e) Agreements and the Application to Stay the Prosecution of the Accused, Together with Certain Other Issues Raised at the Status Conference on 10 June 2008, para 72.

upheld on appeal with the only exception that the discontinuation of the case was lifted should the Prosecutor deliver the necessary material to the defence in due course.[197] As the Prosecutor managed to attain the consent of most providers of information and disclosed the material to the defence, the case could and did go ahead.

We can conclude that confidentiality agreements as foreseen in Art. 54 (3) (e) ICCSt are strictly restricted for 'springboard material'; that is, evidence which will lead to new evidence, and can only be implemented by way of exception.[198]

b. Mode 2: cooperative *(1) General considerations* The second mode of implementing investigative measures is 'cooperation' under Part IX. For this reason Art. 54 (2) (a) ICCSt refers explicitly to Part IX ICCSt. It would have been preferable that Art. 54 (2) ICCSt phrases 'State Party' as does Art. 86 ICCSt, in order to clarify that cooperation with State Parties is different from cooperation with non-State Parties.

Under Art. 93 (1) ICCSt the cooperating state must comply with the request of the Court and provide the warranted assistance. Yet the fulfilment of the duty must be in conformity with the relevant national law (*see* also Art. 99 (1) ICCSt). The respect for the sovereignty of the State Party, which is expressed in this provision, is—from the view of the Rome Statute's compromise—logical and commendable.[199] However it binds the powers of the international Prosecutor to the general rules of cooperation in criminal matters in international relations. The relationship between the Prosecutor and the Member State is thus not a hierarchical one but operates on the principle of equality on a vertical basis.

On the other side, the national states need to assimilate and harmonize their national procedural law to the Rome Statute in order to be in a position to comply with the contractual obligations and fulfil the duties vis-à-vis the ICC. The states are in no position to refuse cooperation with regard to their national law.[200] Should however the request be in conflict with fundamental legal principles of general

[197] ICC *Prosecutor v Lubanga*, AC, ICC-01/04-01/06-1486 (OA 13), 21 October 2008, Judgment on the Appeal of the Prosecutor against the Decision of Trial Chamber I entitled 'Decision on the Consequences of Non-Disclosure of Exculpatory Materials Covered by Article 54(3)(e) Agreements and the Application to Stay the Prosecution of the Accused, Together with Certain Other Issues Raised at the Status Conference on 10 June 2008'.

[198] *See* also K Ambos, 'Confidential Investigations (Article 54(3)(e) ICC Statute) vs. Disclosure Obligations: The Lubanga Case and National Law', 12 *New Criminal Law Review* (2009) 543–68; and R Katzman, 'The Non-Disclosure of Confidential Exculpatory Evidence and the Lubanga Proceedings: How the ICC Defence System Affects the Accused's Right to a Fair Trial', 8 *Northwestern JIHR* (2009) 77.

[199] Triffterer/*Kreß/Prost*, Art. 93 MN 9.

[200] Ibid.

application in the national state, the ICC and the Member State should solve the issue by entering into a dialogue according to Art. 93 (3) ICCSt.[201]

(2) The list of measures Art. 93 (1) ICCSt gives a list of different measures, pertaining to all sorts of situations.[202] There is no precise order in this enumeration,

Lit. a): A Member State needs to execute a request by the ICC Prosecutor to identify a person and ascertain his or her whereabouts. The provision comprises not only the suspect but also witnesses.[203] A second duty pertains to the location of (moveable) items.[204]

Lit. b): The second litera refers again to two different duties: the Member State needs to take evidence upon the request of the ICC. The ICCSt gives an example: the taking of a testimony under oath. A second duty is the production of evidence which is already existing. Also here the ICCSt mentions examples: expert opinions and reports. The examples given here underline the importance of witness testimony or expert opinions in the eyes of the drafters of the ICCSt. The scope of the provision is somehow unclear. A rather broad view would apply lit. b) to all forms of evidence taking, and would also comprise medical examinations, blood samples, or electronic surveillance.[205] This view however conflicts with a systematic interpretation or Art. 93 (1) ICCSt, as it would render lit. h) and l) more or less meaningless.[206] It is therefore preferable to adopt a more narrow interpretation and limit the scope of lit. b) to witness testimony. It must be noted that Art. 55 ICCSt applies to the conduct of questioning (see following).

Lit. c): This sub-paragraph in effect specifies lit. b) with regard to the questioning of the suspect and thus clarifies that in contrast to a witness, the suspect cannot be compelled to give testimony.[207] Also here Art. 55 ICCSt and its paragraph (2) in particular applies.

Lit. d): The national state is obliged to serve documents if the ICC so warrants. These documents could be writs, judicial documents, or any other documentation, which the state needs to transfer to a specified person.[208] An example would be a summons to appear according to Art. 58 (7) ICCSt.

---

201 In greater detail, J Meißner, *Die Zusammenarbeit mit dem Internationalen Strafgerichtshof nach dem Römischen Statut* (CH Beck 2003) 214 *et subs.*

202 *See* also Boas/Bischoff/Reid/Taylor, *ICL III*, 107 *et subs.*

203 G Sluiter, *International Criminal Adjudication and the Collection of Evidence: Obligations of States* (Intersentia 2002) 242.

204 J Meißner, *Die Zusammenarbeit mit dem Internationalen Strafgerichtshof nach dem Römischen Statut* (CH Beck 2003) 191.

205 *See* ibid, 192.

206 Triffterer/*Kreß/Prost*, Art. 93 MN 14.

207 J Meißner, *Die Zusammenarbeit mit dem Internationalen Strafgerichtshof nach dem Römischen Statut* (CH Beck 2003) 192.

208 Triffterer/*Kreß/Prost*, Art. 93 MN 20.

Lit. e): The Member State must support persons who appear voluntarily as witnesses or experts before the ICC. The ICC is disallowed to request the use of force in transferring the person to the Court.[209]

Lit. f): This sub-paragraph connects to lit. e) in that it addresses a specific situation of persons who appear at the ICC. Lit. f) pertains to persons whom are being held in custody by the Member State. In this case the Member State needs to cooperate with the ICC by transferring the person temporarily to The Hague in accordance with Art. 93 (7).

Lit. g): The ICC may request a Member State to conduct on-site examinations. Exhumations and examinations of grave sites are mentioned explicitly as the most common examples in this regard.[210]

Lit. h): This provision requires assistance by searching and seizure in a rather broad way. The procedure itself is left to the Member States' national laws.[211]

Lit. i): The ICC may under this sub-paragraph request the production of any record or document within the possession of the national state. The request must identify the required documents as precisely as possible. This should guarantee that the national state may actually fulfil its international obligation towards the ICC and should at the same time prevent 'fishing expeditions' by the ICC.[212]

Lit. j): This provision aims at preserving the evidence for the ICC prosecution in general. It differentiates between witnesses—whether or not they are victims of the alleged crimes—and other evidence. Witnesses require protection and other (material) evidence needs preservation. The ICCSt does not specify the measures that are to be implemented in either way. Both the ICC and the Member State are therefore free to adopt such measures which are most effective under the circumstances of the individual case.[213]

Lit. k): The final specified measure is one to prepare for a later forfeiture by the ICC as a penalty in the case of a guilty verdict according to Art. 77 (2) (b) ICCSt. In order to guarantee the effectiveness of a forfeiture, the ICC may request Member States to identify, trace, freeze, or seize proceeds, property, and assets of the suspect. These are preliminary measures and therefore without prejudice to the rights of *bona fide* third parties.[214]

Lit. l): The final subparagraph contains a severability clause in the sense of a 'catch-all' provision.[215] It is in the very nature of a provision of this type that

---

[209] Ibid, Art. 93 MN 21.

[210] Ibid, Art. 93 MN 25.

[211] Ibid, Art. 93 MN 26

[212] J Meißner, *Die Zusammenarbeit mit dem Internationalen Strafgerichtshof nach dem Römischen Statut* (CH Beck 2003) 197 *et subs.*

[213] Triffterer/*Kreß/Prost*, Art. 93 MN 28; J Meißner, *Die Zusammenarbeit mit dem Internationalen Strafgerichtshof nach dem Römischen Statut* (CH Beck 2003) 199.

[214] J Meißner, *Die Zusammenarbeit mit dem Internationalen Strafgerichtshof nach dem Römischen Statut* (CH Beck 2003) 200.

[215] Triffterer/*Kreß/Prost*, Art. 93 MN 32; J Meißner, *Die Zusammenarbeit mit dem Internationalen Strafgerichtshof nach dem Römischen Statut* (CH Beck 2003) 190, 203.

the wording is vague and generalizing to a great extent. There are, however, serious doubts whether lit. l) goes beyond what is bearable with a view to the rule of law. These doubts are based in the fact that the provision does in no way specify the measures which can be requested, neither on the level of the ICC nor on that of the national state. The only requirement on the international level is that the measure must assist the investigation or prosecution of crimes within the ICC's jurisdiction. On the national level, it must be ensured that national law does not prohibit the requested measure. These conditions are fine as long as the ICC does not request the execution of a qualified investigative measure. Should the request necessitate coercive means towards an individual, the national state needs a precise legal basis, otherwise there will be a human right's violation. This is undisputed from a human rights point of view and will be elaborated further below with a view to the human rights jurisprudence. In these cases the precondition foreseen in lit. l) must be read *vice versa*: it does not suffice that the request is not prohibited by national law, rather it is the other way round: the requested measure must be allowed by national law.

As a result, we would have to differentiate. In case of a simple investigative measure which is requested by the ICC, the Member State has to comply as long as there is no prohibition in the national law. For example, the Member State must assist the ICC in establishing a video link to The Hague from the location of the witness.[216]

In the case of a qualified investigative measure, the State can only act on the basis of a national legal norm authorizing the requested measure. For example, the Member State can only produce a blood sample or impose a medical examination like forensic testing, and only deploy electronic surveillance on the basis of a specific national norm.

(3) Exception in Art. 99 (4) ICCSt There is one exception to the general principle that the Prosecutor is unable to conduct investigations on the territory of a state directly: Art. 99 (4) ICCSt. According to this provision, the Prosecutor can enter the territory of a state.[217] This is a highly controversial provision as it conflicts with the principle of state sovereignty in an obvious way.[218]

The provision is to be seen as an 'anticipated consent' for ICC prosecutors to conduct investigations which violate neither individual rights nor state sovereignty apart from the mere entering of the ICC agent on the territory of the Member State in his or her official capacity. Therefore it is a form of 'cooperation' but only

216 Triffterer/*Kreß/Prost*, Art. 93 MN 33.

217 *See* J Meißner, *Die Zusammenarbeit mit dem Internationalen Strafgerichtshof nach dem Römischen Statut* (CH Beck 2003) 249.

218 *See* Triffterer/*Kreß/Prost*, Art. 99 MN 1-5, 15.

as regards non-invasive measures,[219] and ontologically different from the power of the Pre-Trial Chamber according to Art. 57 (3) (d) ICCSt.[220]

The list presented by Art. 99 (4) ICCSt is not exclusive but only exemplary.[221] Two situations are mentioned explicitly: (1) interviewing or taking of evidence from a person on a voluntary basis, and (2) examination of a public site or other public place, without modification. However, the scope of the norm remains very limited indeed. Whereas the inspection of a cemetery would be justified, conducting an exhumation of a mass grave would not. This would be a form of search and thus infringe the principle of territorial integrity of the State.[222] The Prosecutor would need a specific justification for this measure.

(4) Procedure to be applied The Rome Statute is open as far as the procedure to be adopted when entering into a cooperation scenario according to Part IX. Art. 93 (1) ICCSt speaks of the Court that requests cooperation. But who represents the Court in this regard? One option would be that the Prosecutor him/herself could file such a request. A Chamber would be involved in the process only if the requested State complains against the legality of the cooperation in accordance with Regulation 108 (1) RegC. Another option would be that the Pre-Trial Chamber, and after confirmation of the charges the Trial Chamber according to Art. 61 (11) ICCSt, is responsible for issuing 'orders and warrants' as may be required for the purpose of the investigation by virtue of Art. 57 (3) (a) ICCSt upon the request of the Prosecutor.[223] Orders and warrants issued under this provision would be transmitted to the State by Art. 87 (1) ICCSt. The latter is the avenue to be followed for two reasons: (1) the request is supported by a higher authority, and (2) the coercive measure—notwithstanding national procedural law—will be authorized by judges. However, according to Rule 176 (2) RPE ICC, the Prosecutor is perfectly able to file a request to a Member State him/herself. At least as regards qualified investigative measures, the Prosecutor should refrain from asking for cooperation under Part IX him or herself and apply for a warrant with the (Pre-)Trial Chamber first according to Art. 57 (3) (a) ICCSt.

According to Art. 87 (1) ICCSt, the request will then be transmitted to the state through (traditional) diplomatic channels or through any other appropriate channel, which the State Party has approved, which might be considerably shorter and thus more efficient compared to the cumbersome diplomatic

[219] R Rastan, 'Testing Co-Operation: The International Criminal Court and National Authorities', 21 *LJIL* (2008) 431, 437 *see*ms to be of the view that Art. 99 (4) ICCSt is closely related to Art. 57 (d) ICCSt and is systematically speaking at the wrong place.

[220] *See* Triffterer/*Kreß*/*Prost*, Art. 99 MN 25.

[221] R Rastan, 'Testing Co-Operation: The International Criminal Court and National Authorities', 21 *LJIL* (2008) 431, 437; Triffterer/*Kreß*/*Prost*, Art. 99 MN 20.

[222] Triffterer/*Kreß*/*Prost*, Art. 99 MN 19 and 22.

[223] *See* Triffterer/*Guariglia*/*Harris*/*Hochmayr*, Art. 57 MN 15.

routes.[224] Details as concerns the language of the request and the information on the changes in the channels of communications are contained in Rules 177–180 RPE ICC.

c. Mode 3: non-consensual In cases where the Prosecutor can neither operate by consent nor achieve cooperation with the member state in which he or she intends to deploy an investigation measure, the only remaining option is that under Art. 57 (3) (d) ICCSt. This way is only feasible if the Member State is unable to execute the request for cooperation. In this case it is within the competence of the Pre-Trial Chamber to authorize the specific investigative step on the territory of a Member State. The provision of Art. 57 (3) (d) ICCSt presupposes the absence of a domestic state organ which would be competent to authorize the measure itself. It does not apply where the state is able, but unwilling, to cooperate. It is thus a 'failed state -scenario which the Statute envisages.[225]

Under these circumstances the provision does not contain an exception to the principle of state consent under the Statute in the strict sense, but applies to a setting where the respective state cannot formulate any will at all.

If the state is in general able to cooperate but is unwilling to do so, the Prosecutor's hands are bound.[226] The only option for the ICC to react to such unwillingness on the side of the Member State would be to make a finding of non-compliance and refer the matter to the ASP or the Security Council.[227] Whether or not political pressure will be effective is highly uncertain and in any case precious time has already been lost.

The formal procedure for a request according to Art. 57 (3) (d) ICCSt is laid down in Rule 115 RPE. The Prosecutor must address the Pre-Trial Chamber in writing and ask for authorization of a certain measure to be employed in the territory of the State Party in question. Should the Chamber be satisfied that the request is well founded, it will issue a reasoned order which may also contain specific procedures to be followed in carrying out the collection of evidence.

224 *See* Triffterer/*Kreß/Prost*, Art. 87 MN 5 *et subs.*, who report on the discussion at the Preparatory Committee stage and the difficulties in finding the right way as many States would prefer the diplomatic routes, which would give them more political influence.

225 R Rastan, 'Testing Co-Operation: The International Criminal Court and National Authorities', 21 *LJIL* (2008) 431, 438.

226 *See* Triffterer/*Guariglia/Harris/Hochmayr*, Art. 57 MN 13; Boas/Bischoff/Reid/Taylor, *ICL III*, 107.

227 M Brubacher, 'Prosecutorial Discretion within the International Criminal Court', 2 *JICJ* (2004) 71, 91 *et subs*. Experiences at the ICTY show, that a complaint to the UN SC is usually not followed by any activity on the side of this organ. ASP is not empowered to deploy sanctions against a Member State.

Considering that the state in question must be 'failed', it is surprising that Rule 115 RPE ICC requests that the State Party concerned is informed and is invited to submit its views. Even a hearing may be held on the Chamber's own initiative or at the request of either the Prosecutor or the Member State. The provision thus shows respect for state structures, even if they are only rudimentary. In order not to lose too much time, it is submitted that the Pre-Trial Chamber should not invest much time in requesting a state authority which might still be in place, when the overall situation is that of a failed state.

The order issued by the Pre-Trial Chamber authorizing the investigative steps serves as an authorization on both levels: (1) it replaces the state's consent, and (2) justifies the infringement of the individual's rights.

6. *Interfering with rights of the individual*

The infringement of the individual's sphere needs further consideration. As we have seen above, 'qualified investigative measures' are in need of a specific authorization in order to avoid human rights violations on the side of the individual. There are mainly two requirements: first, the interference with the private sphere needs to have a basis in the law, and second, the specific measure in general needs to be authorized by a judge. Considering these general conditions, we will now take a closer look into different qualified investigative measures like a. searching, b. seizure, c. forensic testing, d. electronic surveillance, and e. data collection.

a. Searching If the investigating personnel wish to search the suspect's private accommodation and/or office, a special justification is needed, as the measure would otherwise infringe the right to privacy. In the major human rights treaties, the right to privacy entails the protection of the private and family life and of the home (see Art. 17 ICCPR and Art. 8 ECHR). One can easily derive from the case law of the Strasbourg authorities that searching private premises falls within the ambit of respect for the home, notwithstanding difficulties in defining the terms precisely.[228] The question however is, whether or not business premises are subject to human rights protection.

In substance both the HRC and the ECtHR have widened the scope of the protection of privacy and hold that business premises do indeed come within the ambit of the protection.[229] There are mainly two reasons. (1) The term 'private life' cannot be reduced to the inner circle of intimacy. Private life encompasses also the creation of relations with the outside world, which generally takes place within the sphere of

[228] *See* eg, ECtHR *Chappell v UK*, Judgment, 30 March 1989, Series A No. 152, para 51; *Niemitz v Germany*, Judgment, 16 December 1992, Series A No. 251-B, para 29; *Funke v France*, Judgment, 25 February 1993, Series A No. 256-A, para 48. For further analysis *see* C Safferling, *Towards an International Criminal Procedure* (OUP 2003) 151 *et subs*.

[229] *See* HRC General Comment 16 (Article 17), para 5; ECtHR *Niemitz v Germany*, Judgment, 16 December 1992, Series A No. 251-B, para 29.

professional life. (2) It is often impossible to differentiate between the private and the professional sphere. In order to avoid arbitrary discrimination, both must be brought under the protection of the 'right to privacy'.[230] The ECtHR has extended the right to privacy also to legal persons and corporations.[231]

However, no violation of the right to privacy will take place as long as the investigators have a legitimate aim in a democratic society in order to justify the invasions of a person's home. A number of exceptions are foreseen in Art. 8 (2) ECHR. Even if criminal investigation is not mentioned in the catalogue given in Art. 8 ECHR explicitly, a search can be justified if conducted in order to prevent disorder and crime in the interest of national security, public safety, and the protection of the morals, rights, and freedoms of others. As the criminal justice system aims at preventing disorder and crime and serves the public safety in that it urges for security under the law, crime investigation can be seen as a legitimate aim to justify entry into the private dwelling or the business premises of an individual.[232]

In addition, the searching must be anticipated within the law and must be strictly necessary in a democratic society; that is, the measure must be proportionate. The underlying law must in itself conform to human rights and must not be 'too lax and full of loopholes'.[233] Accordingly the law must be sufficiently clear with regards to the foreseeability of the investigative measure and with regard to the separation of powers.[234]

The power to search is not explicitly mentioned in the law of the ICTY. In Rule 39 (i) and (ii), the Prosecutor is entitled to collect evidence and conduct on-site investigations and may undertake such matters as may appear necessary for completing the investigation. Bassiouni finds that these provisions are even broader than the prosecutorial powers of Art. 18 Statute and gives no guidance whatsoever on the standards to be applied.[235]According to the present author's interpretation, these norms must be read in conjunction with Rule 39 (iv) and Rule 54. The prosecutor must request such orders as may be necessary from a Trial Chamber or a judge, if the measures he or she wishes to apply constitute an infringement of human rights. The

230 In greater detail: C Safferling, *Towards an International Criminal Procedure* (OUP 2003) 153 *et subs.*

231 *See* ECtHR *Chappel v UK*, Judgment, 30 March 1989, Series A No. 152, para 25, 63; *STÉS Colas Est et al. v France*, Judgment, 16 April 2002, Appl. No. 37971/97, para 41.

232 For a more extensive discussion of this issue *see* C Safferling, *Towards an International Criminal Procedure* (OUP 2003) 155 *et subs.*

233 ECtHR *Funke v France*, Judgment, 25 February 1993, Series A No. 256-A, para 57. *See* also HRC General Comment 16 (Article 17), paras 1–2.

234 *See* ECtHR *Rekvenyi v Hungary*, Judgment, 20 May 1999, Rep. 1999-III, para 59; *Malone v UK*, Judgment, 2 August 1984, Series A No. 82, paras 67–8; *Sunday Times v UK*, Judgment, 26 April 1979, Series A No. 30, paras 29 and 49. *See* also J Meyer-Ladewig, *Europäische Menschenrechtskonvention* (2nd edn, Nomos 2006) Art. 8 MN 38.

235 C Bassiouni and P Manikas, *The Law of the International Criminal Tribunal for the Former Yugoslavia* (Transnational Publishers 1995) 872–3.

substantive conditions the judge must find fulfilled are those outlined above; that is, that there must be reasonable grounds for believing that there is relevant evidentiary material on the premises.[236]

Furthermore, the Prosecutor may, in urgent cases, request any state to seize physical evidence, as stated in Rule 40 (ii). In the latter case, the legal basis for invasion of a person's privacy must be considered in the light of the domestic law of that state. In the former case, the legal justification for the interference with privacy must be seen in the Rule of Procedure itself. As further elaboration is lacking, the Prosecutor has to comply with the necessities that derive directly from human rights law. In particular, it is submitted here that any entry into people's premises needs the authorization of a judge as contemplated in Rule 39 (iv).

b. Seizure Seizure is closely related to search. If the Prosecutor has found evidentiary material, for example, by way of searching a premise, s/he might want to confiscate this material in order to present it as evidence in court. In English law, traditionally, the powers of seizure are wider than those of search. The only condition for lawful seizure is lawful entry.[237] In German law, in contrast, seizure must be authorized by a judge just like a search warrant, according to § 98 Code of Criminal Procedure.

It must be borne in mind, that seizure constitutes an infringement of the right to property; that is, the right to peaceful enjoyment of property as, for example, protected by Art. 1 Prot. 1 ECHR. Yet this infringement is only of a temporary nature. As soon as the reasons for confiscation cease to apply, the property must be given back to the owner. Therefore justification is needed only for this temporary removal. Yet the general requirements for human rights interference apply, which means there needs to be a legal basis and a legal procedure to be followed, and the seizure must be proportionate. Therefore any item or document can only be seized, if the Prosecutor is convinced that it will assist the investigation and that the material will otherwise not be available for trial.[238]

At the ICTY the Prosecutor is authorized to seize evidentiary material under Rule 39 (i), (ii), and (iv). It is submitted here that the legal basis for seizure of material is to be seen in this rule. However, prior authorization by a judge or a Trial Chamber is necessary. The conditions are the same as those required by human rights norms. If the prosecutor requests a state to seize material, which s/he is empowered to do under Rule 40 (ii), the national authorities must apply their domestic law. What

[236] Compare the test applied by the ICTY President in *Prosecutor v Delalić et al.*, TC, IT-96-21-T, 11 November 1996 Decision on the Prosecutor's Motion for the Production of Notes Exchanged between Zejnil Delalić and Zdravko Mucić, paras 38 and 39.

[237] *See* C Safferling, *Towards an International Criminal Procedure* (OUP 2003) 161 with further references.

[238] Ibid, 162.

is not quite clear is the fact that Rule 39 (i) speaks of collecting evidence, whereas Rule 40 (ii) uses the words 'seize physical evidence'.

c. **Forensic testing** For the purposes of scientific evidence, the offender is often asked to submit to a blood test or similar medical or biological tests. These modern methods of genetic analysis and the like are used alongside the more 'classical' forms of identification, like the taking of fingerprints, photographs, and so forth. Normally, the aim of these measures is to identify the suspect but this is not the only aim; they may also assist in clarifying factual circumstances of the case; for example, the blood-alcohol concentration or a person's mental state. Virtually no problems arise in this connection as long as the suspect cooperates with the investigator. Things become difficult as soon as the suspect refuses to cooperate. Are there ways and means of forcing him or her to submit to these measures?

(1) Applicable human rights norms According to the definition of 'private life' found before, the measures discussed here fall within the ambit of the 'right to privacy'. These acts intrude upon the physical or moral integrity of the individual. In the case of *Costello-Roberts v UK* the ECtHR found, on the other hand, that not every interference with the corporal integrity of the individual constitutes an interference with Art. 8 ECHR.[239] It is not quite clear what the court intended to say with this statement. *Frowein* and *Peukert*, however, point out that interference by state organs always falls within the ambit of Art. 8 ECHR, which is especially true of forced identity measures.[240] In *McVeigh, O'Neill and Evans v UK*, the ECommHR accepted this view, in general, concerning identification measures.[241] It also conceded in *X v Netherlands*, that forced blood tests fall within the scope of Art. 8 ECHR.[242] Medical, especially psychiatric, testing to assess the suspect's state of mind is problematic. In this case, the outcome of the psychiatric test may prejudice the outcome of the trial.

(2) Justification for the interference As an intrusion upon the 'right to privacy', forced identity and other measures require justification. In *McVeigh, O'Neill and Evans v UK*, the ECommHR held that the Convention must allow these measures, if interpreted according to current conditions. The special threat that emerges from terrorist activities makes special countermeasures to combat these activities unavoidable. The case was concerned with the gathering and keeping of personal information to fight against terrorism. However, the ECommHR's decision only looked into terrorist activities. Outside the special circumstances of terrorist activities, it could still be argued that the general practice of keeping

[239] ECtHR *Costello-Roberts v UK*, Judgment, 25 March 1993, Series A No. 247-C, para 36.

[240] J Frowein and W Peukert, *Europäische Menschenrechtskonvention* (3rd edn, NP Engel 2009) Art. 8, No. 7.

[241] ECommHR *McVeigh, O'Neill and Evans v UK*, Report 18 March 1981, Appl. Nos 8022, 8025, 8027/77, DR 25, 15 at 49.

[242] ECommHR *X v Netherlands*, Decision 4 December 1978, Appl. No. 8239/78, 16 DR, 184.

records would be unjustified.[243] Once more we must distinguish between two issues: preventive measures taken in order to combat crime and terrorism, and the repressive measures taken in order to investigate a crime and collect evidentiary material. The justification for the former, which is not of interest here, is clear; the 'prevention of crime' as found in the text of the Convention. The justification for the second is not so clear. Why must the suspect tolerate a blood test to ascertain his or her blood group or analyse his or her DNA? But again we could say that it is in the public interest that the true offender is found.

A 'genetic fingerprint' provides much stronger evidence to support a suspicion. The innocent person, on the other hand, profits from this measure, because suspicion against him or her vanishes. The suspect therefore has to tolerate the infringement because of higher public interests.

d. Electronic surveillance Recent developments in the field of electronic surveillance have led to considerable problems in many Western legal systems. Many judicial decisions have been issued by the highest national and international courts. *Locus materiae* is once again the 'right to privacy', as first held by the ECtHR in *Klaas v Germany*.[244] Attacks on this right via electronic surveillance devices take many forms. Not only do the investigators wire-tap, but the latest developments also make discussion about the legitimacy of using video surveillance necessary. The question, however, remains the same: to what extent are public authorities justified in invading the private sphere of the suspect? To illustrate the situation, we will look at telephone tapping in greater detail.

(1) The national states States have shown a tendency to increase investigators' powers over the last few decades or so in order to meet the challenges of organized crime and terrorism. This is the case even in Germany, where the limits drawn by the Constitution linger. The right to privacy in Art. 13 GG has suffered major restrictions. In the UK, a different course of development can be observed. There has never been and still is no right to privacy, apart from the law that protects a person's proprietary rights.[245] Once more, control over police activity was only gained by rules of evidence established by the courts or through the supervision of senior police officers.[246] After the Police and Criminal Evidence Act (PACE 1984), the law con-

[243] L Loucaides, 'Personality and Privacy under the European Convention of Human Rights', 61 *BYIL* (1990) 175 at 187.

[244] ECtHR *Klaas v Germany*, Judgment, 6 September 1978, Series A No. 28.

[245] *Malone v Metropolitan Police Comr* (No. 2) [1979] Ch 344, [1979] 2 All ER 620. The discussion about whether or not to introduce a right to privacy is still unresolved in the UK. Whilst implementation of the ECHR into British domestic law makes Art. 8 ECHR applicable in domestic courts, and according to the former Lord Chief Justice, Lord Bingham, has made new legislation superfluous, the press in particular fear the threat of a strict privacy regime established by the judges and are therefore calling for a Parliamentary Act, which they hope will lay down more liberal rights. At the time of writing the Freedom of Information Bill has still not been enacted as it is still heavily disputed.

[246] L Leigh, *Police Powers in England and Wales* (2nd edn, Butterworth 1985) 255.

cerning telephone surveillance changed—or rather came into existence in the form of the Interception of Communications Act (1985). Since then, a warrant issued by the Home Minister has been necessary. This warrant will be granted if considered necessary in the interests of national security, to prevent or detect serious crime, or to safeguard the economic well-being of the state. Interception of telecommunication is somehow the *ultima ratio*; that is, reserved for when other so-called ordinary means have failed. This Act reflects prior practice but introduces a tribunal of five lawyers who review complaints of persons who consider their telecommunications have been intercepted.[247] Save for such interception of telecommunications, no other aural or visual surveillance is regulated by statute. Home Office guidelines govern other such devices.[248] What is certainly questionable in this context is authorization solely by the executive organs. No independent authority, no third person, is involved in the prior review of the planned action. As I have argued before with regard to searching and detaining, *ex ante* control through authorization by an independent judge is desirable from a human rights perspective.

(2) Human rights bodies Several cases have been submitted to the European procedure with little success from the applicant's point of view. In *Klaas*, the ECtHR declared surveillance compatible with Art. 8 (II) ECHR; for the sake of 'national security', it is necessary, in a democratic society, for police powers to be modernized to keep up with advanced espionage and terrorism in Europe. The pertinent German law has been equipped with safeguarding and reviewing procedures satisfying the ECtHR. A special review organ outside the main judicial system has been created to deal with complaints; the complaining person can, however, still access the BVerfG in respect of a violation of his or her basic right to privacy. Although the ECtHR indicated that normal judicial control would be preferable,[249] the procedure under German law fulfilled the Court's arguably rather low threshold test of whether or not possible abuse can be excluded or remedied.[250]

In *Malone v UK*, the ECtHR found a violation that then led to the change in English tapping law as discussed above. The case was concerned with 'metering'; that is, recording the numbers dialed, and the time and duration of each call. As English law did not anticipate a legal base for this device at that time, the ECtHR declared the interception incompatible with Art. 8 (2) ECHR.[251] In two French cases, the ECtHR further elaborated on this issue. In the cases of *Kruslin*[252] and *Huving*,[253] the necessity for precise legal provisions was stressed because intrusion

[247] Interception of Communications Act 1985, s 7.

[248] L Leigh, *Police Powers in England and Wales* (2nd edn, Butterworth 1985) 252.

[249] L Loucaides, 'Personality and Privacy under the European Convention of Human Rights', 61 *BYIL* (1990) 175, 187.

[250] ECtHR *Klaas v Germany*, Judgment, 6 September 1978, Series A No. 28, para 50.

[251] ECtHR *Malone v UK*, Judgment 2 August 1984, Series A No. 82, para 72.

[252] ECtHR *Kruslin v France*, Judgment 24 April 1990, Series A No. 176-A.

[253] ECtHR *Huving v France*, Judgment 24 April 1990, Series A No. 176-B.

into the private sphere is a particularly sensitive issue; '[i]t is essential to have clear, detailed rules on the subject, especially as the technology available for use is continually becoming more and more sophisticated'.[254] A violation was found in both cases; the authorizing legal norm must be in accordance with the rule of law;[255] that is, it must lead to predictability (Vorhersehbarkeit) and legal certainty (Bestimmtheitsgebot), which means that if the law permits a margin of appreciation, it must indicate the scope of that discretion.[256] The decisions found a violation of Art. 8 with regard to the requirement that the interference must be 'in accordance with the law'. The Government was condemned not because of what it did but because of how it proceeded. In *Lüdi v Switzerland*, the legal basis for the telephone tapping was indisputable. The ECtHR, without wasting many words, recognized the whole procedure as necessary in a democratic society for the prevention of crime, thus denying a violation of Art. 8ECHR.[257]

Possibly the most interesting case is *A v France*, as it deals with a clever investigation method, the 'telephone trap'.[258] Basically, the trick is to find an acquaintance or accomplice of the suspect, induce him or her to call the suspect, and entice the latter into a conversation about the crime, while the police are listening and taping the whole conversation. The French Government contested the applicability of Art. 8 ECHR on two grounds; first, the conversation was recorded on the initiative of one of the interlocutors and, second, the preparation of a crime is of public interest and therefore does not fall within the private sphere. The ECtHR rebutted this argument, but relied for its final reasoning on the undisputed respect for 'privacy of correspondence'.[259] Once again, however, intrusion did not have a legal basis in French law and was therefore declared unjustifiable with regard to Art. 8 (2) ECHR.[260] The fact that the European authorities rejected the argument that the right to privacy was not concerned remains very important. Although the police are not directly involved, because a private person dials the number and holds the conversation, the latter takes place with the knowledge, and often on the initiative, of investigators using police facilities. It is *de facto*

[254] ECtHR *Kruslin v France*, Judgment 24 April 1990, Series A No. 176-A, para 33.

[255] In *Huving v France*, Judgment 24 April 1990, Series A No. 176-B, paras 28–9, the ECtHR found, overruling the ECommHR, that well-established case law must also be taken into consideration in civil law countries. Law was given a 'substantive' meaning. The differences between common and civil law countries should, in the opinion of the Court, not be overemphasized. This decision is questionable with regard to civil law jurisdiction.

[256] ECtHR *Kruslin v France*, Judgment 24 April 1990, Series A No. 176-A, para 30; *Malone v UK*, Judgment 2 August 1984, Series A No. 82, paras 67–8; *Sunday Times v UK*, Judgment 26 April 1979, Series A No. 30, para 49.

[257] ECtHR *Lüdi v Switzerland*, Judgment 15 June 1992, Series A No. 238, paras 38–9. The other interesting aspect of the case was the involvement of an undercover agent, who acted as agent provocateur. But neither the use of this agent on its own, nor in conjunction with the tapping, was deemed to be unlawful intrusion of the applicant's privacy. The issue was discussed in greater detail under the auspices of Art. 6 (1) and (3) ECHR.

[258] ECtHR *A v France*, Judgment 23 November 1993, Series A No. 277-B.

[259] Ibid, paras 36–7.

[260] Ibid, paras 38–9.

a police interrogation. The crucial question thus emerges of whether the investigator can legitimately circumvent the conditions governing police interrogation; that is, cautioning the suspect and refraining from placing any undue pressure on him. The question was discussed in some detail before the German Bundesgerichtshof. In the end the court held that such a procedure was not tantamount to a police interrogation; the rules governing the interrogation of suspects were thus not applicable.[261] This rather formal approach was heavily criticized in the literature,[262] and rightly so, in particular from a human rights perspective. The ECtHR been never been content with a formal interpretation of specific legal terms or procedures.

The ECtHR asks whether or not the applicant is substantially affected. Although this material approach does not always benefit the applicant and is certainly disputable when state conduct is being assessed,[263] it complies with the human rights aim of inhibiting abusive and arbitrary treatment of individuals by state authorities.

To sum up: aural or visual surveillance for the sake of criminal investigation is an invasion of the 'right to privacy'. To safeguard proper administration of the investigation, these devices must be authorized by an independent judge. S/he may authorize the intrusive measure if s/he has reasonable grounds to suspect the victim of having committed a serious offence and believes that other less intrusive measures will be ineffective. Situations like the 'telephone trap', which are in effect substantially equivalent to a formal interrogation, must be treated as such; that is, the suspect has to be cautioned.

e. Data collection One question that has already appeared in the discussion of investigating measures needs further elaboration and clarification. When may data collected during an investigation be retained and when must they be destroyed? It is undisputed that the storing and release of information relating to an individual's private life in a secret police register constitutes interference with the person's right to respect for his private life.[264]A justification for storing and release must therefore be found. Three distinct cases can be made: (1) the suspicion is disproved in the course of the investigation, (2) the suspect is convicted and sentenced, and (3) the suspect is acquitted.

In the first case—that is, when the suspicion vanishes in the course of the inquiry—it would seem that all information that has been collected for

[261] *See* BGH Großer Senat, Decision of 13 May 1996, 16 *NStZ* (1996) 502.

[262] *See* eg, C Roxin, 'Zum Hörfallen-Beschluss des Großen Senats für Strafsachen, 17 *NStZ* (1997) 18.

[263] As seen before in *Huving v France*, Judgment 24 April 1990, Series A No. 176-B, paras 28–9, the ECtHR allowed case law to be an adequate legal basis for state interference with a citizen's privacy.

[264] ECtHR *Leander v Sweden*, Judgment 26 May 1987, Series A No. 116, para 48. As this case pertained to national security, the ECtHR lowered the *Malone* quality control of the law as regards foreseeability and accessibility and found no violation of Art. 8 ECHR.

investigating purposes must be destroyed. The suspicion was apparently wrong; the invasion of the suspect's private sphere, although justified at the time as a necessary means of investigation, is now illegitimate and no longer necessary in a democratic society. The question has arisen once before the European organs, namely, in *Friedl v Austria*. The dispute was settled amicably and struck off the list, after having been conceded by the ECommHR.[265] In the opinion of the ECommHR, the interference was minor and therefore justified. As a general justification, the Commission referred to the need to prevent crime in modern society. *Friedl* was photographed and his identity was established and stored by the police in the course of investigations into offences against the Road Traffic Act arising in connection with a demonstration by homeless persons in Vienna.

While the complaint concerning the photographs was completely rejected as not within the scope of privacy,[266] the remaining complaints were understood to establish a 'relatively slight interference'. The information was kept separate from the 'proper' criminal files in a general administrative file and not entered into the data-processing system. As such, it was considered necessary in a democratic society for the prevention of disorder and crime.[267] This is certainly an extensive interpretation of what is necessary in a democratic society.

In the second case, namely, if the suspect has been convicted, the prevention of further crime is certainly an issue. The suspect has been convicted by a competent tribunal of committing a criminal offence. The presumption of innocence has thus been rebutted. As the danger of repetition can never be totally ruled out, the investigating authorities may, for a certain period of time, store and retain information. The test for establishing the length of this period is tripartite: first, the nature and seriousness of the offence plays a major role, especially the question of how dangerous it was and still is for society. For example, a cold-blooded killer who mainly works for organized crime is far more dangerous for the community than a woman who stabbed her husband to death and deeply regretted her action. Second, the amount of punishment plays a role. The sentence mirrors the seriou-

---

[265] ECommHR *Friedl v Austria*, Report 19 May 1994; ECtHR *Friedl v Austria*, Judgment 31 January 1995, Series A No. 305-B.

[266] Ibid, paras 49–52. The justification cited was the fact that the photographs had been taken in a public place, and therefore did not constitute an invasion of the 'inner circle' of privacy, their purpose being to record the situation and the character of the demonstration. This is rather difficult to follow, as there does not seem to be any necessity for the police to have a photograph of every demonstrator.

[267] Ibid, para 67. How does this prevent disorder and crime? By deterring potential demonstrators or denying persons who are found in the files the right to participate in further demonstrations? Certainly, it is not as threatening to have one's personal data stored in an administrative file as in a police file. But when a person who is already 'known' to the institutions applies for permission to hold a demonstration, and the application must be filed with the administration, would the record not be found and have consequences for the decision? Would this person not be stigmatized by the mere fact that his name appears in the records?

ness of the offence. Third, the danger of repetition must be assessed. There is no need to store personal data about the released prisoner, if and when repetition can be excluded.

The last case involves acquittal of the suspect by a competent tribunal. In one European case, this question arose in a slightly different context. The applicant was acquitted of murdering his wife and applied for compensation for one year's detention on remand.[268] The claim was rejected on the grounds that not all suspicion had been banished, that there was still room for arguing in favour of the suspect's guilt and that the acquittal was based on a 7:1 vote, which proved that the jurors only gave the defendant the benefit of the doubt. This reasoning is not convincing. Leaving aside the question of whether the state must grant compensation for this kind of detention anyway, state authorities are prohibited from giving a second verdict on the guilt of the suspect after his or her acquittal. Either there are grounds for reopening the trial or the presumption of innocence is still applicable. Assumptions that differ from the court's findings on the guilt of the accused are therefore not permissible. If the investigating body stores records of acquitted persons for further inquiries, it is presuming that the court's decision was wrong. Furthermore, the danger of a suspect being presumed guilty increases if records of his/her previous behaviour are kept with the investigating authorities. He or she is stigmatized for already having had contact with the police and judiciary. For very good reasons this is avoided by criminal proceedings before a jury in English and American law, as the personal circumstances and character evidence of the defendant are irrelevant for the question of guilt or innocence.

f. Summary It has been shown that investigative measures, which concern the right to privacy as a human right of an individual—other than arrest and detention which will be dealt with in the following chapter—cannot be executed by the ICC Prosecutor in a direct way. As a matter of fact he or she needs to overcome the problem of state sovereignty first, which can be done by consent, on the basis of the cooperation regime of Part IX of the ICCSt, or in a very limited way also against the will of the respective state. In any case, the Prosecutor also needs authorization of the infringement of the individual's human rights. . The analysis of the right to privacy regarding the investigative measures of search, seizure, electronic surveillance, forensic testing, and data collection, has shown that in any case a judge must authorize the interference. In many states this will be provided for by national law, which is to be applied in a case of cooperation under Part. IX. However, there is no guarantee for the Prosecutor that indeed the national law follows this avenue. It is therefore preferable that the Prosecutor approaches the Pre-Trial Chamber (or after the Confirmation of the charges, the Trial Chamber) and requests the issuance of a

[268] ECtHR *Sekanina v Austria*, Judgment 25 August 1993, Series A No. 266-A.

warrant according to Art. 57 (3) (a) ICCSt. In that case the ICC warrant will carry the authority for the interference with individual rights.

D. The Rights of the Suspect (*Alena Hartwig*)

The suspect is the most sought-after person during the entire inquiry. A statement from him or her could change, accelerate, or perhaps even end, the Prosecutor's investigation. The suspect is the person, and s/he might well be the only person with the exception of the victim, who knows what really happened. To make the suspect speak is thus the initial primary aspiration of every investigator. Yet there is one major obstacle in his or her path; the suspect cannot be compelled to make a statement. Indeed s/he has a right to remain silent. This is not the only restriction placed upon the Prosecutor regarding the questioning of suspects during the course of his or her investigation. The Prosecutor is also bound by the provisions set down in Art. 55 ICCSt, which aim to protect those subject to or involved in the investigation, from human rights abuses.[269]

The first paragraph of Art. 55 ICCSt refers to 'persons' in general—that is, it is applicable, not only to suspects, but also to other persons involved in the investigation, such as witnesses—whereas Art. 55 (2) ICCSt specifically addresses the questioning of a suspect and thus has a more limited scope.[270] Rule 111 (2) RPE ICC places both the Prosecutor and national authorities under a duty to give 'due regard' to the rights contained in Art. 55 (1) ICCSt whilst conducting their interrogations. Moreover, Art. 54 (1) (c) ICCSt explicitly places the Prosecutor under a general duty to 'fully respect the rights of persons arising under [the ICC] Statute' in the course of his or her investigation. Finally, Regulation 36 *et subs.* of the Regulations of the Office of the Prosecutor contain specific provisions regarding the questioning of persons.

Naturally a suspect must also be informed of his or her rights. Thus, Art. 55 (2) ICCSt and Regulation 41 RegP require the investigating authority to inform a suspect of his or her rights.

At the ICTY and the ICTR, the rights of suspects are laid down in Rule 42 of the respective rules of procedure and evidence. Whilst far from as detailed as Art. 55 ICCSt, the provision nonetheless sets down important safeguards to protect suspects during an investigation. Rule 42 has been criticized insofar as it is only directed at the Prosecutor.[271] However, Rule 37 (B) states that the Prosecutor's

[269] Art. 55 ICCSt is also referred to as a 'mini-human rights convention for the period before trial', *see* Triffterer/*Hall*, Art. 55 MN 1.

[270] *See* also S Zappalá, *Human Rights in International Criminal Proceedings* (OUP 2003) 78 *et subs.*

[271] V Creta, 'The Search for Justice in the Former Yugoslavia and Beyond: Analyzing the Rights of the Accused Under the Statute and RPE of the ICTY', 20 *Houst J Int'l L* (1998) 381, 405 and

duties also apply to staff members or other persons under the direction of the Prosecutor. Hence those acting under the authority of the prosecutor are also obliged to inform the suspect of specific rights prior to questioning.

I. Right to remain silent

One of the basic guarantees with respect to the questioning of a suspect is the right to remain silent. The suspect is under no obligation to give a statement regarding the allegations and questions put to him or her by the prosecutor, but can refuse to comment on them. The right permits the suspect to remain silent, without the fear of incriminating inferences being later drawn from that silence. This guarantee is closely linked to the privilege against self-incrimination, the maxim of *nemo tenetur se ipsum prodere.* The privilege implies that the suspect may not be compelled to testify against him/herself in order to provide the authorities with information that may later be used against him or her. The right to remain silent protects the suspect from undue pressure or coercion by the prosecuting authorities and further safeguards him or her from the acquisition of evidence against or without his or her will, as well as contributing to the prevention of miscarriages of justice.[272] Beyond that, the right to silence reinforces the principle that the investigating authorities must prove their case without the suspect incriminating him/herself.[273]

The right to freedom from self-incrimination is laid down in Art. 14 (3) (g) ICCPR and Art. 8 (2) (g) AmCHR. The ECHR lacks such an explicit provision. However, equal protection against self-incrimination, including the right to remain silent, can be derived from the general maxim of Art. 6 (1) ECHR, which guarantees the right to a fair trial as a whole.[274] Further, the right to remain silent is closely related to the presumption of innocence in Art. 14 (2) ICCPR, Art. 6 (2) ECHR.[275] This connection plainly shows that the burden of proof rests upon the prosecution, and

J Falvey, 'United Nations Justice or Military Justice: Which is the Oxymoron?', 19 *Fordham Int'l L J* (1995) 475, 492.

272 ECtHR *Funke v France*, Judgment 25 February 1993, Series A No. 256-A, para 44; *Murray v United Kingdom*, Judgment 8 February 1996, Rep. 1996-I, para 45. According to the Judgments in *Funke* and *Murray*, the ECtHR understands the privilege against self-incrimination primarily as a protection of the will of the suspect to remain silent. For further interpretations, *see* M Redmayne, 'Rethinking the Privilege Against Self-Incrimination', 27 *Oxford Journal of Legal Studies* (2007) 209 at 3D; A Butler, 'Funke v. France and the Right against Self-Incrimination', 11 *CLF* (2000) 461, 482; ECtHR *Saunders v United Kingdom*, Judgment 17 December 1996, Rep. 1996-VI, Dissenting Opinion of Judge Martens, para 9 *et subs.*

273 G Abernathy and B Perry, *Civil Liberties under the Constitution* (6th edn, Univ. South Carolina Press 1993) 84.

274 ECtHR *Murray v United Kingdom*, Judgment 8 February 1996, Rep. 1996-I, para 45; *Saunders v United Kingdom*, Judgment 17 December 1996, Rep. 1996-VI, para 68 ('... there can be no doubt that the right to remain silent... and the privilege against self-incrimination are generally recognized international standards which lie at the heart of the notion of a fair procedure under Article 6').

275 ECtHR *Weh v Austria*, Judgment 8 April 2004, para 46; P Mahoney, 'The Right to a Fair Trial in Criminal Matters under Article 6 ECHR', 4 *Jud Stud Inst J* (2004) 107, 121.

that the suspect cannot be compelled to cooperate with the investigating authorities. However, neither the ICCPR nor the ECHR explicitly prohibit the drawing of adverse inferences from a suspect's silence. In *Murray*, the ECtHR ruled that an infringement of Art. 6 ECHR is only given where a conviction is based *solely or mainly* on the silence.[276] Adverse inferences may, on the contrary, be drawn in situations in which the prosecution has established a case against a suspect and an explanation from him can be expected.[277] Where there is rather little evidence against a person, adverse inferences may not be drawn from silence.[278] The Human Rights Committee, on the other hand, stated that the drawing of adverse inferences violate several provisions of Art. 14 ICCPR.[279]

Art. 55 ICCSt. contains a twofold safeguard for suspects. Firstly, Art. 55 (1) (a) ICCSt provides that a person 'shall not be compelled to incriminate himself or herself or to confess guilt'. This right stems directly from the *nemo tenetur* principle enshrined in Art. 14 (3) (g) ICCPR. Secondly, Art. 55 (2) (b) ICCSt. states that a suspect who is about to be questioned shall have the right 'to remain silent, without such silence being a consideration in the determination of guilt or innocence'. This provision derives from the privilege against self-incrimination and the presumption of innocence.[280]

Embedded in Art. 55 (2) (b) ICCSt, the prohibition to draw adverse inferences from the silence of a suspect explicitly and unambiguously states that such silence is irrelevant for the determination of guilt or innocence. In this respect, the provision exceeds current international human rights norms. This increased level of protection is, however, made slightly relative through another gap in the Statute: as opposed to other provisions governing the right to silence, the warning given to a suspect, that any statement may be used in evidence, is missing in the Rome Statute.[281] Insofar as the initial hope existed that this would be clarified in the Rules of Procedure and Evidence or in the Regulations of the Court, it can only be said that this hope has yet to be realized.

At the ICTY and the ICTR, the right of the suspect to remain silent is provided for in Rule 42 (A) (iii) of the Rules of Procedure and Evidence. This part

---

[276] ECtHR *Murray v United Kingdom*, Judgment 8 February 1996, Rep. 1996-I, para 47.

[277] Ibid. The Court confirmed these principles in *Averill v United Kingdom*, Judgment 6 June 2000, Rep. 2000-VI, para 44 *et subs*.

[278] ECtHR *Telfner v Austria*, Judgment 20 March 2001, para 17 *et subs*.

[279] CCPR/C/79/Add. 55, 27 July 1995: 'The Committee notes with concern that the provisions of the Criminal Justice and Public Order Act of 1994 . . . whereby inferences may be drawn from the silence of persons accused of crimes, violates various provisions in article 14 of the Covenant . . . .'

[280] The presumption of innocence is contained in Art. 66 ICCSt. In spite of its systematic position, the presumption also applies to suspects and not only to accused persons.

[281] C Safferling, *Towards an International Criminal Procedure* (OUP 2003) 124; Triffterer/*Hall*, Art. 55 MN 12.

of the provision was included in 1995, based on the generally weak position of a suspect who is about to be questioned and the fundamental importance of this guarantee.[282] It follows that a suspect may not be induced to assist the Prosecution in proving the case against him/her.[283] The suspect must be cautioned that any statement s/he makes may be used in evidence. The duty of the Prosecutor to inform the suspect in a language s/he understands is also explicitly stated.[284]

Neither the statutes nor the respective rules of procedure and evidence prohibit the drawing of adverse inferences from a suspect's silence. Nonetheless, the Chambers at the ICTY and the ICTR have ruled that the exercise of the right to remain silent is not to be seen as an implication of guilt.[285] This approach has been applied without exception.[286]

The incorporation of Rule 42 (A) (iii) has ensured that the right to remain silent, as provided for in internationally recognized human rights, is sufficiently safeguarded.

II. Notification of charge

A suspect can only exercise his/her right to freedom from self-incrimination if s/he is aware of the fact that s/he is under suspicion and that s/he is in a situation where s/he may need to make use of this right. Hence, the suspect must be duly informed that s/he is actually under suspicion and notified that s/he is being questioned for this reason. Furthermore, the allegations against him/her must also be disclosed to him/her.

Art. 14 (3) (a) ICCPR, Art. 6 (3) (a) ECHR and Art. 8 (2) (b) AmCHR, all use similar wording to describe a suspect's right to be informed promptly and in detail of 'the nature and cause of the charge against him'. A comparable provision is found in the articles governing the liberty and security of persons. For example, Art. 9 (2) ICCPR and Art. 5 (2) ECHR also state that a detainee must be informed promptly of the reasons for his/her detention. However, the difference between

[282] J Jones and S Powles, *International Criminal Practice* (3rd edn, OUP 2003) 502 under 8.1.33.

[283] ICTY *Prosecutor v Boškoski and Tarčulovski*, AC, IT-04-82, 4 October 2005, Decision on Johan Tarčulovski's Interlocutary Appeal on Provisional Release.

[284] *See* also ICTY *Prosecutor v Delalić et al.*, AC, IT-96-21, 20 February 2001, Judgment, para 551: 'As long as a suspect is clearly informed... in a language he or she understands, the Prosecution fulfils its obligations.'

[285] ICTY *Prosecutor v Delalić et al.*, TC, IT-96-21, 19 January 1998, Decision on the Prosecution's Oral Request for the Admission of Exhibit 155 into Evidence and for an Order to Compel the Accused, Zdravko Mucić, to Provide a Handwriting Sample, paras 46, 50; *Prosecutor v Kupreškić et al.*, TC, IT-95-16,14 January 2000, Judgment, para 339; *Prosecutor v Brđanin*, TC, IT-99-36, 1 September 2004, Judgment, para 24; ICTR *Prosecutor v Niyitegeka*, TC, ICTR-96-14-T, 16 May 2003, Judgment and Sentence, para 46.

[286] J Jones and S Powles, *International Criminal Practice* (3rd edn, OUP 2003) 594 under 8.5.94.

these legal provisions is clear; liberty and security of person only relate to the process of detention. The detainee must be put in a position from which s/he is able to challenge the legality of his/her detention. A person suspected of a criminal offence needs to prepare his/her defence against the criminal allegations.[287] Art. 9 (2) ICCPR therefore relates to Art. 9 (4) ICCPR, which guarantees a detainee the opportunity of challenging the lawfulness of his/her detention. Art. 14 (3) (a) ICCPR serves to ensure the right to prepare the defence as laid down in Art. 14 (3) (b) ICCPR. Since the issue involves criminal law and is a matter of vital importance to the suspect, this right must be expressed in a more precise and detailed manner.[288] For this reason Art. 9 (2) ICCPR specifies that detained persons must be informed of the reason for their arrest and persons suspected of a criminal offence must be informed 'in detail' of the 'nature and cause' of the charges brought against them.[289]

European human rights bodies differentiate between the 'nature' and 'cause' of the allegation. The former refers to the 'legal grounds', the latter to the material facts upon which the allegation is based.[290] The drafting history of Art. 14 (3) (a) ICCPR allows the same interpretation to be given to this provision.[291] Regarding the information required to be submitted, the European organs have in practice allowed relatively few details to suffice.[292] Based on a purposive approach, the term is interpreted to include such information deemed necessary to enable a proper preparation of a defence. When adopting this approach it does not seem mandatory for the interrogator to reveal all the evidence upon which the allegations are based.[293] In *Brozicek* the ECtHR held that the obligation to inform the suspect is satisfied where the offences are listed with references to the relevant rules and the date, place, and name of the victim are mentioned.[294]

Art. 55 (2) (a) ICCSt addresses the right of the suspect to be informed of the fact that s/he has come under suspicion; that is, of his/her status as a suspect, prior to being questioned. This guarantee is not nearly as detailed as Art. 67 (1) (a) ICCSt, which is directed at the accused.[295] Nonetheless, its purpose is to inform a person

---

[287] D Harris *et al.*, *Law of the European Convention on Human Rights* (2nd edn, OUP 2009) 307.

[288] M Nowak, *International Covenant on Civil and Political Rights* (2nd edn, Engel 2005) Art. 14 MN 38.

[289] This gradual difference was also emphasized by the EComHR in *Nielsen v Denmark*, Appl. No. 343/57, 15 March 1960, 2 YB 412 at 462.

[290] ECtHR *Pélissier and Sassi v France*, Judgment 25 March 1999, Rep. 1999-II, para 51.

[291] *See* E/CN.4/SR, 156 the comments of the USA and Yugoslavia (p 11), France and the UK (p 12).

[292] D Harris *et al.*, *Law of the European Convention on Human Rights* (2nd edn, OUP 2009) 308.

[293] P Van Dijk *et al.*, *Theory and Practice of the European Convention on Human Rights* (4th edn, Intersentia 2006) 632.

[294] ECtHR *Brozicek v Italy*, Judgment 19 December 1989, Series A No. 167, para 42.

[295] Art. 67 (1) (a) ICCSt is more specific in this regard and its contents even goes beyond human rights requirements.

that there are grounds to believe that he or she has committed a crime, to illustrate the seriousness of the situation, and to alert the person concerned that he or she ought to consider the need for legal assistance at this stage.[296] When confronting a suspect with the allegations against him/her, the suspect must be informed of the crimes s/he is believed to have committed and of their criminal classification. It follows that s/he has a right to be informed of at least the *nature* of the charges. The provision lacks any explicit reference to the disclosure of the *cause* of the allegations and thereby the conduct upon which the assertions are based. This information or at least parts of it may, however, be communicated to the suspect during the course of questioning, as a necessary prerequisite for the Prosecutor to gain greater knowledge of the context of the allegations. Nonetheless, the extent to which particulars of the cause of the charges are revealed remains within the discretion of the person questioning the suspect.

Unfortunately, the provision also fails to include further elements of the respective human rights guarantees, such as a reference to the language, the scope, and the promptness of the information to be rendered to the suspect.

At the *ad hoc* Tribunals, Art. 21 (4) (a) ICTYSt, Art. 20 (4) (a) ICTRSt merely grant the accused the explicit right to be informed of the nature and cause of the charges. No such guarantee is specified for the suspect. Although neither Art. 18 (3) ICTYSt, Art. 17 (3) ICTRSt nor Rules 42 RPE ICTY, 43 RPE ICTR contain a respective right of the suspect, it seems logical and indeed necessary to extend the applicability of this right, laid down for the accused, to the investigation phase and the questioning of a suspect.

E. Pre-Trial Detention of the Suspect (*Alena Hartwig*)

I. Pre-trial detention under the issuance of a warrant of arrest pursuant to Art. 58 (1) ICCSt

The ICCSt provides alternative methods to ensure a person's presence before the Court. The most effective means is the issuance of a warrant of arrest, leading up to the arrest and surrender of the person sought, followed by his or her pre-trial detention.

1. Procedural questions

According to Art. 58 (1) ICCSt responsibility for the issuance of a warrant of arrest lies with the Pre-Trial Chamber. A warrant may be issued any time after the initiation of an investigation by the Prosecutor pursuant to Art. 53 ICCSt.

[296] Triffterer/*Hall*, Art. 55 MN. 11.

Upon the application of the Prosecutor, the Pre-trial Chamber examines the evidence or other information submitted by the Prosecutor and renders a decision on whether or not to issue a warrant of arrest. The Prosecutor is not bound by any specific prerequisites regarding the type and amount of evidence or information s/he presents, but may decide freely on what s/he deems necessary for the Pre-Trial Chamber to issue a warrant of arrest. Only when satisfied that the requirements of Art. 58 (1) ICCSt are fulfilled, will the Pre-Trial Chamber issue a warrant.

At the ICTY and the ICTR, the confirmation of the indictment is a precondition for the issuance of a warrant of arrest (Art. 19 ICTYSt, Art. 18 ICTRSt). An indictment will only be confirmed if the Prosecutor is able to establish a *prima facie* case against the suspect. If the judge of the Trial Chamber, to whom the indictment has been transmitted, confirms the indictment, the Prosecutor will then request the issuance of a warrant of arrest on the basis of the confirmation.

Whilst Art. 58 (2) ICCSt stipulates the details required in the Prosecutor's application,[297] Art. 58 (3) ICCSt sets out the necessary contents of a warrant of arrest. As well as information to identify the person concerned, the warrant of arrest must also contain specific reference to the crimes for which the person's arrest is sought and the relevant underlying facts.

2. *Requirements for the issuance of a warrant of arrest*

Art. 58 (1) ICCSt lays down the requirements for the issuance of an arrest warrant and the pre-trial detention of the suspect at the seat of the Court. These are two-fold. Firstly, there must be reasonable grounds to believe that the person has committed a crime within the jurisdiction of the Court.[298] Secondly, there must be a specific ground, as listed in Art. 58 (1) (b) ICCSt, which necessitates the detention of the suspect. The word 'and' means that both requirements must be fulfilled. Hence, a mere suspicion that a crime has been committed is not sufficient for the issuance of an arrest warrant and the detention of the suspect.

a. Reasonable suspicion First and foremost, there must be reasonable grounds to believe that the person, for whom the warrant is to be issued, has committed a crime within the jurisdiction of the Court. The examination of this requirement involves two steps. Firstly, there must be reasonable grounds to believe that crimes pursuant to Art. 5 ICCSt have been committed, and secondly, there must be reasonable grounds to believe that the person whose arrest is being sought is criminally responsible for the commission of those crimes.

Neither the Statute nor the Rules of Procedure and Evidence provide any further definition of the term 'reasonable grounds to believe'. The fact that the Rome

---

[297] *See* also Regulation 53 RegP.

[298] Art. 58 (1) (a) ICCSt.

Statute refers to other standards of suspicion or proof, besides 'reasonable grounds to believe', is of some help. For instance, Art. 55 (2) ICCSt speaks of 'grounds to believe' regarding the applicability of specific rights to persons who are about to be questioned. Art. 61 (7) ICCSt refers to 'substantial grounds to believe' for the confirmation of charges. Ultimately, Art. 66 (3) ICCSt provides that for a conviction, the Court must be convinced of the guilt of the accused 'beyond reasonable doubt'. Reflecting upon these provisions, one can identify a system of different standards of suspicion and proof. 'Reasonable grounds to believe' is a higher standard than mere 'grounds to believe' as found in Art. 55 (2) ICCSt, but constitutes a lower standard than the 'substantial grounds to believe' of Art. 61 (7) ICCSt.[299] A general classification of the standards of suspicion and proof becomes apparent. Moreover, this systematization illustrates that the issuance of a warrant of arrest and the subsequent pre-trial detention of the suspect are procedural steps to be held strictly separate from the process of the confirmation of charges.

According to the Appeals Chamber of the ICC, for there to be 'reasonable grounds to believe' there need not be certainty as to whether the person committed the alleged crimes.[300] The threshold of 'reasonable grounds to believe' therefore does not require that only one reasonable conclusion can be drawn from the evidence presented by the Prosecutor. Rather, a certain probability that the person committed the alleged crimes is sufficient to fulfil the standard of 'reasonable grounds to believe'. In other words, the evidence need not be so overwhelming that the conduct of proceedings can be considered definite. In general, the requirement of 'reasonable grounds to believe' in Art. 58 (1) ICCSt is to be equated with the prerequisite of 'reasonable suspicion' in Art. 5 (1) (c) ECHR.[301]

Art. 5 (1) (c) ECHR allows the deprivation of a person's liberty, where there is reasonable suspicion that he or she has committed an offence. In accordance with the structure of Art. 5 (1) (c) ECHR, the element of 'reasonable suspicion' is not a general requirement for pre-trial detention, additional to a separate ground for the deprivation of liberty. Rather, it is a sufficient ground for detention itself, without any further prerequisites being necessary for the lawfulness of the interference with the right to liberty. The requirement of 'reasonable suspicion' implies 'the existence of facts or information which would satisfy an objective observer that the person concerned may have committed the offence'.[302] The suspicion does not have to

---

299 ICC *Prosecutor v Al Bashir*, AC, ICC-02/05-01/09-73, 3 February 2010, Judgment on the Appeal of the Prosecutor against the 'Decision on the Prosecution's Application for a Warrant of Arrest against Omar Hassan Ahmad Al Bashir', para 30.

300 Ibid, para 31 *et subs*.

301 Ibid.

302 ECtHR *Fox, Campbell and Hartley v United Kingdom*, Judgment 30 August 1990, Series A No. 182, para 32; *Labita v Italy*, Judgment 6 April 2000, Rep. 2000-IV, para 155.

suffice for an indictment of the person. However, 'sufficient facts or information which would provide a plausible and objective basis for a suspicion'[303] must exist.

Unlike the legal provisions at the ICC, there is no specific provision governing the initial deprivation of liberty, by way of pre-trial detention, at the *ad hoc* Tribunals. Instead, the arrest and surrender of a person to the seat of the Court is automatically followed by his or her detention (Rules 64, 65 RPE ICTY/ICTR). The legitimacy of pre-trial detention stems from the judicial confirmation of the indictment, which is required at the *ad hoc* Tribunals for the issuance of a warrant of arrest, which in turn is a prerequisite for pre-trial detention. Art. 19 (1) ICTYSt, Art. 18 (1) ICTRSt require the Prosecutor to establish a *prima facie* case. Once this has been achieved, the judge responsible confirms the indictment and may thereafter issue a warrant of arrest (Art. 19 (2) ICTYSt, Art. 18 (2) ICTRSt). A *prima facie* case, as a basis for the confirmation of the indictment and the issuance of an arrest warrant, is principally understood to be 'a credible case which would (if not contradicted by the Defence) provide a sufficient basis to convict the accused on the charge'.[304] The *prima facie* case serves as an indirect implementation of a standard of suspicion required for the pre-trial detention of the accused person. It is somewhat higher than the standard of 'reasonable grounds to believe' at the ICC, due to the fact that it relates to the confirmation of the indictment.

b. Necessity of the arrest In addition to the requirement of reasonable suspicion, Art. 58 (1) (b) ICCSt specifies that the arrest of the person must appear necessary. Only when at least one of the three grounds listed in Art. 58 (1) (b) ICCSt is established will an arrest be considered to be necessary. According to the principle of proportionality the interference with a person's liberty must always be proportional. It follows that an arrest is only legitimate where the reasons for the arrest outweigh the civil liberties of the person concerned. This, as well as the use of the word 'or' in Art. 58 (1) (b) ICCSt, illustrates the exhaustive character of the grounds listed. It follows that, where none of these grounds can be shown, the arrest is, by implication, deemed not necessary and therefore unlawful.

Difficulties arise with the word 'appears'. The ICC provisions offer no further guidance on when an arrest *appears* necessary. The Appeals Chamber has interpreted the term to refer to the mere *possibility* of a ground for detention being realized.[305] This somewhat broad approach must be seen in the context of the

---

303 ECtHR *Murray v United Kingdom*, Judgment 28 October 1994, Series A No. 300-A, para 63.

304 ICTY *Prosecutor v Milošević*, TC, IT-02-54, 24 May 1999, Decision on Review of Indictment and Application for Consequential Orders, para 4; *Prosecutor v Stanišić and Simatović*, TC, IT-03-69, 16 December 2005, Decision on Prosecution Motion for Leave to Amend the Amended Indictment, p. 3.

305 ICC *Prosecutor v Katanga and Chui*, AC, ICC-01/04-01/07-572, 9 June 2008, Judgment in the Appeal of Mathieu Ngudjolo Chui of 27 March 2008 against the Decision of Pre-Trial Chamber I on the Application of the Appellant for Interim Release, para 21.

determination of the risks referred to in Art. 58 (1) (b) ICCSt, which inevitably involves an element of prediction.[306] Hence the standard of the word 'appears' is rather low.

Due to the legal situation at the *ad hoc* Tribunals, as described above, all that is required for the initiation of pre-trial detention is the establishment of a *prima facie* case in order to confirm the indictment. No additional conditions need be fulfilled. The necessity of the restriction of liberty is not an issue in the pre-trial phase of the proceedings. Other grounds for detention, apart from the requirement of suspicion, may become relevant at later stages of the proceedings, when the question of continued detention is at issue.

(1) To ensure the person's appearance at trial The first ground for detention, which relates to the risk of flight, is set down in Art. 58 (1) (b) (i) ICCSt. The arrest of a person appears necessary to ensure his or her appearance at trial. In practice the utmost importance is attached to this ground. Amongst other criteria the international contacts and the financial as well as the professional background of the suspect are the primary considerations for the evaluation of the risk of flight.[307] Further relevant factors include the possibility to exercise influence due to the past and present political position of the person, as well as the availability of a necessary network, which may assist with the required connections and means to flee.[308] With regard to the warrant of arrest against *Al Bashir*, the necessity to ensure his appearance at trial was justified due to the refusal of the Government of Sudan to cooperate with the Court.[309] On the whole, the ICC's evaluation of the grounds for detention in the decisions to issue a warrant of arrest is rather vague. More detailed analysis is undertaken by the Court when justifying the continued detention.

The risk of flight is the third possible ground for detention listed in Art. 5 (1) (c) ECHR. As reasonable suspicion that the person has committed a crime is by itself enough to justify detention, less importance is attached to the risk of flight. Nonetheless, the ECtHR, when evaluating the risk of flight, refers to several criteria, such as the personality of the person, his/her home, assets, morals, and the severity of the possible sentence.[310]

---

[306] *See* ICC *Prosecutor v Lubanga*, AC, ICC-01/04-01/06-824, 13 February 2007, Judgment in the Appeal of Mr. Thomas Lubanga Dyilo against the Decision of Pre-Trial Chamber I entitled 'Décision sur la demande de mise en líberté provisoire de Thomas Lubanga Dyilo', para 137.

[307] ICC *Prosecutor v Bemba*, PTC III, ICC-01/05-01/08-14, 10 June 2008, Decision on the Prosecutor's Application for a Warrant of Arrest against Jean-Pierre Bemba Gombo, para 87.

[308] Ibid, para 89.

[309] ICC *Prosecutor v Al Bashir*, PTC I, ICC-02/05-01/09-3, 4 March 2009, Decision on the Prosecution's Application for a Warrant of Arrest against Omar Hassan Ahmad Al Bashir, para 228 *et subs*.

[310] ECtHR *Smirnova v Russia*, Judgment 24 July 2003, Rep. 2003-IX, para 60.

(2) To prevent the obstruction of the investigation or the court proceedings Art. 58 (1) (b) (ii) ICCSt is aimed at preventing the destruction of evidence, the intimidation of victims and witnesses as well as collusion with accomplices. Its scope includes all kinds of behaviour capable of jeopardizing the conduct of the investigation and with that the proceedings as a whole. Where the person concerned has already dispersed documents on his/her activities or exerted pressure on witnesses prior to the issuance of a warrant of arrest, such behaviour serves as a strong indicator that there is a danger of further interference with the investigation and/or proceedings.[311] Under certain circumstances, the mere possibility of such behaviour occurring is considered to be sufficient to justify an arrest on this ground.[312] In addition to the position of power and the possibility of influencing others, contact with external actors is of further relevance.[313]

The ECHR does not allow for the initiation of pre-trial detention based on the danger of interference with the investigation or court proceedings. This ground is only of relevance for the justification of continued pre-trial detention.

(3) To prevent the commission of further crimes The third ground for arrest is aimed at preventing the commission of further crimes. Art. 58 (1) (b) (iii) ICCSt refers to two alternatives. Firstly, the person shall be hindered from continuing to commit the same crime ('*that* crime'). Secondly, the provision is aimed at preventing the commission of further crimes within the jurisdiction of the court ('or a related crime'), arising out of the same circumstances. Having only been mentioned once, in the decision on the warrant of arrest against *Al Bashir*,[314] this ground for arrest has found little consideration in the ICC jurisprudence to date.

Art. 5 (1) (c) ECHR refers to the prevention of further crimes as the second possible ground for the deprivation of liberty. Considering this rather extensive wording, it must be noted that not every kind of preventative detention may be legitimized on this ground. Instead, there must be a real possibility of the person committing further offences.[315] Contrary to the wording of Art. 58 (1) (b) (iii) ICCSt, it is not mandatory under the ECHR that the crimes committed and possible future crimes are related.

---

[311] ICC *Prosecutor v Harun and Kushayb*, PTC I, ICC-02/05-01/07-1, 27 April 2007, Decision on the Prosecution Application under Article 58 (7) of the Statute, para 129 *et subs*.

[312] ICC *Prosecutor v Al Bashir*, PTC I, ICC-02/05-01/09-3, 4 March 2009, Decision on the Prosecution's Application for a Warrant of Arrest against Omar Hassan Ahmad Al Bashir, para 233.

[313] ICC *Prosecutor v Katanga and Chui*, PTC I, ICC-01/04-01/07-4, 6 July 2007, Decision on the Evidence and Information Provided by the Prosecution for the Issuance of a Warrant of Arrest for Germain Katanga, para 63.

[314] ICC *Prosecutor v Al Bashir*, PTC I, ICC-02/05-01/09-3, 4 March 2009, Decision on the Prosecution's Application for a Warrant of Arrest against Omar Hassan Ahmad Al Bashir, para 235 *et subs*.

[315] ECtHR *Eriksen v Norway*, Judgment 27 May 1997, Rep. 1997-III, para 86; *Ciulla v Italy*, Judgment 22 February 1989, Series A No. 148, para 40.

II. Provisional arrest or arrest and surrender pursuant to Art. 58 (5) ICCSt

In Art. 58 (5), 92 ICCSt, the Rome Statute provides for the possibility of the provisional arrest of a person In this case, the warrant of arrest has already been issued. Only the request for surrender is not available yet. This provision is aimed at avoiding the prolonged procedure of formally requesting the arrest and surrender of a person in urgent cases.[316] The content of a request for provisional arrest is specified in Art. 92 (2) ICCSt. After the arrest of the person, the Court must within sixty days submit a request for surrender with supporting documents thereof (Rule 188 RPE ICC). Otherwise, the person may be released pursuant to Art. 92 (3) ICCSt.

The possibility for provisional arrest at the *ad hoc* Tribunals is laid down in Rule 40 (i) RPE ICTY.[317] According to this Rule it is the Prosecutor who requests a state to provisionally arrest a suspect. This role allocation is due to the procedure applicable at the *ad hoc* Tribunals. Here, a warrant of arrest can only be issued after the confirmation of the indictment (Art. 19 ICTYSt, Art. 18 ICTRSt). This procedure would take too long in urgent cases.[318] The decision of whether to request the provisional arrest of a suspect rests with the Prosecutor and is not subject to judicial supervision.[319]

III. Arrest proceedings in the custodial state

After a warrant of arrest has been issued by the Pre-Trial Chamber, the Court may, in accordance with Art. 89, 91 ICCSt, send out a request for the arrest and surrender of the person being sought to any state upon whose territory he or she is believed to be located. The required content of such a request is specified in Art. 91 (2) ICCSt. In addition to a copy of the arrest warrant, the request shall contain information describing the person, as well as documents and information necessary to enable the state to carry out the process of surrender. Upon receipt of the request, the state concerned shall take immediate steps to arrest the person sought (Art. 59 (1) ICCSt). According to Art. 59 (2) ICCSt, after being arrested the person shall promptly be brought before the competent judicial authority.[320] This authority shall determine, in accordance with the law of that

---

[316] An urgent case constitutes the risk of flight of the person to be arrested, *see* Triffterer/*Kreß/Prost*, Art 92 MN 3.

[317] Rule 40 (A) (i) RPE ICTR.

[318] These are the imminent risks of flight, the intimidation of victims and witnesses or the destruction of evidence, *see* V Morris and M Scharf, *An Insider's Guide to the International Criminal Tribunal for the Former Yugoslavia, Vol I* (Transitional Publishers 1998) 196; W Sharp, 'International Obligations to Search for and Arrest War Criminals: Government Failure in the Former Yugoslavia?', 7 *Duke Journal of Comparative and International Law* (1997) 411, 442.

[319] Critical in this respect K Gallant, 'Securing the Presence of Defendants before the ICTY: Breaking with Extradition', 5 *CLF* (1994) 557, 584; C Bassiouni and P Manikas, *The Law of the International Criminal Tribunal for the Former Yugoslavia* (Transnational Publishers 1996) 874.

[320] This provision serves as an implementation of the human right to 'be brought promptly before a judge or other officer' as laid down in Art. 5 (3) ECHR, Art. 9 (3) ICCPR.

state, whether the warrant applies to the arrested person, whether the arrest was carried out correctly, and whether the rights of the person have been respected.[321] Furthermore, pursuant to Rule 117 (1) RPE ICC, the person arrested has the right to receive a copy of the arrest warrant. The content and scope of the judicial procedure following arrest is governed by national law.[322] The person arrested has the right to apply to the competent national authority for interim release (Art. 59 (3) ICCSt). However, Art. 59 (4) ICCSt specifically states that the national authority shall make no considerations on whether the arrest warrant was properly issued by the Court. The national judge therefore has no power to render a decision on the lawfulness of the arrest. Rule 117 (3) RPE ICC makes further clear that the Pre-Trial Chamber is the only authority vested with the power to do so. Where the arrested person applies to the competent national authority for interim release, the ICC must be notified of such an application in accordance with Art. 59 (5) ICCSt. The Court then has the power to make recommendations on the issue, to which the national authority 'shall give full consideration' before reaching its decision. Although these recommendations are not strictly binding, the wording of Art. 59 (5) ICCSt illustrates their importance and the duty to take full account of them. Where the national authority decides to release the arrested person, the Pre-Trial Chamber may request periodic reports (Art. 59 (6) ICCSt, Rule 117 (5) RPE ICC). The fact that national authorities retain competence to decide whether or not to release the person arrested on the request of the Court can be seen as a great concession to national states.

As far as the *ad hoc* Tribunals are concerned, the primacy of the Tribunal over national states becomes evident. The main provision in this context is Rule 55 RPE ICTY, according to which a copy of the arrest warrant, the indictment, and a statement of the rights of the accused must be transmitted to the state concerned. Pursuant to Rule 56 RPE ICTY the national state 'shall act promptly and with all due diligence'. There is no provision allowing a national judge to release the person before his or her transfer to the Tribunal. Pursuant to Rule 57 RPE ICTY, detention in the custodial state after arrest is mandatory. Moreover, Rule 58 RPE ICTY provides that the duty to cooperate laid down in Art. 29 ICTYSt, Art. 28 ICTRSt prevails over all national law on the surrender or transfer of persons.

IV. Interim release

Alongside the question of the initiation of pre-trial detention under an arrest warrant, the issue of the continued deprivation of liberty is of the utmost importance

[321] It can be said that the phrase 'the law of that State' refers to the law that has been introduced in order to comply with the obligations of the Rome Statute. *See* M El Zeidy, 'Critical Thoughts on Article 59 (2) of the ICC Statute', 4 *JICJ* (2006) 448, 453 on that issue.

[322] Ibid, 454 *et subs.*

for the detained person. Indeed, many theoretical as well as practical questions arise from the issue of whether the detainee should be released or further detained.

1. Initial request upon first appearance

After the suspect has been surrendered to the Court by the custodial state, he or she shall appear promptly before the Pre-Trial Chamber pursuant to Rule 121 RPE ICC. At this first appearance the person has the right to apply, by way of oral motion, for interim release. Written requests are only necessary for applications made after the first appearance before the Court (Rule 118 (3) RPE ICC). Rule 118 (1) RPE ICC requires the Pre-Trial Chamber, after having sought the views of the Prosecutor, to reach a decision on the interim release of the detainee without delay. A closer look at the requirements and the content of the examination follows below.

2. Application for interim release

Either in addition to or independent of a request for interim release at the first appearance before the Court, the detainee may also apply for interim release after his/her initial appearance. Art. 60 (2) ICCSt governs the question of the continuation of detention. This provision is applicable to the first request for interim release (either at the initial appearance or afterwards) and sets out the requirements for a continued deprivation of liberty. The person may only be further detained if the Pre-Trial Chamber is satisfied of the presence of the conditions set out in Art. 58 (1) ICCSt. This means that the requirements necessary to legitimize the arrest must still be met at this later stage. Art. 60 (3) ICCSt relates to subsequent decisions on interim release, following the decision on the first application pursuant to Art. 60 (2) ICCSt. The applicability of paragraph 3 is triggered by the first decision of the Pre-Trial Chamber on the request for interim release of the person.[323] This ruling of the Pre-Trial Chamber is the object of periodic review, carried out in accordance with Art. 60 (3) ICCSt. Where there has been a change of circumstances the Pre-Trial Chamber may modify its previous ruling on release or detention if the circumstances so require.

It follows that the first decision on the continuation of detention is, pursuant to Art. 60 (2) ICCSt, reached by considering the requirements laid down in Art. 58 (1) ICCSt, whilst subsequent decisions constitute a review of the Art. 60 (2) ICCSt decision, which may only be deviated from where a change of circumstances so requires (Art. 60 (3) ICCSt). The purpose of these provisions is to

[323] The decision on the issuance of a warrant of arrest is not considered to fulfil the requirement of a 'ruling', as is stated by Art. 60 (3) ICCSt. Art. 60 (3) ICCSt is only applicable if the Pre-Trial Chamber made a decision in accordance with Art. 60 (2) ICCSt. *See* ICC *Prosecutor v Lubanga*, AC, ICC-01/04-01/06-824, 13 February 2007, Judgment on the Appeal of Mr Thomas Lubanga Dyilo against the Decision of Pre-Trial Chamber I entitled 'Décision sur la demande de mise en líberté Provisoire de Thomas Lubanga Dyilo', para 95 *et subs.*

ensure that (1) a person is only detained if the requirements of Art. 58 ICCSt are met, and (2) s/he is detained only for the period in which these requirements are given.[324]

Rule 65 RPE ICTY governs provisional release at the *ad hoc* Tribunals. Because Rule 64 RPE ICTY states that an accused shall be detained upon arrival at the Tribunal, Rule 65 RPE ICTY only provides for release under special conditions. It is not a multi-stage procedure, such as that laid down in the Rome Statute.

3. Requirements for continued detention

The following section examines the requirements necessary to legitimize the continued deprivation of liberty. Alongside the conditions expressly laid down in the statutes, specific procedural questions such as the burden of proof shall also be examined.

a. Continuing existence of the requirements of Art. 58 (1) ICCSt For the continuation of the deprivation of liberty to be lawful, the condition of reasonable grounds to believe and the element of necessity—that is, Art. 58 (1) (b) (i)–(iii) ICCSt—must be fulfilled. This applies, without question, to the first decision on the release or further detention of a detainee pursuant to Art. 60 (2) ICCSt. Whereas these requirements must be decided upon a new, independent of the decision on a warrant of arrest, the object of a periodic review in accordance with Art. 60 (3) ICCSt is to assess whether the underlying circumstances have changed. This means that at least with regard to a decision in accordance with Art. 60 (2) ICCSt, the requirements of Art. 58 (1) ICCSt must be assessed and affirmed.

(1) Reasonable grounds to believe The requirement of suspicion that the person has committed a crime within the jurisdiction of the Court is taken to be constantly satisfied. In decisions pursuant to Art. 60 (2) ICCSt, following the issuance of a warrant of arrest, the Pre-Trial Chambers have assumed that this condition continues to be fulfilled.[325] This is also true of subsequent decisions under Art. 60 (3) ICCSt, where the Chambers merely examine whether there has been a change in the circumstances by evaluating the facts and evidence presented by the parties.[326] After the charges against a person have been confirmed, the continuing existence of suspicion is simply assumed. In Art. 61 (7) ICCSt, the standard of suspicion required for the confirmation of charges is 'substantial grounds to believe'. It follows that, where the Pre-Trial Chamber has determined 'substantial grounds to believe' that the person has committed a crime within the Court's jurisdiction,

[324] ICC *Prosecutor v Katanga and Chui*, PTC I, ICC-01/04-01/07-330, 18 March 2008, Decision on the Powers of the Pre-Trial Chamber to Review *proprio motu* the Pre-Trial Detention of Germain Katanga, p 9.

[325] ICC *Prosecutor v Katanga and Chui*, PTC I, ICC-01/04-01/07-426, 21 April 2008, Decision on the Conditions of Pre-Trial Detention of Germain Katanga, p 6.

[326] ICC *Prosecutor v Bemba*, PTC II, ICC-01/05-01/08-403, 14 April 2009, Decision on Application for Interim Release, para 40.

the lower standard of 'reasonable grounds' is also fulfilled. In decisions on the issue, the assumption of reasonable grounds is not further elaborated upon.[327]

(2) To ensure the person's appearance at trial In practice, Art. 58 (1) (b) (i) ICCSt is the most important reason for the continuation of detention. Amongst the criteria that have been developed in the case law of the Chambers are aspects that have influenced the decision on the issuance of an arrest warrant. The Appeals Chamber in *Bemba Gombo* elaborated upon the different considerations to be taken into account when determining the risk of flight,[328] the first of which is the gravity of the charges and the length of the sentence in the case of conviction. It is known that the probability of a person trying to evade justice rises in proportion to the consequences of conviction.[329] The gravity of the crimes with which a person is charged is not by itself sufficient to justify the continuation of detention, but is an important aspect which must be seen together with other factors.[330] After the charges have been confirmed, the risk of flight is considered to be higher than at the pre-trial stage.[331] Additional factors are the political and professional position, the availability of a network of international contacts and the financial resources of the person concerned. An aspect weighing in favour of the detainee is supportive and cooperative behaviour towards the Court.[332] The weight attached to the criterion of 'strong family ties' by the Pre-Trial Chamber in *Bemba Gombo*[333]

---

[327] ICC *Prosecutor v Lubanga*, PTC I, ICC-01/04-01/07-426, 14 February 2007, Review of the 'Decision on the Application for the Interim Release of Thomas Lubanga Dyilo', p 6; *Prosecutor v Katanga and Chui*, TC II, ICC-01/04-01/07-794, 12 December 2008, Second Review of the Decision on the Conditions of Detention of Germain Katanga, para 9.

[328] ICC *Prosecutor v Bemba*, AC, ICC-01/05-01/08-631, 2 December 2009, Judgment on the Appeal of the Prosecutor against Pre-Trial Chamber II's 'Decision on the Interim Release of Jean-Pierre Bemba Gombo and Convening Hearings with the Kingdom of Belgium, the Republic of Portugal, the Republic of France, the Federal Republic of Germany, the Italian Republic, and the Republic of South Africa'.

[329] ICC *Prosecutor v Katanga and Chui*, AC, ICC-01/04-01/07-572, 9 June 2008, Judgment in the Appeal by Mathieu Ngudjolo Chui of 27 March 2008 against the Decision of Pre-Trial Chamber I on the Application of the Appellant for Interim Release, para 21.

[330] ICC *Prosecutor v Lubanga*, AC, ICC-01/04-01/07-824, 13 February 2007, Judgment on the Appeal of Mr. Thomas Lubanga Dyilo against the Decision of Pre-Trial Chamber I entitled 'Décision sur la demande de mise en liberté Provisoire de Thomas Lubanga Dyilo', para 136.

[331] ICC *Prosecutor v Katanga and Chui*, TC II, ICC-01/04-01/07-750, 19 November 2008, Second Review of the Decision on the Application for Interim Release of Mathieu Ngudjolo, p 7.

[332] ICC *Prosecutor v Bemba*, AC, ICC-01/05-01/08-631, 2 December 2009, Judgment on the Appeal of the Prosecutor against Pre-Trial Chamber II's 'Decision on the Interim Release of Jean-Pierre Bemba Gombo and Convening Hearings with the Kingdom of Belgium, the Republic of Portugal, the Republic of France, the Federal Republic of Germany, the Italian Republic, and the Republic of South Africa', para 79 *et subs*.

[333] ICC *Prosecutor v Bemba*, PTC II, ICC-01/05-01/08-475, 14 August 2009, Decision on the Interim Release of Jean-Pierre Bemba Gombo and Convening Hearings with the Kingdom of Belgium, the Republic of Portugal, the Republic of France, the Federal Republic of Germany, the Italian Republic, and the Republic of South Africa, para 68. This decision was the first to grant interim release to a detainee at the ICC. The Appeals Chamber in its judgment of December 2009 reversed the decision of the Single Judge and ordered the continued detention of Mr Bemba.

has been made relative by in a subsequent decision of the Appeals Chamber of 2 December, 2009. Furthermore, great weight is given to specific guarantees that the person will appear for trial. These guarantees must appear to be 'sufficient' in light of the grave charges and the length of a possible sentence.[334] In particular the guarantees of states are of great importance. Requests for interim release have been denied mainly because of the absence of such guarantees.[335] The overall analysis made by the Court of the risk of flight can be said to be most profound and detailed, having developed extensively over the past few years. The Chambers are fully aware of the element of prediction necessarily involved in determining this risk and the need to balance different factors against each other.

At the *ad hoc* Tribunals, Rule 65 (B) RPE ICTY stipulates that the Trial Chamber must be 'satisfied that the accused will appear for trial'. More emphasis has been placed on this ground for release after the amendment of Rule 65 RPE ICTY in 1999 (or 2003 for the ICTR), which lead to the deletion of the requirement of 'exceptional circumstances'. Just as at the ICC, the assessment of the risk of flight can only be determined by way of prediction and an analysis of various factors. The relevant criteria and their respective weight depend upon the circumstances of each particular case. Amongst them are: (1) whether the accused surrendered voluntarily to the Court, (2) the guarantee of the state to which the accused seeks to be released, and (3) the personal guarantees of the accused himself.[336] Other factors to be taken into consideration when deciding the question of release are the gravity of the crimes and the length of a possible sentence,[337] the circumstances of the arrest of the accused,[338] the willingness to cooperate with the Tribunal,[339] and the existence of humanitarian reasons at later stages of the proceedings.[340]

(3) To prevent the obstruction of the investigation or court proceedings The danger of obstruction is the second reason to justify the continued detention of a person in

[334] ICC *Prosecutor v Katanga and Chui*, TC II, ICC-01/04-01/07-965, 17 March 2009, Third Review of the Decision on the Application for Interim Release of Mathieu Ngudjolo, para 8.

[335] ICC *Prosecutor v Bemba*, PTC II, ICC-01/05-01/08-475, 14 April 2009, Decision on Application for Interim Release, para 48.

[336] For further details *see* ICTY *Prosecutor v Brđanin and Talić*, TC, IT-99-36, 25 July 2000, Decision on Motion by Radoslav Brđanin for Provisional Release, para 17; *Prosecutor v Stanišić*, AC, IT-04-79, 17 October 2005, Decision on Prosecution's Interlocutory Appeal of Mićo Stanišić's Provisional Release, para 21 *et subs.*; *Prosecutor v Haradinaj et al.*, TC, IT-04-84, 6 June 2005, Decision on Ramush Haradinaj's Motion for Provisional Release, para 34; *Prosecutor v Popović et al.*, TC, IT-05-88, Decision on Drago Nikolić's Request for Provisional Release, para 16.

[337] ICTY *Prosecutor v Ademi*, TC, IT-01-46, 20 February 2002, Order on Motion for Provisional Release, para 25; *Prosecutor v Mrđa*, TC, IT-02-59, 15 April 2002, Decision on Darko Mrđa's Request for Provisional Release, para 35.

[338] ICTY *Prosecutor v Mrđa*, TC, IT-02-59, 15 April 2002, Decision on Darko Mrđa's Request for Provisional Release, para 35.

[339] ICTY *Prosecutor v Krajišnik*, TC, IT-00-39, 8 October 2001, Decision on Momčilo Krajišnik's Notice of Motion for Provisional Release, para 21.

[340] ICTR *Prosecutor v Karemera et al.*, AC, ICTR-98-44, 8 December 2009, Decision on Mathieu Ngirumpatse's Appeal against Decision on Remand on Provisional Release, para 15.

accordance with Art. 60 (2) and Art. 58 (1) (b) ICCSt. Where victims or witnesses have already been intimidated or even killed, evidence thereof is clearly disadvantageous for the release of the detainee.[341] But attempts to obstruct the proceedings are not a mandatory requirement. What matters is the mere possibility of the person exercising his or her influence upon victims or witnesses. According to the wording of Art. 58 (1) (b) ICCSt ('*appears* necessary') it suffices that the person has the potential, by way of contact to the outside world, and sufficient means, to influence others. The probability of an obstruction occurring clearly rises after the process of confirmation of charges, during which the person may obtain knowledge of the identities of victims and witnesses.[342] This requirement is even fulfilled if supporters of the detainee are deemed capable of possible interference.[343] On the other hand, the Single Judge in *Bemba Gombo* held that this danger must be linked 'to [a] specific act or conduct' on the part of the detainee.[344] The issue of the endangerment of victims or witnesses is also closely connected to the stability of the state concerned. The Pre-Trial Chamber has, on the grounds of an instable security situation in the country concerned, regarded victims and witnesses to be in possible danger and ruled that detention had to be upheld unless the security situation changed.[345] An important aspect in this regard is the person's authority and position of power and his or her ability to take influence.[346] Finally, it must be noted that the wording of Art. 58 (1) (b) (ii) ICCSt is not restricted to influencing victims and witnesses, but also covers the destruction of evidence.

The *ad hoc* tribunals deal with the danger of obstruction in a more careful way. Throughout the process of disclosure the identities of victims and witnesses are revealed, but it is not concluded that a released accused automatically poses a danger to them.[347] The mere possibility of influencing victims and witnesses does not suffice; instead concrete evidence that the accused might pose a danger to them

[341] ICC *Prosecutor v Lubanga*, PTC I, ICC-01/04-01/06-586, 18 October 2006, Decision on the Application for the Interim Release of Thomas Lubanga Dyilo, p 6.

[342] ICC *Prosecutor v Katanga and Chui*, TC II, ICC-01/04-01/07-794, 12 December 2008, Second Review of the Decision on the Conditions of Detention of Germain Katanga, para 13.

[343] ICC *Prosecutor v Katanga and Chui*, PTC I, ICC-01/04-01/07-426, 21 April 2008, Decision on the Conditions of the Pre-Trial Detention of Germain Katanga, p 7.

[344] ICC *Prosecutor v Bemba*, PTC II, ICC-01/05-01/08-475, 14 August 2009, Decision on the Interim Release of Jean-Pierre Bemba Gombo and Convening Hearings with the Kingdom of Belgium, the Republic of Portugal, the Republic of France, the Federal Republic of Germany, the Italian Republic, and the Republic of South Africa, para 72.

[345] ICC *Prosecutor v Katanga and Chui*, PTC I, ICC-01/04-01/07-345, 27 March 2008, Decision on the Application for Interim Release of Mathieu Ngudjolo Chui, p 9.

[346] Whereas this factor may also be considered to elaborate on the risk of flight, it may in some cases be an indication for the danger of obstruction. *See* ICC *Prosecutor v Bemba*, PTC III, ICC-01/05-01/08-321, 16 December 2008, Decision on Application for Interim Release, para 38.

[347] ICTY *Prosecutor v Brđanin and Talić*, TC, IT-99-36, 25 July 2000, Decision on Motion by Radoslav Brđanin for Provisional Release, para 19. For the ICTR *see* D Rearick, 'Innocent until Alleged Guilty: Provisional Release at the ICTR', 44 *Harv Int'l L J* (2003) 577, 582.

is required.[348] Rule 65 (B) RPE ICTY does not refer to the destruction of evidence as a ground for detention. This reasoning is only covered by Rule 40*bis* (B) RPE ICTY, where the provisional detention of a suspect is ordered by a judge.

(4) To prevent the commission of crimes So far no specific criteria have been developed regarding the further commission of crimes by the person concerned. This being the third and last ground for (continued) detention, more weight has been attached to the previous reasons. In a decision in *Bemba Gombo*, the Single Judge held that specific information must be available to allow the assumption that the person might commit the same or a related crime.[349] Also of relevance is the stability of the current situation in the country concerned, here the Central African Republic.

Recourse might be taken to the jurisprudence of the ECtHR, which has specified different criteria to indicate the danger of repetition of the offence, such as 'the very prolonged continuation of reprehensible activities, the huge extent of the loss sustained by the victims and the wickedness of the person charged', as well as the network of contacts the person might utilize.[350] The mere reference to the past history of a person does, however, not justify detention.

b. Views of the relevant state Rule 119 (3) RPE ICC provides that the Pre-Trial Chamber shall seek the views of, among others, 'any relevant State' before releasing a person. Regulation 51 RegC specifies this to be the host State and the State to which the person seeks to be released. Bearing in mind that the ICC is dependent upon the cooperation of states, this requirement is rather formal, but nonetheless elementary. Rule 185 RPE ICC places the host State of the Court—that is, the Netherlands—in the case of the release of a person from custody, under the duty to facilitate the transfer and the departure of that person. For this reason the ICC and the Netherlands have concluded a 'Headquarters Agreement', of which Article 47 specifies the assistance required in the case of interim release.

As far as the views of the State to which the person seeks to be released are concerned, the Single Judge in *Bemba Gombo,* intending to hold the hearing afterwards, ruled that a decision to release a person may even be taken in the absence of such a hearing.[351] The Appeals Chamber, on the other hand, noted that the

[348] M DeFrank, 'ICTY Provisional Release: Current Practice, a Dissenting Voice, and the Case for a Rule Change', 80 *Texas Law Review* (2002) 1429, 1437.

[349] ICC *Prosecutor v Bemba*, PTC II, ICC-01/05-01/08-475, 14 August 2009, Decision on the Interim Release of Jean-Pierre Bemba Gombo and Convening Hearings with the Kingdom of Belgium, the Republic of Portugal, the Republic of France, the Federal Republic of Germany, the Italian Republic, and the Republic of South Africa, para 76.

[350] ECtHR *Matznetter v Austria*, Judgment 10 November 1969, Series A No. 10, para 9; *Contrada v Italy*, Judgment 24 August 1998, Rep. 1998-V, para 58.

[351] ICC *Prosecutor v Bemba*, PTC II, ICC-01/05-01/08-475, 14 August 2009, Decision on the Interim Release of Jean-Pierre Bemba Gombo and Convening Hearings with the Kingdom of Belgium, the Republic of Portugal, the Republic of France, the Federal Republic of Germany, the Italian Republic, and the Republic of South Africa, para 88.

identification of a state willing to accept the person, must necessarily take place prior to a decision on release.[352]

c. **Burden of proof** In order to determine the burden of proof, we must look at the wording of the respective articles governing the detention of the suspect. Art. 58 (1) ICCSt refers to the requirements for arrest and detention in a positive manner, that is, it does not provide for *release* under certain circumstances, but conversely states that *detention* is only possible if specific requirements are met. The ICC system with its two requirements (suspicion and necessity) lays the burden of proof upon the Prosecutor. This is recognized and applied in the decisions of the Chambers.[353]

However, when it comes to decisions pursuant to Art. 60 (2) ICCSt, the Chambers' approach corresponds to a reversal of the burden of proof. Here, the Pre-Trial Chambers constantly refer to the decisions on the issuance of a warrant of arrest, without examining the requirements of Art. 58 (1) ICCSt anew. Rather, the detained person is put in a situation where he or she has to rebut the existence of facts warranting detention.[354] This constitutes a reversal of the burden of proof.[355]

At the ICTY and the ICTR, the burden of proof rests with the accused. This is foremost due to the wording of Rule 65 RPE ICTY which states that '[r]elease may be ordered... only if it [the Trial Chamber] is satisfied that...'. Thus, detention being the rule, the requirements for *release* must be specially proven. It follows that here the burden of proof rests with the accused and indeed in practice this is the approach adopted by the Chambers of the Tribunals.[356] This reversal

[352] ICC *Prosecutor v Bemba*, AC, ICC-01/05-01/08-631, 2 December 2009, Judgment on the Appeal of the Prosecutor against Pre-Trial Chamber II's 'Decision on the Interim Release of Jean-Pierre Bemba Gombo and Convening Hearings with the Kingdom of Belgium, the Republic of Portugal, the Republic of France, the Federal Republic of Germany, the Italian Republic, and the Republic of South Africa', para 106 *et subs*.

[353] ICC *Prosecutor v Katanga and Chui*, PTC I, ICC-01/04-01/07-330, 18 March 2008, Decision on the Powers of the Pre-Trial Chamber to Review *proprio motu* the Pre-Trial Detention of Germain Katanga, p 6. *See* also C Muller, 'The Law of Interim Release in the Jurisprudence of the International Criminal Tribunals', 8 *ICLR* (2008) 589, 621.

[354] See eg, ICC *Prosecutor v Katanga and Chui*, AC, ICC-01/04-01/07-572, 9 June 2008, Judgment in the Appeal by Mathieu Ngudjolo Chui of 27 March 2008 against the Decision of Pre-Trial Chamber I on the Application of the Appellant for Interim Release, para 26; *Prosecutor v Bemba*, PTC III, ICC-01/05-01/08-80-Anx, 20 August 2008, Decision on Application for Interim Release, para 52.

[355] ICC *Prosecutor v Bemba*, AC, ICC-01/05-01/08-323, 16 December 2008, Judgment on the Appeal of Mr. Jean-Pierre Bemba Gombo against the Decision of Pre-Trial Chamber III entitled 'Decision on Application for Interim Release', Dissenting Opinion of Judge Georghios M. Pikis, para 26; G Knoops, *Theory and Practice of International and Internationalized Criminal Proceedings* (Kluwer Law International 2007) 150.

[356] ICTY *Prosecutor v Jokić*, TC, IT-01-42/1, 20 February 2002, Order on Miodrag Jokić's Motion for Provisional Release, para 18; *Prosecutor v Ljubičić*, TC, IT-00-41, 26 July 2005, Decision on Second Application for Provisional Release, para 17.

of the burden of proof stands in clear contrast with internationally recognized human rights principles, such as the presumption of innocence and the maxim contained in Art. 9 (3) ICCPR that detention shall not be the general rule but the exception.[357]

d. Legal consequences of the decision The Rome Statute expressly stipulates the legal consequences following the evaluation of the prerequisites for detention. Art. 60 (2) ICCSt provides that the Pre-Trial Chamber 'shall release the person, with or without conditions' if it is not satisfied that the conditions set down in Art. 58 (1) ICCSt are met. Only where they are fulfilled may the person be detained further. It follows that the decision on whether to release the person or not is not of a discretionary nature. Once the Chamber has found that the preconditions for detention are not met, the person must ('shall') be released.[358] This conclusion is supported by the interpretation of the requirements of Art. 58 (1) ICCSt as constituting an exhaustive list, as argued above.

In contrast to this, the consequences of an examination under Art. 60 (3) ICCSt are of a discretionary nature. The provision states that the Chamber '*may* modify its ruling as to detention, release or conditions of release'.[359] As a prerequisite to this, the Chamber must be satisfied that there has been a change in the circumstances which require a modification. However, the wording conflicts with the intention of the drafters of the Rome Statute, as expressed in other parts of the ICCSt. It is hard to believe that the drafters intended to grant the Pre-Trial Chamber complete discretion regarding the release or detention of the suspect. The discretion may be appropriate where the change of circumstances require a mere modification of the conditions of detention. However, where the requirements of Art. 58 (1) ICCSt are no longer fulfilled due to a change in circumstances, the Chamber's discretion must surely come to an end, release being the only logical option. Any other interpretation would conflict with the fundamental idea of Art. 60 (3) ICCSt and Rule 118 RPE-ICC. The purpose of these provisions is to guarantee that a person's detention is restricted to those periods in which the requirements of Art. 58 (1) ICCSt are met. In other words, the conditions of Art 58 (1) ICCSt must be fulfilled and a person should only be detained for as long as the conditions are actually met. When they are no longer met he or she must be released.

Contrary to the Rome Statute's clear specification with binds the ICC Chambers, the wording of Rule 65 (B) RPE-ICTY/ICTR ('Release may be ordered...') grants

[357] This is also criticized by Judge Robinson in ICTY *Prosecutor v Krajišnik*, TC, IT-00-39, 8 October 2001, Decision on Momčilo Krajišnik's Notice of Motion for Provisional Release, Dissenting Opinion of Judge Patrick Robinson, para 24.

[358] *See* also ICC *Prosecutor v Lubanga*, AC, ICC-01/04-01/06-824, 13 February 2007, Judgment on the Appeal of Mr. Thomas Lubanga Dyilo against the Decision of Pre-Trial Chamber I entitled 'Décision sur la demande de mise en líberté Provisoire de Thomas Lubanga Dyilo', para 134.

[359] Own emphasis added.

the judges discretion regarding the issue of release. Hence, even if the accused is able to satisfy the Chamber of the fulfilment of the conditions of release, the Chamber has discretion whether or not to actually grant release. In conjunction with the word 'only', it becomes evident that the requirements specified in Rule 65 (B) RPE-ICTY/ICTR are necessary but that release may nonetheless be denied. This conflicts with internationally recognized human rights, which provide for a deprivation of liberty only in specific cases or on explicit grounds and in accordance with a procedure prescribed by law (Art. 5 (1) ECHR, Art. 9 (1) ICCPR). Furthermore, the provisions of the *ad hoc* Tribunals also conflict with the presumption of innocence and the maxim that detention shall not be the rule (Art. 9 (3) ICCPR). However, in practice where the conditions for release have been fulfilled, the ICTY and ICTR have rarely made use of their discretion to deny release.[360]

4. Periodic review by the Pre-Trial Chamber

Art. 60 (3) ICCSt and Rule 118 (2) ICCRPE provide for a periodic review of detention. The Pre-Trial Chamber may review its ruling on release or detention, either on its own initiative or at the request of the Prosecutor or the detained person.

According to Art. 60 (3) ICCSt and Rule 118 (2) ICCRPE the Pre-Trial Chamber is obliged to review its ruling periodically, at least every 120 days.

Regarding the authority of the Pre-Trial Chamber to initiate a review *proprio motu*, it is noteworthy that this competence applies independent of a decision pursuant to Art. 60 (2) ICCSt. Whilst the Appeals Chamber in *Lubanga* held that Art. 60 (3) ICCSt only applied where a decision under Art. 60 (2) ICCSt precedes,[361] the Pre-Trial Chamber in *Katanga* stated that it had the power to review detention, even though a decision pursuant to Art. 60 (2) ICCSt had not been passed on this point.[362]

The review of detention may also take place on the basis of a request of the Prosecutor or the detained person. This possibility is not restricted in a timely manner, the provisions allowing such a request 'at any time'.

The subject of the Chamber's review is the 'ruling on release or detention'; in other words, the question whether the conditions of Art. 58 (1) ICCSt still remain valid

[360] For cases in which release was denied, although the conditions were fulfilled *see*: ICTY *Prosecutor v Prlić et al.*, TC, IT-04-74, 2 December 2008, Decision on the Accused Praljak's Motion for Provisional Release, paras 22, 23, 32; *Prosecutor v Gotovina et al.*, TC, IT-06-90, 27 February 2009, Decision on Motion for Provisional Release of Ivan Čermak, para 10.

[361] ICC *Prosecutor v Lubanga*, AC, ICC-01/04-01/06-824, 13 February 2007, Judgment on the Appeal of Mr. Thomas Lubanga Dyilo against the Decision of Pre-Trial Chamber I entitled 'Décision sur la demande de mise en líberté Provisoire de Thomas Lubanga Dyilo', para 94 *et subs*.

[362] ICC *Prosecutor v Katanga and Chui*, PTC I, ICC-01/04-01/07-222, 21 February 2008, Decision Concerning Pre-Trial Detention of Germain Katanga, p 6; *Prosecutor v Katanga and Chui*, PTC I, ICC-01/04-01/07-330, 18 March 2008, Decision on the Powers of the Pre-Trial Chamber to Review *proprio motu* the Pre-Trial Detention of Germain Katanga, p 7 *et subs*.

and therefore justify the continued deprivation of liberty.[363] However, this does not mean that the evaluation of the requirements of Art. 58 (1) ICCSt shall take place *ab initio*.[364] Rather, the Chamber must examine the circumstances referred to in the previous ruling on release or detention and decide, on a summary basis, whether they still exist. The Chamber may then modify its ruling if it is satisfied that the underlying circumstances have changed.[365]

Neither the statutes nor the rules of the *ad hoc* Tribunals refer to the review of detention, let alone grant a right to review. The ICTR in the proceedings against *Jean Bosco Barayagwiza* adopted the human rights guarantee of *habeas corpus* for the review of detention and formally recognized it as customary law.[366] In subsequent cases both the ICTR and ICTY followed this approach. The request of the accused for review of detention follows the procedure and rules set out for 'other motions' in Rule 73 or Rule 72 A (i), D (i) RPE-ICTY/ICTR.[367] These options are not particularly promising and do not live up to human rights standards.[368]

V. Conditional release

If the Pre-Trial Chamber is satisfied in accordance with Art. 60 (2), (3) ICCSt that the requirements of Art. 58 (1) ICCSt are no longer fulfilled, it may set conditions restricting liberty when ordering the release of the person. Rule 119 (1) RPEICC provides for a non-exhaustive list[369] of possible conditions. The imposition of conditions is aimed at minimizing or negating the risks addressed in Art. 58 (1) (b) ICCSt. If the release of the person would involve one of the risks listed, conditions

---

[363] ICC *Prosecutor v Bemba*, AC, ICC-01/05-01/08-962, 19 November 2010, Judgment on the Appeal of Mr. Jean-Pierre Bemba Gombo against the Decision of Trial Chamber III of 28 July 2010 entitled 'Decision on the Review of the Detention of Mr. Jean-Pierre Bemba Gombo Pursuant to Rule 118 (2) of the Rules of Procedure and Evidence', para 52.

[364] Ibid, para 53.

[365] 'The requirement of "changed circumstances" imports either a change in some or all of the facts underlying a previous decision on detention, or a new fact satisfying a Chamber that a modification of its prior ruling is necessary', *see* ICC *Prosecutor v Bemba*, AC, ICC-01/05-01/08-631, 2 December 2009, Judgment on the Appeal of the Prosecutor against Pre-Trial Chamber II's 'Decision on the Interim Release of Jean-Pierre Bemba Gombo and Convening Hearings with the Kingdom of Belgium, the Republic of Portugal, the Republic of France, the Federal Republic of Germany, the Italian Republic, and the Republic of South Africa', para 60.

[366] ICTR *Prosecutor v Barayagwiza*, AC, ICTR-97-19, 3 November 1999, Decision, paras 88, 89; ICTY *Prosecutor v Milošević*, TC, IT-02-54, 8 November 2001, Decision on Preliminary Motions, para 38.

[367] For further differentiation *see* ICTY *Prosecutor v Nikolić*, AC, IT-94-2, 9 January 2003, Decision on Notice of Appeal, Dissenting Opinion of Judge Shahabuddeen, para 11 *et subs*.

[368] *See* G McIntyre, 'Defining Human Rights in the Arena of International Humanitarian Law: Human Rights in the Jurisprudence of the ICTY', in: G Boas and W Schabas (eds), *International Criminal Law Developments in the Case Law of the ICTY* (Kluwer Law International 2003) 193, 208 *et subs*.

[369] H Friman, 'Investigation and Prosecution', in: R Lee (ed), *The International Criminal Court—Elements of Crimes and Rules of Procedure and Evidence* (Transnational Publishers 2001) 493, 520.

of release may be imposed.[370] However, the Appeals Chamber in *Bemba* found that under certain circumstances it may impose conditions unconnected to this aim.[371] This means that even if there is no fear that the person released might act in a way described by Art. 58 (1) (b) ICCSt, the respective Chamber may still impose conditions restricting liberty.

Before releasing the person and imposing conditions, the Pre-Trial Chamber shall seek the views of the Prosecutor and the detainee, as well as any relevant state and, most notably, the victims who have communicated with the Court in the respective case (Rule 119 (3) RPE ICC).

In accordance with Rule 119 (4) RPE ICC, the Pre-Trial Chamber may issue a warrant of arrest after the release if it is convinced that the person has failed to comply with the imposed conditions.

At the *ad hoc* Tribunals conditions may be imposed pursuant to Rule 65 (C) RPE ICTY/ICTR. This rule expressly aims at reducing the risk of flight and securing the protection of others. Unlike Rule 119 (1) RPE ICC, Rule 65 (C) RPE ICTY/ICTR does not contain a catalogue of specific conditions restricting liberty. The practice of the Tribunals has shown that the conditions imposed are diverse, but similar to the possibilities listed in Rule 119 (1) RPE ICC.[372] Contrary to the 'two-tiered examination' referred to in *Bemba*, the wording of Rule 65 (C) RPE ICTY/ICTR suggests that the conditions imposed must correspond with the grounds for detention and the purpose of imprisonment. Nonetheless, on occasions irrelevant considerations have been taken into account.[373]

To-date, none of the persons detained at the ICC has been released. Hence, there is currently no example of the Court's practice regarding the imposition of conditions. However, the mere possibility of imposing conditions restricting liberty must be regarded with caution in light of the human rights issues at stake. Generally such conditions may be imposed to avoid the more severe measure of pre-trial detention, if the same purpose can be achieved by their imposition. But if the requirements of

---

370 ICC *Prosecutor v Bemba*, AC, ICC-01/05-01/08-631, 2 December 2009, Judgment on the Appeal of the Prosecutor against Pre-Trial Chamber II's 'Decision on the Interim Release of Jean-Pierre Bemba Gombo and Convening Hearings with the Kingdom of Belgium, the Republic of Portugal, the Republic of France, the Federal Republic of Germany, the Italian Republic, and the Republic of South Africa', para 105.

371 Ibid. The Chamber speaks of a 'two-tiered examination' in this respect.

372 ICTY *Prosecutor v Ademi*, TC, IT-01-46, 20 February 2002, Order on Motion for Provisional Release, para 40; *Prosecutor v Šainović et al.*, TC, IT-05-87, 4 July 2007, Decision on Ojdanić for Temporary Provisional Release, para 9; *Prosecutor v Haradinaj et al.*, TC, IT-04-84, 6 June 2005, Decision on Ramush Haradinaj's Motion for Provisional Release, para 53.

373 This is criticized in ICTY *Prosecutor v Haradinaj et al.*, AC, IT-04-84, 10 March 2006, Decision on Ramush Haradinaj's Modified Provisional Release, Joint Dissenting Opinion of Judge Shahabuddeen and Judge Schomburg, paras 2 *et subs*. *See* also C Muller, 'The Law of Interim Release in the Jurisprudence of the International Criminal Tribunals', 8 *ICLR* (2008) 589, 612 *et subs*.

Art. 58 (1) ICCSt are no longer fulfilled, the legitimacy of the further infringement of personal liberty seems questionable. It follows that the Chamber's ruling as to whether the requirements for detention pursuant to Art. 58 (1) (b) ICCSt are fulfilled or not must also apply to other measures, such as conditions restricting liberty.

F. Victims' Participation

Following the general agenda of the Rome Statute and the political comprise on which it is based, victims need to be able to present their views and concerns at any stage of the proceedings. Whereas Art. 68 (3) ICCSt as the fundamental norm in this regard leaves the question of when the victims may participate relatively open, the RPE mention three specific instances in which their participation is feasible at the pre-trial stage. (1) Art. 15 (3) ICCSt and Rule 50 RPE determine, that victims can take part in the procedure for authorization by the Pre-Trial Chamber of the commencement of the investigation pursuant to Art. 15 (3) ICCSt. (2) Rule 59 (1) (b) RPE allows victims to participate in a proceeding under Art. 19 (3) ICCSt concerning question of jurisdiction and admissibility. (3) According to Rule 119 (3) RPE victims can participate in a proceedings concerning the release of the accused pending or during trial. (4) Finally, victims' participating according to Art. 68 (3) ICCSt is according to the ICC jurisprudence imperative throughout the proceeding.

I. Participation in the proceedings under Art. 15 (3) ICCSt

At this stage, there is no investigation underway. According to Art. 15 (3) ICCSt the Prosecutor must at first seek the authorization of the Pre-Trial Chamber for the opening of an investigation. At this early stage of the procedure it is rather difficult to foresee victim participation as the actual scope of the crime or crimes is still to be investigated so that it will regularly be unclear, who is or can be seen as a victim.

The onus is on the Prosecutor supported by the Victims and Witnesses Unit (VWU) to inform the victims known to him or her or to the Victims and Witnesses Unit. S/he must do so unless he or she is of the opinion that the information would pose a danger to the integrity of the investigation or the life or well-being of victims and witnesses.[374] S/he must report to the Pre-Trial Chamber (Regulation 87 (1) RegC). In general the Rules foresee a procedure in writing and only in exceptional circumstances will a hearing be held. Therefore the victims may make representations in writing. In the first proceeding at the ICC concerning Art. 15 (3) ICCSt, the Victim Participation and Reparation Unit submitted the report on the victims' representation.

[374] S De Gurmendi and H Friman, 'The Rules of Procedure and Evidence of the International Criminal Court', 3 *YB Int'l Hum L* (2000) 157, 183.

It is interesting to note that whereas Art. 68 (3) ICCSt limits victim participation to those victims whose personal interests are affected, Art. 15 (3) ICCSt contains no such restraint.[375]

This difference can be explained by referring to what has been said at the beginning. At this early stage the status of a victim in the sense of Art. 68 (3) ICCSt cannot be determined. In fact Art. 15 (3) ICCSt refers to a different term of 'victim', namely the victim of a 'situation'. Having said that, it must be stated that nevertheless the definition of Rule 85 RPE applies also at this stage.[376]

Yet victim participation at this stage should not be mistaken as only fulfilling the urge for information on the crimes committed on the side of the Prosecutor; that is, that victims are in fact only witnesses.[377] Representations made by victims at this stage do carry political weight and have an impact on the decision of the Chamber. It must thus be seen as a real right to participation. This has been proved in the first and thus far only decision on Art. 15 ICCSt in the situation concerning Kenya. At the stage of the Art. 15 ICCSt decision the considerable number of 406 statements were handed over to the Court by victims, of which 396 in the end fulfilled the requirements of the definition of victims according to Rule 85 RPE.[378] In considering the gravity of the crime, which is part of the reasonable basis test to be applied here (*see* p 222), the Chamber stated that it considers the victims representations as a 'significant guidance for the Chamber's assessment'.[379] And indeed the victims' report is taken into consideration in order to corroborate the Prosecutors allegations on a permanent basis.[380] In fact, as a result of the victim's representation the Chamber broadens the temporal scope of the investigation beyond the original request of the Prosecutor to investigate in relation to the post-election violence in Kenya in 2007/2008.[381]

The Pre-Trial Chamber must inform the victims who have made representations about the outcome of the proceedings.

---

375 Boas/Bischoff/Reid/Taylor, *ICL III*, 314.

376 *See* E Chaitidou, 'Rechtsprechungsübersicht: Aktuelle Entwicklungen am Internationalen Strafgerichtshof', 4 *ZIS* 2010, 726, 734.

377 Reading Triffterer/*Bergsmo/Pejic*, Art. 15 MN 24 one could indeed get this impression.

378 ICC *Situation in the Republic of Kenya*, Victims Participation and Reparation Unit, ICC-01/09-17-Corr-Red, 29 March 2010, Public Redacted Version of Corrigendum to the Report on Victims' Representations [ICC-01/09-17-Conf-Exp-Corr] and annexes 1 and 5.

379 *See* ICC *Situation in the Republic of Kenya*, PTC, ICC-01/09, 31 March 2010, Decision Pursuant to Article 15 of the Rome Statute on the Authorization of an Investigation into the Situation in the Republic of Kenya, para 62.

380 *See* ibid, para 196.

381 Ibid, paras 203–7.

II. Participation under Art. 19 (3) ICCSt

As we have already seen, challenges to the jurisdiction of the Court or the admissibility of a case will be ruled on by the Pre-Trial Chamber (or after the confirmation decision the Trial Chamber) according to Art. 19 ICCSt. The proceeding is in writing (Rule 59 (2) RPE), whereas the Chamber may, if it considers necessary, hold a hearing (Rule 58 (2) RPE).[382] The victims must be informed of the challenges according to Rule 59 (1) RPE by the Registry, which selects the persons according to Rule 59 (1) (b) RPE and informs those persons or their legal representatives who have already been in contact with the Court. This strategy is certainly a pragmatic one, but is considerably narrower compared to the victim selection according to Art. 15 (3) ICCSt. One possible explanation for this modification can be seen in the fact that the situation in Art. 19 ICCSt is much more advanced compared to the authorization of an investigation according to Art. 15 ICCSt. The investigation has already begun and the victim who has already communicated with the Court suffers a loss, if the proceeding will be terminated. The interest in the continuation of the prosecution on the side of the victim which has already shown interest in the process is affected and therefore it has a right to be heard.[383] This is the reason why the participation of the victim is not dependant on an extra determination of their personal interests. Personal interests are affected in that the proceeding, in which the respective victim has made a representation, might be halted.[384] However the questions concerning jurisdiction and admissibility are largely technical questions, which do as such not affect the position of a victim. The gravity of the crime as in Art. 17 (1) (d) ICCSt is the only instance on which the victims may have a direct impact.

In the Lubanga case, the Pre-Trial Chamber has interpreted the defendant's application for release as a challenge according to Art. 19 (2) (a) ICCSt and consequently informed the victims and invited them together with the state to file observations within a period of time of one month.[385] Three victims did submit observation arguing—not wholly surprisingly—in favour of jurisdiction of the Court, to which the defence was allowed to reply.[386] Pre-Trial Chamber I dismissed the challenged according to Art. 19 (2) ICCSt.[387]

---

[382] *See* Triffterer/*Hall* Art. 19 MN 20.

[383] In greater detail: C Safferling, 'Das Opfer völkerrechtlicher Verbrechen: Die Stellung der Verbrechensopfer vor dem Internationalen Strafgerichtshof', 115 *ZStW* (2003) 352, 373 *et subs.*

[384] Misleading in this regard Boas/Bischoff/Reid/Taylor, *ICL III*, 315.

[385] ICC *Prosecutor v Lubanga*, Presidency, ICC-01/04-01/06-206, 24 July 2006, Decision Inviting the Democratic Republic of the Congo and The Victims in the Case to Comment on the Proceedings Pursuant to Article 19 of the Statute, pp 3–4.

[386] ICC *Prosecutor v Lubanga*, PTC, ICC-01/04-01/06-359, 28 August 2006, Decision on the Defence's Request to File a Reply.

[387] ICC *Prosecutor v Lubanga*, PTC, ICC-01/04-01/06-512, 3 October 2006, Decision on the Defence Challenge to the Jurisdiction of the Court Pursuant to article 19 (2) (a) of the Statute.

III. Participation under Rule 119 (3) RPE

A third mode of victim participation is foreseen in Rule 119 (3) RPE. This is concerned with conditional release of the accused. Before the Pre-Trial Chamber may impose or amend any conditions restricting liberty, the victims need to be heard next to the Prosecutor, the person concerned and any relevant state. Again Art. 68 (3) ICCSt is not applicable here, however, the requirement that personal interests of the victim have to be affected is circumscribed in a specific way in this provision. Only those victims will be admitted who have already communicated with the Court and who would be at risk as a result of the release or the condition imposed. Whereas the first condition is a rather formal one and independent from registration as victim according to Art. 68 (3) ICCSt, the latter is at the discretion of the Chamber and is based on a prognosis established by the Chamber as to the potential risks likely to confront a victim.[388]

In the *Lubanga* case, victims were allowed to participate in proceedings referring to pre-trial detention from the very beginning. Victims' representative thereby observed that a release would endanger the entire prosecution process and in fact lead to impunity of the accused. In addition they alleged, that release would strengthen the cause of some paramilitary groups in Ituri (Congo) and thus encourage them to resume fighting.[389] One can say that the victims did not bring forward issues which are related to their personal situation but argue very much on an abstract level; that is, acting in support of the Prosecutor's responsibility to fight impunity. This is supported by the Pre-Trial Chamber I as a consequence of the general aim of the ICCSt to integrate victims into the process.[390]

When at the trial stage the release of Lubanga was discussed, victims' representatives argued in a similar way and the Trial Chamber took due recourse to the observations presented to the Chamber, even if the Chamber ordered the release.[391]

IV. The influence of Art. 68 (3) ICCSt on the pre-trial stage

1. Situations

The ICC Pre-Trial Chamber I has extended victims' participation to the entire investigation stage. It has done so by referring to the overall aim of victim

[388] Boas/Bischoff/Reid/Taylor, *ICL III*, 315.

[389] *See* ICC *Prosecutor v Lubanga*, PTC, ICC-01/04-01/06-530-tEN, 9 October 2006, Observations of Victims a/0001/06, a/0002/06 and a/003/06 in Respect of the Application for Release Filed by the Defence, para 11 *et subs.* In the consequence the application for release was dismissed, *see* ICC *Situation in the Democratic Republic Republic of Congo*, TC, ICC- 01/04-01/06-586-tEN, 18 October 2006, Decision on the Application for the Interim Release of Thomas Lubanga Dyilo.

[390] ICC *Situation in the Democratic Republic of Congo*, PTC, ICC-01/04-101, 17 January 2006, Public Redacted Version. Decision on the Applications for Participation in Proceedings of VPRS 1, VPRS 2, VPRS 3, VPRS 4, VPRS 5, and VPRS 6, paras 53, 63.

[391] *See* ICC *Prosecutor v Lubanga*, TC, ICC-01/04-01/06-1418, 2 July 2008, Decision on the Release of Thomas Lubanga Dyilo, paras 15–21.

participation: '[T]he Statute grants victims an independent voice and role in proceedings before the Court. It should be possible to exercise this independence, in particular, vis-à-vis the Prosecutor of the International Criminal Court so that victims can present their interests.'[392]

The Pre-Trial Chamber therefore extended the right to participate for the victim to the 'situation' stage of the investigation; that is, to that phase of the proceedings where no individual suspect has been identified. Even if the reference to Art. 6 ECHR is misleading and cannot justify the extensive interpretation of Art 68 (3) ICCSt adopted by the Pre-Trial Chamber, the main argument rests on the 'personal interest' of the victims are affected at the pre-trial stage, because the identification of the person who is criminally responsible is essential for the victim:

> The right to present their views and concerns and to file material pertaining to the ongoing investigation stems from the fact that the victims' personal interests are affected because it is at this stage that the persons allegedly responsible for the crimes from which they suffered must be identified as a first step towards their indictment. The close link between the personal interests of the victims and the investigation is even more important in the regime established by the Rome Statute, given the effect that such an investigation can have on future orders for reparations pursuant to article 75 of the Statute.[393]

The Appeals Chamber had to intervene at this stage after enormous criticism of the Pre-Trial Chamber's ruling[394] and adopted a more restrictive approach.[395] It held that Art. 68 (3) ICCSt would not encompass participation of the victims at the 'situation' stage as this stage does not qualify as a 'judicial proceeding' in the meaning of Art 68 (3) ICCSt. The structure of the ICCSt gives to the Prosecutor the sole authority to conduct investigations and does not foresee the victim as a co-Prosecutor so to speak. Even if the reasoning of the Appeals Chamber is rather axiomatic and lacks convincing arguments, it is, after all, correct and was at that stage long overdue.[396]

---

[392] ICC *Situation in the Democratic Republic of Congo*, PTC, ICC-01/04-101-tEN-Corr, 17 January 2006, Public Redacted Version. Decision on the Applications for Participation in Proceedings of VPRS 1, VPRS 2, VPRS 3, VPRS 4, VPRS 5, and VPRS 6, para 51; *see* also G Gordon, 'Toward an International Criminal Procedure: Due Process Aspirations and Limitations', 45 *Colum J Transnat'l L* (2007), 635, 696 *et subs.*

[393] ICC *Situation in the Democratic Republic of Congo*, PTC, ICC-01/04-101-tEN-Corr, 17 January 2006, Public Redacted Version. Decision on the Applications for Participation in Proceedings of VPRS 1, VPRS 2, VPRS 3, VPRS 4, VPRS 5, and VPRS 6, para 72.

[394] *See* eg, J de Hemptinne and F Rindi, 'ICC Pre-Trial Chamber Allows Victims to Participate in the Investigation Phase of Proceedings', 4 *JICJ* (2006) 342.

[395] ICC *Situation in the Democratic Republic of Congo*, AC, ICC-01/04-556, OA4, OA5, OA 6, 19 December 2008, Judgment on Victim Participation in the Investigation Stage of the Proceedings in the Appeal of the OPCD against the Decision of Pre-Trial Chamber I of 7 December 2007 and in the Appeals of the OPCD and the Prosecutor against the Decision of Pre-Trial Chamber I of 24 December 2007, para 56 *et subs.*

[396] *See* also Boas/Bischoff/Reid/Taylor, *ICL III*, 321.

In 'situations', victim participation is possible only under the auspices of Art. 15 (3) ICCSt, as discussed above.

2. Cases

Despite the ruling by the Appeals Chamber on the participation in situations, the question arises whether participation is allowed in cases. Such participation can be derived from Art. 68 (3) ICCSt in instances which do not fall under one of the special provisions discussed above (Art. 19 (3) ICCSt or Rule 119 (3) RPE). '[I]t must be clarified that victims are not precluded from seeking participation in any judicial proceedings, including proceedings affecting investigations, provided their personal interests are affected by the issues arising for resolution.'[397]

The Appeals Chamber leaves it up to the Pre-Trial Chamber to determine the 'judicial proceedings' which come within the ambit of Art. 68 (3) ICCSt. The ICCSt indeed gives little guidance in this matter. As one commentator rightly observes: 'In essence, each case is a blank page upon which victims' participatory rights have yet to be written. The scope of that participation is left to the discretion of the individual Chamber.'[398]

Despite all the uncertainty it must be emphasized that in any case the prerequisites of Art. 68 (3) ICCSt apply. This means that victims need to prove that their 'personal interests' are affected. According to the current case law of the ICC Appeals Chamber, victims must re-apply for the right to participate at each stage of the proceedings—that is, the pre-trial stage, the trial stage, and the appeals stage—stating the relevant grounds for their claim.[399] Therefore the victim must prove his or her personal interests and how they are affected in particular by a judicial proceeding at the pre-trial stage. The effects of this are most visible in the question of how victims should be allowed to participate at the confirmation stage. This issue will be discussed later.

---

[397] ICC *Situation in the Democratic Republic of Congo*, AC, ICC-01/04-556, OA4, OA5, OA 6, 19 December 2008, Judgment on Victim Participation in the Investigation Stage of the Proceedings in the Appeal of the OPCD against the Decision of Pre-Trial Chamber I of 7 December 2007 and in the Appeals of the OPCD and the Prosecutor against the Decision of Pre-Trial Chamber I of 24 December 2007, para 56

[398] Boas/Bischoff/Reid/Taylor, *ICL III*, 322 *et subs.*

[399] ICC *Prosecutor v Lubanga*, AC, 01/04-01/06 (OA7), 13 February 2007, Judgment on the Appeal of Mr. Thomas Lubanga Dyilo against the Decision of Pre-Trial Chamber I entitled 'Décision sur la demande de mise en liberté provisoire de Thomas Lubanga Dyilo', para 44; dissenting on this point Judge Sang Hyun Song, according to whom the authorization to participate applies to all stages of the proceedings. Such authorization may however be rescinded or modified by the Court; *See* Dissenting Opinion of Judge Sang-Hyun Song Regarding the Participation of Victims, at p. 55 *et seq.*

7

THE CONFIRMATION PROCEEDINGS

The confirmation stage is placed between the investigation phase and the trial. It is the 'linking interface' between the prosecutor's investigations and the trial.[1] At some point in time someone must decide whether or not the case is serious enough to be brought before a judge or a bench in order to proceed with a fully fledged criminal trial. This is because the criminal justice system follows an accusatory structure,[2] which is an outcome of the principle of the separation of powers, according to which the court (judiciary) must be institutionally separated from the prosecution (executive branch).[3] When and by whom the decision to transfer the case from the prosecutor to the judge is taken, is dealt with differently in different legal system. The *ad hoc* Tribunals and the ICC have their own respective systems, which will be looked at in the following.[4]

There is another matter, which at least functionally belongs to the confirmation stage: the issue of disclosure of evidence. Even though the subject of disclosure may arise at almost any time during the proceedings, disclosure serves the preparation of the trial and is therefore connected to the confirmation stage, after which the case is sent to trial.

A. Confirmation Proceedings

At the Nuremberg trial, the confirmation stage was not totally absent, yet it was rather rudimentary in nature. It was the Committee for the Investigation and Prosecution of Major War Criminal, consisting of the four Chief Prosecutors of the Allied Powers, which improved the indictment and the evidence and lodged the

---

[1] K Ambos and D Miller, 'Structure and Function of the Confirmation Procedure before the ICC from a Comparative Perspective', 7 *ICLR* (2007) 335, 336.

[2] *See* Boas/Bischoff/Reid/Taylor, *ICL III*, p 178.

[3] *See* Chapter 4 for more detail.

[4] From a comparative perspective: C Safferling, *Towards an International Criminal Procedure* (OUP 2003) 172 *et subs.*; K Ambos and D Miller, 'Structure and Function of the Confirmation Procedure before the ICC from a Comparative Perspective', 7 *ICLR* (2007) 335, 349–358.

indictment together with the accompanying documents with the judges pursuant to Art. 14 (1) (c) and (d) IMTSt.

The confirmation process is perhaps the most 'distinct' mark of the ICC procedure.[5] According to the Rome Statute it takes place before a Pre-Trial Chamber consisting of three judges, to which the Presidency has assigned the situation (Regulation 46 (2) RegC). Such Pre-Trial Chambers are composed by the Presidency of the ICC as permanent Chambers (Regulation 46 RegC).[6] The Presiding Judge of the Pre-Trial Chamber plays the predominant role during these proceedings.

Both the Prosecutor and the suspect participate in the confirmation proceedings. The latter is called 'the person' or 'the person concerned' throughout the Rome Statute and the RPE ICC. This rather complicated wording supports the view that the formal 'charge' is issued not by the Prosecutor, but by the Pre-Trial Chamber through the confirmation decision. This means that the person concerned; that is, the suspect, becomes the person charged only after the confirmation decision has been rendered.[7] It is interesting to note that in the case of the SCSL Rule 47 (H) (ii) RPE SCSL explicitly states that the 'suspect' becomes the 'accused' upon approval of the indictment.

No article in the Statutes or rule in the Rules of Procedure and Evidence of the *ad hoc* Tribunals make provision for a confirmation hearing like Art. 61 (7) ICCSt. The procedure to confirm the indictment is a mere review of the charges, pursuant to Art. 19 (1) ICTYSt and Art. 18 (1) ICTRSt. The Statute of the SCSL does not include any provision concerning the review of an indictment.

At the ICTY as well as at the ICTR, a single judge may review the indictment transmitted by the Prosecutor. Before compiling the indictment, the latter must determine whether the '*prima facie* case' threshold has been achieved (Art. 18 (4) ICTYSt and Art. 17 (4) ICTRSt). Upon the submission of the indictment a single judge may confirm or dismiss this finding. Rule 47(B) RPE ICTY/ICTR stipulates that the Prosecutor shall transmit the indictment if he or she is satisfied that 'there is sufficient evidence to provide reasonable grounds for believing that a suspect has committed a crime within the jurisdiction of the Tribunal'. This threshold is higher than the standard provided in Art. 19 (1) ICTYSt and Art. 18 (1) ICTRSt.

At the ICTY, Judge McDonald addressed this issue in the review of the indictment against Kordić *et al.* by drawing on the formulation used by the International Law

5 M Miraglia, 'Admissibility of Evidence, Standard of Proof, and Nature of the Decision in the ICC Confirmation of Charges in Lubanga', 6 *JICJ* (2008) 489, 490.

6 *See* also Chapter 4, this book.

7 Sometimes the wording is not consistent. Triffterer/*Shibahara*/*Schabas*, Art. 61 MN 16 phrases 'the person charged' from the beginning of the confirmation proceedings; Similarly K Ambos and D Miller, 'Structure and Function of the Confirmation Procedure before the ICC from a Comparative Perspective', 7 *ICLR* (2007) 335, 340.

Commission in its Draft Statute for the ICC: '[A] *prima facie* case for this purpose is understood to be a credible case which would (if not contradicted by the Defence) be a sufficient basis to convict the accused on the charge.'[8]

In any case, the contradictory wording only affects the determination of the Prosecutor (Art. 18 (4) ICTYSt and Art. 17 (4) ICTRSt) and not the finding of the judge reviewing the indictment. The text of Rule 47(E) RPE ICTY clearly determines that the judge may apply 'the standard set forth in Article 19, paragraph 1, of the Statute';[9] the same wording is included in Rule 47(E) RPE ICTR.

Rule 47 RPE SCSL does not contain any such requirements and only provides two prerequisites for the judge which he or she may take into account in order to determine whether or not to approve the indictment:

> (i) the indictment charges the suspect with a crime or crimes within the jurisdiction of the Special Court; and
>
> (ii) that the allegations in the Prosecution's case summary would, if proven, amount to the crime or crimes as particularised in the indictment.

The wording of the RPE SCSL may lead to the confirmation of indictments which are partially unfounded because of its low standard.[10]

The Prosecutor for the ICTY submitted various indictments against Slobodan Milošević between 1999 and 2001. Subsequently, the suspect was arrested on 1 April 2001 by Serbian authorities and transferred to the ICTY on 29 June 2001. On 3 July 2001 he appeared for the first time before the court and the last review of the indictment took place only four month later. Judge May also applied the above-mentioned standard in the Milošević case regarding it to be the last so-called 'Bosnia' indictment.[11] It comprises two pages and sixteen paragraphs. This illustrates that the 'review' approach adopted by the ICTY and ICTR enables a speedy trial without violating other rights of the accused.

Without exceeding the above-mentioned threshold of the *prima facie* case, Judge Riad in his review of the indictment against Ratko Mladić and Radovan Karadžić used the expression 'sufficient evidence to provide reasonable grounds for believing'.[12]

---

[8] ICTY *Prosecutor v Kordić et al.*, Judge McDonald, IT-95-14, 10 November 1995, Decision on Review of the Indictment; Extract from the Yearbook of the International Law Commission, Vol II, UN Doc A/49/10 (1994), p 48; *see* further C Safferling, *Towards an International Criminal Procedure* (OUP 2003) 182.

[9] H Krieger, *The Kosovo Conflict and International Law: an Analytic Documentation 1974–1999* (CUP 2001) 518.

[10] C Rose, 'Troubled Indictments at the Special Court for Sierra Leone', 7 *JICJ* (2009) 353, 357.

[11] ICTY *Prosecutor v Milošević*, Judge May, IT-02-54, 22 November 2001, Decision on Review of Indictment, para 11.

[12] ICTY *Prosecutor v Mladić and Karadžić*, Judge Riad, IT-95-18-I, 16 November 1995, Review on the Indictment.

In another case before the ICTY, Judge Sidhwa based the entire review of the indictment on the meaning of the expression '*prima facie* case'. He held that '[t]o constitute reasonable grounds, facts must be such which are within the possession of the Prosecutor which raise a clear suspicion of the suspect being guilty of the crime. It predicates that all the ingredients of the offence are covered.'[13]

During his analysis of the expression, Judge Sidhwa conducted an in-depth analysis of the various national and international provisions regarding the confirmation of the indictment or charges. He clearly favoured the 'confirmation hearing' approach, where the accused has the opportunity to be heard regarding the charges brought against him.

Notably, the warrant of arrest will only be issued after the indictment has been reviewed (Art. 19 (2) ICTYSt and Art. 18 (2) ICTRSt and Rule 47(H)(i) RPE ICTY/ICTR) and the charges therewith confirmed.

The ICC does not use the term 'indictment' but refers to charges. Pursuant to Art. 61 (1) ICCSt the Prosecutor presents the 'charges' to the Pre-Trial Chamber, which holds a hearing in order to confirm or decline to confirm these (Art. 61 (7) ICCSt). The charges are submitted to the Pre-Trial Chamber in the 'Document containing the charges' (DCC). We have looked at the difficulties in defining the term 'charge' earlier. We now turn to discuss the procedure followed by the Pre-Trial Chamber when confirming the charges.[14] We will differentiate between the proceedings before the confirmation (1), the actual confirmation hearing (2), and after the hearing, but before the opening of the trial (3). Finally we will take a look at the cases before the ICC and how the different Pre-Trial Chambers have dealt with the Statute and Rules in this regard (4).

I. Procedure before the confirmation hearing

One of the prerequisites required to initiate the confirmation process is the presence of the suspect at the ICC. As soon as the person appears before the Court, be it upon surrender or voluntarily, the Pre-Trial Chamber sets a date for the confirmation hearing pursuant to Art. 60 (1) ICCSt and Rule 121 (1) RPE ICC. The first appearance of the suspect before the Pre-Trial Chamber must take place immediately ('promptly') upon his/her arrival in The Hague. According to Art. 61 (1) ICCSt the confirmation hearing must be held within a 'reasonable time' after the first appearance. During this time, various steps must be taken.

The Prosecutor must prepare the DCC. The person concerned must then be informed of the charges and prosecution evidence, pursuant to Art. 61 (3) ICCSt.

---

[13] ICTY *Prosecutor v Rajić*, Judge Sidhwa, IT-95-12-I, 29 August 1995, Review on the Indictment, p 8.

[14] A rather short introduction into that stage is given by Boas/Bischoff/Reid/Taylor, *ICL III*, 247.

The complex question of how disclosure works at this stage is discussed later. According to Art. 61 (3) ICCSt and Rule 121 (2) RPE ICC the Pre-Trial Chamber oversees this process. No later than thirty days before the date of the hearing the Prosecutor must present the DCC and his evidence to the Pre-Trial Chamber and to the person concerned (Rule 121 (3) RPE ICC). Nonetheless, the OTP may continue the investigation and may amend or withdraw charges in accordance with Art. 61 (4) ICCSt. In the case of an amendment the person concerned as well as the Pre-Trial Chamber must be informed no later than fifteen days before the confirmation hearing (Art. 61 (4) ICCSt, Rule 121 (4) RPE ICC).

If the Prosecutor decides to withdraw charges, s/he must, according to Art. 61 (4) ICCSt, give reasons for this. There are several reasons, why the Prosecutor might wish to withdraw charges. For one, s/he might change his/her opinion and find that a charge is not supported by sufficient evidence.[15] However, at the ICC this insufficiency may only stem from new evidence found after the DCC has been filed with the Pre-Trial Chamber. Otherwise the Prosecutor would have acted in violation of Arts 53 (2) and 61 (1) ICCSt, under which s/he must, before filing the DCC, be of the opinion that enough evidence is available to support reasonable grounds to believe that a crime, according to Art. 5 ICC, has indeed been committed.

Secondly, the Prosecutor might withdraw a charge due to a (new) prosecutorial strategy. The ICTY Prosecutor has often taken this course of action in order to refer the case to a national jurisdiction.[16] A withdrawal might also be part of a plea agreement[17] or a specific trial strategy.[18]

Similarly, the OTP must inform the Chamber and the person concerned of new evidence, which the Prosecutor wishes to rely upon at the hearing, no later than fifteen days before the hearing (Rule 121 (5) RPE ICC). Likewise, the person concerned must provide a list of evidence s/he intends to present in response to the charges, to the Pre-Trial Chamber, no later than fifteen days before the date of the confirmation hearing. The Pre-Trial Chamber will then forward the list to the OTP (Art. 61 (6) ICCSt; Rule 121 (6) RPE ICC). Amended charges and new evidence brought forward by the Prosecutor may be countered by evidence which the person concerned has presented to the Pre-Trial Chamber at some stage before the hearing.[19]

[15] *See* eg, ICTR *Prosecutor v Rusatira*, ICTR-2002-80-I, 14 August 2002, Decision on the Prosecutor's *Ex Parte* Application for Leave to Withdraw the Indictment.

[16] ICTY *Prosecutor v Sikirica et al.*, IT-95-8-I, 5 May 1998, Order Granting Leave for Withdrawal of Charges Against Jamjić, Kondić, Lajić, Saponja, Timarac.

[17] As to the 'plea', *see* p 438 *et subs*.

[18] Boas/Bischoff/Reid/Taylor, *ICL III*, 197.

[19] There is no time limit indicated in the Statute or Rules concerning the filing of a response to amended charges or new evidence. Rule 121 (6) RPE ICC does not even specify that the PTC shall in such a case transmit the list to the OTP. As the OTP is allowed to submit amendments or new evidence up to fifteen days before the hearing, the person concerned has only two weeks to prepare

During this process the person may be assisted or represented by counsel (Rule 121 (2) (a) RPE ICC). Indeed legal representation is essential, as the person concerned is confronted with serious allegations which will be reviewed in a public hearing before a bench of three judges. It is also important to respect the time limits. According to Rule 121 (8) RPE ICC, charges or evidence presented too late will not be taken into consideration.

The Prosecutor and the person concerned may submit written statements to the Pre-Trial Chamber concerning issues of fact and law no later than three days before the hearing, pursuant to Rule 121 (9) RPE ICC. The provision explicitly refers to grounds for excluding criminal responsibility under Art. 31 (1) ICCSt. The exclusionary rule contained in Rule 121 (8) RPE ICC, however, does not apply to statements referring to a criminal defence. Although not stated explicitly, the structure of Rule 121 RPE ICC makes it clear that the rule excluding evidence submitted too late does not apply. Rule 121 (9) RPE ICC is placed after the exclusionary rule in Rule 121 (8) RPE ICC and can thus not be limited by this prior rule.

According to Rule 121 (10) RPE ICC the Registry creates and maintains a record of all proceedings before the Pre-Trial Chamber. It follows that this record will so far contain the DCC together with a list of the evidence to be presented by the Prosecutor, the objections and the list of evidence by the person concerned, and also any amendment or new evidence and any other statement brought before the Pre-Trial Chamber. The Prosecutor or the person concerned, as well as victims participating in the proceedings and their representatives, may consult the record.[20]

The complexity of the preparation of the hearing necessitates a status conference, which is held by the Pre-Trial Chamber (Rule 121 (2) (b) RPE ICC).

II. Procedure at the confirmation hearing

The framework that is given for the confirmation hearing by the Statute is rather sketchy. Under Art. 61 (5) and (6) ICCSt, the Prosecutor presents evidence to support the DCC and the person concerned may object to the charges, challenge the Prosecutor's evidence and present evidence him or herself. It follows that the proceedings are—in contrast to the UN tribunals—adversarial in nature.[21] This is also shown by the fact that according to Rule 122 (9) RPE ICC applies *mutatis mutandis* to the confirmation hearing.

Yet due to the fact that the Registry holds a record containing all the documents and lists of evidence upon which the parties wish to rely, the Pre-Trial Chamber is

---

his objection. If this proves to be too short a period of time, s/he needs to apply for the hearing to be postponed under Rule 121 (7) RPE ICC.

[20] Triffterer/*Shibahara*/*Schabas*, Art. 61 MN 15.

[21] C Kreß, 'The Procedural Law of the International Criminal Court in Outline: Anatomy of a Unique Compromise', 1 *JICJ* (2003) 603, 610.

in a position to lay down a rather precise schedule for the hearing and the presentation of the evidence (see Rule 122 (1) RPE ICC) and should thus be able to manage the hearing rather rigorously.

1. Preliminary issues

At the beginning of the hearing, the Presiding Judge will ask the officer of the Registry to read out the DCC which has been filed by the Prosecutor (Rule 122 (1) RPE ICC). Thereafter, two issues are addressed. First, any question concerning jurisdiction or admissibility shall be raised and may be discussed during the confirmation hearing in accordance with Rule 58 RPE ICC (*see* Rule 122 (2) RPE ICC). Secondly, the Prosecutor and the person concerned must raise any objections or observations they may have concerning the proper conduct of the proceedings (Rule 122 (3) RPE ICC). These issues will then be discussed in an adversarial manner (Rule 122 (5) RPE ICC).This may lead to a separation of the issues from the actual confirmation hearing, which will then be adjourned (Rule 122 (6) RPE ICC). The Pre-Trial Chamber will, if necessary, decide on these issues before the confirmation hearing (Rule 122 (7) RPE ICC). It must be noted that objections from the parties concerning the conduct of the proceedings before the confirmation hearing will not be heard at a later stage (Rule 122 (4) RPE ICC).

2. On the merits of the charges

Once these preliminary issues have been dealt with, the Pre-Trial Chamber will proceed with the actual confirmation hearing and assess the merits of the charges. The final threshold for the Prosecutor is to establish substantial grounds to believe that the person committed the crime charged. In order to achieve this, s/he must present sufficient evidence. S/he may rely on documentary or summary evidence and need not call the witnesses expected to testify at the trial (Art. 61 (5) ICCSt).

The defence may then present its arguments; that is, (a) object to the charges; (b) challenge the evidence presented by the Prosecutor; and (c) present own evidence (Art. 61 (6) ICCSt). In order to put the parties on an equal footing, the defence should also be allowed to rely on documentary or summary evidence, if it so wishes.

At the end of the hearing OTP and the person concerned may make final observations (Rule 122 (8) RPE ICC).

3. Presence of the person concerned

As a rule, the person concerned must be present at the confirmation hearing. The Pre-Trial Chamber will adopt measures in order to ensure his or her presence according to Rule 123 RPE ICC. In the ordinary course of events the person's presence will be secured by the arrest warrant or summons to appear, which is executed before the confirmation procedure is initiated. Yet according to Art. 61

(2) ICCSt, there are two situations in which a hearing may be held in the absence of the person concerned:

(a) The person is in custody at the ICC, but has submitted a written request and waived his or her right to be present (see Rule 124 RPE ICC). In that case the Pre-Trial Chamber must be satisfied that the person understands the right to be present at the hearing and the consequences of the waiver. Notwithstanding the waiver, the person can always submit written observations to the Chamber. The Pre-Trial Chamber may also permit the person to observe the hearing from outside the courtroom via communications technology.

(b) The person has fled or cannot be found even though all reasonable steps have been taken to secure his or her presence at the Court. In that case the Pre-Trial Chamber must ensure that an arrest warrant has been issued and that all reasonable measures have been taken to locate and arrest the person sought (Rule 123 (3) RPE ICC). The wording of these provisions does not clarify whether the holding of the confirmation hearing *in absentia* is possible only if the person concerned has at some stage been in the custody of the Court or whether it is also applicable where that person has never been in touch with the Court.[22] It is suggested that the former is correct. Three grounds support this view. First, as expressed in Art. 63 ICCSt the Rome Statute is based on the presumption that there will be no trial *in absentia*. The ICC furthermore depends heavily on the presence of the suspect, as illustrated by Arts 58–60 ICCSt, which demonstrate that the initial proceedings before the Court also require the presence of the person concerned. Second, it is unclear what should be achieved by holding a confirmation hearing in the absence of the person concerned. Whereas at the ICTY the Rule 61 Procedure leads to an international arrest warrant,[23] this is not the case at the ICC, even if the Art. 61 (2) ICCSt Procedure is often compared to the Rule 61 RPE ICTY Procedure.[24] Third, should the person concerned be transferred to The Hague after the confirmation of the charges, a new confirmation hearing must be held. Not to do so would be unfair, since the person concerned would not have had a chance to raise objections to the charges at the confirmation stage. Keeping in mind that a person who absconds, after being in custody at the Court, after all does so voluntarily and thus implicitly waives his or her right to be present and raise objections, a confirmation hearing in his or her absence seems justified. The case could then be sent to the Trial Chamber as soon as the person sought is surrendered to the Court (Rule 126 (3) RPE ICC).

In any case the Pre-Trial Chamber must, should it decide to hold a confirmation hearing, also decide whether or not the person may be represented by counsel,

[22] Triffterer/*Shibahara/Schabas*, Art. 61 MN 9.

[23] *See* C Safferling, *Towards an International Criminal Procedure* (OUP 2003) 243–5 for a critical appraisal of the Rule 61 Procedure at the ICTY.

[24] *See* eg, C Kreß, 'The Procedural Law of the International Criminal Court in Outline: Anatomy of a Unique Compromise', 1 *JICJ* (2003) 603, 611, and Triffterer/*Shibahara/Schabas*, Art. 61 MN 7.

(Art. 61 (2) ICCSt, Rule 125 (1) RPE ICC). Where the Pre-Trial Chamber has decided that counsel should represent the person concerned, counsel may carry out the rights of the person concerned on his or her behalf, (Rule 126 (2) RPE ICC). Should the Chamber rule against a hearing *in absentia*, the confirmation of the charges may not take place until the person is available to the Court, (Rule 125 (3) RPE ICC). In any event it can review the decision at any time, be it at the request of the Prosecutor or *proprio motu*. 'Where the person concerned is available, the Pre-Trial Chamber will order him to appear' (Rule 125 (4) RPE ICC).

4. The decision

The decision must relate separately to each individual charge contained in the DCC and not to the DCC in its entirety. According to Art. 61 (7) ICCSt the Pre-Trial Chamber has three different options. It can:

(a) Confirm a charge and commit the person for trial on the charges as confirmed. In that case the person may be called 'the charged';

(b) Decline to confirm a charge, in which case the Prosecutor may return to the Pre-Trial Chamber with additional evidence and ask for confirmation once more, pursuant to Art. 61 (8) ICCSt;[25] or

(c) Adjourn the hearing and request the Prosecutor to either provide further evidence or consider amending the charges, as the evidence presented appears to establish a different crime under Art. 5 ICCSt.

As the Chamber must decide each charge separately, the DCC can thus be confirmed in parts, rejected in other parts, and the Prosecutor may also be required to consider amending some parts. Where the Chamber confirms some charges and adjourns the proceedings relating to the other charges, the person concerned will not be committed to trial until the Pre-Trial Chamber has ruled on all the charges. In that case, Rule 127 RPE ICC provides that the OTP be set a specific time limit to provide further evidence or amend the charges.

Should the Pre-Trial Chamber decline to confirm the charges, any warrant that was previously issued with respect to such charges will cease to have effect according to Art. 61 (10) ICCSt. This is true in particular with regard to an arrest warrant, which means that the person concerned must be released from pre-trial detention immediately after the Pre-Trial Chamber has declined confirmation.[26] This practical consequence might pose a real threat to the prosecution process and may lead

[25] This is rather unfortunate for the person concerned as he or she does not receive a definite decision. Even if the situation does not fall within the ambit of double jeopardy (*ne bis in idem*) according to Art. 20 ICCSt, it bears many similarities. It is hoped that the OTP will use this right to submit charges against the same person a second, and maybe even a third and a fourth time, restrictively. Otherwise the Pre-Trial Chamber should consider disciplinary measures because of a misuse of procedural rights.

[26] Triffterer/*Shibahara*/*Schabas*, Art. 61 MN 22.

to the Prosecutor refraining from having a second go at establishing substantial grounds, as permitted under Art. 61 (8) ICCSt.

The threshold for each charge is the determination of substantial grounds to believe that the person concerned committed the crimes charged in the DCC. It is unclear from the wording whether the evidence brought forward by the defence will have any effect on the Chamber's decision.[27] However, it would be rather pointless to hold an adversarial, that is, *inter parte,* hearing as opposed to *ex parte* proceedings and then disregard the arguments of the defence. After all, the person concerned should be afforded protection against charges made up out of thin air.[28]

The Chamber must deliver its decision within sixty days from the date the confirmation hearing ends, as stated in Regulation 53 RegC. The decision must be in writing and address all the charges contained in the DCC. It is at this moment that the suspect is actually charged. The confirmed charges constitute the final indictment, so to speak.[29] The DCC read together with the Confirmation Decision of the Pre-Trial Chamber contain the actual charges for which a trial will be set.

The Prosecutor, the person charged, and his or her counsel must therefore all be notified of the decision (Rule 129 RPE ICC). The decision together with the entire record of the proceedings before the Pre-Trial Chamber is then transmitted to the Presidency. At this point the confirmation stage ends, concluding the work of the Pre-Trial Chamber and terminating its competence for the case.

III. After confirmation

Upon the confirmation of the charges, the Presidency will constitute a Trial Chamber and refer the case to it. It transmits the decision of the Pre-Trial Chamber together with the record of the proceedings to the Trial Chamber (Rule 130 RPE ICC).[30]

However, even after confirmation the Prosecutor will continue to investigate and might find new charges or may want to withdraw charges. This seems to be a standard proceeding in international criminal procedure.[31] While a mere amendment of the charges might not be of great detriment to the person charged, and can be permitted by the Pre-Trial Chamber according to Art. 61 (9) 1 ICCSt, the Prosecutor may not simply add further charges or substitute the original charges with more serious ones. In that case the person charged must be placed in a position to exercise his right under Art. 61 (6) ICCSt. Hence the Pre-Trial Chamber must hold a new hearing.

---

[27] Critical in this regard Triffterer/*Shibahara/Schabas*, Art. 61 MN 17.

[28] *See* Boas/Bischoff/Reid/Taylor, *ICL III*, 183.

[29] Ahlbrecht/*Kirsch*, MN 1425.

[30] As to the differences in the constitution of the Pre-Trial Chamber and the Trial Chamber, *see* Chapter 4, this book.

[31] *See* Boas/Bischoff/Reid/Taylor, *ICL III*, 187.

Art. 61 (9) ICCSt furthermore states that after the trial has commenced the Prosecutor may withdraw the charges only with the permission of the Trial Chamber. We can conclude *e contrario* that the Prosecutor is not allowed to amend the charges at the trial stage.[32]

B. Confirmation Hearings in Practice

To-date, the Pre-Trial Chamber has rendered five decisions concerning situations in the Democratic Republic of the Congo (DRC), the Central African Republic (CAR), and Sudan. So far the confirmation decisions have concerned seven persons, against whom the Prosecutor has brought various charges before the court. We will now proceed to analyse each individual case in chronological order to illustrate the development in the decision-making process of the Pre-Trial Chambers.

I. Situation in the Democratic Republic of the Congo

In 2002, a conflict between groups of Hema ethnicity and groups of Lendu and Ngiti ethnicities broke out in the Ituri district about the allocation of land and the appropriation of its natural resources.[33] The situation in the DRC was assigned to Pre-Trial Chamber I on 5 July 2004.[34]

1. Thomas Lubanga Dyilo[35]

The suspect, the alleged leader of the *Union de Patriotes Congolais* (UPC), one of the Hema ethnicity groups. and from September 2002 until at least the end of 2003, alleged commander-in-chief of the *Forces Patriotique pour la Libération du Congo* (FPLC), was the first person to face a confirmation hearing before the ICC. The Prosecutor charged him with conscripting and enlisting children under the age of fifteen years into an armed group and using them to participate actively in hostilities in the period from July 2002 to the end of 2003.

The warrant of arrest against Thomas Lubanga Dyilo was issued on 10 February 2006 by Pre-Trial Chamber I. The suspect was arrested and extradited by the Congolese authorities to The Hague on 17 March 2006 and appeared three days later before the court; that is, on 20 March 2006. The confirmation hearing was held

[32] Triffterer/*Shibahara*/*Schabas*, Art. 61 MN 21.

[33] ICC *Prosecutor v Lubanga*, PTC, ICC-01/04-01/06-803-tEN, 14 May 2005, Decision on the Confirmation of the Charges, para 1 *et subs.*

[34] ICC *Situation in the Democratic Republic of Congo*, Presidency, ICC-01/04-01, 5 July 2004, Decision Assigning the Situation in the Democratic Republic of Congo to the Pre-Trial Chamber I.

[35] For a detailed examination of the substantive legal issues regarding the *Lubanga* decision *see* eg, T Weigend, 'Intent, Mistake of Law and Co-Perpetration in the Lubanga Decision on the Confirmation of the Charges', 6 *JICJ* (2008) 471 and O Bekou, 'Prosecutor v Thomas Lubanga Dyilo—Decision on the Confirmation of Charges', 8 *HRLR* (2008) 343.

from 9–28 November 2006. More than ten months after his first appearance before the court, Pre-Trial Chamber I issued its decision on the confirmation of charges on 29 January 2007. It comprises 157 pages and is divided into seven chapters.

During the preparation phase the Pre-Trial Chamber rendered various decisions regarding different legal matters. The Chamber noted in this regard that 'if in the future, the Prosecution filed dozens of Rule 81 applications concerning thousands of pages, it would be difficult for the Court to reconcile the application of the Appeals Chamber's guiding principles with the requirement that proceedings be conducted expeditiously.'[36]

This statement of the Pre-Trial Chamber followed two decisions of the Appeals Chamber, regarding several items included in the list of evidence of the Prosecutor. These items could not be taken into account by the Pre-Trial Chamber when rendering its decision on the confirmation of the charges. Only the exculpatory parts contained in the above-mentioned evidence could be included.[37] The *Lubanga* decision dealt with the following four main issues challenged by the parties:

(1) Among other things, the defence challenged the admissibility of evidentiary items seized from the home of a person who was detained at the time of the seizure and therefore not present during the operation. A Congolese appeals court ruled the evidence to be inadmissible, because of breaches of the Congolese Code of Procedure and infringements of international human rights law. The Pre-Trial Chamber ruled that it 'is not bound by decisions of national courts on evidentiary matters'.[38] Furthermore, regarding the principle of proportionality and the violation of internationally recognized human rights pursuant to Art. 69 (7) ICCSt, it stated that a balance between the seriousness of the violations and the rights of the accused to a fair trial must be reached.

(2) Regarding a defence challenge against the admissibility of anonymous hearsay evidence the Pre-Trial Chamber held that 'there is nothing in the Statute or the Rules which expressly provides that evidence which can be considered hearsay from anonymous sources is inadmissible per se.'[39]

The defence had argued that the redacted statements were anonymous hearsay evidence, because of the lack of access to the sources. According to the Chamber, this kind of evidence would grant only low probative value if not corroborated by other evidence.[40]

[36] ICC *Prosecutor v Lubanga*, PTC, ICC-01/04-01/06-803-tEN, 14 May 2005, Decision on the Confirmation of the Charges, para 54.

[37] Ibid, para 55.

[38] Ibid, para 69.

[39] Ibid, para 101.

[40] Ibid, para 103; the PTC took the same view as the ECtHR in its decision *Doorson v The Netherlands*, Judgment 26 March 1996, Rep. 1996-II.

(3) Conversely, the Prosecutor challenged the admissibility and the probative value regarding some of the evidence presented by the defence. On 24 November 2006 the defence filed a request to withdraw evidence from their own list. The Pre-Trial Chamber determined in its decision that 'nothing in the Statute or the Rules empowers parties to withdraw evidence included in their List of Evidence.'[41] Such a provision would undermine the obligation of the Chamber to determine whether the 'substantial grounds to believe' threshold has been achieved.[42]

(4) Within the frame of the material elements of the crimes charged, the court discussed the characterization of the armed conflict. The Prosecutor assumed in the DCC that the conflict in Ituri was of non-international character, while the defence argued that the conflict was of an international nature. In principle, the classification of the armed conflict was not essential, because Art. 8 ICCSt provides for criminal responsibility for the use of child soldiers in both an international as well as an internal conflict.[43] Notably, the Chamber ruled that during the period of July 2002 to June 2003 the conflict in Ituri was of an international character, because of the intervention of Uganda and its 'overall control'[44] over the territory concerned. This finding was based on a decision of the ICJ.[45] The ICJ stated that the establishment of a 'provisional governor' by Uganda was a substitution of the authority of the government of the Democratic Republic of the Congo by the Ugandan authority[46] and that therefore, the 'overall control' requirement was achieved. While confirming the charges, the Pre-Trial Chamber changed this legal fact without the consent of the Prosecutor.

2. Germain Katanga and Mathieu Ngudjolo Chui[47]

The two persons concerned were leading members of the military forces of Lendu and Ngiti ethnicity in the conflict in the district Ituri, which opposed the UPC. Germain Katanga was the alleged military leader of the *Force de Résistance Patriotique en Ituri* (FRPI) and Mathieu Ngudjolo Chui was the alleged leader of the *Front de Nationalistes et Intégrationnistes* (FNI).

The Prosecutor charged both suspects with crimes against humanity, in particular murder, rape, and sexual slavery, as well as with the war crimes of using children

---

[41] Ibid, para 140.

[42] Ibid, para 142.

[43] For an international armed conflict *see* Art. 8 (2) (b) (xxvi) ICCSt and for an internal conflict *see* Art. 8 (2) (e) (vii) ICCSt.

[44] The 'overall control' test was established in the *Tadić* judgment: ICTY *Prosecutor v Tadić*, AC, IT-94-1-A, Judgment 15 July 1999, para 120 *et subs.*

[45] ICJ *DRC v Uganda*, Armed Activities on the Territory of the Congo, Judgment 19 December 2005, Rep. 908, para 160.

[46] Ibid, para 174 *et subs.*

[47] For a detailed analysis of the substantive legal issues regarding the *Katanga and Chui* decision *see* eg, T Weigend, 'Perpetration through an Organization, The Unexpected Career of a German Legal Concept', 9 *JICJ* (2011) 91 and R Rastan, 'Review of the ICC Jurisprudence 2008', 7 *Northwestern JIHR* (2009) 261.

under the age of fifteen years to participate actively in hostilities, directing an attack against a civilian population, wilful killing, destruction of property, pillaging, sexual slavery, and rape.

The warrant of arrest against Gemain Katanga was issued on 2 July 2007. The suspect was arrested and extradited to The Hague by the Congolese Authorities on 17 October 2007, and appeared before the court four days later. The warrant of arrest against Mathieu Ngudjolo Chui was issued on 6 July 2007. Until his arrest on 6 February 2008, he was a member of the governmental military forces. The confirmation hearing for the case was held from 27 June to 18 July 2008. The decision on the confirmation of charges was issued on 26 September 2008; that is, more than eleven months after Gemain Katanga first appeared before court. The decision encompasses 226 pages and is divided into four chapters.

In this decision the Pre-Trial Chamber, which was often criticized for its practice of requesting the Prosecutor to provide further evidence, clarifies its position by arguing: '[t]he purpose of the confirmation hearing is to ensure that no case proceeds to trial without sufficient evidence to establish substantial grounds to believe that the person committed the crime or crimes with which he has been charged. This mechanism is designed to protect the rights of the Defence against wrongful and wholly unfounded charges'.[48]

Beyond that it stated that the confirmation hearing 'should not be seen as a "mini trial" or a "trial before the trial" ',[49] because the evidentiary threshold must not exceed the 'substantial grounds to believe' requirements.[50]

The evidence is presented only for the purpose of confirming the charges, bearing in mind that every decision regarding the admissibility of a particular item 'will not preclude a subsequent determination of the admissibility of that same evidence later in the proceedings',[51] that is, the Trial Chamber can exercise its power and function without being bound by any finding of the Pre-Trial Chamber.

Defence counsel of Germain Katanga challenged the admissibility of the *process-verbal d'audition*. The suspect was interrogated on 20 January 2006 in Kinshasa (DRC) without being represented by counsel. The defence counsel argued that this constituted a violation of the internationally recognized human rights of Germain Katanga and beyond that amounted to a breach of the constitution of the DRC.[52] Regarding the latter, the Pre-Trial Chamber ruled, as it did in the *Lubanga* case,[53]

---

[48] ICC *Prosecutor v Katanga and Chui*, PTC, ICC-01/04-01/07-717, 30 September 2008, Decision on the Confirmation of Charges, para 63.
[49] Ibid, para 64.
[50] Ibid, para 62.
[51] Ibid, para 71.
[52] Ibid, para 79.
[53] *See* p 327.

that it was not bound 'by the decisions of national courts on evidentiary matters'.[54] Regarding the second legal issue, the court, following the case law of the ECtHR,[55] held that if the person concerned has the possibility to be represented by counsel in a later stage of proceedings, his right to a fair hearing is not violated. Hence, the *process-verbal d'audition* was admissible for determining the confirmation of the charges.

During the confirmation hearing the Prosecutor declared that he no longer intended to rely on the *process-verbal d'audition* as evidence. The Chamber held that this would undermine the power of the Pre-Trial Chamber to determine whether the 'substantial grounds to believe' threshold is achieved. Each item included in the list of evidence of the Prosecutor can only be ruled inadmissible by a decision of the Chamber and cannot be withdrawn by the Prosecutor.[56] As mentioned above in the *Lubanga* case, the same applies to the defence list of evidence.[57]

Furthermore, the defence objected to interviews of minor witnesses conducted without the consent of their parents or guardian. Dismissing the challenge, the Pre-Trial Chamber held that 'no statutory provision makes the prior consent of a parent or a guardian a condition for a child's testimony'.[58]

The defence of Mathieu Ngudjolo Chui challenged the statement of a witness who died during the investigation phase, by arguing that the evidence would not be available at the trial stage. The line of argument went as follows: since the Trial Chamber will hold the evidence to be inadmissible, it should also be rendered inadmissible by the Pre-Trial Chamber.[59] Deciding as a single judge, Judge Steiner ruled that 'she [ie the Pre-Trial Chamber, CS] is neither competent to decide on admissibility of the evidence at trial nor is the confirmation hearing the appropriate stage of proceedings to hold a debate on the admissibility of evidence at trial'.[60]

Both defence teams objected to the evidence provided by the Legal Representatives of the Victims as well as the use of the victims' application as corroborating evidence. The Chamber held that victims' applications are not classified as evidence and therefore cannot be rendered inadmissible.[61]

---

[54] Ibid, para 87.

[55] ICC *Prosecutor v Katanga and Chui*, PTC, ICC-01/04-01/07-717, 30 September 2008, Decision on the Confirmation of Charges, para 94 *et subs.*

[56] Ibid, para 89 *et subs.*

[57] *See* p 328.

[58] ICC *Prosecutor v Katanga and Chui*, PTC, ICC-01/04-01/07-717, 30 September 2008, Decision on the Confirmation of Charges, para 146.

[59] Ibid, para 186 *et subs.*

[60] ICC *Prosecutor v Katanga and Chui*, PTC, ICC-01/04-01/07-496, 22 May 2008, Decision on the Defences' Application to Leave to Appeal the 'Decision on the Admissibility for the Confirmation Hearing of the Transcripts of Interview of Deceased Witness 12', p 8.

[61] ICC *Prosecutor v Katanga and Chui*, PTC, ICC-01/04-01/07-717, 30 September 2008, Decision on the Confirmation of Charges, para 229 *et subs.*

Regarding the character of the conflict, the Pre-Trial Chamber decided that the armed conflict concerned was of an international character, because of the direct involvement of Uganda,[62] as mentioned above in the *Lubanga* decision.

II. Situation in the Central African Republic

Jean-Pierre Bembo Gombo[63] The suspect was the alleged president and commander-in-chief of the *Mouvement de libération du Congo* (MLC) and is a national of the DRC. In August 2002, Ange-Félix Patassé, the president of the Central African Republic, a neighbouring country of the DRC, solicited military support from Jean-Pierre Bemba Gombo, averting a coup led against him by François Bozizé. The troops of the MLC were involved in the armed conflict in the Central African Republic from 26 August 2002 until at least 15 March 2003. The Prosecutor charged Jean-Pierre Bemba Gombo with the crimes against humanity of murder, rape, and torture, and the war crimes of murder, rape, torture, outrages upon personal dignity, and pillaging.

The situation in the Central African Republic was assigned to Pre-Trial Chamber III on 19 January 2005.[64] The warrant of arrest against Jean-Pierre Bemba Gombo was issued on 23 May 2008 and he was arrested by the Belgian authorities on 24 May 2008. His transfer to The Hague took place on 3 July 2008 and one day later the suspect appeared for the first time before the court. The confirmation hearing was held from 12–15 January 2009 and the decision on the confirmation of charges was issued on 15 June 2009, more than eleven months after his first appearance before the court. The decision of Pre-Trial Chamber III comprises 186 pages and is divided into six chapters.

It begins with an analysis of the evidentiary threshold for the confirmation hearing; that is, for the decision on the confirmation of the charges, pursuant to Art. 61 (7) ICCSt. The Chamber noted that

> [t]he drafters of the Statute established three different, progressively higher evidentiary thresholds for each stage of the proceedings under article 58(1), 61(7) and 66(3) of the Statute. The nature of these evidentiary thresholds depends on the different stages of the proceedings and is also consistent with the foreseeable impact on the relevant decisions on the fundamental human rights of the person charged.[65]

---

62 Ibid, para 236.

63 For an in-depth analysis regarding substantive law issues in the decision on the confirmation of charges *see* K Ambos, 'Critical Issues in the Bemba Confirmation Decision', 22 *LJIL* (2009) 715, and D Bedermann, 'International Criminal Law—Mens Rea—Intent and Guilty Knowledge', 104 *AJIL* (2010) 241.

64 ICC *Situation in the Central African Republic*, Presidency, ICC-01/05-1, 19 January 2005, Decision on Assigning the Situation in the Central African Republic to the Pre-Trial Chamber III.

65 ICC *Prosecutor v Bemba*, PTC, ICC-01/05-01/08-424,15 June 2009, Decision Pursuant to Article 61(7)(a) and (b) of the Rome Statute on the Charges of the Prosecutor Against Jean-Pierre Bemba Gombo, para 27.

Regarding the 'substantial grounds to believe' standard for the pre-trial stage, the Chamber held that

> the Prosecutor needs to provide not all but only sufficient evidence which allows the Chamber to determine whether there are substantial grounds to believe that the suspect committed each of the crimes charged. Therefore, the Chamber is of the view that the expression 'include, but... not limited to' does not infringe the rights of the Defence at this stage.[66]

Furthermore, the Pre-Trial Chamber determined that its discretionary power regarding the assessment of evidence is limited to 'the relevance, probative value, and admissibility of each piece of evidence'.[67]

The Prosecutor based his charge of the crime against humanity of torture on the allegation that 'the same criminal conduct can be prosecuted under two different counts, namely the count of torture as well as the count of rape, the acts of rape being the instrument of torture.'[68]

The Pre-Trial Chamber rejected this cumulative charging approach, based on the finding that this 'is detrimental to the rights of Defence since it places an undue burden on the Defence.'[69] The implementation of this approach is only possible if the charged person's conduct refers to two different crimes; that is, where each of the crimes requires an additional material element not contained in the other.[70] The count of rape requires the invasion of the body of a person which is not contained in the count of torture, but conversely the crime of torture does not require any further material element and therefore, 'the act of torture is fully subsumed by the count of rape'.[71] On this reasoning, the Chamber declined to confirm the counts of war crimes of torture and outrages upon personal dignity.[72]

Beyond that, the Pre-Trial Chamber determined the general principles regarding the DCC: '[A] DCC must state the material facts underpinning the charges and that the material facts underpinning the charges shall be specific enough to clearly inform the suspect of the charges against him or her'.[73]

It follows, that the person concerned was not in the position to prepare his defence properly because of the difficulties arising from the lack of precision regarding the crime of torture.[74]

66 Ibid, para 66.
67 Ibid, para 61 *et subs.*
68 Ibid, para 199.
69 Ibid, para 202.
70 Ibid, para 202.
71 Ibid, para 205.
72 Ibid, paras 291 and 302.
73 Ibid, para 208.
74 Ibid, para 209.

Already in the preparation phase before the confirmation hearing, the Pre-Trial Chamber rendered a decision concerning the adjournment of the hearing, noting that 'the evidence submitted appeared to establish a different crime within the jurisdiction of the Court and requested the Prosecutor to consider submitting to the Chamber an amended document containing the charges addressing article 28 of the Statute as a possible mode of criminal responsibility.'[75]

Furthermore, the Chamber stated that analysing whether the criminal conduct of Jean-Pierre Bemba might fall under Art. 28 ICCSt depends on the inapplicability of Art. 25 (3) a ICCSt; that is, the individual criminal responsibility of the perpetrator as co-perpetrator. Hence, only if the requirements of the latter are not met, may the Chamber examine the provision of Art. 28 ICCSt.[76]

Beyond that, the Pre-Trial Chamber determined the concepts of *dolus* contained in the Statute. According to the Chamber, the Statute provides only two forms of *dolus*; that is, *dolus directus* first degree and *dolus directus* second degree. Every further form of *dolus*, for example, *dolus eventualis* or recklessness, is not contained in the legal text of the Statute.[77] Regarding Art. 28 ICCSt, the Pre-Trial Chamber noted that Art. 30 (3) ICCSt is not applicable because the crime does not stem from the acts of the perpetrator. In cases involving command responsibility, the perpetrator does not fulfil his or her duty to supervise and/or control his or her subordinates and as a consequence he commits a crime which falls within the jurisdiction of the court.[78]

III. Situation in Darfur, Sudan

The three persons concerned in the situation in Sudan were charged with having conducted the same crime; that is, attacking members of the peacekeeping mission of the African Union Mission in Sudan in the region of Darfur on 29 September 2009. In the course of this attack twelve members of the African Union Mission in MGS Haskanita died and eight were seriously injured. The conflict in the Darfur region between the government of Sudan and various rebel groups broke out in August 2002 and continues until this day.[79] The ICC Presidency assigned the situation of Sudan to the Pre-Trial Chamber I on 21 April 2005.[80]

---

[75] Ibid, para 15.
[76] Ibid, para 342.
[77] Ibid, para 360.
[78] Ibid, para 479.
[79] ICC *Prosecutor v Garda*, PTC, ICC-02/05-02/09-243-Red, 8 February 2010, Decision on the Confirmation of Charges, para 15 *et subs*.
[80] ICC *Situation in Darfur, Sudan*, Presidency, ICC-02/05-1, 21 April 2005, Decision Assigning the Situation in Darfur, Sudan to Pre-Trial Chamber I.

1. Bahar Idris Abu Garda

At the time of the attack, the suspect was the alleged Vice President, Secretary General, and second-commander-in-chief of the Justice and Equality Movement (JEM), one of the rebel groups fighting against the government of Sudan. He has been the chairman of the United Resistance Front (URF) since January 2008.[81] The Prosecutor charged Bahar Idris Abu Garda with war crimes committed in an internal conflict; in particular violence to life, intentionally directed attack against personnel, installations, material, units, and vehicles involved in a peacekeeping mission and pillaging.[82]

The summons to appear was issued on 7 May 2009 by Pre-Trial Chamber I. On 18 May 2010 the suspect appeared voluntarily for the first time before the court and the confirmation hearing took place from 19 to 29 October 2009. The decision on the confirmation was rendered on 8 February 2010; that is, more than eight months after Bahar Idris Abu Garda's first appearance before the court. It encompasses 103 pages and is divided into five chapters.

The Chamber held, regarding the 'substantial grounds to believe' threshold and its limits that 'at no point should Pre-Trial Chambers exceed their mandate by entering into a premature in-depth analysis of the guilt of the suspect. The Chamber, therefore, shall not evaluate whether the evidence is sufficient to sustain a future conviction.'[83]

Furthermore the Chamber stated that 'inconsistent, ambiguous or contradictory evidence may result in the Chamber reaching a decision not to confirm the charges. Such conclusion would not, however, be based on the application of the principle of *in dubio pro reo* to the assessment of the probative value of the evidence presented by the Prosecutor at this stage of the proceedings.'[84]

This determination by the Pre-Trial Chamber resulted in it declining to confirm the charges against Bahar Idris Abu Garda, on the grounds of evidentiary lacunae to prove his individual criminal responsibility. No evidence contained in the DCC served as proof that the person concerned bore criminal responsibility, neither as a direct perpetrator nor as an indirect co-perpetrator.[85]

Consequently, the Prosecutor filed an application for leave to appeal the decision on the confirmation of charges. Dealing with the issues raised by the Prosecutor by itself, the Pre-Trial Chamber clearly noted that '[t]he decision on the confirmation of the charges was intentionally excluded by the drafters of the Statute

[81] ICC *Prosecutor v Garda*, PTC, ICC-02/05-02/09-243-Red, 8 February 2010, Decision on the Confirmation of Charges, para 2.

[82] Ibid, para 1.

[83] Ibid, para 40.

[84] Ibid, para 43.

[85] Ibid, para 232.

from the categories of decisions which may be appealed directly to the Appeals Chamber.'[86]

In the pre-trial phase the Chamber issued various decisions, *inter alia* regarding the participation of victims. It held that 'victims shall be enabled to fully participate on the debate held at the confirmation hearing, bearing in mind its limited scope.'[87]

In other words, the rights of victims to participate in the pre-trial stage are only limited by the rights of the accused to a fair and impartial trial. The court must find a balance between these two opposing interests.[88]

Judge Tarfusser in his separate opinion pointed out the difficulties which arise by an unnecessary in-depth determination of the objective and subjective elements of a crime. In the present case, the Chamber analyzed every single issue in a very detailed way and hence, Judge Tarfusser noted that 'the Prosecution's failure to establish a proper connection between a given event and a given individual makes any analysis of the presence of the objective and subjective elements of criminal responsibility a mere academic debate.'[89]

Furthermore, he concluded that 'the Chamber is obliged to refrain from conducting such analysis by a fundamental principle of judicial economy: *frustra probatur quod probatum non relevat*'[90] and moreover, such an analysis would lead to prejudice in related cases and would, therefore, constitute a breach of the rights of the accused to a fair and impartial trial.[91]

2. *Abdallah Banda Abakaer Nourain and Saleh Mohammad Jerbo Jamus*

Abdallah Banda Abakaer Nourain was the alleged commander-in-chief or general commander of a splinter group of the above-mentioned JEM.[92] The second suspect, Saleh Mohammad Jerbo Jamus was the alleged operations room commander of the Sudan Liberation Movement-Unity Command (SLA-Unity).[93] The Prosecutor charged both suspects with the same war crimes with which Bahar Idris Abu Garda (see earlier) had been charged.

---

[86] ICC *Prosecutor v Garda*, PTC, ICC-02/05-02/09-267, 23 April 2010, Decision on the 'Prosecution's Application for Leave to Appeal the "Decision on the Confirmation of the Charges"', p 5.

[87] ICC *Prosecutor v Garda*, PTC, ICC-02/05-02/09-136, 6 October 2009, Decision on Victims' Modalities of Participation at the Pre-Trial Stage of the Case, para 7.

[88] Ibid, para 8.

[89] ICC *Prosecutor v Garda*, PTC, ICC-02/05-02/09-243-Red, 8 February 2010, Decision on the Confirmation of Charges, Separate Opinion of Judge Cuno Tarfusser, para 7.

[90] Ibid.

[91] Ibid.

[92] ICC *Prosecutor v Banda and Jerbo*, PTC, ICC-02/05-03/09-121-Corr-Red, 7 March 2011, Corrigendum of the 'Decision on the Confirmation of Charges', para 141.

[93] Ibid, para 142.

The summonses to appear were issued on 27 August 2009. Both persons concerned appeared for the first time before the court on 17 June 2010 and the confirmation hearing took place on 8 December 2010; that is, approximately six months after their first appearance. The decision on the confirmation of the charges comprises seventy five pages and is divided into ten chapters.

At the beginning of the proceedings, the Registry reported having problems finding an interpreter for the language of Zaghawa, spoken by the two persons concerned. On 28 September 2009, he requested in his report to the court a postponement of the confirmation hearing, because the training of qualified interpreters, although already commenced, would take at least six months.[94]

Consequently, the two suspects waived their right to be present at the confirmation hearing. The defence announced the willingness to waive this right in a joint submission filed together with the Prosecutor. Subsequently, the Pre-Trial Chamber held that 'the Defence only expressed the willingness of the suspects to waive their right to be present at the confirmation hearing without submitting any written request pursuant to rule 124(1) of the Rules nor anticipating the submission of any request'.[95]

In the joint submission, the defence submitted that it did not challenge any of the items included in the DCC. Regarding the admissibility of the evidence the Pre-Trial Chamber therefore noted that

> the proceedings leading to the confirmation hearing are not provided for the sole benefit of the parties. The aim of the procedural framework laid down in the Statute is to allow the facts alleged by the Prosecutor as forming the basis of the most serious criminal offences to be presented in full whenever either the interests of justice, which are paramount, or the interests of the victims, which are also critical, so require.[96]

Moreover, regarding the scope of the confirmation hearing the Chamber commented that 'the relationship between the pre-trial phase and the trial phase of the proceedings goes beyond the filtering of cases by the Pre-Trial Chamber for the benefit of the Trial Chamber.'[97]

Furthermore, the Pre-Trial Chamber rejected the 'agreed facts' in the joint submission, because 'the parties failed to submit a specific list of agreed-upon and uncontested facts'[98] and therefore deemed that it had to 'adopt a cautious approach'

---

[94] ICC *Prosecutor v Banda and Jerbo*, PTC, ICC-02/05-03/09-74, 29 September 2010, Report on the Registrar on Zaghawa Interpretation to be Provided During the Confirmation of Charges Hearing.

[95] ICC *Prosecutor v Banda and Jerbo*, PTC, ICC-02/05-03/09-81, 22 October 2010, Decision Postponing the Confirmation Hearing and Setting a Deadline for the Submission of the Suspects' Written Request to Waive their Rights to Attend the Confirmation Hearing, para 9.

[96] ICC *Prosecutor v Banda and Jerbo*, PTC, ICC-02/05-03/09-121-Corr-Red, 7 March 2011, Corrigendum of the 'Decision on the Confirmation of Charges', para 45.

[97] Ibid, para 32.

[98] Ibid, para 47.

when determining whether the 'substantial grounds to believe' standard has been achieved.[99]

The Chamber was mindful of the close relationship of the present case to the confirmation hearing of Bahar Idris Abu Garda and decided to 'refrain from revisiting issues or discussing arguments which were exhaustively addressed in that decision'.[100]

This statement indicates how an overly in-depth approach could lead to prejudice, as stressed by Judge Tarfusser in his separate opinion in the *Garda* decision.[101]

C. The Nature of Confirmation

Having stated the law and practice concerning the confirmation proceedings at the ICC, the question might be posed: 'what is the true nature of this part of the process?' Nowhere has this question so far been raised. Based on a functional approach, the answer to this question is decisive for the interpretation of the law and the analysis of the practice which has developed so far.

I. Unsolved questions

Neither the Statute nor the Rules oblige the Pre-Trial Chamber to give a reasoned decision when confirming the charges, much less a decision of more than one hundred pages. Indeed, as the decision is not even reviewable on appeal, there is no reason for the Chamber to do so.[102] Such extensive reasoning could, on the contrary, negatively influence the perception of the trial judges.[103]

What is also unclear is the question of the true nature of the confirmation decision. Is the confirmation *de facto* an amendment to the DCC? Would it then be fair to say that the DCC represents nothing more than the preliminary or provisional charges?[104] Does the DCC lose its provisional character by the confirmation and thereafter contain the 'final' charges?[105] But what if the charges differ? Is there a final DCC and, if so, who is responsible for drafting it?

The nature of the confirmation hearing is equally uncertain. Does it consist of a 'mini-trial', with a full in-depth evaluation of the evidence? The Pre-Trial

[99] Ibid.

[100] Ibid, para 23.

[101] ICC *Prosecutor v Garda*, PTC, ICC-02/05-02/09-243-Red, 8 February 2010, Decision on the Confirmation of Charges, Separate Opinion of Judge Cuno Tarfusser, para 7.

[102] Rightly stated by M Miraglia, 'Admissibility of Evidence, Standard of Proof, and Nature of the Decision in the ICC Confirmation of Charges in Lubanga', 6 *JICJ* (2008) 489, 500.

[103] Concerns in this regard were aired by M Miraglia, 'Admissibility of Evidence, Standard of Proof, and Nature of the Decision in the ICC Confirmation of Charges in Lubanga', 6 *JICJ* (2008) 489, 498 *et subs*.

[104] Ahlbrecht/*Kirsch*, MN 1415.

[105] Ibid, MN 1425.

Chambers have acted as though this was indeed intended and have decided issues such as the admissibility of evidence according to Art. 69 (7) ICCSt, which is systematically not applicable at the pre-trial stage.[106] Any decision taken by the Pre-Trial Chamber will most certainly not be binding upon the Trial Chamber, as the Pre-Trial Chamber itself stated, after almost ten pages of discussion.[107] The in-depth analysis of the evidence carried out by the Pre-Trial Chambers, in which they considered both incriminating and exonerating evidence, equals that of a Trial Chamber's judgment concerning the guilt of the accused.[108] Moreover, can a Pre-Trial Judge claim to be searching for the truth and order the production of additional evidence pursuant to Art. 64 (6) (d) ICCSt?

At the end of the day it has to be decided whether the confirmation of charges hearing is the little sister of the trial, or whether it merely bears the function of filtering out cases which are obviously without merit. In the latter case the hearing can be considerably shortened and the decision should not be reasoned.

It has been said that 'much will depend upon the workload of the ICC and how it interprets its broad evidentiary provisions'.[109] If the workload is leading to procedural and substantive decisions, this is not a good start for the ICC. Workload develops at random. Thus, any decision based on workload is arbitrary. We need to find a reasonable answer to the unsolved questions and must therefore turn to analyse the function of the confirmation stage in the context of the criminal proceedings.

II. The aim of the confirmation process

In order to find an answer to the question of the nature of the confirmation process we need to analyse its function and purpose. Two issues are relevant in this regard. The Statute establishes a variety of threshold requirements as the case moves along. According to Art. 61 (7) ICCSt, the confirmation decision requires sufficient evidence to establish substantial grounds to believe that the person committed the crimes charged. Firstly, this threshold needs to be put into the context of similar threshold requirements in the system of the ICC. Secondly, based on this analysis, an overall evaluation of the aim and function of the confirmation stage within the ICCSt must be undertaken.

---

[106] This has not been made an issue by the Pre-Trial Chamber, ICC *Prosecutor v Lubanga*, PTC, 29 January 2007, Confirmation Decision, para 70 *et subs.*

[107] ICC *Prosecutor v Lubanga*, PTC, 29 January 2007, Confirmation Decision, para 90; *see* also M Miraglia, 'Admissibility of Evidence, Standard of Proof, and Nature of the Decision in the ICC Confirmation of Charges in Lubanga', 6 *JICJ* (2008) 489, 494.

[108] M Miraglia, 'Admissibility of Evidence, Standard of Proof, and Nature of the Decision in the ICC Confirmation of Charges in Lubanga', 6 *JICJ* (2008) 489, 499.

[109] G Boas, 'Developments in the Law of Procedure and Evidence at the ICTY and the ICC', 12 *CLF* (2001) 167, 183.

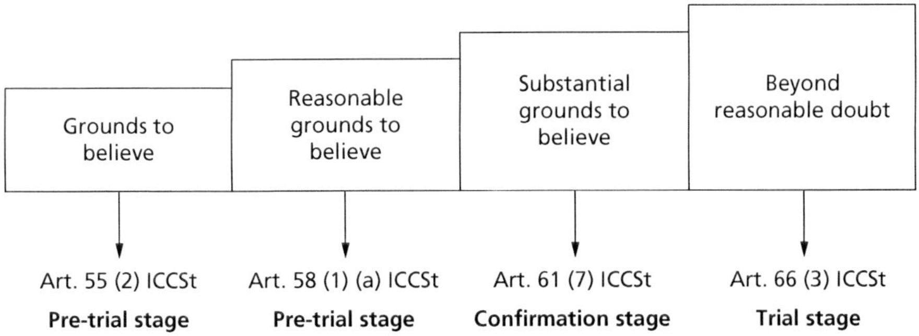

Figure 7.1 The threshold requirements

1. The threshold requirement

Art. 61 (7) ICCSt provides that for the charges to be confirmed, the Pre-Trial Chamber shall determine whether there is sufficient evidence to establish substantial grounds to believe that the person committed each of the crimes charged.

The Rome Statute refers to various evidentiary thresholds at different stages of the proceedings. The first can be found in Art. 55 (2) ICCSt, which requires 'grounds to believe' for the applicability of additional rights to persons during an investigation; that is, rights in addition to the ones stipulated in Art. 55 (1) ICCSt. Furthermore, Art. 58 (1) (a) ICCSt requires 'reasonable grounds to believe' that the person has committed a crime within the jurisdiction of the Court in order for an arrest warrant to be issued. The standard of 'substantial grounds to believe' is necessary for the confirmation of the charges under Art. 61 (7) ICCSt. Lastly, Art. 66 (3) ICCSt requires the Court to be convinced of the guilt of the accused 'beyond reasonable doubt' in order to convict the accused. Thus, a 'four stage-model' of different evidentiary thresholds can be established as shown by Figure 7.1.

The threshold of 'substantial grounds to believe' is higher than the ones referred to in Arts 55 (2), 58 (1) (a) ICCSt, but lower than 'beyond reasonable doubt'.[110]

In order to determine the exact meaning of 'substantial grounds to believe', the Pre-Trial Chambers of the ICC first looked at the purpose of the respective evidentiary thresholds and that of the confirmation hearing. The Pre-Trial Chamber in *Lubanga* found that the purpose of the confirmation hearing was limited to 'committing for trial only those persons against whom sufficiently compelling charges going beyond mere theory or suspicion have been brought', thus protecting

[110] *See* M Miraglia, 'Admissibility of Evidence, Standard of Proof, and Nature of the Decision in the ICC Confirmation of Charges in Lubanga', 6 *JICJ* (2008) 489 at 495; *see* also K Ambos and D Miller, 'Structure and Function of the Confirmation Procedure before the ICC from a Comparative Perspective', 7 *ICLR* (2007) 335 at 345 *et subs.*

the rights of the defence 'against wrongful and wholly unfounded charges'.[111] In *Katanga and Ngudjolo Chui,* the Chamber clarified that the confirmation hearing had a limited scope and must be seen as a 'means to distinguish those cases that should go to trial from those that should not go to trial'.[112] Besides the purpose of protecting the suspect from wrongful prosecution, a further aim of the confirmation hearing is to ensure judicial economy.[113] Nonetheless, it should in no case be seen as a 'mini-trial' or a 'trial before the trial'.[114] It has also been stated that it is not the Pre-Trial Chamber's task to evaluate whether there is sufficient evidence to sustain a future conviction.[115]

After having elaborated on the position of the standard of 'substantial grounds to believe' amongst the other evidentiary thresholds and the purpose of the confirmation hearing, the Pre-Trial Chamber in the *Lubanga* case, as a 'forerunner' for future decisions on this issue, relied upon internationally recognized human rights jurisprudence.[116] The Chamber cited definitions of the concept of 'substantial grounds to believe' in which the term was deemed to mean 'substantial grounds have been shown for believing' and 'strong grounds for believing'. In addition to a reference thereupon, the Pre-Trial Chamber in the *Bemba* case also referred to the literal meaning of the term 'substantial' as 'significant' or 'solid'.[117]

The Pre-Trial Chamber in the *Lubanga* case accordingly defined the threshold of 'substantial grounds to believe' to mean that the Prosecution 'must offer concrete and tangible proof demonstrating a clear line of reasoning underpinning its specific allegations'.[118] So far, the Chambers have applied this standard in all other

[111] ICC *Prosecutor v Lubanga*, PTC,ICC-01/04-01/06, 29 January 2007, Decision on the Confirmation of Charges, para 37.

[112] ICC *Prosecutor v Katanga and Ngudjolo Chui*, PTC, ICC-01/04-01/07, 25 April 2008, Corrigendum to the Decision on Evidentiary Scope of the Confirmation Hearing, Preventive Relocation and Disclosure under Article 67 (2) of the Statute and Rule 77 of the Rules, para 6.

[113] ICC *Prosecutor v Bemba*, PTC, ICC-01/05-01/08, 31 July 2008, Decision on the Evidence Disclosure System and Setting a Timetable for Disclosure between the Parties, para 15, 19 ('filtering function'). *See* also O Bekou, 'Prosecutor v Thomas Lubanga Dyilo—Decision on the Confirmation of Charges', 8 *HRLR* (2008), 343 at 344.

[114] ICC *Prosecutor v Katanga and Chui*, PTC, ICC-01/04-01/07–717, 30 September 2008, Decision on the Confirmation of Charges, para 64. *Ambos*, however, states that the confirmation of charges may lead to a strong presumption of the guilt of the accused, *see* K Ambos, 'The Structure of International Criminal Procedure: "Adversarial", "Inquisitorial" or "Mixed"', in: M Bohlander (ed), *International Criminal Justice: A Critical Analysis of Institutions and Procedures* (Cameron May 2007) 429, 456.

[115] ICC *Prosecutor v Abu Garda*, PTC, ICC-02/05-02/09, 8 February 2010, Decision on the Confirmation of Charges, para 40.

[116] Confirmation Decision (fn 111), para 38.

[117] *Prosecutor v Bemba*, PTC, ICC-01/05-01/08, 15 June 2009, Decision Pursuant to Article 61 (7) (a) and (b) of the Rome Statute on the Charges of the Prosecutor Against Jean-Pierre Bemba Gombo, para 29.

[118] Confirmation Decision (fn 111), para 39.

confirmation decisions, as they have not seen a compelling reason to deviate from its application.

The Statutes of the *ad hoc* Tribunals require the establishment of a *prima facie* case by the Prosecutor for the confirmation of the indictment (Art. 19 (1) ICTYSt, Art. 18 (1) ICTRSt). The standard of a *prima facie* case is understood to be 'a credible case which would (if not contradicted by the Defence) be a sufficient basis to convict the accused on the charge'.[119] By comparing the *prima facie* standard and the threshold of substantial grounds to believe, it can be said that the latter requires a higher standard of proof. In spite of the fact that the definition of a *prima facie* case includes the wording 'sufficient basis to convict', this by no means provides for a standard 'beyond reasonable doubt'. Upon closer examination, the *prima facie* case is quite similar to 'reasonable grounds to believe' in Art. 58 (1) (a) ICCSt.[120]

At the ICC, the Pre-Trial Chamber must be 'reasonably persuaded'[121] by significant and solid evidence that the person has committed the crimes charged. In addition, the *prima facie* case of the *ad hoc* Tribunals refers to a credible case which is not contradicted by the defence, whereas at the ICC confirmation hearing the Prosecution and the Judges are confronted with submissions of the defence. Thus, at the ICC the Prosecution has to establish a case with strong evidence sustaining the assumption that the person has committed the crimes charged even though contradicted by the defence.

2. *The function of confirmation in the context of the entire criminal proceedings*

The confirmation process is systematically placed between the investigation stage and the trial. Its purpose is to determine whether the case should be sent to trial.[122] 'The confirmation hearing is the trial of the work of the Prosecutor at the pre-trial stage not the trial of the accused, is this work good and strong enough to begin a trial?'[123]

The confirmation hearing thus has the function of a filter in the form of a judicial review of the prosecution's allegations.[124] The work of the Prosecutor is put

119 ICTY *Prosecutor v Kordić et al.*, Prosecutor, IT-95-14-I, 10 November 1995, Decision on Review of the Indictment, p 3.

120 M Miraglia, 'Admissibility of Evidence, Standard of Proof, and Nature of the Decision in the ICC Confirmation of Charges in Lubanga', 6 *JICJ* (2008) 489 at 498. A different view is taken by D Natanda Nsereko, 'Prosecutorial Discretion before National Courts and International Tribunals', 3 *JICJ* (2005) 124 at 140.

121 Cassese/Gaeta/Jones/*Marchesiello*, Commentary on the Rome Statute, 1231 at 1245.

122 Triffterer/*Shibahara*/*Schabas*, Art. 61 MN 1.

123 G Bitti, 'Two Bones of Contention Between Civil and Common Law: The Record of the Proceedings and the Treatment of a Concursus Delictorum', in: H Fischer, C Kreß, S R Lüder (eds), *International and National Prosecution of Crimes Under International Law* (Berlin Verlag 2001) 273, 277.

124 *See* Boas/Bischoff/Reid/Taylor, *ICL III*, 183; K Ambos and D Miller, 'Structure and Function of the Confirmation Procedure before the ICC from a Comparative Perspective', 7 *ICLR* (2007) 335, 341: primary aim of the confirmation is to act as a check and balance on the prosecutor.

under early scrutiny for two reasons, one being of a normative character, the other political: (1) to protect 'the rights of the defence against wrongful and wholly unfounded charges',[125] and (2) to avoid the prosecutor from becoming a kind of superpower.[126]

The confirmation process must be seen in the context of the pre-trial procedure in its entirety, which was designed to 'increase fairness and efficiency through a process of winnowing'.[127] Confirmation was indeed envisaged as a tool to expedite prosecution by organizing the charges and the evidence,[128] and in particular by avoiding lengthy discussion on disclosure issues later at trial.[129] By inspecting the Prosecutor's allegations, the charges are to be clarified by the Pre-Trial Chamber in order to specify the topic of the trial to follow. This indeed might not be as easy to achieve as it seems in international criminal proceedings, as the crimes charged cover both a macro and a micro perspective and both need to be adequately addressed.[130]

To sum up, the Confirmation stage fulfils the following functions. (1) Control of the Prosecutor, (2) protection of the rights of the defence, (3) enhancing fairness and expediting prosecution, and (4) finalizing the issues for trial.

III. Summary and conclusions

The charging process at the ICC is rather ambiguous and highly complex. What is quite worrying is the practical outcome. The final charges are contained in the DCC read in conjunction with the Pre-Trial Chamber's confirmation decision. If, as has been the case, the Pre-Trial Chamber is content to modify the DCC, it is not only the person charged who will be confused. The OTP and even the Trial Chamber may find it difficult to determine the exact scope and content of the charges as confirmed. Trial Chamber II therefore ordered the Prosecutor to produce a document, which contains the charges as amended by the Confirmation

[125] ICC *Prosecutor v Katanga and Chui*, PTC, ICC-01/04-01/07-717, 30 September 2008, Decision on the Confirmation of Charges, para 63.

[126] The Rome Statute foresees a whole set of mechanisms to exercise control over the Prosecutor, which can be seen as a sign of political distrust in the institution of an independent international prosecutor altogether, *see* C Safferling, *Towards an International Criminal Procedure* (OUP 2003) 79–86. *See* also K Ambos and D Miller, 'Structure and Function of the Confirmation Procedure before the ICC from a Comparative Perspective', 7 *ICLR* (2007) 335, 349.

[127] *See* Boas/Bischoff/Reid/Taylor, *ICL III*, p 248.

[128] G Bitti, 'Two Bones of Contention Between Civil and Common Law: The Record of the Proceedings and the Treatment of a Concursus Delictorum', in: H Fischer, C Kreß, S R Lüder (eds), *International and National Prosecution of Crimes Under International Law* (Berlin Verlag 2001) 273, 277, explaining the original French proposal.

[129] K Ambos and D Miller, 'Structure and Function of the Confirmation Procedure before the ICC from a Comparative Perspective', 7 *ICLR* (2007) 335, 348.

[130] C Möller, 'Das Vorverfahren im Strafprozess vor dem Internationalen Straftribunal für das ehemalige Jugoslawien ('Pre-Trial and Preliminary Proceedings'), in: S Kirsch (ed), *Internationale Strafgerichtshöfe* (Nomos 2005) 19, 52.

Decision of the Pre-Trial Chamber.[131] It seems a little unfortunate, to put it mildly, that the OTP is called upon to interpret the Confirmation Decision for the Trial Chamber. Obviously the prosecution will be tempted to interpret the decision in the light of its own interests. The defence was not heard on this issue.

This brings us to several conclusions.

In 2001 there was still some enthusiasm about the confirmation regime at the ICC, which was praised for its 'tough rules'.[132] Things change somewhat as the law moves out of the texts and into practice! The confirmation stage is deemed far too complex and is detrimental to a fair trial for several reasons. Even if the purpose of confirmation is to protect the suspect from unfounded allegations, the procedure is far too lengthy, especially where the person concerned is in pre-trial detention. The Pre-Trial Chamber should avoid staging a 'mini-trial'[133] and refrain from commenting on any legal question which might arise.[134] It is wholly unnecessary to develop an entirely new definition of the mental element-requirements in Art. 30 ICCSt. Similarly questions concerning an error of law[135] or a systematic approach to the question of perpetration according to Art. 25 ICCSt are also issues that do not fall within the scope of the Pre-Trial Chamber's competence.[136] Further, it is unnecessary to discuss command responsibility under Art. 28 ICCSt in depth at the pre-trial stage.[137] To embark on a legal discourse with the Trial Chamber just for the sake of it, and elaborate on highly dogmatic questions regarding substantive law in 150 pages and more makes a mockery of the interests of the person charged, who wants, and indeed has a right to the speedy processing of his or her case.

It is also unnecessary to question the admissibility of every piece of evidence presented by the Prosecutor. The question of admissibility of evidence according to Art. 69 (7) ICCSt is not an issue to be decided by the Pre-Trial Chamber. The pre-trial judges can in general assume that the evidence is admissible and decide whether or not the case shall be continued on that basis. Only if the Prosecutor relies on evidence which was evidently constructed or obviously obtained by the

[131] ICC *Prosecutor v Katanga and Chui*, TC II, ICC-01/04-01/07-1547-tENG,21 October 2009, Decision on the Filing of a Summary of the Charges by the Prosecutor.

[132] G Boas, 'Developments in the Law of Procedure and Evidence at the ICTY and the ICC', 12 *CLF* (2001) 167, 182–3.

[133] Held by the ICC *Prosecutor v Katanga and Chui*, PTC, ICC-01/04-01/07-717, 30 September 2008, Decision on the Confirmation of Charges, para 64. This has proven to be pure lip-service.

[134] M Miraglia, 'Admissibility of Evidence, Standard of Proof, and Nature of the Decision in the ICC Confirmation of Charges in Lubanga', 6 *JICJ* (2008) 489, 500 *et subs*.

[135] As was the case in ICC *Prosecutor v Lubanga*, PTC, 29 January 2007, Confirmation Decision, para 304 *et subs*.

[136] As was the case in ICC *Prosecutor v Lubanga*, ibid, para 318 *et subs*.

[137] As was the case in ICC *Prosecutor v Bemba*, PTC II, ICC-01/05-01/08-424, 15 June 2009, decision Pursuant to Article 61(7)(a) and (b) of the Rome Statute on the Charges of the Prosecutor against Jean-Pierre Bemba Gombo, para 402 *et subs*.

serious violation of human rights of the person concerned could the Pre-Trial Chamber conclude that there will be no case to answer and deny confirmation. By doing this the Pre-Trial Chamber would fulfil its duty to protect the person concerned from false allegations.

The Pre-Trial Chamber should furthermore refrain from modifying the charges *at libitum* or adding new charges.[138] It is either a 'yes' or a 'no', or a request to the Prosecutor to amend the charge. Adding new charges evidently conflicts with the objective of the confirmation hearing to protect the interests of the defendant.[139]

At the end of the confirmation process the scope of the allegations, which establish the issues of the trial to follow, must be crystal clear to all participants. It is during the pre-trial stage that the 'not infrequent failure of the Prosecution to identify its case clearly' is to be remedied.[140] It is suggested that the Pre-Trial Chamber concludes its decision with a list of the confirmed charges, thereby unequivocally setting the issues to be determined at trial.

D. Disclosure of Evidence (*Lars Büngener*)

The term 'disclosure of evidence', used in a narrow or 'technical' sense, refers to a procedure which is rooted in the adversarial system of criminal procedure: the uncovering of collected evidence or other material by a party of the trial, usually to the other party, but occasionally also to the bench or to the public. In the Roman-Germanic criminal procedure, the term is unknown. Here, the prosecutor prepares a 'dossier' containing all relevant evidence, incriminating as well as exculpatory. This dossier is handed to the defendant as well as to the Court, meaning that all participants in the trial have (ideally) the same information.[141]

In international criminal procedure, the 'dossier' approach did not get underway. The historic dominance of the adversarial system led to the implementation of a 'disclosure regime', which has undergone various changes over time. The question of how to inform the suspect about the allegations and their evidentiary basis rises in the context of the preparation for trial. That it must be done is a human rights prerequisite. As such Art. 67 (1) (b) ICCSt, which guarantees the right of the

[138] A different view is taken by K Ambos and D Miller in 'Structure and Function of the Confirmation Procedure before the ICC from a Comparative Perspective', 7 *ICLR* (2007) 335, 360. The authors wish to apply Regulation 55 RegC and adopt the principle of *iura novit curia* to this question. Even if it is conceded that the prosecution would be more efficient, it is not quite clear how this approach could fit the functional approach which shared with the authors. The function of the Pre-Trial Chamber at this stage is to control the Prosecutor and not to collaborate with him/her.

[139] Rightly put forward by Triffterer/*Shibahara/Schabas*, Art. 61 MN 5.

[140] I Bonomy, 'The Reality of Conducting a War Crimes Trial', 5 *JICJ* (2007) 348, 352.

[141] The approaches in the Roman Germanic legal systems vary; *see* Khan/Buisman/Gosnell/*Gibson/Lusiaá-Berdou* 306, at note 5.

defence to adequate time and facilities for the preparation of the defence, apparently directly grants a right to disclosure.[142]

Next we will address this complex issue at first from a principles viewpoint, (1) arguing that disclosure fulfils three main purposes: (a) disclosure is warranted by several human rights provisions, (b) it aids the procedural management, and (c) it supports the truth-finding aspect of the criminal procedure. Thereafter we will look at the disclosure requirements for the different participants, namely the Prosecutor (2), the defence (3), and the Court (4), before we scrutinize the role of the victim towards disclosure (5). Nowadays disclosure is also a technical question, because at international courts and tribunals, IT solutions prevail (6).

I. Introduction

In international criminal justice, the procedural feature of disclosure has existed from the first day up until now. This is striking in at least two ways. First and foremost, in 1945, statutory rules of disclosure were, with few exceptions, nonexistent in national jurisdictions.[143] The traditional jurisprudence in the USA and the UK (being the two most influential countries for the development of the Rules of Procedure for the IMT) was of the view that there was, under common law, no strict legal obligation of any of the parties to reciprocal disclosure in criminal trials.[144] It thus comes as a surprise that, at least to some extent, the IMT Rules of Procedure put the prosecution, and the prosecution alone, under an obligation to disclose to the defendants all documents accompanying the indictment thirty days before the trial. The second surprise may be seen in the very existence of a complex disclosure regime in the RPE ICC. As has been argued before, one can observe a clear shift of international criminal procedure towards the Continental European inquisitorial system.[145] Admittedly, the procedure of the ICC still has various adversarial elements. Yet with the Prosecutor being committed to the (material) truth and obliged to investigate incriminating and exonerating circumstances equally (Art. 54 (1) (a) ICCSt), it would have meant but a small step to give up the complex disclosure regime and introduce an (arguably simpler) dossier approach. However, this was not done.

---

142 *See* ICC *Prosecutor v Lubanga*, PTC (Single Judge), ICC-01/04-01/06-102, 15 May 2006, Decision on the Final System of Disclosure and the Establishment of a Timetable, para 53: 'Hence, while articles 67 (1) (b) and 67 (2) of the Statute and rule 77 of the Rules impose on the Prosecution the obligation to disclose to the Defence before the confirmation hearing those materials that are potentially exculpatory or are otherwise material for the Defence's preparation for the confirmation hearing..., as well as para 73: 'In respect of the materials which the Prosecution must disclose to the Defence under articles 67 (1) (b) and 67 (2) of the Statute and rule 77 of the Rules and which neither party intends to use at the confirmation hearing....

143 *See* as to the history of disclosure generally, and instructively, W LaFave, J Israel, N King, and O Kerr, *Criminal Procedure* (3rd edn, Thomson/West 2007–2009) Chapter 20.1.

144 Ibid, Chapter 20.1 (a).

145 *See* p 52.

As stated at the beginning of this chapter, the term 'disclosure' in a formal sense can be described as the uncovering of evidence and other information between the parties of legal proceedings before and during these proceedings.[146]

In international criminal jurisdictions, however, the disclosure of evidence has developed into something which must be understood more broadly, for it includes not only the parties, but the court as well. Before we look at the disclosure regime in international criminal procedure in greater detail, we need to clarify the purpose of disclosure of evidence.

We can differentiate at least three aspects concerning the purpose of disclosure: the human rights aspect (1), the procedural or trial management aspect, which relates to the efficiency of the proceedings (2), and the truth finding aspect (3).

1. The human rights aspect

Today, disclosure in criminal proceedings tends to be seen primarily in relation with the protection of the accused's rights as regards criminal trials; that is, with his or her fair trial guarantees.[147] Most authors and human rights bodies relate disclosure to the accused's rights of information and the facilities for the preparation of the defence. These rights are part of the minimum guarantees of the major human rights conventions as in Art. 14 (3) (a) and (b) ICCPR, and Art. 6 (3) (a) and (b) ECHR. The right to information as concerns the charges and adequate time and facilities for the preparation of the defence, is usually cited when it comes to disclosure issues. In relation to disclosure, some authors appear to stress the first provision—information of the accused[148]—while many merely cite the second one—adequate time and facilities for the preparation of the defence.[149] The two provisions are obviously closely linked to each other: a proper preparation of the defence is impossible without knowing the charges in detail; the same is true if the charges are known but the defence lacks the time and facilities for preparation.[150] However, disclosure *stricto sensu* is indeed more closely linked to the *facilities* for the preparation of the defence, whereas the information on the charges refers more to the indictment or charges.[151] Disclosure usually takes place *after* the charges are

[146] The term 'discovery' is mostly used synonymously, compare P Matthews and H Malek, *Disclosure* (3rd edn, Sweet & Maxwell 2010); M Lynch, 'Closure and Disclosure in Pre-Trial Argument', 5 *Human Studies* (1982) 285, 291.

[147] *See* eg, H Brady, *Disclosure of Evidence* (Transnational Publisher 2001) 403.

[148] S Zappalà, *Human Rights in International Criminal Proceedings* (OUP 2003) 119.

[149] *See* eg, S Stavros, *The Guarantees for Accused Persons under Article 6 of the European Convention on Human Rights* (Nijhoff 1993) 178 *et subs.*, 182; D Rzepka, *Zur Fairness im deutschen Strafverfahren* (Klostermann 2000) 63; C Safferling, *Towards an International Criminal Procedure* (OUP 2003) 194 *et subs.*; J Frowein and W Peukert, *Europäische Menschenrechtskonvention* (3rd edn, Engel 2009) Art. 6 MN 185.

[150] *See* also S Stavros, *The Guarantees for Accused Persons under Article 6 of the European Convention on Human Rights* (Martinus Nijhoff Publishers 1993) 168.

[151] As to the indictment or the 'document containing the charges' *see* p 244 *et subs.*

formulated and refers to pieces of evidence and factual information which go beyond the contents of an indictment.[152] In fact, the right to information *serves* the right to preparation.[153] Obviously, there is also a close link with the time granted for the preparation of the defence, because a disclosure of evidence which does not take place with sufficient time before the hearing is relatively useless.

However, the disclosure of evidence is also often linked to the accused's right to an adversarial trial.[154] This term is not to be found explicitly in the ECHR, but has been recognized by the ECtHR.[155] What the ECtHR calls the 'right to an adversarial trial' is, at least, very similar to what would be called the 'right to be heard'[156] in the Continental European legal tradition.[157] Indeed, the Court has indicated this conclusion in, for example, *Kamasinski v Austria*, when it made the English phrase, 'right to be heard' equivalent to the French term 'le principe du contradictoire'.[158]

The right to be heard also implies a right to information, in order to be able to make an informed choice as to whether and how the accused should try to influence the decision of the court. Also, the 'right to access to the dossier' as known in the Continental European legal tradition, which for its part forms the 'Continental counterpart' to disclosure, is often, at least partially, derived from this right to be heard.[159] Similarly the principle of 'equality of arms', which is in substance identical

---

[152] *See* also ECommHR, *Ofner v Austria*, Application No. (524/59), 3 Yearbook 322, 19 December 1960.

[153] *See* also ECommHR, *Haase v Federal Republic of Germany*, Application No. 7412/76, Report 12 July 1977, para B (a), p 27; and *Jespers v Belgium*, Application No. 8403/78, Report, 14 December 1981, para 56. *See* also J Frowein and W Peukert, *Europäische Menschenrechtskonvention* (3rd edn, Engel 2009); and also: HRC *OF v Norway*, Communication No. 158/1983, 26 October 1984, para 5.5.

[154] *See* eg, D Harris, M O'Boyle, E Bates, and C Buckley, *The Law of the European Convention on Human Rights* (2nd edn, OUP 2009) 254 *et subs.*; Jakobs, White, and Ovey, *The European Convention on Human Rights* (5th edn, OUP 2010) 156 *et subs.*; *see* also S Trechsel and S Summers, *Human Rights in Criminal Proceedings* (OUP 2006) 92 *et subs.*

[155] *See* ECtHR *Brandstetter v Austria*, Series A No. 212, Judgment, 28 August 1991, paras 66 and 67.

[156] As, eg, in Art. 103 (1) of the Basic Law for the Federal Republic of Germany (*Grundgesetz*): 'In the courts every person shall be entitled to a hearing in accordance with law.'; *see* also § 33 German Code of Criminal Procedure (*Strafprozessordnung*).

[157] Compare also S Trechsel and S Summers, *Human Rights in Criminal Proceedings* (OUP 2006) 89. *See* for a comparison of the right to be heard with the principle of equality of arms for Germany also C Safferling, 'Audiatur et altera pars—die prozessuale Waffengleichheit als Prozessprinzip?', 24 *NStZ* (2004) 181.

[158] ECtHR, *Kamasinski v Austria*, Application No. 9783/82, Judgment, 19 December 1989, para. 102. *See* also R Esser, *Auf dem Weg zu einem europäischen Strafverfahrensrecht* (DeGruyter 2002) 406; *see* also: *Edwards v UK*, Application No. 13071/87, Judgment, 16 December 1992, para 36; *Rowe and Davis v UK*, Application No. 28901/95, Judgment, 16 February 2000, para 60.

[159] 18 BVerfGE 399, 404; 62 BVerfGE 338; Löwe/Rosenberg/*Lüderssen* StPO, § 147 MN 2; H Schäfer, 'Die Grenzen des Rechts auf Akteneinsicht durch den Verteidiger', 4 *NStZ* (1984) 204; in this sense apparently also S Trechsel and S Summers, *Human Rights in Criminal Proceedings* (OUP 2006) 89.

to the right to be heard or the right to an adversarial trial,[160] can be invoked to support the necessity to disclosure of evidence as has been done by some authors.[161]

Finally, the right to an expeditious trial can be invoked.[162] Disclosure of evidence has proved to be a very efficient tool in shortening trials. Therefore, disclosure by the prosecution can definitely be said to be supporting the right to an expeditious trial of the accused.

A different question arises as concerns disclosure by the defence: can an accused or the defence, in support of the right to an expeditious trial, be forced to disclose evidence? From a formalistic point of view, given the fact that the accused enjoys the privilege against self-incrimination,[163] one may be tempted to answer this question in the negative right away. On the other hand, as we will see, all international courts and tribunals, as well as all major national jurisdictions, know disclosure duties of the defence.

2. *The procedural management aspect*

By the procedural management,[164] which is closely related to the aspect of an expeditious trial which we have just looked at, we mean the tendency of disclosure to reduce surprises at trial and thus to also reduce the overall time required for it. This consequence of shortening the legal proceedings was, at the beginning of the historical development of the disclosure regime, maybe not expressly desired, but indeed warmly welcomed by legal practitioners—defendants who are allowed to see the sheer mass of evidence the prosecution has are often much more likely to make confessions or enter a guilty plea,[165] which saves time and money for everyone involved. Lack of disclosure, in turn, often leads to delays in the proceedings. Some disclosure provisions, such as the obligation of the defence to disclose evidence in relation with the defence of alibi or special defences (such as lack of mental responsibility) certainly point to the purpose of shortening the trial. The procedural management aspect may thus also be seen as part of the general system of effective criminal justice.[166]

---

[160] In further detail p 410 *et subs.*

[161] R Cryer, H Friman, D Robinson, and E Wilmshurst, *An Introduction to International Criminal Law and Procedure* (2nd edn, CUP 2010) 381.

[162] In further detail p 383 *et subs.*

[163] *See* right to silence p 287 *et subs.*

[164] Also called like this by, eg, the Prosecutor of the ICC, and endorsed by Trial Chamber I, *see*, ICC, *Prosecutor v Lubanga*, TC I, ICC 01/04-01/06-1235, 20 March 2008, Decision on Defence Disclosure, para 20.

[165] To be sure, a guilty plea may also obstruct the truth-finding function of criminal proceedings—for this reason, many jurisdictions have safeguards against false guilty pleas; *see* eg, Rule 11 (b) (3) Federal Rules of Criminal Procedure, which requires that a 'factual basis' for the plea must exist. The risk of involuntarily entering false guilty pleas, however, is reduced by full disclosure, *see* K McMunigal, 'Disclosure and Accuracy in the Guilty Plea Process', 40 *Hastings Law Journal* (1989) 957, 969.

[166] *See* also, eg, Sunderland in G Ragland, *Discovery before Trial* (Callaghan and Co 1932), at p iii: 'It is probable that no procedural process offers greater opportunities for increasing the

3. *The truth-finding aspect*

Truth-finding has been declared as one of the main goals of criminal procedure.[167] Disclosure, we hold, adds to this aspect. At first glance, this seems to be contrary to the original intention of the Anglo-American tradition. As *Wigmore*, even up until the 3rd edition of his treatise on evidence of 1940, concisely and poignantly put it:

> To require the disclosure to an adversary of the evidence that is to be produced, would be repugnant to all sportsmanlike instincts. Rather permit you to preserve the secret of your tactics, to lock up your documents in the vault, to send your witness to board in some obscure village, and then, reserving your evidential resources until the final moment, to marshal them at the trial before your surprised and dismayed antagonist, and thus overwhelm him. Such was the spirit of the common law; and such in part it still is.[168]

However, even before the turn of the twentieth century, there were voices from common law practitioners, which point in the opposite direction—opposing the combative character of the criminal trial and instead calling for a 'neutral' prosecutor.[169] The history and development of the disclosure of evidence in national and international systems show that historically, the truth-finding aspect played a crucial role in the expansion of disclosure. Throughout the nineteenth and until the middle of the twentieth century we find explicit references to truth-finding in debates about disclosure; especially in the American discourse accompanying the liberalization of disclosure in the 1960s.[170]

On the international level, ICTY Judge McDonald acknowledged this fact when stating:[171]

> The modern approach, and one embraced by the Rules of the International Tribunal, is to facilitate full disclosure of all relevant facts to enhance the truth-finding process

efficiency of the administration of justice than that of discovery before trial.'; as well as Auld LJ, Review of the Criminal Courts of England and Wales (2001), hereinafter: Auld Report, Chapter 10, para 115: 'Advance disclosure by the prosecution serves two main purposes. The first is its contribution to a fair trial looked at as a whole. The second is its contribution to the efficiency, including the speed, of the pre-trial and trial process and to considerate treatment of all involved in it' (footnote omitted).

167 *See* p 55 *et subs.*

168 J H Wigmore, *A Treatise on the Anglo-American System of Evidence in Trials at Common Law*, Vol. 6, (3rd edn, Little, Brown, 1940) § 1845, p 375 *et subs.*

169 H Chaplin, 'Reform in Criminal Procedure', 7 *HLR* (1895) 189, 199 *et subs.*

170 *See* eg, US Supreme Court, *Brady v Maryland*, 373 US 83, 83 SCt 1194, USMd 1963 and the writings of one of the most influential Supreme Court Justices in this regard: W Brennan, 'The Criminal Prosecution: Sporting Event or the Quest for Truth?' 3 *Washington University Law Quarterly* (1963) 279; and later: W Brennan, 'The Criminal Prosecution: Sporting Event or the Quest for Truth? A Progress Report, 68 *Washington University Law Quarterly* (1990) 1.

171 *See* ICTY *Prosecutor v Tadić*, TC, IT-94-1-T, 27 November 1996, Separate and Dissenting Opinion of Judge McDonald on Prosecution Motion for Production of Defence Witness Statements, para 11.

that is at the core of all criminal justice systems. This approach does not contravene the equality of arms principle contained in the ICCPR and the ECHR.[172]

...By this statement, the Chief Justice of the High Court of Australia reveals his predisposition toward the production of all relevant evidence that will aid the court in arriving at the truth. This concept lies at the heart of my decision.[173]

...Indeed, the search for truth is so paramount that after the proceedings before a Trial Chamber or the Appeals Chamber have been concluded, Rule 119 [RPE ICTY, the author] authorises the parties to file a motion with that Chamber to review its judgement if a new fact has been discovered which was not known to the moving party at the time of the proceeding.[174]

II. Disclosure by the Prosecutor

In modern times, the disclosure duties of the prosecution compared to those of the defence are generally more ample. The reasons for this are obvious: the defendant is protected by the principle that the burden of proof lies on the prosecution, therefore the latter is primarily responsible for the gathering of the evidence and, accordingly, its disclosure; at the same time, the prosecution enjoys massive advantages in the facilities for the gathering of evidence, like investigators, the obtaining of search warrants, wire taps, etc.

From an historical viewpoint, like in the national systems,[175] we can state that the disclosure duties of the prosecution have widened over time.

1. Nuremberg

The Nuremberg IMT, as has been seen before,[176] was well aware of the concept of fairness towards the accused. Yet the disclosure regime provided by the IMTSt and the Rules was rather thin. Even if Art. 16 (a) IMTSt states that the defendants were to be handed a copy of the Indictment together with all the documents lodged with the Indictment in reasonable time before the trial, it was unclear to what extent evidentiary material had to be included.[177] However, German defence lawyers did, in principle, get access to evidentiary documents although they were never admitted

---

[172] Ibid, para 6.

[173] Ibid, para 18.

[174] Ibid, para 39.

[175] Compare, once again, W LaFave, J Israel, N King, and O Kerr, *Criminal Procedure*, (3rd edn, Thomson/West 2007–2009) Chapter 20.1.

[176] *See* p 11 *et subs.*

[177] The Soviets and French favoured a dossier system, whereas the Americans wanted to restrict the indictment to the utmost minimum. In the end, apparently some lists of evidence were handed over together with the indictment, *see* V von der Lippe, *Nürnberger Tagebuchnotizen* (Knapp 1951) 35. Dr von der Lippe was an assistant to Dr Siemers, defense counsel for the defendant Raeder. The exact content of the lists, however, is unclear.

to the Prosecution archives.[178] It was mostly the President of the IMT, Sir Geoffrey Lawrence, who insisted on disclosure, which in his eyes was fundamental for the fairness of the trial. On 22 November 1945 when the presentation of evidence began, he stated: 'The Tribunal has heard with great satisfaction of the steps which have been taken by the Chief Prosecutors to make available to defending counsel the numerous documents upon which the Prosecution rely, with the aim of giving to the defendants every possibility for a just defense.'[179]

However, as American prosecutor Telford Taylor later noted: 'It soon emerged that this matter had not been satisfactorily resolved.'[180] Often the President of the IMT intervened on behalf of the German defence counsel and in some cases, though not always, demanded that each one was to be served with a copy of relevant documentary evidence, whereas the US prosecution team previously adopted a procedure of only depositing some copies in the 'Defendant's Information Center'.[181] In the view of the defence, the situation concerning the disclosure of evidence by the prosecution was often desperate. In his diary, von der Lippe uses such expressions as 'war' or 'battle' of documents. Telford Taylor later admitted that the archives should have been opened to all counsel—which clearly would have been contrary to common law at that time—but that mistrust towards the German counsel put a stop to such a procedure.[182] In any case, he states, that too much time was wasted to sort out the needs of a trial in this regard.[183]

2. Ad hoc *Tribunals*

Differing from the IMT system, the Rules of Procedure and Evidence of the *ad hoc* Tribunals contain a somewhat sophisticated disclosure regime. Following the Anglo-American tradition, at the *ad hoc* Tribunals, disclosure by the Prosecutor represents the most significant category of disclosure. The types of material which the Prosecutor has to disclose to the defence can be divided into four categories: supporting material and prior statements of the accused (Rule 66 (A)), witness statements (Rule 66 (B)), exculpatory material (Rule 68), and other material evidence, such as books and tangible objects (Rule 67 (C)). While most of these provisions can be traced back to American law,[184] the inclusion of the obligatory disclosure of exculpatory material

[178] This was despite several attempts made by defence counsel, *see* C Haensel, 'The Nuremberg Trial Revisited', 13 *DePaul Law Review* (1963–1964) 248, 256; O Kranzbühler, 'Nuremberg Eighteen Years Afterwards', 14 *DePaul Law Review* (1964–1965) 333, 336; H Laternser, 'Looking Back at the Nuremberg Trials with Special Consideration of the Processes against Military Leaders', 8 *Whittier Law Review* (1986–1987) 557, 561 *et subs.*

[179] IMT Protocols II, 29.

[180] T Taylor, *The Anatomy of the Nuremberg Trials* (Bloomsbury 1993) 165.

[181] *See* eg, IMT Protocols II, 183 *et subs.*

[182] T Taylor, *The Anatomy of the Nuremberg Trials* (Bloomsbury 1993) 627.

[183] Ibid.

[184] Compare Morris/Scharf, *An Insider's Guide to the International Criminal Tribunal for the Former Yugoslavia, vol. 1* (Hotei Publishing 1995) 177.

appears worth mentioning here, since it is still not to be found in American statutory law. In light of the mentioned jurisprudence of the international human rights authorities, it would appear logical that the *ad hoc* Tribunals had to implement an obligatory disclosure of exculpatory material. In procedural regimes adhering to the Continental tradition, the finding of exculpatory material is comprised in the investigation duties of the prosecutor,[185] and thus treated like any other evidence (which means that it must be included in the dossier). The fact that the Rules of the *ad hoc* Tribunals contain such an obligation is, nevertheless, quite surprising. In the traditional adversarial system on which the *ad hoc* Tribunals criminal procedure is based, it is still primarily the task of the defence to gather exculpatory evidence.[186] Even though a certain practice concerning the disclosure of exculpatory material under constitutional law has developed,[187] the US Supreme Court has still denied a general constitutional right to disclosure in criminal cases.[188]

The Appeals Chamber of the ICTY, for its part, has emphasized that the disclosure of exculpatory material is 'fundamental to the fairness of proceedings before the Tribunal, and considerations of fairness are the overriding factor in any determination of whether the governing Rule has been breached'[189] and that '[t]he prosecution's obligation under Rule 68 is not a secondary one, to be complied with after everything else is done; it is as important as the obligation to prosecute.'[190]

3. ICC

As is the case at the *ad hoc* Tribunals as well as in national jurisdictions, also at the ICC the Prosecution carries the main burden of disclosure obligations. In contrast to the *ad hoc* Tribunals, however, the disclosure regime of the ICC is contained both in the ICC Statute and the Rules. The Statute and the Rules thus need to be applied jointly.[191] The RPE ICC must be seen as norms which for their part form and shape the content of the more general ICCSt articles.[192]

---

185 *See* eg, § 160 (2) StPO (German Code of Criminal Procedure).

186 ICTY *Prosecutor v Blagojević et al.*, TC II, IT-02-60-PT, 12 December 2002, Joint Decision on Motions Related to Production of Evidence, para 26.

187 Eg, the disclosure of so-called 'Brady-material' in the USA, *see* US Supreme Court *Brady v Maryland*, 373 US (1963) 83.

188 US Supreme Court *Weatherford v Bursey*, 429 US (1977) 545, 559.

189 ICTY *Prosecutor v Krstić*, AC, IT-98-33-A, 19 April 2004, Appeals Judgment, para 180.

190 ICTY *Prosecutor v Kordić and Čerkez*, Pre-Appeal Judge, IT-95-14/2-A, 11 May 2001, Decision on Motions to Extend Time for Filing Appellant's Briefs, para 14.

191 In the beginning, the ICC occasionally based its rulings on disclosure issues on the Rome Statute alone; that is, on Art. 61 (3) (b) and Art. 67 (1) (b) ICCSt, *see* ICC *Prosecutor v Lubanga*, PTC (Single Judge), ICC-01/04-01/06-54, 23 March 2006, Decision Requesting Observations of the Prosecution and the Duty Counsel for the Defence on the System of Disclosure and Establishing an Interim System of Disclosure, p 3

192 *See* also ICC *Prosecutor v Lubanga*, AC, ICC-01/04-01/06-773 (OA 5), 14 December 2006, Judgment on the Appeal of Mr Thomas Lubanga Dyilo against the Decision of Pre-Trial Chamber I entitled 'Second Decision on the Prosecution Requests and Amended Requests for Redactions under Rule 81', Separate Opinion by Judge Georghios M. Pikis, p 25, para 4.

(1) The Rome Statute In contrast to the respective Statutes of the *ad hoc* Tribunals, the Rome Statute makes, on several occasions, explicit reference to disclosure. Though leaving most of the details of disclosure to the Rules of Procedure and Evidence, the Statute addresses, roughly speaking, three aspects of disclosure. These comprise the procedural disclosure rights of the accused, and limitations to disclosure, due to witness protection, and the protection of security interests of national states and third parties.

A particular feature of the ICC's procedural law, which has already been analysed above,[193] is the two-stage approach of its criminal procedure. The drafters of the ICC opted for a system with two separate public and oral procedures: the confirmation of the charges according to Art. 61 ICCSt, held before a pre-trial chamber, and the trial according to Art. 62 *et subs.*, which is staged before a trial chamber. In contrast to the *ad hoc* Tribunals, the ICC thus has, as it were, *two* pre-trial stages (before the confirmation hearing as opposed to *after* the confirmation hearing, but *before* the trial). This occasionally makes it a little more complicated to determine at what time and to what extent disclosure must take place. Hereinafter, for reasons of clarity, we will, when appropriate, discriminate between 'pre-confirmation' and 'pre-trial' disclosure.

The first mention of disclosure contained in the Statute can be seen in the duty of the Prosecutor to submit to the accused, together with the document containing the charges, 'information' on the evidence on which the Prosecutor intends to rely at the confirmation hearing, Art. 61 (3) (b) ICCSt, which is followed by an affirmation of the competent Pre-Trial Chamber to rule on any issues on the matter of disclosure at this stage.[194]

Another central provision is the duty of the Prosecutor to disclose exculpatory evidence, which also proved to be a very important aspect in the disclosure regime of the *ad hoc* Tribunals. The drafters of the ICCSt, however, obviously considered this disclosure duty important enough to include it in the Statute itself, in the same Article, though in a separate paragraph, as the fair trial rights of the accused (Art. 67 (2) ICCSt). The formulation thus not merely stipulates an obligation of the Prosecution, but indeed a positive right of the accused.[195] Flanked by the duty of the Prosecutor not only to disclose but also to actively investigate exonerating circumstances (Art. 54 (1) (a) ICCSt), Art. 67 (2) ICCSt demonstrates a strong case of the drafters of the ICC for both fairness and truth-finding.

The same holds true for Art. 64 (3) (c) and (6) (d) ICCSt, which reiterate the power of the Trial Chamber to rule on disclosure issues before it and is thus in parallel

193 *See* p 316 *et subs.*

194 This is further elaborated by Rule 121 RPE-ICC; *see* for more details on this p 369 *et subs.*

195 *See* also S Zappalà, 'The Rights of the Accused', in A Cassese, P Gaeta, and J Jones (eds), *The Rome Statute of the International Criminal Court: A Commentary* (OUP 2002) 1319, 1352.

with Art. 61 (3). Art. 64 (6) (b) and (d) ICCSt, in turn, reaffirm the power of the Trial Chamber to order the attendance of witnesses as well as the production of evidence *ex officio*, even exceeding the material already collected and presented by the parties.[196] This reaffirms the view that the Court has been provided with far-reaching inquisitorial powers by the ICC legislator.

Aspects limiting disclosure, however, have also found their way into the Statute. Directly after the rights of the accused as enumerated in Art. 67 ICCSt follow the rights of victims and witnesses. Art. 68 (5) ICCSt serves as a counterweight to prosecution disclosure if the safety of victims and witnesses is at stake. Art. 54 (3) (e) represents a consequence of the *ad hoc* Tribunals' experience that international trials can hardly be conducted satisfactorily if states and international organizations are unwilling to share information. This is closely related with the aspect of the protection of national security interests, as elaborated in Arts 72, 73, 93, and 99 ICCSt.

(2) The Rules of Procedure and Evidence The particulars of the disclosure regime at the ICC are, however, regulated in the Rules of Procedure and Evidence of the ICC. Most of the relevant provisions are to be found in Chapter 4 ('Provisions relating to various stages of the proceedings'), Section II; that is, Rules 76–84 of the RPE ICC ('Disclosure').

(1) Incriminating evidence Rule 76 and 77 RPE ICC Rule 76 RPE ICC regulates disclosure pertaining to prosecution witnesses. The names of witnesses whom the Prosecutor intends to call to testify shall be made available to the defence together with copies of any prior statements of these witnesses both in the original language and in a language which the accused fully understands. The disclosure obligation is subject to the protection and privacy of the victims and witnesses as foreseen by Art. 68 (5) ICCSt.

Despite the fact that the wording of this provision relates to pre-trial disclosure only, it is also applicable to the pre-confirmation stage *mutatis mutandis*.[197] In the case of pre-confirmation disclosure, particular attention has to be paid to possible prejudice of ongoing investigations as expressed by Rule 81 (2) RPE

[196] It is to be noted that the Appeals Chamber of the ICC has expressed the view that this wording envisions that 'the right to lead evidence pertaining to the guilt or innocence of the accused... lies primarily with the parties', *see* ICC *Prosecutor v Lubanga*, AC, ICC-01/04-01/06-1432 (OA 9, OA 10), 11 July 2008, Judgment on the Appeals of The Prosecutor and The Defence against Trial Chamber I's Decision on Victims' Participation of 18 January 2008, para 93.

[197] ICC *Prosecutor v Lubanga*, AC, ICC-01/04-01/06-568, 13 October 2006, Judgment on the Prosecutor's Appeal against the Decision of Pre-Trial Chamber I entitled 'Decision Establishing General Principles Governing Applications to Restrict Disclosure Pursuant to Rule 81 (2) and (4) of the Rules of Procedure and Evidence', para 34.

ICC in a general manner.[198] In that case the Prosecutor is obliged to disclose the evidence, but may do so summarily or in the form of redacted versions. Redactions pose, without doubt, a milder form of interfering with the right of the suspect to be informed properly compared to total non-disclosure.[199] Rule 76 (1) RPE ICC covers also names and statements of witnesses whom the Prosecutor intends to rely on without calling the witness in person.[200] As regards so-called 'pre-assessment interviews', in which the witness, before testifying, is examined in order to decide whether or not s/he should testify, the ICC held that they are not witness statements, but may qualify as exculpatory evidence or fall under Rule 77.[201]

It is questionable whether the Prosecutor must also disclose prior statements of the accused as there is no provision in the RPE ICC determining this matter. Mostly these statements will fall within the scope of Art. 67 (2) ICCSt (exculpatory evidence) and thus need to be disclosed.

Rule 77 refers to the inspection of material in possession or control of the Prosecutor. Not much relevance should be attributed to the fact that the language of the rule speaks of 'inspection' rather than of 'disclosure'. 'Inspection' must be interpreted to comprise the handing over of copies of those materials which the defence, after or during inspection, requests.[202] The question of relevance of the material for the defence is to be answered extensively and must be interpreted as also comprising material which may serve to impeach witnesses and may thus be of use in cross-examination.[203] The obligation to disclosure pertains also to the identity of 'intermediaries', who serve as a liaison between investigators and witnesses.[204] In *Lubanga*, this issue led to a serious controversy between the Trial Chamber and the Prosecutor, who was not willing to disclose the identity of intermediaries, even if

[198] ICC *Prosecutor v Lubanga*, AC, ICC-01/04-01/06-774 (OA 6), 14 December 2006, Judgment on the Appeal of Mr Thomas Lubanga Dyilo against the Decision of Pre-Trial Chamber I entitled 'Second Decision on the Prosecution Requests and Amended Requests for Redactions under Rule 81', para 35 *et subs*.

[199] The view that the possibility of redactions can be inferred from Rule 81 (2) RPE-ICC has been applied generally by the ICC, *see* eg, ICC *Prosecutor v Lubanga*, TC I, ICC-01/04-01/06-2190-Red, 10 December 2009, Redacted Decision on the Application to Disclose the Identity of Intermediary 143, para 20.

[200] ICC *Prosecutor v Lubanga*, PTC (Single Judge), ICC-01/04-01/06-102, 15 May 2006, Decision on the Final System of Disclosure and the Establishment of a Timetable, para 93 *et subs*.

[201] ICC *Prosecutor v Bemba*, TC III, ICC-01/05-01/08-750-Conf, 9 April 2010, Public Redacted Version of 'Decision on the Defence Request for Disclosure of Pre-interview Assessments and the Consequences of Non-disclosure', para 33.

[202] ICC *Prosecutor v Lubanga*, PTC (Single Judge), ICC-01/04-01/06-102, 15 May 2006, Decision on the Final System of Disclosure and the Establishment of a Timetable, para 113 *et subs*.

[203] *See* ICC *Prosecutor v Lubanga*, TC I, ICC-01/04-01/06-2624, 12 November 2010, Decision on the Scope of the Prosecution's Disclosure Obligations as Regards Defence Witnesses.

[204] ICC *Prosecutor v Lubanga*, TC I, ICC-01/04-01/06-2434-Red2, 31 May 2010, Redacted Decision on Intermediaries, para 139 b.

the Chamber ordered him to doing so. This finally culminated in a temporary stay of proceedings in the *Lubanga* trial.[205]

According to the ICC Appeals Chamber, even material which is not directly related to the case but rather tends to explain the overall situation in a conflict scenario may be 'material' in the sense of Rule 77.[206]

(2) Exculpatory evidence, Art. 67 (2) ICCSt, Rule 83 RPE ICC The Prosecutor must investigate incriminating and exonerating circumstances equally according to Art. 54 (1) (a) ICCSt. The Prosecutor's prerogative of assessment as to whether evidentiary material is 'exculpatory' in the sense of Art. 67 (2) ICCSt carries with itself a corresponding duty. This means that s/he must carefully assess every piece of evidence vis-à-vis every reasonably conceivable line of defence. If in such a case a line of defence is revealed at a late stage of the proceedings and could not be reasonably foreseen, the trial may have to continue without the (then) unavailable evidence, and quite possibly might still have to be considered to be fair. This, however, is for the Court to decide, and must indeed be done on a case-by-case basis.[207]

The disclosure obligation pertains to all material which shows or tends to show the innocence of the accused, mitigate the guilt of the accused, or may affect the credibility of the Prosecution's evidence. Information on the criminal record of a witness on whom the Prosecutor intends to rely, also falls within the scope of this provision, as it is relevant for evaluating the reliability of the witness.[208]

The Prosecutor is dispensed of the duty to disclose in case of admissions of facts regarding potentially exculpatory evidence, whereby the evidence itself would not need to be disclosed anymore, in the interest, for example, of witness protection.[209]

---

[205] *See* ICC *Prosecutor v Lubanga*, TC I, ICC-01/04-01/06-2517-Red, 8 July 2010, Redacted Decision on the Prosecution's Urgent Request for Variation of the Time-Limit to Disclose the Identity of Intermediary 143 or Alternatively to Stay Proceedings Pending Further Consultations with the VWU.

[206] *See* eg, ICC *Prosecutor v Lubanga*, AC, ICC-01/04-01/06-1432 (OA 9, OA 10), 11 July 2008, Judgment on the appeals of The Prosecutor and The Defence against Trial Chamber I's Decision on Victims' Participation of 18 January 2008, para 76–82; the decision dealt with material which showed the use of child soldiers in the situation of the DRC in general, without being specifically connected with the charges against Mr Lubanga. S Swoboda, 'The ICC Disclosure Regime', 19 *CLF* (2008) 449, 454 appears to hold that this is only the case *after* the confirmation hearing; in our opinion, there is no compelling reason why this should not apply to pre-confirmation disclosure as well.

[207] ICC *Prosecutor v Lubanga*, AC, ICC-01/04-01/06-1432 (OA 9, OA 10), 11 July 2008, Judgment on the Appeals of The Prosecutor and The Defence against Trial Chamber I's Decision on Victims' Participation of 18 January 2008, para 53. *See* also B Kuschnik, 'International Criminal Due Process in the Making: New Tendencies in the Law on Non-Disclosure in the Proceedings of the ICC', 9 *ICLR* (2009) 157, 161 *et subs.*; and W Schabas, *ICC* (CUP 2010) 819 *et subs.*

[208] ICC *Prosecutor v Katanga and Chui*, PTC, ICC-01/04-01/07-717, 30 September 2008, Decision on the Confirmation of Charges, paras 181, 214.

[209] ICC *Prosecutor v Lubanga*, TC I, ICC-01/04-01/06-1295, 24 April 2008, Decision on Disclosure Issues, Responsibilities for Protective Measures and other Procedural Matters, para 90 *et subs.* The issue evolved mainly around witnesses who would refuse to cooperate with the Court

Furthermore, Art. 67 (2) ICCSt is inapplicable if the Prosecutor and the defence counsel have reached an agreement or the Prosecutor has withdrawn the factual allegations or charges concerning the relevant material.[210] However, summaries of exculpatory evidence do not meet the Prosecutor's disclosure obligation.[211]

III. Disclosure by the Defence

The main burden of disclosure lies on the prosecution as has been said before. However, there are situations in which the defence for its part is obliged to disclose certain material to the prosecution. Defence disclosure mainly relates to 'special defences', such as alibi[212] or mental incapacity. Its main purpose appears to be to secure an expeditious trial, by enabling the prosecution to adequately prepare its case, as well as the mentioned truth finding functionality.

1. The IMT at Nuremberg

As much as the President of the IMT aided defence counsel by insisting on disclosure by the Prosecution, he also requested the defence to lay open its evidence and defence strategy:

> At the conclusion of the case for the Prosecution, the defendants' counsel will be invited to submit to the Tribunal the evidence they propose to call; but they will be strictly confined to the names of the witnesses and the matters to which their evidence will be relevant, and this submission must not be in the nature of a speech. Is that clear? In case there should be any misunderstanding, what I have just said will be posted up on the board in the defendants' Counsel Room so that you can study it there.[213]

Before the defence case started, defence counsel and Prosecution agreed on a procedure regarding disclosure of both life and documentary evidence, which was decided on by the Tribunal on 18 February 1946.[214] Most of the discussions which

for security concerns. Judge Blattmann dissented: *Prosecutor v Lubanga*, TC I, ICC-01/04-01/06-1295-US-Exp-Anxl, 28 April 2008, Separate and Dissenting Opinion of Judge Blattmann attached to Decision on Disclosure Issues, Responsibilities for Protective Measures and other Procedural Matters, para 17 *et subs*. Judge Blattmann instead proposes a 'normal' approach allowing redactions, which could be lifted upon application by the defence to the Chamber, *see* ibid, para 26.

[210] ICC *Prosecutor v Lubanga*, TC I, ICC-01/04-01/06-1401, 13 June 2008, Decision on the Consequences of Non-disclosure of Exculpatory Materials Covered by Art. 54 (3) (e) Agreements and the Application to Stay the Prosecution of the Accused, together with Certain Other Issues Raised at the Status Conference on 10 June 2008, para 6; *see* also W Schabas, *ICC* (OUP 2010) 818.

[211] ICC *Prosecutor v Katanga* and *Chui*, TC I (Single Judge), ICC-01/04-01/07-621, 20 June 2008, Decision on Article 54 (3) (e) Documents Identified as Potentially Exculpatory or Otherwise Material to the Defence's Preparation for the Confirmation Hearing, paras 67–76.

[212] 'Alibi' is not mentioned in the ICCSt as a ground for excluding criminal liability. It means evidence tending to show that by reason of the presence of the accused at a particular place at a particular time he was not at the place where the offence is alleged to have been committed, *see* J Sprack, *Criminal Procedure* (12th edn, OUP 2008) 20.62.

[213] IMT Protocols III, 335 (10 December 1945).

[214] IMT Protocols VII, 516.

would follow in the courtroom were about the admissibility of evidence as the Prosecution was allowed to challenge the relevance of the defence evidence on the basis of the disclosure long before it was presented in court on the basis of Art. 24 (d) IMTSt.[215] The defence had not been granted (or not taken) this opportunity during the Prosecution case; however, the IMT used its discretion in a rather broad way in favour of the defendants.[216]

2. *The* ad hoc *Tribunals*

At the very beginning, the judges at the ICTY had contemplated a 'modern' approach towards disclosure, requiring disclosure from both parties.[217] Indeed, the first President of the ICTY, Judge Antonio Cassese, stated in 1994: 'We have made considerable efforts to put both the prosecution and the defence on the same footing, with full disclosure of documents and witnesses by both sides, so as to safeguard the rights of the accused and ensure a fair trial. In this respect we have made a conscious effort to make good the flaws of Nuremberg and Tokyo.'[218]

However, in the original version of the Rules, the defence would only be obliged to disclose its intent to rely on 'special defences', such as alibi or mental incapacity. Other disclosure obligations would arise only regarding material evidence such as documents, tangible objects, etc., and only if the defence would, for its part, request the disclosure of corresponding material from the Prosecution ('reciprocal disclosure', which was the original heading of Rule 67).[219] But in the course of existence of the *ad hoc* Tribunals, disclosure obligations of the defence have been broadened considerably, especially as far as the ICTY is concerned.[220] Since 2008, Rule 67 establishes similar disclosure duties for the defence compared to those of the Prosecution, including the names and addresses of witnesses and, particularly, their statements.

3. *The ICC*

The ICC Statute, while containing disclosure obligations of the Prosecutor, does not contain any explicit notion of defence disclosure which would go beyond the general right of the respective Chambers to order the production of evidence pursuant to Arts 64 (6) (b), (d), 69 (3) ICCSt. The Rules, however, lay down a defence

[215] *See* eg, IMT Protocols VIII, 161 *et subs.*

[216] *See* C Safferling and P Graebke, 'Strafverteidigung im Nürnberger Hauptkriegsverbrecherprozess: Strategien und Wirkungen', 123 *ZStW* (2011) 47, 70.

[217] C Kamardi, *Die Ausformung einer Prozessordnung sui generis durch das ICTY unter Berücksichtigung des Fair-Trial-Prinzips* (Springer 2009) 315.

[218] Statement by the President Made at a Briefing to Members of Diplomatic Missions IT/29, 11 February 1994. Summary of the Rules of Procedure of the International Criminal Tribunal for the Former Yugoslavia, printed in V Morris *and* M Scharf, *An Insider's Guide to the International Criminal Tribunal for the Former Yugoslavia* (Hotei Publishing 1995) 649, 650.

[219] At the ICTR and the SCSL, it still is.

[220] *See* also Khan/Buisman/Gosnell/*Gibson/Lusiadá-Berdou* 306, 338 *et subs.*

disclosure regime. We can distinguish four different provisions within the Rules which specifically deal with disclosure by the defence: (a) Rule 78, which partially mirrors disclosure by the Prosecutor regarding documents, tangible objects etc. according to Rule 77; (b) Rule 79 (1)–(3), which deal with alibi and grounds for excluding criminal responsibility, (c) Rule 80, which specifically deals with grounds for excluding responsibility under Art. 31 (3) ICCSt, and (d) Rule 79 (4), which allows the Chamber to order the disclosure of 'any other evidence', and may thus serve as a residual clause.

Obviously, defence disclosure can conflict with the accused's rights to remain silent and his or her privilege against self-incrimination as provided for in Arts 67 (1) (g), 55 (1) (a), (2) (b) ICCSt. Since the Statute is higher in rank than the Rules, the latter must be read subject to the former (Art. 51 (5) ICCSt). The same holds true for the Regulations of the Court, which are even lower in rank than the Rules (Regulation 1 (1) RegC), nevertheless on the face of it, Regulation 54 RegC significantly widens the potential disclosure and notification duties of the defence.[221] Generally, the ICC Chambers have emphasized that, given the fact that the person concerned has the right to remain silent and s/he cannot be forced to disclose evidence even in his or her favour,[222] disclosure can only be required in limited circumstances.[223]

---

[221] Regulation 54 RegC Status conferences before the Trial Chamber

At a status conference, the Trial Chamber may, in accordance with the Statute and the Rules, issue any order in the interests of justice for the purposes of the proceedings on, *inter alia*, the following issues:

- (a) The length and content of legal arguments and the opening and closing statements;
- (b) A summary of the evidence the participants intend to rely on;
- (c) The length of the evidence to be relied on;
- (d) The length of questioning of the witnesses;
- (e) The number and identity (including any pseudonym) of the witnesses to be called;
- (f) The production and disclosure of the statements of the witnesses on which the participants propose to rely;
- (g) The number of documents as referred to in Art. 69, para 2, or exhibits to be introduced together with their length and size;
- (h) The issues the participants propose to raise during the trial;
- (i) The extent to which a participant can rely on recorded evidence, including the transcripts and the audio and video record of evidence previously given;
- (j) The presentation of evidence in summary form;
- (k) The extent to which evidence is to be given by an audio or video link;
- (l) The disclosure of evidence;
- (m) The joint or separate instruction by the participants of expert witnesses;
- (n) Evidence to be introduced under Rule 69 as regards agreed facts;
- (o) The conditions under which victims shall participate in the proceedings;
- (p) The defences, if any, to be advanced by the accused.

[222] To enforce the disclosure of *incriminating* material would obviously additionally infringe upon the accused's privilege against self-incrimination.

[223] *See* eg, ICC *Prosecutor v Lubanga*, TC I, ICC-01/04-01/06-1235, 20 March 2008, Decision on Disclosure by the Defence, para 27 *et subs.*, as well as ICC *Prosecutor v Bemba*, PTC III, ICC-01/05-01/08-55, 31 July 2008, Decision on the Evidence Disclosure System and Setting a Timetable for Disclosure between the Parties, para 30 *et subs.*

(a) Rule 78 RPE ICC represents a parallel provision vis-à-vis Rule 77 containing the corresponding disclosure duty of the Prosecutor. Substantially, Rule 78 relates to the same material as Rule 77 (books, documents, photographs, and other tangible objects). In contrast to Rule 77 RPE ICC, there is no 'materiality' test, which is understandable, given the fact that the defence is not bound to present or 'rely on' any evidence during the confirmation hearing or the trial.[224] In contrast to the disclosure regime of the *ad hoc* Tribunals, the disclosure obligations by the defence was always conceived of as independent from the corresponding duty of the Prosecutor, so there was no reciprocity intended. The only prerequisite for the application of Rule 78 is thus the fact that the defence is planning to use the material 'as evidence for the purposes of the confirmation hearing or the trial'.

(b) Rule 79 RPE ICC pertains to 'special defences'[225] such as alibi and grounds for excluding criminal responsibility as contained in Art. 31 (1) ICCSt. This is a rather far-reaching obligation on the side of the defence, as it pertains not only to mental disease and intoxication as foreseen in Art. 31 (1) (a) and (b) ICCSt, but also to circumstances like self-defence or duress according to Art. 31 (c) and (d) ICCSt.[226] In contrast to Rule 76, however, the defence counsel needs to provide the Prosecutor with the statements of the witnesses. Rule 79 (1)–(3) RPE ICC has as yet not been specifically applied by the ICC, for none of the accused have invoked any grounds for excluding criminal responsibility up to now.

(c) Rule 80 RPE ICC pertains to the procedure to be followed when a ground for excluding mental responsibility according to Art. 31 (3) ICCSt is to be considered. In contrast to Art. 31 (1) ICCSt, Art. 31 (3) deals with grounds for excluding criminal responsibility which are not contained in the Statute but may be derived from the sources of law as contained in Art. 21 ICCSt. The purpose of Art. 31 (3) ICCSt is largely unclear. Allegedly, the norm does not pertain to specific 'defences' in domestic legal systems, but to grounds excluding criminal liability which are based on public international law, like military necessity, reprisals, and the inherent right to self-defence as contained in Art. 51 UN Charter.[227] In any case such an unlikely submission brought forward by the defence would certainly give rise to major discussions. This is the reason why in this event the defence shall give notice both to the Trial Chamber[228] and the Prosecutor to have sufficient time to adequately

[224] *See* also ICC *Prosecutor v Bemba*, PTC III, ICC-01/05-01/08-55, 31 July 2008, Decision on the Evidence Disclosure System and Setting a Timetable for Disclosure between the Parties, para 30 *et subs*.

[225] This terminology stems from the Anglo-American tradition and is (intentionally) not used by the Statute; compare K Ambos, *Der Allgemeine Teil des Völkerstrafrechts: Ansätze einer Dogmatisierung* (Duncker and Humblot 2002) 825 *et subs*. with further references.

[226] The *ad hoc* Tribunals' disclosure regime was not as strict towards the defence, *see* Rule 67 (B) (i) (b) RPE-ICTY which only referred to 'special defences'.

[227] *See* W Schabas, *ICC* (OUP 2010) 492 *et subs*.

[228] Interestingly, the Pre-Trial Chamber is obviously considered incompetent to treat this issue and discuss grounds excluding criminal responsibility from outside the ICCSt.

prepare for the argument. Rule 80 RPE ICC has apparently not been applied by the ICC up to now.

(d) Finally, Rule 79 (4) RPE ICC refers to other evidence which is to be disclosed upon an order by a Chamber. Considering the heading of the Rule 79, this subparagraph clearly refers to defence disclosure. It appears as a rather dangerous 'catch-all' provision which can easily come into conflict with the rights of a person concerned to remain silent and his or her privilege against self-incrimination as provided by Arts 67 (1) (g), 55 (1) (a), (2) (b) ICCSt; this holds true especially with the accompanying provision of the already mentioned Regulation 54 RegC. Trial Chamber I had to deal with this provision and indeed made the connection to Regulation 54 RegC. The judges also saw the dangerous potential regarding the rights of the suspect and attempted to develop a 'proportionality approach'.[229] As this proportionality test is related to the Prosecutor's disclosure obligations in particular regarding exonerating materials, the Chamber is *de facto* developing 'reciprocal disclosure duties', which the Rome Statute actually tried to avoid. If the defence, however, chooses to remain silent, Rule 79 RPE ICC should have no scope of application.

IV. Exceptions and limitations to disclosure

Disclosure must be considered the general rule, non-disclosure the exception.[230] Any non-disclosure of evidence must thus be based on a specific ground.[231]

1. *The* ad hoc *Tribunals*

Rule 66 (A) mentions Rules 69 and 53 RPE ICTY as inherent limits: Rule 69 is concerned with the protection of victims and witnesses and its impact on disclosure. The protection of victims and witnesses is generally one crucial aspect of disclosure limitation, and was, in fact, one of the main arguments against disclosure in legal history. The provision determines that in exceptional circumstances the competent Chamber (or judge) may order the non-disclosure of the identity of a victim or witness who may be in danger or at risk. This implies the non-disclosure of the witness statements from that person, at least as long as the witness statement allows drawing conclusions as to the identity of the witness.

[229] ICC *Prosecutor v Lubanga*, TC I, ICC 01/04-01/06-1235, 20 March 2008, Decision on Defence Disclosure, paras 33–5.

[230] This principle has been endorsed by the ICC Judges, *see* ICC *Prosecutor v Lubanga*, AC, ICC-01/04-01/06-568, 13 October 2006, Judgment on the Prosecutor's Appeal against the Decision of Pre-Trial Chamber I entitled 'Decision Establishing General Principles Governing Applications to Restrict Disclosure pursuant to Rule 81 (2) and (4) of the Rules of Procedure and Evidence', para 39; ICC *Prosecutor v Katanga*, AC, ICC-01/04-01/07-475 (OA), 13 May 2008, Judgment on the Appeal of the Prosecutor against the Decision of Pre-Trial Chamber I entitled 'First Decision on the Prosecution Request for Authorisation to Redact Witness Statements', para 70.

[231] *See* also B Kuschnik, 'International Criminal Due Process in the Making: New Tendencies in the Law on Non-Disclosure in the Proceedings of the ICC', 9 *ICLR* (2009) 157, 166.

The case of Rule 53 RPE ICTY is slightly different. Systematically, Rule 53 is still closely connected with the indictment—it is contained in Part 5, Section 1 of the Rules ('Indictments'), after Rule 52, which states that indictments, in principle, are public documents. This fact can be explained by the historical development of the provision, which original referred to 'indictments' only. Now, referring to *any* document, it is from a systematic or contextual viewpoint a little 'out of place'. The same holds true for the specific link between Rule 66 (A) and Rule 53 RPE ICTY: basically the two provisions do not have much to do with each other, since Rule 53 deals with disclosure to the public, whereas Rule 66 deals with disclosure to the defence. The identification of a witness, for instance, is a fundamental necessity for the preparation of the defence, in particular, for the preparation of cross-examination. On the other hand, the public disclosure of documents which allow the identification of a witness might put that witness into danger and does not advance the defence of the accused.[232] Thus, measures according to Rule 53 may well go hand in hand with Rule 66 RPE ICTY.

Under the current wording of Rule 66 (C) RPE ICTY, the prosecution's disclosure obligations according to Rule 66 (A) are subject to secrecy and security reservations pursuant to Rule 66 (C). This is true for all three of the tribunals, ICTY, ICTR, and SCSL.

Limits to disclosure are also contained in Rule 70 RPE ICTY/ICTR/SCSL. Rule 70 (A) pertains to internal documents prepared by the party, its assistants, or representatives. Rule 70 (B)-(E) is about confidential information given to the Prosecutor, but is by virtue of Rule 70 (F) applicable also to the defence upon order by the Chamber. However, this provision is restricted to material which is used to generate new evidence.[233] The rule was invoked in the case of the testimony of US General Wesley Clark, who had been the Commander of the NATO forces during the air campaign against Yugoslavia in 1999.[234]

Another limit to disclosure, which, of course, only applies to defence disclosure, is established by the lawyer-client privilege as laid down in Rule 97 RPE ICTY/ICTR/

[232] ICTY *Prosecutor v Milošević*, TC, IT-02-54, 19 February 2002, Decision on Prosecution Motion for Provisional Protective Measures, para 32; endorsed in ICTY *Prosecutor v Ojdanić*, TC, IT-99-37-PT, 7 June 2002, Decision on Prosecution's Motion for Order of Non-disclosure to Public of Supporting Materials Disclosed Pursuant to Rule 66 (A) (i), para 3.

[233] ICTY *Prosecutor v Blaškić*, TC I, IT-95-14-T, 11 November 1997, Decision of Trial Chamber I on the Prosecutor's Motion for Video Deposition and Protective Measures, para 10.

[234] ICTY *Prosecutor v Milošević*, TC, IT-02-54-T, 30 October 2003, Confidential Decision on Prosecution's Application for a Witness Pursuant to Rule 70 (B); and ICTY *Prosecutor v Milutinović et al.*, TC, IT-05-87-T, 16 February 2007, Second Decision on Prosecution Motion for Leave to Amend its Rule 65*ter* Witness List to Add Wesley Clark, para 26; *see* for references and on the issue of Rule 70 in the trials against *Milošević* and *Milutinović* in detail E O'Sullivan and D Montgomery, 'The Erosion of the Right to Confrontation under the Cloak of Fairness at the ICTY', 8 *JICJ* (2010) 528 *et subs.*

SCSL. Such a privilege is recognized as a general principle of international law.[235] These privileges will be discussed later in the context of the law of evidence.[236]

2. *The ICC*

The applicable provisions of the ICC know the same basic categories of exceptions and limitations to disclosure as the *ad hoc* Tribunals; that is, internal documents, witness protection, and state security interests. Most of them are contained in Rule 81 RPE ICC, which refers to different provisions of the Rome Statute; also, there is the highly important exception to disclosure of confidential material according to Rule 54 (3) (e), to which Rule 82 RPE ICC refers. Finally, privileged communication according to Rule 73 RPE ICC represents an exception to disclosure which is not contained in Section II ('Disclosure') of Chapter 4 of the Rules, but in Section 1 ('Evidence').

(1) Rule 81 (1) RPE ICC refers to internal documents. The provision is modelled after Rule 70 (A) RPE ICTY. The provision was discussed in connection with the demand of some of the ICC Chambers that the OTP produce a 'table of incriminating evidence' or an 'in-depth analysis chart'.[237] Such a document has been held not to constitute an internal paper covered by Rule 81 (1) RPE ICC:

> it is based on material that has been filed as part of the prosecution's disclosure obligations; furthermore, it is a necessary and proportionate procedural tool that assists in revealing the prosecution's case against the accused, notwithstanding the resources that will be necessary for its completion.[238]

Other than that, the Prosecution apparently also tried to persuade the Court that the so-called pre-assessment interviews conducted before an actual witness interrogation were internal documents according to Rule 81 (1) RPE ICC; this was, rightly, denied by Trial Chamber III.[239]

(2) Rule 81 (2) RPE ICC pertains to prejudice of ongoing investigations which could be warranted by disclosing sensitive material. Rule 81 (2) clearly origi-

---

[235] *See* M Benzing, *Das Beweisrecht vor internationalen Gerichten und Schiedsgerichten in zwischenstaatlichen Streitigkeiten* (Springer 2010) 426 *et subs.* with further references.

[236] *See* following, Chapter 8, p 463 *et subs.*

[237] *See* ICC *Prosecutor v Katanga and Chui*, OTP, ICC-01/04-01/07-982, 23 March 2009, Prosecution's Application for Leave to Appeal the 'Order Concerning the Presentation of Incriminating Evidence and the E-Court Protocol', para 25; *Prosecutor v Bemba*, OTP, ICC-01/05-01/08-656, 15 December 2009, Prosecution's Submissions on the Trial Chamber's 8 December 2009 Oral Order Requesting Updating of the In-Depth-Analysis Chart, para 9. Indeed, this is a good example of the intertwinement of disclosure and truth-finding.

[238] ICC *Prosecutor v Bemba*, TC III, ICC-01/05-01/08-682, 29 January 2010, Decision on the 'Prosecution's Submissions on the Trial Chamber's 8 December 2009 Oral Order Requesting Updating of the In-Depth-Analysis Chart', para 26.

[239] ICC *Prosecutor v Bemba*, TC III, ICC-01/05-01/08-750-Conf, 9 April 2010, Public Redacted Version of 'Decision on the Defence Request for Disclosure of Pre-interview Assessments and the Consequences of Non-disclosure', para 35.

nates from Rule 66 (C) RPE ICTY. Obviously, Rule 81 (2) RPE ICC can be a very powerful tool in the hands of the Prosecutor for the purposes of reaching non-disclosure. Crucial issues in the practice of the ICC appear to be the general capability of Rule 81 (2) RPE ICC to provide for redactions in material which must be otherwise disclosed. Most of the judges of the ICC agree on the fact that Rule 81 (2) RPE ICC provides a legal basis for redactions in material which must be disclosed, even though the provision does not explicitly state so. The judges thus do not necessarily determine, as the wording of Rule 81 (2) RPE ICC suggests, *whether* certain material must be disclosed, but rather *how much of it*.[240]

The test as to whether and to what extent redactions can be granted according to Rule 81 (2) RPE ICC applied by the ICC Appeals Chamber is one of proportionality; the Chamber emphasizes that the defence must be given the right to be heard, and that redactions must be strictly necessary to prevent possible prejudice of further or ongoing investigations.[241] The Appeals Chamber refuses to take a definitive position, and rather retains a case-by-case approach.

(3) Rule 81 (3) and (4) RPE ICC deal with the confidentiality provisions of the Rome Statute in Arts 54 (3) (f),[242] 57 (functions and powers of the Pre-Trial Chamber), 64 (functions and powers of the Trial Chamber), 72 (national security issues), and 93 (confidentiality issues arising with the cooperation of states), and the safety requirements for victims and witnesses according to Art. 68 ICCSt. Sub-rule (3) relates to protective measures, which are already in place; sub-rule (4), in turn, refers to protective measures which are about to be taken. In the jurisprudence of the ICC, sub-rule (4) has been applied in a large number of instances, whereas it appears that sub-rule (3) has not gained much significance. The Appeals

[240] *See* only *Prosecutor v Lubanga*, ICC-01/04-01/06-773 (OA 5), Judgment on the Appeal of Mr Thomas Lubanga Dyilo against the Decision of Pre-Trial Chamber I entitled 'First Decision on the Prosecution Requests and Amended Requests for Redactions under Rule 81' as well as ICC-01/04-01/06-774 (OA 6) Judgment on the Appeal of Mr Thomas Lubanga Dyilo against the Decision of Pre-Trial Chamber I entitled 'Second Decision on the Prosecution Requests and Amended Requests for Redactions under Rule 81', Appeals Chamber, both dated 14 December 2006; as well as ICC *Prosecutor v Katanga*, AC, ICC-01/04-01/07-475 (OA), 13 May 2008, Judgment on the Appeal of the Prosecutor against the Decision of Pre-Trial Chamber I entitled 'First Decision on the Prosecution Request for Authorisation to Redact Witness Statements', and Judgment on the Appeal of Mr Germain Katanga against the Decision of Pre-Trial Chamber I entitled 'First Decision on the Prosecution Request for Authorisation to Redact Witness Statements', Appeals Chamber, both dated 13 May 2008.

[241] ICC *Prosecutor v Katanga*, AC, ICC-01/04-01/07-475 (OA), 13 May 2008, Judgment on the Appeal of the Prosecutor against the Decision of Pre-Trial Chamber I entitled 'First Decision on the Prosecution Request for Authorisation to Redact Witness Statements', paras 68–73. *See* B Kuschnik, 'International Criminal Due Process in the Making: New Tendencies in the Law on Non-Disclosure in the Proceedings of the ICC', 9 *ICLR* (2009) 157, 168 *et subs*.

[242] Art. 54 (3) (e) ICCSt information is covered by Rule 82 RPE ICC.

Chamber maintains that the test to be applied to Rule 81 (4) is the same as for Rule 81 (2).[243] Different categories of persons have appeared in need to protection, including identity protection of prosecution staff,[244] 'potential' prosecution witnesses,[245] persons who have been victimized but in a different context than the case at hand and who do not take part in the proceedings as participating victims,[246] or 'innocent third parties'.[247] Once more, the Appeals Chamber proves its flexible approach to restrictions on disclosure.[248] In any case, and in contrast to the *ad hoc* Tribunals, sub-rule (4) makes clear that non-disclosure of the identity of witnesses *during* trial is impossible.

(4) Rule 81 (5) and (6) RPE ICC give some guidance as regards the practical application of Art. 68 (5) ICCSt, the non-disclosure due to witness protection. Sub-rule (5) pertains to prosecution witnesses whereas sub-rule (6) is concerned with the same protection for defence witnesses. Art. 68 (5) ICCSt specifically applies to any point in time 'prior to the commencement of the trial', thus chiefly the confirmation hearing, and basically enables the Prosecutor to submit summaries of evidence instead of the evidence itself; the provision appears to be connected with Art. 61 (5) ICCSt, which also allows the Prosecutor to rely on documentary or summary evidence at the confirmation hearing. The fact that, in turn, Rule 81 (5) RPE ICC refers to both the confirmation hearing and the trial, may be regarded as superfluous, since from Art. 68 (5) ICCSt we can conclude *e contrario* that in any case, material can be retained only until the commencement of the trial. It appears possible that *adequate* disclosure according to Rule 81 (5) RPE ICC entails that disclosure must actually take place at a point in time *sufficiently* before the trial.

(5) Rule 82 refers to the confidentiality agreements pursuant to Art. 54 (3) (e) ICCSt as the specific disclosure rule. The provision has caused considerable controversy up to now, as the Prosecutor made rather excessive use of confidentiality

[243] ICC *Prosecutor v Katanga*, AC, ICC-01/04-01/07-475 (OA), 13 May 2008, Judgment on the Appeal of the Prosecutor against the Decision of Pre-Trial Chamber I entitled 'First Decision on the Prosecution Request for Authorisation to Redact Witness Statements', para 59.

[244] Ibid, para 89 *et subs.*

[245] Ibid, para 45 *et subs.* The Appeals Chamber based its decision in this regard (also) on Rule 81 (2); in any case, as mentioned, it applies the same test under sub-rule (2) and sub-rule (4).

[246] ICC *Prosecutor v Katanga and Chui*, AC, ICC-01/04-01/07-521 (OA 5), 27 May 2008, Judgment on the Appeal of Mr Mathieu Ngudjolo against the Decision of Pre-Trial Chamber I entitled 'Decision on the Prosecution Request for Authorisation to Redact Statements of Witnesses 4 and 9', para 34.

[247] ICC *Prosecutor v Katanga*, AC, ICC-01/04-01/07-475 (OA), 13 May 2008, Judgment on the Appeal of the Prosecutor against the Decision of Pre-Trial Chamber I entitled 'First Decision on the Prosecution Request for Authorisation to Redact Witness Statements', para 43 *et subs.*

[248] *See* for more, once again, B Kuschnik, 'International Criminal Due Process in the Making: New Tendencies in the Law on Non-Disclosure in the Proceedings of the ICC', 9 *ICLR* (2009) 157, 171 *et subs.*

agreements with international organizations in the situation of the DRC. It must be kept in mind that Art. 54 (3) (e) ICCSt does not allow the witholding of material which the Prosecutor intends to rely on but only such material with which the Prosecutor intends to generate new evidence (so-called 'lead'or 'springboard' evidence).[249] The Prosecutor had, as a matter of standard procedure, acquired large amounts of evidence, among which there were many documents containing exculpatory evidence. Since the confidentiality agreements also forbade the Prosecutor to disclose these documents to the Trial Chamber, the latter was unable to exercise its functions under, among other provisions, Art. 67 (2) ICCSt. Finally, after lengthy to-ing and fro-ing regarding whether or not the Prosecutor would get the consent of the information providers to disclose the evidence, Trial Chamber I stayed the proceedings, grounded on the accused's right to a fair trial, and on the fact that the relevant evidence was kept secret from the Chamber itself as well.[250] The decision was, as far as the latter reasoning is concerned, upheld by the ICC Appeals Chamber,[251] and has been extensively analysed by legal scholars.[252]

The argument focuses mainly on the question of whether one needs to differentiate between *obtaining* the information and *how to use* it. The Prosecutor interpreted Art. 54 (3) (e) ICCSt to refer not to the *kind* of evidence, but to the *use* of it. Reading Art. 54 (3) (e) in conjunction with Art. 93 (8)(b) ICCSt and Rule 82 (1) RPE ICC, it held that often, at the moment of the reception of the evidence, the prosecution will not know exactly whether the material itself has evidentiary value or will only provide lead evidence. The Prosecutor was, according to his interpretation, thus free to receive any kind of material, but restricted regarding the use of it.[253]

[249] ICC *Prosecutor v Lubanga*, TC I, ICC-01/04-01/06-1401, 13 June 2008, Decision on the Consequences of Non-disclosure of Exculpatory Materials Covered by Art. 54 (3) (e) Agreements and the Application to Stay the Prosecution of the Accused, Together with Certain Other Issues Raised at the Status Conference on 10 June 2008, para 71 *et subs.*

[250] Ibid, para 92 *et subs.*

[251] ICC *Prosecutor v Lubanga*, AC, ICC-01/04-01/06-1486 (OA 13), 21 October 2008, Judgment on the Appeal of the Prosecutor against the Decision of Trial Chamber I entitled 'Decision on the Consequences of Non-disclosure of Exculpatory Materials Covered by Article 54(3)(e) Agreements and the Application to Stay the Prosecution of the Accused, Together with Certain Other Issues Raised at the Status Conference on 10 June 2008'.

[252] *See* eg, K Ambos, 'Confidential Investigations (Article 54(3)(e) ICC Statute) vs. Disclosure Obligations', 12 *New Criminal Law Review* (2009) 543; S Swoboda, 'The ICC Disclosure Regime', 19 *CLF* (2008) 449; B Kuschnik, 'International Criminal Due Process in the Making: New Tendencies in the Law on Non-Disclosure in the Proceedings of the ICC', 9 *ICLR* (2009) 157; A Whiting, 'Lead Evidence and Discovery Before the International Criminal Court: The Lubanga Case', 14 *UCLA Journal of International Law and Foreign Affairs* (2009) 207.

[253] ICC *Prosecutor v Lubanga*, ICC-01/04-01/06-1446-Anx1 (OA 13), 24 July 2008, Prosecution's Document in Support of Appeal against Decision to Stay Proceedings, para 6 *et subs.*

The Appeals Chamber apparently did not want to follow the interpretation of the Trial Chamber that Art. 54 (3) (e) ICCSt may only be invoked to obtain lead evidence, and resorted to the fundamental notion that the Chamber must have the opportunity to rule on the issue, and that this may not be prevented by confidentiality agreements.[254]

The consequences, however, are impressively shown by the course of the events in the *Lubanga* case. Taken seriously, this interpretation makes Art. 54 (3) (e) dysfunctional in its application; the practical arguments brought forward by the Prosecutor are certainly right. The only solution appears to be more or less along the lines of the decision of the Appeals Chamber: the Prosecutor must use Art. 54 (3) (e) ICCSt cautiously, and at all times ensure that the confidentiality agreements do not cover the Chamber dealing with the matter, so that it can exercise its controlling functions, particularly as far as Art. 67 (2) ICCSt is concerned.

In any case, the warning shot of Trial Chamber I did not go unheard; the providers of the confidential information were ultimately persuaded to consent to the disclosure of the material to the Chamber; and the Prosecutor has since become more cautious.[255]

(6) Rule 73 pertains to privileged communication and information which form part of the relationships between clients and lawyers and other groups of persons where communication can reasonably be expected to be confidential. In principle, the Rome Statute recognizes these privileges according to Art. 69 (5) ICCSt, as do most national jurisdictions. The substance of the norm will be discussed as a question of the law of evidence.[256]

---

[254] ICC *Prosecutor v Lubanga*, AC, ICC-01/04-01/06-1486 (OA 13), 21 October 2008, Judgment on the Appeal of the Prosecutor against the Decision of Trial Chamber I entitled 'Decision on the Consequences of Non-disclosure of Exculpatory Materials Covered by Article 54 (3) (e) Agreements and the Application to Stay the Prosecution of the Accused, Together with Certain Other Issues Raised at the Status Conference on 10 June 2008'.

[255] Compare ICC *Prosecutor v Bemba*, ICC Case No. 01/05-01/08, Status Conference 7 October 2009, Transcript, ICC-01/05-01/08-T-14-ENG ET WT 07-10–2009, p 21, l. 16–p 22, l. 1:

'PRESIDING JUDGE FULFORD:... Article 54(3)(e), an article with [sic] Judge Odio Benito and myself and Judge Blattmann will never forget. Now have all of the issues on Article 54 (3) (e) now been resolved? We are aware that there have been four reports provided to the Chamber, the last of which was on 12 November 2008, in which at paragraph 10 it was suggested that all of the relevant information providers had consented to lift the redactions on all the relevant material. Now, that therefore seems to make Article 54 (3) (e) a non-issue, but I wish to make sure that that is truly the position.

MS. KNEUER: Your Honour, that reflects the situation correctly. All items were disclosed and no further items under Article 54 (3) (e) were collected.

PRESIDING JUDGE FULFORD: That demonstrates that no two trials are the same, Ms Kneuer.'

[256] *See* following, p 506.

V. Disclosure and the bench

The influence of courts within the disclosure proceedings is growing both at the national and the international level. A modern concept of disclosure of evidence seems to attribute a key factor to the judges. A bench, who is in the end the organ that will convict or acquit,[257] has a strong tendency to involve itself in the disclosure process and guarantee a high level of information to the judges regarding the material which is disclosed between the parties. Before looking at the considerable amount of jurisprudence which has already been produced by the ICC in this regard, we will consider the relevant development at the *ad hoc* Tribunals.

1. Ad hoc *Tribunals*

The judges of the tribunals recognized that disclosure, not only between the parties but also the communication of evidence to the court itself, has clear advantages as regards trial management and judicial economy. Some important reforms to this end came, like Rule 94*bis*, in the summer of 1998.[258] The most significant reforms were the introduction of the Pre-Trial Judge (Rule 65*ter* RPE-ICTY) as well as the Pre-Trial and Pre-Defence Conferences (Rules 73*bis* and *ter*) RPE-ICTY/R.

The Pre-Trial Judge is in charge of most of the issues that arise between the parties during the pre-trial phase, among them with disclosure according to Rules 66 and 67 RPE ICTY.[259] Other than that, Rules 65*ter* and 73*bis* and *ter* are quite closely related to 'disclosure to the Chamber', or, for that matter, communication of information to the Chamber before the trial.

Rule 73*bis* RPE ICTR as well as Rule 65*ter* (E) in conjunction with Rule 73*bis* RPE ICTY basically require the Prosecutor to lay out his or her case in considerable detail, including witness lists, and summaries of the facts on which they will testify. The material must also be supplied to the defence. The latter, in turn, according to Rule 65*ter* (F) RPE ICTY, must answer, laying out the nature of the defence, and regarding which matters it takes issue with the Prosecutor and in what way. It is, according to Rule 63*ter* (L) RPE ICTY, collected by the Pre-Trial Judge in a file, which is then transmitted to the Trial Chamber. The same, according to Rule 73*ter* RPE ICTR, and Rule 63*ter* (G) in conjunction with Rule 73*ter* RPE ICTY, happens after the prosecution case, when the defence, in the so-called defence

---

[257] This was called the 'judging element' before, *see* p 55 *et subs*.

[258] ICTR: 8 June 1998, ICTY: 10 July 1998 (13th revision). *See* regarding the efforts to enhance the judicial economy of the Tribunals also Report of the Expert Group to Conduct a Review of the Effective Operation and Functioning of the International Tribunal for the Former Yugoslavia and the International Criminal Tribunal for Rwanda, UN Doc. A/541634, 22 November 1999, as well as the critical remarks of D Mundis, 'Improving the Operation and Functioning of the International Criminal Tribunals,' 94 *AJIL* (2000) 759–773.

[259] Rule 65*ter* (C) RPE ICTY as of rev. 44: 'The pre-trial Judge shall be entrusted with all of the pre-trial functions set forth in Rule 66, 67, Rule 73*bis* and Rule 73*ter*, and with all or part of the functions set forth in Rule 73.'

conference, must provide an outline of its case, again including a list of witnesses and summaries of the facts on which they will testify.

Another rather elegant way to unfold material has been developed predominantly by the ICTR judges on the basis of Rules 54 and 98 RPE ICTY/ICTR. While Rule 54 contains the general power of the competent Trial Chamber to make decisions concerning the proceedings as necessary, Rule 98 RPE ICTY/ICTR[260] provides for the Chamber to request the production of additional evidence from the parties. It thus implies the specific empowerment of the Trial Chamber to extend the evidence for the trial on its own accord. While this power is somewhat unusual in Anglo-American jurisdictions, it has always been a 'feature' of international procedural frameworks and is an indispensable right for any judge working in a Romano-Germanic procedural system, as it is a means of truth-finding.[261]

In the *Akayesu* case, the Trial Chamber ordered the prosecution to 'submit all available written witness statements to the Chamber in the case and that all such statements to which reference had been made by either the Prosecutor or the defence shall be admitted as evidence and form part of the record.'[262]

This was the starting point of a practice by which the ICTR Trial Chambers regularly rely on Rule 98—both *proprio motu* and upon request of the defence.[263]

This practice is a good example of the ever-growing tendency of involvement of the bench in the disclosure proceedings and indeed proves the close connection between disclosure and truth-finding. The Court makes use of a rule which contextually has not got anything to do with disclosure in order to, on the one hand, make information available to a party of the proceedings, while itself taking advantage of this information for truth-finding purposes on the other. In fact, some of these decisions even literally refer to 'disclosure according to Rule 98'.[264]

2. ICC

(1) Pre-confirmation disclosure

Art. 61 (3) ICCSt together with Rule 121 RPE ICC attach an influential position to the Pre-Trial Chamber regarding disclosure issues in the pre-confirmation stage.

260 As to the differences of these two provision *see*: Khan/Buisman/Gosnell/*Gibson/Lusiaá-Berdou* 306, at note 185.

261 *See* ICTY *Prosecutor v Blaškić*, TC I, IT-95-14, 25 March 1999, Decision of Trial Chamber I in Respect of the Appearance of General Enver Hadžihasanović: 'in order to ascertain the truth in respect of the crimes of which the accused has been charged'; *see* also Arts 17 (b), (c) and 24 (f) IMTSt, Art. 11 (a) to (c) IMTFESt; Art. 64 (6) (b) and (c) ICCSt, Rule 140 (2) (b) RPE ICC; §§ 244 (2), 238 (1) StPO (German Code of Criminal Procedure).

262 ICTR *Prosecutor v Akayesu*, TC I, ICTR-96-4-T, 28 January 1997, Decision by the Tribunal on its Request to the Prosecutor to Submit the Written Witness Statements.

263 *See* Khan/Buisman/Gosnell/*Gibson/Lusiaá-Berdou* 306, 345 *et subs*. with further references.

264 *See* eg, ICTR *Prosecutor v Karera*, TC, ICTR-01-74-T, 1 September 2006, Decision on the Defence Motion for Additional Disclosure (Rule 98).

Yet the ICC Pre-Trial Chambers are somewhat undecided how to understand these provisions properly.

Whereas the Single Judge of Pre-Trial Chamber I adopted a restricted view saying that the Chamber only need to know evidence which the parties intend to rely on at the confirmation hearing and that disclosure to the Chamber would mainly take place via the record envisaged by Rule 121 (10) RPE ICC.[265] Pre-Trial Chamber III opines that the reference to 'all evidence' in Rule 121(2)(c) RPE ICC implies that communication to the Chamber comprises all the evidence disclosed between the parties and that it is not limited to the evidence which the parties intend to rely on or to present at the confirmation hearing.[266] Pre-Trial Chamber III thus attributes even to pre-confirmation disclosure a truth-finding aspect next to the trial management and human rights protection aspect.[267] Furthermore the Chamber requested that the Prosecutor file an 'in-depth analysis chart',[268] concerning each and every piece of evidence communicated to the Chamber, stating what it is, whether it is incriminating, (potentially) exculpatory or mixed, and in what way it is relevant to the case and the charges; that is, which element of crime is to be proved by it.[269]

Meanwhile, the practice of demanding an in-depth analysis chart has been taken over in the trial proceedings in the *Katanga* case using the term 'table of incriminating evidence',[270] and, as already mentioned regarding the question whether the

---

[265] ICC *Prosecutor v Lubanga*, PTC I (Single Judge), ICC-01/04-01/06-102, 15 May 2006, Decision on the Final System of Disclosure and the Establishment of a Timetable, para 41–3, 64. This jurisprudence was confirmed in *Prosecutor v Abu Garda*, PTC I, ICC-2/05-02/09-35, 15 July 2009, Second Decision on Issues Relating to Disclosure, Pre-Trial Chamber I, and attached Partly Dissenting Opinion of Judge Cuno Tarfusser, ibid, p 21 *et subs.*, who favours the approach of Pre-Trial Chamber III in *Bemba*.

[266] ICC *Prosecutor v Bemba*, PTC III, ICC-01/05-01/08-55, 31 July 2008, Decision on the Evidence Disclosure System and Setting a Timetable for Disclosure Between the Parties, paras 10, 43.

[267] Ibid, para 15.

[268] Similar to the analysis chart briefly mentioned in the context of Rule 81 (1), *see* p 363.

[269] ICC *Prosecutor v Bemba*, PTC III, ICC-01/05-01/08-55, 31 July 2008, Decision on the Evidence Disclosure System and Setting a Timetable for Disclosure Between the Parties, para 64 *et subs*, *see* in this regard also the Annex to the decision: 'Case "The Prosecutor v. Jean-Pierre Bemba Gombo", Technical protocol ("e-Court Protocol") for the Provision of Evidence, Material and Witness Information in Electronic Form for the Confirmation of Charges', ICC-01/05-01/08-55-Anx 31-07-2008.

[270] *See* ICC *Prosecutor v Katanga and Chui*, TC II, ICC-01/04-01/07-1337, 13 March 2009, Order concerning the Presentation of Incriminating Evidence and the E-Court Protocol, para 11: 'In order to better assist the Chamber and to enable each Defence Counsel to prepare their case effectively, the Prosecution is hereby ordered to submit an analytical table of all the evidence it intends to use during the trial. The table shall be based on the charges confirmed and follow the structure of the Elements of crimes. An example is attached in Annex A to this decision. This table will be referred to as the "Table of Incriminating Evidence".'

in-depth analysis chart falls into Rule 81 (1) RPE ICC, in the trial proceedings against *Bemba* as well.[271]

(2) Pre-trial disclosure

The question whether the Trial Chamber should get to see any evidence before the start of the trial has been left unanswered by the drafters of the Statute and the Rules. Whereas Rule 121 (10) RPE ICC obliged the Registrar to maintain a full record of the proceedings before the Pre-Trial Chamber, this record is being transmitted to the Trial Chamber by virtue of Rule 131 RPE ICC. However, the Chamber itself is not mentioned amongst those who can consult the record nor does any other provision clarify the role of the record at trial, another piece of 'constructive ambiguity' within the procedural regime of the ICC.[272]

The Trial Chambers have more or less continued the practice of the Pre-Trial Chambers. Thus the Trial Chamber in the *Katanga* case noted that it has access to the record of the proceedings before the Pre-Trial Chamber and requested, as has been mentioned before, the Prosecutor to produce a 'table of incriminating evidence' structured by the elements of crimes and file all the evidence referred to in the table with the Registry.[273]

As seen above, the *Bemba* Pre-Trial Chamber originally had taken the most extensive view as to what should be communicated to the Chamber, and ordered that *all* evidence disclosed should be filed with the Registry. Additionally, the Prosecutor was to provide an in-depth analysis chart, at first, regarding all evidence, including exculpatory evidence and Rule 77 material. This, however, later changed in that the in-depth analysis chart was only to refer to incriminating evidence.[274] It is unclear how this change of mind came about. As with the above-mentioned cases of *Lubanga* and *Katanga*, this practice apparently continued after the confirmation of the charges, meaning that the order once put in place by the Pre-Trial Chamber, and the 'work instructions' given to the Registry and the parties, just went on, absent any new order of the Trial Chamber which was now in charge of the matter. This means that evidence apart from incriminating evidence would be disclosed *inter partes* only, with

[271] ICC *Prosecutor v Bemba*, TC III, ICC-01/05-01/08-682, 29 January 2010, Decision on the 'Prosecution's Submissions on the Trial Chamber's 8 December 2009 Oral Order Requesting Updating of the In-Depth Analysis Chart'.

[272] H Brady, 'Setting the Record Straight: A Short Note on Disclosure and "the Record of the Proceedings",' in: H Fischer, C Kreß, and S Lüder (eds), *International and National Prosecution of Crimes Under International Law: Current Developments* (Berlin Verlag 2001) 261, 272.

[273] ICC *Prosecutor v Katanga and Chui*, TC II, ICC-01/04-01/07-1337, 13 March 2009, Order Concerning the Presentation of Incriminating Evidence and the E-Court Protocol, paras 24 and 25.

[274] ICC *Prosecutor v Bemba*, PTC III, ICC 01/05-01/08-232, 10 November 2008, Decision on the Submission of an Updated, Consolidated Version of the In-depth Analysis Chart of Incriminatory Evidence, para 8.

the Chamber, however, being notified of the transaction between the parties.[275] The Trial Chambers are thus, in any case, informed of at least the incriminating evidence beforehand.

VI. Disclosure and victims

The importance of the victims in the Rome Statute has already been discussed.[276] As victims have, under certain circumstances, the right to participate in the proceedings, it does not surprise that they also take part in the disclosure process between the parties.

As far as the confirmation proceedings are concerned, we note that Rule 121 (10) RPE ICC indeed confers upon the victims the right to consult the record of the proceedings, which, as we have seen, contains at least the evidence on which the parties intend to rely at the confirmation hearing. For the trial proceedings, Rule 131 confers the same right upon the victims. Thus we can speak of 'disclosure to the victims' as soon as victims get to see the evidence which is disclosed between the parties.

In the relevant jurisprudence of the ICC, Trial Chamber I stated that generally the victims should have access only to the public filings contained in the record,[277] but that if their personal interests are related to specific confidential material contained in the record and this material is relevant to their participation, 'consideration shall be given to providing this information to the relevant victim or victims, so long as it will not breach other protective measures that need to remain in place.'[278]

It is quite clear that the victims should not be able to inspect material in the possession or control of the defence. However, to grant the victims access to material in possession of the Prosecutor and to lift the confidentiality of certain material does not appear necessary.

The far-reaching participation rights granted to victims before the ICC have led to the question whether the participating victims should also be under an obligation to disclose (exculpatory) material to the accused on fairness grounds.[279]

To be sure, the procedural framework of the ICC does not foresee such a duty, which is also the main reason why the Chambers of the Court have answered

[275] *See* ICC *Prosecutor v Bemba*, ICC Case No. 01/05-01/08, Status Conference Transcript, 7 October 2009, p 17, lines 10–22.

[276] *See* p 169 *et subs.*

[277] *See* also O Abo Youssef, *Die Stellung des Opfers im Völkerstrafrecht* (Schulthess 2008) 115.

[278] ICC *Prosecutor v Lubanga*, TC I, ICC-01/04-01/06-1119, 18 January 2008, Decision on Victims' Participation, para 106.

[279] *See* ICC *Prosecutor v Katanga and Chui*, Defence, ICC-01/04-01/07-1618, 10 November 2009, Defence for Germain Katanga's Additional Observations on Victims' Participation and Scope Thereof, para 3.

this question in the negative. The Trial Chamber in *Katanga and Ngudjolo Chui* pointed out that there can be no duty of the victims to disclose evidence, because there is no specific right for them to present evidence, either.[280]

Whether the victims are obliged to disclose exculpatory evidence in their possession has been an issue before the Appeals Chamber. Such a claim must be denied. The victim is certainly not bound to objectivity. This task rests with the Prosecutor by virtue of Art. 54 (1) (a) ICCSt.[281]

A final question concerning victims could be raised in the sense of whether the identity of participating victims must be revealed to the accused. Considering the strong position of the victims, a 'faceless' second prosecutor must be avoided under all circumstances. The weighing of safety and security of victims and their right to participate on the one hand and the fundamental guarantee of a fair trial for the accused on the other, however, has not been brought to a clear conclusion. Trial Chamber I is inclined to decide on a case-by-case basis.[282] The only absolute parameter according to Trial Chamber I is that the Chamber must always know the victim's true identity. In our view this is not enough. Anonymous allegations are inherently unfair.[283]

VII. Electronic disclosure

Compared to the 1940s and the administration of disclosure in Nuremberg via hardcopies, in recent years IT solutions have been developed to handle the vast amount of material to be disclosed. The modern courtroom is dominated by computers, and communication is organized through electronic databases.[284] At the *ad hoc* Tribunals the Prosecutor is to fulfil his or her disclosure obligations in an electronically searchable form by virtue of Rule 68 (ii) RPE ICTY and Rule 68 (B) RPE ICTR. The Prosecutor gives to the defence access to the electronic database which is called the 'Electronic Disclosure Suite' (EDS). Yet to transform the complex disclosure system into access modalities has proven difficult and in a way hard to control.[285] Another issue, which gave rise to criticism, is the undifferentiated use between incriminating and exculpatory material. The Appeals Chamber ruled that

280 ICC *Prosecutor v Katanga and Chui*, TC II, ICC-01/04-01/07-1788, 22 January 2010, Decision on the Modalities of Victim Participation at Trial, para 105.

281 ICC *Prosecutor v Katanga and Chui*, AC, ICC-01/04-01/07-2288 (OA 11), 16 July 2010, Judgment on the Appeal of Mr Katanga Against the Decision of Trial Chamber II of 22 January 2010 entitled 'Decision on the Modalities of Victim Participation at Trial', paras 48, 81, and 85.

282 ICC *Prosecutor v Lubanga*, TC I, ICC-01/04-01/06-1119, 18 January 2008, Decision on Victims' Participation, para 131.

283 *See* also the critical remarks in C Safferling, 'The Role of the Victim in the Criminal Process: A Paradigm Shift in National German and International Law?' 11 *ICLR* (2011) 183, 213.

284 *See* also Boas/Bischoff/Reid/Taylor, *ICL III*, 233.

285 *See* the critical remarks by one defence lawyer, M Karnavas, 'Gathering Evidence in International Criminal Trials—The View of the Defence Lawyer', in: M Bohlander (ed), *International Criminal Justice: A Critical Analysis of Institutions and Procedures* (Cameron May 2007) 75, 100.

the Prosecutor cannot fulfil his or her obligation under Rule 68 to disclose exculpatory material simply by giving the defence access to the entire evidence collection in a searchable format and leave it up to the defence counsel to analyse the material. The Prosecutor must analyse the exculpatory value of the material himself and notify the defence of its existence.[286]

At the ICC, 'Ringtail' software for trial management is in use which also provides for an electronic disclosure system. Apparently until now the system did not cause major difficulties, as the parties have praised it as being the 'most convenient' format for disclosure.[287]

VIII. Conclusion

Disclosure is one of the most intriguing, complex, and time-consuming procedural issues in international criminal procedure. The right to be informed of the evidence supporting the allegations and the right to have adequate time and facilities assemble the human rights basis of disclosure. Yet the modern concept of disclosure cannot be understood without taking into due account its procedural management aspect. At the same time, disclosure also serves the finding of the truth, which after all is one of the main rationales of criminal procedure.

The IMT has been an important starting point regarding disclosure, even though from a modern perspective, the trial would hardly be considered fair. On the other hand, in the context of its time as American Chief Prosecutor Robert Jackson said, the defence received 'much more than any citizen of the United States gets on trial in the courts of the United States'.[288]

The *ad hoc* Tribunals started out with a disclosure system which strongly resembled the American system at the time. However, the judges of the *ad hoc* Tribunals have, over time, created a rather different disclosure regime, which not only demands massive disclosure by the defence but also include the Chambers in the disclosure procedure. The truth-finding aspect of disclosure seems to have been one of the driving forces behind these amendments next to the urge to expedite the proceedings.

The ICC, building on the developments and experience of the *ad hoc* Tribunals, is equipped with the most comprehensive disclosure system. While the RPE ICC leave much more room for defence disclosure, the jurisprudence of the Court also demonstrates that the ICC judges are willing to pay respect to the rights of the

---

[286] ICTR *Prosecutor v Karemera et al.*, AC, ICTR 98-44-AR73.7, 20 June 2006, Decision on Interlocutory Appeal Regarding the Role of the Prosecutor's Electronic Disclosure Suite in Discharging Disclosure Obligations, para 10.

[287] *See* ICC *Prosecutor v Lubanga*, PTC I (Single Judge), ICC-01/04-01/06-102, 15 May 2006, Decision on the Final System of Disclosure and the Establishment of a Timetable, para 68, where notice is taken on the parties' agreement to use the IT solution regarding disclosure.

[288] IMT Protocols II, 438.

accused, which they demonstrated particularly in the proceedings against *Lubanga*, when they stayed the proceedings twice. Due to the fact that the Registry maintains records of both the pre-trial and the trial proceedings and that the judges have access to these records in preparation for the hearings, the disclosure practice at the ICC has moved considerably close to the 'dossier' approach of Continental provenience; the mentioned 'in-depth-analysis chart' and 'table of incriminating evidence' point in this direction too. This proves nothing more than the fact that the judge, who is not only the procedural manager of the case, but also needs to pass the judgment, warrants full knowledge of the case in order to base his or her decision to the greatest extent possible on the true and complete facts of the case.

E. Victim's Participation

The participation of a victim in a case is only permitted if the victim can show that he has suffered harm from the alleged crimes contained in the DCC.[289] The victim must demonstrate a causal link between him or herself and the perpetrator.[290] In addition the victim must prove that his or her personal interests are affected by the confirmation hearing in order to be invited to participate pursuant to Art. 68 (3) ICCSt. It has already been stated that the normative framework of the ICC is silent as to the scope of victim participation and the applicable procedure.[291] This is true, in particular, of the confirmation stage. Victim's participation at this stage rests on the overall provisions of Art. 68 (3) ICCSt and Rules 89–93 RPE ICC. It is not surprising under these circumstances that in all of the confirmation hearings that have been held at the ICC to-date, the participation of victims has in each case taken a slightly different shape. However in all five hearings, in the cases against Lubanga, Katanga and Chui, Bemba, Garda, and Banda and Jerbo, victims have been admitted and have participated in the proceedings.

In *Lubanga,* Pre-Trial Chamber I stressed that the confirmation stage is essential for the entire prosecution process and that victims' participation could contribute to the prosecution.[292] However, it did not say how and why this is the case, and how, as is alleged by the Chamber, victims' participation supports the prosecution better than the victims' statements brought forward by the Prosecutor as witness testimony under Art. 61 (5) ICCSt. The only substantial reason given for victim

[289] ICC *Prosecutor v Lubanga*, PTC I, ICC-01/04-01/06-462-tEN, 22 September 2006, Decision on the Arrangements for Participation of Victims a/0001/06, a/0002/06 and a/0003/06 at the Confirmation Hearing, p 5.

[290] *See* ICC *Prosecutor v Lubanga*, TC I, ICC-01/04-01/06-1813,8 April 2009, Decision on 'Indirect Victims'; and Boas/Bischoff/Reid/Taylor, *ICL III*, 322.

[291] *See* Chapter 4, p 173 *et subs.*

[292] ICC *Prosecutor v Lubanga*, PTC I, ICC-01/04-01/06-462-tEN, 22 September 2006, Decision on the Arrangements for Participation of Victims a/0001/06, a/0002/06 and a/0003/06 at the Confirmation Hearing, p 5.

participation at this stage lies in the fact that the victims would subsequently be able to obtain reparations for the harm suffered. Furthermore, it was stressed that the Rome Statute 'is distinctive in the importance it affords to the participation of victims in proceedings'.[293]

As two of the three victims applied for anonymity, the Pre-Trial Chamber withheld their identity from the defence, but as a consequence granted to them the following rather limited participatory rights: (1) access to public documents, and (2) presence at public hearings only. (3) Their representatives were allowed to make opening and closing statements, but they were not permitted to add additional evidence or question witnesses. (4) Where they wished to intervene at the public hearing, the Chamber would decide on a case-by-case basis.[294]

These limitations on the participatory rights granted by Rule 91 RPE ICC were said to be based on the 'fundamental principle prohibiting anonymous accusations'.[295]

In the case of Katanga and Chui, Single Judge Steiner, of Pre-Trial Chamber I, put stressed that the role of the victim is autonomous vis-à-vis the Prosecutor and that victims must be granted an independent voice in the proceedings.[296] She then differentiated between anonymous and other victims,[297] holding that whereas due to their anonymity, participation can and will be limited in the case of anonymous victims, other victims will not be limited in their participatory rights under Rule 91 RPE ICC. As a result, the legal representatives of the non-anonymous victims were permitted to: (1) access confidential records, (2) make submissions regarding prosecution and defence evidence, (3) examine such evidence at the hearing, (4) examine witnesses, (5) attend all sessions, (6) make oral and written submission on all issues, and (7) file written motions, responses, and replies on all matters not specifically prohibited by the Rome Statute and the Rules. Victims were only excluded from *ex parte* proceedings.[298]

Pre-Trial Chamber III, Judge Kaul acting as Single Judge, in the case against *Bemba* adopted a comparatively restricted view and deviated from Judge Steiner, in that he granted only a limited set of participatory rights to victims. He argued against differentiating between anonymous and non-anonymous victims, as victims in

[293] Ibid, p 6.

[294] ICC *Prosecutor v Lubanga*, PTC I, ICC-01/04-01/06-462-tEN, 22 September 2006, Decision on the Arrangements for Participation of Victims a/0001/06, a/0002/06 and a/0003/06 at the Confirmation Hearing, p 7 *et subs.*

[295] Ibid, p 8.

[296] ICC *Prosecutor v Katanga and Chui*, PTC I, ICC-01/04-01/07-474, 13 May 2008, Decision on the Set of Procedural Rights Attached to Procedural Status of Victim at the Pre-Trial Stage of the Case, para 155 *et subs.*

[297] Ibid, para 165 *et subs.*, 182; 171 *et subs.*

[298] Ibid, paras 124–42.

need of protection would thereby be discriminated against.[299] Judge Kaul granted the following participatory rights: (1) presence at public confirmation hearings, (2) access to public documents in the record, (3) access to public evidence contained in the record, (4) access to public transcripts, (5) notification of all decisions and filings, (6) oral submissions subject to leave of the Chamber, and (7) where the Chamber deems it appropriate, the submission of written statements. The Chamber did not rule upon whether victims' representatives are permitted to question witnesses, as no witnesses were heard at the confirmation hearing in *Bemba*. Participatory rights were thus at first restricted to a right to be informed, notified, and be present. Any procedural activities regarding oral or written submission were to be decided on a case-by-case evaluation of the Chamber. Prior to the confirmation hearing, the OPCV filed a request to extend these rights. Judge Kaul reacted sharply and complained of a tendency to disregard the letter, spirit, and guidance provided by his previous decision.[300]

In all of the five named confirmation hearings the victims, through their representatives, participated in the proceedings in a manner authorized by the respective Pre-Trial Chamber. Yet the scope of the participatory rights of victims is still unclear. In any case it is urged that a restricted approach regarding victim participation at the confirmation stage should be taken. As has been argued throughout this chapter, the Pre-Trial Chambers have a tendency to inflate the confirmation stage to the detriment of the person charged. Yet the confirmation stage should not be seen as a 'mini-trial', but merely as a filter to avoid unnecessary proceedings and false accusations. Broad participatory rights on the side of the victims would go against this underlying rationale and unnecessarily delay the decision. The potential of streamlining the pre-trial process should be used.[301] And, indeed, steps should be taken 'to prevent the confirmation hearing from taking the form of a first trial'.[302]

[299] ICC *Prosecutor v Bemba*, PTC III, ICC-01/05-01/08-320, 12 December 2009, Fourth Decision on Victims' Participation, paras 99–110.

[300] ICC *Prosecutor v Bemba*, PTC III, ICC-01/05-01/08-349, 8 January 2009, Sixth Decision on Victims' Participation Relating to Certain Questions Raised by the Office of Public Counsel for Victims, para 13.

[301] *See* also M Harmon, 'The Pre-Trial Process as a Means of Ensuring an Expeditious Trial', 5 *JICJ* (2007) 370, who argues in favour of a tightly managed pre-trial phase in order to speed up the entire prosecution process with a view to the ICTY.

[302] C Kreß, 'The Procedural Law of the International Criminal Court in Outline: Anatomy of a Unique Compromise', 1 *JICJ* (2003) 603, 610.

8

THE TRIAL

The trial is the core of the entire prosecution process. At its end, the question of the individual criminal responsibility of the accused will be answered and the amount of punishment—upon a guilty verdict—will be determined. The rules for the procedure, which will in the end lead to the answer, vary greatly according to national legal systems. They depend heavily on the cultural heritage and the socio-historical circumstances. As we have seen, international criminal procedure has no such basis to rely upon, so it must be construed in such a way that is acceptable to world society, and to the societies particularly affected by international criminal trials.

The legal framework for the trial before the ICC is marked by Arts 62–76, which constitute Part VI of the Rome Statute headed 'The trial'. These articles are accompanied by Rules 131–144 RPE ICC of Chapter 6: Trial procedure. It is interesting to note that despite the fact that the trial is the core of the entire proceedings, its normative framework is somewhat limited, and much is left to be decided by the judges in the course of the process.

Before entering into a discussion of the course of the procedure in detail, it is thus necessary to establish a set of principles, derived from human rights law, as a yardstick for the structure of the trial (below, A). We will then look at how the trial is prepared (B) and how it is conducted (C). The rules concerning evidence will be discussed separately (D), as they establish the backbone of the verdict, which will then be addressed (F). In between (E) a summary is provided concerning witness protection. At the end of this chapter we will take another look at victim participation at this stage (G).

A. Principles of the Trial

More than any other area of the law, it seems, criminal procedure is dominated by principles.[1] This is certainly the case for German criminal procedure, where every

[1] S Negri, 'The Principle of Equality of Arms and the Evolving Law of International Criminal Procedure', 5 *ICLR* (2005) 513, 570 with further references.

book on the subject must elaborate on these principles, which are often called *Prozessmaximen*.[2] In some regards the situation in US law is similar as constitutional rights, for example, the due process clause in the Fourteenth Amendment, heavily influence the criminal procedure.[3] From an international perspective, these maxims are mostly interrelated with human rights law. These rights and principles influence the entire prosecution process as we have already seen in the previous stages of this study. Yet the trial is the place, where all other measures and previous proceedings appear as preliminary stages with the sole purpose to prepare the main hearing concerning the guilt of the accused person. This is why the principles of the trial must materialize at this stage in a particular way, when all preparatory means are being tested, weighed, and evaluated as to whether they will legitimize the conviction and punishment. It has been said that these principles are somewhat academic and indeed are observed by experienced judges instinctively.[4] With all due respect, this is rather dangerous. It should be monitored very closely as to whether this 'instinct' conforms to the human rights provisions and principles. Moreover these principles are not only to be observed by the judges, but also by the Prosecution and the Registry.

In the following I have identified eight principles. Most of these are to a greater or lesser extent expression of the overall principle of a 'fair trial'. Trial fairness is a common maxim, which is easily proclaimed but hard to define precisely. I will start with a critical analysis of the fair trial principle and continue by looking at other more concrete principles pertaining to the trial.

I. Fair trial

Fair trial is the core concept and principle of a criminal trial according to modern discussion of criminal procedure.[5] 'Thus, since it is a commonly shared opinion that justice is achieved only by processes which are perceived as fair and impartial adherence to procedural fairness as a means to the realization of substantive equality becomes the critical test of international courts' legitimacy and credibility.'[6]

This development has been fostered by the human rights jurisprudence, in particular that of the ECtHR.[7] Without this, the word 'fairness' would probably not

---

2 *See* K Volk, *Grundkurs StPO* (7th edn, CH Beck 2010) § 18 MN 1.

3 *See* P Hay, *US-Amerikanisches Recht* (CH Beck 2000) MN 604.

4 *See* I Bonomy, 'The Reality of Conducting a War Crimes Trial', 5 *JICJ* (2007) 348, 351.

5 *See* in general: D J Harris, 'The Right to a Fair Trial in Criminal Proceedings as a Human Right', 16 *International & Comparative Law Quarterly* (1967) 355.

6 S Negri, 'The Principle of Equality of Arms and the Evolving Law of International Criminal Procedure', 5 *ICLR* (2005) 513, 514; *see* also A Fichtelberg, 'Fair Trials and International Courts: A Critical Evaluation of the Nuremberg Legacy', 28 *Criminal Justice Ethics* (2009).

7 *See* R Esser, *Auf dem Weg zu einem europäischen Strafverfahrensrecht* (DeGruyter 2002) 400 *et subs.*

have met the same level of acceptance even in Continental Europe. It is interesting to note, that the German language does not have a proper synonym and 'fairness' has found its way into the language as a foreign word in particular in the field of a sporting event in the sense of 'fair play'.[8]

The IMTSt contained only a few provisions on procedure. However, Part IV of the IMTSt was headed 'Fair Trial for Defendants' and Art. 16 IMTSt laid down the procedure which should ensure fairness vis-à-vis the accused.[9] Much has been written about whether the Nuremberg trial could be considered as a fair trial.[10] Whereas the Prosecutors—not surprisingly—considered the trial to have been fair,[11] doubts were raised by defence counsels.[12]

The IMT was under the particular duty to expedite proceedings according to Art. 18 IMTSt. Therefore defence rights were sometimes taken back for the purpose of speeding up the trial. However, with particular regard to disclosure rights, the IMT practice went beyond the US or British law on disclosure.[13]

Today the tensions are even higher.[14] Expediency of the trial is one major issue at modern tribunals. Disclosure rules have caused many problems with regards to trial fairness as was discussed in Chapter 7.[15] The greatest challenge concerning fairness is connected to rights of witnesses and victims as regards their protection and possible participation as foreseen at the ICC.

Yet a fair trial is a prerequisite for justice: 'A fair trial is the only means to do justice. If no fair trial can be held, the object of the judicial process is frustrated and the process must be stopped.'[16]

---

[8] G Radbruch, *Der Geist des Englischen Rechts* (Vadenhoeck and Ruprecht 1956) 15.

[9] It is interesting to note, that the official translation of the IMTSt into the German language did not use the word 'fair', but 'gerecht' meaning 'just' and translates 'ensure fair trial for the defendants' as 'Zwecks Wahrung der Rechte des Angeklagten' meaning 'in order to observe the rights of the accused'.

[10] *See* D Luban, 'Fairness to Rightness: Jurisdiction, Legality, and the Legitimacy of International Criminal Law', *Georgetown Law Faculty Working Papers* (2008)13 available at: <http://scholarship.law.georgetown.edu/fwps_papers/67>; P Kirsch, 'Applying the Principles of Nuremberg in the International Criminal Court', 6 *Wash U Global Studies L Rev* (2007) 501.

[11] *See* eg, R H Jackson, Report to the President by Mr Justice Jackson, October 7, 1946 (Department of State 1949) p 437 *et subs.*; *see* also T Taylor, *The Anatomy of the Nuremberg Trials* (Bloomsbury 1993) 627 *et subs.*; stressing in particular the extraordinary situation as regards the crimes and the post-war situation in Germany.

[12] *See* O Kranzbühler, 'Nuremberg Eighteen Years Afterwards', 14 *DePaul Law Review* (1964–1965) 333 *et subs.* also C Safferling and P Graebke, 'Strafverteidigung im Nürnberger Hauptkriegsverbrecherprozess: Strategien und Wirkungen', 123 *ZStW* (2011) 47 with further references.

[13] *See* Chapter 7 C.

[14] *See* O Lagodny, 'Legitimation und Bedeutung des ständigen Internationalen Strafgerichtshofes', 113 *ZStW* (2001) 800, 803.

[15] *See* Chapter 7 B.

[16] ICC *Prosecutor v Lubanga*, AC, ICC-01/04-01/06-772, 14 December 2006, Judgment on the Appeal of Mr. Thomas Lubanga Dyilo against the Decision on the Defence Challenge to the Jurisdiction of the Court Pursuant to Article 19 (2) (a) of the Statute of 3 October 2006, para 37.

But what does procedural 'fairness' mean? Is there a general standard of 'fairness'? Or is every jurisdiction, indeed every court, called upon to develop its own concept of trial fairness?[17] Is 'fairness' relative to the procedural system at the individual courts and tribunals?

In general, we can agree with *Zappalá*, who has held that: 'Fairness is the standard for assessing the behavior of public authorities towards the individual against whom criminal charges are laid and who is then subjected to criminal prosecution.'[18]

To find out what the standard is, one ought to look first at human rights law.

1. *Human rights law*

Human rights documents do not speak of a 'fair trial' but rather acknowledge a right to a 'fair hearing' to the person charged, Art. 14 (1) ICCPR and Art. 6 (1) ECHR. In particular, the jurisprudence of the ECtHR has emancipated itself from the English wording of the Convention's text.[19] It has turned the right to a fair trial into one of the most fundamental legal principles as part of the *ordre public* and closely connected this to the principle of the rule of law.[20]

Despite this prominence, a clear definition is lacking. The systematic approach which has developed is such that Art. 14 (3) ICCPR and Art. 6 (3) ECHR respectively contain minimum guarantees for the accused.[21] Yet a violation of one of the minimum guarantees in the eyes of the ECtHR does not automatically warrant the conclusion that the trial has been unfair.[22] An 'overall examination' as to whether the trial 'as a whole' was unfair, is to follow.[23] However, this does not mean that the absence of a violation of a specific minimum guarantee leads to the conclusion that the trial has been fair. It was this understanding of fairness which goes beyond the minimum guarantees' concept, which helped develop a living and dynamic general right, and establish additional aspects like the right to an adversarial hearing, the principle of equality of arms, and the right to a reasoned judgment.[24]

Yet this interpretation has also a critical side to it. The fair trial requirement, as it has developed in the case law of the ECtHR and other bodies, appears sometimes to be an obstacle to further development of procedural rights. The standard test of the ECtHR to apply an 'overall examination' whether or not the proceedings in

---

[17] This seems to be the opinion of Triffterer/*Bitti*, Art. 64 MN 9.
[18] S Zappalá, 'The Rights of Victims *v* the Rights of the Accused', 8 *JICJ* (2010) 137, 149.
[19] *See* ECtHR *Neumeister v Austria*, Judgment 27 June 1968, Series A No. 8.
[20] *See* R Esser, *Auf dem Weg zu einem europäischen Strafverfahrensrecht* (DeGruyter 2002) 401.
[21] *See* S Trechsel and S Summers, *Human Rights in Criminal Proceedings* (OUP 2006) 86.
[22] *See* A Zahar and G Sluiter, *International Criminal Law* (OUP 2007) 293.
[23] *See* also C Safferling, *Internationales Strafrecht* (Springer 2011) § 13 MN 36 *et subs.*
[24] Compare A Zahar and G Sluiter, *International Criminal Law* (OUP 2007) 293.

its entirety can be seen to be 'fair',[25] has added to the vagueness of the rights of the accused.[26]

2. *Tribunals*

Art. 21 ICTYSt and Art. 22 ICTRSt contain the right to a 'fair trial' in a similiar wording as the human rights covenants. In particular the twofold approach of (1) a list of minimum guarantees, and (2) the over 'fairness' requirement can be found in both statutes. In interpreting these rights, the Tribunals have always taken heed of the jurisprudence of the ECtHR.

One general question regarding the implementation of procedural fairness, which has been brought up by the ICTY, is the question of whether the prosecutor can claim unfairness and rely on equal arms vis-à-vis the defence.

In several decisions, different chambers of the ICTY have built a strong case around the hypothesis that fairness, namely the equality of arms requirement, operates on both sides, that is, could also benefit the Prosecutor. As the ICTY Appeals Chamber stated in *Aleksovski*: 'This application of the concept of a fair trial in favour of both parties is understandable because the Prosecution acts on behalf of and in the interests of the community, including the interests of the victims of the offence charged.'[27]

This sentence reveals a clear misunderstanding of the concept of human rights in criminal procedure.[28] This confusion is to a certain extent fuelled by the often invoked principle of equality of arms, which will be discussed later.[29] This principle which has be derived from the 'fair' trial principle, assumes that there are two parties which need to be brought together at the same level. But even the equality of arms principle does not imply a right for the prosecutor.

Trial fairness is a human right for the accused and nothing else. His or her position as both a subject and an object of the proceedings requires protection from the overwhelming power of state authorities. The trial must be just and fair towards the accused.

3. *ICC*

The ICC's legal regime is similar to that of the *ad hoc* Tribunals. Art. 67 (1) ICCSt contains the right to a 'fair hearing' as well as an extended list of minimum guarantees. The drafters of the Statute have amended the list according to the jurisprudence

---

[25] *See* eg, ECtHR *Edwards v United Kingdom*, Judgment 16 December 1992, Series A No. 247-B, para 34 and *Miailhe v France*, Judgment 26 September 1996, Rep. 1996-IV, para 34.

[26] R Esser, *Auf dem Weg zu einem europäischen Strafverfahrensrecht* (DeGruyter 2002) 402 *et subs.*

[27] ICTY *Prosecutor v Aleksovski et al.*, AC, IT-95-14/1-AR73, 16 February 1999, Decision on Prosecutor's Appeal on Admissibility of Evidence, para 23.

[28] Harsh also the criticism of A Zahar and G Sluiter, *International Criminal Law* (OUP 2007) 294: 'An approach which might be perceived as damaging to the legitimacy and credibility of the ICTY.'

[29] *See* p 410 *et subs.*

of the ECtHR and other human rights bodies, and developed a laudable modernized list of minimum guarantees.[30]

To date, it is unclear what the ICC will make of this. The primary responsibility for the fairness of the proceedings rests with the Trial Chamber that must, according to Art. 64 (2) ICCSt, ensure that the trial is 'fair and expeditious and is conducted with full respect for the rights of the accused and due regard for the protection of victims and witnesses.' This brings a whole bouquet of different aspects and dimensions which must be taken into account. The wording implies that fairness and expeditiousness are situated on the same level. Yet the full respect for the rights of the accused and due regards for the protection of victims seem to be on different levels; that is, rights of the accused are on a higher level. In the case of conflict, the rights of the accused shall prevail.

4. Conclusion

Trial fairness is an important yardstick. It is the key to a just, legitimate, and acceptable judgment. Yet at the same time, the concept remains rather vague. Fairness consists of a list of minimum guarantees but must be seen as a dynamic principle, which goes beyond these separate rights. However, the concept of the 'overall examination' of the fairness as applied by the ECtHR is not helpful regarding the development of an international procedural law. An overall examination might be useful for an appeals court or a human rights body. It does not assist in the development of precise rights at the trial level.

Fairness must be seen as an uncompromising concept. A trial is either fair or unfair. It cannot be less fair or fairer.

It must be kept in mind, that 'fairness' is a highly subjective concept, depending to a large extent on the individual understanding of the spectator. Different people will have different views on what still is and what no longer is fair. If such a vague term is used as a legal term, there is a real danger of user-defined, even arbitrary, interpretation. It is thus necessary to develop certain hard criteria as necessary conditions of procedural fairness.

What can be counted amongst these criteria is the necessity to treat the accused not as a pure object of the proceedings, but to meet him/her as a subject of the proceeding and respect his or her human dignity notwithstanding the charges which are brought.

II. Expeditious trial

'Justice delayed is justice denied'.[31] The maxim of an expeditious trial is of enormous importance for the criminal process. The criminological rational behind the

[30] Triffterer/*Schabas*, Art. 67 MN 5 *et subs.* This approach adopted by the PrepCom was accepted without dispute by the delegates at the Rome Conference.

[31] Attributed to William Gladstone (1809–1898), although this attribution is not verifiable. However the maxim has found its way to the reasoning at international tribunals: ICTR *Prosecutor*

maxim is the empirically proven fact that a sanction, which follows immediately after the offence has taken place, has more impact on the culprit and works as a deterrent. From a victimological point of view, a swift legal response might have a greater influence on the healing process.[32]

National courts are in conflict with this provision frequently as is shown by the fact that out of all ECtHR case law, 26 per cent of cases pertain to the right to be tried without undue delay contained in Art. 6 (1) ECHR.[33] In international criminal procedure, the situation seems even worse. The excessive length of periods of pre-trial detention and trials are 'a weak spot in the administration of international criminal justice'.[34] Not only are the cases relatively complex, but language problems and procedural challenges tend to delay the proceedings too.

Before looking at the specifications of the right to a speedy trial, a clarification is necessary: what will be discussed in the following is the 'speedy trial' as a principle of the trial. The scope of application is thus limited to the trial. This means that in this section we will not take issue with the question of whether in an international setting of mass atrocities, more time needs to elapse between the offences and prosecution, as the entire truth might come to light only after some time has passed.[35] This question is related to the legitimacy of international criminal prosecution and is discussed in this context.

1. Human rights law

All major human rights treaties recognize a right to a 'speedy' trial. The terms used are that the accused has a right to be tried without 'undue delay', as in Art. 14 (III) (e) ICCPR, or 'within a reasonable time' according to Art. 6 (I) ECHR and Art. 8 (I) AmCHR, or Art. 7 (I) (d) AfCHPR. Even if the wording is unclear, the provision pertains not only to the beginning of the trial, but comprises the time by which a trial should end and judgment be rendered.[36] The aim of the rule is to protect all parties in court proceedings against excessive procedural delays.[37] The accused has a specific interest in a verdict being given without undue delay. Bearing in mind that his/her reputation is at stake and that s/he

v Bagosora, TC II, ICTR-96-7-T, 17 March 1998, Separate Opinion of Judge Yakov Ostrovsky on the Prosecution's Motion for Adjournment, para 9.

[32] *See* in particular regarding juvenile offenders: F Streng, *Jugendstrafrecht* (2nd edn, CF Müller 2008) § 1 MN 22.

[33] Report of the ECHR, 50 Years of Activity, p 14. Germany alone has been convicted for violating Art. 6 (1) ECHR by undue delays 54 times.

[34] A Zahar and G Sluiter, *International Criminal Law* (OUP 2007) 300.

[35] This is the argument presented by A Whiting, 'In International Criminal Prosecutions, Justice Delayed Can Be Justice Delivered', 50 *Harvard Int'l L J* (2009) 323.

[36] *See* HRC General Comment 13 (Article 14), para 10.

[37] ECtHR *Stögmüller v Austria*, Judgment 10 November 1969, Series A No. 9, para 5.

must be presumed innocent throughout the trial, the proceedings must be conducted in a way that the charged does not remains uncertain of his/her fate for too long.[38]

The right to a speedy trial becomes even more important if the accused is in pre-trial detention, as is regularly the case at international criminal courts.[39] Art. 9 (3) ICCPR and Art. 5 (3) ECHR therefore have separate provisions for the person in detention. The scope of application of these norms is not uncontested.[40] Yet it is recognized as calling for even more expeditious proceedings in order to end the stage of uncertainty for the accused as soon as possible.[41]

Due to the difference in complexity of cases, it is impossible to give absolute time limits for the trial. Some delays are acceptable, while some are not. The ECtHR has developed the following test and established a number of parameters which are relevant here:[42]

The relevant time starts with the 'charge'; that is, the moment the person concerned is formally confronted for the first time with the accusations against him/her. It ends with the final verdict. In considering whether or not the length of the proceedings is reasonable, the complexity of the case has to be taken into account. The complexity is derived from the volume of evidence,[43] the number of defendants or charges,[44] the need to obtain expert witness or testimony from people abroad,[45] or indeed, the intricacy of the legal issues involved. It could thus be necessary for the prosecution and the court to reduce the number of charges in order to enhance the manageability of the case and shorten the proceeding.[46]

On the other side, however, the obstacles presented by the defendant must be taken into account. Deliberate obstruction of the prosecution cannot be blamed on the judicial authorities.[47] But this is a fine line. As the defendant need not cooperate

[38] ECtHR *Wemhoff v Germany*, Judgment 27 June 1968, Series A No. 7, para 18.

[39] *See* Chapter 5 A.

[40] For a discussion in detail *see* C Safferling, *Towards an International Criminal Procedure* (OUP 2003) 251 *et subs.*

[41] ECtHR *Abdoella v Netherlands*, Judgment 25 November 1993, Series A No. 248-A, para 24; *Čevizović v Germany, Judgment* 29 July 2004, Appl. No. 49746/99; *see* also J Meyer-Ladewig, *Europäische Menschenrechtskonvention—EMRK: Handkommentar* (Nomos 2006) Art. 5 MN 36 with further references.

[42] *See* eg, ECtHR *Metzger v Germany*, Judgment 31 May 2001, Rep. 2001-XII; *Bock v Germany*, Judgment 29 March 1989, Series A No. 150.

[43] ECtHR *Boddaert v Belgium*, Judgment 12 October 1992, Series A No. 235-D, para 37 *et subs.*

[44] ECtHR *Eckle v Germany*, Judgment 15 July 1982, Series A No. 51, para 79 *et subs.*

[45] ECtHR *Neumeister v Austria*, Judgment 27 June 1968, Series A No. 8, para 21.

[46] This was suggested in the case ECtHR *Eckle v Germany*, Judgment 15 July 1982, Series A No. 51, para 84.

[47] Ibid, para 82.

with the prosecution s/he cannot be compelled to do so by referring to the speedy trial requirement.[48]

In summary the ECtHR adopts the following criteria:

(1) The significance of the issue for the defendant, for example, the person detained has a greater interest in expeditious proceedings.
(2) The complexity of the case.
(3) The conduct of the defendant himself.
(4) The conduct of state officials concerned with the case.

2. Tribunals

Art. 21 (4) (c) ICTYSt and Art. 20 (4) (c) ICTRSt state that the accused has the right to be tried 'without undue delay'. The wording of Art. 17 (4) (c) SCSLSt is similar. As the wording of the respective norms mirrors the human rights conventions mentioned above, the UN judges have always respected the ECtHR for the interpretation of the Tribunals' statutes.[49] Furthermore the Appeals Chamber has held that the speedy trial principle is not at the disposition of the accused. S/he cannot waive this right. The Tribunal is responsible for a process without undue delays.[50]

In order to speed up the proceedings, which was even more relevant after the Completion Strategy was in place, the Tribunals developed several specific mechanisms to expedite the proceedings.[51] These lead to modifications in the pre-trial phase in particular, which was recognized as essential for the proper preparation and management of the trial.[52]

Therefore, amendments to the indictment brought forward by the Prosecutor according to Rule 50 RPE ICTY do not justify a delay in the proceedings.[53] A Pre-Trial Judge was introduced by Rule 65*ter* RPE ICTY, who should manage the case from early on.[54] The role of the Pre-Trial Judge will be discussed

[48] ECtHR *König v Germany*, Judgment 28 June 1978, Series A No. 28, para 111—this case concerned civil proceedings but the findings are nevertheless valid for a criminal case also.

[49] *See* eg, ICTY *Prosecutor v Blaškić*, TC, IT-95-14-T, 14 December 1996, Denying a Motion for Provisional Release.

[50] ICTY *Prosecutor v Kvočka et al.*, AC, IT-98-30/1, 25 May 2001, Decision on Interlocutory Appeal by the Accused Zoran Zigic against the Decision of Trial Chamber I dated 5 December 2000, para 19 *et subs*.

[51] *See* eg, G Boas, 'Developments in the Law of Procedure and Evidence at the ICTY and the ICC', 12 *CLF* (2001) 167, 168–70 for the early stages of the ICTY; also S Bourgon, 'Procedural Problems Hindering Expeditious and Fair Justice', 2 *JICJ* (2004) 526, 527 *et subs*.

[52] *See* eg, M Harmon, 'The Pre-Trial Process as a Means of Ensuring an Expeditious Trial', 5 *JICJ* (2007) 370.

[53] ICTY *Prosecutor v Kordić and Čerkez*, TC, IT-95-14-2, 28 January 1998, Decision on the Prosecutor's Motion to Hold Pre-Trial Motions in Abeyance.

[54] This was developed by the decision in ICTY *Prosecutor v Kunarac et al.*, TC, IT-96-23 and 23/1, 18 June 1998, Order Appointing a Pre-Trial Judge.

in further detail later on.[55] Statements and motions should be introduced in writing and a hearing would only be held in exceptional circumstances.[56] At the trial phase, the Trial Chamber can limit the time for the parties to present their respective cases.[57]

The decision as to whether there has been an undue delay or not is to be taken on a case-by-case basis.[58] The ICTR Appeals Chamber has developed a list of parameters which mirrors the above-mentioned ECtHR case law. These parameters are:

(1) the length of the delay,
(2) the complexity of the proceedings,
(3) the conduct of the parties,
(4) the conduct of the relevant authorities and, as an additional requirement,
(5) the prejudice to the accused, if any.[59]

In case of an extreme delay on the side of the Prosecutor the Appeals Chamber of the ICTR held that as a last resort the trial could be halted and the charges be dropped. In that case a retrial would be disallowed.[60]

3. ICC

At the ICC the right to a speedy trial is contained in Art. 64 (2) and 67 (1) (c) ICCSt and repeats Art. 14 (3) (e) ICCPR.[61] The ICC has set itself too ambitious a goal when it was stated in the Court Capacity Model that the average trial should not last more than three years.[62] Today the proceedings suffer in particular from the extensive confirmation stage, which is shown by the following tables:

---

[55] *See* pp 421, 489.

[56] *See* ICTY *Prosecutor v Krnojelac*, TC, IT-97-25-T, 24 February 1999, Decision on the Defence Preliminary Motion on the Form of the Indictment, para 65 *et subs.*

[57] ICTY *Prosecutor v Blaškić*, TC, IT-95-14-T, 17 December 1997, Decision on the Length of the Proceedings and the Time Allocated to the Parties to Present their Evidence. *See* also ICTY *Prosecutor v Blaškić*, TC, IT-95-14-T, 3 March 2000, Judgment, para 53 *et subs.*

[58] ICTR *Prosecutor v Kanyabashi*, TC II, ICTR-96-15-I, 23 May 2000, Decision on the Extremely Urgent Motion on Habeas Corpus and for Stoppage of Proceedings.

[59] ICTR *Prosecutor v Mugiraneza*, AC, ICTR-99-50-AR73, 27 February 2004, Decision on Prosper Mugiraneza's Interlocutory Appeal from Trial Chamber II-Decision of 2 October 2003 Denying the Motion to Dismiss the Indictment, Demand Speedy Trial and for Appropriate Relief.

[60] ICTR *Prosecutor v Barayagwiza*, AC, ICTR-97-19-AR72, 3 November 1999, Decision, para 102 *et subs.*; *see* also ICTR *Prosecutor v Mugiraneza*, TC II, ICTR-99-50-I, 2 October 2003, Decision on Prosper Muguiraneza's Request Pursuant to Rule 73 for Certification to Appeal Denial of his Motion to Dismiss for Violation of Article 20 (4) (c) of the Statute, Demand for Speedy Trial and Appropriate Relief.

[61] There was some argument in the preparatory phase of the ICCSt to ameliorate the language of the provision; yet in the end the text was retained; *see* Triffterer/*Schabas*, Art. 67 MN 26 with further references.

[62] *See* Report on the Court Capacity Model, Document ICC-ASP/5/10, para 23.

Table 8.1 Timeline of *Prosecutor v Thomas Lubanga*

Prosecution application for a warrant of arrest	12 January 2006
Warrant of arrest:	
Issued under seal	10 February 2006
Unsealed	17 February 2006
Surrender to the Court and transfer to the Detention Centre in The Hague	17 March 2006
First appearance before Pre-Trial Chamber I	20 March 2006
Confirmation of charges hearing	9–28 November 2006
Decision on the confirmation of the charges	29 January 2007
Commencement of trial	26 January 2009

Table 8.2 Timeline of *Prosecutor v Germain Katanga*

Prosecution application for a warrant of arrest	25 June 2007
Warrant of arrest:	
Issued under seal	2 July 2007
Unsealed	18 October 2007
Surrender to the Court and transfer to the Detention Centre in The Hague	17 October 2007
First appearance before Pre-Trial Chamber I	22 October 2007
Confirmation of charges hearing	27 June–18 July 2008
Decision on the confirmation of the charges	26 September 2008
Commencement of trial	24 November 2009

Table 8.3 Timeline of *Prosecutor v Jean-Pierre Bemba Gombo*

Prosecution application for a warrant of arrest	9 May 2008
Warrant of arrest:	
Issued under seal	23 May 2008
Unsealed	24 May 2008
Request to the Kingdom of Belgium for provisional arrest	23 May 2008
Arrest from the Belgian authorities	24 May 2008
Warrant of arrest replacing (23 May 2008)	10 June 2008
Request to the Kingdom of Belgium for arrest and surrender	10 June 2008
Transfer and surrender	3 July 2008
Initial appearance before Pre-Trial Chamber III	4 July 2008
Confirmation of charges hearing	12–15 January 2009
Decision on the confirmation of the charges	15 June 2009
Commencement of trial	22 November 2010

The ICC should also adopt a last resort in terminating the proceedings in case of an inexcusable delay on the side of the Prosecutor. This sword of Damocles should help OTP structure its work and thus expedite investigation and prosecution, a responsibility which rests largely with the Prosecutor.[63]

[63] A Zahar and G Sluiter, *International Criminal Law* (OUP 2007) 302.

4. Conclusion

War crime trials are not of such a special nature that the human rights criteria which have been developed over many years cannot be applied in evaluating the length of the proceedings.[64] Yet parameters, like the complexity of the case, are influenced by several factors which are typical for war crimes trials. For example, dealing with traumatized victims is difficult, the finding of evidence in circumstances of war is highly dangerous, prosecution may take place many years after the alleged crime occurred, and often in a country far from the seat of the trial. The Tribunals and the ICC have always adhered to this principle and take into account ECtHR case law when considering delays in the process. Yet they have stretched human rights standards as far as possible, so that sometimes reference to them appears to offer no more than pure lip service.[65]

One argument, often brought forward when discussing the length of proceedings, is the lack of financial resources.

The principle of a speedy trial must be related to other procedural maxims. An expedited trial is a corollary of the general fairness requirement.[66] It is also an expression of the presumption of innocence, as the defendant's status of uncertainty should be resolved as quickly as possible. However, there are other rights of the accused which would—objectively—lead to a delay in the process. But these rights, like the right to adequate time and facility to prepare the defence, cannot as such justify a delay. The urge to speed up the proceedings is in conflict with the quest for truth. Prosecution must be both speedy and efficient.

In that regard, the ICTY has been criticized after the completion strategy was set in place for having thrown the baby out with the bath water, and shifted the focus of criminal procedure to the lengths of trials only.[67] And at least one judge has expressed his concerns regarding the fairness of the trials and the rights of the accused, which are threatened by a one-sided emphasis of the speedy conclusion of trials.[68]

---

[64] The ECommHR had to delay with such a situation in the case *Jentzsch v Germany* Report 30 November 1970, 14 *YB* (1971) 876. The facts of the case can be found in the decision on admissibility, 19 December 1967, 10 *YB* (1967) 218. The Commission found that six years in pre-trial detention before the trial eventually commenced were compatible with the Convention.

[65] Very critical as regards the work of the UN tribunals: A Zahar and G Sluiter, *International Criminal Law* (OUP 2007) 302.

[66] D McGoldrick, *The Human Rights Committee: Its Role in the Development of the International Covenant on Civil and Political Rights* (2nd edn, OUP 1994) XX.

[67] *See* eg, G Boas, *The Milošević Trial: Lessons for the Conduct of Complex International Criminal Proceedings* (CUP 2007) 64, who observes a certain obsession at the ICTY to conclude the trials speedily.

[68] *See* ICTY *Prosecutor v Milošević*, AC, IT-02-54-AR73.4, 21 October 2003, Dissenting Opinion of Judge David Hunt on Admissibility of Evidence in Chief in the Form of Written Statement (Majority Decision Given 30 September 2003), para 20.

III. Public trial

The trial must be a public one. A liberal and democratic legal system cannot allow criminal prosecution to take place in secret, as the lack of control would open the field to unfairness, abuse, and arbitrariness.[69] Also, a public trial safeguards the independence of the judiciary in the sense of a separation of powers. Justice shall be made transparent and accessible to everyone.[70] At the same time, publicity sometimes poses a danger to either the accused or other participants in the trial, like the witnesses or victims. The principle of a public trial cannot be seen as an absolute right and its merits must thus be weighed up against other interests and principles.[71] Yet there must always be a possibility for the general public to exercise control over the procedure as such. We will see in the following how human rights law and international criminal tribunals deal with these dilemmas.

Before doing this, I want to mention two public groups of key relevance. The press plays an important role in making the public aware of the proceedings. The presence of the press in the courtroom is a special guarantee for the safeguarding of 'fairness'. Therefore, even if the interest of the general public is great, and the facilities of a courthouse limited, some seats must always be reserved for journalists.[72] It is, after all, their responsibility to inform the general public about the trial.

Another group of persons who merit special attention are trial monitors. In some international tribunals, in particular in Sierra Leone and Cambodia, but also in some national courts, as in Germany, specially trained monitors observe the trial and report to the general public by posting weekly reports on the internet. Monitors watch over the adherence to international 'fair trial' standards and prepare protocols for academic analysis. These monitors are mostly seen as part of the general public but would deserve a status similar to the press, as they fulfil a special duty to the public which goes beyond mere information dissemination.

1. Human rights law

The principle of a public trial is embodied in Art. 14 (1) ICCPR, Art. 6 (1) ECHR, and Art. 8 (5) AmCHR. However, these norms are accompanied by a whole variety of exceptions. For example, Art. 14 (1) 3 ICCPR states:

> The press and the public may be excluded from all or part of a trial for reasons of morals, public order (*ordre public*) or national security in a democratic society, or when the interest of the private lives of the parties so requires, or to the extent strictly

[69] As stated by the ICTY *Prosecutor v Tadić*, TC, IT-94-1-T, 10 August 1995, Decision on the Prosecutor's Motion Requesting Protective Measures for Victims and Witnesses, para 32.

[70] *See* eg, HRC General Comment 13 (Article 14), para 6.

[71] *See* also C Safferling, *Towards an International Criminal Procedure* (OUP 2003) 226 *et subs.*

[72] D McGoldrick, *The Human Rights Committee: Its Role in the Development of the International Covenant on Civil and Political Rights* (2nd edn, OUP 1994) 403.

necessary in the opinion of the court in special circumstances where publicity would prejudice the interests of justice; but any judgement rendered in a criminal case or in a suit at law shall be made public except where the interest of juvenile persons otherwise requires or the proceedings concern matrimonial disputes or the guardianship of children.

a. Publicizing the decision There is a clear separation between the public hearing on the one hand and the public pronouncement of the judgment on the other. As regards the latter, there is only one exception to the publicity: the interests of juvenile persons. Even if there were good reasons to hold the hearing behind closed doors, the 'result' of the proceedings; that is, the decision, must be made public.[73] The deposition of the decision with the registry will satisfy the public pronouncement requirement as long as the decision is publicly accessible.[74] This will put the public in a position to exercise control *ex post*, even if the ongoing trial was unsupervised.

b. Publicizing the hearing The exceptions to the publicity of the hearing are far more complex. All in all there are five. The public may be excluded for the protection of: (a) morals, (b) public order (*ordre public*), (c) national security, (d) in the interest of the private lives of the parties, or (e) if it is strictly necessary in the opinion of the court in circumstances where publicity would prejudice the interests of justice.

Three cases seem to be most relevant during the criminal procedure. (1) Order in the courtroom must be upheld and, if necessary, by excluding the public from the hearing, (2) sensitive information concerning national security must be protected, and (3) the accused, victims, and witnesses could need protection which could be provided by excluding the audience from the courtroom.

(1) Concerning the order in the courtroom justification of holding an in-camera hearing might be based on the 'protection of public order' requirement. Even if the term '*ordre public*' usually pertains to something more fundamental, as the general constitutional principles of society, it has been argued that the prevention of disorder in the courtroom comes under this exception.[75] Also the jurisprudence of the ECtHR points into this direction.[76]

---

[73] *See* eg, M Nowak, *UN Covenant on Civil and Political Rights: CCPR Commentary* (2nd edn, Engel 2005) Art. 14 MN 28.

[74] *See* eg, ECtHR *Axen v Germany*, Judgment 8 December 1983, Series A No. 72.

[75] *See* eg, M Nowak, *UN Covenant on Civil and Political Rights: CCPR Commentary* (2nd edn, Engel 2005) Art. 14 MN 25.

[76] *See* eg, ECtHR *Le Compte, van Leuven and De Meyere v Belgium*, Judgment 23 June 1981, Series A No. 43; *Campbell and Fell v United Kingdom*, Judgment 28 June 1984, Series A No. 80.

(2) The term 'national security' in Art. 14 (1) ICCPR has been supplemented by the words 'in a democratic society'.[77] This means that this exception cannot be invoked by the government at liberty, but can be reviewed by the court. Yet in international criminal law, national security issues are at stake at a much more frequent rate compared to purely national trials prosecuting ordinary crimes as will be discussed later.

(3) Finally, the protection of the persons involved in the trial can justify excluding the public from the hearing. This is true for the accused. In particular the juvenile offender falls within the scope of this exception.[78] Also in cases of sexual offences, the private and family life of the accused might be affected in such a way that the public could be excluded.[79]

Concerning the protection of the victim, it is doubtful whether justification could be based on the 'interests of the private lives of the parties', as technically speaking a victim is not a party to the proceedings.[80] I would thus suggest that the protection of both victims and witnesses comes within the ambit of the final ground for justification mentioned in Art. 14 (1) ICCPR, namely that 'publicity would prejudice the interests of justice'. Even if this provision can only applied in special circumstances and even if the exclusion of the public must be strictly necessary in the opinion of the court, this clause embraces all cases in which conflicting rights and principles need to be balanced against the right to a public hearing.

It must be kept in mind that the exceptions pertain not only to the question of whether or not the public can be excluded. The principle of publicity of trial also demands that the exclusion of the public shall be as short as possible and shall only be applied as long as strictly necessary. In general, this means that the exclusion of the public is only justified as long as the danger prevails. To exclude the public from the entire trial is only justified in proceedings against juvenile offenders.

2. *Tribunals*

The *ad hoc* Tribunals recognize the principle of a public trial amongst other rights of the accused in Art. 21 (2) ICTYSt, Art. 20 (2) ICTRSt, and Art. 17 (2) SCSLSt. The tribunals adopt this principle by holding public hearings and inviting the public to sit in the visitors' gallery, by broadcasting the hearings over the internet, by publishing decisions and submissions of the parties, and by providing trial transcripts on the internet.[81] Yet the Chamber may order the exclusion of the public

[77] *See* C Safferling, *Towards an International Criminal Procedure* (OUP 2003) 230 for further references concerning the drafting history.

[78] In Art. 6 (1) ECHR the juveniles are mentioned explicitly.

[79] ECommHR *X v Austria*, Appl No 1913/63, 2 Digest 428.

[80] In greater detail *see* C Safferling, *Towards an International Criminal Procedure* (OUP 2003) 233 *et subs*.

[81] *See* Boas/Bischoff/Reid/Taylor, *ICL III*, 267.

according to Art. 20 (4) ICTYSt, Art. 19 (4) ICTRSt and Rule 79 RPE SCSL. Indeed, the right of the accused to be tried in public is *expressis verbis* limited by the protection of the rights and interests of victims and witnesses. Art. 22 ICTYSt and Art. 21 ICTRSt foresee *in camera* proceedings for this reason, further elaborated in Rules 75 (B) (ii) and 79 ICTY RPE.

The Rules provide further exceptions in Rule 79 ICTY RPE. For reasons of (i) public order or morality, (ii) safety, security of non-disclosure of the identity of a victim or witness, and (iii) the protection of the interests of justice, the press, which is mentioned separately, and the public may be excluded from all or part of the proceedings. Similarly, Rule 79 RPE SCSL anticipates closed sessions for reasons of (i) national security, (ii) protection of victims and witnesses, and (iii) interests of justice.

Obviously, the Tribunals' provisions mirror the human rights norms without them being congruent. At some point they seem even more vague than their respective human rights equivalent. This is particularly regrettable as the Statute and Rules of the Tribunals are silent concerning the application of the exceptions. The prerequisites for exclusion of the public remain unclear.[82] However, the jurisprudence of the ICTY shows, that the judges have—on a case-to-case basis[83]—rightly adopted a restrictive interpretation of the law concerning closed sessions and held that those were only justified if no other measure would provide the degree of protection required.[84] Therefore it has been held, that the 'national security interests' will not be at the discretion of the state, but will be reviewed by the Court.[85] Also frequently, the facial distortion of the broadcast image of the witness was considered a less restrictive measure instead of a closed session.[86] The ICTY has also developed a unique feature in order to protect the witness at risk and at the same time uphold the publicity of the trial. Instead of going into closed session, which is anticipated in the Statute and Rules, the trial might also go into private session. Whereas in a closed session the public is excluded from following the trial altogether, in a private

[82] The concept is also blurred by the fact that Rule 75 (B) RPE ICTY refers to Rule 79, whereas Rule 79 (A) (ii) refers to Rule 75. A vicious circle which was not resolved by the many amendments to the RPE, *see* C Safferling, *Towards an International Criminal Procedure* (OUP 2003) 238.

[83] ICTY *Prosector v Mrkšić et al.*, TC II, IT-95-13/1-PT, 9 March 2005, Decision on Confidential Prosecution Motions for Protective Measures and Nondisclosure and Confidential Annex A, pp 4–5.

[84] ICTY *Prosecutor v Tadić*, TC II, IT-94-1-T,31 July 1996, Decision on the Prosecutor's Motion Requesting Protective Measures for Witness 'R', para 7. Similarly *Prosecutor v Blaškić*, TC I, IT-95-14-PT, 10 July 1997, Decision of Trial Chamber I on the Prosecutor's Requests of 5 and 11 July 1997 for Protection of Witnesses, para 12.

[85] ICTY *Prosecutor v Blaškić*, AC, IT-95-14-AR108*bis*, 29 October 1997, Judgment on the Request of the Republic of Croatia for Review of the Decision of Trial Chamber II of 18 July 1997, para 65.

[86] ICTY *Prosecutor v Tadić*, TC II, IT-94-1-T, 31 July 1996, Decision on the Prosecutor's Motion Requesting Facial Distortion, and *Prosecutor v Tadić*, TC II, 12 November 1996, IT-94-1-T, Decision on the Prosecutor's Motion to Withdraw Protective Measures for Witness K.

session, the audio is turned off but no blinds are drawn. Therefore the public can see what is happening behind the bullet-proof glass, but cannot hear.[87]

3. ICC

At the ICC, Art. 74 (5) ICCSt declares that the judgment or a summary therefore must be delivered in open court.[88] Furthermore Art. 64 (7) and 67 (1) ICCSt anticipate a public trial as the general rule. Yet closed sessions are designed for the protection of the accused, witnesses, and victims (as of Art. 68 (2) ICCSt), and also for the protection of confidential or sensitive information. It appears that the number of exceptions is rather limited compared to the human rights requirements. The protection of juveniles is not necessary, as the jurisdiction *ratione personae* of the ICC does not embrace persons under the age of eighteen, according to Art. 26 ICCSt.

a. For protection purposes Art. 68 (1) and (2) ICCSt and Rule 88 (1) RPE ICC name a list of scenarios in which a closed session would be justified:

- In cases where the safety, physical and psychological well-being, dignity, and privacy of victims and witnesses is at risk,
- in the case of a victim of sexual violence,
- in the case of a child as a victim or witness,
- in the case of an elderly person,
- in the case of a traumatized victim.

A hearing on a motion requesting the exclusion of the public according to Art. 68 (2) ICCSt may also be held *in camera* according to Rule 88 (2) RPE ICC. Also a hearing on other protective measures for victims and witnesses may be held in closed session according to Rule 87 (3) RPE ICC. Finally, a special norm is to be found in Rule 72 (2) RPE ICC. In a case of sexual violence, if evidence concerning consent of the victim is in question, the Chamber may hold a hearing *in camera* when ruling on the admissibility of such evidence.

As can be seen from the few cases the ICC is prosecuting to date, these rules are applied in a rather profligate way. Not only are many hearings held totally or partially *in camera*, but as early as the second day of the first trial of the newly established ICC, in the case against Thomas Lubanga on 27 January 2009, the Chamber applied Rule 88 RPE ICC and had part of the hearing in closed session,[89] also decisions are often published in severely redacted versions.[90]

---

[87] Compare Boas/Bischoff/Reid/Taylor, *ICL III*, 268.

[88] *See* also p 524 for details.

[89] ICC *Prosecutor v Lubanga*, TC I, ICC-01/04-01/06-T-109-ENG, 27 January 2009, Transcript Hearing (Open Session), p 55.

[90] Triffterer/*Schabas*, Art. 67 MN 11.

b. Confidentiality purposes Art. 64 (7) ICCSt is rather vague when referring to sensitive or confidential information. The source of the confidentiality is not laid down in detail. Indeed there may be several sources. It might be based on a privilege as contained in Rule 73 RPE ICC. Along with the lawyer-client relationship, several professional privileges are enumerated in Rule 73 (3) RPE ICC.

States may furthermore apply for protective measures, including the exclusion of the public, in respect of the protection of its servants or agents and the protection of confidential or sensitive information according to Art. 68 (6) ICCSt. A more detailed norm embracing confidential or sensitive information[91] is to be found in the disclosure regime. Confidentiality might be derived from 'national security interests' of sovereign states as foreseen in Art. 72 (7) (a) (i) ICCSt. Under these circumstances it is not only possible to exclude the public and hold the hearing *in camera,* it is also possible to exclude other parties and have an *ex parte* hearing. It is highly questionable what exactly falls under the remit of security interests, and it ought not surprise that states tend to adopt a rather broad understanding of this term.[92] However, truth-finding in criminal trials is severely hampered by imposing vast national security limits. It is thus submitted that the term should be read in a narrow way, pertaining to threats which affect the country as a whole and relate to the use of force, or threat of force, against the political independence or territorial integrity of the state.[93] The ICC would be well advised to follow the ICTY jurisprudence in this regards and insist on its power to determine whether or not the national security interests are concerned. In doing this, the ICC may hold an *ex parte* hearing.

4. Conclusion

The publicity of the trial is an important human rights provision. In international criminal procedure, the accused has a right to a public trial. However, the Statutes of the Tribunals as well as the Rome Statute place equal weight on the need to protect victims and witnesses. Therefore, there are extensive possibilities to exclude the public in order to protect the life, the well-being, or the privacy of witnesses and victims. In almost every international trial, restrictive measures have been applied but despite these, witnesses have been threatened, assaulted, or killed for having testified.[94]

The principle of a public trial is not severely restricted by these options. Indeed principles always need to be balanced with other principles and interests. In this instance, the security of the witnesses and victims need to be weighed against the requirement for a public trial. In the course of this consideration, however, the general

[91] Triffterer/*Donat-Cattin*, Art. 68 MN 34 conclude that both terms are congruent.
[92] *See* Triffterer/*Dixon/Duffy/Hall*, Art. 72 MN 6-7.
[93] Ibid, Art. 72 MN 7 with further references.
[94] *See* Boas/Bischoff/Reid/Taylor, *ICL III*, 267 with further references in footnote 97.

aim towards publicity of the trial must not be abolished. As has been expressed by Judge Fulford at the first Status Conference in the Lubanga case before the ICC: 'we [ie the Trial Chamber] propose to scrutinise very carefully each and every occasion when it is suggested that there should be a departure from the principle of open justice.'[95]

As long as the public is still in a position to monitor the trial and exercise democratic control over the judges in an overall sense, I do not see a violation of the principle of publicity. In particular, the decisions and judgments need to be made public, so that the public can be informed and can supervise the judiciary.

IV. Defendant's presence at trial

The accused has a right to be present at trial. A 'trial *in absentia*' is generally conceived of as being unfair. Even if not all national legal systems recognize such trials, although Continental European criminal procedural law is broadly familiar with some sort of trial *in absentia*,[96] international criminal procedure following Anglo-American law in this regard insists on the presence of the accused at trial.

This was not always the case. The case against Martin Bormann at the IMT in Nuremberg was conducted without the accused being present pursuant to Art. 12 IMTSt. Indeed Bormann, who was represented by counsel, was sentenced *in absentia* to death by hanging. It was discovered later that he was already dead at the time of the trial.[97] His legal counsel, Dr Friedrich Bergold, often complained that without contact with his client he was not in a position to investigate exculpatory evidence properly.[98] The case against Bormann was delayed until the end of the parent trial, in order to give more time to prepare the defence.[99] Nevertheless, Bergold fought a losing battle, not least due to a tendency of the other accused to put the blame on Bormann, who after all was not present to oppose.[100] Even as Bergold tried to prove the death of the defendant by witness testimony, the IMT judges were not willing to terminate proceedings against Bormann.[101]

---

95 *See* ICC *Prosecutor v Lubanga*, TC I, ICC-01/04-01/06-T-50-ENG, 4 September 2007, Transcript Status Conference, p 6.

96 *See* C Safferling, *Towards an International Criminal Procedure* (OUP 2003) 241 *et subs.* for several examples. *See* also C Laue, 'Die Hauptverhandlung ohne den Angeklagten', *Juristische Arbeitsblätter* (2010) 294–7.

97 Bormann died on 2 May 1945. His corpse was only found in 1972.

98 IMT Protocols XIV, 625 and XVII, 287.

99 A further submission to delay the case was however denied, IMT Protocols XVII, 272.

100 *See* eg, IMT Protocols XIV, 625.

101 *See* IMT Protocols XVII, 489.

1. *Human rights law*

Art. 14 (3) (d) ICCPR foresees a right of the defendant to be tried in his or her own presence. Even if it is not contained in the ECHR explicitly, the right to be present is inherent in Art. 6 ECHR as a whole, with regard to the object and purpose of this article.[102] The right to be present is essential for a fair and just trial for three reasons: (1) the accused has the right to be heard, (2) s/he has a right to defend himself adequately, and (3) his/her presence is necessary for the truth-finding purpose to confront the accused with the evidence and the testimony of witnesses.[103]

Yet the right to be present is not guaranteed in absolute terms. The reasons for the absence of the defendant have to be taken into account. In the interests of a proper administration of justice, a trial *in absentia* might be permissible.[104] The HRC has given the 'waiver' of the right to be present as an example for such an exception. In any case, the rights of the defence must be strictly observed, even if the absence of the accused is permissible in exceptional circumstances.[105] It is highly questionable if an adequate defence can be observed at all, if the defendant has never appeared, and has never been in contact with counsel. The case against Bormann is a good example for this. Therefore it is necessary that should the defendant appear at some later time, then s/he must be able to obtain a new determination of the merits of the charge. This means that the entire trial must be repeated from the beginning as an appeals procedure is not sufficient in this regard.[106] This might be different if the accused is excluded from the trial hearing for some limited time only for reasons of upholding order in the courtroom.

2. *Tribunals*

The UN Tribunals relate to Art. 14 (3) (d) ICCPR and prohibit trials *in absentia*, Art. 21 (4) (d) ICTYSt, Art. 20 (4) (d) ICTRSt and Art. 17 (4) (d) SCSLSt.[107] The accused has a right to be present in the courtroom. Yet the Tribunals have two exceptions: (1) waiver, and (2) disruption.

The accused can waive the right to be present in the courtroom if this decision is 'free and unequivocal', fully informed, and s/he is continuously represented by counsel.[108] These prerequisites have been applied in a rather broad way as the ICTR

---

[102] ECtHR *Brozicek v Italy*, Judgment 19 December 1989, Series A No. 167, para 45, and *Colozza v Italy*, Judgment 12 February 1985, Series A No. 89, para 27.

[103] *See* ECtHR *Van Geyseghem v Belgium*, Judgment 21 January 1999, Rep. 1999-I; *Krombach v France*, Judgment 13 February 2001, Rep. 2001-II.

[104] *See* C Safferling, *Towards an International Criminal Procedure* (OUP 2003) 242–3.

[105] *See* HRC *Mbenge v Zaire* Doc. A/38/40, p. 134; and HRC General Comment 13 (Article 14), para 11.

[106] *See* ECtHR *Colozza v Italy*, Judgment 12 February 1985, Series A No. 89, paras 29–30.

[107] *See* also the Report of the Secretary-General Pursuant to Paragraph 2 of Security Council Resolution 808 (1993), S/25704, 3 May 1993, para 101.

[108] ICTR *Prosecutor v Nahimana et al.*, AC, ICTR-99-52-A, 28 November 2007, Judgment, para 109.

interpreted the declaration of the accused Barayagwiza that his trial was a show trial and never attended an implicit waiver.[109] At the ICTY some accused have offered their written consent to the trial continuing in their absence, which seems unproblematic.[110]

The second reason for a trial *in absentia* is constant disruption of the proceedings on the side of the accused. If and when the accused intentionally and continuously interrupts the ongoing trial, the judges may remove him/her from the courtroom, after s/he has been warned. The accused forfeits the right to be present by such undue behaviour.[111] A video-link should be made available so that the accused is in a position to follow the trial from outside the courtroom in such instances.[112]

A different scenario arises if the accused suffers from a long-term illness and is thus prohibited from being physically present in the courtroom. It has been upheld that the right to physical presence is not being compromised by participation via video-link.[113] Therefore, in the case of unintentional disruption of the trial by illness, trial must be delayed. Yet if the disruption is 'substantial' and all other reasonable means have been exhausted, the trial could continue in the absence of the accused in order to assure a reasonably expeditious trial.[114]

In that case, the chamber must apply measures to safeguard the accused's right to follow the trial and participate in the proceedings. The accused must therefore be in a position to communicate freely with counsel and to address the court at any time.[115] This would mean that the trial should be broadcast to the accused and the proceedings must be interrupted at regular intervals to give the accused time to consult and instruct his or her legal representative in the courtroom.

However, if the health of the accused degrades constantly, or his/her mental capacity diminishes to such an extent that s/he cannot follow the proceedings, instead of continuing in the absence of the accused, the prosecution should be halted and the proceedings against such a person terminated.[116] At the IMT in Nuremberg,

---

[109] ICTR *Prosecutor v Nahimana et al.*, AC, ICTR-99-52-A, 28 November 2007, Judgment, para 99–107.

[110] ICTY *Prosecutor v Popović et al.*, TC, IT-05-88-T, 28 April 2009, Trial Transcript, p 33312.

[111] ICTY *Prosecutor v Milošević*, AC, IT-02-54AR73.7, 1 November 2004, Decision on Interlocutory Appeal of the Trial Chamber's Decision on the Assignment of Defence Counsel, para 13.

[112] *See* Boas/Bischoff/Reid/Taylor, *ICL III*, 274.

[113] ICTR *Prosecutor v Zigiranyirazo*, AC, ICTR-2001-73-AR73, 30 October 2006, Decision on Interlocutory Appeal, para 12.

[114] ICTY *Prosecutor v Stanišić and Simatović*, AC, IT-03-69-AR73.2, 16 May 2008, Decision on Defence Appeal of the Decision on Future Course of Proceedings, para 15, 18–19.

[115] ICTY *Prosecutor v Stanišić and Simatović*, TC I, IT-03-69-PT, TC, 29 May 2009, Decision on Start of Trial and Modalities for Trial, para 13.

[116] The line is difficult to draw. In recent cases in Germany, concerns regarding age and frailty of alleged Nazi criminals were put aside in favour of prosecution. *See* S Beck, 'Does Age Prevent Punishment? The Struggles of the German Juridical System with Alleged Nazi Criminals:

this was done in the case of Gustav Krupp. Due to his illness and age, the charges were dropped and no proceeding *in absentia* took place.[117] The judges were almost prepared to release Rudolf Hess due to his state of mind (amnesia), but because he declared himself fit to stand trial, it continued in his presence.[118] Later on as doubts were raised as to the mental fitness of Hess,[119] the IMT constantly denied reviewing its prior decision again.[120]

It should be mentioned that Rule 61 RPE ICTY provided for a hearing which took place without the suspect. Yet this review of the indictment which was invoked only five times in the early jurisprudence of the ICTY,[121] resulted in the issuance of an international arrest warrant and did not constitute a proper trial. As soon as the suspect appeared at the ICTY, a trial proceeding was initiated.[122]

3. ICC

Art. 63 (1) ICCSt expresses the prohibition of a trial *in absentia*.[123] The accused 'shall be present during trial'. Art. 67 (1) (d) ICCSt contains the defendant's right to be present at trial. Both provisions are limited by Art. 63 (2) ICCSt which gives the Chamber the power to remove the accused if s/he continues to disrupt the trial. The trouble must be repetitive and persistent.[124] The accused can only be removed, if all other means to uphold order in the courtroom have been exhausted. In particular the accused must be warned that s/he might be removed from the courtroom should s/he not adopt his or her behaviour. The procedure to be adopted in such a case is similar to that at the Tribunals. The person removed must be put in a position to follow the trial from the outside of the courtroom and communicate with counsel if s/he so wishes. The duration of the removal must be kept to the minimum possible.

Commentary on the Criminal Proceedings against John Demjanjuk and Heinrich Boere', 11 *GLJ* (2010) 347–66.

[117] *See* eg, V. von der Lippe, *Nürnberger Tagebuchnotizen* (Knapp 1951) 20, 23.

[118] IMT Protocols II, 548. *See* also W Harris, *Tyranny on Trial* (3rd edn, Southern Methodist UP 1999) 31.

[119] Eg, by the US psychologist Gustave Martin Gilbert, *see* G Gilbert, *Nuremberg Diary* (Da Caop Press 1995) 213.

[120] And even in the Judgment the judges emphasized Hess's fitness, IMT Protocols I, 189, 320 *et subs*.

[121] ICTY *Prosecutor v Nikolić*, TC, IT-94-2-R61, 20 October 1995, Review of Indictment Pursuant to Rule 61 of the Rules of Procedure and Evidence; *Prosecutor v Martić*, TC, IT-95-11-R61, 8 March 1996, Decision; *Prosecutor v Mrkšić, Radić and Šljivančanin*, TC, IT-95-13-R61, 3 April 1996, Review of the Indictments Pursuant to Rule 61 of the Rules of Procedure and Evidence; *Prosecutor v Rajić*, TC, IT-95-12-R61, 13 September 1996, Review of the Indictment pursuant to Rule 61 of the Rules of Procedure and Evidence; *Prosecutor v Karadžic and Mladić*, TC, IT-95-5-R61 and IT-95-18-R61, 11 July 1996, Review of the Indictments pursuant to Rule 61 of the Rules of Procedure and Evidence.

[122] For a more detailed analysis of these reviews *see* C Safferling, *Towards an International Criminal Procedure* (OUP 2003) 243–5.

[123] Ibid, 245–50.

[124] Triffterer/*Schabas*, Art. 63 MN 15.

Although the Rome Statute does not contain an explicit provision on the waiver of the right to be present, the ICC should accept such a concept, despite the wording of Art. 63 (1) ICCSt. There is no necessity to delay the proceeding in a case where the informed accused voluntarily waives his or her right to be present at trial as long as there is legal representation in the courtroom.

There are some provisions in the ICC law which allow an *ex parte* hearing; that is, without the accused and counsel. According to Art. 72 (7) ICCSt such a hearing might be staged for the protection of national security information. Furthermore, Rule 74 (4) RPE ICC foresees an *ex parte* deliberation with the prosecution of the question whether a witness who might incriminate him or herself could be given an assurance that his or her testimony will be kept confidential and not be used in subsequent proceedings before the Court. Finally, Rule 88 (2) RPE ICC provides for an *ex parte* hearing in order to consider the implementation of special protective measures to a traumatized victim.

4. *Conclusion*

The right to be present at trial is not only a right in the classical sense. It is a general principle of international criminal procedure that there is no trial *in absentia*.[125] Yet this principle is not absolute.[126] Either by waiver or by forfeiture, the trial might continue without the accused being present. However, this avenue is only open for the Chamber in exceptional circumstances, and must be kept as short as possible. In addition, the accused must have the opportunity to follow the proceedings from the outside of the courtroom. Counsel, who must in any case attend the trial, must be able to communicate with the client at all times.

V. Oral trial

The trial has to be oral. This principle is closely connected to the maxim of a public trial. The modern trial is not a secret one based solely on reviewing documents. The importance of this principle stems from the fact that there is, at least in Continental Europe, no 'strong tradition' of oral presentation of evidence at trial.[127] Prior to the French Revolution the conviction was based solely on paper; that is, in the file.[128] It was thus a major achievement of the Enlightenment to eliminate secret trials and establish that the charge together with the evidence against the accused have to be made public and read out loud so that the public can exercise democratic control over the trial. The development in England was more cognizant of the oral trial

---

[125] *See* Triffterer/*Schabas*, Art. 63 MN 11.

[126] *See* Boas/Bischoff/Reid/Taylor, *ICL III*, 272.

[127] *See* A Zahar and G Sluiter, *International Criminal Law* (OUP 2007) 314 *et subs.*; T Vormbaum, *Einführung in die moderne Strafrechtsgeschichte* (Springer 2008) 100 *et subs.*; C Safferling, *Towards an International Criminal Procedure* (OUP 2003) 5–9 as to the historic development.

[128] K Volk, 'Napoleon und das deutsche Strafrecht, 31 *Juristische Schulung* (1991) 281.

principle, as trial by jury and cross-examination presuppose the oral presentation of the accusation and the evidence.[129]

The oral trial principle requires also that the judgment may only be based on facts and issues which are heard in court and on which the accused has a chance to comment.[130]

In the Nuremberg trial, the principle of an oral trial was respected but was balanced with the duty to expedite proceedings as foreseen in Art. 18 IMTSt. Justice Jackson applied to the judges on 22 March 1946 to treat all the documentary material which has been translated as having been read out already.[131] The defence lawyers objected, because the prosecution had spent months reading the documents and it would be unfair if the defence were not allowed to do the same.[132] The IMT decided that whenever a party wants to rely on a document as evidence, a summary should be presented, and the Court be directed to important passages.[133]

1. *Human rights law*

The principle of an oral trial is not spelt out in human rights treaties literally but is implied by several sentences about the fair trial norms.[134] First, orality is a corollary of the public trial as it would otherwise not make sense to invite the public to the trial.[135] Secondly, the right to examine or have witnesses examined, provided for in Art. 14 (3) (e) ICCPR and Art. 6 (3) (d) ECHR can only be fulfilled via oral confrontation of the witness.[136] Both the HRC and the ECtHR have found a violation of the principle of a public hearing in instances where proceedings took place only in writing.[137] The oral trial principle is particularly important if questions of facts are involved. In appeals proceedings in which only points of law are contested, a hearing might not be indispensable.[138]

2. *Tribunals*

There is no explicit provision in the Tribunals' respective Statutes that the trial must be oral by nature. However, as the procedural law at the Tribunals is based on the

---

[129] In greater detail: C Safferling, *Towards an International Criminal Procedure* (OUP 2003) 9–14.

[130] K Volk, *Grundkurs StPO* (7th edn, CH Beck 2010) § 18 MN 25.

[131] IMT Protocols IX, 726.

[132] Ibid, 729 *et subs.*

[133] Ibid, 742.

[134] S Stavros, *The Guarantees for Accused Persons under Article 6 of the ECHR* (Brill 1993) 189.

[135] D J Harris, M O'Boyle, and C Warbrick, *Law of the ECHR* (LexisNexis 1995) 218.

[136] C Safferling, *Towards an International Criminal Procedure* (OUP 2003) 240.

[137] *See* HRC *Touron v Uruguay* Doc. A/36/40, 120; ECtHR *Fredin v Sweden* (No. 2), Judgment 23 February 1994, Series A No. 283-A, paras 21–2.

[138] *See* ECtHR *Fredin v Sweden* (No. 2), Judgment 23 February 1994, Series A No. 283-A, paras 21–2.

human rights requirements of a fair and public trial, and on an adversarial examination of the evidence (Rule 85 RPE ICTY), it is presumed that the trial is oral (*see* also Rules 90 (A) RPE ICTY/ICTR/SCSL).[139] Case law shows that the UN judges operate on this assumption when a document or an exhibit is to be admitted to the trial through a witness.[140] In addition, the opposing party must be in a position to cross-examine or present oral argument regarding documents or exhibits.[141] Only under exceptional circumstances may public documents be admitted as evidence from the bar,[142] or written statements from witnesses might be admissible under Rules 89 (F) and 92*bis* RPE ICTY. As concerns the latter, these written statements are not allowed in order to prove acts and conduct of the accused. Written testimony can thus only pertain to circumstantial information.[143] The Appeals Chamber has adopted a broad approach and admitted written evidence as long as the witness was present and could have confirmed his or her statement.[144] This approach was heavily criticized for adopting a far too utilitarian approach and neglecting principled considerations of fairness.[145] In general however, non-oral evidence will not carry the same evidentiary weight as oral testimony.[146] We can thus conclude that the ICTY and the other Tribunals consider the orality of the trial as a general requirement of a fair proceeding.

3. ICC

The situation at the ICC is similar to that at the UN Tribunals. There is no explicit norm stating that the trial be oral. Yet those human rights incorporated in Art. 67 ICCSt presuppose an oral hearing for the determination of the guilt of the person charged.[147] The ICCSt expresses a preference for *viva voce*, or live, testimony, in Art. 69 (2).[148] Whereas summary evidence instead of witness testimony

---

[139] Similarly A Zahar and G Sluiter, *International Criminal Law* (OUP 2007) 315.

[140] ICTY *Prosecutor v Strugar*, TC II, IT-01-42-T, 9 September 2004, Decision II on the Admissibility of Certain Documents, para 9.

[141] ICTY *Prosecutor v Milošević*, TC III, IT-02-S4-T, 12 February 2004, Decision on Prosecution Motion for Admission of Witness Statement of Investigator Bernard O'Donnell in *lieu* of Viva Voce Testimony Pursuant to Rules 54 and 92*bis*, p 3.

[142] ICTY *Prosecutor v Galić*, TC I, IT-98-29-T, 11 September 2002, Decision on the Admission into Evidence of Documents Tendered from the Bar Table by the Prosecutor, p 3.

[143] *See* J Nemitz, 'Die Hauptverhandlug unter besonderer Berücksichtigung des Beweisrechts', in: S Kirsch (ed), *Internationale Strafgerichtshöfe* (Nomos 2005) 53, 66.

[144] ICTY *Prosecutor v Milošević*, AC, IT-02-54-AR73.4, 30 September 2003, Decision on Interlocutory Appeal on the Admissibility of Evidence-in-Chief in the Form of Written Statements, para 16.

[145] *See* ICTY *Prosecutor v Milošević*, AC, IT-02-54-AR73.4, 21 October 2003, Dissenting Opinion of Judge David Hunt on Admissibility of Evidence in Chief in the Form of Written Statements, para 8.

[146] ICTY *Prosector v Naletilić and Martinović*, TC, 31 March 2003, IT-98-34-T, Judgment, para 12; J Nemitz, 'Die Hauptverhandlug unter besonderer Berücksichtigung des Beweisrechts', in: S Kirsch (ed), *Internationale Strafgerichtshöfe* (Baden-Baden 2005) 53, 59.

[147] C Safferling, *Towards an International Criminal Procedure* (OUP 2003) 240.

[148] Boas/Bischoff/Reid/Taylor, *ICL III*, 352 *et subs.*

has been admitted at the confirmation stage,[149] these decisions by the Pre-Trial Chamber should be considered as exceptions pertaining only to the confirmation hearing, which—according to the opinion offered here—should be a summary proceeding.[150]

4. *Conclusion*

Even if human rights norms do not state explicitly that the trial must be an oral one, the orality principle is inherent in several fair trial requirements. Most importantly, only in the case of an oral trial can the public exercise its right and duty to a democratic control of the prosecution.

The Tribunals and the ICC respect this principle in general. Nevertheless, there is an increasing tendency at the ICTY to allow written statements and thus speed up the proceedings. However, the comparatively cautious approach adopted by the ICC judges with a view to written testimony might also be due to the fact that they do not feel such an enormous time pressure compared to the *ad hoc* Tribunals' backlog yet.[151] Their dangerous willingness to rely on written statements might increase with rising pressure on the time spent at trial. Even if it is necessary to approve exceptional circumstances in which written evidence needs to be admitted—which will be discussed at a later stage—it is necessary to adhere to the general principle of a oral trial in order to render public control possible.

VI. Presumption of innocence

The presumption of innocence is perhaps the most important provision, a cardinal principle[152] of the modern, liberal, criminal prosecution. Its aim is to safeguard the compliance with and the prevalence of the rule of law in contrast to the *fama publica*, or political interests, as the basis for a criminal sanction. Justice Jackson expressed the presumption of innocence before his assignment to act as the US Chief Prosecutor in Nuremberg addressing the American Society of International Law in Washington DC: 'That is one of the risks that are taken whenever trials are commenced. The ultimate principle is that you must put no man on trial under the forms judicial proceedings if you are not willing to see him freed if not proven guilty.'[153]

---

[149] ICC *Prosecutor v Lubanga*, PTC, ICC-01/04-01/06-517, 4 October 2006, Decision Concerning the Prosecution Proposed Summary Evidence, p 3 *et subs.*

[150] *See* Chapter 5 B.

[151] Opined by Boas/Bischoff/Reid/Taylor, *ICL III*, 356.

[152] *See* F Jacobs and R White, *The European Convention on Human Rights* (2nd edn, OUP 1996) 150.

[153] R H Jackson, 'The Rule of Law amongst Nations', 19 *Temple Law Quarterly* (1945–46) 135, address delivered before the American Society of International Law, Washington DC, 14 April 1945.

The Nuremberg trial was based on this credo despite the fact that the Soviet opinion deviated considerably. The Soviet delegation operated on the conviction that the guilt of the twenty one defendants present at Nuremberg before the IMT was already determined. The trial, according to the Soviet opinion, had merely the aim of fulfiling the political will, which was expressed in the Moscow Declaration of November 1943, and attributing the sentence according to the individual responsibility of the accused. The dissenting opinion of the Russian judge, Nikitschenko, expresses this attitude.[154]

Yet the presumption of innocence has many aspects, which we need to look at in greater detail.[155]

1. Human rights law

It ought not surprise that the principle of presumed innocence is contained in all the major human rights treaties, for example, in Art. 14 (2) ICCPR and Art. 6 (2) ECHR, in Art. 8 (2) AmCHR and Art. 7 (1) (b) AfCHPR. It has consequences for the institution of criminal proceedings, in particular for the independence and impartiality of the judiciary, as has been discussed above.[156] At the trial stage, the presumption of innocence has three different aspects: (1) it relates to the burden of proof, (2) it also relates to the requirement of the proof of guilt, and (3) it influences the behaviour of court or other public officials.

a. Burden of proof Both the ICCPR regime and the ECHR require that the burden of proof is on the prosecution and any doubt shall benefit the accused.[157] We will not go into further detail as concerns the common law–civil law divide in that regard. The differences are marginal and do not touch on the general principle, that it is the state which must prove the guilt of the accused, and the onus of proof of innocence must never lie with the defendant.[158]

The ECtHR has issued a number of decisions in which this principle has been jeopardized by differentiating between a presumption of facts and a presumption of guilt. Only the latter falls under the prohibition of Art. 6 (2) ECHR.[159]

---

[154] IMT Nuremberg, Vol 1, 342. *See* also M Bazyler, 'The Role of the Soviet Union in the International Military Tribunal at Nuremberg', in: H Reginbogin and C Safferling (eds), *The Nuremberg Trials: International Criminal Law Since 1945* (Saur 2006) 42.

[155] *See* in summary Triffterer/*Schabas*, Art. 66 MN 2.

[156] *See* Chapter 4.

[157] *See* HRC General Comment 13 (Article 14) para 7; and ECtHR *Barberà, Messeguè and Jabardo v Spain*, Judgment 6 December 1988, Series A No. 147, para 77. *See* also R Esser, *Auf dem Weg zu einem europäischen Strafverfahrensrecht* (DeGruyter 2002) 403 *et subs.*; S Zappalà, *Human Rights in International Criminal Procedure* (OUP 2003) 91.

[158] In further detail as regards the different approaches and how to solve them, *see* C Safferling, *Towards an International Criminal Procedure* (OUP 2003) 257 *et subs.*

[159] *See* ECommHR *X v United Kingdom*, Decision, 19 July 1972, Appl. No. 5124/71, 42 CD 135; ECtHR *Salabiaku v France*, Judgment 7 October 1988, Series A No. 141-A; *Pham Hoang v France*, Judgment 25 September 1992, Series A No. 243.

According to the Strasbourg case law, legal presumption is not prohibited on a general basis, as long as the defendant has a fair chance to rebut the presumption, and as long as the court does refrain from any automatic reliance on the presumption. This jurisprudence is regrettable and has been rightly criticized as perverting the presumption of innocence by putting the onus of proof *de facto* onto the accused.[160]

It must be kept in mind that the ECtHR is often reluctant to intervene vigorously into the laws of the Member States. It has therefore developed the methodological doctrine of the overall-fairness evaluation. The Strasbourg judges will always look at the situation as a whole considering the gravity of the violation, the importance of the human right that risks being violated, and the performance of the national authorities.[161] A state will thus only be convicted for having violated the convention if the individual's right is *de facto* 'extinguished'.[162]

b. Proof of guilt A second question connected to the presumption of innocence is that of the standard of proof required for a conviction; that is, the standard required to refute the presumption of innocence. The standard often invoked is 'proof of guilt of the accused beyond reasonable doubt'.[163] Despite differences in terminology and despite a missing clarification by the ECtHR, which relies heavily on the domestic law and the principles of weighing evidence it contains, and exercises nothing more than a control of misuse and arbitrariness,[164] the threshold for reasonable doubt can be seen as generally accepted in democratic societies.

The content of the principle is not specified any further. Taken literally, doubts are obviously allowed, as only 'reasonable' doubts would destruct the prosecution case. What constitutes reasonableness in this context is certainly elusive[165] and cannot be derived from human rights provisions. We will have to come back to this point later, when discussing the law at the international courts and Tribunals.

---

[160] *See* eg, also R Esser, *Auf dem Weg zu einem europäischen Strafverfahrensrecht* (DeGruyter 2002) 743.

[161] *See* ECtHR *Jalloh v Germany*, Judgment 11 July 2006, Rep. 2006-IX, para 95 *et subs.*; *Khan v United Kingdom*, Judgment 12 May 2000, Rep. 2000-V, para 34 and *Allan v United Kingdom*, Judgment 5 November 2002, Rep. 2002-IX, para 42 concerning Art. 6 ECHR.

[162] ECtHR, *Heaney and McGuiness v Ireland*, Judgment 21 December 2000, Rep. 2000-VII, para 57 *et subs.*

[163] *See* eg, HRC General Comment 13 (Article 14), para 7, disregarding the fact that the formula has been deliberately rejected in the drafting history of the ICCPR, *see* E/CN.4/365; E/CN.4/SR.156, 6.

[164] For further discussion *see* C Safferling, *Towards an International Criminal Procedure* (OUP 2003) 259 *et subs.* with references.

[165] *See* Boas/Bischoff/Reid/Taylor, *ICL III*, 385.

c. **Conduct of officials** In informal findings prior to the judgment, the court must refrain from presuming the guilt of the accused.[166] Therefore it is enough for a violation of the presumption of innocence 'that there is some reasoning suggesting that the court regards the accused as guilty.'[167] In such a case the impartiality of the judges would be severely hampered.[168]

The presumption of innocence does not only pertain to the court but also to other state officials. All state authorities must treat the suspect as if he or she were innocent until the presumption is refuted by the judgment of the competent court. Even if the state is obliged to inform 'the public about criminal investigations in progress, but it requires that they do so with all discretion and circumspection necessary if the presumption of innocence is to be respected.'[169]

Ministers or high-ranking officers must therefore refrain from commenting on an ongoing trial.

The presumption of innocence has yet another side to it. The authority of the judiciary might be damaged if the accused is treated as guilty in the media. The state must prevent such a situation because Art. 6 (2) ECHR requires the state to protect the suspect from prejudicial influence on his/her prosecution and the protection against unlawful attacks on honour and reputation as provided for in Art. 17 ICCPR.[170] The outcome of a trial is for the court to determine and not for the media. Should journalists interfere in this regard, the state may and must react accordingly and suppress inadmissible commentaries.[171] A trial by media must under all circumstances be avoided.[172]

2. *Tribunals*

The presumption of innocence is contained in Art. 21 (3) ICTYSt, Art. 30 (3) ICTRSt and Art. 17 (3) SCSLSt and is accepted by the Tribunals as a leading principle of procedural law.[173] As concerns the onus of proof, ICTY jurisprudence recognizes that the onus of proof of the guilt of the accused rests on the Prosecution throughout the case.[174]

---

166 *See* also S Trechsel, *Human Rights in Criminal Proceedings* (OUP 2005) 163.

167 ECtHR *Minelli v Switzerland*, Judgment 25 March 1983, Series A No. 62, para 37.

168 *See* A Zahar and G Sluiter, *International Criminal Law* (OUP 2007) 302.

169 ECtHR *Allenet de Ribemont v France*, Judgment 10 February 1995, Series A No. 308, para 38.

170 A Zahar and G Sluiter, *International Criminal Law* (OUP 2007) 302.

171 ECtHR *Time Newspaper v United Kingdom*, Judgment 5 March 1999, Series A No. 30, para 63; *Worm v Austria*, Judgment 29 August 1997, Rep. 1997-V, para 50.

172 *See* also R Esser, *Auf dem Weg zu einem europäischen Strafverfahrensrecht* (DeGruyter 2002) 718.

173 *See* ICTR *Prosecutor v Ntuyahaga*, TC, ICTR-98-40-T, 18 March 1999, Decision on the Prosecutor's Motion to Withdraw the Indictment.

174 ICTY *Prosecutor v Delalić et al.*, TC II, IT-96-21-T, 19 August 1998, Decision on the Prosecution's Alternative Request to Reopen the Prosecution's Case, para 20.

With regard to the standard of proof for the conviction, the Tribunal adopts the standard of proof 'beyond reasonable doubt'. Yet Rule 85 (A) (2) RPE ICTY/ICTR/SCSL refers only to the majority of the Trial Chamber who need to be satisfied that the accused is guilty. The 'reasonable doubt' requirement relates to the individual judge and not to the chamber as a whole. Even if majority verdicts are traditionally the practice of courts in common law states, it is questionable whether this culture should be transferred to the chambers of international courts and Tribunals. The difficulties are described by the following: if two judges have no doubts, but one judge is not convinced, could it be said that the doubts of this one judge are unreasonable, solely because the other two judges have no doubts? In the present author's view, the majority rule, if adapted to the question of guilt, constitutes a violation of the presumption of innocence, and the chambers should always speak with one voice. In matters of the interpretation of the law, dissenting opinions and majority decisions do not pose the same dangers, and could aid the further development of international criminal law both in substantive and in procedural aspects.[175]

The third aspect of the presumption of innocence, that is, the conduct of officials and media, has also given rise to discussions at the UN Tribunals. To uphold the reputation of the accused and protect him/her as innocent seems most difficult to achieve. Several accused have had to suffer from undue scrutiny of their personality in the media before or pending trial.[176]

3. ICC

Art. 66 ICCSt containing the presumption of innocence is a much more advanced norm compared to the human rights provisions. In the first paragraph the general principle is mentioned, according to which everyone is presumed innocent until proven guilty before the Court in accordance with the applicable law.[177] The following provisions address two of the discussed consequences of the presumption of innocence, namely that the onus of proof needs to be on the prosecutor (Art. 66 (2) ICCSt), and that the standard of proof is proof beyond reasonable doubt (Art. 66 (3) ICCSt).

a. Onus of proof It has been said that the ICCSt does not contain any provision establishing 'reverse onus'.[178] Yet the Statute goes even further and provides for an explicit right of the accused not to have imposed on him or her any reversal of the burden of proof or any onus of rebuttal in Art. 67 (1) (i) ICCSt.[179] This marks a new development in procedural law making. By this additional norm the ICCSt

[175] In greater detail: C Safferling, *Towards an International Criminal Procedure* (OUP 2003) 262–3.

[176] *See* S Zappalà, *Human Rights in International Criminal Procedure* (OUP 2003) 85–6.

[177] Triffterer/*Schabas*, Art. 66 MN 10.

[178] Ibid, Art. 66 MN 18.

[179] Ibid, Art. 66 MN 19.

prevents the judges from reversing the onus by case law. Such a scenario might arise with a view of 'defences'; that is, grounds for excluding criminal liability. One of the reasons why the term 'defences' was avoided in the Rome Statute is to be seen in the danger, that the onus to proof the factual circumstances of a 'defence' is quite easily been transferred to the accused.[180] An example, which has arisen at the ICTY, could be the plea of insanity.[181] If we—as did the ICTY Trial Chamber—operate on the assumption that every person is mentally sane and capable of understanding the law and the trial, one could quickly conclude that the accused who wants to defend himself by referring to his state of mind, must deliver proof for his mental insanity according to Art. 31 (1) (a) ICCSt. Art. 67 (1) (d) ICCSt would prohibit such a ruling.[182] In case the defendant does indeed raise a mental disease as the reason for eluding criminal responsibility, the Prosecutor must show that the accused was at the time of the deed in full control of his/her conduct to conform to the requirements of the law.[183]

Similarly one could come to the conclusion that a commander is responsible for the crimes committed by his subordinates according to Art. 28 (1) ICCSt, unless he can show that s/he did not and could not have known of the misbehaviour on the side of his or her subordinates and unless s/he can provide proof that s/he has taken all necessary and reasonable measures to prevent or repress the commission of the crimes or to submit the matter to prosecution. Also here, it is submitted, that it is not the commander who needs to exculpate him or herself, but the onus is on the prosecutor to prove that the commander failed to fulfil the Art. 28 ICCSt requirements.[184]

b. Standard of proof The Rome Statute contains the 'reasonable doubt' requirement in Art 66 (3) ICCSt. As has been shown before, there are several standards of evidence throughout the ICCSt concerning the beginning of an investigation (Art. 53 ICCSt): the issuance of an arrest warrant (Art 58 (1) ICCSt), and the confirmation hearing (Art. 61 (7) ICCSt).[185] Looking at these as a rising scale, the 'reasonable doubt' requirement would certainly be on the top of the scale, demanding the highest degree of proof.[186]

Two other provisions are of interest in this regard. Art. 74 (2) ICCSt states that the decision can only be based on evidence which has been presented at the hearing.

---

180 *See* A Zahar and G Sluiter, *International Criminal Law* (OUP 2007) 362.

181 *See* ICTY *Prosecutor v Delalić et al.*, TC, IT-96-21-T, 16 November 1998, Judgment, para 1157–60.

182 *See* also K Volk, *Grundkurs StPO* (7th edn, CH Beck 2010) § 18 MN 18.

183 A different approach is given by Triffterer/*Schabas*, Art. 66 MN 20, who opines that such a burden would be an impossible task for the Prosecutor.

184 Differently again Triffterer/*Schabas*, Art. 66 MN 21, who states, that Art. 28 ICC contains an effective reversal of the onus of proof.

185 *See* p 339.

186 *See* also Triffterer/*Schabas*, Art. 66 MN 23.

The emphasis of this provision lies on the fact that the judges must rest their decision on the entire evidence which was presented.[187] Art. 74 (3) ICCSt further states that judges should attempt to achieve unanimity, but may also take a decision by majority. As has been said before, the majority rule is difficult with a view to the standard necessary in order to rebut the presumption of innocence.[188] For the reasons given above, unanimity, in particular as regards the question of guilt or innocence, is preferable.[189]

c. Conduct of officials Members of the ICC must under all circumstances refrain from utterances which would presume the guilt of the suspect. This is particularly true for the judges who must avoid casting any shadow on their independence and impartiality. As the ICC is an independent international institution itself, it is difficult for it to influence other bodies that might comment on the guilt of a suspect, as these are beyond the reach of the ICC. The same is true for the media. In a national context the executive branch of government is in a much better position to protect the accused from undue allegation prior or pending trial.[190] As with the UN Tribunals, the ICC can only influence other people or the media by putting strong emphasis on the respect for the suspect and on the importance of the presumption of innocence. Should the misconduct happen before the ICC, the contempt of court regime might be set into action.

4. Conclusion

The presumption of innocence in its three forms, onus of proof, standard of proof, and conduct of officials, is widely accepted as a general principle of criminal procedure and is complied with at international criminal courts only in parts. In particular as regards the reversal of the onus of proof on the defendant, the ICTY and the ICC go beyond the relatively lax approach which can be observed at the ECtHR. The ECtHR jurisprudence should not be adopted. As has been shown, the ECtHR operates on an overall fairness evaluation in order to respect the sovereignty of the national state. The situation at the ICC is different. Respect for the Member States' sovereignty is not necessary in this regard.[191] The ICC does not control domestic legal systems, but is in search of a procedural order which suits both efficiency and human rights.

Even if the formula that a conviction requires proof beyond reasonable doubt of the guilt of the accused is vague, it is a commonly accepted standard and should thus

[187] Based on proposals by France and Germany, *see* C Safferling, *Towards an International Criminal Procedure* (OUP 2003) 264 with references.

[188] *See* also Triffterer/*Schabas*, Art. 66 MN 28, who raises the question but in the end endorses—in a rather positivistic way—the Statute.

[189] C Safferling, *Towards an International Criminal Procedure* (OUP 2003) 264.

[190] Triffterer/*Schabas*, Art. 66 MN 27.

[191] Differently Triffterer/*Schabas*, Art. 66 MN 22, who advises the ICC to turn to the ECtHR's restriction of the presumption of innocence.

be adhered to. Yet extensive use of the possibility to pass judgments by majority, as foreseen in Art. 23 (2) ICTYSt and Art. 74 (5) ICCSt, must be guarded against. Proof beyond reasonable doubts means that all judges of the chamber should be convinced of the guilt of the accused.

Protection against attacks from the media is difficult to guarantee by international Tribunals.[192] Tribunals do not have the ability and competences to influence other officials and the media apart from the 'contempt of court' regime.[193] The chambers do have the responsibility to behave in an impeccable way towards the accused, to emphasize the importance of the presumption of innocence as a general principle of criminal justice, and to demand the media to show respect for the human rights of the suspect.

VII. The principle of equality of arms

'Equality of arms' is a well-known international legal principle.[194] International courts have derived this principle from the fair trial requirement as contained in Art. 14 (1) ICCPR and Art. 6 (1) ECHR,[195] and have held that it is also implied in the 'right to confront' according to Art. 14 (3) (d) ICCPR and Art. 6 (3) (d) ECHR.[196] Scholars have attributed much force to this principle. It was seen as the minimum threshold requirement for any judicial proceeding to be considered fair and consistent with human rights: 'Indeed, the duty incumbent upon international courts to secure equality and procedural balance between the parties is amplified when related to proceedings involving the protection of individuals.'[197]

Also attempts were made to establish the equality of arms as the main structural principle of criminal procedure not only of the trial proceedings but also of the investigation.[198] At the very least it was determined as a pre-condition for any adversarial structured trial.[199]

[192] A Zahar and G Sluiter, *International Criminal Law* (OUP 2007) 303.

[193] *See* Chapter 10.

[194] S Negri, 'The Principle of Equality of Arms and the Evolving Law of International Criminal Procedure', 5 *ICLR* (2005) 513, 514; ICTY *Prosecutor v Aleksovski*, AC, IT-9S-14/l-AR73, 16 February 1999, Decision on Prosecutor's Appeal on Admissibility of Evidence, para 23.

[195] ICTY *Prosecutor v Kordić and Čerkez,* AC, IT-95-14/2-A, 11 September 2001, Decision on the Application by Mario Cerkez for Extension of Time to File his Respondent's Brief, para 5; *Prosecutor v Tadić*, AC, IT-94-1-A, 15 July 1999, Judgment, para 48; ICTR *Prosecutor v Kayishema and Ruzindana*, AC, ICTR-9S-1-A, 1 June 2001, Judgment (Reasons), para 67.

[196] ICTY *Prosecutor v Delalić et al.*, TC II, IT-96-21-T, 4 February 1998, Decision on the Prosecution's Motion for an Order Requiring Advance Disclosure of Witnesses by the Defence, para 45; *Prosecutor v Kupreškić et al.*, AC, IT-95-16-AR73.3, 15 July 1999, Decision on Appeal by Dragan Papic against Ruling to Proceed by Deposition, para 24.

[197] S Negri, 'The Principle of Equality of Arms and the Evolving Law of International Criminal Procedure', 5 *ICLR* (2005) 513, 514.

[198] *See* K Ambos, 'Der EGMR und die Verfahrensrechte', 115 *ZStW* (2003) 583.

[199] *See* S Kirsch, 'The Trial Proceeding before the ICC', 6 *ICLR* (2006) 275, 284.

Despite its general acceptance and recognition, and despite its alleged metaphorical strength, the concept lacks clarity when applied to specific situations. Indeed it distorts other specific rights which are mentioned as rights of the accused in Art. 14 ICCPR or Art. 6 ECHR.[200]

Taken literally, the principle assumes a trial being similar to a fight, in which the parties need to be equipped with the same weapons in order for the battle to be considered fair. This image might be fitting to a private law action, where plaintiff and defendant stand on equal footing, but a criminal trial is surely shaped by a structural inequality between the state, represented by the prosecutor, and the citizen; that is; the accused.[201] Besides, the martial expression with reference to war and battle should be set aside as being unworthy of any liberal criminal procedural system. I would therefore prefer to abandon the principle altogether as it adds nothing to other much more precise rights, namely the right to be heard by the court or tribunal, the right to have adequate time and facility to prepare the defence, and the right to call and examine witnesses.[202]

In international criminal procedure the principle of equality of arms has played an enormous role. Thus the IMT in Nuremberg was heavily criticized, in particular by the German defence lawyers, as a mockery regarding equality of arms.[203] Indeed, judging from the structural and quantitative data, the situation was almost grotesque: twenty seven senior and fifty four junior defence counsels defended twenty two accused and six accused organizations. In contrast the American delegation alone consisted of 2000 members, there were 170 British staff, twenty four Soviet personnel, and about a dozen French lawyers.

In modern international criminal trials, the situation is not much different, and we ought to ask ourselves what 'equality of arms' can mean under these circumstances.

1. *Human rights law*

The principle of equality of arms cannot be found *expressis verbis* in any of the major human rights codifications. Neither Art. 6 of the European Convention on Human Rights (ECHR), nor Art. 14 of the International Covenant on Civil and Political Rights (ICCPR) make reference to the concept. Yet it is generally

---

200 *See* in greater detail C Safferling, 'Audiatur et altera pars—die prozessuale Waffengleichheit als Prozessprinzip?', 24 *NStZ* (2004) 181.

201 S Zappalá, 'The Rights of Victims *v* the Rights of the Accused', 8 *JICJ* (2010) 137, 149: 'To consider that equality implies that all parties to the trial must be treated on an equal footing is to misinterpret the requirements of fairness and equality'.

202 In greater detail: C Safferling, 'Audiatur et altera pars—die prozessuale Waffengleichheit als Prozessprinzip?' 24 *NStZ* (2004) 181.

203 O Kranzbühler, *Rückblick auf Nürnberg* (Zeit-Verlag 1949) 6 *et subs.*

accepted that equality of arms is a corollary to the right to a 'fair trial'.[204] The early jurisprudence of the European Commission on Human Rights took a rather formal approach to the principle of equality of arms interpreting it to comprise merely the defendant's right to be heard, if the prosecution had the opportunity to present its case.[205] In more recent decisions, the European Court of Human Rights has substantially expanded the remit of the equality principle. It has held that the right of the accused to confront a witness according to Art. 6 (3) (d) ECHR is based on the necessity to establish 'full equality of arms' between prosecutor and defendant regarding witness testimony.[206] Similarly the defendant must be allowed to present a scientific expert in his/her favour if the expert witness, who has been named by the court or by the prosecutor, is not neutral.[207]

The principle of equality of arms has also 'some application to the pre-trial proceedings'.[208] The right to legal assistance during the questioning at the investigation stage is necessitated by the equality principle,[209] as is the disclosure of inculpatory material in order to prepare for an effective defence at trial or for a *habeas corpus* appeal.[210] During the investigation, however, equality of arms cannot be seen as the governing principle, as this phase is inherently inquisitorial in nature. A fair balancing of powers is necessary only as far as the evidence gathering has prejudicial value to the later trial.

The 'equality of arms' principle as interpreted by the ECtHR is thus a mainly formal principle.[211] Each party to the trial must have a chance to take notice of and comment on evidence and statements filed by the opposite side.[212]

2. *Tribunals*

At the UN tribunals the principle of equality of arms has been recognized and applied in several cases. Both the ICTY and the ICTR have held that the equality of arms principle obligates a judicial body to ensure that neither party is put at a

---

[204] *See* eg, UN HRC *Morael v France*, Communication No. 207/1986, 28 July 1989, UN Doc. CCPR/8/Add/1, 416.

[205] Leading cases on this issue: ECHR *Ofner v Austria*, Appl. No. 524/59, Report 23 November 1962, 6 YB, 680 and *Hopfinger v Austria*, Appl. No. 617/59, Report 23 November 1962, 6 *YB*, 680.

[206] ECtHR *Barberà v Spain*, Judgment 6 December 1988, Series A No. 146, 67, 78 and in a civil lawsuit *Dombo Beheer BV v Netherlands*, Judgment 27 October 1993, Series A No. 273.

[207] ECtHR *Brandstetter v Austria*, Judgment 28 August 1991, Series A No. 211, 59.

[208] ECtHR *Lietzow v Germany*, Judgment 13 February 2001, para 44; *Schöps v Germany*, Judgment 13 February 2001, para 44 and *Garcia Alva v Germany*, Judgment 13 February 2001, para 39.

[209] ECHR *Murray v United Kingdom*, Appl. No. 18731/91, Reports 1996-I, 70.

[210] ECtHR *Edwards v United Kingdom*, Judgment 16 December 1992, Series A No. 247-B; *Brogan et al. v United Kingdom*, 29 November 1988, Series A No. 145-B, para 65.

[211] A different view is taken by K Ambos, *Internationales Strafrecht* (2nd edn, CH Beck 2007) §10 MN 14.

[212] *See* R Esser, *Auf dem Weg zu einem Europäischen Strafverfahrensrecht* (DeGruyter 2002) 411.

disadvantage when presenting its case.[213] Art. 20 (1) ICTYSt is to be interpreted according to Art. 14 (1) ICCPR and Art. 6 (1) ECHR. Thus the equality of arms principle is implied in the Tribunals' respective Statutes.[214] As the responsibility for the observance of the procedural maxim lies with the judges, the principle applies only to circumstances within the control of the Tribunal.[215] Furthermore the Tribunals have ruled that it is one consequence of the equality of arms principle to give to the defence adequate time and facility for preparation of the defence.[216] In this context the 'equality of arms' principle is most prominently referred to with a view to disclosure rules, which aim at allowing the defence the same level of access to information as the Prosecutor.[217] The disclosure regime is discussed above.[218]

Rule 85 (A) RPE ICTY illustrates a clear equality of arms in the presentation of evidence. This is the case because the defence is entitled to present its case in an identical manner to the Prosecutor. The defence is entitled to examine and re-examine its own witnesses, as is the prosecution.[219]

Yet there is one major issue which is critical as regards the implementation of the principle of equality of arms in the law of the UN Tribunals: The visible structural inequality between prosecutor and defence, as has already been criticized in the Nuremberg trial.[220]

Taking note of the structural inequality of the prosecutor's office on the one hand and the defence on the other, the Appeals Chamber rushes to add that 'equality of arms' does not amount to material equality between the parties in terms

[213] ICTY *Prosecutor v Kordić and Čerkez*, AC, IT-95-14/2-A, 17 December 2004, Judgment, para 175; *Prosecutor v Tadić*, AC, IT-94-1-A, 15 July 1999, Judgment, para 48; ICTR *Prosecutor v Kayishema and Ruzindana*, AC, ICTR-95-1-A, 1 June 2001, Judgment (Reasons), para 69.

[214] ICTY *Prosecutor v Kordić and Čerkez*, AC, IT-95-14/2-A, 17 December 2004, Judgment, para 175; *Prosecutor v Tadić*, AC, IT-94-1-A, 15 July 1999, Judgment, para 44.

[215] ICTY *Prosecutor v Tadić*, AC, IT-94-1-A, 15 July 1999, Judgment, para 49; ICTR *Prosecutor v Kayishema and Ruzindana*, AC, ICTR-9S-1-A, 1 June 2001, Judgment (Reasons), para 73.

[216] ICTY *Prosecutor v Kordić and Čerkez*, AC, IT-95-14/2-A, 17 December 2004, Judgment, para 175. *See* also ICTY Manual on Developed Practices (2009), 182, regarding access to IT for the accused in order to prepare his/her defence, and 211 as regards facilities in the form of administrative and logistical support from the Tribunal for the defence.

[217] *See* eg, ICTY *Prosecutor v Tadić*, TC, TC II, IT-94-1-T, 27 November 1996, Separate Opinion of Judge Vohrahon Prosecution Motion for Production of Defence Witness Statements; *see* also S Negri, 'The Principle of Equality of Arms and the Evolving Law of International Criminal Procedure', 5 *ICLR* (2005) 513, 560 *et subs.*; G McIntyre, 'Equality of Arms—Defining Human Rights in the Jurisprudence of the International Criminal Tribunal for the Former Yugoslavia', 16 *LJIL* (2003) 269, 272 *et subs.*

[218] *See* Chapter 7 D.

[219] ICTY *Prosecutor v Delalić et al.*, TC II, IT-96-21-T, 1 May 1997, Decision on the Motion on Presentation of Evidence by the Accused, Esad Landzo, para 29.

[220] P Wald, 'The International Criminal Tribunal for the Former Yugoslavia Comes of Age: Some Observations on Day-To-Day Dilemmas of an International Court', 5 *Washington University Journal of Law & Policy* (2001) 87, 105; S Kirsch, 'The Trial Proceeding before the ICC', 6 *ICLR* (2006) 275, 284 *et subs.*

of financial and/or human resources.[221] The Appeals Chamber chose—again—a rather formal approach in saying: 'The principle of equality of arms would be violated only if either party is put at a disadvantage *when presenting its case.* In the circumstances of this case, the Appeals Chamber finds that the Appellant cannot rely on the alleged inadequacy of funds during the pre-trial stage to establish such a disadvantage'.[222]

This approach has been rightly criticized as being premature and damaging the visibility of procedural fairness.[223] Because of the gross inequality between prosecutor and defendant in their respective ability to prepare their case, it has been argued that the ICTY should adopt a more normative approach and abolish the formal interpretation of the principle.[224] This would mean that the judges should take on more responsibility as regards the abilities of the defence, and should seek to influence the proceedings more actively. As the parties of the trial do not begin as direct equals, the desired equality has to be keenly and creatively constructed and the defence be brought to the same level as the prosecutor.[225]

What has also raised criticism is the tendency of the ICTY to reduce the scope of application of the principle of equality of arms in international criminal procedure compared to national procedural regimes. The reason given is the lack of means of execution on the side of international Tribunals. Whereas in national law the prosecuting authorities can rely on the police force to assist in executing orders and warrants, in international law prosecutors need to rely on state cooperation.[226] Yet it remains unclear why the ICTY Appeals Chambers considers this to be an issue of inequality between prosecutor and defence. Rather it would seem that both parties, prosecution and defence, suffer from insufficient cooperation of national agencies.[227] Besides, national courts prosecuting international crimes are confronted with exactly the same problem when evidence need to be collected abroad.

The jurisprudence of the ICTY is thus a good example for the unsuitability of the principle of equal arms for criminal trials. Because this concept is so unclear, it can be used against the interests of the accused in order to enhance the efficiency of the proceeding for the prosecution.

---

221 ICTR *Prosecutor v Nahimana, Barayagwiza, Ngeze*, AC, ICTR-99-52-A, 28 November 2007, Judgment, para 220 with further references.

222 *See* ICTY *Prosecutor v Milutinović et al.*, AC, IT-99-37-AR73.2, 13 November 2003, Decision on Interlocutory Appeal on Motion for Additional Funds, para 24 (emphasis added).

223 Critically Ahlbrecht/*Kirsch*, MN 1290.

224 G McIntyre, 'Equality of Arms—Defining Human Rights in the Jurisprudence of the International Criminal Tribunal for the Former Yugoslavia', 16 *LJIL* (2003) 269, 272.

225 Ibid, 269, 320.

226 ICTY *Prosecutor v Tadić*, AC, IT-94-1-A, 15 July 1999, Judgment, para 51 *et subs.*

227 A Zahar and G Sluiter, *International Criminal Law* (OUP 2007) 294.

3. ICC

The ICC Statute, based on the experiences of the *ad hoc* Tribunals, must be read as incorporating the principle of equality of arms in Art. 67 ICCSt.[228] Equality is addressed in the Statute regarding the disclosure rules in Arts 64 (3) (c) and 67 (2) ICCSt.

A major achievement has been reached in the pre-trial phase. The Pre-Trial Chamber will assist the suspect and the defence counsel in gathering evidence by issuing orders and warrants as necessary according to Art. 57 (3) (b) ICCSt. The right to have adequate time and facilities to prepare for the defence as enshrined in Art. 67 (1) (d) ICCSt is thus made operational.[229] Even if the defence is not an organ of the court—in contrast to the Prosecutor—the Chambers must and will provide assistance regarding the preparation of the defence. The ICCSt to a certain extent heals the criticism which was brought forward against the UN tribunals as discussed above and assigns to the Chamber a much more active role in furthering the defence interests.[230] However, ideally this power should not be invoked too often, as it would seem unnecessary as long as the prosecutor fulfils his/her obligation according to Art. 54 (1) (a) ICCSt as an objective organ of the court, collecting both incriminating and exculpating evidence.

In contrast, it has been said that Art. 99 (4) ICCSt contains a blatant breach of the equality of arms principle. The power to conduct onsite investigations under the Cooperation Regime of Part IX pertains only to the Prosecutor whereas the defence cannot compel a state to cooperate.[231]

For the time being the 'equality of arms' principle has not been made an issue in the jurisprudence of the ICC. It will, however, as soon as more cases are brought to the trial stage.

4. Conclusion

'Full equality between parties to criminal proceedings is an idle aspiration from a practical perspective', as stated in *Zahar/Sluiter*.[232] It is probably not even that. Equality should not even be intended. Due to the enormous differences in their respective positions, their procedural functions, their interests, and their resources, equality as regards 'procedural weapons' would simply not be enough. It is preferable

[228] It is interesting to note, that one of the main advocates of the equality of arms principles, K Ambos, does not mention this principle in his book on international criminal law as being relevant for the procedure at the ICC or the Tribunals, *see* K Ambos, *Internationales Strafrecht* (2nd edn, CH Beck 2007) § 8 MN 19–49.

[229] *See* Triffterer/*Guariglia/Harris/Hochmayr*, Art. 57 MN 17 *et subs.*; S Kirsch, 'The Trial Proceeding before the ICC', 6 *ICLR* (2006) 275, 288.

[230] *See* p 420 *et subs.*

[231] *See* A Zahar and G Sluiter, *International Criminal Law* (OUP 2007) 295.

[232] Ibid, 293.

to refer a high amount of protection to the defendant by enhancing the rights of the accused and have these safeguarded by the judges.

The constant struggle between Prosecutor and Defence, between crime control and due process, gives the duty to observe and preserve an equal equilibrium to the judges. Their main interest should be to assist the defence and 'show [themselves] extremely willing to assist the defence in gaining access to witnesses, wherever possible'.[233]

Even if the concept of equality of arms has been widely used in criminal law cases, it has no place in criminal procedure, as it has thus far been of no service in developing a precise structural concept which would enhance the fairness of the trial, and it has not been seen to add any value to the procedural problems international Tribunals are facing. Yet the principle itself continues to be praised: 'It is general and undisputed opinion that "equality of arms" is a key element of the due process of law.'[234]

I doubt that equality of arms is or even could be a key element of trial fairness. Quite the contrary is true. Equality of arms does not add anything to existing rights of the accused, which are contained not only in the major human rights treaties but also in Art. 67 ICCSt, Art. 20 ICTYSt, and Art. 19 ICTRSt. The right to be heard, the right to have adequate time and facility to prepare the defence, and the right to call and examine witnesses are the key rights for a fair trial.[235] Relating these rights to a higher principle of equality of arms runs the risk that these rights will in fact be restricted, as has been the case at the ICTY through the purely formal interpretation of equality.[236]

Furthermore its military wording implies a trial which consists of a battle between prosecutor and defence.[237] Resembling a real fight or a 'trial by ordeal' of ancient times[238] is unseemly for a liberal criminal law and incompatible with the presumption of innocence.

VIII. Immediate trial

Immediacy of the trial is one of the principles pertaining to the law of evidence. The evidence presented at trial should always be the one most proximate to the

[233] J Jones, 'The Gamekeeper Turned Poacher's Tale', 2 *JICJ* (2004) 486, 493.

[234] S Negri, 'The Principle of Equality of Arms and the Evolving Law of International Criminal Procedure', 5 *ICLR* (2005) 513, 569.

[235] *See* C Safferling, 'Audiatur at altera pars—die prozessuale Waffengleichheit als Prozessprinzip?', 24 *NStZ* (2004) 181, 187 *et subs.*

[236] *See* U Kohlbacher, *Verteidigung und Verteidigungsrechte unter dem Aspekt der 'Waffengleichheit'* (Schulthess 1979) 2 and J Renzikowski, '"Fair Trial" im Strafprozess', in: D Dölling *et al.* (eds), *Jus humanum: Grundlagen des Rechts und Strafrecht—Festschrift für E-J Lampe* (DeGruyter 2003) 791, 802.

[237] G Radburch, *Der Geist des Englischen Rechts* (Vadenhoeck and Ruprecht, 1956) 15 *et subs.* writing as an observer about English law.

[238] *See* C Safferling, *Towards an International Criminal Procedure* (OUP 2003) 6, 10.

actual event and relate to the facts of the case directly. Indirect or mediated evidence is not as reliable as direct and immediate evidence. This principle furthermore implies that the trial is the core of the quest for the truth. Pre-trial stages such as investigation or confirmation are preparatory parts of the prosecution process and do not carry the same weight as the trial. Therefore, a witness has to testify at trial even if s/he has previously delivered his or her testimony before a prosecutor. The most prominent expression of this principle is to be found in Sec. 250 of the German Code of Criminal Procedure: 'If the evidence is based on what a person has seen or heard, this person must be examined during the main hearing. The examination shall not be replaced by the reading of a record of a prior examination or a written statement.'

In Nuremberg, the prosecution case rested mainly on documentary evidence and only a few witnesses testified. Several witness statements were furthermore introduced into the trial by way of affidavit. This is, in general, contrary to the principle of an immediate trial. However, this course of action was justified by the enormous amount of unequivocal direct documentary evidence produced by the prosecutors proving the guilt of the accused that it seemed unnecessary to hear more witnesses than strictly necessary.[239]

In modern criminal procedure the principle of an immediate trial is largely contested by the question of whether hearsay evidence is admissible or not. Hearsay witnesses cannot testify on the actual facts of the case according to their own perception, but can report what someone else told them. This kind of testimony is thus indirect. In Anglo-American criminal procedure such a witness is, in general, excluded from entering the witness box, whereas in Continental Europe there is no such exclusionary rule.[240] Yet there is the principle of an immediate trial which permits tackling hearsay from a different angle.

1. Human rights law

In human rights law we do not find a positive codification of the principle of an immediate trial. The issue is mostly discussed in connection with the right to confrontation according to Art. 14 (3) (e) ICCPR and Art. 6 (3) (d) ECHR and with hearsay evidence. Neither the ICCPR nor the ECHR exclude hearsay evidence on a general basis. They are concerned mainly with whether the proceeding was fair in its entirety and whether the accused had a chance to defend him or herself. The right to confrontation is a vehicle of fairness, which says that the defendant must have had the opportunity to pose questions to the witness. A direct confrontation with the witness is however only feasible if the witness

---

[239] This prosecutorial strategy was criticized for being too clinical, *see* eg, L Douglas, 'History and Memory in the Courtroom: Reflections on Perpetrator Trials', in: H Reginbogin and C Safferling (eds), *The Nuremberg Trial: International Criminal Law Since 1945* (Saur 2006) 89.

[240] C Safferling, *Towards an International Criminal Procedure* (OUP 2003) 306 *et subs.*

himself is present. The right to confrontation thus presupposes the principle of the immediacy of the trial. We will come back to the consequences of this principle for the law of evidence later.

2. *Tribunals*

There is no explicit mentioning of the principle of immediacy in the Statutes and Rules of the Tribunals. Yet several norms and decisions deal with issues related to this principle. In particular hearsay evidence, that is, ; indirect evidence, has caused a whole list of decisions. It is therefore a general rule that witnesses need to testify in the presence of the accused, see Rule 89 (F) ICTY RPE, Rule 90 (A) ICTR RPE. The Trial Chambers have made clear that the right to confront the witness according to Art. 21 (4) (e) ICTYSt and Art. 20 (4) (e) ICTR RPE can only be duly exercised if the witness is a direct witness. With a hearsay witness, cross-examination cannot help to test the reliability of the testimony.[241] In that case the chamber must scrutinize the probative value of the statement in a special way.[242] We can conclude from these decisions that the *ad hoc* Tribunals prefer direct evidence to indirect evidence, and thus accept the principle of immediacy of the trial.[243]

However, for the purpose of expediting proceedings, the ICTY has accepted many exceptions to this general rule as the judges were often satisfied with written testimony.[244]

3. *ICC*

The Rome Statute anticipates the immediacy of the trial in Art. 69 (2) ICCSt explicitly, when it states: 'testimony of a witness will be given in person'. Yet this general rule is followed by a number of exceptions, including audio and video broadcasting, recorded evidence, or even written statements. The parameters of how to apply these exceptions are not laid down in the Statute and raise some doubts.[245] Nevertheless, the general principle must be observed, which is expressed by the fact that the final sentence of Art. 69 (2) ICCSt refers to the rights of the accused which must be respected.

---

[241] ICTY *Prosecutor v Blaškić*, TC I, IT-95-14-T, 21 January 1998, Decision on Standing Objection of the Defence to the Admission of Hearsay with No Inquiry as to its Reliability, para 29.

[242] ICTY *Prosecutor v Kordić and Čerkez*, AC, IT-95-14/2-AR73.5, 21 July 2000, Decision on Appeal Regarding Statement of a Deceased Witness, para 24.

[243] *See* also ICTY *Prosecutor v Rajić*, TC, IT-95-12-R61, 13 September 1996, Review of the Indictment Pursuant to Rule 61 of the Rules of Procedure and Evidence, para 23.

[244] S Kay, 'The Move from Oral Evidence to Written Evidence', 2 *JICJ* (2004) 495; S Bourgon, 'Procedural Problems Hindering Expeditious and Fair Justice', 2 *JICJ* (2004) 526, 530 *et subs*. Both are very critical towards this development. *See* also R Cryer, H Friman, D Robinson, and E Wilmshurst, *An Introduction to International Criminal Law and Procedure* (2nd edn, CUP 2010) 467.

[245] G Boas, 'Developments in the Law of Procedure and Evidence at the ICTY and the ICC', 12 *CLF* (2001) 167, 181–3.

One of these is the right to confrontation, which is worded in the same way as in the major human rights treaties. In Art. 67 (1) (e), the first sentence is identical with Art. 14 (3) (e) ICCPR. However, hearsay evidence is not excluded on a general basis. On the contrary, the presiding judge is in a position to determine the 'mode and order of questioning witnesses and presenting evidence' according to Regulation 43 RegC. Cross-examination may be feasible but is not obligatory, as is made clear by the wording of Rule 140 (2) RPE ICC.

4. *Conclusion*

The principle of the immediacy of trial stems mainly from the German legal system. It is not mentioned explicitly in the human rights treaties nor in the Statutes of international courts and Tribunals. Yet it is implied in several other norms, in particular the right of the accused to confront the witness against him/her. To test the reliability of the witness by questioning is not possible in the case of an indirect witness; that is, a hearsay witness. We conclude therefore that there is a general principle that the trial must be based on direct, that is, immediate evidence. This does not mean that judges are generally forbidden from hearing indirect testimony. Yet if they do, the violation of the principle of the immediacy of the trial must be counterbalanced by strict necessity and compensated by a reduced probative value of the testimony in question.

The principle of the immediate trial serves the procedural truth finding as it forces the prosecution to present the best and most reliable source; that is, the direct witness. At the same time it enables the public and oral trial. Therefore, the judgment can only be based on evidence which was presented and discussed at the hearing.[246] The right to confront the witness puts the accused on a similar footing with the prosecutor. It is thus a guarantor of a 'fair trial'.

The principle of the immediacy of the trial unfolds at the hearing of the evidence at trial. It influences the questions of when and how hearsay evidence can be admissible, of how to deal with both deceased and most vulnerable witnesses. These topics will be discussed later.

B. Preparing for Trial

As soon as the President of the ICC constituted a Trial Chamber for a case according to Art. 61 (11) ICCSt and Rule 130 RPE, or assigns a case to a previously constituted Trial Chamber according to Art. 64 (3) ICCSt, the process enters its trial stage.[247] But before the trial itself starts, there is an interim stage which serves

[246] K Ambos, *Internationales Strafrecht* (2nd edn, CH Beck 2007) § 8 MN 41.

[247] *See* K Ambos and D Miller, 'Structure and Function of the Confirmation Procedure before the ICC from a Comparative Perspective', 7 *ICLR* (2007) 335, 338. The Rome Statute differentiates

as preparation of the trial proceeding. The preparation for trial is in itself a part of the trial process and should not be mistaken for the pre-trial stage. Whereas at the pre-trial stage the topic of the later trial is carved out and finally confirmed by a Pre-Trial Chamber, the Trial Chamber is now called upon to guarantee the 'fair and expeditious conduct of the proceedings' (Rule 132 PRE). The preparation for trial thus serves the proper management of the process and helps avoid excessive delays of the proceedings.

Looking at the cases which have reached the trial stage at the ICC to date it is rather obvious that what has been named an interim stage can be a rather arduous and long struggle between the Chamber and other participants. For example, in the *Lubanga* case, the charges were confirmed on 29 January 2007 but the trial did not open until 26 January 2009 almost two years later. In *Katanga and Chui*, the trial opened on 24 November 2009, fourteen months after the Confirmation decision of 26 September 2008, and Bemba's trial was opened on 22 November 2010, some seventeen months after Confirmation of 15 June 2009.

The method of doing this is the 'status conference', which is envisaged as a mandatory exercise of the Trial Chamber in Rule 132 (1) RPE ICC. Despite this, however, the concept of 'preparation for trial' remains rather open. This is the case despite the fact that the question of who manages the case, how it is to be managed, and to what extent it is to be managed, touch upon the heart of the criminal trial process: the role of the judge. The more the judge takes responsibility for the conduct of the trial and does not leave it entirely up to the prosecution and the defence to present their respective cases, the more the judges need to know about the facts of the case and about the evidence. This knowledge, however, changes the position of the trial judges dramatically. We will come back to these questions shortly.

Before looking at the ICC, we turn to look at the practice of the UN Tribunals. The concept of pre-trial conferences was developed there and will without doubt influence the ICC.

The pre-trial phase at the ICTY differs hugely from that of the ICC. After a modest confirmation process (*see* earlier Chapter 7), the original intention of the ICTY drafters was that the trial chamber should conduct the trial on the basis of the indictment. Yet as with the Rome Conference and the adoption of the ICCSt, the judges at the ICTY amended the RPE ICTY and introduced a Pre-Trial Judge and Pre-Trial Conferences. In July 1998 Rules 65*bis*, 73*bis*, and 73*ter* RPE ICTY were introduced, Rule 65*ter* followed in 2000.

---

between the concept of 'constituting' and 'assignment', without being clear about the consequences. As to the drafting history, *see* Triffterer/*Bitti*, Art. 64 MN 11.

According to Rule 65*bis* (1) ICTY RPE Status Conferences are mandatory even 120 days after the initial appearance of the accused at the Tribunal and are held by either the Pre-Trial Judge or the Chamber.[248]

For the pre-trial procedure a Pre-Trial Judge (PTJ) is being appointed according to Rule 65*ter* RPE ICTY. S/he is under a duty to construct a 'work plan' containing terms and obligations of parties and time limits. The 'work plan' supervision is delegated to a Senior Legal Officer, who confers with the parties and reports to the PTJ and back to the parties.[249]

The prosecutor is obliged to file: (i) a final version of the pre-trial brief, (ii) a list of the prosecution witnesses, and (iii) a list of the exhibits the prosecution intends to rely on as evidence according to Rule 65*ter* (E) RPE ICTY.

Similarly, the defence must file a pre-trial brief addressing both factual and legal issues according to Rule 65*ter* (F) RPE ICTY. The defence must also set out the general nature of the accused's defence, and is obliged to identify the matters in the prosecutor's pre-trial brief, which the defence disputes and give reasons for disputing. A witness list and the defence exhibits must only be submitted after the closure of the prosecution case by virtue of Rule 65*ter* (G) RPE ICTY.

In case of non-compliance with their respective pre-trial obligations Rule 65*ter* (N) RPE ICTY foresees sanctions to be imposed by the Trial Chamber, for example, the exclusion of evidence from trial.

On the basis of the pre-trial briefs, the PTJ according to Rule 65*ter* (H) RPE ICTY classifies the issues both factual and legal as disputed and undisputed. S/he may consult with the parties in order to avoid misunderstandings, Rule 65*ter* (I) PRE ICTY, when putting together his/her record, which is then transferred to the Trial Chamber, including transcripts, minutes of the meetings, and prosecution and defence filings, Rule 65*ter* (L) RPE ICTY.

This file, assembled and presented by the PTJ, will be the basis of the Pre-Trial Conference which convenes on invitation by the Trial Chamber in order to prepare for trial according to Rule 73*bis* RPE ICTY, which found its present form on 17 July 2003 and was supposed to be the most efficient tool for the management

[248] C Möller, 'Das Vorverfahren im Strafprozess vor dem Internationalen Straftribunal für das ehemalige Jugoslawien ("Pre-Trial and Preliminary Proceedings")', in: S Kirsch (ed), *Internationale Strafgerichtshöfe* (Nomos 2005) 19, 49.

[249] *See* also M Harmon, 'The Pre-Trial Process at the ICTY as a Means of Ensuring Expeditious Trials', 5 *JICJ* (2007) 377, 384–8, discussing the different types of Conferences: Rule 65*ter*-Conferences, Status Conferences and Pre-Trial Conferences. The author quite rightly points to the problem that the Senior Legal Officer lacks the competence to decide matters. A serious discussion about the relevant issues of the case and the possibility to delimit the range of the indictment will thus not take place.

of the proceedings.[250] The Trial Chamber may limit the number of witnesses[251] and determine the time available for examination; indeed, the Chamber has the power over the information available to it through the file to reorganize the prosecution case according to its own evaluation of the case and reduce the number of counts.[252] The same procedure will be adopted *mutatis mutandis* regarding the defence case in the Pre-Defence Conference according to Rule 73*ter* RPE ICTY.

The ICTY law thus shows an unmistakable deviation from the common law approach of a passive judge.[253] The judge gains the role of a trial manager and controls the preparation of the trial in order to expedite proceedings.[254]

This development is also mirrored in the law of the ICTR and the SCSL. According to Rule 65*bis* RPE SCSL/ICTR, the Trial Chamber or a designated PTJ may call a status conference with the aim of expediting trial proceedings. To that end Rule 73*bis* RPE SCSL/ICTR obliges the Trial Chamber or PTJ to hold a pre-trial conference at which the prosecution may be ordered to file a prosecution pre-trial brief on the facts and the law of the case, a statement of matters contesting both fact and law together with a list of prosecution witnesses and exhibits.[255] The prosecution may even be ordered to provide copies with written statements of each prosecution witness. As a consequence the Trial Chamber can reduce the estimated time allowed for each prosecution witness and reduce the number of prosecution witnesses. The defence is put under a similar obligation, and a Pre-Defence Conference takes place according to Rule 73*ter* RPE SCSL/ICTR.

The Tribunals thus have set into place a system which is well equipped to distil only matters in dispute in advance of the trial and prepare for litigation. Yet it seems that the potential for speeding up the lengthy proceedings dormant in these rules are seldom invoked.[256] This might be due to the fact that the judges are more or less rooted in common law practice, which is generally hostile towards judges' involvement in the planning of the trial. It might also be due to the fact that the

---

[250] C Möller, 'Das Vorverfahren im Strafprozess vor dem Internationalen Straftribunal für das ehemalige Jugoslawien ("Pre-Trial and Preliminary Proceedings")', in: S Kirsch (ed), *Internationale Strafgerichtshöfe* (Nomos 2005) 19, 50.

[251] *See* Boas/Bischoff/Reid/Taylor, *ICL III*, 244 with further references.

[252] As has been the cases: ICTY *Prosecutor v Šešelj*, TC I, IT-03-67-PT, 8 November 2006, Decision on the Application of Rule 73*bis*; *Prosecutor v Milutinović et al.*, TC, IT-05-87-T, 11 July 2006, Decision on Application of Rule 73*bis*. In the *Karadžić* case, the Prosecutor was threatened with shortening the case if he, the Prosecutor, did not do so himself: *Prosecutor v Karadžić*, TC, IT-95-5/18-PT, 22 July 2009, Order to the Prosecution under Rule 73*bis* (D), para 5.

[253] G Boas, 'Developments in the Law of Procedure and Evidence at the ICTY and the ICC', 12 *CLF* (2001) 167, 172–4 (with a view to Rule 65*bis* RPE ICTY).

[254] ICTY *Prosecutor v Krajišnik*, TC, IT-00-39, 1 August 2001, Decision on Motion for the Clarification in Respect of Application of Rule 65*ter*, 66 (B) and 67 (C).

[255] ICTR *Prosecutor v Ndayambaje et al.*, TC II, IT-96-8-T, 14 December 2001, Decision on the Prosecutor's Motion to Modify her List of Exhibits.

[256] G Higgins, 'Fair and Expeditious Pre-Trial Proceedings: The Future of International Criminal Trials', 5 *JICJ* (2007) 394, 398 *et subs.*; *see* also Boas/Bischoff/Reid/Taylor, *ICL III*, 243.

ICTY judges are widely inexperienced regarding the role of the PTJ and are thus reluctant to rely on his or her services.[257]

At the ICC, the Trial Chamber is under the obligation to organize the trial. Art. 64 (3) ICCSt expresses precisely this in three different ways:

(a) the Chamber needs to confer with the parties and adopt such procedures as are necessary to facilitate the fair and expeditious conduct of the proceedings,
(b) determine the language or languages to be used at trial, and
(c) provide additional disclosure if necessary.

The question of disclosure of evidence has been dealt with in a separate chapter (Chapter 7). The determination of the languages to be used is connected to Art. 50 ICCSt and Rule 41 RPE ICC pertaining to the working languages only.[258] The right of the accused to be informed of the charges in a language s/he fully understands and speaks remains untouched by the decision as to the working languages.

In the following we will focus on the first of the named issues: the obligation of the Trial Chamber to communicate with parties in order to manage and organize the trial in such a way that the proceedings will be fair and expeditious. This communication is dependent on four different issues: (I) its formal method seems to be embodied in the so-called Status Conference; (II) however the parties have the option to submit motions to the chamber and thus communicate their interests to the judges; (III) apparently the 'record', which has been collected during pre-trial phase by the Registry, in particular of the confirmation hearing, plays an important role; (IV) finally, the Trial Chamber has the power to join or sever proceedings against more than one accused according to Art. 64 (5) ICCSt.

I. Status conferences

The Statute does not mention the term Status Conference, but in the Rules of Procedure and Evidence we find a differentiation between two types of Status conferences: (a) a mandatory Status Conference concerning the setting of the date for trial according to Rule 132 (1) RPE ICC, and (b) other Status Conferences which may be held in order to facilitate the fair and expeditious conduct of the proceedings according to Rule 132 (2) RPE ICC. As we will see, the practice at the ICC does not follow this rather artificial and inefficient differentiation.

[257] M Harmon, 'The Pre-Trial Process at the ICTY as a Means of Ensuring Expeditious Trials', 5 *JICJ* (2007) 377, 389–92.
[258] In detail: Triffterer/*Bitti*, Art. 64 MN 13.

As regards the form of the Status Conference, Regulation 30 RegC gives broad discretion to the judges. Therefore, a Status Conference might take the form of a hearing but it could also take the form of a written procedure, where the participants submit written statements to the Chamber.

1. Mandatory Status Conference

The only issue to be discussed at the mandatory Status Conference is the date of the trial. This conference has to be held 'promptly' after the case has been referred to the Trial Chamber. It is unclear who is invited to participate. Whereas it is obvious that the Prosecutor and the defendant have to attend as the main actors in the trial, it is questionable whether victims and their representatives or state representatives should also take part.[259]

According to the wording of Rule 132 (1) RPE ICC, it is more likely that other participants of the trial hearing need to absent themselves from this conference. These participants are merely informed of the trial date, and cannot influence the date or ask for postponement.

2. Other Status Conferences

Other questions concerning the organization of the trial apart from the date are to be dealt with in a separate Status Conference according to Rule 132 (2) RPE ICC. A lengthy but not exhaustive list of possible issues to be discussed during such a conference is contained in Regulation 54 RegC, which states:

> Regulation 54 Status conferences before the Trial Chamber
>
> At a status conference, the Trial Chamber may, in accordance with the Statute and the Rules, issue any order in the interests of justice for the purposes of the proceedings on, *inter alia*, the following issues:
>
> (a) The length and content of legal arguments and the opening and closing statements;
> (b) A summary of the evidence the participants intend to rely on;
> (c) The length of the evidence to be relied on;
> (d) The length of questioning of the witnesses;
> (e) The number and identity (including any pseudonym) of the witnesses to be called;
> (f) The production and disclosure of the statements of the witnesses on which the participants propose to rely;
> (g) The number of documents as referred to in article 69, paragraph 2, or exhibits to be introduced together with their length and size;
> (h) The issues the participants propose to raise during the trial;

[259] *See* Triffterer/*Bitti*, Art. 64 MN 12.

(i) The extent to which a participant can rely on recorded evidence, including the transcripts and the audio and video record of evidence previously given;
(j) The presentation of evidence in summary form;
(k) The extent to which evidence is to be given by an audio- or video-link;
(l) The disclosure of evidence;
(m) The joint or separate instruction by the participants of expert witnesses;
(n) Evidence to be introduced under rule 69 as regards agreed facts;
(o) The conditions under which victims shall participate in the proceedings;
(p) The defences, if any, to be advanced by the accused.

It is obvious that the judges were inspired by the practice of the UN Tribunals, when drafting this list, and they added a few more topics. The ICC judges have added at least one more: the condition of the detention of the accused.[260] The power of the judges to manage the trial proceeding pertains not only on structural or quantitative questions as to the lengths or the statements, and the number of documents but embraces also the definition of issues to be discussed—including 'defences' to be advance by the accused,[261]—the manner of the presentation of the evidence, and the form of participation by the victims. Even if the power of judges to limit the number of witnesses of the parties or the crime sites is missing from this list, the authority to do so could still be based on Regulation 54 RegC.[262] Given the fact that the Pre-Trial Chamber should already have made the case manageable during the confirmation of the charges, a further reduction of any aspect of the case should not be necessary. If the practice at the ICC proves differently and the Pre-Trial Chambers fail to shape cases appropriately, the Trial Chambers will take over this responsibility.

Whereas Rule 132 (2) RPE ICC speaks only of the 'parties', that is, defence and prosecution, who are invited to participate in Status Conferences, Regulation 54 RegC interprets the Rules in a broad way, referring to 'participants' instead. Looking at the list put forward, it would make sense to allow victims' representatives to be present at the conference, as their position might be an issue.[263] Also representatives of states could take part in the Status Conference, if specific state interests are of concern. These might be[264] questions of admissibility and jurisdiction, the protection of agents or servants, and confidential information, including matters of national security. Furthermore, it might be sensible to have the Registry

260 ICC *Prosecutor v Bemba*, TC III, ICC-01/05-01/08-T-18-Red-ENG, 8 December 2009, Transcript Status Conference, p 1.

261 The terminology is highly unfortunate as the Rome Statute itself does not use the term 'defences' for very good reasons, *see* C Safferling, *Internationales Strafrecht* (Springer 2011) § 5 MN 11.

262 A different view is taken by Boas/Bischoff/Reid/Taylor, *ICL III*, 248 who opine that the ICC judges do not have direct procedural authority to limit the number of witnesses or fix the number of crime sites.

263 *See* Triffterer/*Bitti*, Art. 64 MN 12, which states that representatives of victims may also certainly attend in accordance with Regulation 54 (o).

264 *See* list given by Triffterer/*Bitti*, Art. 64 MN 12.

present at the Conference in order to resolve any technical issues, such as problems with IT or translations. The Office of the Public Counsel for Victims should also be invited to participate.

3. Evaluation

The Status Conference is an important tool to prepare for the trial. It should be used in order to achieve as much clarity as possible on disputed issues. Possibly the gravest difficulty for an international trial is the vast amount of information available combined with multiple charges. As has been argued, the pre-trial phase should be used to determine the topic of the trial and to shape the charges accordingly. At the trial phase the main focus should be on the actual management of the presentation of evidence, yet this obligation is not on the Trial Chamber alone. The Prosecutor representing the public interest is also obliged to attain clarity, as s/he is bound by the principle of a speedy trial.[265] It is difficult when parties throw as much material as possible at the Chamber, and expect the judges to 'sort it out'.[266]

It is highly inefficient to have several and separate conferences for the date and for other issues. The judges should use their inherent powers to organize the trial and the preparation for trial and combine the question of the setting of the date with other issues as to the management of the proceedings. Under these circumstances it would be advisable to adopt the rather informal approach, which is mirrored in Regulation 30 RegC regarding the conduct of the Status Conferences, in order to gain as much positive effect for the organization of the formal presentation of evidence, and thus help speed up the proceedings.

Looking at the Status Conferences which have taken place at the ICC thus far, it becomes obvious that the judges indeed take this liberty and unfold a rather result-oriented approach to the Status Conferences. From the first Status Conference in the Lubanga case, assembled by Trial Chamber I, the English Judge Fulford presiding, on 4 September 2007 onward, the question of setting a date has been connected to other issues regarding the investigation, disclosure and so on. Indeed, it appears that it might be impossible to discuss a specific date before these other questions have been solved. The Chambers have also developed a practice of issuing a list of questions they would like to see addressed at a Status Conference to the participants.[267]

Furthermore from Lubanga onwards, the Status Conference has been used to read out the charges as confirmed by the Pre-Trial Chamber to the defendant. This is

---

[265] *See* p 383 *et subs.*

[266] I Bonomy, 'The Reality of Conducting a War Crimes Trial', 5 *JICJ* (2007) 348, 352.

[267] *See* eg, ICC *Prosecutor v Lubanga*, TC I, ICC-01/04-01/06, 18 July 2007, Request for Submissions on the Subjects that Require Early Determination; *Prosecutor v Katanga/Chui*, TC II, ICC-01/04-01/07-747-tENG, 13 November 2008, Order Instructing the Participants and the Registry to Respond to Questions of Trial Chamber II for the Purpose of the Status Conference (Article 64 (3) (a) of the Statute).

done in order to satisfy the duty to inform the defendant according to Art. 64 (8) (a) and Art. 67 (1) (a) ICCSt, and give to the defendant the opportunity to enter a plea of guilty or not guilty according to Art. 65 ICCSt. Even if it is be reasonable to do this, the Chambers should be careful not to be too permissive in interpreting the Statute. The articles quoted refer to the beginning of the trial hearing. A status conference is not a trial hearing, but a preparatory and informal meeting. Therefore, the charges must be read out at the 'commencement' of the trial again and the defendant be given the opportunity to respond to them.[268]

Looking at the ICC practice adopted by the Trial Chambers, Status Conferences are widely used and often take more time than initially assumed.

II. Pre-trial motions

Another and more formal way to communicate between the parties and the Chamber are pre-trial motions.[269] The law at the ICC foresees a variety of such motions as follows.

The parties may request postponement of the date of the trial according to Rule 132 (1) RPE ICC. The date is set by the Chamber, and must take due regard to the right of the accused to adequate time for preparation, the efficiency of the proceedings, and the principle of a speedy trial.

According to Rule 133 RPE ICC motions challenging admissibility of the case of jurisdiction of the ICC can be raised by the accused, by a state, which has jurisdiction over a case, or by the Prosecutor according to Art. 18 and 19 ICCSt.[270] Such motions shall be heard and decided first according to Rule 58 (1) RPE ICC.[271]

Most relevant for the preparation of the trial proceedings is Rule 134 (1) RPE ICC. The prosecutor or the defence may raise any issue concerning the conduct of the proceedings on which the applicant wishes a decision to be made by the Trial Chamber. The procedure to be applied in dealing with such a motion is adversarial in nature; that is, the 'opposite' party has to have the opportunity to file a response.

---

[268] Judge Fulford was mindful of the differences in the form of the hearing. ICC *Prosecutor v Lubanga*, TC I, ICC-01/04-01/06, 4 September 2007, Transcript Status Conference, p 3. Also TC II emphasized the difference: *Prosecutor v Katanga/Chui*, TC II, ICC-01/04-01/07-747-tENG, 13 November 2008, Order Instructing the Participants and the Registry to Respond to Questions of Trial Chamber II for the Purpose of the Status Conference (Article 64 (3) (a) of the Statute), para 8.

[269] P Lewis, 'The Rules of Procedure and Evidence of the International Criminal Court: Confirmation Hearing to Trial', in: H Fischer, C Kreß, and S R Lüder (eds), *International and National Prosecution of Crimes under International Law: Current Developments* (Berlin Verlag 2001) 219, 228.

[270] *See* Chapter 5.

[271] *See* also Triffterer/*Bitti*, Art. 64 MN 12.

According to Rule 134 (2) RPE ICC the Prosecutor and the defence may raise objections or present observations on proceedings conducted after the confirmation hearing. Any issue that took place before that must be raised before the Pre-Trial Chamber and cannot be invoked later; *see* Rule 122 (4) RPE ICC.[272]

At this point, and following thorough scrutiny of the prosecution's case, the defence might request further investigation be conducted or further evidence be produced by the Trial Chamber by virtue of Art. 64 (6) (d) ICCSt.[273] As the Court is not obliged to extend the presentation of evidence on any matter that is relevant for the finding of the truth, but has the authority to order the production of evidence, the onus is on the defence to point out to the Chamber relevant factors which are missing in the Prosecutor's case. It might be detrimental to the interests of the defence that the Prosecutor has a right to file a response and possibly persuade the judges of the irrelevance of the material requested by the defence.

Finally, the Chamber may also rule on the question of expert evidence.[274] According to Regulation 44 (2) RegC, the Chamber may direct the joint instruction of an expert by both the defence and the prosecution. After receipt of an expert report, a party may request the instruction of a further expert by virtue of Regulation 44 (3) RegC.

These motions, after all, refer to issues which might be dealt with in a Status Conference. The Chambers should invite participants to contribute to a Status Conference and try to issue the necessary orders *en bloc*. This would enhance transparency of the proceedings and add to the speeding up of the trial. This appears to be the case, as can been seen from the tactics adopted by the ICC Trial Chamber thus far.

III. Record

As has been said, one of the main differences between Continental European and Anglo-American criminal procedure is that the former relies mainly on a 'dossier', which is known to the professional judges and serves as a basis for the proceeding and the presentation of evidence, whereas the latter relies on the parties for the presentation of evidence and prefers the judge to be unaware of the facts of the case prior to the hearing.

Whereas nowhere in the Rome Statute is the Prosecutor obliged to put together a 'file' containing all the facts and evidence of the case, the Registry builds up a 'record' of the proceedings (Regulation 21 RegR), which at the end of the day resembles a 'file' akin to Continental practice, and this is used in the preparation for trial.

---

272 Triffterer/*Bitti*, Art. 64 MN 12.
273 *See* Ahlbrecht/*Kirsch* MN 1422.
274 *See* Ahlbrecht/*Kirsch* MN 1423.

According to Rule 121 (10) RPE ICC 'the Registry shall create and maintain a full and accurate record of all proceedings before the Pre-Trial Chamber, including all documents transmitted to the Chamber pursuant to this rule'. Amongst these documents is all the disclosure material, which becomes part of the record by virtue of Rule 121 (2) RPE ICC. At this stage, the fate of the record is rather simple as it can be of service to the Prosecutor, the person charged, and the victims or their legal representatives, to the extent they are permitted to the proceedings pursuant to Rules 89 to 91 RPE ICC. These participants may consult the record and thus be informed for the confirmation hearing according to Rule 121 (10) RPE ICC.

At the end of the confirmation process, the Registry will have collected everything that was material to the pre-trial phase and placed it into the record. Next, the Presidency refers the case to a Trial Chamber according to Rule 130 RPE ICC. However, together with this referral the entire record maintained by the Registrar is transmitted to the Trial Chamber, as is ordered by Rule 130 RPE ICC.[275]

Whereas the record may help the Prosecutor, the defence, the victims, and their representatives, as well as representatives of states participating in the proceedings prepare as they may consult the record according to Rule 131 RPE ICC, it is doubtful what happens to the record in the Trial Chamber; this is not mentioned in Rule 131 RPE ICC.[276] Are the judges allowed to use the record for the preparation of the trial proceeding? The ICC law is deliberately silent in this regard.[277] What would be the pros and cons of allowing the record to be so used?

A judge who knows the facts of the case is certainly in a better position to manage the case. S/he can make his or her independent judgment on the focal points of the facts, the evidence, and the law, and does not depend on what the parties tell him. Having knowledge of the facts and circumstances would put the judge in a much better position to evaluate the urgency of victim or witness protection or other confidentiality issues.

But how independent is the information the judges receive through the record? As the record pertains to the confirmation process, it will certainly have an emphasis on the incriminating evidence.[278] It might even be that for some tactical reasons, the defence did not raise any objection during the confirmation stage at all. Consequently, the record will be rather one-sided. If the judges base the trial

[275] Rules 130 and 131 RPE ICC are unclear as regards the responsibility for the record. The record is 'transmitted' to the Trial Chamber, but it is 'maintained' by the Registry.

[276] Ahlbrecht/*Kirsch* MN 1416; *see* also S Kirsch, 'The Trial Proceedings before the ICC, 6 *ICLR* (2006) 275, 279 *et subs.*

[277] As to the drafting history, *see* H Brady, 'Setting the Record Straight: A Short Note on Disclosure and "the Record of the Proceedings"', in: H Fischer, C Kreß, and S R Lüder (eds), *International and National Prosecution of Crimes under International Law: Current Developments* (Berlin Verlag 2001) 261–73.

[278] S Bourgon, 'Procedural Problems Hindering Expeditious and Fair Justice', 2 *JICJ* (2004) 526, 530 *et subs.*

on such a biased pool of information, it could be argued, that this would result in a violation of the principle of presumption of innocence.[279]

However, to expose the judges to materials yet to be presented in evidence does not necessarily lead to pre-judgement or partiality on their side. The professionalism of the judges is a guarantee that the presumption of innocence will be respected.[280] Furthermore, it seems that the Rome Statute's approach towards an active judge who may order the production of evidence *proprio motu* (Art. 64 (6) (d) ICCSt), warrants a judge who has greater responsibility for the finding of the truth and should thus have enhanced knowledge of the facts and circumstances of the case. As has been said, this knowledge could also work as a form of control of the prosecutor.[281] The case against Lubanga has shown that such control is important and necessary.

Balancing the pros and cons regarding the question of whether the judge should have knowledge of the record, the answer has to be 'yes'.[282] As long as the judges are aware of the circumstances of how the record came about, one should trust their professionalism. Also, if it is true that the judge is working towards finding the truth together with prosecutor and defence, all should progress towards this goal at the same speed. Consequently, the record does indeed fulfil a similar function to a 'file' in a Continental prosecution.

There is one final issue to be addressed. The record pursuant to Rule 121 (10) RPE ICC pertains only to the proceedings before the Pre-Trial Chamber. But what happens to evidence which was disclosed after the date of the confirmation decision? Will this be included in the record or is the record incomplete and thus unreliable?[283]

The answer is to be found in Rule 137 RPE ICC, headed 'record of the trial proceedings'. According to this rule, the Registrar makes and preserves a full and accurate record of all proceedings. As the wording of the rule embraces 'all proceedings' it is submitted that this can only mean that the Registrar continues to service the record, stemming originally from the confirmation proceeding, and adds new material to it as the proceedings progress. As 'all proceedings' are to be covered, material which is being disclosed after the confirmation decision should be made part of the record.

---

[279] *See* p 403 *et subs.*

[280] ICTY *Prosecutor v Blagojević et al.*, AC, IT-02-60-AR73, IT-02-60-AR73.2, IT-02-60-AR73.3, 8 April 2003, Decision, para 29.

[281] *See* W Schomburg, 'Wahrheitsfindung im Internationalen Gerichtssaal', *Vereinte Nationen* (2009) 3.

[282] *See* also C Kreß, 'Vorbemerkungen Vor III 26 ("Internationaler Strafgerichtshof")', in: H Grützner, P G Pötz, and C Kreß (eds), *Internationaler Rechtshilfeverkehr in Strafsachen* (CF Müller 2002) MN 136.

[283] *See* S Kirsch, 'The Trial Proceedings Before the ICC', 6 *ICLR* (2006) 275, 279 *et subs.*

The practice at the ICC has developed in that direction, yet with one caveat. The obligation to record the evidence disclosed after the confirmation pertains only to incriminating evidence presented by the Prosecutor. Potentially exculpatory material and the Rule 77 material are only disclosed to the defence upon notification to the Chamber but not filed to the record.[284]

We can thus conclude that in principle a Continental style 'file' has been developed at the ICC by means of the record, yet it results in an 'attenuated' record regime, focusing on incriminating evidence.

IV. Joinder and severance

International criminal law and procedure has to deal mostly with crimes involving several suspects and multiple charges.[285] As the situational context is similar, it might be both efficient and wise to try several people in one trial. It is more efficient because the presentation of evidence concerning circumstantial questions will be valid for several accused at the same time and duplications could be avoided, while witnesses and victims are being spared the distress of attending several trials; it is wise as the political environment, the number of the crimes and, indeed, the entire panorama of the incidents will come to light more easily than in the case where only isolated offences are being discussed.[286]

The Nuremberg Trial against the major German war criminals is a good example in this regard. The allied powers had assembled twenty four persons who should be held responsible for crimes that could not be attributed to a specific geographical setting and would thus have to be tried by common enterprise. This policy was developed in the Moscow Declaration in November 1943, made between Roosevelt, Churchill, and Stalin. As a result the charges covered a rather wider range from crimes against peace and crimes of conspiracy, to incitement to commit war crimes and crimes against humanity, to the forced labour programme. Under modern circumstances such a trial could never be concluded within a year, as was the Nuremberg trial, lasting from 20 November 1945 to 1 October 1946. In the subsequent trials—which we have seen were not international trials *strictu sensu*—the accused were pooled by their professional positions,[287] the types of crimes,[288] or the location of the crimes charged.[289]

---

[284] *See* the discussion between the presiding Judge Fulford and Ms Kneuer representing the Prosecutor in the Bemba case: ICC *Prosecutor v Bemba*, TC III, ICC-01/05-01/08-T-14-ENG ET, 7 October 2009, Transcript Status Conference, p. 17.

[285] *See* above Chapter 2 for an analysis of this special context.

[286] *See* Boas/Bischoff/Reid/Taylor, *ICL III*, 198.

[287] Like the 'Doctors' Trial', the 'Jurist Trial', the 'Ministries Trial', or the 'High Command Case'; see W Harris, *Tyranny on Trial* (Southern Methodist University Press 1999) 546 *et subs.*

[288] Like the 'Einsatzgruppen Trial'.

[289] As done in the Dachau Trials, the Bergen-Belsen Trials, or later in the so-called Auschwitz Trial in Germany.

Nowadays, the complexity of both the incidents and the procedure often advise against a joinder of several cases. A case with too many persons involved will turn out to be unmanageable and at the end prove to be inefficient.[290]

Thus, it is necessary for reasons of efficiency and fairness to be able to both join cases and sever cases as seems adequate. In international criminal procedure there are provisions foreseeing both concepts.

1. Joinder

At the UN Tribunals one can differentiate two strategies. (1) the concept of indicting more than one accused, and (2) joining trials of multiple accused charged under different indictments. Concept (1) is specifically authorized by Rule 48 RPE ICTY/ICTR and Rule 48 (a) RPE SCSL. The ICTY and ICTR followed this road frequently.[291] The few accused at the SCSL were indicted separately but joined later invoking concept (2). The relevant legal question is, according to Rule 48 RPE ICTY/ICTR, whether the events relate to the same 'transaction'. According to Rule 2 (A) RPE ICTY a transaction is defined as: 'a number of acts or omissions whether occurring as one event or a number of events, at the same or different locations and being part of a common scheme, strategy or plan'.

Sometimes suspects would be indicted in separate instruments, because investigations developed at a different speed or the policy of transferring suspects to The Hague would necessitate a differentiated strategy, and the Prosecutor would later request the merger of two or more indictments into a single joint indictment as the basis of a single trial against several accused persons. Of course, also the Completion Strategy urged the Tribunals to combine cases.[292]

The test the chamber reviewing the request to joinder would be as follows: (1) do the rules allow the joinder of the indictments; that is, do the events *prima facie* relate to the same 'transaction' according to Rule 48 RPE ICTY/ICTR,[293] and (2) should the Chamber nevertheless deny joinder according to its discretion? This discretion was exercised by submitting to the following parameters:

> (a) the joinder of the Accused would avoid duplication of the presentation of evidence related to underlying crimes and to some extent to the criminal responsibility of several of the Accused; minimise hardship to witnesses; and would be in the interests of judicial economy, since, on the basis of the Prosecution's submissions, the

[290] As emphasized by Boas/Bischoff/Reid/Taylor, *ICL III*, 198.

[291] To give one example each: ICTY *Prosecutor v Naletilić and Martinović*, IT-98-34-I, 18 December 1998, Indicment; ICTR *Nyiramasuhuko and Ntahobali*, ICTR-97-21-I, 26 May 1997, Indictment.

[292] *See* Boas/Bischoff/Reid/Taylor, *ICL III*, 202.

[293] *See* ICTY *Prosecutor v Milutinović et al.*, TC, IT-03-70-PT, 8 July 2005, Decision on Prosecution Motion for Joinder. In this case reference was made to the *prima facie* case of all of the accused being part of a joint criminal enterprise.

length of one joint trial is likely to be significantly shorter than the combined period necessary for two separate trials;

(b) that no basis has been identified for concluding that joinder would create a conflict of interest or otherwise prejudice the right of any of the Accused to a fair and expeditious trial, and no basis has been advanced to persuade the Trial Chamber that it is not able to manage the conduct of a joint trial adequately; moreover, the Trial Chamber is confident that by applying existing Rules of Procedure and Evidence, it will be able to ensure to the Accused a fair and expeditious trial;

(c) that there is no indication that a joint trial could not start in December 2005 or January 2006, the anticipated date for the start of trial in the *Milutinović et al.* case.[294]

Operating with a considerably smaller number of accused, the SCSL has combined the indictments into three trials altogether relying on similar argument as developed by the UN Tribunals.[295]

According to Art 64 (5) ICCSt the Trial Chamber at the ICC has the *proprio motu* authority to join or sever proceedings in respect of charges against more than one accused. It has been held that the ICC will consider the practice at the UN Tribunals in particular Rules 48 and 72 RPE ICTY when applying this provision.[296] Indeed, in the sole decision on joinder made to-date in the case against *Katanga and Chui*,[297] the Chamber applied the same factors that were emphasized by the Tribunals and the SCSL.[298]

The allegations against the two suspects pertain to the same incident, the joint attack on the village of Bogoro. Furthermore, the Pre-Trial Chamber relied on its threefold obligation to: (a) take appropriate measures to protect the safety, physical and psychological well-being, dignity, and privacy of victims and witnesses pursuant to Arts 57 3(c) and 68 of the Statute, (b) to respect the rights of the accused according to Art. 67 ICCSt and (c) to guarantee fair and expedited

294 Ibid (reference omitted); *see* also ICTR *Prosecutor v Bagosora et al.*, TC I, ICTR-98-41-T, 27 March 2006, Decision on Request for Severance of Three Accused. Similarly ICTY *Prosecutor v Delalić et al.*, TC II, IT-96-21-T, 25 September 1996, Decision on the Motion of the Accused Delalić to Be Tried Separately from his Co-Accused. The request has been denied by the Chamber. Leave to appeal was not granted.

295 *See* eg, SCSL *Prosecutor v Norman*, SCSL-2003-08-PT; *Prosecutor v Fofana*, SCSL-2003-11-PT; *Prosecutor v Kondewa*, SCSL-2003-12-PT, 27 February 2004, Decision and Order on Prosecution Motions for Joinder, referring frequently to the UN Tribunal's Case Law. In greater detail *see* Boas/Bischoff/Reid/Taylor, *ICL III*, 204–6. As regards the accused at the SCSL *see* Chapter 1, p 32 *et subs*.

296 *See* Triffterer/*Bitti*, Art. 64 MN 19.

297 ICC *Prosecutor v Katanga and Chui*, PTC I, ICC-01/04-01/07-257, 10 March 2008, Decision on the Joinder of the Cases against Germain Katanga and Mathieu Ngudjolo Chui.

298 *See* Boas/Bischoff/Reid/Taylor, *ICL III*, 206.

proceedings.[299] On this basis the Pre-Trial Chamber developed the following check-list:

(i) joinder enhances the fairness as well as the judicial economy of the proceedings because, in addition to affording to the arrested persons the same rights as if they were being prosecuted separately, joinder:

(a) avoids having witnesses testify more than once and reduce expenses related to those testimonies;

(b) avoids duplication of the evidence; and

(c) avoids inconsistency in the presentation of the evidence and would therefore afford equal treatment to both arrested persons;

(ii) joinder minimises the potential impact on witnesses, and better facilitate the protection of the witnesses' physical and mental well- being; and

(iii) concurrent presentation of evidence pertaining to different arrested persons does not per se constitute a conflict of interests.[300]

In weighing these interests against the general prevalence of the Statute in favour of joint trials, the Chamber decided to proceed accordingly and combine the trials of the two persons as the defence could not establish inappropriateness of the joinder in these cases.[301]

2. Severance

As regards severance of trials Rule 136 RPE ICC foresees that those jointly accused shall be tried together unless the Trial Chamber orders separate trials in order to avoid serious prejudice to the accused, to protect the interests of justice, or because one accused has made an admission of guilt in accordance with Art. 65 ICCSt. This rule has been interpreted by the Pre-Trial Chamber in *Katanga and Chui* as forming the presumption in favour of joint proceedings.[302]

At the Tribunals similar rules applied, *see* Rule 82 RPE ICTY/ICTR/SCSL. Most requests for separate trials have been denied because chambers see the interests of justice best protected by joint trials.[303] Severance was ordered, however, if due to ill health of one of the co-accused the trial would be delayed considerably and would thus conflict with the right of the other co-accused to be tried without undue delay.[304] A similar situation might arise, if one or more of the accused were not

299 ICC *Prosecutor v Katanga and Chui*, PTC I, ICC-01/04-01/07-257, 10 March 2008, Decision on the Joinder of the Cases against Germain Katanga and Mathieu Ngudjolo Chui, p 6.

300 Ibid, p 8 (reference omitted).

301 Boas/Bischoff/Reid/Taylor, *ICL III*, 206.

302 ICC *Prosecutor v Katanga and Chui*, PTC I, ICC-01/04-01/07-257, 10 March 2008, Decision on the Joinder of the Cases against Germain Katanga and Mathieu Ngudjolo Chui, p 8 *et subs*.

303 ICTY *Prosecutor v Popović et al.*, TC, IT-05-88-PT, 26 June 2006, Decision on Severance of Case against Milorad Trbić, p 3.

304 Eg, ICTY *Prosecutor v Brđanin and Talić*, TC II, IT-99-36-T, 20 September 2002, Decision on Prosecutor's Oral Request for the Separation of Trials, para 26–9.

present to stand trial at the seat of the Tribunal.[305] In any case the chambers expected that proof of a serious prejudice to a specific right of an accused, mostly the right to be tried without undue delay, could be demonstrated.[306]

The ICC judges will most certainly rely on the Tribunals' jurisprudence, and rightly so. In particular if one takes into account that the witnesses and victims are spared the necessity of testifying several times if trials are conducted jointly, there must be strong evidence that the rights of the accused are seriously hampered if no separation of the trials is ordered. This was also the rationale of Rule 136 RPE ICC attached to it by the drafters.[307]

V. Summary

The preparation for trial takes place after the charges have been confirmed and before the trial starts. This interim phase is directed by the Trial Chamber to which the case has been assigned. It is mostly concerned with putting together the trial calendar and the designing of the presentation of evidence at trial. Whereas the Prosecutor and the Pre-Trial Chamber, in confirming the charges, have carved out the theme of the trial, the parties need to agree with the Trial Chamber on how to proceed. Conferring in Status Conferences largely accomplishes this.

The dominant role of the Trial Chamber in managing the proceedings should be respected and advanced. Having obtained full knowledge of the case and the proceedings thus far through the 'record',[308] the Trial Chamber can evaluate the weaknesses and strengths of the Prosecution case by itself and plan accordingly.

The possible strength of the Trial Chamber is at the same time the greatest loophole in the ICCSt.[309] The Rome Statute gives to the Trial Chamber the authority to dominate the trial, direct the parties, and conduct its own investigation. However, the Rome Statute does not at the same time attribute full responsibility for the 'quest for truth' to the trial judges. The text of the Statute leaves it to the discretion of the Chamber to decide how much it actually wants to be involved in the search for the truth as an active player, or whether it prefers to stand back and watch the parties perform.[310]

---

[305] ICTR *Prosecutor v Bizimana and Nzabonimana*, TC I, ICTR-98-44-I, 7 November 2008, Decision on Prosecution Motion for Severance and Amendment of Indictment, para 5.

[306] ICTR *Prosecutor v Karemera, Ngirupatse and Nzirorera*, TC III, ICTR-98-44-T, 10 September 2009, Decision on Remand Regarding Continuation of Trial, para 6.

[307] *See* Triffterer/*Bitti*, Art. 64 MN 19.

[308] *See* p 92.

[309] Critical in this regard S Kirsch, 'The Trial Proceedings before the ICC', 6 *ICLR* (2006) 275, 279 *et subs*.

[310] *See* also T Weigend, 'Should We Search for the Truth, and Who Should Do it?' 36 *North Carolina Journal of International Law and Commercial Regulation* (2011) 389, 408 *et subs*.

Consequently, there is a responsibility gap. The failure of the Rome Statute on this point might prove detrimental to the rights of the accused, as s/he cannot rely on the Trial Chamber to ask the right questions in his or her favour. However, his or her fate might depend thereon, in particular if the defendant is lacking resources for investigating himself.

This responsibility gap must be filled either by obliging the Trial Chamber to decide in advance which way it wants to try the case, which would probably lead to different strategies being adopted by different chambers in different cases, or-preferably—by placing the responsibility for searching for the truth squarely on the Trial Chamber. The overall development of international criminal procedure points in the latter direction.[311] Most judges would probably see themselves as being part of the quest for the truth. However, the crucial point is that the judges are not only part of this quest, but its driving force and the body that will be held responsible in case of failure. The 'inquisitorial element', which has been identified as one of the relevant factors of the role of the judge, should be attributed to the ICC judge and thereby close the responsibility gap described.[312]

C. The Structure of the Trial

Before looking at the trial structure of the ICC in detail we have to address a couple of preliminary issues. These are the questions of whether the trial consists of one or of two 'acts' (below I.1), and whether, and to what extent, the trial incorporates the entering of a 'plea' of guilty or not guilty on the side of the accused (below I.2).

I. Preliminary issues that may influence structure

1. The two-act system

The structure of the trial is not a straightforward issue. The two main systems followed in most of the world, Anglo-American and Continental European, follow different ideas of how to structure a criminal trial. On the Continent, there is only one act: conviction and sentencing are combined, in the sense that from the beginning of the trial the possible sanction is at issue. In the Anglo-American tradition there are two separate stages; in the first half, the case is presented and discussed with the sole intention of proving the guilt of the accused. Only in the second part, after the conviction, are the circumstances that are relevant to the extent of the penalty presented and disputed.

The original reason for this separation was the fact that the question of guilt had to be considered by a jury, while determination of the punishment could easily be left

---

311 *See* C Safferling, *Towards an International Criminal Procedure* (OUP 2003) 220–5.

312 As to consequences on appeal *see* p 535 *et subs*.

to the judge. The phenomenon of the jury was discussed earlier and it was shown then that a jury is unnecessary from a human rights perspective and that there is no 'right to a jury'. So we are faced with the interesting question of whether or not separation of guilt and punishment is still appropriate, or whether it is outdated. It is argued here that separation still makes sense and indeed supports protection of, and fairness towards the accused.

If there is a separate second stage for sentencing, the accused's personal details, his or her background, occupation, and income, his or her position as regards previous convictions, are of no interest in the first part of the procedure. There, commission of the criminal offence is the only issue that is under scrutiny. In a single-stage trial, on the other hand, all of the above matters will be mentioned before guilt is established. This of course has the advantage that the judge gets the complete picture relying not only on the circumstances of the act as such but comprising also the personality of the accused, his or her character, previous convictions, and dangerousness.

The pros and cons of both approaches are easily enumerated. Whereas the Continental system allegedly does more justice to the individual guilt of the perpetrator by taking his or her personality into account, it leads at the same time to serious concerns regarding the presumption of innocence and the protection of the privacy of the accused.[313] A separation of the questions of the guilt of the offender and of the amount of punishment to be imposed thus seems to be preferable from a human rights perspective.[314]

It does not surprise that the *ad hoc* Tribunals, which are modelled according to the Anglo-American system, originally followed the two-act structure. However, this split system turned out to be a rather time-consuming enterprise. For example, Dusko Tadić was convicted by Trial Chamber II on 7 May 1997[315] and the sentencing judgment was handed down two months later on 14 July 1997.[316] As the conviction was modified on appeal,[317] the trial chamber had to revisit its sentencing decision and issued a new judgment on 11 November 1999.[318] The appeal against this sentencing judgment was finally served on 26 January 2000.[319] Thus in order

[313] For a discussion in detail *see* C Safferling, *Towards an International Criminal Procedure* (OUP 2003) 270.

[314] It should be noted that even in Germany we often find a separate guilt-finding stage being exercised informally. *See* H Schöch and W Schreiber, 'Ist die Zweiteilung der Hauptverhandlung praktikabel?', 11 *Zeitschrift für Rechtspolitik* (1978) 457.

[315] ICTY *Prosecutor v Tadić*, TC II, IT-94-1-T, 7 May 1997, Opinion and Judgment.

[316] ICTY *Prosecutor v Tadić*, TC II, IT-94-1-T, 14 July 1997, Sentencing Judgment.

[317] ICTY *Prosecutor v Tadić*, AC, IT-94-1-A, 15 July 1999, Judgment.

[318] ICTY *Prosecutor v Tadić*, TC II, IT-94-1-T*bis*-R117, 11 November 1999, Sentencing Judgment.

[319] ICTY *Prosecutor v Tadić*, AC, IT-94-1-A and IT-94-1-A*bis*, 15 July 1999, Judgment in Sentencing Appeals.

to speed up the proceedings, Rule 87 C RPE ICTY was amended in that regard. Since 10 July 1998 the Trial Chamber will issue one single judgment containing both the verdict as to the guilt of the offender and, in the case that this is positive, determine the penalty to be imposed with regard to the convictions in respect of the charges.

The ICC in contrast adheres to the two-act system and separates the question as to the guilt of the offender from the question of the sentence to be imposed. This is laid down on the one hand in Art. 65 ICCSt, and in the provisions pertaining to the sentencing on the other, which are Arts 74 and 76 ICCSt.

2. *The guilty plea*

Another issue, which has consequences on the structure of the trial, is the question of how much influence is attributed to the 'confession' of the accused. One special phenomenon of the Anglo-American system in this regard is the 'guilty plea'. The accused has the option of pleading guilty before the hearing starts. If s/he does so, the first stage of the trial becomes superfluous. No more proof is needed to establish the guilt of the defendant. With the guilty plea, the defendant seems to be automatically waiving his or her rights under the human rights treaties: as far as the establishing of the facts is concerned, no more defence is needed (Art. 14 (3) (b) and (d) ICCPR), no more witnesses need to be examined (Art. 14 (3) (e) ICCPR), and the right to appeal is severely limited (Art. 14 (5) ICCPR).[320] The enormous practicality and speedy termination of the proceedings have been put forward as having advantages here.[321] The possibility of pleading guilty enables the prosecuting agencies to focus on important issues and liberates them from the tiring work of detailed judicial scrutiny of the charges.

The plea is necessarily foreign to the Continental system of criminal procedure because it cannot be reconciled with its maxim of truth finding. In Continental proceedings a confession does not have the result of terminating the procedure; it merely constitutes one strand of evidence among others.

The ICTY once more follows the Anglo-American tradition and foresees two trial stages, despite the fact that no jury is involved. On his or her initial appearance before the Trial Chamber, the accused must enter a plea of guilty or not guilty (Rule 62 RPE ICTY). In the case of a guilty plea, the trial proceeds immediately to its second stage and the hearing only concerns the appropriate sentence (Rule 100 RPE ICTY[322]). A plea of guilty concerning allegations of crimes against humanity

[320] N Clark, 'Plea Bargaining at the ICTY: Guilty Pleas and Reconciliation', 20 *EJIL* (2009) 415, 418.

[321] Compare eg, J Hatchard, B Huber, and R Vogler, *Comparative Criminal Procedure* (BIICL 1996) 224–5.

[322] Rule 100 was amended to clarify this case during the 11th Plenary Meeting of the Judges, 25 June 1996. It now contains an explicit reference to cases involving a guilty plea.

(Art. 5 ICTYSt) was entered by Erdemović. The Trial Chamber I was satisfied that the plea was made voluntarily, in full cognizance of the nature of the charge and its consequences, and was unequivocal, and sentenced the defendant to ten years' imprisonment.[323]

However, Erdemović appealed against this judgment and in particular against his guilty plea. The Appeals Chamber delivered its decision on 7 October 1997, overruling the Trial Chamber with regard to the plea on the following grounds: Erdemović pleaded guilty to the counts of crimes against humanity (Art. 5 ICTYSt) in the belief that this was the lesser charge compared to the alternative indictment of a violation of the laws or customs of war (Art. 3 ICTYSt). This proved to be erroneous. The Trial Chamber made a considerable effort to define crimes against humanity as the gravest and most serious crime imaginable, deserving the severest punishment. Had Erdemović been aware of the situation, he would most probably have entered a different plea. For the Appeals Chamber, the guilty plea was therefore not an informed one and the defendant was given the opportunity to plea again with full knowledge of both the nature of the charges against him and the consequences of his plea before another Trial Chamber.[324] For these reasons, Erdemović then pleaded guilty to the charge of a violation of the laws or customs of war on 14 January 1998, whereupon the prosecutor withdrew the alternative count of a crime against humanity. The Trial Chamber gave a second sentencing judgment on 5 March 1998, reducing the sentence to five years, having found Erdemović's second plea voluntary, informed, and unequivocal.[325]

In order to avoid similar inconveniences in the future, the Fourteenth Plenary Session adopted Rule 62*bis*, where it laid down the conditions for a valid guilty plea.[326]

The discussions concerning the Rome Statute where thus influenced by two sets of arguments: (1) a situation like the one in which Erdemović found himself is to be avoided under all circumstances, and (2) from a truth-finding perspective the guilty plea can prove counterproductive if the decision whether or not to stage a trial is left entirely up to the accused. The Rome Statute thus, even if it did not abolish the 'plea' proceedings entirely, departed substantially from the Anglo-American structure. According to Art. 65 ICCSt, the accused does not enter a guilty plea but rather admits this guilt. The term 'guilty plea' was deliberately avoided.[327] The Trial Chamber must in this case still evaluate whether

---

[323] ICTY, *Prosecutor v Erdemović*, TC I, IT-96-22-T, 29 November 1996, Sentencing Judgment, para 10–14.

[324] ICTY *Prosecutor v Erdemović*, AC, IT-96-22-A, 7 October 1997.

[325] ICTY *Prosecutor v Erdemović*, TC II, IT-96-22-T, 5 March 1998, para 23. For a more detailed description *see* Boas/Bischoff/Reid/Taylor, *ICL III*, 216–21.

[326] 14th Plenary Session on 12 November 1997.

[327] Boas/Bischoff/Reid/Taylor, *ICL III*, 225.

this voluntary admission is supported by the facts of the case. This is strongly reminiscent of the Continental way dealing with a confession.[328] However, the procedure which is to be followed is rather complicated and will be looked at below in greater details.

3. Plea bargaining

In a system where the discretionary powers of the prosecutor are wide, in which two parties line up in order to present their respective hypotheses, and in which a guilty plea will not be questioned as to its truthfulness, it is natural that these parties can craft a deal in advance and agree upon what to present to the judges and what to leave aside.[329] Thus a murder charge can be traded for a guilty plea to a charge of manslaughter and—possibly—a genocide charge for a charge of war crimes. This is what is called charge bargaining. The prosecution might also offer a specific sentence in return for a guilty plea, which would be called sentence bargaining.[330] For a Continental lawyer such an approach is foreign for principled reasons. As the main purpose of the criminal trial is to discover the truth, a deal concerning this truth is unthinkable. Yet for many years plea bargaining has found strong support amongst judges, prosecutors, and defence lawyers even on the Continent. Its persuasiveness comes from its power to speed up the proceeding and reduce the workload of all participants considerably.

The practice of plea bargaining enjoys wide recognition at the ICTY and has been used, both in the form of charge and of sentence bargaining,[331] in particular in order to speed up the trials and fulfil the necessities of the completion strategy.[332] This was not always the case.[333] Only on 13 December 2001 was Rule 62*ter* RPE ICTY adopted which would allow for plea bargaining.[334] Since then about one-third of all

---

[328] *See* C Safferling, *Towards an International Criminal Procedure* (OUP 2003) 276.

[329] For a short history of plea-bargaining and the ideological underpinnings *see*: N Amoury Combs, 'Copping a Plea to Genocide: The Plea Bargaining of International Crimes', 151 *U Pa L Rev* (2002) 1, 12 *et subs.*, 50 *et subs.*

[330] *See* for the differentiation between charge and sentence bargaining: R Pati, 'The ICC and the Case of Sudan's Omar Al Bashir: Is Plea Bargaining a Valid Option?', 15 *UC Davis J Int'l L and Pol'y* (2009) 265, 282 *et subs.* with further references.

[331] Charge bargaining was first accepted in the case ICTY *Prosecutor v Plavšić*, IT-00-39 and 40-PT, 7 March 2002, Amended Consolidated Indictment; and *Prosecutor v Plavšić*, TC, IT-00-39 and40/1-S, 20 December 2002, Decision Granting Prosecution's Motion to Dismiss Counts 1, 2, 4, 5, 6, 7, and 8 of the Amended Consolidated Indictment. The only charge which remained was one of persecution as a crime against humanity; the other counts of genocide and crimes against humanity were dropped.

[332] *See* A Zahar and G Sluiter, *International Criminal Law* (OUP 2007) 42.

[333] It was ruled out by the former President A Cassese as not admitted by the ICTY's law prior to this amendment, *see* V Morris and M P Scharf, *An Insider's Guide to the ICTY* (1995) ii, 649, 652.

[334] *See* for a more detailed description of Rule 62*bis*: Boas/Bischoff/Reid/Taylor, *ICL III*, 221–4.

convictions were secured by plea bargaining,[335] a 'triumph of pragmatism' indeed.[336] Whereas the ICTR has evidently the same Rules as the ICTY, guilty pleas have terminated the trial in only about sixteen out of every hundred cases.[337]

Yet plea bargaining has caused some discussion at the ICTY:[338] It is an issue as to whether a guilty plea, which is part of a plea bargaining, can be seen as a mitigating factor in the sentencing decision.[339] Its nature as a negotiated 'confession' raises serious doubts as to whether it can add to the reconciliation process in the societies concerned.[340] It is also doubtful whether the truth finding is enhanced by plea bargaining notwithstanding the fact that the ICTY has frequently held exactly this.[341] At the very least, neither the Chambers nor the public can assert whether what was agreed upon in the plea agreement coincides with the factual truth.[342]

It is generally questionable whether plea bargaining is an adequate method of administering justice in international criminal trials.[343] Considering that plea agreements are seldom used with serious crimes in national jurisdictions it seems not acceptable to act otherwise confronted with the gravest offences which shock the conscience of mankind.[344] The argument in favour of plea bargaining for reason of efficiency of the proceedings is one of convenience but not of substance.[345] A different answer to the problem of administering

335 R Henham and M Drumbl, 'Plea Bargaining at the International Criminal Tribunal for the Former Yugoslavia', 16 *CLF* (2005) 53.

336 N Jørgensen, 'The Genocide Acquittal in the Sikirica Case before the International Criminal Tribunal for the Former Yugoslavia and the Coming of Age of the Guilty Plea', 15 *LJIL* (2002) 407.

337 *See* Triffterer/*Guariglia*/*Hochmayr*, Art. 65 MN 13.

338 M P Scharf, 'Trading Justice for Efficiency: Plea-Bargaining and International Tribunals', 2 *JICJ* (2004) 1070, 1074.

339 This has been generally accepted by ICTR *Prosecutor v Kambanda*, AC, ICTR-97-23-A, 19 October 2000, Judgment, para 120, 122, 126.

340 ICTY *Prosecutor v Nikolić*, TC, IT-94–2-S, 18 December 2003, Sentencing Judgment; *see* also: N Clark, 'Plea Bargaining at the ICTY: Guilty Pleas and Reconciliation', 20 *EJIL* (2009) 415 and R Henham, 'Plea Bargaining and the Legitimacy of International Trial Justice: Some Observations on the Dragan Nikolic Sentencing Judgment of the ICTY', 5 *ICLR* (2005) 601.

341 ICTY *Prosecutor v Deronjić*, TC II, IT-02-61-S, 30 March 2004, Sentencing Judgment, para 236. Very critical in this regard the dissenting opinion of Judge Schomburg.

342 This was admitted by the Trial Chamber II: ICTY *Prosecutor v Nikolić*, TC, IT-94–2-S, 18 December 2003, Sentencing Judgment, para 122.

343 As for the US criminal justice system and the role of plea bargaining, *see* US Supreme Court *Santobello v New York*, 404 US 257, 260 (1971).

344 N Amoury Combs, 'Copping a Plea to Genocide: The Plea Bargaining of International Crimes', 151 *U Pa L Rev* (2002) 1 analysing the national context and comparing it to the international level. *See* also A Petrig, 'Negotiated Justice and the Goals of International Criminal Tribunals', 8 *Chi-Kent J Int'l & Comp L* (2008) 1, 19 *et subs* analysing the duty to prosecute on the international level; *see* also R Pati, 'The ICC and the Case of Sudan's Omar Al Bashir: Is Plea Bargaining a Valid Option?', 15 *UC Davis J Int'l L & Pol'y* (2009) 265, 322.

345 A Petrig, 'Negotiated Justice and the Goals of International Criminal Tribunals', 8 *Chi-Kent J Int'l & Comp L* (2008) 1, 29 *et subs.*

properly would be to fund the Court in an adequate way so that it can fulfil its mandate.[346]

At the ICC luckily a rather cautious approach prevailed regarding plea bargaining. In Art. 65 (5) ICCSt this fact found its expression in that any agreement between the Prosecutor and the defence concerning either the modification of charges, the admission of guilt, or the expected penalty, will not be binding on the Court. However, negotiations between the Prosecutor and the defence are thus not ruled out.[347] Whether and to what extent an agreement reached between these two parties will influence the proceedings before the Chambers will depend heavily upon the willingness of the judges to intervene.[348] As much as the judges can influence the confirmation of the charges at the pre-trial stage pursuant to Art. 61 (7) ICCSt, and as much as the judges can require additional evidence to be produced at the trial stage pursuant to Art. 64 (6) ICCSt, they are not forced to do so. As has been discussed before, the judges are not as such responsible for the truth finding.[349] Judges could just as well satisfy themselves with the charges as bargained between prosecution and defence and desist from inquiring about the whole truth of the event.[350]

Budgetary limits could raise the attraction of plea agreements as a means to terminate cases quickly.[351] Because of the procedural practice at the *ad hoc* Tribunals, it is likely that plea bargaining will play some role at the ICC also.[352] Despite of all the criticism raised against plea bargaining both at the national and the international level, all the participants in the prosecution process always yielded to temptation based on the practicality of a 'deal'. It would be utterly unrealistic to assume that things would turn out differently at the ICC. One additional class of player however could make a difference: the victims. Because of their involvement into the trial process, it could become more difficult for the 'parties' to bargain behind closed curtains.[353] It might then not be enough to point to the effect of the guilty plea that

---

346 *See* M P Scharf, 'Trading Justice for Efficiency: Plea-Bargaining and International Tribunals', 2 *JICJ* (2004) 1070, 1080; also: M Bohlander, 'Plea-Bargaining before the ICTY', in: R May *et al.* (eds), *Essays on ICTY Procedure and Evidence in Honour of Gabrielle Kirk McDonald* (Kluwer 2001) 151, 159.

347 Indeed, as has been rightly pointed out, the wording of Art. 65 (5) presupposes the existence of such negotiations, *see* Triffterer/*Guariglia/Hochmayr*, Art. 65 MN 40.

348 This is rightly stressed by Boas/Bischoff/Reid/Taylor, *ICL III*, 226 *et subs.*

349 *See* Chapter 2, p 131 *et subs.*

350 *See* M Bohlander, 'Plea-Bargaining before the ICTY', in: R May *et al.* (eds), *Essays on ICTY Procedure and Evidence in Honour of Gabrielle Kirk McDonald* (Kluwer 2001) 151, 157.

351 This realistic danger is described by R Pati, 'The ICC and the Case of Sudan's Omar Al Bashir: Is Plea Bargaining a Valid Option?', 15 *UC Davis J Int'l L & Pol'y* (2009) 265—the author sees plea bargaining as not an 'insurmountably great injustice' at the ICC.

352 Argued by Boas/Bischoff/Reid/Taylor, *ICL III*, 214.

353 The problems of the plea bargaining for the victims have been stressed by: R Pati, 'The ICC and the Case of Sudan's Omar Al Bashir: Is Plea Bargaining a Valid Option?', 15 *UC Davis J Int'l L & Pol'y* (2009) 265, 287.

'the victims of [the] crimes were spared the emotional burden of having to testify at trial'.[354] Victims might insist on the searching for the entire truth.

II. The structure of the trial at the ICC

The actual structure of the trial is not the core issue of the Rome Statute. It is mainly Art. 64 (8) ICCSt which gives the basic parameters for the trial. Accordingly, the trial begins with the reading out of the confirmed charges, Art. 64 (8) (a) ICCSt.[355] Upon the presentation of the charges the accused is to be given the opportunity to make an admission of guilt or plead not guilty. The structure of the rest of the trial is mainly for the presiding judge to decide, for it is he or she who has to ensure that the proceeding is conducted in a fair and impartial manner, Art. 64 (8) (b) ICCSt.

It is interesting to note that according to Rule 140 (1) RPE ICC a rather non-hierarchical alternative is foreseen. In the event that the Presiding Judge does not give directions, the parties; that is, the Prosecutor and the defence, shall agree on the order and manner in which the evidence shall be submitted to the Trial Chamber. If this does not work, the authority will in the end be referred back to the Presiding Judge. The intention of the RPE ICC is rather unclear in this regard. All options are permitted.[356]

The Rome Statute follows a two-act system, that is, the guilt of the accused is dealt with in a proceeding, which is separate from that concerning the sentencing. The first act of the trial is again twofold. The first stage comprises the question of admission of guilt and the consequences thereof. The second stage consists of the presentation of evidence, if a full-blown trial is warranted. We will look at these stages as three different phases: phase 1: the guilty plea, phase 2: the presentation of evidence, and phase 3: the sentencing.

1. *Phase 1: Guilty plea*

The trial starts with the reading of the charges as confirmed by the Pre-Trial Chamber. This is more or less a formal act, as the accused knows the allegations, which are being raised against him/her, from the status conferences held in preparation of the trial. The accused should then state whether s/he pleads not guilty or whether s/he wants to make an admission of guilt (not of facts) according to Art. 65 ICCSt.

Even if Art. 64 (8) and Art. 65 ICCSt relate the admission to the beginning of the trial stage, there is no reason why the accused should not have the right to admit

354 As did the ICTY *Prosecutor v Todorović*, TC, IT-95-9/1-S, 31 July 2001, Judgment, para 70.

355 *See* p 420 *et subs.*, concerning the preparation stage.

356 Ahlbrecht/*Kirsch*, MN 1371, who argues in favour of a swift clarification of the many questions arising out of this openness.

his/her guilt after the trial has already entered its second stage, the presentation of the evidence. The Trial Chamber will in that case speed up prosecution by following Art. 65 ICCSt.[357] It becomes more difficult if the accused wants to admit his/her guilt before that. There are two problems connected to this question. One is that the Pre-Trial Chamber, confirming the charges according to Art. 61 ICCSt, has no authority to opt for an abbreviated procedure according to Art. 65 ICCSt as it does not possess the power to convict.[358] The second issue is the fact that the 'charges' containing the allegations are only available after the confirmation decision. Before the charges are finalized, there is no formal allegation to which the accused could admit his guilt. Therefore, it is impossible to implement the Art. 65 ICCSt proceeding before the beginning of the trial. In the event that the person concerned is conscience-stricken, s/he can of course cooperate with the OTP and thereby speed up the entire proceeding during the investigation stage and the confirmation process. A formal admission of guilt however is only allowed after the beginning of the trial.[359]

In case of an admission, the Trial Chamber will scrutinize the validity of this admission and test whether the admission is supported by the facts of the case. There are four options at the discretion of the Chamber, which follow:[360]

(1) Convict the accused on that basis (Art. 65 (2) ICCSt);
(2) Reject the admission and proceed with the (ordinary) trial (Art. 65 (3) ICCSt);
(3) Despite the general acceptance of the confession order the presentation of additional evidence (Art. 65 (4) (a) ICCSt); or
(4) Despite a valid confession reject the admission and order an ordinary trial (Art. 65 (4) (b) ICCSt).

We will look at the validity test and the support by facts as well as the option to proceed with the trial despite a valid admission in greater detail.

a. Validity of the admission of guilt The Rome Statute ties in with the ICTY practice concerning the guilty plea. Pursuant to Art. 65 (1) ICCSt, preconditions for the validity of the admission of guilt are as follows:

(a) the accused must understand the nature and consequence of the admission of guilt, and
(b) the admission must be voluntary and be made after sufficient consultation with defence counsel.

357 *See* Triffterer/*Guariglia/Hochmayr*, Art. 65 MN 15 *et subs.*
358 *See* again ibid, Art. 65 MN 16.
359 Ibid.
360 *See* Boas/Bischoff/Reid/Taylor, *ICL III*, 226.

(a) The admission of guilt pertains to the charges and not the actual facts. The admission of guilt is not a confession in the Continental European sense. Thus the Chamber must satisfy itself that the accused understands the 'nature', ie the elements of the crime, the legal requirements, the gravity of the 'charges', and the possible penalties. Furthermore, the accused must be aware of the 'consequences' of his/her admission, that is, the waiver of his procedural rights.

(b) The admission of guilt is voluntary, if it is free from any form of threat, coercion, duress, or any form of improper promise.[361] The requirement of consultation with counsel should act as a guarantee for the voluntariness in this sense. Despite its systematic place within Art. 65 (1) ICCSt, the requirement of consultation with counsel should also help to safeguard the knowledge of the accused concerning the nature and consequence of the admission of guilt. The question of how much consultation is 'sufficient' is to be answered on a case-by-case basis. It depends on the complexity of the charges, the capacities of the accused and the amount of influence which has already taken place from prosecuting agencies. This requirement is evidently connected to the right of a suspect or accused according to Art. 55 (1) (a) and Art. 67 (1) (g) ICCSt not to incriminate him/herself.[362]

The requirement of counsel consultation has another element to it: defence counsel is thereby made responsible for any failures in this regard. Consequently, allegations of ineffective assistance of counsel could be raised.[363]

b. Supporting facts Even if the admission of guilt was informed and voluntary and took place after sufficient consultation with counsel, it is only 'valid' in the sense of Art. 65 ICCSt, if it is supported by facts.[364] Art. 65 (1) (c) (i)–(iii) ICCSt differentiates between three points of reference determining the facts that are relevant here.

First, the admission of guilt has to conform to the facts 'contained in the charges'. As we have seen, a 'charge' encompasses a factual side, specifying the natural act, time, and place as well as the victim.[365] Secondly, the statement of the accused needs to comply with the facts which are contained in the material presented by the Prosecutor, and which has been accepted by the accused. The material presented in support of the charges in the DCC is that which is meant by Art. 61 (3) (b) ICCSt.[366] It is however necessary that the accused accepts this material. Finally,

[361] Triffterer/*Guariglia/Hochmayr*, Art. 65 MN 25.
[362] Ibid.
[363] *See* Boas/Bischoff/Reid/Taylor, *ICL III*, 225 *et subs.*
[364] Ahlbrecht/*Kirsch*, MN 1426.
[365] *See* Chapter 5 B.
[366] The language of Art. 65 (1) (c) (ii) ICCSt speaks of material which 'supplements' the charge instead of 'support'. This differentiation in wording should not be given much attention; *see* Triffterer/*Guariglia/Hochmayr*, Art. 65 MN 29.

the Chamber needs to find congruence between the admission of guilt and any other evidence presented by the Prosecutor or the accused. In that case the facts need not have been approved by the accused.[367]

In the event that the Chamber is content with the admission, it may convict the accused on this basis according to Art. 65 (2) ICCSt and enter into the sentencing procedure according to Art. 76 ICCSt. Art. 66 (3) ICCSt should be applicable here, which means that the Chamber must be convinced of the guilt of the accused 'beyond a reasonable doubt'.

If the Chamber is not satisfied with the material and evidence before it, it proceeds according to Art. 65 (3) ICCSt. The admission of guilt is in that case to be considered as not having been made; that is, the case is to be put into the *status quo ante*. It is for the Chamber to decide whether to remit the case to another Trial Chamber.[368] It would do so if the proceedings on the admission of guilt have damaged the impartiality of the judges.

c. Further evidence despite valid admission of guilt Should the Trial Chamber be of the opinion that the admission of guilt is valid and is also supported by the facts as required by Art. 65 (1) ICCSt, it may still proceed as foreseen in Art. 65 (4) ICCSt and request more evidence from the Prosecutor or order the application of ordinary trial procedure, if the interests of justice so require. Before deciding on this issue the Chamber hears the view of the Prosecutor and of the defence according to Rule 139 (1) RPE ICC.

This is a rather problematic provision, which to a certain extent punctures the idea of the abbreviated procedure in case of an admission of guilt. I cannot see why this provision establishes 'an important link between the civil law and the common law approach on guilty pleas'[369] for two reasons. First, the provision of Art. 65 (4) ICCSt pertains only to a situation in which the Trial Chamber is satisfied with the admission of guilt as being both valid and supported by the facts. Secondly, the further proceeding is not necessary for the determination of the guilt of the accused, but only for reasons of the interests of justice. Therefore, there is a real danger that the accused is made an object of the proceeding, having to suffer a prolonged procedure for some higher goal; that is, 'interests of justice'. Neither common law nor civil law would endorse such an outcome for the accused.

Therefore, it seems hard to justify these 'extra' proceedings according to Art. 65 (4) ICCSt. It can only be achieved by interpreting the 'interests of justice' as the

[367] The wording of the Statute is clear in this regards; *see* again Triffterer/*Guariglia/Hochmayr*, Art. 65 MN 29.

[368] Triffterer/*Guariglia/Hochmayr*, Art. 65 MN 36. A previous draft used the word 'shall' instead of 'may'. It was thus the intention of the drafter to leave this decision in the discretion of the Trial Chamber.

[369] Argued by Triffterer/*Guariglia/Hochmayr*, Art. 65 MN 37.

'interests of the victims'. Indeed the victims' interests are mentioned explicitly in this provision.[370] Assuming that the victims have an interest in establishing an all-embracing record and have an interest in having their voices heard in a public forum,[371] one could balance the interest of the accused to have a speedy trial with these interests of the victims and conclude that in special scenarios, additional evidence underpinning the admission of guilt, would be welcomed.[372] I would suggest the ICC embark down this avenue according to Art. 65 (4) (a) ICCSt only in exceptional circumstances and avoid an 'unnecessarily lengthy hearing' under Art. 65 ICCSt.

d. A full trial and rejection of admission Reasons for an ordinary trial are even harder to retrieve in cases in which the admission of guilt is valid and supported by the facts. But Art. 65 (4) (b) ICCSt allows this, if a more complete presentation of the facts is required in the interests of justice, in particular the interests of the victims. The trial is in such a case not necessary for the determination of the guilt of the accused. The accused has admitted his/her guilt, and his/her plea is credible and conforms to the facts. If in such a case a full trial is ordered, this trial is obviously conducted for other reasons than to convict the accused according to his/her guilt. At the end of the day, the trial, which will be staged according to Art. 65 (4) (b) ICCSt, equals a judge-led truth commission. In any case, if the Chamber decides to have an ordinary trial despite a valid admission of guilt is must remit the case to another Trial Chamber, otherwise the trial would become a mockery, as the judges are clearly already convinced of the guilt of the accused.

Of course this reading of Art 65 ICCSt is based on the basic assumption that any case in which the judges doubt the truthfulness of the admission of guilt comes within the remit of Art. 65 (3) ICCSt. The only case relevant for Art. 65 (4) (b) ICCSt would be a separation of trial against several accused, which will be discussed below. The question of whether the decision of the Trial Chamber to reject the admission of guilt is reviewable on appeal will be discussed later.[373]

e. Partial admission A situation might arise in which the accused admits his/her guilt, but only to some of the 'charges', and plead not guilty to the remaining charges. There could be two answers to this setting: either the Chamber accepts the partial charge and convicts for these immediately while proceeding

370 Under these circumstances it seems odd that the victims are not invited to present their views as they are not mentioned in Rule 139 (1) RPE ICC. If victims' interests and participation is been taken serious, the victims' representatives should be heard according to the general rule of Art. 68 (3) ICCSt.

371 A Petrig, 'Negotiated Justice and the Goals of International Criminal Tribunals', 8 *Chi-Kent J Int'l & Comp L* (2008) 1, 23 *et subs.*, analysing the victims interests with a view to a guilty plea.

372 Triffterer/*Guariglia/Hochmayr*, Art. 65 MN 38.

373 *See* Chapter 5 E.

with an ordinary trial concerning the remaining charges, or the Chamber proceeds with the ordinary trial and consider the admission of guilt together with the other evidence presented in the course of the trial.[374] I would suggest that it is preferable to follow the latter course, mainly for two reasons: (1) to have split trials against one accused should be avoided, as it would complicate the proceedings unnecessarily, and (2) the scenario is one of the cases of the application of Art. 65 (4) (b) ICCSt, where the interests of justice require a full trial. The Chamber should question the reasons for the accused to admit his/her guilt to some and plead not guilty to other charges. For this matter an ordinary trial is necessary.

In a scenario where several accused are tried jointly and one accused admits his or her guilt, the Chamber should separate his or her trial according to Rule 136 (1) RPE ICC and proceed in the abbreviated trial form of Art. 65 (2) ICCSt.[375]

2. *Phase 2: Presentation of evidence*

After the Trial Chamber has read out the charges as confirmed by the Pre-Trial Chamber, and has satisfied itself that the accused understands these charges properly, and after the accused has been given the opportunity to admit his/her guilt according to Art. 65 ICCSt or plead not guilty, the trial enters into the next stage: the presentation of evidence.

a. Structure of the trial The order and the manner in which the evidence is being presented depend on the individual Trial Chamber (see Rule 140 (1) RPE ICC).[376] At the *ad hoc* Tribunals the rules laying down the structure of the trial were more straightforward. Analogous to these rules, the structure of the trial at the ICC could or maybe even should be as follows:

(1) Opening Phase[377]
- Opening Statement of Prosecutor
- Opening Statement of Defence

(2) Presentation of Evidence[378]
- case-in-chief by the Prosecutor
- case-in-chief by the Defence
- Rebuttal by Prosecution

374 *See* Triffterer/*Guariglia/Hochmayr*, Art. 65 MN 32.

375 Ibid, Art. 65 MN 33.

376 On example can be found at ICC *Prosecutor v Katanga and Chui*, TC II, ICC-01/04-01/07-1665, 20 November 2009, Direction for the Conduct of the Proceedings and Testimony in Accordance with Rule 140, by Presiding Judge Bruno Cotte.

377 *See* Rule 84 RPE ICTY.

378 *See* Rule 85 RPE ICTY.

- Rejoinder by Defence
- additional evidence as ordered by the Trial Chamber (Art. 64 (6) (d) ICCSt)

(3) Closing Phase (Rule 141 RPE ICC)[379]

- Closing Statement by the Prosecutor
- Closing Statement by the Defence

The opening phase and the presentation of evidence could be conducted in such a way that the defence makes its opening statement after the Prosecutor has finished his or her case; that is, given his opening address and presented his or her evidence. In particular, English law has developed this method[380] and this is the way in which the *ad hoc* Tribunals operate (*see* Rule 98 RPE SCSL, Rule 98*bis* RPE ICTY/ICTR).[381] It has at least one advantage. Should the prosecutor fail to submit a conclusive string of evidence to buttress his or her hypothesis and establish the guilt of the accused beyond a reasonable doubt, the defence could enter a motion of 'no case to answer'.[382] Should the Trial Chamber decide in favour of the defence, the trial would be terminated without the defence having to present evidence.

The test which is being applied is elaborated on in the *Celebici* Appeal[383] and confirmed in the *Jelisić* Appeal:[384] '[t]he test applied is whether there is evidence (if accepted) upon which a reasonable tribunal of fact *could* be satisfied beyond reasonable doubt of the guilt of the accused on the particular charge in question'.

There are thus three criteria, which are relevant at that point:

(1) the standard of proof is the same as for the conviction of the accused. Therefore, the prosecutor's evidence, if accepted, must prove the guilt of the accused beyond reasonable doubt. This seems logical, as the defence case which would follow will not harden the prosecutor's case; indeed, quite the contrary will be the case.

(2) The test is a hypothetical one. The prosecution evidence is not tested according to admissibility and reliability. This again is plausible, as the analysis of the evidence in this regard could not enhance the prosecution case.

---

379 *See* Rule 86 RPE ICTY.

380 *See* J Sprack, *Criminal Procedure* (12th edn, OUP 2008) 20.48–55.

381 ICTY *Prosecutor v Orić*, TC, IT-03-68-T, 8 June 2005, Trial Transcript, p 9032–33; *Prosecutor v Sikirica, Došen and Kolundžija*, TC, IT-95-8-T, 3 September 2001, Judgment on Defence Motions to Acquit, para 172; *Prosecutor v Kordić and Čerkez*, TC, IT-95-14/2-T, 6 April 2000, Decision on Defence Motions for Judgment of Acquittal. In all cases the accused persons were acquitted for some charges whereas other allegations were upheld and the trial continued on this limited number of charges.

382 P Robinson, 'Rough Edges in the Alignment of Legal Systems in the Proceedings at the ICTY', 3 *JICJ* (2005) 1037, 1046 *et subs.*

383 ICTY *Prosecutor v Delalić et al.*, AC, IT-96-21-A, 20 February 2001, Judgment, para 434.

384 ICTY *Prosecutor v Jelisić*, AC, IT-95-10-A, 5 July 2001, Judgment, para 37 (emphasis in original).

(3) The judges must not predict whether they *would* convict. They must guess whether any chamber *could* convict. To put it into a negative test: the judges must be satisfied that under no circumstances would a reasonable tribunal convict on the particular charge in question.

This test is to be applied on the different charges individually. As a result, the accused might be acquitted for some charges whereas the trial would continue on the remaining charges.[385]

There is no reason why at the ICC a Trial Chamber should not accept a similar motion of 'no case to answer' even if it is not foreseen in the relevant provisions explicitly.[386] Even if one could say that the Pre-Trial Chamber fulfils a similar function, in that it evaluates the evidence presented by the prosecutor in the confirmation hearing, a situation could arise at the trial in which after the main prosecution case, the evidence presented by the prosecution faltered in cross-examination and the guilt of the accused seems wholly unlikely. Even if the Pre-Trial Chamber found 'substantial grounds to believe' that the accused has indeed offended as charged, the standard to be applied at the trial stage is reasonably higher and could thus not be met in the eyes of the trial chamber. Acquitting mid-trial would then raise the efficiency of the proceeding in its entirety and spare the accused unnecessary hardship and costs.

Likewise the accused could at the end of the prosecution case enter a guilty plea (as at the *ad hoc* Tribunals) or admit his/her guilt according to Art. 65 ICCSt. In that case there would be no defence case-in-chief. The Chamber would proceed immediately to the determination of the sentence.[387]

b. Form of presentation of evidence The form of presenting the evidence is anything but optional and interchangeable. Indeed we are confronted here with one of the crucial differences between the Continental European and Anglo-American trial system.

(1) Witness testimony in the inquisitorial system If we take the German system of criminal procedure as an example, we note first of all that the presiding judge leads the questioning of the witness (*see* §§ 238 (1) and 240 (1) German Code of Criminal Procedure). Pursuant to § 69 German Code of Criminal Procedure the

[385] *See* Boas/Bischoff/Reid/Taylor, *ICL III,* 289 with particular attention to the different wording used regarding 'charge' or 'count'.

[386] *See* K Khan and R Dixon (eds), *Archbold International Criminal Courts: Practice, Procedure and Evidence* (3rd edn, Sweet and Maxwell Ltd 2009) 8–80. A different view is allegedly taken by Boas/Bischoff/Reid/Taylor, *ICL III*, 288.

[387] *See* p 438 *et subs.*, and p 461 *et subs*. Compare Boas/Bischoff/Reid/Taylor, *ICL III*, 287.

examination which follows is separated in two stages: (1) the report, and (2) the questioning.[388]

The witness must be given a chance to give his/her testimony free of interruptions by questions.[389] Thereby, the judges can observe what the witness recalls and what s/he states upon 'coaching' by the court.[390]

The presiding judge will admit questions by the prosecutor, the accused, and the defence counsel, thus conducting the questioning pursuant to § 240 German Code of Criminal Procedure. Civil party is also allowed to pose questions.[391] These questions serve the truth-finding process in that they help test the witness, detecting contradictions, and ensure his or her statement is precise.[392] The right to confrontation as contained in Art. 6 (3) (d) ECHR is thereby fulfilled.[393]

In § 239 German Code of Criminal Procedure, formal cross-examination is also foreseen. As a matter of fact, however, this norm is almost never invoked.[394] This is largely due to the fact that cross-examination is foreign to German criminal procedure.[395] Indeed, neither the prosecutor nor the defence would be interested in nor be prepared to take on the full presentation of evidence.[396] Yet one has to state that in most German courtrooms the questioning of a witness is conducted by way of informal cross-examination in that judges, prosecutor, defence, and civil party are on equal footing in questioning a witness and that the provision of § 240 (2) German Code of Criminal Procedure is applied extensively.[397]

One important maxim of German Criminal Procedure is the fact that the accused is not a witness.[398] This is understood to be a corollary of the right of the accused to be silent.[399] As s/he cannot be forced to cooperate with the prosecution and even has the right to lie to the court, no pressure is to be put onto him or her at all.[400] As a witness s/he would be obliged to tell the truth and be put under oath. The German Criminal Procedural Code thus does not allow the accused to testify as a witness in order to prevent unnecessary stress and pressure for him/her.

---

388 3 BGHSt 281: this separation is mandatory.

389 38 BVerfGE 105.

390 *See* 3 BGHSt 281, 284.

391 *See* L Meyer-Goßner, *Strafprozessordnung* (54th edn, CH Beck 2011) § 240 MN 3.

392 K Volk, *Grundkurs StPO* (7th edn, CH Beck 2008) § 21 MN 19.

393 L Meyer-Goßner, *Strafprozessordnung* (54th edn, CH Beck 2011) § 240 MN 1.

394 Ibid, § 239 MN 1; K Volk, *Grundkurs StPO* (7th edn, CH Beck 2008) § 21 MN 19.

395 *See* eg, C Roxin/B Schünemann, *Strafverfahrensrecht: Ein Studienbuch* (26th edn, CH Beck 2009) § 44 MN 24.

396 L Meyer-Goßner, *Strafprozessordnung* (54th edn, CH Beck 2011) § 239 MN 1.

397 Ibid, § 239 MN 2.

398 *See* 10 BGHSt 8, 10.

399 *See* p 287 *et subs*.

400 K Volk, *Grundkurs StPO* (7th edn, CH Beck 2008) § 21 MN 1.

(2) Cross-examination in the adversarial system In the adversarial system, where the presentation of the evidence is to be conducted by the parties, namely the prosecutor and the defence, cross-examination is the backbone of witness testimony. *Wigmore* called the cross-examination the greatest engine ever invented for the discovery of the truth.[401] The US Supreme Court gives its constitutional blessing stating that it follows from the Sixth Amendment that the Government may not rely on witnesses without submitting them to cross-examination.[402]

Yet 'cross-examination' is not to be confused with the human right of the accused to 'examine' the witnesses against him/her as contained in Art. 6 (3) (d) ECHR and Art. 14 (3) (d) ICCPR. It is not to be mistaken as a simple right of the defence to put questions to the witness. The term 'cross-examination' stands for a special technique of presenting witnesses as evidence at trial.

The presentation of the witness consists of different stages:

(1) Direct examination or examination-in-chief;

(2) Cross-examination;

(3) Redirect examination or re-examination.

The idea of this mode of presentation is to edit the evidence for the jury and dissect the case into easily digestible portions. In direct examination the prosecutor will lead the witness to support his/her hypothesis as to the guilt of the accused. In cross-examination the opponent counsel will try to cast enough doubt on either the person of the witness or on his/her statement such as to render the witness untrustworthy or the evidence unreliable. The primary issue is not to establish the truth but to falsify the prosecution case. On re-examination the primary examiner will try to minimize the damage done to his/her case on cross-examination.

The accused cannot be compelled to testify; however, s/he is a perfectly competent witness to testify, if s/he so wishes. If s/he enters the witness-box,[403] s/he is in general to be treated like any other witness with two important exceptions:[404] (a) s/he cannot claim the privilege against self-incrimination concerning the misconduct s/he is being prosecuted for, and (b) evidence of bad character is generally admitted. These two exceptions make the testimony of the accused fairly unattractive or even dangerous for the outcome of the trial, as the prosecutor can potentially destroy

[401] Wigmore, quoted by Lidstone in J A Andrews (ed), *Human Rights in Criminal Procedure: A Comparative Study* (Brill 1982) 93.

[402] US Supreme Court *Alford v US* 282 US 687 (1931).

[403] S/he is not allowed to give his/her testimony from the 'dock', but must be seated in the 'witness box', *see Farnham Justices ex parte Gibson* [1991] Crim LR 642.

[404] J Sprack, *A Practical Approach to Criminal Procedure* (12th edn, OUP 2008) 20.58–59.

the positive image painted by direct examination through cross-examining the accused.

(3) Witness examination in international proceedings In Nuremberg the presentation of evidence followed the Anglo-American structure and the presentation of evidence rested in the responsibility of the parties. Thus, cross-examination by the adversary party was an important procedural tool pursuant to Arts 16 (e) and 24 (e) IMTSt.

One of the most impressive and memorable cross-examinations in Nuremberg was that of Rudolf Höss, the former commander at Auschwitz concentration camp.[405] He was called into the witness box by counsel for Kaltenbrunner, Dr Kurt Kauffmann, in order to deculpate his superior, the accused Kaltenbrunner. He should give evidence that only very few people indeed knew of the gas chambers and the systematic extermination, and that the death squads consisted only of some sixty men.[406] On cross-examination by Col. Amen the witness confirmed what he had stated in an affidavit gained by Whitney Harris before, that about three million Jews were exterminated at Auschwitz concentration camp.[407] For the first time the Holocaust in all its brutality and monstrosity was made known to the public. This indeed took place by way of cross-examining the witness.[408]

Many of the accused at Nuremberg appeared as witnesses before the court. They did not have to. According to the IMTSt, the defendants could also make an unsworn statement to the Tribunal without subjecting himself to cross-examination. The drafter of the IMTSt made this concession to the Continental system.[409] If however they chose to appear as witnesses, they were consequently cross-examined by prosecution; seldom could the positive image the counsel was attempting to draw in direct examination be upheld under scrutiny of prosecution counsel. Only Albert Speer managed to bluff the court and make the judges believe he did not know about the 'final solution'.[410] The cross-examination of Hermann Göring, who was the most senior person in the dock, by the US Chief Prosecutor Justice Robert H Jackson, was at the time and later often dramatized and was treated like the ultimate showdown between 'good' and 'evil'. Indeed Göring took the liberty of not only answering Jackson's questions but elaborating excessively in order to explain

405 *See* W R Harris, *Murder by the Millions. Rudolf Hoess at Auschwitz* (Robert H Jackson Center 2005).

406 IMT Protocols XI, 396 *et subs.*

407 Ibid, 414 *et subs.*; *see* also W Harris, 'Tyranny on Trial', in: H Reginbogin and C Safferling (eds), *The Nuremberg Trials: International Criminal Law since 1945* (Saur 2006) 100, 102.

408 C Safferling, 'German Participation in the Nuremberg Trials and its Implications for Today', in: B A Griech-Polelle (ed), *The Nuremberg War Crimes Trial and its Policy Consequences for Today* (Nomos 2009) 33–43.

409 *See* Jackson Report (1949) XI.

410 *See* C Safferling and P Graebke, 'Strafverteidigung im Nürnberger Hauptkriegsverbrecherprozess: Strategien und Wirkungen', 123 *ZStW* (2011) 47, 63 *et subs.*

the situation of the German people from his perspective. Despite Jackson's objections the Court let Göring and his political statements pass,[411] which is very unusual in cross-examination. When Jackson, who admittedly was not an experienced cross-examiner, informed the Court that the cross-examination is not the place for political statements,[412] he was right. During examination-in-chief the defendant has the chance to state what s/he wants to state. The Court however followed the argument of defence counsel Strahmer, who claimed that the accused must be given the time to explain the answer properly. Jackson adjusted his strategy and the next day Göring saw himself confronted with one document after the next and he had to admit that he had signed them.[413] The *gloire* of the day before turned to dust.[414]

The IMT, despite its clear tendency towards the Anglo-American trial structure, consisted of all four Allied Powers, two of whom were used to Continental trials. In addition, the German defence counsels were not used to cross-examination. It should therefore not surprise that at some points the IMT practice deviated from the pure Anglo-American procedural system. We can also conclude from the Nuremberg Trial that judges who are themselves obliged to decide the case, tend to be more active and take the liberty to intervene in the presentation of evidence, than those judges who merely control the presentation of the evidence for the jury.[415]

The first impression, which we gained by looking at several instances at the IMT, is confirmed by the practice at the *ad hoc* Tribunals. Originally, the Statutes were drafted according to an Anglo-American blueprint. Thus, the respective parties present evidence and the witness is submitted to cross-examination. Rule 85 (B) RPE ICTY speaks of 'examination-in-chief, cross-examination, and re-examination', which must be allowed in each case. Rule 90 (H) RPE ICTY regulates cross-examination in that it limits its scope to the subject matter of the examination-in-chief, matters affecting the credibility of the witness and other matters relevant for the case of the cross-examining party. A vivid discussion has arisen whether the cross-examiner may confront the witness with prior inconsistent statements.[416] Despite the vagueness of the RPE in this matter, such questioning must be allowed in order to test the reliability of the witness, which is after all the

[411] *See* IMT Protocols IX, 567 *et subs.*

[412] Ibid, 563 *et subs.*

[413] K Kastner, *Von den Siegern zur Rechenschaft Gezogen* (Hoffmann 2001) 139; W Harris, 'Tyranny on Trial', in: H Reginbogin and C Safferling (eds), *The Nuremberg Trials: International Criminal Law since 1945* (Saur 2006) 100, 102.

[414] C Safferling and P Graebke, 'Strafverteidigung im Nürnberger Hauptkriegsverbrecherprozess: Strategien und Wirkungen', 123 *ZStW* (2011) 47, 70.

[415] *See* also Chapter 1, p 54 *et subs.*

[416] E M DiPardo, 'Caught in a Web of Lies: Use of Prior Inconsistent Statements to Impeach Witnesses before the ICTY', 31 *Boston College International and Comparative Law Review* (2008) 277, 284 *et subs.* (arguing in favour of a solution similar to the US Federal Rule of Evidence 613 and the rule developed by the Supreme Court in *Harris v New York*, 401 US 222, 224 [1971]).

aim of cross-examination.[417] However, if the use of prior witness statements impede the fairness of the trial, their use must not be permitted.[418]

At any time a judge may pose a question to the witness, Rule 85 (B) RPE ICTY, so as has been said, the Trial Chamber largely controls cross-examination.[419] In practice, a written summary of the testimony is handed over to the Chamber before the witness is heard *viva voce*.[420] This shows how eager judges are to gain control over cross-examination.[421] It should not surprise that this development was fuelled by the former German Judge Schomburg.[422]

According to Rule 85 (C) RPE ICTY the accused may appear as witness. It is left to his or her discretion as to whether he or she wishes to do so and if so, when to testify. S/he cannot be compelled to testify at all.[423]

In general the Chambers accept the traditional aim of cross-examination, that is, extract further information and—most importantly—to cast doubt on the narrative of the story presented in direct examination.[424] Yet the further development shows that the judges attribute to cross-examination the ability to find the truth. This, as has been said, is after all the overall aim of the taking of evidence.[425] If this is the case, a judge must at any time be in a position to bring forward questions which s/he considers relevant for the quest for the truth. Indeed, s/he would be obliged to do so, otherwise s/he would knowingly base judgment on an incomplete factual basis.

At the ICC the normative situation is even more complex. As the ICCSt was drafted as a compromise and was intended to establish a unique international procedural

417 *See* eg, ICTY *Prosecutor v Mrkšić*, TC II, IT-95-13/1-T, 9 October 2006, Decision Concerning the Use of Statements Given by the Accused, para 30 (in this case prior statements of the accused were admitted).

418 As has happened in the case ICTY *Prosecutor v Simić et al*, TC II, IT-95-9-T, 11 March 2011, Reasons for Decision on Prosecution's Motion to Use Telephone Interviews. In this case the Prosecutor intended to rely on telephone interviews which were conducted with one defendant, who at the time was not aware of the charges against him.

419 G Boas, 'Developments in the Law of Procedure and Evidence at the ICTY and the ICC', 12 *CLF* (2001) 167, 175.

420 *See* for some examples, V Tochilovsky, *Jurisprudence of the International Criminal Courts* (Wolf Legal Publishers 2006) 225.

421 S Bourgon, 'Procedural Problems Hindering Expeditious and Fair Justice', 2 *JICJ* (2004), 526, 530 *et subs*.

422 *See* ICTY *Prosecutor v Stakić*, TC II, IT-97-24-PT, 25 November 2002, Trial Transcript, available at <http://www.icty.org/x/cases/stakic/trans/en/021125ED.htm>.

423 *See* ICTR *Prosecutor v Bagosora et al.*, TCI, ICTR-98-41-T, 11 January 2005, Decision on Motion to Compel Accused to Testify Prior to Other Defence Witnesses, para 5; ICTY *Prosecutor v Kordić and Čerkez*, TC III, IT-95–1412-PT, 9 March 1999, Decision on Prosecutor's Motion on Trial Procedure, p. 4.

424 *See* ICTY *Prosecutor v Delalić et al.*, TCII, IT-96-21-T, 1 May 1997, Decision on the Motion on Presentation of Evidence by the Accused, Esad Landzo, para 22.

425 *See* Judge Schomburg: ICTY *Prosecutor v Stakić*, TC II, IT-97-24-PT, 25 November 2002, Trial Transcript, available at <http://www.icty.org/x/cases/stakic/trans/en/021125ED.htm>.

order, a clear commitment to one or the other way of witness examination was avoided.

In Rule 140 (2) RPE ICC the Anglo-American style of witness testimony is being presented as an optional way. It reads as follows:

> 2. In all cases, subject to Article 64, paragraphs 8 (b) and 9, article 69, paragraph 4, and rule 88, sub-rule 5, a witness may be questioned as follows:
>
> (a) A party that submits evidence in accordance with article 69, paragraph 3, by way of a witness, has the right to question that witness;
> (b) The prosecution and the defence have the right to question that witness about relevant matters related to the witness's testimony and its reliability, the credibility of the witness and other relevant matters;
> (c) The Trial Chamber has the right to question a witness before or after a witness is questioned by a participant referred to in sub-rules 2 (a) or (b);
> (d) The defence shall have the right to be the last to examine a witness.

The way in which here words like 'cross-examination' or 'direct examination' are avoided has an almost comical touch to it. Yet it is clear, that (2) (a) refers to examination-in-chief, and (2) (b) to cross-examination. Why re-examination has been omitted is unclear. Following the development at the ICTY, (2) (c) allows for the judges to intervene but only before or after the questioning by the Prosecutor or defence counsel and not at the time of the questioning. Taken verbatim this would mean that a judge may not interrupt counsel while questioning a witness, and a judge may only question a witness once, before *or* after the parties' examination. It is doubtful whether these restrictions were really intended as it would mean that the ICC Judge is much more limited in his/her inquisitorial competences than his/her ICTY colleagues. Under these circumstances it must be hoped that the ICC judges would disregard Rule 140 (2) RPE ICC and rather follow a more informal approach to the question of witnesses.

The ICCSt is more cautious towards the accused appearing as witness. According to Art. 67 (1) (h) ICCSt the accused has the right to make an unsworn oral or written statement in his or her defence. This could mean several things.[426]

(1) It could mean that his/her right to make an unsworn statement at the same time disallows the accused from testifying as a witness on his behalf (*argumentum e contrario*).
(2) One could also argue that the accused retains his/her right to enter the witness box, swear to the truth, submit to cross-examination, and run the risk of being prosecuted for perjured testimony by virtue of Art. 74 (2) ICCSt,[427] yet if s/he chooses not to do so, s/he may submit an unsworn

426 *See* also Triffterer/*Schabas*, Art. 67 MN 48 *et subs.*
427 *See* p 563 *et subs.*

statement. The judges shall in that case accept this statement as evidence the truthfulness and weight of which they must evaluate by other means than cross-examination and oath.

Whereas opinion (1) would favour a Continental procedural order,[428] opinion (2) is attributable to an Anglo-American approach, enlarging the narrow view that only sworn statements count as evidence at trial.

It is typical for the ICCSt to be caught between two stools. It is most likely that the drafters intended to comprise all possible options, which of course renders the system arbitrary to a certain extent. According to the functional–normative approach which is being followed in this book it would not matter so much that the accused has these two options: (1) access the witness box and submit to cross-examination, and (2) issue an unsworn statement. It would be necessary however to ensure that the accused will not suffer any disadvantage depending on the options s/he chooses to follow. Therefore, an unsworn statement must in general have the same evidentiary value as a sworn testimony. The difference however lies in the way in which the reliability and truthfulness is being tested. In the case of a testimony under oath, this test is being conducted by way of cross-examination. In the case of an unsworn statement the evaluation must be effected by other means, like circumstantial evidence and indirect evidence. Either way, the judges must identify their reasons why they did or did not believe the defence plea by the accused.

(4) Witness proofing A question which needs to be addressed when talking about witnesses in a criminal trial is that of whether or not and to what extent may a witness be prepared for his/her testimony. There are several ways of preparation imaginable. First, a witness who might have travelled a long way and is unfamiliar with the surroundings, might be shown around the courtroom in order to get him/her accustomed to the room, the technical equipment, and the seating arrangements. Secondly, a witness might be briefed as regards the procedural idiosyncrasies; that is, who poses the questions, what are the rights of the witness, and what is the meaning of the 'oath'. Thirdly, the party for whom the witness appears speaks with the victim prior to his/her appearance in court and prepares him or her for his or her testimony. This might go as far as a proper 'rehearsal' of the examination-in-chief combined with the attempt to anticipate the issues the opponent party might raise at cross-examination.

The first two stages described above are widely uncontested. The need to familiarize the witness with the surroundings and the procedure is necessary, as the witness might come from a social environment in which court proceedings do not play an important role. It is also necessary to protect the witness and ensure the proper

[428] Compare p 54 *et subs.*

understanding of his or her rights or even grant some kind of counselling for the time of his/her testimony. These steps can be staged by an independent body like the Registry, so that the parties do not need to get involved.

The third step, the substantial preparation of a witness through a party, which is often called 'witness proofing' is a different matter, and one highly contested.

At the *ad hoc* Tribunals witness proofing is being practised on a permanent basis, even if neither aim nor scope are obvious.[429] The ICTY has in the leading case against *Limaj*[430] and later[431] repeatedly held that the proofing of a witness is necessary for the full discovery of the truth. The necessity for a preparation of the witness is explained by the need of the witness to be informed about the indictment. Evidently prosecutors have been in contact with the witness and interviewed him/her during the investigation stage. However, that was at a time when the indictment was not yet drafted. Thus in advance of his/her testimony at trial the witness needs to be directed as to the actual charges. Despite a common definition of 'witness proofing' the Trial Chambers have attempted to limit the scope to adjusting inconsistencies arising from prior statements of the same or of other witnesses and to refreshing the witness' memory, while ruling out training or tampering with a witness. The SCSL follows a similar avenue.[432] On the basis of the *Limaj* decision the OTP at the ICTY issued 'Proofing Guidelines', which entail a rather broad approach to witness proofing but have never been challenged by a chamber.[433]

The ICC deviated from this approach adopted by the *ad hoc* Tribunals and prohibited 'witness proofing'. In the case against *Lubanga* the Pre-Trial Chamber[434] held that it does not see itself bound by the practice of the *ad hoc* Tribunals in that matter by virtue of Art. 21 ICCSt. Looking at the ICCSt and the Rules the Pre-Trial Chamber found that a 'familiarization' of the witness with the surroundings and the layout of the court is not only admissible but mandatory for

---

[429] R Karemaker, B Don Taylor, and T W Pittman, 'Witness Proofing in International Criminal Tribunals: A Critical Analysis of Widening Procedural Divergence', 21 *LJIL* (2008) 683, 685 *et subs.*; W Jordash, 'The Practice of "Witness Proofing" in International Criminal Tribunals: Why the International Criminal Court Should Prohibit the Practice', 22 *LJIL* (2009) 501, 503 *et subs.*

[430] ICTY *Prosecutor v Limaj et al.*, TC II, IT-03-66-T, 10 December 2004, Decision on Defence Motion on Prosecution Practice of 'Proofing' Witnesses, para 2–3.

[431] ICTY *Prosecutor v Milutinović et al.*, TC III, IT-05-87-T, 12 December 2006, Decision on Ojdanić Motion to Prohibit Witness Proofing, para 16; similarly ICTR *Prosecutor v Karemera et al.*, TC III, ICTR-98-44-T, 15 December 2006, Decision on Defence Motions to Prohibit Witness Proofing, para 11 *et subs.*

[432] In greater detail: W Jordash, 'The Practice of "Witness Proofing" in International Criminal Tribunals: Why the International Criminal Court Should Prohibit the Practice', 22 *LJIL* (2009) 501, 509 *et subs.*

[433] Prosecution Response to *Haradinaj* Submissions on the Procedure for the Proofing of Prosecution Witnesses, 21 March 2007, paras 22, 44 and the Guidelines in the Annex.

[434] ICC *Prosecutor v Lubanga*, PTC I, ICC-01/04-01/06-679, 8 November 2006, Decision on the Practices of Witness Familiarisation and Witness Proofing.

ensuring the well-being of the witness. As the safety of the witness is within the competence of the court, it is not for the Prosecutor to 'familiarize' the witness. This exercise will be undertaken by the Victims and Witnesses Unit. Witness proofing in the meaning of a substantial preparation of the witness, however, is inadmissible. It concluded that in several jurisdictions tampering with the witness would be considered unethical or even unlawful, so there is no general rule of international law allowing witness proofing as alleged by the ICC Prosecutor.

The Trial Chamber concurred one year later.[435] As concerns the familiarization process, however, the Trial Chamber held that a witness is 'not a witness for the court' and not for one or the other party. Yet the witness will have been chosen by one of the parties who thus has a better knowledge and understanding for the needs of the witness. It is therefore advisable that the Victims and Witnesses Unit cooperate with the respective party in familiarizing the witness with the ICC and its procedure.[436]

As regards the witness proofing the Trial Chamber stressed further the differences between the *ad hoc* Tribunals and the ICC in particular as regards the role of the Prosecutor. According to Art. 54 (1) (a) ICCSt the ICC Prosecutor has to investigate in an objective manner. Witness proofing might be detrimental to this novel role compared to the *ad hocs*.[437] Furthermore, the Chamber weighed the advantages and disadvantages witness proofing might have for the quest of the truth. It arrived at the conclusion that witness proofing is more likely to distort the truth as it might easily be misused as a 'rehearsal' of the live testimony.[438]

The practice to be adopted is as follows:[439] The only contact the witness has with the Court is through the VWU. The party who has called the witness to the bench will advise the VWU as to the familiarization process. It will further provide to the VWU any prior statement of the witness. The VWU processes these documents to the witness who may use them to refresh his/her memory before testifying. After the familiarizing has ended, no contact between the party and the witness is allowed. Witness proofing is thus prohibited.

---

[435] ICC *Prosecutor v Lubanga*, TC I, ICC-01/04-01/06-1049, 30 November 2007, Decision Regarding the Practices Used to Prepare and Familiarise Witnesses for Giving Testimony at Trial.

[436] Ibid, para 34.

[437] Ibid, para 45.

[438] Ibid, para 51. It has been argued that misuse can be prevented by rules of professional conduct, *see* Boas/Bischoff/Reid/Taylor, *ICL III*, 286 *et subs*.

[439] *See* ICC *Prosecutor v Lubanga*, TC I, ICC-01/04-01/06-1049, 30 November 2007, Decision Regarding the Practices Used to Prepare and Familiarise Witnesses for Giving Testimony at Trial, para 53–7.

Not all commentators have welcomed these decisions of the ICC.[440] Methodologically, the ICC has in that case entered the avenue to further emancipation from the *ad hoc* Tribunals. It has strengthened the maxim that the search for the truth is the governing principle of any procedural step.[441] Rendering largely irrelevant previous or national concepts of criminal procedure the risks and the pros need to be analysed from the functional perspective adopted by the ICC. In doing this, the ICC arrived at the conclusion that witness proofing adds little to the truth 'but risks much'.[442]

It is interesting to note, however, that the *ad hoc* Tribunals did not find it necessary to reconsider its approach towards witness proofing after the ICC's chambers' verdict.[443] The practice of witness proofing at the *ad hoc* Tribunals is well embedded into the overall procedural system. In particular, the mandatory cross-examination makes good for many risks identified by the ICC judges as being connected to witness proofing.[444] Indeed, much relies on the competence of the adversary party and the courtroom skills of the counsel to detect and unfold constructed testimony.[445] The ICC takes a different route, as cross-examination is not mandatory as has been shown above.[446] A more cautious approach towards witness proofing is therefore more than apt for the ICC legal regime.

c. **Summary** It remains largely unclear which line the Trial Chambers at the ICC will take. Even if the trial structure, as proposed above, is adhered to, the potential dormant in Art. 64 (6) (d) ICCSt is still to be seized. However, what can be derived from the practice adopted by the ICC Chambers thus far is that fact that the judges are not willing to follow any traditional national system or previous *ad hoc* Tribunals' experience. The ICC is directed towards the aims of finding the truth and this loosens the bonds of any traditional system. Its perception is much more functionally directed towards this very aim. In that

---

440 W Jordash, 'The Practice of "Witness Proofing" in International Criminal Tribunals: Why the International Criminal Court Should Prohibit the Practice', 22 *LJIL* (2009) 501, 520 *et subs.* (a step in the right direction).

441 *See* also K Ambos, '"Witness Proofing" before the International Criminal Court: A Reply to Karemaker, Taylor, and Pittman', 21 *LJIL* (2008) 911, 912.

442 W Jordash, 'The Practice of "Witness Proofing" in International Criminal Tribunals: Why the International Criminal Court Should Prohibit the Practice', 22 *LJIL* (2009) 501, 523.

443 In greater detail as to the arguments brought forward, *see* R Karemaker, B Don Taylor, T W Pittman, 'Witness Proofing in International Criminal Tribunals: A Critical Analysis of Widening Procedural Divergence', 21 *LJIL* (2008) 683, 689.

444 This cathartic effect is also doubtful as has been argued by Ambos, *see* K Ambos, '"Witness Proofing" before the International Criminal Court: A Reply to Karemaker, Taylor, and Pittman', 21 *LJIL* (2008) 911, 915 *et subs.* with further references.

445 As to the controlling effect of cross-examination in this regard, *see* R Karemaker, B Don Taylor, and T W Pittman, 'Witness Proofing in International Criminal Tribunals: A Critical Analysis of Widening Procedural Divergence', 21 *LJIL* (2008) 683, 695 *et subs.*

446 *See* p 419 and Rule 140 RPE ICC. This has allegedly been overlooked by R Karemaker, B Don Taylor, and T W Pittman, 'Witness Proofing in International Criminal Tribunals: Response to Ambos', 21 *LJIL* (2008) 917, 918.

manner we can observe that the ICC neither puts the judge into the overall leading position nor does it stick to the formality of direct examination and cross-examination derived from a party-driven system. The ICC concept is one of communication and cooperation in the search for the truth. It might be that under these circumstances different Chambers adopt different trial structures.[447] It is possible that one Chamber may even vary its approach on a case-to-case basis.

However, as has also been observed before, this approach has at least one rather worrying danger: the responsibility gap. This far it is unclear who at the end of the day bears the responsibility for the search of the truth. Who is responsible for determining that all the evidence necessary for the determination of the truth has been heard? It is submitted here that the Chamber itself must take on responsibility. This means that on appeal the allegation might be raised that the Chamber has not heard all the evidence necessary but failed to inquire the incident properly.

3. *Phase 3: Determination of the sentence*

After the decision on the question of guilt, the trial enters into the final stage, in which the sentence is being determined. Whereas the determination of guilt is a binary system, in which only a 'yes' or a 'no' is admitted as an outcome, the sentencing stage is rather more complex. The chamber must undertake a process of hearing evidence concerning the gravity of the crime and the individual circumstances of the convicted person and impose a sentence of imprisonment upon weighing the different aspects.[448] The guilt of the offender has to be 'translated' into a numeric system of years of imprisonment. We are not concerned with the actual process of weighing, neither in the outcome. Several books have been written about this issue.[449] What we are concerned with is the procedure which is to be applied in order to find the answer to this complicated question.

Whereas the law at the ICTY is somehow doubtful as Art. 24 (1) ICTYSt refers to the general practice in the former Yugoslavia, in practice the judges have tried to rely on 'general principles of criminal law' and the few precedents which were available

[447] *See* also P Robinson, 'Rough Edges in the Alignment of Legal Systems in the Proceedings at the ICTY', 3 *JICJ* (2005) 1037, 1057.

[448] An analysis of how this is being done in Germany in English language is available by: F Streng, 'Sentencing in Germany—Basic Questions and New Developments', 8 *GLJ* (2007) 153–72.

[449] I Hühnerbein, *Die Straftatenkonkurrenz im Völkerstrafrecht* (Duncker and Humblot 2005); F Melloh, *Einheitliche Strafzumessung in den Rechtsquellen des ICC-Statuts* (Duncker and Humblot 2010); J Nemitz, *Strafzumessung im Völkerstrafrecht* (Nomos 2002); id, 'Sentencing in the Jurisprudence of the International Criminal Tribunals for the Former Yugoslavia and Rwanda', in: H Fischer, C Kreß, and S R Lüder (eds), *International and National Prosecution of Crimes under International Law: Current Developments* (Berlin Verlag 2001) 605.

on the international level.[450] According to Rule 100 RPE ICTY the parties may submit any material relevant in order to assist the Trial Chamber in determining the appropriate sentence. In most cases this was done by hosting an additional hearing even if this not foreseen in the law concerning the *ad hoc* Tribunals.[451] Yet in order to speed up the proceeding, the ICTY judges changed the rules in 1998 and since then demand the parties to present sentencing evidence at the end of the trial, Rule 85 (A) (vi) RPE ICTY/ICTR. Rule 100 RPE ICTY applies only in cases of a guilty plea on the side of the accused. Consequently, the ICTY Chambers issue only one single judgment containing both the guilty verdict and the sentence.[452]

According to Art. 76 ICCSt the Trial Chamber will take into account all the evidence presented at the previous stage in deciding on the sentence. However, it might—and regularly will—be necessary to hear additional evidence in a separate hearing according to Art. 76 (2) ICCSt and Rule 143 RPE ICC.[453] It will be necessary because the substance of the inquiry differs from the determination of guilt in the first phase of the trial. The parameters which are important for the determination of the sentence are laid down in Art. 78 (1) ICCSt and are further elaborated in Rule 145 RPE ICC. The basis of the decision on the sentence is to be seen in the culpability of the offender. This is reflected first in the gravity of the crime and the personal circumstances of the convicted person. In addition mitigating and aggravating circumstance need to be taken into consideration, Rule 143 (2) RPE ICC.[454] As the age, education, and the social and economic condition of the convicted person have not been an issue during the first part of the trial, evidence concerning these matters will be presented to the Chamber in a new hearing. It might thus be necessary to include psychiatric and psychological reports and to hear from the convicted person (again).[455]

Whether or not the ICC will stage a pre-sentencing hearing or follow the ICTY in hearing sentencing evidence at the end of the trial is still unclear. Both ways are in accordance with the ICC Statute and Rules. One major advantage of having a separate sentencing procedure from the accused's point of view is that s/he is freer to speak if the guilty verdict has already been passed, and a conflict with the freedom from self-incrimination is avoided.[456] A separate hearing would thus be preferable from a human rights point of view.

[450] *See* ICTY *Prosecutor v Erdemović*, TC 1, IT-96-22-T, 29 November 1996, Sentencing Judgment, para 40 stating that the reference to the practice in the former Yugoslavia actually meant a reflection of general principles of law.

[451] *See* also C Safferling, *Towards an International Criminal Procedure* (OUP 2003) 315.

[452] *See* also Boas/Bischoff/Reid/Taylor, *ICL III*, 290 *et subs.*

[453] *See* Triffterer/*Schabas*, Art. 76 MN 3 *et subs.*, who argues that a separate hearing may strengthen the 'right to silence' of the accused during trial.

[454] For a further discussion as to the substantive law *see* C Safferling, *Internationales Strafrecht* (Springer 2011) § 5 MN 115 *et subs.*

[455] Triffterer/*Schabas*, Art. 76 MN 8.

[456] *See* Boas/Bischoff/Reid/Taylor, *ICL III*, 291.

D. Evidence (*Hilde Farthofer*)

There are only a few articles and rules included in the Rome Statute and its Rules of Procedure and Evidence concerning the prerequisites for submitting evidence; for example, requirements for admissibility. Commonly, the trial is inherently based on evidence tendered by the Prosecutor, by the defence, or by a witness. Hence, the categorization and the associated evaluation of evidence is a very important part of the trial. The rights of the accused can easily be restricted by, for example, extending the opportunity to take judicial notice of an adjudicated fact by the Court. Furthermore, when a single piece of evidence has been declared admissible, its probative force will be weighed by the judges at the end of proceedings.

For the purposes of this chapter, first, evidence which can be submitted will be categorized and analysed. Following that, the concept of taking judicial notice or at least accepting unproven evidence for the purpose of judicial economy will be discussed. The next part deals with the requirements of admissibility of evidence. Finally, the specific groups of persons who are granted relative or absolute testimonial or professional privilege by the legal framework of the ICC will be examined in detail.

I. Different forms of evidence

The two main categories of evidence, according to Art. 69 ICCSt, are testimonial and documentary evidence. Each category is subdivided into different forms and, consequently, the requirements posed for evidence, in particular regarding admissibility, differ widely. Therefore, it would be counterproductive to list every item which is permitted to be used as evidence, pursuant to the Rome Statute and the Rules of Procedure and Evidence. Trial Chamber I proceeds on the assumption that 'the drafters of the Statute framework have clearly and deliberately avoided proscribing certain categories or types of evidence, a step which would have limited—at the outset—the ability of the Chamber to assess evidence "freely".'[457]

As stated, one power granted by the judges is the free assessment of all evidence submitted by the parties, pursuant to Rule 63 (2) RPE ICC. Any finding by the Trial Chamber is clearly understandable because Art. 69 (2) ICCSt only refers to the testimony of a witness, recorded testimony of a witness, documents, and written transcripts. The wording does not specify what type of item is permissible to admit into evidence and what type is excluded. In the following, the main categories will be analysed *inter*

[457] ICC *Prosecutor v Lubanga*, TC I, ICC-01/04-01/06-1399, 13 June 2008, Decision on the Admissibility of Four Documents, para 24.

alia with regard to the purpose for which the particular evidence can be introduced into the trial.

At the Nuremberg trials, the right to free evaluation of evidence had already been established in Art. 19 IMTSt and, furthermore, the Statutes and the Rules of Procedure and Evidence of the *ad hoc* Tribunals do not limit the admission of evidence by specifying the type. Rule 89 (C) RPE ICTY/ICTR/SCSL notes clearly that 'any... evidence' can be used to prove the guilt or innocence of the accused. The same provision is included in Rule 87 RPE ECCC.

1. Testimonial evidence

The existing hierarchical order between different types of evidence is pointed out by the first words in Art. 69 (2) ICCSt. Hence, the preferred evidence at trial is the live testimony of a witness. Only if there are exceptional reasons will the Chamber accept, for example, a written statement or a prior recorded statement of a witness. The general principle of oral testimony should be considered when dealing with evidence before international courts, but it is limited by the protection of the rights of the two main actors affected by a trial and its outcome, the accused and the witness.[458]

The accused has the right to due process. This encompasses, for example, the right to examine the witness who submits incriminating evidence against him or her. As a minimum safeguard, this should always be respected, according to Art. 67 (1) (e) ICCSt, if it is not in opposition to the right to life and security of the witness. Notably, nowhere in the text of the Rome Statute or the Rules of Procedure and Evidence is the word 'cross-examination' used. This emphasizes that the accused has the right to question the witness testifying against him/her but does not mean that he or she automatically has the right to cross-examine.[459] Examination by the prosecutor, by the defence, and in particular, by the judges—also when conducted at different times—is the main requirement for permission to submit a written statement as evidence, pursuant to Rule 68 (a) RPE ICC.[460]

In contrast, Rule 85 (B) RPE ICTY determines that examination-in-chief, cross-examination, and re-examination should be allowed in each case. Cross-examination is limited to the subject matter of the evidence-in-chief and matters affecting the credibility of a witness. Rule 90 (H) (ii) RPE ICTY points out the purpose of cross-examination of a witness; that is, to put questions on issues on which the testimony is contradictory.[461] The opportunity to cross-examine a

---

458 *See* Chapter 8, p 400.

459 C Safferling, *Towards an International Criminal Procedure* (OUP 2003) 283 *et subs.*; *see* also Chapter 8, p 453.

460 Discussed later on in detail, Chapter 8, p 477.

461 ICTY *Prosecutor v Brđanin and Talić*, TC II, IT-99-36-T, 22 March 2002, Decision on 'Motion to Declare Rule 90 (H) (ii) Void to the Extent it is in Violation of Article 21 of the Statute of

witness must be separated from the request to recall a witness. In *Nyiramasuhuko et al.*, the Chamber stated that '[t]he recall of a witness should be granted only in the most compelling of circumstances where further evidence is of significant probative value and not of a cumulative value'.[462]

Regarding the rights of the witness, the Court has to enforce adequate measures to protect witnesses as well as victims, according to Art 68 (1) ICCSt. The Chamber concerned must take all necessary steps in order to establish the security and well-being of the witness and of persons in close relationship to him or her. For this purpose, the Registry has created a Victims and Witnesses Unit,[463] pursuant to Art. 43 (6) ICCSt, which recommends appropriate protection measures for prosecution as well as defence witnesses, according to Art. 68 (4) ICCSt. In particular, the nature of the crime must be taken into account by the Court, for example, matters of sexual violence, as well as the specific concerns of individual witness, such as close relationships to victims of the crime in question.

Before testifying, according to Art. 69 (1) ICCSt, the witness must give a solemn declaration before the Court. Thereby he or she confirms that the content of his or her testimony will be truthful and that he or she will fully answer the questions.[464] The Trial Chamber in *Lubanga* decided that: 'Rule 74 is a long and complicated provision, and for any witness—and particularly young former child soldiers who are unlikely previously to have been inside a courtroom—it would be extremely difficult to understand and thereafter to react appropriately to a judicial explanation of the operation of this Rule...'[465]

According to Rule 90 (A) RPE ICTY and Rule 90 (B) RPE ICTR, the witness has to give the solemn declaration before commencing testimony. The wording of the declaration is similar to the formulation in Rule 66 (1) RPE ICC. Rule 90 (B) RPE SCSL includes two options for the declaration, one of which includes an oath on the Bible.

The Court is allowed to make exceptions to this principle, pursuant to Rule 66 (2) RPE ICC, if the witness does not completely understand the meaning of testifying under oath. This is an important point regarding witness testimonies in cases of involvement of children, as for instance during criminal prosecutions for the

the International Tribunal' by the Accused Radoslav Brđanin and on 'Rule 90 (H) (ii) Submissions' by the Accused Momir Talić, para 12.

462 ICTR *Prosecutor v Nyiramasuhuko et al. (Kanyabashi and Nsabimana)*, TC II, IT-98-42-T, 28 October 2008, Decision on Kanyabashi's and Nsabimana's Motions to Cross-examine Prosecution Witness QA on Additional Topics, para 25.

463 *See* Chapter 8, p 516.

464 The exact wording can be found in Rule 66 (1) RPE ICC: 'I solemnly declare that I will speak the truth, the whole truth and nothing but the truth.'

465 ICC *Prosecutor v Lubanga*, TC I, ICC-01/04-01/06-T-110-ENG, 28 January 2009, Transcript, p 2.

recruitment of child soldiers. In particular, the age of the witness may cause a problem regarding the undertaking associated with a solemn declaration. A legally valid submission of an oath requires that the person concerned knows that he or she must tell the truth, but also that he or she knows what impact a lie or an incomplete answer could have for him or her. Refraining from the solemn declaration, pursuant to Art. 69 (1) ICCSt and Rule 66 (1) RPE ICC, does not necessarily mean inadmissibility of testimony. According to Rule 66 (2) RPE ICC, the Trial Chamber has the power to accept such testimonial evidence if the person, for example, is a child who is mature enough to understand that he or she must tell the truth and merely describes his or her own experiences. The same difficulties may occur with an elderly person who cannot follow the explanation why he or she must give a solemn declaration before testifying. In such cases, too, the exclusion or the admission of such testimony lies within the discretion of the Court.

Rule 90 (B) RPE ICTY and Rule 90 (C) RPE ICTR/SCSL provide the same exception exclusively for children, that is, to refrain from an solemn declaration when testifying at the *ad hoc* Tribunals. Furthermore, the first words of Rule 90 (C) RPE SCSL, namely 'every adult witness', clearly point out that a child need not testify under oath. Notably, Rule 24 (2) RPE ECCC provides a list of persons who do not have to testify under oath, for example, a father or sister of the charged person, and also a child under the age of fourteen.

In *Karadžić* the prosecution witness list comprised seventy-seven witnesses for various purposes, including journalists and expert witnesses for background information about the history, and military analysis.[466] Bearing in mind the importance of witnesses for the establishment of the truth in cases where mass atrocities have been committed, the hierarchy, that is, primarily live testimony, thus seems highly reasonable.

a. Witness As mentioned, witnesses should give their testimony *viva voce* before the Court. The Appeals Chamber in *Bemba* rightly determined that the first sentence of Art. 69 (2) ICCSt 'makes in-court personal testimony the rule, giving effect to the principle of orality'[467] and the Trial Chamber in *Katanga and Chui* clearly noted that the principle of oral testimony is 'one of the key principles of trials before the ICC'.[468]

According to Rule 89 (F) RPE ICTY, a witness must testify directly and, only if it is in the interest of justice, the Chamber may allow a statement in written

[466] ICTY *Prosecutor v Karadžić*, IT-95-5/18-1, 29 June 2011, OTP Witness Information.

[467] ICC *Prosecutor v Bemba*, AC, ICC-01/05-01/08-1386, 3 May 2011, Judgment on the Appeals of Mr. Jean-Pierre Bemba Gombo and the Prosecutor against the Decision of Trial Chamber III entitled 'Decision on the Admission into Evidence of Materials Contained in the Prosecution's List of Evidence', para 76.

[468] ICC *Prosecutor v Katanga and Chui*, TC II, 25 May 2011, ICC-01/04-01/07-2954, Decision on Defence Request to Admit into Evidence Entirety of Document DRC-OTP-1017.0572, para 4.

form. Until now, the Rules of Procedure and Evidence of the other *ad hoc* Tribunals have not dealt with this issue in such an explicit form but encompass in Rule 90 (A) RPE ICTR/SCSL the formulation that a witness shall be heard directly.[469] This wording implies the principle of oral testimony without clearly establishing a hierarchy between live testimony, written statements, and transcripts.

In specific circumstances the Chamber is able to make an exception from this guiding principle. According to Rule 67 (3) RPE ICC and Art. 69 (2) ICCSt, the Court can accept testimony by means of audio or video-link technology if it is necessary for the safety, the physical and psychological well-being, dignity, and privacy of the witness.[470]

According to Rule 75 (B) (iii) RPE ICTY/ICTR/SCSL, the Chamber can order 'one-way closed circuit television' to protect the well-being of witnesses and victims. Use of this technology may be justified by the mental condition of the witness. According to Rule 81*bis* RPE ICTY, the technological measures can be requested by one of the parties as well as ordered *proprio motu* by the Court. In *Karadžić*, the Chamber reiterated three criteria to meet, also mentioned in other decisions of ICTY:

> (i) [t]he witness must be unable, or have good reasons to be unwilling, to come to the Tribunal;
>
> (ii) the witness's testimony must be sufficiently important to make it unfair to the requesting party to proceed without it; and
>
> (iii) the accused must not be prejudiced in the exercise of his or her right to confront the witness.[471]

The use of testimony via video conference enshrined in Rule 26 RPE ECCC is limited to such cases where it is not 'seriously prejudicial to, or inconsistent with defence rights'.

During testimony by means of audio or video-link technology, an officer of the Registry must be at the location of the witness. This procedure should guarantee that the witness testifies truthfully and without being influenced by a third party. The use of this technology is not undisputed in cases when it is permitted that all three parties to the trial—the prosecutor, the defence, and the judges of the chamber—

---

469 In the first version of the Rules of Procedure and Evidence of the ICTY in 1994, Rule 90 (A) RPE ICTY read in the following way: 'Witnesses shall, in principle, be heard directly by the Chambers.' This provision was abolished in the version of 19 January 2001.

470 Listing several protection measures which the Court can apply to safeguard witnesses if their life or security is endangered, C Safferling, *Towards an International Criminal Procedure* (OUP 2003) 279 *et subs.*

471 ICTY *Prosecutor v Karadžić*, TC, IT-95-5/18-T, 22 July 2010, Decision on Prosecution's Motion for Testimony to be Heard via Video-conference Link, para 6.

have the opportunity to question the witness.[472] Specifically, in the case of a child witness or a witness who is also a victim of a crime of sexual violation, the Court should try to prevent secondary victimization and should allow such technology-based testimony. Nevertheless, it should remain an exception to general face-to-face questioning.

However, the Rules of Procedure and Evidence include limitations when questioning a witness who is concurrently a victim of sexual violence, for example the 'credibility, character or predisposition to sexual availability of a victim or a witness cannot be inferred by reason of the sexual nature of the prior or subsequent conduct of a victim or witness', according to Rule 70 (d) RPE ICC. Moreover, before the defence can submit evidence to challenge a crime of sexual violence on the basis, for example, of the supposed consent of the alleged victim, it must notify the Court of its intention and prove the relevance of the evidence for the particular case, pursuant to Rule 72 (1) RPE ICC.

In general, a witness called before the Court appears voluntarily but if not the Court has the opportunity to issue a subpoena. With very few exceptions,[473] all witnesses can be compelled to testify before the ICC. However, a point of criticism regarding the execution of such a subpoena is the lack of any means of implementation by the Court. It must rely on the 'voluntary' cooperation of a state and has no opportunity to compel the state, for example, to surrender a witness to the Court. Pursuant to Rule 65 RPE ICC, a witness appearing before the Court has the duty to answer any question posed by the 'other' side; that is, a witness of the defence must also answer the questions posed by the prosecution. If he or she refuses to perform his or her obligation after a warning, the Court can charge the witness, according to Art. 71 ICCSt, with deliberate refusal to comply with a court order.[474]

Pursuant to Rule 54 RPE ICTY/ICTR/SCSL, both parties can request the issue of summon or subpoena to compel a witness to appear before the Court. A summons as well as a subpoena are a means of last resort; that is, they should only be issued if the necessary information cannot be obtained by other means.[475] Some years ago, the Rules of Procedure and Evidence of the ICTY were amended and now according to Rule 54*bis* RPE ICTY, states have an obligation to implement an issued summons on their territory. Regarding the other tribunals, the Court has no power to constrain states to cooperate in

[472] Khan/Buismann/Gosnell/*Rohan,* 533 *et subs.*

[473] To the privileges granted by some professional groups *see* Chapter 8, p 506.

[474] *See* Chapter 10, p 567.

[475] *See* ICTY *Prosecutor v Halilović*, AC, IT-01-48-AR73, 21 June 2004, Decision on the Issuance of Subpoenas, para 7 and ICTY *Prosecutor v Milošević*, TC, IT-02-54-T, 9 December 2005, Decision on Assigned Counsel Application for Interview and Testimony of Tony Blair and Gerhard Schröder, para 41.

particular, to extradite their own nationals or to compel state officials to testify before the Court.[476]

b. Self-incriminating testimony Testifying before a Court always carries a risk for the witness of self-incrimination, in particular if the witness is the accused who testifies before the Court. The accused has the right to remain silent[477] and therefore cannot be compelled to testify, pursuant to Art. 67 (1) (g) ICCSt. Therefore, an important source for establishing the truth cannot be used as evidence. This right is not absolute and some courts are ready to balance it against the establishment of an effective judiciary. Nevertheless, one should deal with this issue carefully because it cannot be expected that the accused will tell the truth and thereby put him or herself at risk of conviction. Therefore, the value of an accused's testimony is highly questionable.

The same scenario is provided for in the procedural law of the ICTY, pursuant to Art. 21 (4) (g) ICTYSt; that is, the accused cannot be compelled to testify before the Court. The Trial Chamber rightly pointed out that '[t]wo of the three accused in the present case, namely Haradin Bala and Isak Musliu, did not give evidence at trial. The Chamber has not, of course, attached any probative relevance to their decision.'[478]

According to Rule 85 (C) RPE ICTY, the accused may appear as a witness in his or her own defence if he or she wishes to do so. Furthermore, in the same above-mentioned decision the Trial Chamber clearly noted that 'Fatmir Limaj . . . testified in his own defence before the Chamber. He did so before any other Defence witnesses were called, which counts in his favour in the assessment of credibility.'[479]

In order to circumvent a sanction for false testimony which emerges from a testimony under oath, the accused has the right to make an unsworn written or oral statement in his or her defence, according to Art. 67 (1) (h) ICCSt.[480] Confronting this provision with the wording in Rule 66 (3) RPE ICC, it becomes clear that the right of the accused to testify without giving a solemn declaration is an exception to the rule. This approach is particularly unusual for lawyers in the common law tradition because in their national legal systems such testimony would be inadmissible. In contrast, in the civil law tradition the accused never gives testimony under oath.[481]

---

476 For further information on the practice of the *ad hoc* Tribunals in dealing with this issue, *see* Khan/Buismann/Gosnell/*Azarnia* 582 *et subs.*

477 *See* Chapter 6, p 287.

478 ICTY *Prosecutor v Limaj, Bala and Musliu*, TCII, IT-03-66-T, 30 November 2005, Judgment, para 22, *see* also ICTY *Prosecutor v Orić*, TC II, IT-03-68-T, 21 October 2004, Order Concerning Guidelines on Evidence and the Conduct of Parties during Trial Proceedings, para 5.

479 ICTY *Prosecutor v Limaj, Bala and Musliu*, TCII, IT-03-66-T, 30 November 2005, Judgment, para 22.

480 *See* Chapter 8, p 456.

481 Triffterer/*Schabas*, Art. 67 MN 48.

As a minimum guarantee, the content of Art. 14 (3) (g) ICCPR determines that the accused '[can]not be compelled to testify against himself or to confess guilt'. Rule 84*bis* (A) RPE ICTY provides that 'the accused may, if he or she so wishes, and the Trial Chamber so decides, make a statement...'. Moreover, the accused shall not be compelled to make a solemn declaration and shall not be examined on the content of a statement. The wording makes clear that it is not for the accused alone to decide if he or she wants to make an initial comment on the indictment, because the Chamber has the power to reject such a statement. None of the other *ad hoc* Tribunals provide such a possibility for the accused in their Rules of Procedure and Evidence.

According to Art. 55 (2) ICCSt, before questioning in the course of investigation is carried out, the Prosecutor has to inform the alleged perpetrator about the suspicion against him or her. If the investigating staff of the OTP fail to do so the statement obtained will be rendered inadmissible, pursuant to Art. 69 (7) ICCSt.[482] Furthermore, the person concerned must be informed about the right to remain silent and the right to request legal assistance. Of course, it is up to the suspect to decide if he or she wants to waive the right to be counselled. Rule 112 (1) RPE ICC includes a list of prerequisites to be complied with during the questioning, *inter alia* that it shall be video- or audio-recorded. The Prosecutor must follow the procedure, pursuant to Rule 112 (1) RPE ICC, although exceptions are permitted if the circumstances render regular conduct impossible and, at the very least, a written transcript must be produced.

In *Halilović* the Chamber noted that a prior statement by the accused could not be declared admissible because the statement was obtained by questioning him as a witness, and therefore not under the requirements of Rule 42 (A) (iii) RPE ICTY. In the course of investigations, the person concerned voluntarily gave a statement to the prosecution which years later ended up at the bar table as incriminatory evidence. In its decision, the Chamber did not clearly note that the admissibility of such evidence would breach the right of the accused against self-incrimination but instead referred to Rule 43 RPE ICTY. The suspect was questioned contrary to the prescribed way of proceeding; that is, without audio- or video-recording the testimony. The accused did not waive his right to remain silent because he testified as a witness and, hence, had no opportunity to challenge the content of the statement.[483] The Appeals Chamber later confirmed the finding of the Trial Chamber.

According to Rule 66 (3) RPE ICC, before starting to testify, all witnesses have to be informed of the offences included in Art. 70 (1) (a) ICCSt; that is, of contempt

[482] ICC *Prosecutor v Katanga and Chui*, TC II, ICC-01/04-01/07-2635, 17 December 2010, Decision on the Prosecutor's Bar Table Motion, para 61 *et subs*.

[483] ICTY *Prosecutor v Halilović*, TC I, IT-01-48-T, 8 July 2005, Decision on Motion for Exclusion of Statement of Accused, para 24 *et subs*. For further information *see* S Luzzati, 'On the Admissibility of Statements Made by the Defendant Prior to Trial', 8 *JICJ* (2010) 221, 224 *et subs*.

of court.[484] If the issue of self-incrimination becomes official for the first time during a hearing, the Chamber must interrupt the testimony and has to provide the opportunity for the witness to obtain legal advice, pursuant to Rule 74 (10) RPE ICC. The Trial Chamber decided to recommend to former child soldiers who were now over the age of eighteen that 'the relevant lawyers must... provide appropriate advice to their clients as regards self-incrimination'[485] in advance of giving testimony. The reasoning was that the Court could not guarantee that testimony would not be used in prosecuting them by the national courts in the Democratic Republic of Congo.

If the problem is already known, the prosecutor, the defence, the accused, or the witness must immediately inform the Chamber about the possibility of self-incrimination and request an *in camera* hearing, non-disclosure of the identity of the witness concerned, and non-disclosure of the content of the evidence, pursuant to Rule 74 (7) RPE ICC. Generally, the request will be posed by the party on whose behalf the witness is testifying.

Another possibility for the witness avoiding the consequences of self-incriminatory testimony might be to negotiate in advance an agreement with the prosecution. Such an agreement may lead to the inadmissability of incriminatory evidence against the witness or to a plea bargain resulting in a reduced sentence.[486]

In order to facilitate the testimony of a witness, the Court has the power to guarantee that the testimony and its content will be kept confidential and will not be used directly or indirectly against the person concerned, according to Rule 74 (2) and (3) (c) RPE ICC. Before guaranteeing this testimonial privilege to the witness, the Court should hear the Prosecutor. Rule 74 (5) RPE ICC includes a list of reasons which the Court may take into account in order to decide a specific case; for example, the importance of the testimony or the nature of the alleged incrimination. After examining the legal situation in the Democratic Republic of Congo regarding the testimony of former child soldiers, the Trial Chamber in *Lubanga* pointed out that: 'the only way that the court can give a truly effective assurance to any of the witnesses who are to come that they will not be prosecuted for previous crimes on account of his or her testimony is to implement Rule 74(2) with all of the attendant difficulties that would follow over the lack of a public trial.'[487]

Rule 90 (E) RPE ICTY/ICTR/SCSL permits a witness to refuse to answer questions which involve a risk of self-incrimination. The Court may compel a witness

[484] In detail *see* Chapter 10.

[485] ICC *Prosecutor v Lubanga*, TCI, ICC-01/04-01/06-T-113-ENG, 30 January 2009, Transcript, p 9.

[486] Khan/Buisman/Gosnell/*Rohan* 526.

[487] ICC *Prosecutor v Lubanga*, TC I, ICC-01/04-01/06-T-113-ENG, 30 January 2009, Transcript, p 9.

to make a statement but the testimony obtained cannot be used to prosecute that witness. Rule 28 RPE ECCC includes a similar provision with the further proviso that the Court may give formal assurance to the person concerned. In deciding this issue, the Court should balance the importance of the testimony for the efficient prosecution and the right of the witness not to testify against him or herself. However, the testimony can be used to prosecute the witness for the offence of giving false testimony.

In addition, the Chamber must take into consideration the personal relationship between the witness and the accused. According to Rule 75 (1) RPE ICC, the Court should not request a witness to incriminate a family member. In other words if the witness is a spouse, a child, or a parent of the accused, he or she should not be compelled to incriminate the family member but, nevertheless, the witness can choose to do so.

In proceedings before *ad hoc* Tribunals, the potential incrimination of a family member cannot be used as justification for a witness not to testify or not to answer certain questions. The right of witnesses to object to make a self-incriminating statement is not extended to the incrimination of family members. This right is restricted presuming that it would serve the interests of establishing the truth. As mentioned, one cannot assume that a witness will tell the truth if this would lead to the conviction of a family member. For that reason it does not seem the right approach to undermine the rights of the accused and the witness in order to make the truth-finding process more effective.

c. Rule 82 RPE ICC witness An exception of all the above-mentioned provisions is a witness who testifies under Rule 82 RPE ICC. He or she cannot be compelled to answer any question relating to the origin of material submitted by that witness or to give any additional information if the witness objects due to reasons of confidentiality, according to Rule 82 (3) RPE ICC.

This testimonial privilege is based on the principle provided in Art. 54 (3) ICCSt[488] and aims at facilitating cooperation between the prosecution and, for example, intergovernmental organizations like the UN or governments to hand over relevant information which can affect the interests of the provider. The testimony of a representative of the supplier cannot be requested by any party to the trial because the only way to obtain such testimony would be by consent.[489]

The same exception is determined in Rule 70 (D) RPE ICTY/ICTR/SCSL. This provision clearly shows the political interests which have found their way into the legal framework of the *ad hoc* Tribunals as well as of the ICC because the regulation

[488] *See* disclosure, Chapter 7, p 344.
[489] For more details on privileges *see* Chapter 8, p 510.

is based on the consideration that national political and security interests are valued higher than the interests of the community as a whole.

The provision also affects the rights of the accused. He or she has the opportunity to challenge information as well as to examine the testimony of a witness, testifying under Rule 82 RPE ICC, but does not have the right to cross-examine that witness on the origin of the information provided or on any other subject due to confidentiality.

Under to Rule 70 (E) RPE ICTY/ICTR/SCSL, the accused has the right to challenge any evidence, regardless of the provider. Without knowing the original source of evidence, it will be quite hard to produce counter-evidence or to challenge the credibility of the source. On that account, the provision should be applied with caution because of the potential risk of infringing the rights of the accused. One has to bear in mind that in this regard, abuse is inherent. In general, the Prosecutor is obliged to disclose all material to the defence but this information cannot be subject to disclosure and, therefore, exculpatory evidence can also be affected.[490]

d. Expert witness The ICTY provides a definition of the term 'expert witness'. Thus, it is widely accepted 'to be a person whom by virtue of some specialised knowledge, skill or training can assist the trier of fact to understand or determine an issue in dispute (and to that end testifies)'.[491] The ICTR further stated on this issue that an expert witness is a witness 'whose testimony is intended to enlighten the Judges on specific issues on a technical nature, requiring special knowledge in a specific field'.[492]

The fields where expertise is needed as evidence in court to make the information available and more understandable are multifarious, in particular regarding the background of an ongoing conflict. The following list is not exhaustive, but gives some indication of what kinds of fields might require expert opinion: historic, linguistic, forensic, military, psychiatric, legal, and technical.

According to Regulation 44 (1) RegC, the Office of the Registrar should create and maintain a list of experts. The list should be available for every participant and organ of the Court. Neither the OTP nor the defence is forced to select their experts from the list but if they choose someone from outside the list, they must provide the necessary professional information about the person concerned so that the Chamber can evaluate his or her qualifications for the specific purpose.[493] The

490 *See* Chapter 7, p 350.

491 ICTY *Prosecutor v Galić*, TC, IT-98-29-T, 3 July 2002, Decision Concerning the Expert Witnesses Ewa Tabeau and Richard Philipps, p 2 *et subs.*

492 ICTR *Prosecutor v Akayesu*, TC I, ICTR-96-4-T, 9 March 1998, Decision on a Defence Motion for the Appearance of an Accused as an Expert Witness, p 1.

493 ICC *Prosecutor v Katanga and Chui*, TC II, ICC-01/04-01/07-1515, 9 October 2009, Decision on the Disclosure of Evidentiary Material Relating to the Prosecutor's Site Visit to Bogoro on 28, 29 and 31 March 2009 (ICC-01/04-01/07-1305, 1345, 1360, 1401, 1412 and 1456), para 3.

instruction of the expert can occur jointly or separately by the Prosecutor and the defence or *proprio motu* by the Chamber. The Trial Chamber stated in this regard[494] that it would 'favour, where possible, the joint instruction of expert witnesses' by reasoning that this would obviously save costs and time.[495]

Neither the Rome Statute nor the Rules of Procedure and Evidence provide a specific regulation providing requirements regarding the testimony of expert witnesses. Thus, the above-mentioned provisions regarding a witness also apply to the testimony of an expert witness. Also the expert must issue a solemn declaration at the beginning of his or her examination and the opposing party has the right to question him or her and, further, to provide a different expert witness to counter the opponent's expert.[496] In contrast to other witnesses, the party who admitted the expert witness into evidence has to examine his or her curriculum vitae before asking substantive questions. In the course of that examination all publications, books, and articles of the expert as well as his or her position in specific professional circles will be relevant and can be a matter for examination by the opposing party.

The ICTY Trial Chamber stated clearly that the party calling the expert witness must provide proof that the expert witness has the necessary knowledge, skills, and training in the area needed and, furthermore, is giving 'his or her expert opinion in full transparency of the established or assumed facts'.[497] This does not mean that the expert must possess first-hand knowledge to be qualified to testify before the Court.[498]

In *Stanišić and Župljanin* the Chamber decided that a close relationship between the party calling on his or her expertise and the expert witness does not make the expertise inadmissible, even if that witness was engaged in 'the investigation or preparation of the Prosecution or Defence case'.[499] The Chamber reasoned that the opposing party has the possibility of challenging the credibility, reliability, and relevance of the expertise during cross-examination.[500] In national procedural

494 ICC *Prosecutor v Lubanga*, TC I, ICC-01/04-01/06-1069, 10 December 2007, Decision on the Procedure to be Adopted for Instructing Expert Witnesses, para 16.

495 Ibid, para 14.

496 ICTY *Prosecutor v Milošević*, TC, IT-02-T, 1 March 2006, Decision on the Admissibility of Expert Report of Kosta Cavoski, p 2; the Trial Chamber ruled that the defence expert witness 'is at least as relevant to the proceedings as Professor Budding's expert report'.

497 ICTY *Prosecutor v Galić*, TC, IT-98-29-T, 3 July 2002, Decision Concerning the Expert Witnesses Ewa Tabeau and Richard Philipps, p 2.

498 ICTY *Prosecutor v Popović et al.*, AC, IT-05-88-AR73.2, 30 January 2008, Decision on Joint Defence Interlocutory Appeal Concerning the Status of Richard Butler as an Expert Witness, para 29.

499 ICTY *Prosecutor v Stanišić and Župljanin*, TC II, IT-08-91-T, 29 September 2010, Decision Pursuant to Rule 94*bis* Accepting Ewan Brown and Affirming Ewa Tabeau as Prosecution Expert Witnesses, and Written Reasons for the Oral Ruling Accepting Andreas Riedlmayer as an Expert Witness, para 10.

500 Ibid, paras 10 and 12; and ICTY *Prosecutor v Milošević*, TC, IT-02-54-T, 1 March 2006, Decision on Admissibility of Expert Report of Kosta Cavoski, p 2.

law, for example in Germany, any close contact between one of the parties and the expert witness would induce a suspicion of bias and subsequently would lead to rejection of that person as an expert witness.[501]

The ICTR adopted another approach by holding that an expert witness 'must... be impartial in the case' and that a person 'who is accused by the Tribunal for crimes related to those with which [the accused] is charged and, under similar counts, cannot be assured'.[502]

Contrary to a 'normal' witness, an expert witness can attend proceedings inside the courtroom to provide 'assistance to the Accused'[503] as well as to the Prosecutor by analysing the testimony of other witnesses. Before testifying, the expert must give a written statement to the contracted party and, subsequently, this report has to be disclosed to the other parties in the trial.[504] All expert reports[505] are based on personal opinions and findings and therefore can be challenged. One has to bear in mind that the expert report as well as the expert witness come within the category of hearsay evidence because of course he or she was not present when the incident occured and instead examines the situation retrospectively.[506] Notably, such evidence is admissible before the Court but can be challenged by the opposing party in the course of the proceedings.

2. *Documentary evidence*

The term 'documentary evidence' is neither defined in the Rome Statute nor in its Rules of Procedure and Evidence. In *Musema* the Trial Chamber of the ICTR gave a definition of the notion 'document' and noted in this context that:

> the term 'document' is interpreted broadly, being understood to mean anything in which information of any description is recorded. This interpretation is wide enough to cover not only documents in writing, but also maps, sketches, plans, calendars, graphs, drawings, computerized records, mechanical records, electro-magnetic records,

[501] During the trial against a Rwandan citizen charged with genocide before the Higher Regional Court of Frankfurt, the Court challenged one of the proposed expert witnesses for bias due to close contact between the expert and the accused and his family, pursuant to §§ 74 (1), 24 (2) German Code of Criminal Procedure.; *see* International Research and Documentation Centre War Crimes Trials, Monitoring Report 2, 9 February 2011, p 5 available at <http://www.uni-marburg.de/icwc/monitoring/monitoringolgfrankfurt>.

[502] ICTR *Prosecutor v Akayesu*, TC, ICTR-96-4-T, 9 March 1998, Decision on a Defence Motion for the Appearance of an Accused as an Expert Witness, p 2 (emphasis added).

[503] ICTY *Prosecutor v Karadžić*, TC, IT-95/5/18-T, 14 June 2011, Decision on Accused's Request for Assistance of Defence Expert in the Courtroom During Testimony of Expert Witness Theunens, para 4.

[504] If it cannot complied with the time limit, fixed by the Chamber, the party concerned has to justify the delay; ICC *Prosecutor v Katanga and Chui*, TC II, ICC-01/04-01/07-1515, 9 October 2009, Decision on the Disclosure of Evidentiary Material Relating to the Prosecutor's Site Visit to Bogoro on 28, 29 and 31 March 2009 (ICC-01/04-01/07-1305, 1345, 1360, 1401, 1412 and 1456), para 4.

[505] *See* Chapter 8, p 481.

[506] *See* Chapter 8, p 495.

digital records, databases, sound tracks, audio-tapes, video-tapes, photographs, slides and negatives.[507]

Contrary to this, in some national legal systems, for example in Austria,[508] audio- or video-recorded evidence, if not a recorded questioning, comes within ostensible evidence (*Augenscheinbeweis*) and not within documentary evidence and, therefore, the term 'documentary evidence' will not be universally interpreted so broadly.

The main purpose of the introduction of documentary evidence into trial is not to prove the acts and conduct of the accused charged in the indictment but rather to prove circumstances; for example, the history of the region where an armed conflict took place or other background information which could help the Court to gain a better understanding of the events which led to the charges.

The practice of reverting mainly on documentary evidence had already been implemented in the course of the Nuremberg Trials. The Court declared admissible the use of affidavits as well as the use of summaries of recorded testimony regardless of the availability of the witness concerned.[509] This approach is also highly questionable when it is used to expedite the trial because it puts the rights of the accused to examine the witness testifying against him/her in jeopardy.

The formulation 'acts and conduct of the accused' is defined as 'deeds and behaviour of the accused'[510] and therefore, does not comprise criminal acts or conduct of other persons who are individually responsible for the committed crimes.[511]

A difference regarding the probative force of proof is the time and the purpose of origin. Inherently, contemporaneous documents, for example military orders or reports produced by members of a peacekeeping mission during an armed conflict, are accepted as authentic and the content as truthful. Understandably, it is believed that the person who produced the document had not noticed at the moment of its creation that it may later be used as evidence at trial.[512] The presumption of its

---

507 ICTR *Prosecutor v Musema*, TC, ICTR-l96-13-A, 27 January 2000, Judgment, para 53.

508 § 149 (1) Austrian Code of Criminal Procedure.

509 C Safferling and P Graebke, 'Strafverteidigung im Nürnberger Hauptkriegsverbrecherprozess: Strategien und Wirkung', 123 *ZStW* 47, 58 *et subs.* and 74.

510 ICTY *Prosecutor v Karadžić*, TC, IT-95-5/18-T, 10 November 2009, Decision on Prosecution's First Motion for Admission of Statements and Transcripts into Evidence in Lieu of *Viva Voce* Testimony Pursuant to Rule 92*bis* (Witnesses for Eleven Municipalities), para 5.

511 Ibid.

512 The Trial Chamber decided in *Lubanga* that primary school records are 'created contemporaneously to the events the record (*viz.* the enrolment of students)' and therefore, 'are, prima facie, probative of the issue just described'; ICC *Prosecutor v Lubanga*, TC I, ICC-01/04-01/06-2595-Red, 17

veracity remains until a successful rebuttal. This approach interferes with the right of the accused to a fair trial and, therefore, the Court has to deal cautiously with this issue and should not lose sight of the overall picture.

Another matter are documents which are produced after the event, for example for preparation of court proceedings. This kind of evidence has to be corroborated or has to be introduced by a witness, otherwise the Court must examine carefully if the evidence fulfils the requirements of admissibility, in particular if it is evidence from a reliable source.

In the following, documentary evidence is divided into five main groups: (a) written statements or transcripts, (b) impeachment documents, (c) court documents, (d) reports, books, and other documents, and (e) forensic evidence and other expert reports. Bear in mind that these categories overlap and, therefore, the requirements of more than one group will potentially be met by the same piece of evidence.

a. Written statements or transcripts According to Rule 68 RPE ICC, the Court can 'allow the introduction of previous recorded audio or video testimony of a witness, or the transcript or other documented evidence of this testimony'. The provision includes two limitations. Firstly, only if the prosecution as well as the defence has had the possibility to examine the witness is the statement admissible. If this requirement is not fulfilled, the admission of the statement depends on the approval of the witness concerned that the transcript can be read out at trial or the recorded testimony played. Secondly, the witness must be presented in court and, consequently, is available to answer questions of the parties to the trial if necessary.

Rule 89 (F) RPE ICTY allows rendering admissible not only live testimony by a witness but also a written statement or transcript 'where the interests of justice allow'.[513] According to Rule 92*bis* (C) RPE ICTY, the Chamber has discretionary power to decide after a hearing if the cross-examination of the witness is necessary or if the written statement will be admissible without live testimony.[514]

In addition, under Rule 92*bis* (A) RPE ICTY/ICTR/SCSL, the content of a written statement may not concern the acts or conduct of the accused but,

November 2010, Redacted Decision on the Defence Request for the Admission of 422 Documents, para 70.

513 Rule 89 was amended to speed up the proceedings before the ICTY. *See,* for the relationship between the above-mentioned rules, O Kwon, 'The Challenge of an International Criminal Trial as Seen from the Bench', 5 *JICJ* (2007) 360, 365 *et subs.*, supporting the implementation of the opportunity also to accept written statements and transcripts as evidence.

514 *See* eg, ICTY *Prosecutor v Karadžić,* TC, IT-95-5/18-T, 10 November 2009, Decision on Prosecution's First Motion for Admission of Statements and Transcripts into Evidence in Lieu of *Viva Voce* Testimony Pursuant to Rule 92*bis* (Witnesses for Eleven Municipalities).

rather—as described in Rule 92*bis* (A) (i) RPE ICTY/ICTR but notably not in the Rules of Procedure and Evidence of the SCSL—might consist of a general or statistical analysis of the ethnic composition of the population or might relate to issues of the character of the accused. The arguments for and against admission of a written statement listed in Rule 92*bis* are not exhaustive.[515]

According to Rule 92*ter* RPE ICTY/SCSL, a transcript or written statement of a witness is admissible if the judges are satisfied that the three listed prerequisites are met; that is: (1) the witness is present in court; (2) the judges can cross-examine the witness; and (3) the witness has given a declaration that the content of the transcript or written statement reflects his or her personal experiences. Pursuant to Rule 92*bis* (B) RPE ICTY, the Chamber has discretion to dispense with attendance of the witness at Court, if he or she attests that the content of the written statement is truthful and correct. The issue of the declaration must be witnessed by a person authorized in accordance with national law or by the Presiding Officer appointed by the Registrar. The provision mainly concerns circumstances where a witness had just testified in one trial and will testify on the same issues again. The Chamber might refrain from renewed testimony if the cross-examination in the previous trial was conducted properly.[516] The provision of Rule 92*bis* RPE ICTY clearly puts the rights of the accused in jeopardy because the rights of the defence are restricted by refusing adequate opportunity to challenge the admitted evidence.

Rule 68 RPE ICC does not really fit the case when the witness is deceased or unobtainable, for example after a video interview with investigators of the Prosecutor but without involvement of the defence. Art. 56 ICCSt provides the possibility for preserving the testimony of a witness by informing the Pre-Trial Chamber of the impending death of the witness concerned. In *Katanga and Chui* the Trial Chamber had to deal with two deceased witnesses. The testimony of one of the witnesses was audio-video recorded. The Chamber stated that the defence as well as the judges could view the tapes and therefore convince themselves of the demeanour of the witness, and if all other requirements were met, it would be admissible at trial.[517] The second witness gave a manuscript to the Prosecutor. This manuscript was written shortly after the attack in Bogoro and contained information about the historical background of the

---

[515] ICTY *Prosecutor v Karadžić*, TC, IT-95-5/18-PT, 15 October 2009, Decision on Prosecution's Third Motion for Admission of Statements and Transcripts of Evidence in Lieu of *Viva Voce* Testimony Pursuant to Rule 92*bis* (Witnesses for Sarajevo Municipality), para 7.

[516] Opposing this discretionary power of the Chamber, P Robinson, 'Rough Edges in the Alignment of Legal Systems in the Proceedings at the ICTY', 3 *JICJ* (2005) 1037, 1044 *et subs*.

[517] ICC *Prosecutor v Katanga and Chui*, TC II, ICC-01/04-01/07, 16 November 2009, Prosecution's Consolidated Response to 'Defence Objections to Admissibility in Principal and in Substance' (ICC-01/04-01/07-1558) and 'Requête de la Défense en vue d'obtenir une décision d'irrecevabilité des documents liés aux témoins décédés référencés sous les numéros T-167 et T-258' (ICC-01/04-01/07-1556), para 19 *et subs*.

armed conflict in the Democratic Republic of Congo as well as of the alleged role of the accused within the FNI[518]-FRPI.[519] The Chamber decided that the manuscript was a contemporaneous document and hence admissible until its rebuttal.[520]

Commonly, this kind of evidence is admissible but probably has lesser probative value if it is not corroborated by other testimony or documentary evidence. The Trial Chamber noted in *Bemba* regarding the use of written statements of witnesses that: 'the introduction of such prior-recorded testimony remains an option which should be adopted only in specific and exceptional circumstances.'[521]

Documentary evidence also encompasses diaries as, for example, submitted by a witness in *Katanga and Chui*,[522] or affidavits, written statements which were carried out before a notary or a person with similar responsibility as, for example, submitted by the defence in *Lubanga*.[523]

In contrast, the Rules of Procedure and Evidence of the *ad hoc* Tribunals deal explicitly with the event when a witness dies before testifying or is no longer available. According to Rule 92*ter* (A) (ii) RPE ICTY/SCSL and Rule 92*bis* (C) (ii) RPE ICTR, the Chamber has to balance the circumstances in which the statement or transcript was made and must come to the conclusion that there are reasonable indicia that the source is reliable. Before rendering a statement of a deceased witness admissible, the Chamber must divide the statement into parts and must evaluate every part individually, and not just the statement as a whole.[524] Furthermore, Rule 92*bis* RPE ICTR stipulates that the decision of the Court should be made on a case-by-case basis.[525]

518 Front Nationalistes et Intégrationnistes.

519 Force de Résistance Patriotique en Ituri.

520 ICC *Prosecutor v Katanga and Chui*, TC II, ICC-01/04-01/07, 16 November 2009, Prosecution's Consolidated Response to 'Defence Objections to Admissibility in Principal and in Substance' (ICC-01/04-01/07-1558) and 'Requête de la Défense en vue d'obtenir une décision d'irrecevabilité des documents liés aux témoins décédés référencés sous les numéros T-167 et T-258' (ICC-01/04-01/07-1556), para 20 *et subs*.

521 ICC *Prosecutor v Bemba*, TC III, ICC-01/05-01/08-886, 16 September 2010, Decision on the 'Prosecution Application for Leave to Submit in Writing Prior-Recorded Testimonies by CAR-OTP-WWWW-0032, CAR-OTP-WWWW-0080, and CAR-OTP-WWWW-0108', para 7; in the case concerned the Trial Chamber III decided that all three witnesses have to testify *viva voce* because it would be prejudicial to the right of the accused if the defence would not have the possibility to examine the witnesses at trial.

522 ICC *Prosecutor v Katanga and Chui*, TC II, ICC-01/04-01/07-T-123-Red-ENG, 25 March 2010, Transcript, p 42.

523 ICC *Prosecutor v Lubanga*, TC I, ICC-01/04-01/06-2664-Red, 16 March 2011, Redacted Decision on the 'Troisième requête de la Défense aux fins de dépôt de documents', para 48 *et subs*.

524 ICTY *Prosecutor v Galić*, TC, IT-98-29-T, 2 August 2002, Decision on the Admission into Evidence of Written Statement by a Deceased Witness, Hamdija Cavicić, and Related Report Pursuant to Rule 92*bis* (C).

525 For further information on the development of the guiding principle to hear a witness *viva voce* to the now prevailing practice of accepting written statements *see* P Wald, 'To "Establish Incredible Events by Credible Evidence": The Use of Affidavit Testimony in Yugoslavia War Crimes Tribunal Proceedings', 42 *Harv Int'l L J* (2001) 535–53.

b. Impeachment documents Impeachment documents will be submitted by the opposing party to challenge the credibility of a witness testifying at trial. For this purpose, the impugning party can use all kinds of evidence, for example a military order but also a prior statement given by the same witness during the course of the investigation. The latter is only admissible within certain limits. In *Katanga and Chui*, the Prosecutor presented a prior statement of a witness to that witness, and asked them to read (in silence) a specific passage. Afterwards the prosecution posed questions on that part of the statement. The Chamber rejected a motion by the defence to admit the prior statement as a whole into evidence, although already submitted in parts by the Prosecutor, by noting that it is well-established practice at the ICC 'not to allow prior statements of witnesses who appear before it into evidence'.[526] In the case under consideration, the defence only had the opportunity to use that specific part of the statement during cross-examination.

No limitation regarding the phase of the trial is proposed in the Rome Statute and, therefore, such evidence can be introduced at any phase of trial. In contrast, rebuttal evidence can only be introduced at trial if it relates to a significant issue and it suddenly comes up during evidence by the opposing party.[527]

In *Lubanga*, the defence argued that the prosecution could not submit new incriminating evidence after closure of the prosecution case because the only permitted new evidence tendered by the prosecution could be 'material designed to test or challenge the credibility of a witness or to refresh his memory'.[528] The Trial Chamber disagreed with the defence opinion and noted that '[t]he Rome Statute framework does not apply fixed stages for the presentation of evidence during the trial, and in this the ICC differs from the position in some other courts or tribunals.'[529]

Impeaching documents can be used to challenge the credibility of a witness as well as an accused but only if it does not amount to 'fresh evidence' which has new incriminating value. In addition, the rights of the accused would be violated and, therefore, it is up to the Prosecutor to prove the 'exceptional circumstances' for the introduction of impeaching documents.[530]

526 ICTY *Prosecutor v Katanga and Chui*, AC, ICC-01/04-01/07-2954, 25 May 2011, Decision on Defence Request to Admit into Evidence Entirety of Document DRC-OTP-1017-0572, para 6 *et subs.*

527 ICC *Prosecutor v Lubanga*, TCI, ICC-01/04-01-06-2727-Red, 28 April 2010, Redacted Decision on the Prosecution's Application to Admit Rebuttal Evidence from Witness DRC-OTP-WWWW-0005, para 36 *et subs.*

528 ICC *Prosecutor v Lubanga*, TC I, ICC-01/04-01/06-2403, 24 April 2010, Decision on the 'Requête de la Défense sollicitant l'autorisation d'interjeter appel de la décision orale du 4 mars 2010 autorisant l'utilisation et le dépôt en preuve de trois photographies', para 25.

529 Ibid, para 26.

530 *See* inter alia SCSL *Prosecutor v Taylor*, TC II, SCSL-03-01-T-865, 30 November 2009, Decision on Prosecution Motion in Relation to the Applicable Legal Standards Governing the use and Admission of Documents by the Prosecution During Cross-examination, para 27.

Both parties have the right to challenge the credibility of witnesses of the opposing party as well as their own witnesses. In *Popović et al.*, the Appeals Chamber noted that 'a calling party must seek the permission of the Trial Chamber to impeach its own witness in relation to the credibility' and, furthermore, the cross-examination of the witness of the calling party underlies the control of the Trial Chamber.[531]

c. Court documents The submission of judicial documents can take place for different purposes. The main purpose is to challenge the credibility of a witness who has already testified in another trial but it can also be used, for example, as proof of a recent conviction or acquittal based on the same charges. Unfortunately, the Court does not apply the same caution when dealing with documents from national courts as when dealing with documents from other trial chambers of the ICC or from the *ad hoc* Tribunals.[532] One has to bear in mind that a judgment only reflects the findings of the Court but cannot be used as evidence for the facts on which the judgment is based. Moreover, the Chamber has discretion to take judicial notice of facts originating in decisions or judgments of another Chamber of the ICC.[533]

d. Reports, books, and other documents Other forms of documentary evidence may be reports, books, and so on introduced as evidence at trial. Their main purpose is to give an overview of historical background information and very seldom to prove specific acts or conduct of an accused as charged in the indictment. Such evidence is used for better understanding, for example why an armed attack occurred in which the accused allegedly committed the crimes in question.

In *Lubanga,* about ninety documents were made available by the UN on behalf of the Under Secretary General for Peacekeeping Operations to the Prosecutor, the bulk of them military daily reports. The disclosure of the documents was delayed because of the possible endangerment for the UN Mission in the Republic of Congo.[534] In the majority of cases, the authors of the entries in contemporaneous books or reports are unknown, as with the daily reports in a military logbook, which are written by different persons. Nevertheless, the majority of documents are official records and, therefore, bear sufficient indicia of reliability, for example official

---

[531] ICTY *Prosecutor v Popović et al.*, AC, IT-05-88-AR73.3, 1 February 2008, Decision on the Appeals against Decision on Impeachment of a Party's Own Witness, p 10.

[532] In *Mbarushimana* the defence submitted an order of a German court which is now available on the internet. This document is not redacted and may trespass on data privacy regulations. The court should deal with this issue very cautiously because of its possible negative impact on national trials. (ICC *Prosecutor v Mbarushimana*, Defence, ICC-01/04-01/10–40, 25 January 2011, Supplementary Information in support of the Defence Challenge to the Validity of the Arrest Warrant).

[533] Khan/Buismann/Gosnell/*Nerenberg/Timmermann* 488.

[534] ICC *Prosecutor v Lubanga*, ICC-01/04-01/06-1454-Anx 1, 11 August 2008; in this letter the UN Headquarters agreed to the disclosure of a list of documents.

reimbursement receipts issued by the OTP or a contemporaneously created primary school record.[535]

e. Forensic evidence and other expert reports The last category of evidence tendered at trial encompasses expert reports and forensic evidence. Both forms of evidence are based on scientific arguments and therefore should be used with caution. An expert report is a rendering of the personal opinion of an expert, that is, a person who specializes in a certain field of social, forensic, or other science. As a result, every expert report can be disproved by another expert in the same area.[536]

In *Stanišić and Župljanin* the Chamber defined the criteria that an expert report must meet to be admissible:

- the proposed witness is classified as an expert,
- the expert report or statement meets the minimum standard of reliability,
- the expert report or statement is relevant and of probative value, and
- the content of the expert report or statement falls within the accepted expertise of the expert witness.[537]

Even if all requirements are met and the Court accepts the expert as witness, this does not signify that the report will be automatically admitted into evidence.[538]

The report must contain all sources on which the results are based because otherwise the opposing party will not have the opportunity to review the report properly and to prepare for cross-examination of the expert witness. If the report does not include the source, this will probably affect the admissibility of the report as well as the testimony.

Experts consulted by the International Criminal Court have comprised a wide range of scientific and military fields, for example expert knowledge of the linguistic characteristics of region, the determination of the age of a former alleged child soldier, or a forensic study based on the exhumation of human remains. For the purpose of the trial a written statement can be sufficient if the opposing party does not object to the findings included in the report. As a result the opposing party would waive its right to examine the expert witness face to face.

Pursuant to Rule 94*bis* RPE ICTY/ICTR/SCSL, both parties to the trial have the right to introduce an expert witness to give evidence in the proceedings. The

[535] ICC *Prosecutor v Lubanga*, TC I, ICC-01/04-01/06-2595-Red, 17 November 2010, Redacted Decision on the Defence Request for the Admission of 422 Documents, para 64 and 68 *et subs.*

[536] Khan/Buismann/Gosnell/*Singh* 619 *et subs.*

[537] ICTY *Prosecutor v Stanišić and Župljanin*, TC II, IT-08-91-T, 29 September 2010, Decision Pursuant to Rule 94*bis* Accepting Ewan Brown and Ewa Tabeau as Prosecution Expert Witnesses, and Written Reasons for the Oral Ruling Accepting Andreas Riedlmayer as an Expert Witness, para 11.

[538] ICTY *Prosecutor v Popović et al.*, AC, IT-05-88-AR73.2, 30 January 2008, Decision on Joint Defense Interlocutory Appeal Concerning the Status of Richard Butler as an Expert Witness, para 31.

expert has to give a written statement or report to his or her contracting entity in advance. The time frame for disclosure to other party is different depending on the *ad hoc* Tribunal; thirty days at the ICTY and ICTR, and only fourteen days at the SCSL.

After disclosure the opposing party has three options, pursuant to Rule 94*bis* RPE ICTY/ICTR/SCSL. First, it can accept the written statement and consequently will lose its right to cross-examine the expert witness, according to Rule 94*bis* (C) RPE ICTY/ICTR/SCSL. Secondly, it can file a motion for cross-examination of the expert witness, to challenge the credibility of that witness, and lastly, the defence can challenge the qualification of the expert witness,[539] because of a lack of knowledge in the specific area.

The wide range of fields where expert statements are needed is significant. In *Lubanga*, the Trial Chamber ordered *inter alia* an expert report 'on names and other social conventions in the Democratic Republic of the Congo'.[540] In the course of the proceeding, the Prosecutor as well as the defence will submit various expert reports as evidence, as, for example, in *Katanga and Chui*; *inter alia* the Prosecution submitted an expert report on ballistics[541] and several forensic expert reports on human remains found near to where the alleged attack occurred.[542]

As mentioned earlier, an expert report carried out on a specific issue does not automatically mean that the findings thus obtained are without uncertainty and cannot be disproven. In *Lubanga* a wrist and mandible X-ray were taken from an alleged child soldier to determine his age.[543]

---

539 SCSL *Prosecutor v Brima et al.*, TC II, SCSL-04-16-T, 5 August 2005, Decision on Prosecution Request for Leave to Call an Additional Witness (Zainab Hawa Bangura) Pursuant to Rule 73*bis* (E), and on Joint Defence Notice to Inform the Trial Chamber of its Position vis-à-vis the Proposed Expert Witness (Mrs Bangura) Pursuant to Rule 94*bis*, para 30; the Chamber clearly pointed out that: 'all the above concerns *regarding the qualification of Mrs Bangura* are matters that go to the weight and not admissibility of the evidence, and that can adequately be tested during cross-examination' (emphasis added).

540 ICC *Prosecutor v Lubanga*, Registry, ICC-01/04-01/06-2025-tENG, 3 July 2009, Redacted version of 'Submission of Mr Kambayi Bwatshia's Expert Report'.

541 ICC *Prosecutor v Katanga and Chui*, TC II, ICC-01/04-01/07-1515, 7 October 2009, Decision on the Disclosure of Evidentiary Material Relating to the Prosecutor's Site Visit to Bogoro on 28, 29 and 31 March 2009, para 41 *et subs.* The Trial Chamber decided that the Ballistic Report could not be added to the list of incriminatory evidence of the Prosecution but rather could be helpful for the defence.

542 ICC *Prosecutor v Katanga and Chui*, TC II, ICC-01/04-01/07-1515, 7 October 2009, Decision on the Disclosure of Evidentiary Material Relating to the Prosecutor's Site Visit to Bogoro on 28, 29, and 31 March 2009, para 46 *et subs.* and para 51 *et subs.* The expert reports were directed to analysing the blood stains found inside the Institute of Bogoro and the exhumation and autopsy of human remains found in the vicinity of the Institute. According to opinion of Trial Chamber II, the reports comprised information with only low relevance and therefore, could be used only if the significance of the information prevailed over the procedural implications caused by the late disclosure to the defence.

543 ICC *Prosecutor v Lubanga*, TC I, ICC-01/04-01/06-2472-Red, 11 June 2010, Prosecution's Application for Admission of Documents Related to Witness 297, Pursuant to Article 64(9).

This method is also used in some European countries for age determination of minor asylum seekers and is highly criticized. For example, the German District Court of Braunschweig noted that expertise based only on a wrist X-ray did not suffice to determine the exact age of a person.[544] Regarding determination of age, the German Administrative Court of Düsseldorf referred in its decision to an expert report by a paediatrician who stated that in the case concerned the age determination was not possible because the wrist X-ray of the person concerned led to the conclusion that he was eighteen years old but the examination of his genitalia suggested someone only fourteen years of age.[545]

Similar problems arise with the collection of forensic evidence in cases of mass exhumations and mass autopsies. In general, forensic scientists are not used to dealing with such large-scale crimes, as the example of the former Yugoslavia has shown.[546] There is often a long time between the commission of crimes and the commencement of the forensic investigations. In this time frame the evidence can be contaminated or deliberately faked.[547] Although gathering of forensic evidence is not without difficulties, the obtained evidence is indispensable for the truth-finding process.[548]

3. Facts of common knowledge, adjudicated facts, and agreed facts

The legal framework of the ICC provides limited opportunity for the Court to accept unproven facts as evidence and, furthermore, takes judicial notice of some of those facts.[549] There are three categories of facts concerned: (a) facts of common knowledge, (b) adjudicated facts, and (c) agreed facts.

In *Fofana*, the Trial Chamber of the SCSL clearly noted that Rule 94 RPE ICTY/ICTR/SCSL encompasses three different categories of facts: '(a) facts of common knowledge (94(A)); (b) adjudicated facts from other proceedings before the Court

[544] LG Braunschweig, 30 December 2009, 3 T 1065/08, 3 T 464/09, *Migrationsrecht.net* (20 November 2010) 40, 43, available at <http://www.migrationsrecht.net>.

[545] VG Düsseldorf, 21 June 2007, 13 K 6992/04.A, 4 ANA-ZAR (2007) 29 Doc 738.

[546] M Klinker, 'Forensic Science Expertise for International Criminal Proceedings: an Old Problem, a New Context and a Pragmatic Resolution', 13 *The International Journal of Evidence & Proof* (2009) 102, 112.

[547] The impeccability of forensic evidence is now a matter of common knowledge, in particular at the national level, eg, *see* P Giannelli, 'The Abuse of Scientific Evidence in Criminal Cases: the Need for Independent Crime Laboratories', 4 *Virginia Journal of Social Policy and the Law* (1996–1997) 439–78.

[548] Forensic evidence was the key factor of the conviction of Radislav Krstić, Deputy Commander of the Drina Corps of the Bosnian Serb Army. He was found guilty of aiding and abetting genocide regarding mass-executions in Srebrenica. This would not have been possible without identification of the dead bodies found in mass graves as being the remains of the missing members of the Muslim Population. *See* also M Klinker, 'Proving Genocide, Forensic Expertise and the ICTY', 6 *JICJ* (2008) 447–66.

[549] E O'Sullivan and D Montgomery, 'The Erosion of the Right to Confrontation under the Cloak of Fairness at the ICTY', 8 *JICJ* (2010) 511, 519.

(94(B)); and (c) documentary evidence from other proceedings before the Court (94(B))'.[550] Art. 69 (6) ICCSt does not contain such a categorization of facts and, therefore, the applied classification for the following analysis differs from the one proposed in the jurisdiction of the *ad hoc* Tribunals.

In any case, the Court only accepts facts which do not deal with the acts, conduct, or mental state of the accused because of their considerable impact on the rights of the accused, even if the defence has the opportunity to challenge all proposed facts. Furthermore, it is prohibited to take judicial notice of facts related to the accused; this approach is founded in the right of the accused to confront and examine incriminating evidence.[551] The *ad hoc* Tribunals have established a stringent approach, that is, the defence has no right to challenge a fact which is taken as judicially noticed and, therefore, 'cannot be the subject of further evidence or dispute in the trial.'[552]

a. Facts of common knowledge According to Art. 69 (6) ICCSt, facts of common knowledge do not have to be proven by the submitting party and the Court may take judicial notice of them.[553] Until now, the Court has not taken judicial notice of any fact of common knowledge and, therefore, the phrase 'facts of common knowledge' is not determined regarding the ICC. The reason behind this provision is to reduce the length of trials by avoiding proof for notorious facts which are part of general knowledge.[554] In *Katanga and Chui*, the Trial Chamber explicitly addressed this topic to prosecution and defence before commencing the trial by questioning if any of the parties

550 SCSL *Prosecutor v Norman et al.*, AC, SCSL-2004-14-AR73, 16 May 2005, Fofana—Decision on Appeal Against 'Decision on Prosecution's Motion for Judicial Notice and Admission of Evidence', para 19.

551 Boas/Bischoff/Reid/Taylor, *ICL III*, 365.

552 SCSL *Prosecutor v Norman et al.*, AC, SCSL-2004-14-AR73, 16 May 2005, Fofana—Decision on Appeal Against 'Decision on Prosecution's Motion for Judicial Notice and Admission of Evidence', Separate Opinion of Judge Robertson, para 5.

553 A similar regulation is provided in Art. 13 (d) Charter of the IMT for the Far East, Art. 21 IMT Statute and Rule 94 (A) RPE ICTY/ICTY/SCSL. In contrast, the ECCC clearly stated that 'there is no legal basis in the Law on the Establishment of the ECCC or in the Internal Rules for the Chamber to take judicial notice of adjudicated facts or for facts of common knowledge to be applied before the ECCC'; ECCC *Prosecutor v Nuon et al.*, TC, 002/19-09-2007-ECCC/TC, 4 April 2011, Decision on Ieng Sary's Motions Regarding Judicial Notice of Adjudicated Facts form the Trial 001 and Fact of Common Knowledge being Applied in Case 002, p 3.

554 OTP, 'Informal Expert Paper, Measures Available to the International Criminal Court to Reduce the Length of Proceedings' (2003), para 114; available at <http://www.icc-cpi.int/NR/rdonlyres/20BB4494-70F9-4698-8E30-907F631453ED/281982/length_of_proceedings.pdf>, (visited 14 November 2011).

wanted the Court to take judicial notice, according to Art. 69 (6) ICCSt, of any fact submitted as evidence.[555]

In *Karemera et al.*, the Trial Chamber of the ICTR established a definition for the term 'common knowledge'. According to this, 'the notion encompasses facts that are not reasonably subject to dispute: in other words, commonly accepted or universally known facts, such as general facts of history or geography, or the laws of nature.'[556]

During negotiations for the establishment of the ICC the delegation of the USA argued that the wording of Rule 94 RPE ICTY was not clear enough concerning the meaning of 'facts of common knowledge' and, therefore, they provided a more precise definition to be included in the Rules of Procedure and Evidence of the ICC. 'For example, "facts of common knowledge" can refer not only to well known geographical, temporal, or other phenomena, but also to scientific facts capable of being easily verified, or populations patterns and other social and economic data.'[557]

Until now, there has been no explicit rule dealing with this issue in the Rules of Procedure and Evidence. In its internal expert report, the OTP concluded that the concept of the term 'facts of common knowledge' should be broadened to facilitate the Court to take judicial notice also of facts such as the nature of the conflict or the existence of an armed conflict.[558] The proposals by the USA during negotiations for the establishment of the ICC went even further and opined that the Court should also take judicial notice of 'various regulations of domestic or international law'.[559] One has to bear in mind that the onus of proof shifts from the Prosecutor to the accused and, hence, in particular in criminal proceedings, the issue of judicial notice should be approached carefully. The rights of the accused are largely based on the principle of the presumption of innocence, that is, the prosecution must prove the guilt of an accused and not vice versa, pursuant to Art. 66 ICCSt.[560] This could easily lead to a violation of the fundamental rights of the accused when persisting in the extension of the application of the term 'judicial notice'.

---

555 ICC *Prosecutor v Katanga and Chui*, TC II, ICC-01/04-01/07-747-tENG, 13 November 2008, Order Instructing the Participants and the Registry to Respond the Questions of Trial Chamber II for the Purpose of the Status Conference (article 64 (3)(a) of the Statute), para 11.

556 ICTR *Prosecutor v Karemera et al.*, TC III, ICTR-98-44-T, 11 December 2006, Decision on Appeals Chamber Remand of Judicial Notice, para 10.

557 US Non-Paper of Rules of Investigation, Procedures and Evidence for the International Criminal Court, 21 August 1995, para 90; available at <http://www.legal-tools.org>.

558 OTP, 'Informal Expert Paper, Measures Available to the International Criminal Court to Reduce the Length of Proceedings' (2003) para 114; available at <http://www.icc-cpi.int/NR/rdonlyres/20BB4494-70F9-4698-8E30-907F631453ED/281982/length_of_proceedings.pdf>.

559 US Non-Paper of Rules of Investigation, Procedures and Evidence for the International Criminal Court, 21 August 1995, para 90; available at <http://www.legal-tools.org>.

560 *See* Chapter 8, p 407.

The *ad hoc* Tribunals have ruled that taking judicial notice of facts of common knowledge is not at the Court's discretion. Because of the 'specific, mandatory language of Rule 94 (A) . . . the Trial Chamber has no discretion to determine that a fact, although "of common knowledge", must nonetheless be proven through evidence at trial.'[561] In the same decision the Appeals Chamber recognized genocide as a fact of common knowledge arguing that '[t]here is no reasonable basis for anyone to dispute that'.[562] The application of judicial notice in this form jeopardizes the rights of the accused. Furthermore, the term 'genocide' is a legal characterization and, hence, inadequate to be judicially noticed. For this reason, the Appeals Chamber noted in *Norman et al.* 'that legal conclusions as well as facts which constitute legal findings cannot be judicially noticed'.[563] It might have been better to acknowledge the circumstances of the events in Rwanda in 1994 than to recognize the term 'genocide' as a fact of common knowledge.[564]

b. Adjudicated facts Neither the Rome Statute nor the Rules of Procedure and Evidence contain a provision regarding adjudicated facts. As a measure to enhance the effectiveness of the Court, the internal expert report of the OTP advised that the Chamber should also take judicial notice of adjudicated facts such as the nature of conflict reasoning that this would 'counter defence attempts to delay proceedings by disputing issues that could never be reasonably in dispute'.[565] Until now this issue has not been addressed to the Chamber and, therefore, no decision concerning this has been taken by the Court.[566]

Rule 94 (B) RPE ICTY/ICTR/SCSL explicitly deals with adjudicated facts and documentary evidence from other proceedings that might be judicially noticed by the Court after hearing the parties. The wording of the regulation is not mandatory and, therefore, its application is at the discretion of the Chamber.[567] The purpose

---

561 ICTR *Prosecutor v Karemera et al.*, AC, ICTR-98-44-AR73(C), 16 June 2006, Decision on Prosecutors Interlocutory Appeal of Decision on Judicial Notice, para 23 (emphasis added).

562 Ibid, para 35; for further information *see* R Mamiya, 'Taking Judicial Notice of Genocide? The Problematic Law and Policy of the *Karemera* Decision', 25 *Wisconsin International Law Journal* (2007) 1–22.

563 SCSL *Prosecutor v Norman et al.*, AC, SCSL-2004-14-AR73, 16 May 2005, Fofana—Decision on Appeal Against 'Decision on Prosecution's Motion for Judicial Notice and Admission of Evidence', para 32.

564 R Mamiya, 'Taking Judicial Notice of Genocide? The Problematic Law and Policy of the *Karemera* Decision', 25 *Wisconsin International Law Journal* (2007) 1, 21 *et subs.*

565 OTP, 'Informal Expert Paper, Measures Available to the International Criminal Court to Reduce the Length of Proceedings' (2003), para 114; available at <http://www.icc-cpi.int/NR/rdonlyres/20BB4494-70F9-4698-8E30-907F631453ED/281982/length_of_proceedings.pdf>.

566 S Kirsch, 'The Trial Proceedings before the ICC', 6 *ICLR* (2006) 275, 290; the author takes the view that although there is no provision in the Rome Statute or the Rules of Procedure and Evidence the Chamber has the power to take judicial notice of adjudicated facts and documentary evidence from other proceedings.

567 ICTY *Prosecutor v Milošević*, AC, IT-02-54-AR73.5, 31 October 2003, Separate Opinion of Judge Shahabuddeen Appended to the Appeals Chamber's Decision dated 28 October 2003

behind taking judicial notice of adjudicated facts is to serve judicial economy.[568] Notably, the Chamber can take judicial notice due to a motion by the Prosecutor or the defence but also *proprio motu*.[569]

In *Popović et al.*, the Trial Chamber developed the criteria required for adjudicated facts to be judicially noticed. First, adjudicated facts must be relevant for the current proceedings. The facts must be distinct, concrete, and identifiable, and furthermore should not be altered by the submitting party but, rather, be formulated in the same way as in the original judgment. Moreover, the facts should not be used in a misleading or unclear manner. In addition, the applicant party should not request judicial notice of an entire judgment but rather should determine the exact paragraphs concerned. Further, the facts must not contain characterizations of an essential legal nature[570] and must not be based on an agreement between the parties to the original proceedings.[571] Moreover, the facts must not be related to the acts, mental state, or conduct of the accused and they must not be subject to pending appeal or review.[572]

c. Agreed facts The last category of facts which can be submitted as evidence without being proven is based on an agreement between the Prosecutor, the defence, and the legal representative of the victims. According to Rule 69 RPE ICC, they can agree on facts contained in the charges, on the content of a document, on the expected testimony of a witness, or on a joint selected expert. The Court cannot take judicial notice of the agreed facts but rather can simply accept them. The outcome of the agreement will be introduced during the status conference before the Trial Chamber, according to Regulation 54

on the Prosecution's Interlocutory Appeal against the Trial Chamber's 10 April 2003 Decision on Prosecution Motion for Judicial Notice of Adjudicated Facts, para 6.

568 ICTY *Prosecutor v Milošević*, TC, IT-02-54-T, 16 December 2003, Final Decision on Prosecution Motion for Judicial Notice of Adjudicated Facts, para 11.

569 In *Simić* the Trial Chamber noted that the requested adjudicated fact was not an adequate fact to be judicially noticed but *proprio motu* took judicial notice that Bosnia and Herzegovina proclaimed its independence on 6 March 1992, and the independence was recognized by the European Community and the USA; ICTY *Prosecutor v Simić et al.*, TC, IT-95-9-T, 25 March 1999, Decision on the Pre-Trial Motion by the Prosecution Requesting the Trial Chamber to take Judicial Notice of the International Character of the Conflict in Bosnia-Herzegovina, p 3.

570 Reasoning that the international character of the conflict in Bosnia and Herzegovina is a legal characterization, the Chamber dismissed the motion by the Prosecutor to take judicial notice of this adjudicated fact; ICTY *Prosecutor v Simić et al.*, TC, IT-95-9, 25 March 1999, Decision on the Pre-Trial Motion by the Prosecution Requesting the Trial Chamber to take Judicial Notice of the International Character of the Conflict in Bosnia-Herzegovina, p 3.

571 *Nsengiyumva* filed a motion to request that the Chamber take judicial notice of a fact based on a guilty plea and hence the Chamber dismissed the motion reasoning that 'facts shall not be deemed "adjudicated" if they are based on guilty plea or admissions voluntarily made by an accused during the proceedings.' ICTR *Prosecutor v Bagosora*, AC, ICTR-98-41-A, 29 October 2010, Decision on Anatole Nsengiyumva's Motion for Judicial Notice, para 10.

572 ICTY *Prosecutor v Popović et al.*, TC II, IT-05-08-88-T, 29 September 2006, Decision on Prosecution Motion for Judicial Notice of Adjudicated Facts, paras 5–14.

RegC. Notably, the Trial Chamber has the opportunity to dismiss the agreed facts, reasoning that this would not be in the interests of justice, in particular in the interests of the victims. In *Katanga and Chui*, the prosecutor, the defence, and the legal representatives of the victims reached an agreement on seven of 149 proposed facts.[573]

Under Rule 65*ter* (H) RPE ICTY, it is in the power of the Pre-Trial Judge to accept agreed facts but it is still possible at the trial stage to agree facts. In that case, the court order regarding the agreed facts will be issued by the Trial Chamber which can exercise the function of the Pre-Trial Judge.[574]

According to Art. 21 IMTSt, the Tribunal shall not require proof for facts of common knowledge. Moreover, '[i]t shall also take judicial notice of official governmental documents and reports of the United Nations, including the acts and documents of the committee set up in the various Allied countries for the investigation of war crimes, and the records and findings of military or other Tribunals of any of the United Nations'.

The extent of the opportunity to take judicial notice is clearly broader than provided for in the Rome Statute or the Statutes of the *ad hoc* Tribunals. Again, this imposes an unacceptable burden on the defence and contradicts the principle of the presumption of innocence.

II. Admissibility of evidence

Pursuant to Art. 64 (9) (a) ICCSt, the Trial Chamber has the power to rule on the admissibility or relevance of evidence. Effectively the same wording with more detail can be found in Art. 69 (4) ICCSt, namely with reference to the probative value of evidence and the prejudicial impact of the admission of evidence on the rights of the accused, enshrined in Art. 67 ICCSt.

Under Rule 89 (C) RPE ICTY/ICTR, the Chamber has the power to evaluate any evidence regarding its relevance and its probative value. Remarkably, Rule 89 (C) RPE SCSL is differently formulated, that is, the Chamber may only determine the relevance or irrelevance of a single item tendered in evidence.[575] Thus it is obvious that the ICTY as well as the ICTR have established a twofold test to ascertain admissibility. In *Delalić et al.*, the Chamber pointed out that the wording of the Rules of Procedure and Evidence only support the conclusion that the Trial Chambers of the ICTY should decide on this issue 'in favour of admissibility of evidence as long as the evidence is relevant and is deemed to have probative value

[573] ICC *Prosecutor v Katanga and Chui*, TC II, ICC-01/04-01/07-2681, 3 February 2011, Decision on Agreements as to Evidence, para 2.

[574] ICTY *Prosecutor v Perišić*, TC I, IT-04-81-T, 30 September 2009, Second Decision in Respect of Srebrenica Agreed Facts, p 2.

[575] Boas/Bischoff/Reid/Taylor, *ICL III*, 338.

(Sub-rule 89 (C)), and its probative value is not substantially outweighed by the need to ensure a fair trial (Sub-rule 89 (D)).'[576]

The ICTR had to deal repeatedly with facts of pre-1994 events; that is, events from outside the temporal jurisdiction of the Court. In *Gatete*, the Chamber clearly pointed out that the admission of such evidence is not prohibited *per se* but must fulfil certain requirements to be rendered admissible. Hence, such evidence has to be aimed at:

(i) clarifying a given context, such as providing historical context or background;
(ii) establishing by inference the elements (in particular, criminal intent) of criminal conduct occurring in 1994;
(iii) demonstrating a deliberate pattern of conduct.[577]

The Trial Chamber in *Lubanga* developed a threefold test which the Court had to consider by examining the admissibility or inadmissibility of evidence 'other than oral evidence'.[578] Firstly, the Court had to determine if the evidence tendered was *prima facie* relevant to the specific case,[579] and secondly, the Chamber had to evaluate if that evidence had *prima facie* probative value.[580] Finally, 'the Chamber must, where relevant, weigh the probative value of the evidence against its prejudicial effect'.[581] The criteria mentioned demonstrate the general requirements for the admissibility of evidence. Moreover, even if the wording of the law indicates that either relevance or admissibility must exist, it is obvious that relevance is part of admissibility, pursuant to the jurisdiction of the ICC and, therefore, has to coexist in addition to the other requirements of admissibility; that is, the probative value and the balance between the effectiveness of proceedings and the potential prejudice caused by particular evidence to a fair trial.

A Trial Chamber of the ICTY ruled that there are basic differences between the 'legal admissibility of documentary evidence and the weigh that documentary evidence is given in the courtroom.'[582]

---

[576] ICTY *Prosecutor v Delalić et al.*, TC, IT-96-21-T, 19 January 1998, Decision on the Motion of the Prosecution for the Admissibility of Evidence, para 16 and also ICTY *Prosecutor v Orić*, TC II, IT-03-68-T, 21 October 2004, Order Concerning Guidelines on Evidence and the Conduct of Parties During Trial Proceedings, para 10.

[577] ICTR *Prosecutor v Gatete*, TC III, ICTR-2000-61-T, 3 November 2009, Decision on Defence Motion on Admissibility of Allegations Outside the Temporal Jurisdiction of the Tribunal, para 5.

[578] ICC *Prosecutor v Lubanga*, TC I, ICC-01/04-01/06-2595-Red-Corr, 8 March 2011, Corrigendum to Redacted Decision on the Defence Request for the Admission of 422 Documents, para 39.

[579] ICC *Prosecutor v Lubanga*, TC I, ICC-01/04-01/06-1399, 13 June 2008, Decision on the Admissibility of Four Documents, para 27.

[580] Ibid, para 28.

[581] Ibid, para 31.

[582] ICTY *Prosecutor v Brđanin and Talić*, TC II, IT-99-36-T, 15 February 2002, Order on the Standards Governing the Admission of Evidence, para 16.

1. General requirements

In *Lubanga* the Court clearly noted that 'the Chamber has [been] given a wide discretion to rule on admissibility or relevance and to assess any evidence, subject to the specified issues of "fairness" ',[583] according to Rule 63 (2) RPE ICC. Notably, this discretion is not unlimited; that is, the Chamber cannot render evidence admissible without evaluating it item by item or by substantiating its finding, pursuant to Rule 64 (2) RPE ICC. In *Bemba*, the Appeals Chamber reversed the decision of the Trial Chamber[584] on that account, reasoning that it 'acted outside the legal framework of the Court.'[585] Judge Ozaki went even further in her dissenting opinion to the reversed decision by arguing that the Trial Chamber applied the concept of *prima facie* admissibility which in her opinion 'does not exist in the Rome Statute ("Statute") or in the Rules of Procedure and Evidence ("Rules").'[586] Moreover, she argued that the Chamber creates an 'intermediate stage' when ruling on admissibility which is not foreseen in the legal framework of the ICC.[587] The Chamber should not create a *prima facie* stage for all evidence without evaluating every single item. Such an approach seriously violates the rights of the accused because of the immense burden which would be imposed on the defence. Therefore, the Chamber should not automatically admit or exclude evidence without proper examination.[588]

The Chambers of the ICTY prefer to render evidence admissible than to decline its admission.[589] That notwithstanding, if an item is rendered irrelevant it must be excluded beyond all question 'in the interest of a fair and expeditious trial.'[590] That implies that evidence will not be admitted into evidence without examining its relevance, probative value, and prejudice. Furthermore, the Court has also had

583 ICC *Prosecutor v Lubanga*, TC I, ICC-01/04-01/06-1399, 13 June 2008, Decision on the Admissibility of Four Documents, para 23; emphasis added from the correction in Annex A (1399-Corr-AnxA, p 2).

584 ICC *Prosecutor v Bemba*, TC III, ICC-01/05-01/08-1022, 19 November 2010, Decision on the Admission into Evidence of Materials Contained in the Prosecution's List of Evidence.

585 ICC *Prosecutor v Bemba*, AC, ICC-0/05-01/08-1386, 3 May 2011, Judgment on the Appeals of Mr. Jean-Pierre Bemba Gombo and the Prosecutor against the Decision of Trial Chamber III entitled 'Decision on the Admission into Evidence of Materials Contained in the Prosecution's List of Evidence', para 2.

586 ICC *Prosecutor v Bemba*, TC III, ICC-01/05-01/08-1028, 23 November 2010, Dissenting Opinion of Judge Kuniko Ozaki on the Decision on the Admission into Evidence of Materials Contained in the Prosecution's List of Evidence, para 4.

587 Ibid, para 5.

588 ICC *Prosecutor v Lubanga*, TC I, ICC-01/04-01/06-1399, 13 June 2008, Decision on the Admissibility of Four Documents, para 29.

589 ICTY *Prosecutor v Brđanin and Talić*, TC II, IT-99-36-T, 15 February 2002, Order on the Standards Governing the Admission of Evidence, para 11.

590 ICTY *Prosecutor v Orić*, TC II, IT-03-68-T, 21 October 2004, Order Concerning Guidelines on Evidence and the Conduct of Parties During Trial Proceedings, para 10.

the opportunity to decide on this issue *proprio motu* if it appeared appropriate.[591] Furthermore, the Court clearly pointed out that decisions on admissibility are reversible at a later stage of the proceedings.[592] This also includes the opportunity for the parties involved in the trial to seek the admission of the rejected item at a later stage 'if it is considered to fulfil the requirements of Rule 89 that it be relevant, of probative value, and bear sufficient indicia of authenticity.'[593]

Pursuant to Rule 64 (1) RPE ICC, the admissibility of evidence may be challenged at the time the item is submitted into evidence. Only if the reason for challenging becomes known thereafter, may the party concerned put forward their arguments against the admissibility of evidence. Notably, the Court in *Lubanga* rightly stated that '[i]f a challenge is made to the admissibility of evidence, it appears logical that the burden rests with the party seeking to introduce the evidence.'[594] Generally, the presenting party has more information on the origin of the evidence and, of course, of the credibility and reliability of the source than does the challenging party.

The ICC has adopted the same approach as the ICTY regarding the burden of proof. Thus, the requesting party must prove the relevance and probative value of the tendered evidence. In its guidelines on evidence the Trial Chambers pointed out that there are differences between the prosecution and the defence. While the defence only has to prove the admissibility of its evidence on 'a balance of probabilities'[595] the Prosecutor must prove the relevance, probative value, and reliability of its evidence 'beyond reasonable doubt'.[596]

a. Relevance As mentioned earlier, relevance and admissibility are two different concepts.[597] According to Art. 69 (4) ICCSt, the Chamber may examine the 'relevance or admissibility' of evidence submitted. That implies that the legal framework of the ICC foresees a two-part evaluation carried out by the Chamber at any stage of the process. However, the decisions already made by the Court suggest that it combines the two concepts into one comprehensive approach.[598] In *Katanga and Chui,*

[591] ICTY *Prosecutor v Orić*, TC II, IT-03-68-T, 21 October 2004, Order Concerning Guidelines on Evidence and the Conduct of Parties During Trial Proceedings, p 7.

[592] ICTY *Prosecutor v Orić*, TC II, IT-03-68-T, 21 October 2004, Order Concerning the Guidelines on Evidence and the Conduct of Parties During Trial Proceedings, p 5; ICTY *Prosecutor v Brđanin and Talić*, TC II, IT-99-36-T, 15 February 2002, Order on the Standards Governing the Admission of Evidence, para 17.

[593] ICTY *Prosecutor v Karadžić*, TC, IT-95-5/18-T, 18 July 2011, Decision on Prosecution Bar Table Motion for the Admission of Records of Bosnian Serb organs, para 4.

[594] ICC *Prosecutor v Lubanga*, TC I, ICC-01/04-01/06-1399, 13 June 2008, Decision on the Admissibility of Four Documents, para 25.

[595] ICTY *Prosecutor v Orić*, TC II, IT-03-68-T, 21 October 2004, Order Concerning Guidelines on Evidence and the Conduct of Parties During Trial Proceedings, p 5.

[596] Ibid.

[597] Cf. Triffterer/*Piragoff* Art. 69, MN 37.

[598] Boas/Bischoff/Reid/Taylor, *ICL III*, 339 *et subs.*

the Chamber determined that 'relevance is a legal precondition to admissibility'[599] because relevance means that 'the evidence tendered makes the existence of a fact at issue more or less probable.'[600] Hence, the affirmation of relevance is a logical requirement needed before the Court can deal with the prerequisites of admissibility.

The ICTR follows the same conclusion; that is, evidence is relevant if 'there is connection between the evidence and one or more allegations against the accused charged in the indictment.'[601]

The threshold for relevance is rather low; an item submitted to evidence is irrelevant, only if there is no reasonable link between the evidence and the allegation against the accused. Furthermore, the Chamber in *Katanga and Chui* defined two purposes for evaluating the relevance of evidence. These were the exclusion of irrelevant evidence and the determination of the proposition of why exactly that item was admitted into evidence.[602]

The ICTY has adopted a rather similar approach concerning the threshold of admissibility; that is, it 'should not be set excessively high';[603] the same approach is generally applied by the Chambers of the ICTR.[604]

b. Probative value Evaluating the probative value of evidence, the Chamber must assess reliability and significance, defined in *Bemba* as the 'weight to be attached to the evidence concerned',[605] of a single item on a case-by-case basis. If the tendered evidence is authenticated, it is reliable. In *Katanga and Chui*, the Chamber rightly noted that a confining list of criteria does not exist. There exist only several key factors which depend on the source, the nature, and characteristic of the item of evidence, on its contemporaneousness, on its purpose, and on the independent verification and test of the evidence gathering proceedings.[606] First, documentary evidence has to be evaluated according to this scheme. Regarding written statements of witnesses, the Chamber in *Lubanga* referred to

599 ICC *Prosecutor v Katanga and Chui*, TC II, ICC-01/04-01/07-2635, 17 December 2010, Decision on the Prosecutor's Bar Motion, para 16.

600 Ibid.

601 ICTR *Prosecutor v Gatete*, TC III, ICTR-2000-61-T, 3 November 2009, Decision on Defence Motion on Admissibility of Allegations Outside the Temporal Jurisdiction of the Tribunal, para 3.

602 ICC *Prosecutor v Katanga and Chui*, TC II, ICC-01/04-01/07-2635, 17 December 2010, Decision on the Prosecutor's Bar Table Motion, para 17.

603 ICTY *Prosecutor v Delalić et al.*, TC, IT-96-21, 19 January 1998, Decision on the Motion of the Prosecution for the Admissibility of Evidence, para 20.

604 ICTR *Prosecutor v Rutaganda*, AC, ICTR-96-3-A, 26 May 2003, Judgment, para 382; the Chamber referred in its judgment to ICTR *Prosecutor v Akayesu*, AC, ICTR-96-4-A, 1 June 2001, Judgment, para 286 *et subs.*

605 ICC *Prosecutor v Bemba*, TC III, ICC-01/05-01/08-1022, 19 November 2010, Decision on the Admission into Evidence of Materials Contained in the Prosecution's List of Evidence, para 9.

606 ICC *Prosecutor v Katanga and Chui*, TC II, ICC-01/04-01/07-2635, 17 December 2010, Decision on the Prosecutor's Bar Table Motion, para 27.

the criteria developed by the ICTY. According to this, an item is deemed to be reliable if it is 'voluntary, truthfully and trustworthy, as appropriate.'[607]

According to Rule 89 (E) RPE ICTY/ICTR, the 'Chamber may request verification of the authenticity of evidence'. The Trial Chamber of the ICTY noted that if there are sufficient indicia of reliability, the item will be rendered admissible. However, the authenticity and the proof of authorship will be weighed at the end of the proceedings when the Court finally has to pronounce on the probative value of every item admitted into evidence.[608]

In *Delalić et al.*, the Chamber went even further by defining reliability as 'the invisible golden thread which runs through all the components of admissibility.'[609]

The second criterion is the significance of a specific item to increase the outcome of the investigation of the Court. The evidence may significantly help the Court in two ways. Firstly, it may be helpful by influencing the truth-finding process of the Chamber and, secondly, it may help to prove the reliability of other evidence in the same case.[610]

The probative value of evidence must be separated from the evidentiary value. The former is one of the key factors when determining the admissibility of evidence, while the latter describes the importance of a single item to prove a certain issue. Both have to be evaluated by the Chamber at the end of the trial based on the overall picture which arises from all admitted evidence.[611]

A finding by the Chamber that the tendered evidence is relevant and possesses probative value does not mean that it is automatically admissible until the 'weighing [of] the potential probative value of the evidence against the possible prejudice effect'[612] has been undertaken.

c. **Prejudice** As the Trial Chamber rightly determined in *Lubanga,* any submitted incriminating evidence is at the same time prejudicial to the accused and

[607] ICC *Prosecutor v Lubanga*, TC I, ICC-01/04-01/06-1399, 13 June 2008, Decision on the Admissibility of Four Documents, para 28, referring to ICTY *Prosecutor v Aleksovski*, AC, IT-95-14/1, 16 February 1999, Decision on the Prosecutors Appeal on Admissibility of Evidence, para 15.

[608] ICTY *Prosecutor v Orić*, TC II, IT-03-68-T, 21 October 2004, Order Concerning Guidelines on Evidence and the Conduct of Parties During Trial Proceedings, p 5; ICTY *Prosecutor v Brđanin and Talić*, TC II, IT-99-36-PT, 15 February 2002, Order on the Standards Governing the Admission of Evidence, para 18 *et subs.*

[609] ICTY *Prosecutor v Delalić et al.*, TC, IT-96-21-T, 19 January 1998, Decision on the Prosecution's Oral Request for the Admission of Exhibit 155 into Evidence and for an Order to Compel the Accused Zdravko Mucić, to Provide a Handwriting Sample, para 32.

[610] ICC *Prosecutor v Katanga and Chui*, TC II, ICC-01/04-01/07-2635, 17 December 2010, Decision on the Prosecutor's Bar Table Motion, para 34.

[611] Ibid, para 13.

[612] ICC *Prosecutor v Lubanga*, TC I, ICC-01/04-01/06-1399, 13 June 2008, Decision on the Admissibility of Four Documents, para 41.

therefore the Chamber has to carry out its evaluation carefully.[613] In *Katanga and Chui* the Chamber posed two questions in order to determine the purpose of examining the prejudice of evidence. First, what caused the prejudice, and secondly, what right of the accused or of someone else would be violated by the admission of the evidence.[614] The first question can only be answered on a case-by-case basis because of the infinite opportunities to prejudice the rights of the accused. It depends on 'specific characteristics of the item of evidence and the nature of the alleged prejudice'.[615] The answer to the second question can be found in the wording of Art. 69 (4) ICCSt, that is, the potential impact on a fair trial and on the fair evaluation of the testimony of a witness, enshrined in Art. 67 ICCSt.[616]

In the Chambers of the ICTY, it is general practice not to apply the common law approach regarding the exclusion of evidence. The reasoning therefore is situated in what was called the 'judging element'.[617] Generally in common law systems, evidence will be presented to a jury and the lay juror should be removed from the influence of prejudicial evidence. In international courts the finding will be rendered by professional judges who are trained and qualified to deal with evidence which is perhaps excluded later in the proceedings.[618]

Pursuant to Rule 89 (D) RPE ICTY, the Court has to balance the probative value of a certain item and the rights of the accused to a fair trial. If it comes to the conclusion that the probative value does not justify the restriction of the rights of the accused, it may exclude the evidence. Neither the Rules of Procedure and Evidence of the ICTR nor the SCSL comprise such a limitation.

2. *Hearsay*

There are two different kinds of hearsay evidence. The first are hearsay testimonies; that is, a witness who testifies in court provides information about the experiences of another person, for example for protection reasons. The problem here is that the Chamber must be satisfied not only with the reliability of the witness who testifies but also the source of origin must provide sufficient indicia of reliability to convince the Court. The second form of hearsay evidence is the

613 ICC *Prosecutor v Lubanga*, TC I, ICC-01/04-01/06-1399, 13 June 2008, Decision on the Admissibility of Four Documents, para 30.

614 ICC *Prosecutor v Katanga and Chui*, TC II, ICC-01/04-01/07-2635, 17 December 2010, Decision on the Prosecutor's Bar Table Motion, para 38.

615 Ibid, para 40.

616 *See* Chapter 8, p 489.

617 *See* Chapter 1, p 55.

618 ICTY *Prosecutor v Orić*, TC II, IT-03-68-T, 21 October 2004, Order Concerning Guidelines on Evidence and the Conduct of Parties During Trial Proceedings, para 11; ICTY *Prosecutor v Brđanin and Talić*, TC II, IT-99-36-T, 15 February 2002, Order on the Standards Governing the Admission of Evidence, para 14.

written statement[619] of a witness who is not going to testify before the Court. Arguments for the absence of live testimony might be a deceased or disappeared witness but also a witness who has testified before the Court on the same issue but in another case.[620]

In procedural law, common and civil law rule differently on the admissibility of hearsay evidence. After World War II, the then established courts acting in Nuremberg and Tokyo implemented the opportunity to submit hearsay into evidence.[621] In the inquisitorial system of civil law, hearsay evidence is *prima facie* admissible, whereas in the adversarial system of the common law, this kind of evidence is *per se* inadmissible, with limited exceptions.[622] The reason behind this ruling in common law is to protect jurors from the impact of information from an unreliable source.[623] At the ICC, professional judges who are trained and experienced in handling the different values of evidence have to decide this issue and, hence, the negative impact should be slight. The traditional hearsay rule provides 'that no assertion offered as testimony can be received unless it is or has been open to test by cross-examination or an opportunity for cross-examination'.[624]

In English law, section 114 of the Criminal Justice Act 2003 defines hearsay as

> a statement not made in oral evidence in the proceedings but clearly stated that it is admissible only if
>
> (a) any provision of this Chapter or any other statutory provision makes it admissible,
>
> (b) any rule of law preserved by section 118 [eg public information or *res gestae*] makes it admissible,
>
> (c) all parties to the proceedings agree to it being admissible, or
>
> (d) the court is satisfied that it is in the interests of justice for it to be admissible.[625]

---

619 *See* Chapter 8, p 477, also for the problems concerning implementation of Rule 92*bis* RPE ICTY/ICTR/SCSL.

620 E O'Sullivan and D Montgomery, 'The Erosion of the Right to Confrontation under the Cloak of Fairness at the ICTY', 8 *JICJ* (2010) 511, 513; G Boas, 'Creating Laws of Evidence for International Criminal Law: The ICTY and the Principle of Flexibility', 12 *CLF* (2001) 41, 55 *et subs*.

621 R May and M Wierda, 'Trends in International Criminal Evidence: Nuremberg, Tokyo, The Hague, and Arusha', 37 *Colum J Transnat'l L* (1998–1999) 725, 745 *et subs*.

622 For a narrow analysis of hearsay evidence *see* C Safferling, *Towards an International Criminal Procedure* (OUP 2003) 306 *et subs*.

623 K Fabian, 'Proof and Consequences: an Analysis of the Tadić and Akayesu Trials', 49 *DePaul Law Review* (2000) 981, 1019. In the USA, a study on the influence of hearsay evidence on jurors was carried out. As a concluding remark, it can be mentioned that jurors are highly sceptical against the admission of hearsay evidence into trial. Hence, the reasoning for excluding hearsay evidence in common law systems seems not to be well founded. M Bull Kovera, R Park, S Penrod, 'Jurors Perceptions of Eyewitnesses and Hearsay Evidence', 76 *Minnesota Law Review* (1991–1992) 703, 704 *et subs*.

624 B Garner (ed), *Black's Law Dictionary* (3rd edn, Thomson West 2006) 327.

625 Criminal Justice Act 2003, Part 11.

In civil law systems the admissibility of hearsay evidence is not undisputed. In Germany, in cases where, for example, organized criminal groups are involved, undercover agents are exempted from testifying personally in court but the person who questioned them at the investigation stage introduces their statement as hearsay evidence.[626] This is permitted only as a last resort because of its negative impact on the rights of the accused.

The ECtHR has implemented an approach closer to common law; that is, generally, hearsay evidence is inadmissible with few exceptions because it puts the right of the accused to examine the prosecution witness as well as the witness testifying on his/her behalf enshrined in Art. 6 (3) (d) ECHR in jeopardy.[627] To compensate for the restriction of the rights of the accused, the Court has to examine the process in three steps, according to ECtHR case law.[628]

First, the Court has to determine the reasons for restricting the defence right to confront the witness for the prosecution. In *Doorson*, the ECtHR affirmed the decision of the Amsterdam Court of Appeal not to disclose the identity of witnesses who feared reprisals from the applicant, reasoning that 'drug dealers frequently resorted to threats or actual violence against persons who gave evidence against them'.[629] Therefore, in order to obtain evidence from witnesses whose right of life, liberty, or security enshrined in Art. 8 ECHR is endangered, the limitation of the defence rights does not affect the admissibility of evidence.

Secondly, there is no violation of the right to confront the witness 'if it is established that the handicaps under which the defence laboured were sufficiently counterbalanced by the procedures followed by the juridical authorities'.[630] The procedure sufficiently compensates the restrictions if, for example, defence counsel is present when the witness is questioned and has the opportunity to pose questions.[631]

As a final step, the hearsay evidence has to be corroborated by other evidence and conviction of the accused must not be based on hearsay alone.[632] Of course, this must not go so far that the accused would also have been convicted if the hearsay

[626] C Safferling, 'Verdeckte Ermittler im Strafverfahren—deutsche und europäische Rechtssprechung im Konflikt?', 26 *NStZ* (2006) 75.

[627] ECtHR *Lüdi v Switzerland*, Judgment 15 June 1992, Series A No. 238, para 43 *et subs.*; the ECtHR clearly pointed out that the accused must have the possibility to challenge the witness against him or her, not personally but at least the national court must confront the witness with the allegation brought. In the disputed case the Court showed no intention of questioning the witness, an undercover agent.

[628] C Safferling, 'BVerfG 2 BvR 547/08—Entscheidung der 2. Kammer des 2. Senats vom 8.10.2009', 30 *StV* (2010) 337, 340.

[629] ECtHR *Doorsen v The Netherlands*, Judgment 26 March 1996, Rep. 1996-II, para 71.

[630] Ibid, para 72.

[631] Ibid, para 73; no counterbalance to the procedure could be ascertained in ECtHR *Kostovski v The Netherlands*, Judgment 20 November 1989, Series A No. 166, para 43.

[632] ECtHR *Windisch v Austria*, Judgment 27 September 1990, Series A No. 186, para 24 *et subs.* and ECtHR *AM v Italy*, Judgment 14 December 1999, Rep. 1999-IX, para 25.

evidence was not admissible in terms of the principle *conditio sine qua non*, as such a procedure would be similar to the exclusion of evidence.[633]

However, the ICC has adopted the civil law approach on hearsay evidence. This becomes clear by the wording of Art. 69 (4) ICCSt, where the Chamber has the power to rule on the relevance or admissibility of *any* evidence. Therefore, under certain circumstances hearsay evidence is also admissible even if the Court prefers live testimony. In *Lubanga*, the Chamber referred on this issue to the findings of the ICTY and, thus, implemented the criteria listed in *Aleksovski*.[634]

Pursuant to the above-mentioned ruling of the Appeals Chamber of the ICTY, 'the probative value of a hearsay statement will depend upon the context and character of the evidence in question'.[635] In *Kordić and Čerkez*, the Chamber specified the criteria which have to be taken into account by analysing the evidence tendered: (1) if the statement was given under oath, (2) if it was subject to cross-examination, (3) if it was corroborated by other evidence, (4) if it was 'first hand' or more removed, and (5) if the statement originated contemporaneously with the events or was produced years later.[636]

Furthermore, the Chamber clearly pointed out in *Aleksovski* that even if hearsay evidence is rendered admissible, its evidentiary value will always be lower than the weight of oral testimony in court.[637] As a consequence, it becomes clear that, in principle, hearsay evidence is admissible in proceedings before the ICTY, moreover the Appeals Chamber when affirming the decision, assessed that this 'is well settled practice of the Tribunal'.[638] Until now, the Chambers of the ICTR have applied the same requirements for hearsay evidence as those developed by the ICTY.[639]

---

[633] C Safferling, 'BVerfG 2 BvR 547/08—Entscheidung der 2. Kammer des 2. Senats vom 8.10.2009', 7 *StV* (2010) 337, 340 *et subs*.

[634] ICC *Prosecutor v Lubanga*, TC I, ICC-01/04-01/06-1399, 13 June 2008, Decision on the Admissibility of Four Documents, para 28.

[635] ICTY *Prosecutor v Aleksovski*, AC, IT-95-14/1, 16 February 1999, Decision on Prosecutors Appeal on Admissibility of Evidence, para 15.

[636] ICTY *Prosecutor v Kordić and Čerkez*, AC, IT-95-14/2, 21 July 2000, Decision on Appeal Regarding Statement of Deceased Witness, para 27.

[637] ICTY *Prosecutor v Aleksovski*, AC, IT-95-14/1, 16 February 1999, Decision on Prosecutors Appeal on Admissibility of Evidence, para 15, and also ICTY *Prosecutor v Milošević*, AC, IT-02-54-AR73.2, 30 September 2002, Decision on the Admissibility of Prosecutions Investigator's Evidence, para 18.

[638] ICTY *Prosecutor v Aleksovski*, AC, IT-95-14/1, 16 February 1999, Decision on Prosecutors Appeal on Admissibility of Evidence, para 15; referred to *inter alia* in ICTY *Prosecutor v Brđanin and Talić*, TC II, IT-99-36-T, 15 February 2002, Order on the Standards Governing the Admission of Evidence, para 21, and *Prosecutor v Orić*, TC II, IT-03-68-T, 21 October 2004, Order Concerning Guidelines on Evidence and the Conduct of Parties During Trial Proceedings, p 6.

[639] *See inter alia* ICTR *Prosecutor v Bagosora et al.*, TC I, ICTR-98-41-T, 11 December 2006, Decision on Defence Motion on Admission of Statement of Witness LG-1/U-03 under Rule 92*bis*, the Chamber only denied admissibility in regard with the part of the statement concerning the acts and conduct of the accused.

Submitting such evidence into the proceedings puts the right of the accused to confront his or her accuser, enshrined in Art. 67 (1) (e) ICCSt, in jeopardy and, therefore, the Court has to deal with this with the utmost caution. The prerequisites listed in *Aleksovski* are crucial when analysing hearsay evidence regarding both the ICC as well as the ICTY, in particular the requirement that the statement was 'voluntary, truthful and trustworthy'.[640] Examining the requirements for rendering hearsay evidence admissible, the Chamber should always bear in mind that the legal framework of the ICC is based on the principle of primacy of oral testimony, enshrined in Art. 69 (2) ICCSt.[641] In *Bemba*, Judge Ozaki rightly stated that '[t]he reading of a witness statement can never be a substitute to such observations [as the demeanour of a witness] and live evaluations.'[642]

3. *Exclusionary rule Art. 69 (7) ICCSt*

If the exclusionary rule seems to be mandatory at first sight, evidence which is obtained by infringing international human rights law or the provisions of the Statute of the ICC is not inadmissible *per se*. Exclusion of evidence is restricted to compliance with one of the two requirements listed in Art. 69 (7) (a) and (b) ICCSt, that is, only if 'the violation casts substantial doubt on the reliability of the evidence, or' if 'the admission of the evidence would be antithetical to and would seriously damage the integrity of the proceedings' should evidence be excluded.

In mind that in most national legal frameworks there is a legal guarantee that only lawfully obtained evidence can be used by the prosecution against an accused.[643] This restricts the ways and means of how the investigating officers can obtain evidence for later use at trial.[644] Hence, the process of collecting evidence must satisfy a minimum standard which allows the conduct of a fair trial regarding the reliability of obtained evidence and its prejudicial impact on the process as a whole.

The Chamber may exclude evidence which is obtained by violating the Statute of the ICC or of internationally recognized human rights, according to Art. 69 (7)

---

640 ICTY *Prosecutor v Aleksovski*, AC, IT-95-14/1, 16 February 1999, Decision on Prosecutors Appeal on Admissibility of Evidence, para 15

641 ICC *Prosecutor v Bemba*, AC, ICC-01/05-01/08-1386, 3 May 2011, Judgment on the Appeals of Mr Jean-Pierre Bemba Gombo and the Prosecutor against the Decision on Trial Chamber III entitled 'Decision on the Admission into Evidence of Materials Contained in the Prosecution's List of Evidence', para 74 *et subs*.

642 ICC *Prosecutor v Bemba*, TC III, ICC-01/05-01/08-1028, 23 November 2010, Dissenting Opinion of Judge Kuniko Ozaki on the Decision on the Admission into Evidence of Materials Contained in the Prosecution's List of Evidence, para 23 (emphasis added).

643 For an overview of different national legal approaches regarding the exclusionary rule *see* J Murray, 'Assessing Allegations: Judicial Evaluation of Testimonial Evidence in International Tribunals', 10 *Chi J Int'l L* (2010) 769.

644 Triffterer/*Piragoff* Art. 69 MN 59.

ICCSt. The violation of the Rules of Procedure and Evidence is not encompassed and, therefore, cannot trigger the exclusion of evidence. In its decisions on this issue, the Chambers referred *inter alia* to the ECHR and in particular, to the findings of the *ad hoc* Tribunals.[645]

Art. 6 ECHR enshrines the rights of the accused to a fair trial but does not explicitly deal with the issue of excluding evidence, for example, obtained by torture or by an unlawful seizure of the property of the suspect. Art. 3 ECHR prohibits the use of torture, inhuman, or degrading treatment and punishment. Thus, this conduct must not be carried out against the suspect or any potential witness in order to obtain information and, if it occurs, the evidence thus obtained must be excluded. With certain additions, very similar wording can be found in Art. 5 African Charter on Human Rights, in Art. 7 ICCPR, and in Art. 5 (2) Inter-American Convention on Human Rights. Furthermore, the ECHR provides in Art. 8 the right of everyone 'to respect for his private and family live, his home and his correspondence'. This right is likewise enshrined in Art. 17 ICCPR and Art. 11 Inter-American Convention on Human Rights. This leads to the conclusion that evidence obtained by an unlawful seizure of property of a suspect violates internationally recognized human rights law and, therefore, may be excluded. According to Art. 8 (2) ECHR, this right can be lawfully restricted and is not therefore absolute, and thus the violation of the right enshrined in Art. 8 (1) ECHR must be disproportionate.[646]

The legal framework of the *ad hoc* Tribunals provides for, in Rule 95 RPE ICTY/ICTR, the exclusion of evidence under rather similar requirements to those provided in Art. 69 (7) ICCSt. Evidence which is obtained by coercion or other conduct which leads to an infringement of the freedom of choice of a witness or the accused cannot be used as evidence at trial. Rule 95 RPE SCSL is not formulated in such a clear manner; it only provides that any evidence shall be inadmissible if its 'admission would bring the administration of justice into disrepute'.

In *Delalić et al.*, the Chamber pointed out that if a statement was made voluntarily, the burden of proof 'is on the Prosecutor'.[647] Furthermore, 'the Trial Chamber is the guardian of the procedural and substantive rights of the Accused'.[648] However, regarding irregular seizure of the home of an accused, the Court decided that

[645] ICC *Prosecutor v Kantanga and Chui*, TC II, ICC-01/04-01/07-2635, 17 December 2010, Decision on the Prosecutor's Bar Table Motions, para 60; for a comprehensive overview of internationally recognized human rights regarding the exclusion of evidence *see* C Safferling, *Towards an International Criminal Procedure* (OUP 2003) 309 *et subs.*

[646] ECtHR *Miailhe v France*, Judgment 25 February 1993, Series A No. 256, para 39.

[647] ICTY *Prosecutor v Delalić et al.*, TC, IT-96-21, 2 September 1997, Decision on Zdravko Mucic's Motion for the Exclusion of Evidence, para 42.

[648] ICTY *Prosecutor v Orić*, TC II, IT-03-68-T, 21 October 2004, Order Concerning Guidelines on Evidence and the Conduct of Parties During Trial Proceedings, p 8.

'minor breaches of procedural rules'[649] cannot lead to the exclusion of evidence because such an approach would not be in the interest of justice.[650] Furthermore in *Brđanin*, the Chamber pointed out that in examining if evidence should be excluded, it must weigh the gravity of the charges brought against the accused and the alleged violation of the law.[651]

Art. 67 ICCSt constitutes *lex specialis* to the general requirements of admissibility, in particular regarding potential prejudice to the rights of the accused. Moreover, the Chamber stated in *Lubanga* that the exclusionary rule 'represents a clear exception to the general approach',[652] and therefore, 'it is impermissible to introduce this further factor, namely adding the probative value of the evidence as a criterion of admissibility'.[653] However, it becomes clear that the Chamber does not take the same line in interpreting the general prerequisites of admissibility.[654] In *Bemba*, the Trial Chamber noted that the only difference between the provisions in Art. 69 (4) ICCSt and Art. 69 (7) ICCSt is that the 'latter provision... is the only situation in which the Chamber has a duty to make a ruling on admissibility'.[655] This finding does not conform with Rule 63 (3) RPE ICC; that is, that the Chamber 'shall rule' on challenges on admissibility concerning the exclusionary rule, pursuant to Art. 69 (7) ICCSt.

Until now, the Court has had to deal with two cases on the exclusion of evidence, according to Art. 69 (7) ICCSt. In *Lubanga*, the Trial Chamber had to decide on the admissibility of evidence obtained by an unlawful seizure which infringed the right to privacy of another person than the accused.[656] The question of whether a violation occurred does not depend on the person whose rights were infringed but how far the interference affects the right to a fair trial as a whole.[657] According to the Chamber, the search was disproportionate because

[649] ICTY *Prosecutor v Delalić et al.*, TC, IT-96-21, 9 February 1998, Decision on the Tendering of Prosecution Exhibits 104–8, para 20.

[650] Ibid, para 21.

[651] ICTY *Prosecutor v Brđanin*, IT-99-36-T, 3 October 2003, Decision on the Defence 'Objection to Intercept Evidence', para 8, reaching to the same finding ICTY *Prosecutor v Karadžić*, IT-95-5/18-T, 30 September 2010, Decision on the Accused's Motion to Exclude Intercepted Conversations, para 10.

[652] ICC *Prosecutor v Lubanga*, TC I, ICC-01/04-01/06-1981, 24 June 2006, Decision on the Admission of Material from the 'Bar Table', para 34.

[653] Ibid, para 43.

[654] *See* Chapter 8, p 489, as to the difficulties caused by the threefold test and the different interpretation of the terms relevance, probative value (reliability and significance), and prejudice.

[655] ICC *Prosecutor v Bemba*, TC III, ICC-01/05-01/08-1022, 19 November 2010, Decision on the Admission into Evidence of Materials Contained in the Prosecution's List of Evidence, para 18.

[656] ICC *Prosecutor v Lubanga*, TC I, ICC-01/04-01/06-1981, 24 June 2006, Decision on the Admission of Material from the 'Bar Table', para 38; the Pre-Trial Chamber I had come to the same conclusion ICC-01/04-01/06-803-tEN, 29 January 2007, Decision on the Confirmation of Charges, para 82.

[657] Ibid, para 37.

the authorities seized many documents unrelated to the criminal offence against the alleged suspect. This finding will not be sufficient to exclude the evidence concerned due to the fact that the Court must be satisfied that one of the options determined in Art. 69 (7) (a) or (b) ICCSt is met.

The Pre-Trial Chamber noted in its decision on the confirmation of charges that the reliability of evidence, enshrined in Art. 69 (7) (a) ICCSt, was not affected by the unlawful seizure, and the Trial Chamber affirmed this reasoning.[658] Hence the second option had to be examined. A wide range of concerns must be balanced to justify the exclusion of evidence, pursuant to Art. 69 (7) (b) ICCSt, because the seriousness of the crimes for which the Court is authorized to render justice does not permit exclusion of evidence solely to discipline the Prosecutor or national investigating officers.[659] In this particular case, the Chamber concluded that the violation: (1) did not amount to a serious infringement of the fair trial standards; (2) did not directly violate the rights of the accused but instead the rights of a third person; and (3) was carried out by Congolese authorities and not by a member of the OTP.[660] In conclusion, the Court stated that the admission into evidence of the seized items did not 'seriously damage the integrity of the proceedings', albeit the precondition, that is, the violation of a fundamental international recognized human right, was satisfied.[661]

The second case in which the Trial Chamber had to deal with the exclusionary rule enshrined in Art. 69 (7) ICCSt was *Katanga and Chui*. The appellant filed a motion against the admission into evidence of his prior statement made during interrogation by the national authorities of the military court in Kinshasa on 20 January 2006. The defence argued that the presence of counsel during the questioning was denied, albeit the accused requested the assistance of his defence counsel.[662] Notably, the Trial Chamber based its finding on the following internationally recognized human rights law regarding the right to be assisted by a lawyer of choice.

This right is stipulated in Art. 6 (c) ECHR, Art. 7 (c) African Charter on Human Rights, and Art. 8 (2) (d) Inter-American Convention on Human Rights. The ECtHR has clearly stated that the right to be assisted by counsel can be restricted 'for good cause'.[663] The permission to restrict this right must be examined on

---

658 ICC *Prosecutor v Lubanga*, PTC I, ICC-01/04-01/06-803-tEN, 29 January 2007, Decision on the Confirmation of Charges, para 85.

659 ICC *Prosecutor v Lubanga*, TC I, ICC-01/04-01/06-1981, 24 June 2006, Decision on the Admission of Material from the 'Bar Table', para 42 *et subs*.

660 Ibid, para 47.

661 The Trial Chamber affirmed the abovementioned decision by referring to it on another occasion; ICC *Prosecutor v Lubanga*, TC I, ICC-01/04-01/06-2589, 21 October 2010, Decision on the 'Prosecution's Second Application for Admission of Documents from the Bar Table Pursuant to Article 64(9)', para 29 *et subs*.

662 ICC *Prosecutor v Katanga and Chui*, TC II, ICC-01/04-01/07-2635, 17 December 2010, Decision on the Prosecutor's Bar Table Motion, para 56.

663 ECtHR *Öcalan v Turkey*, Judgment 12 May 2005 (Grand Chamber), Rep. 2005-IV, para 131.

a case-by-case basis 'in the light of the entirety of the proceedings'.[664] Due to the long period during which the suspect was denied access to his lawyer, the self-incriminating statements made by the suspect at the time, and their crucial role for his conviction, the Court concluded that Art. 6 (3) (c) ECHR had been breached.[665]

In *Delalić et al.*, the Court argued that if the national legal framework does not provide the right to be counselled, the Court is not bound by those provisions, pursuant to Rule 89 (A) RPE ICTY and, therefore, evidence obtained by breaching the law of the Court must be excluded as evidence. The Chamber argued that 'the Austrian rights of the suspect are so fundamentally different from the rights under the International Tribunal's Statute and Rules as to render the statement made under it inadmissible'.[666]

Referring to the findings of the ECtHR, the Chamber argued that the ECHR requires only that the suspect is granted access to his lawyer, and therefore defence counsel need not be present during questioning to protect the rights of the accused. Nevertheless, the Chamber came to the conclusion that the rights of the accused were violated because of the lack of adequate legal advice before interrogation, and hence the prior statement could not be admitted into evidence.[667] The Chamber did not conclusively determine which option given in Art. 69 (7) ICCSt was satisfied, but it can be assumed that the absence of a lawyer, at the pre-trial stage, puts the integrity of the proceeding in jeopardy by causing irretrievable prejudice to the rights of the accused.[668]

Of particular concern is the order of the Co-Investigating Judges of the ECCC on the admission into evidence of statements obtained by torture or potentially obtained by torture. Notably, in the legal framework of the ECCC no regulation similar to the exclusionary rule, enshrined in Art. 69 (7) ICCSt, exists. Rule 21 (3) RPE ECCC only provides for a regulation regarding the inadmissibility of statements obtained by the use of 'inducement, coercion or threats' when conducted by officials of the ECCC. The Judges argued that this provision was not applicable to evidence obtained by torture conducted by members of the Communist Party of Kampuchea.[669] Pursuant to Rule 87 (3) (d) RPE ECCC, the Chamber can refuse

[664] ECtHR *Öcalan v Turkey*, Judgment 12 May 2005 (Grand Chamber), Rep. 2005-IV, para 131.

[665] Ibid.

[666] ICTY *Prosecutor v Delalić et al.*, TC, IT-96-21, 2 September 1997, Decision on Zdravko Mucić's motion for the exclusion of evidence, para 52.

[667] ICC *Prosecutor v Katanga and Chui*, TC II, ICC-01/04-01/07-2635, 17 December 2010, Decision on the Prosecutor's Bar Table Motion, para 61 *et subs.*

[668] *See* Chapter 8, p 499.

[669] ECCC *Prosecutor v Ieng*, Co-Investigating Judges, 002/19–19-09-2007-ECCCC-OCIJ-D130/8, 28 July 2009, Order on use of statements which were or may have been obtained by torture, para 17.

the admission of evidence which is 'not allowed under the law', that is, under the national law as well as under all law enshrined in international treaties signed and ratified by Cambodia. The Convention against Torture and other Cruel, Inhuman and Degrading Treatment or Punishment (CAT) is one of the international contracts which the Court has to take into account in deciding on the admissibility of evidence.

In requesting the exclusion of the evidence concerned, the defence argued that statements made under torture could only be used against direct perpetrators and then only in cases where it would be used as proof that torture was committed, according to the wording of Art. 15 CAT.[670] Furthermore, the defence noted that statements made under torture are not reliable, and therefore cannot be used as evidence for the truth of their content.[671] Deciding on the defence request, the Co-Investigating Judges pointed out that a restrictive interpretation of Art. 15 CAT would 'allow those who are accused of torture to use the law designed to prevent torture to shield themselves from liability',[672] because the above-mentioned provision had to be read in the light of Art. 31 (3) (b) of the Vienna Convention on the Law of Treaties, that is, every treaty has to be interpreted 'in good faith'. According to the order, statements made under torture can be submitted into evidence to prove that, for example, a person whose name was given as a result of torture, was subsequently detained and was also subject to torture.[673] The Judges dismissed the request by the defence.

Another issue in this regard is the admissibility of statements obtained by torture or threat of torture in order to obtain further incriminating evidence, for example the precise position of the body of a murder victim.[674] In Germany in the course of criminal investigations regarding an abducted child, a deputy chief of police ordered his subordinate to threaten the suspect with torture and, if necessary, if the person concerned did not disclose the whereabouts of the child, to carry this

[670] ECCC *Prosecutor v Ieng*, Defence, 002-19-09-2007-ECCC-OCIJ-D130, 11 February 2011, Defence Request for Exclusion of Evidence Obtained by Torture, para 55.

[671] *A and Others v Secretary of the State for the Home Department* (No. 2) [2005] UKHL 71, para 16.

[672] ECCC *Prosecutor v Ieng*, Co-Investigating Judges, 002/19–19-09-2007-ECCCC-OCIJ-D130/8, 28 July 2009, Order on Use of Statements which were or may have been Obtained by Torture, para 24; M Scharf, 'Tainted Provenance: When, if Ever, should Torture Evidence be Admissible?', 65 *Washington & Lee Law Review* (2008) 129, 159; the author considered that if in the abovementioned case the evidence obtained by torture will be rendered inadmissible this would 'lead to absurd and unreasonable result.'

[673] ECCC *Prosecutor v Ieng*, Co-Investigating Judges, 002/19–19-09-2007-ECCCC-OCIJ-D130/8, 28 July 2009, paras 23 and 27, against broadening the exception included Art. 15 CAT: D McKeever, 'Evidence Obtained through Torture before the Khmer Rouge Tribunal, Unlawful Pragmatism?', 8 *JICJ* (2010) 615, 617 *et subs.*

[674] For an overview of international jurisdiction on the use of evidence obtained by torture and its admission into evidence *see* T Thienel, 'The Admissibility of Evidence Obtained by Torture under International Law', 17 *EJIL* (2006) 349, 356 *et subs.*

out. As a consequence, the suspect disclosed the whereabouts of the child and one day later confessed to the killing.[675] The Frankfurt am Main Regional Court noted that the treatment was a prohibited method of interrogation, pursuant to § 136a German Code of Criminal Procedure, and thus all statements made by the accused, even when not made under threat, were inadmissible. The exclusion of evidence comprised all further statements by the suspect in view of the continuing effect of the torture (*Fortwirkung*), caused by the lack of 'qualified instruction' (*qualifizierte Belehrung*). This effect could have been avoided by explaining to the suspect that his prior statements were obtained illegally and, therefore, were inadmissible.[676]

However, the Court rejected the exclusion of all evidence obtained as a consequence of the statements (*Fernwirkung*), for example the body of the child.[677] The 'fruit of the poisonous tree' doctrine implies that all evidence obtained as a result of using illegal methods of investigation are excluded as evidence. The exclusionary rule restricts not only the confession made under threat or coercion but also all evidence as a result thereof. The US Supreme Court pointed out that:

> The essence of a provision forbidding the acquisition of evidence in a certain way is that not merely evidence so acquired shall not be used before the Court but that it shall not be used at all. Of course this does not mean that the facts thus obtained become sacred and inaccessible. If knowledge of them is gained by an independent source they may be proved like any others, but the knowledge gained by the Government's own wrong cannot be used by it in the way proposed.[678]

The decision of the German court is not undisputed,[679] because of the perils associated with the refusal to apply the 'fruit of the poisonous tree' doctrine. The ECtHR affirmed that a breach of Art. 3 ECHR had occured but it could not approve a violation of Art. 6 (1) and (3) ECHR, that is, an infringement of the fair trial standards. The national court compensated for the breach of Art. 3 ECHR by excluding the statements made by the applicant.[680]

This approach is rather questionable because if the 'fruit of the poisonous tree' concept is not strictly implemented, the persons who carry out investigation are always at risk of breaching human rights law when balancing considerations of legally protected values. The deputy chief of the Frankfurt police and his subordinate were prosecuted and convicted. However, the case shows that on the one hand, the national court condemned the inhuman treatment carried out by the investigating officers, but on the other hand there was a clear lack of conse-

---

675 LG Frankfurt/M., 9 April 2003, 5/22 Ks 3490 Js 230118/02, 6 *StV* (2003) 325, 326.

676 Ibid, 325, 326.

677 Ibid, 325.

678 US Supreme Court *Silverthorne Lumber Co. v US*, 251 U.S. 385 (1920).

679 T Weigend, 'Anmerkung zu LG Frankfurt/M., 9 April 2003–5/22 Ks 3490 Js 230118/02', 8 *StV* (2003) 436, 439 *et subs.*

680 ECtHR *Gäfgen v Germany*, Judgment 1 June 2010 (Grand Chamber), App. No. 22978/05, para 147 *et subs.*

quences for the police officers who breached those human rights and therefore the ECtHR rightly noted that: '[s]uch punishment, which is manifestly disproportionate to a breach of one of the core rights of the Convention, does not have the necessary deterrent effect in order to prevent further violations of the prohibition of ill-treatment in future difficult situations.'[681]

Using evidence obtained unlawfully, for example, by an illegal seizure or other means, irretrievably infringes the rule of law and therefore this Pandora's Box should never be opened by any of the parties at court.[682]

III. Privileges

Commonly, the Chambers of the ICC have discretion to rule on any evidence and may also request additional evidence from the parties to the trial. This general rule is not unlimited; Art. 69 (5) ICCSt and Rule 73 RPE ICC comprise exceptions. Protecting relationships based on confidentiality from being published during the course of a public hearing, and more specifically to guard content of communications between those involved, is based on the premise that the truth should be established but not any price. This approach is recognized in most countries and is reaffirmed in the text of Art. 69 (5) ICCSt.[683]

The legal framework of the *ad hoc* Tribunals only provides privilege for the lawyer–client relationship. The other categories have been developed by case law.

In the following, the different categories of relationships and the extension of their protection will be discussed in detail. Inherently, the privileges are divided into testimonial and professional privileges. On no account may the former be compelled to testify at trial. In addition, protection of the latter includes communications between the parties concerned. The classification of testimonial and professional privileges will not be discussed because of many overlaps between both categories.

1. Legal counsel–client privilege

Rule 73 (1) RPE ICC enshrines protection of communication between lawyer and client. First, the meaning of the term 'lawyer' has to be defined. Only communications between the lawyer, that is, the attorney and the person working under his or her oversight, is protected. It is not undisputed that, for example, an investigator of the defence team falls under this definition.[684] One has to

---

[681] ECtHR *Gäfgen v Germany*, Judgment 1 June 2010 (Grand Chamber), App. No. 22978/05, para 124.

[682] Agree in opinion G Jerouschek and R Kölbel, 'Folter von Staats wegen?' 12 *JZ* (2003) 613.

[683] W Schabas, *ICC* (OUP 2010) 845 *et subs.*

[684] The Trial Chamber at the ICTY stated that communication with a legal adviser who is not approved by the Registry falls under the lawyer–client privilege if he or she respects the obligation of counsel working with the tribunal. ICTY *Prosecutor v Šešelj*, TC II, IT-03-67-PT, 9 May 2003,

bear in mind that the task of the investigator lies in the search for exculpatory evidence and in order to accomplish this duty he or she must have information available which is potentially incriminating for the accused. Not to extend the protection to this group of persons would lead to the circumvention of the right of protection of the confidential relationship between lawyer and client and, furthermore, to a violation of the right to equality of arms[685] between the parties to the trial.

There are only two opportunities listed in Rule 73 (1) RPE ICC which would lead to the disclosure of confidential information. Firstly, the client can consent to disclosure, but this approval must be given in writing, according to Rule 73 (1) (a) RPE ICC and, secondly, the client can voluntarily disclose the confidential information to a third person. By doing so he or she waives the right to protection of his or her confidential information because the third person can voluntarily testify on his or her knowledge or can be compelled to testify on the content of the confidential information, pursuant to Rule 73 (1) (b) RPE ICC.

Rule 97 RPE ICTY/ICTR is formulated in the same manner as Rule 73 (1) ICCSt, and therefore provides the same two options for losing protection of confidential communications between lawyer and client. Rule 97 (3) RPE SCSL provides another possibility for waiving the right of non-disclosure. If the client makes allegations of ineffective assistance against his or her lawyer, all communications relevant to the case have to be disclosed. A similar provision can be found in Art. 13 (B) (iii) Code of Professional Conduct for Counsel appearing before the International Tribunal.[686]

Notably at the ICTY, the counsel may disclose confidential information in order to prevent a criminal act which may lead to 'the death or substantial bodily harm of any person'. The same provision is included in the Code of Professional Conduct for Defence Counsel[687] at the ICTR.

The Code of Professional Conduct for Counsel[688] acting before the ICC does not enshrine such an exception. Art. 8 Code of Conduct only provides that counsel may disclose confidential information related to the lawyer–client relationship when ordered by the Court, according to Rule 76 *et subs.* RPE ICC concerning the issue of disclosure.

Decision on Prosecution's Motion for Order Appointing Counsel to Assist Vojislav Šešelj with his Defence, para 29.

685 *See* Chapter 8, p 410.

686 IT/125 REV.3, 22 July 2009.

687 Code of Professional Conduct for Defence Counsel, ASP/4/Res.1, 2 December 2005, Art. 8.

688 Code of Professional Conduct for Defence Counsel, ASP/4/Res.1, 2 December 2005.

2. *Self-incriminating testimony*

Of course, the right of the accused as well as of a witness not to testify against him or herself is a testimonial privilege. The group mentioned in Rule 75 (1) RPE ICC belongs to the same category, that is, witnesses should not be compelled to testify against family members. The right of the accused and the witness not to make incriminating statements against themselves and the right of a witness not to testify against family members have already been discussed.[689]

3. *Other confidential relationships*

In examining whether a privilege other than the lawer–client privilege should be granted a specific relationship, the Chamber must consider the prerequisites enshrined in Rule 73 (2) RPE ICC. The class of relationship concerned has to satisfy a threefold test to be protected: (1) the communications made in the course of the relationship must be grounded on confidentiality and this results in expectations of privacy and non-disclosure; (2) confidentiality is an inherent part of the relationship; and (3) weighing the pros and cons of the privilege, the Chamber must determine that, for the purpose of the legal framework of the ICC, recognition of the privilege is more important than establishing the truth.

The professional relationships listed in Rule 73 (3) RPE ICC should be recognized as privileged if there are no reasons against it; that is, the Court does not have to examine in detail the relationship before declaring it confidential. The list is not conclusive and, therefore, it lays in the discretionary power of the Chamber to determine on a case-by-case basis a particular relationship as worthy of protection.

As mentioned, neither the Statutes of the *ad hoc* Tribunals nor their Rules of Procedure and Evidence encompass a privilege for communications between medical professionals and their patients. The now adopted approach on this issue is developed by jurisprudence, mainly from the ICTY.

Among the professional relationships listed in Rule 73 (3) RPE ICC are, of course, the relationship between a medical doctor, a psychiatrist, or a psychologist and their patients which is clearly based on confidentiality. Only this link and therefore the communications between the patient and his or her medical practitioner are protected, according to Rule 73 (2) RPE ICC.

However, Rule 73 (3) RPE ICC stipulates the right that communications of relationships 'in particular, those related to or involving victims' should be granted protection from being made public. Attention should be paid to the meaning of the term 'medical doctor' because in its literal sense it would not comprise the staff of, for example, a hospital. Therefore, it is highly recommendable to

[689] *See* Chapter 8, p 469.

interpret it equally to the above-mentioned definition of the term 'lawyer', that is, it should encompass not only the medical doctor but rather all medical staff who are under his or her supervision and are involved in the medical care of the person concerned.

In *Stanišić/Simatović*, the Trial Chamber clearly pointed out that 'the transparent medical reporting should not unnecessarily encroach on the privacy rights of the Accused or third persons.'[690] That implies that not only the relationship between victims and witnesses and their medical professionals will be protected but under certain circumstances also the relationship of the accused to his medical doctor. If the health of the accused is the reason for a violation of the right of other accused to an expeditious trial, the medical report of this accused loses its privilege.[691]

Rather ambiguous is the term 'counsellor' in this regard because of its various meanings. Does the term refer only to a legal counsellor of an accused who has decided to defend him- or herself or should the notion be interpreted more broadly and also include a military counsellor or, for example, the investigator? Until now, the question has not arisen in the course of proceedings before the ICC and, therefore, a response is still awaited. A solution can, however, be found on a case-by-case basis. The Court should only interfere in any relationship of the accused or of a victim or a witness if it is in the interest of justice. Rendering its decision, the Chamber must balance with utmost caution the need for such interference with efficient prosecution and the right to privacy of the person concerned. Hence, also the relationship of a spiritual consultant should be protected.

Another professional group listed in Rule 73 (3) RPE ICC is the clergy. In particular, the Chamber should take into account that 'communications made in the context of a sacred confession where it is an integral part of the practice of that religion', is protected. However, the Christian religion is the only one in which sacred confession is practised and in which the clergy form an essential part of the practice of religion. A stringent interpretation of Rule 73 (3) RPE ICC would beyond doubt lead to discrimination of other religions such as Islam or Buddhism. One may ask whether, for example, the request of a witness to an Imam for a *fatwa*, that is, a religious judgment which can be ruled on by each Islamic judge in the world without a personal relationship between them, would be sufficiently based on confidentiality because it lacks the prerequisites of a sacred confession and is therefore not as worthy of protection as a confession in the Catholic

[690] ICTY *Prosecutor v Stanišić and Simatović*, TC I, IT-03-69-T, 6 July 2009, Decision on Urgent Defence Request for Further Submissions of Psychiatric Medical Expert and Decision on Defence Motion to Redact Medical Reports.

[691] ICTR *Prosecutor v Karemera et al.*, TC III, ICTR-98-44-T, 28 August 2009, Decision on motion for Disclosure of Medical Information and Extension of Time, para 10.

religion. Until now the ICC has not had to rule on this issue but perhaps this question will arise during the trials in Libya.[692]

4. Officials of the UN

The privilege of officials of the UN is not based on the Statute or its Rules of Procedure and Evidence but rather on the Convention on the Privileges and Immunities of the United Nations[693] (hereinafter: Convention). According to Art. V Section 18 (a) Convention, the official is privileged 'from legal process in respect of words spoken and written and all acts performed by them in their official capacity'. That implies that the Court cannot compel any official of the UN to testify at trial. Notably, pursuant to Art. V Section 20 Convention, this privilege should only be granted to an official for the benefit of the UN and not on the basis of personal interests.

In 2004, the ICC and the UN concluded an agreement on their relationship.[694] Pursuant to Art. 15 (2) Negotiated Relationship Agreement between the International Criminal Court and the United Nations (hereinafter: Agreement), the UN has the right to take all necessary measures, including non-disclosure of documents, to ensure the safety and security of its officials and their families. This provision should not be used carelessly because of its negative impact on proceedings before the ICC, as the case of *Lubanga*[695] clearly showed. This provision combined with the safeguards enshrined in Art. 54 (3) ICCSt were used in order to restrain from disclosure of exculpatory material to the defence. Art. 16 Agreement includes the obligation for the UN to cooperate with the ICC, that is, if the Court requests the testimony of an official of the UN, it should make all efforts in order to waive the privilege.[696]

Also the *ad hoc* Tribunals has had to deal with difficulties resulting from information which was supplied by the UN based on a confidential agreement. In *Brima et al.*, the Trial Chamber rendered a decision that a UN Human Rights officer could be compelled to give information about his sources in the course of

[692] On 26 June 2011 Pre-Trial Chamber I issued a warrant of arrest against Muammar Gaddafi, the head of state of Libya, his son Saif Al-Islam Gaddafi, the *de facto* prime minister, and Abdullah Al-Senussi, Colonel of the Libyan forces for the alleged commission of crimes against humanity. Subsequent events in Libya have revised this situation.

[693] A/RES/22(1), 13 February 1946.

[694] Negotiated Relationship Agreement between the International Criminal Court and the United Nations (hereinafter: Agreement), *see* also Chapter 1, p 51.

[695] ICC *Prosecutor v Lubanga*, TC I, ICC-01/04-01/06-1401, 13 June 2008, Decision on the Consequences of Non-disclosure of Exculpatory Materials Covered by Article 54 (3) (e) Agreements and the Application to Stay the Prosecution on the Accused, Together with Certain Issues Raised at the Status Conference on the 10 June 2008.

[696] In the case of *Lubanga*, not only the UN official whose right not to testify was waived by the UN, but also the UN counsellor who has to be presented during testimony of a UN official, had to take an oath; ICC *Prosecutor v Lubanga*, PTC I, ICC-01/04-01/05-T-37-EN, 15 November 2006, Transcript, p 5.

his testimony at Court. Prior to that, the UN had waived parts of his immunity.[697] The Court ruled that the Prosecutor could not guarantee the confidentiality of the information. Subsequently, the Appeals Chamber quashed that decision by stating that the Prosecutor has to assert the confidentiality of information and only if the Trial Chamber is not satisfied does it have the right to question the assertion. Thus, the threshold for the assertion should be very low.[698]

5. *Privilege on non-disclosure of state security information*

Generally, Member States of the Rome Statute must cooperate with officials of the Court, in particular with the Prosecutor, pursuant to Art. 86 ICCSt. However, the state may refuse to cooperate in order to protect national security information from being disclosed. Art. 72 ICCSt deals with the opportunities to find a solution between the interests of justice and the national security interests of the state concerned. According to Art. 72 (2) ICCSt, this provision also applies if a court order against a state official to appear and to testify before Court is produced. As mentioned, the Court has no power of self-assertion; that is, it cannot compel a state to comply.

In *Blaskić*, the Appeals Chamber affirmed the decision of Trial Chamber II regarding the concerns of Croatia that the disclosure of requested documents would prejudice its national security by quoting the following from the decision: '[A] State invoking a claim of national security as a basis for non-production of evidence requested by the International Tribunal, may not be exonerated from its obligation by a blanket assertion that its security is at stake. Thus, the State has the onus to prove its objection.'[699]

However, the Appeals Chamber pointed out that the disclosure of information which might bring the national security interests into jeopardy should not be claimed without sufficient cause. Furthermore, the Court should provide measures safeguarding the information and should order an *in camera ex parte* hearing.[700] Hence, the ICTY clearly noted that the Court also has the power to order the

[697] SCSL *Prosecutor v Brima et al.*, TC II, SCSL-04-16–389, 16 September 2005, Decision on the Prosecution's Oral Application for Leave to be Granted to Witness TF1-150 to Testify without Being Compelled to Answer any Questions in Cross-Examination that the Witness Declines to Answer on Grounds of Confidentiality Pursuant to Rule 70 (B) and (D) of the Rules, paras 2 and 18.

[698] SCSL *Prosecutor v Brima et al.*, AC, SCSL-2004-16-AR73, 26 May 2006, Decision on Prosecution Appeal against Decision on Oral Application for Witness TF1-150 to Testify without being Compelled to Answer Questions on Grounds of Confidentiality, para 19; the same approach was adopted by the ICTY Appeals Chamber in ICTY *Prosecutor v Milošević*, AC, IT-02-54-AR108*bis* and 73.3, 23 October 2002, Public Version of the Confidential Decision on the Interpretation and Application of Rule 70.

[699] ICTY *Prosecutor v Blaskić*, TC II, IT-95-14-PT, 18 July 1997, Decision on the Objection of the Republic of Croatia to the Issuance of *subpoena duces tecum*, para 147, cit in ICTY *Prosecutor v Blaskić*, AC, IT-95-14-A, 29 October 1997, Judgment on the Request of the Republic of Croatia for Review of the Decision of Trial Chamber II of 18 July 1997, para 61.

[700] ICTY *Prosecutor v Blaskić*, AC, IT-95-14-A, 29 October 1997, Judgment on the Request of the Republic of Croatia for Review of the Decision of Trial Chamber II of 18 July 1997, para 67.

disclosure of information against national security interests of a state by clarifying that 'to allow national security considerations to prevent the International Tribunal from obtaining documents that might prove of decisive importance to the conduct of trials would be tantamount to undermining the very essence of the International Tribunal's function.'[701]

All international criminal courts deal with atrocities committed during armed conflicts and, therefore, there will always be military information which a state does not wish to have disclosed. The approach of the ICTY goes further by clearly insisting on its inherent power to order states to disclose relevant information. The only option which remains for the state concerned is to request measures in order to safeguard the information in question. The Chambers of the ICC do not have such a power and, thus, depend on the cooperation of the states.

Notably, the state concerned has to be proactive if it realizes that information which would seriously infringe national security interests is to be disclosed. If no satisfactory solution can be found, the state has to claim specific reasons for an absolute ban on the disclosure of the information concerned. The real purpose behind this provision is to enable the access of the Court to relevant information by guaranteeing sufficient safeguards for the national security interests of the state concerned.[702]

6. The ICRC

Rule 73 (4) RPE ICC expressly mentions that no document or other information related to the work of the ICRC should be disclosed, not even by testimony of present or former employees of the ICRC. Only if one of the following circumstances are met can the information be disclosed in the course of the trial: (1) the ICRC does not object to the disclosure in writing or otherwise waives its privilege, and (2) the information concerned is contained in public documents and statements of the ICRC.

If the ICRC objects to the disclosure of certain information, the parties to the trial can seek the same information from other sources, pursuant to Rule 73 (5) RPE ICC. Only if the evidence is of major importance, can the Court contact the ICRC in order to solve the problem. In the course of the negotiation with the ICRC, the Court must have regard for the interests of justice and the victims as well as to the functions of the ICRC, according to Rule 73 (6) RPE ICC.

The question of whether employees of the ICRC could be compelled to testify first emerged in the case of *Simić et al.* before the ICTY. The Trial Chamber argued that the neutrality and impartiality of the ICRC is based on the Geneva Convention and, therefore, all Member States have to respect the special status

[701] ICTY *Prosecutor v Blaskić*, AC, IT-95-14-A, 29 October 1997, Judgment on the Request of the Republic of Croatia for Review of the Decision of Trial Chamber II of 18 July 1997, para 64.

[702] Triffterer/*Dixon/Duffy revised by Hall*, Art. 72 MN 5 *et subs.*

of the ICRC. Furthermore, the function of the ICRC, for example to inspect camps and detention centres, is based on confidentiality and, hence, should not be jeopardized by the Court.[703] Concluding, the Chamber noted that 'the right of non-disclosure of information related to the ICRC's activities in the possession of its employees in judicial proceedings is necessary for the effective discharge by the ICRC of its mandate'.[704]

Remarkably in *Katanga and Chui*, the Trial Chamber extended the protection granted to the ICRC and noted regarding two organizations (the names of which were redacted) that: '[t]here is, [...], no specific legal basis in the Statute or the Rules which mandates the Chamber to protect the neutral image of information providers'[705] but 'the two organisations involved have a legitimate interest [...] that they are seen to be neutral and impartial.'[706] However, '[t]here is a real risk that an innocent act of technical cooperation with the Court or the fact of having provided information to a third party, who subsequently transmitted it to the Court, may, rightly or wrongly, be perceived by some as an act of active collaboration with the Prosecution.'[707]

In contrast, a Trial Chamber of the ICTR rendered a decision that employees of national Red Cross societies are not included in the privilege granted to the ICRC, albeit cooperating with the ICRC. The reason given was that other organizations are not granted the same privilege as the ICRC because they are not mandated by the Geneva Conventions and should not subsequently be protected to such an extent as the ICRC.[708]

7. Journalists working in conflict zones

No privilege against having to testify or to provide information to the Court for journalists working in conflict zones is mentioned in the Statute or in its Rules of Procedure and Evidence. It remains to be seen whether the Chambers of the ICC will follow the finding of the *ad hoc* Tribunals on this issue.

In *Brđanin*, the Trial Chamber issued a subpoena against a journalist from the *Washington Post* because of his unwillingness to testify about an interview he

703 For further information on this issue *see* S Jeannet, 'Recognition of the ICRC's Long-standing Rule of Confidentiality', 838 *IRRC* (2000) 403.

704 ICTY *Prosecutor v Simić et al.*, TC, IT-95-9-PT, 27 July 1999, Decision on the Prosecution Motion under Rule 73 for a Ruling Concerning the Testimony of a Witness, para 73.

705 ICC *Prosecutor v Katanga and Chui*, TC II, ICC-01/04-01/07-2055-Red, 5 May 2010, Decision on the Protection of the Neutral and Impartial Status of Information Providers, para 17.

706 Ibid, para 18.

707 Ibid, para 22.

708 ICTR *Prosecutor v Muvunyi*, TC II, ICTR-2000-55A-T, 15 July 2005, Reasons for the Chamber's Decision on the Accused's Motion to Exclude Witness TQ, para 16.

conducted with the accused. Admittedly, the Chamber noted that the work carried out by journalists has an 'obvious utility in effectively serving to bring to justice those responsible for crimes'.[709] Nevertheless, the Court upheld its decision to compel the journalist to testify. Subsequently, the Appeals Chamber overturned the decision of the Trial Chamber. It reasoned that media personnel should only be compelled to testify in court if two requirements are met, namely that the testimony of the journalist 'is direct and important to the core issue of the case'[710] and the information cannot be obtained through other sources.[711] This decision is not undisputed because it goes further than the rationale solely to protect the confidential source or the person who facilitates the work of the journalist.[712] The goal behind the refusal of the journalist mentioned earlier to appear before the Court was to force the Court to clarify the status of journalists, and to confirm their right to choose whether to testify at trial. In some national legal systems, journalists can be compelled to testify on the content of a recently published article.[713]

In *Taylor*, the Trial Chamber of the SCSL had to deal with a request by the defence that the witness, a journalist, should disclose the identities of people who helped him to cross the border from Liberia to Sierra Leone during the conflict. In its decision, the Chamber pointed out that the term 'source' must be interpreted in a broad sense and, therefore, people who facilitate journalistic work during armed conflict should also be protected.[714]

This implies that, first and foremost, one must distinguish between the information-based privilege and the professional-based privilege.[715] The former deals

[709] ICTY *Prosecutor v Brđanin and Talić*, TC II, IT-99-36-T, 7 June 2001, Decision on Motion to Set Aside Confidential Subpoena to Give Evidence, para 25.

[710] ICTY *Prosecutor v Brđanin and Talić*, AC, IT-99-36-AR73.9, 11 December 2002, Decision on Interlocutory Appeal, para 39; unfortunately, the Appeals Chamber used the term 'war correspondent' not in the sense of Art. 79 Add. Prot. I, ie journalists who are accredited to the armed forces of one of the conflict parties, but determined the term 'war correspondent' as 'individuals who, for any period of time, report (or investigate for the purpose of reporting) from a conflict zone on issues relating to the conflict', para 29.

[711] Boas/Bischoff/Reid/Taylor, *ICL III*, 370.

[712] Crit. Khan/Buismann/Gosnell/*Azarnia* 558; in favour of the decision A Heeger, 'Securing a Journalist's Testimonial Privilege in the International Criminal Court' 6 *San Diego Int'l L J* (2005) 295; the author proposed a legal test for a rule regarding this issue for the ICC; in contrast, categorically rejecting a testimonial privilege for journalists H Tumber, 'Journalists, War Crimes and International Justice', 1 *Media War & Conflict* (2008) 261.

[713] In § 51 (1) (5) German Code of Criminal Procedure a relative privilege for journalists regarding confidential sources is stipulated; whereas in Austria the right to refuse to give evidence for media personnel is established in § 157 (1) (4) Austrian Code of Criminal Procedure, including the prohibition on circumventing this provision.

[714] SCSL *Prosecutor v Taylor*, TC II, SCSL-03-01-T, 6 March 2009, Decision on the defence motion for the disclosure of the identity of a confidential 'source' raised during cross-examination of TF1-355, para 25.

[715] Khan/Buismann/Gosnell/*Azarnia* 557 *et subs.*

with the confidential relationship between the journalist and his or her sources, or between him/her and the people who facilitate his or her work as a journalist. However, the latter deals with the right to freedom of expression enshrined in Art. 19 ICCPR and Art. 10 ECHR. Journalists act as neutral observers in order to gather information and thus should be granted the right to decide if they want to testify. The privilege is not absolute and does not prohibit journalists from testifying voluntarily.

E. Witnesses and Victims Protection: A Summary (*Hilde Farthofer*)

The testimony of witnesses constitutes a cornerstone in trial proceedings based on the principle of oral testimony, as the Trial Chamber in *Katanga and Chui* clearly pointed out.[716] To hear even a small proportion of evidence from persons affected by a crime which in reality aggrieves an entire society necessitates a huge amount of logistical and administrational effort, in particular owing to the circumstance that the seat of the Court is spatially separated from the crime scene. The topic of witness protection and the role of victims has been addressed in several instances in the course of this book. Due to the importance of this issue, however, relevant questions regarding the protection of witnesses and victims as they appear in the context of the ICC will be presented here in summary form.

Especially in cases of large-scale crimes, the protection of witnesses and victims is important for the credibility of the Court, that is, a potential witness will not be willing to testify if he or she has heard that other witnesses have been assassinated owing to a lack of protection measures. Bearing in mind that these persons in general have no opportunity to change their whereabouts, that is, to leave the regional sphere of influence of the alleged perpetrators, special protection for witnesses and victims is needed while, at the same time, the measures taken must not violate the rights of the accused stipulated in Art. 67 ICCSt. The legal basis for the implementation of safety or protection measures is enshrined in Arts 68 (1) and 43 (6) ICCSt. The establishment of a specific protection measure will depend on the circumstance of the individual case and the reasons why the particular witness or victim has to be sheltered.

I. Reasons for protection

There are various reasons why a witness or a victim appearing before the Court has to be protected. These can be divided into three main categories: (1) the inherent

[716] *See* Chapter 8, p 463 and *Prosecutor v Katanga and Chui*, TC II, ICC-01/04-01/07-2954, 25 May 2011, Decision on Defence Request to Admit into Evidence Entirety of Document DRC-OTP-1017.0572, para 4.

risk of retaliatory measures, (2) the risk of new traumatization, and (3) the risk of self-incrimination.

(1) The first category refers not only to natural persons but also to organizations which are working in conflict zones and need to give the impression of neutrality to protect their own staff.[717] Persons who live or work in an area of ongoing armed conflict do not have the opportunity to leave the area and, therefore, are perpetually exposed to the risk of violence from both sides of the opposing parties. '[I]t is assumed that all persons who are known to have contacts with the ICC face a certain degree of risk.'[718]

(2) Rule 86 RPE ICC mentions in particular victims of sexual and gender violence, children, elderly persons, and persons with disabilities. These groups have to be sheltered due to their specific vulnerability against 'second victimization' that questioning before the Court could cause. All parties to the trial have to be aware of their traumatized condition and have to deal with it in a sensible manner. Notably, the Victims and Witnesses Unit, a subsection of the Registry,[719] organizes workshops on this issue for the staff of the Office of the Prosecutor as well as for defence counsel.

(3) Witnesses need legal assistance if they run the risk of making self-incriminating statements. The Victims and Witnesses Unit has to offer support and help in finding proper legal advice in order to protect their rights, according to Rule 17 (2) (b) (i) RPE ICC.[720]

Each of these groups needs other protection measures or a variety of different measures. In the following different protection measures will be examined.

II. Protection measures

According to Art. 68 (1) ICCSt, the Court has to establish appropriate measures to safeguard the 'safety, physical and psychological well-being, dignity and privacy' of witnesses and victims. In principle there are two scenarios where protection is warranted: (a) inside the courtroom, and (b) outside the courtroom. The rights of the accused, which need to be protected throughout prosecution proceedings, are affected only by the first group of protection measures, namely those which have an impact on the course of proceedings.

The Registry via the Victims and Witnesses Unit is responsible for the implementation of all protection and security measures regarding witnesses and victims. One

[717] ICC *Prosecutor v Katanga and Chui*, TC II, ICC-01/04-01/07-2055-Red, 5 May 2010, Decision on the Protection of the Neutral and Impartial Status of Information Providers, para 22.

[718] Registry, Summary Report on the Round Table on the Protection of Victims and Witnesses Appearing Before the International Criminal Court, 29 and 30 January 2009, p 5.

[719] *See* Chapter 4, p 157.

[720] For further information on this issue *see* Chapter 8, p 469.

has to bear in mind that not only are the witnesses of the prosecution endangered due to their testimony, but defence witnesses are also faced with the same risks. However, the Victims and Witnesses Unit describes itself as 'part of a neutral organ and does not assume that the accused (detained person) poses a threat to Office of the Prosecution witnesses'.[721]

1. Inside the courtroom

The protective measures which can be ordered by the Court to be used inside the courtroom are listed in Rule 87 (3) RPE ICC and Regulation 94 RegR. The Prosecutor or the defence can request the application of such measures after they have communicated with the Victims and Witnesses Unit. In any case, a protection measure can only be imposed on a witness or victim with his or her consent and in the case of a child with the consent of the parents or the guardian.

As mentioned above, if a witness is granted certain protection measures, this implies almost automatically the restriction of the rights of the accused. In the following the different protection measures provided for in the legal framework of the ICC will be analysed with an emphasis on of the particular rights of the accused which will be placed in jeopardy.

a. Expunctions The Court has the power to order the redaction of all information of a witness or victim which could lead to his or her identification, pursuant to Rule 87 (3) (a) RPE ICC and Regulation 94 (g) RegR. This includes, for example, the whereabouts and the names of family members of the person concerned[722] but could also lead to an expunction of the entire statement of the witness or victim.

If the name of the person, that is, the identity of the witness, is redacted and thus not disclosed to the defence, the right of the accused to examine a witness testifying against him or her is infringed as well as his right to prepare his case in advance. In this event, the rights of the accused have to be balanced with the rights of the witnesses or victims.[723] The Appeals Chamber rightly noted in *Lubanga* that

> three of the most important considerations for an authorisation of non-disclosure of the identity of a witness pursuant to rule 81 (4) of the Rules of Procedure and Evidence; [are] the endangerment of the witness or of members of his or her family that the disclosure of the identity of the witness may cause; the necessity of the protective measure; and why the Pre-Trial Chamber considered that the measure would

---

[721] Registry, Summary Report on the Round Table on the Protection of Victims and Witnesses Appearing Before the International Criminal Court, 29 and 30 January 2009, p 5.

[722] ICC *Prosecutor v Lubanga*, TC I, ICC-01/04-01/06-2283-Red, 24 February 2010, Redacted Decision on the Prosecution's Request for Non-disclosure of Information in the Statements of Three Individuals Providing Rule 77 Information, para 9.

[723] *See* Chapter 8, p 494.

Table 8.4 Witness and victims protection measures versus rights of the accused

Protection measures	Rights of the accused
Expunctions (Art. 68 (5) ICCSt and Rule 87 (3) (a) RPE ICC) **Pseudonym** (Art. 68 (5) ICCSt and Rule 87 (3) (d) RPE ICC) **Non-disclosure** (Art. 68 (5) ICCSt and Rule 87 (3) (b) RPE ICC)	Right to examine the witness against him or her (Art. 67 (1) (e) ICCSt) and right to prepare his or her case (Art. 67 (1) (b) ICCSt)
Testimony by technical means (eg voice distortion) (Regulation 94 (b) and (c) RegR)	
Testimony by technical means (eg video conference) (Art. 68 (2) ICCSt and Rule 87 (3) (c) RPE ICC)	Right to examine the witness against him or her directly (Art. 67 (1) (e) ICCSt)
Non-public proceedings (Art. 68 (2) ICCSt and Rule 87 (3) (e) RPE ICC)	Right to a public hearing (Art. 67 (1) ICCSt)

not be prejudicial to or inconsistent with the rights of the accused and a fair and impartial trial.[724]

The identities of the witnesses and victims have to be disclosed to the defence shortly before the commencement of trial. The Pre-Trial Chamber has determined that disclosure of the identities of protected witnesses before the confirmation hearing is 'an inadequate solution should the charges be confirmed because the identities of the relevant witnesses still would be disclosed a long time prior to their being called to testify at trial'.[725] The Appeals Chamber quashed the decision stating that at least fifteen days before the confirmation hearing, the identities of the witness or victim must be disclosed to the defence. Of course, the identities of the witnesses and victims in question will never be disclosed to the public and the media if the Court so orders.

Furthermore, the application of protection measures must be proportionate and necessary. In *Lubanga*, the Appeals Chamber stated that:

> The use of the word 'necessary' emphasises the importance of witness protection and the obligation of the Chamber in that respect; at the same time, it emphasises that protective measures should restrict the rights of the suspect or accused only as far as necessary.[726]

[724] ICC *Prosecutor v Lubanga*, AC, ICC-01/04-01/06-773, 14 December 2006, Judgment on the Appeal of Mr. Thomas Lubanga Dyilo against the Decision of Pre-Trial Chamber I entitled 'First Decision on the Prosecution Requests and Amended Requests for Redactions under Rule 81', para 21.

[725] ICC *Prosecutor v Lubanga*, PTC I, ICC-01/04-01/06-437, 15 September 2006, First Decision on the Prosecution Requests and Amended Requests for Redactions under Rule 81, p 8.

[726] ICC *Prosecutor v Lubanga*, AC, ICC-01/04-01/06-568, 13 October 2006, Judgment on the Prosecutor's Appeal against the Decision of the Pre-Trial Chamber I entitled 'Decision Establishing

The principle of proportionality is not expressly stipulated in Art. 68 ICCSt nor in Rule 81 (4) RPE ICC. Nevertheless, it is encompassed in Rule 81 (4) RPE ICC by referring to the rights of the accused. The Court has to counterbalance the infringed rights of the accused and the necessity to protect the witnesses and victims. For this purpose, the Prosecutor may request the Victims and Witnesses Unit to relocate the witness or victim concerned shortly before commencement of trial. If the consent of the person concerned cannot be obtained, but the risk for the witness or victim is disproportionate, the Prosecutor cannot use his or her testimony in the prosecution case.

Remarkably, in its first decisions the Trial Chamber of the ICTY decided that the identities of protected witnesses and victims should never be disclosed to the defence, even during trial.[727] The requirements for the derogation of recognized procedural guarantees are that

(i) there is a real fear for the safety of the witness and his or her family;
(ii) the testimony of the particular witness is of specific importance to the prosecution case;
(iii) there is no *prima facie* evidence that the witness is untrustworthy;
(iv) no protection programme exists or the established programme is ineffective; and
(v) the measure must be necessary, ie no less restrictive measure can protect that particular witness.

b. Pseudonym The identification of the victim can also be protected by using a pseudonym, pursuant to Rule 87 (3) (d) RPE ICC and Regulation 94 (a) RegR. This has the advantage that the parties can question the witness or victim without the risk of accidentally using their real name.[728]

As mentioned above, non-disclosure of the identity of a witness always infringes the rights of the accused because to prepare his or her case without knowing who will testify against him or her upsets the 'equality of arms' principle.[729]

General Principles Governing Applications to Restrict Disclosure pursuant to Rule 81 (2) and (4) of the Rules of Procedure and Evidence', para 37.

[727] ICTY *Prosecutor v Tadić*, TC, IT-95/1-T, 10 August 1995, Decision on the Prosecutor's Motion Requesting Protective Measures for Victims and Witnesses, para 61 *et subs*.

[728] ICC *Prosecutor v Bemba*, Registrar, ICC-01/05-01/08-177-Red, 21 October 2008, Public Redacted Version of ICC-01/05-01/08-177-Conf, Victims and Witnesses Unit's Observations on the Protection Measures in Relation to Witness 029; the Office of the Prosecutor inadvertently disclosed the identity of a witness to the defence and requested protection measures for the person concerned.

[729] For a more detailed analysis of disclosure *see* Chapter 7, p 344 and for the 'equality of arms' principle *see* Chapter 8, p 410.

c. Non-disclosure The Prosecutor, the defence, and all other parties to the trial can be ordered by the Court not to disclose the name or any other information which could lead to the identification of a witness or victim, pursuant to Rule 87 (3) (b) RPE ICC.[730]

Non-disclosure of the names of witnesses puts the rights of the accused in jeopardy and, therefore, the testimony has less probative value.[731] In *Lubanga*, the Court ordered the disclosure of the name of an intermediary, but the Prosecutor failed to comply, reasoning that he was obliged according to Art. 68 ICCSt to protect all persons affected by his investigations. This refusal caused a temporarily halt in proceedings.[732] The Appeals Chamber stated, regarding this issue, that '[t]here is no exception to the general principle that the Prosecutor (or other parties and participants) must follow the orders of the Trial Chamber when it comes to issues of protection.'[733]

d. Testimony by technical means (a) The identity of a witness or a victim can also be covered by use of technical means, as for example, facial distortion (Regulation 94 (b) RegR) and voice distortion (Regulation 94 (c) RegR). Both measures will be used to shelter the witness or victim against potential retaliation. The utilization of such technical means violates the rights of the accused to examine the witness testifying against him or her, therefore the Court should only permit such measures as a means of last resort. As already mentioned, the burden on the defence to prepare the case without any information about witnesses would be immense and, of course, cannot be in the interests of justice.

(b) Technical means can also be applied to enable the testimony of vulnerable witnesses and victims to reduce the risk of secondary victimization. This includes videoconferences (Regulation 94 (f) RegR) and closed-circuit television, pursuant to Rule 87 (3) (c) RPE ICC. The purpose of this is to prevent the person concerned from testifying face-to-face with their alleged perpetrator. The protection of the rights of the victims and witnesses not to be harmed in the course of proceeding must always be respected. In particular, where children are involved, the Court should balance the rights of the most affected actors, the witnesses, victims, and the accused, with great caution.[734]

e. Non-public proceedings The last measure which can be used in the courtroom to protect witnesses or victims is the possibility of holding the hearing *in*

---

[730] For detailed information on the disclosure regime at the ICC *see* Chapter 7, p 352.

[731] *See* Chapter 8, p 494.

[732] *See* Chapter 7, p 355.

[733] ICC *Prosecutor v Lubanga*, AC, ICC-01/04-01/06-2582, 8 October 2010, Judgment on the Appeal of the Prosecutor against the Decision of Trial Chamber I of 8 July 2010 entitled 'Decision on the Prosecution's Urgent Request for Variation of the Time-Limit to Disclose the Identity of Intermediary 143 of Alternatively to Stay Proceedings Pending Further Consultations with the VWU', para 50.

[734] *See* Chapter 8, p 394.

camera or in private session, according to Rule 87 (e) RPE ICC and Regulation 94 (d) and (e) RegR.

The accused has the right to a public hearing under Art. 67 (1) ICCSt. This right will be breached by hearings *in camera* or in private sessions but, it is submitted, this presents an opportunity to protect witnesses and victims which would affect the rights of the accused only minimally.[735]

2. *Outside the courtroom*

Protective measures should not end with the testimony of the witness or victim but rather be implemented if necessary over a longer period. The Registry has to develop a protection programme for witnesses and victims of both sides of the trial, that is, for the Prosecutor as well as for the defence, according to Regulation 96 RegR. Notably, on some occasions the Victims and Witnesses Unit has denied the application of a provisional settlement of a witness which was subsequently carried out by the Office of the Prosecutor itself.[736] This programme includes *inter alia* the resettlement of the person concerned. The application of such measures depends mainly on the consent of the witness or victim concerned.

The application of such a measure will not infringe the rights of the accused because it enables the disclosure of their names and, therefore, the defence can improve its case because it knows who will testify against the accused.

III. Conclusion

The issue of protection will always be in conflict with the rights of one of the parties. If the Court grants protective measures to a prosecution witness, this would almost automatically infringe the rights of the accused. But if the Court decides that the witness or victim will not be subject to protection measures, his or her right of well-being or possibly even his or her right to life will be violated.

The Court has to balance the rights of all participants very carefully and render its decision on a case-by-case basis and not according to a general guideline. However, it must take into account the proportionality and necessity of the protective measures. Each situation brought before the Court will also require a different approach regarding the issue of witness and victim protection.

---

735 *See* Chapter 8, p 394.

736 ICC *Prosecutor v Katanga and Chui*, OTP, ICC-01/04-01/07-398, 16 April 2008, Prosecution's Submission of Information on the Preventive Relocation of Witnesses 132, 163, 238 and 287, para 9.

F. Judgment

The Presiding Judge terminates the submission of evidence. After the closing arguments of the parties and the 'last word' of the defence (Rule 141 RPE ICC), the Chamber retires to deliberate and come to a decision determining the accused's guilt on the basis of the evidence, which was presented at trial. Art. 74 ICCSt uses the term 'decision' rather than 'judgment'. The latter term would be the correct one used in the final determination of guilt of the accused, and was the word used by Art. 26 IMTSt and Art. 23 ICTYSt. 'Decision' is the more general term comprising also intermediate findings of the court.[737] Despite this wording, Art. 74 ICCSt relates to the final judgment and not to any decision.

I. Deliberations

The deliberations are to be held in secret, Art. 74 (4) ICCSt. This is of course necessary for the independence of the judges, otherwise there is the danger that a judge will be put under pressure and endure sanctions. The deliberations shall be concluded 'within a reasonable period of time after the Trial Chamber has retired to deliberate', is said by Rule 142 (1) RPE ICC. The 'reasonableness' correlates with Art. 67 (1) (c) ICCSt and the principle of a speedy trial contained therein.[738]

The relevant point of reference for the deliberations is laid down in Art. 74 (2) ICCSt. The judges must base their evaluation on the evidence presented and discussed before them at trial.[739] This is a corollary of the principle of a public and oral trial, according to which no secret knowledge of the judges may be used. The framework is determined by the charges as presented by the Prosecutor as confirmed by the Pre-Trial Chamber.

It is only the judges that may participate in the deliberations. Other persons are not called upon and thus not legally allowed to convict a person. The judges furthermore must have been present at each stage of the trial and throughout the deliberations. Art. 76 (1) ICCSt contains this provision, which is a logical prerequisite as otherwise the judge would not know the factual basis of his or her decision and would have no direct appreciation of the evidence presented.[740]

---

737 *See* Triffterer/*Triffterer*, Art. 74 MN 11.
738 In greater detail *see* Chapter 8, p 383.
739 The wording 'may...only' expresses the mandatory effect of this provision, *see* Triffterer/*Triffterer*, Art. 74 MN 29.
740 Triffterer/*Triffterer*, Art. 74 MN 12.

The practice at the international tribunals and at the ICC raises some doubt in this regard, as the judges rely heavily on help by legal assistants.[741] Legal assistants may be used to prepare a judgment and clarify questions of law. Yet they cannot aid in evaluating the evidence for two reasons: (1) they are not authorized to do so on the grounds of the ICCSt, and (2) they have most probably not been present during the entire proceedings, so they do not have the same factual knowledge as judges that have. Judges should thus always be wary of how they use legal assistants and choose the subjects they wish them to work on very carefully.

II. Written and reasoned judgment

According to Art. 74 (5) ICCSt the judgment must be in writing and it must be reasoned. The judgment is in one of the working languages, that is, either English or French (*see* Art. 50 (2) ICCSt), and will be translated into the language the accused understands according to Art. 67 (1) (f) ICCSt. Giving reasons for the decision has developed as good practice in international criminal trials. According to Art. 26 IMTSt, the Military Tribunal at Nuremberg was obliged to issue a reasoned judgment, and Art. 23 (2) ICTYSt anticipates that a reasoned opinion must be rendered by the judges.

There are several national jurisdictions in which written and reasoned judgments are not the general rule. This is particular true for states which have a jury system. A jury of twelve women and men is not able to draft a judgment; and beyond this practical argument, juries base their social legitimacy and acceptability on the representative number of laypeople they comprise, and not on their legal expertise.[742]

In international trials a reasoned judgment is obligatory mainly for two reasons; one being normative, the other of a more practical nature.[743] First, the legitimacy and acceptability of a verdict can only come from a convincing argument in a global discourse. The judges must lay open their evidentiary basis. They must establish why evidence was excluded or admitted and they must justify their conviction and explain that no doubts remain as regards the guilt of the accused. The judgment is a means to communicate with global society in general and the specific society concerned, that is, the particular place where the situation at issue occurred. If this is the case, the verdict cannot just be stated; it must also be explained. At least an attempt must be made to make it explicable to the accused, the victims, and other people concerned.

---

[741] P Wald, 'The International Criminal Tribunal for the Former Yugoslavia Comes of Age: Some Observations on Day-To-Day Dilemmas of an International Court', 5 *Washington University Journal of Law & Policy* (2001) 87, 93 *et subs.*

[742] *See* C Safferling, *Towards an International Criminal Procedure* (OUP 2003) 209–16 for further discussion of the jury system.

[743] *See* also Boas/Bischoff/Reid/Taylor, *ICL III*, 378.

Secondly, the judgment must be in writing and reasoned because there must exist the possibility for appeal.[744] The Prosecutor and the defence can only evaluate whether the judgment was materially affected by error of fact of law or procedural error if the judges give reasons for their findings. The right to appeal, as embodied in Art. 14 (6) ICCPR, thus presupposes a written and reasoned judgment.

Both reasons are necessary and sufficient by themselves. The Nuremberg Tribunal handed down a reasoned judgment although no appeal was possible, but the attempt was made to explain the judgment in order to be understood in Germany and elsewhere.

III. Pronouncement

Art. 74 (5) ICCSt orders the judgment to be delivered in open court. Rule 144 (1) RPE ICC declares furthermore that the verdict shall be pronounced in the presence of the accused, the Prosecutor, the victims or their legal representatives, and representatives of states which have participated in the proceedings. As has been seen, the public pronouncement is a human rights' prerequisite.[745] However Art. 74 (5) makes a concession to the efficiency of the proceedings in that the reading of a summary of the judgment is considered sufficient. Considering the lengthy nature of judgments of the international tribunals, this seems reasonable. What is unclear, however, is whether the summary can be delivered before the written judgment is completed. Of course it might be advisable in order to speed up the proceeding to allow the judgment to be pronounced before the written and reasoned draft is available.[746] However, experience from Arusha shows that it can sometimes take more than two years before the written judgment is available. It would therefore be prudent to have a definite time limit for the written judgment to be presented. I would suggest that six months after the public pronouncement of the verdict is an adequate period, otherwise there would be a breach of the principle of a speedy trial as the uncertainty for the accused prevails until a final verdict has been reached on appeal.[747]

IV. Structure of the judgment

As to the structure of the judgment, there is no formal provision of what this ought to be, thus each Tribunal will develop its own 'tradition' in this regard. The structure of the judgments of the *ad hoc* Tribunals thus varies, yet they share certain elements:[748]

744 Triffterer/*Triffterer*, Art. 74 MN 32.
745 *See* Chapter 8, p 391.
746 *See* Triffterer/*Triffterer*, Art. 74 MN 36.
747 *See* Chapter 8, p 389.
748 Similarly: Boas/Bischoff/Reid/Taylor, *ICL III*, 387.

(1) Historical background of the situation and the case at hand;
(2) Introduction and identification of the accused and the charges;
(3) A short procedural history;
(4) Identification of the relevant law regarding both the crimes and the forms of responsibility;
(5) A description and evaluation of the evidence presented to the Chamber;
(6) Application of the law to the facts as derived from the evidence;
(7) A *dispositif* setting forth the verdict for each separate charge.

As separate sentencing proceedings were eliminated at the ICTY and ICTR in 1998, judgments which were handed down after that date contained also an evaluation and application of sentencing factors. At the ICC—as is the case at the SCSL—the sentencing decision will take place in a separate judgment.[749]

V. Reasonable doubts requirements and majority verdicts

The threshold for a conviction (that the judges must be convinced of the guilt of the accused beyond a reasonable doubt) has been discussed elsewhere.[750] The judges must form their conviction by evaluating the 'entire proceedings', as stated in Art. 74 (2) ICCSt. The Statute states that the judges should not look merely at each aspect of hearings individually.[751] Rather, the trial in its entirety is the relevant point of reference. This includes the interrelationship between the individual pieces of evidence, and the appearance of the accused and of the defence counsel.

The judges must decide on every single charge separately according to Rule 142 (2) RPE ICC and if there is more than one accused, they must also decide on the charges against each accused separately, Rule 142 (3) RPE ICC.

The Chamber is called upon to reach unanimity in its decision by virtue of Art. 74 (3) ICCSt, however, should this not be possible, a majority verdict is possible. In that case, there will be a majority judgment and the views of the minority must be included, as foreseen by Art. 74 (5) ICCSt. This is a somewhat surprising norm. Usually the minority will identify itself and issue a (signed) separate and dissenting opinion. This is the way the *ad hoc* Tribunals have operated, Art. 23 (2) ICTYSt, Art. 22 (2) ICTRSt, Art. 18 SCSLSt, Rule 98*ter* (C) RPE ICTY, Rule 88 (C) RPE ICTR/SCSL. On the international level the International Court of Justice may count as a predecessor. Art. 57 ICJSt anticipates the right of any judge to deliver a separate opinion. Likewise, Art. 45 (2) ECHR grants the judges of the ECtHR the

[749] Ibid, 388.
[750] *See* Chapter 8, p 408.
[751] Triffterer/*Triffterer*, Art. 74 MN 26.

right to issue a separate opinion. In many national legal systems, in particular those stemming from an Anglo-Saxon background, dissents are foreseen in the legal proceedings.[752] But even at the Federal Constitutional Court in Germany the justices are allowed to attach dissenting opinions to the majority decision according to Sec. 30 (2) Federal Constitutional Court Act (*Bundesverfassungsgerichtsgesetz*).

Yet these national and international judicial bodies are not criminal courts. These organs do not have the power to deliver a guilty verdict and send a person to prison for a considerable amount of time. Discussing a constitutional question differs immensely from a criminal trial. The effect the ICC achieves by allowing dissenting opinions at the trial level are thus to be analysed very carefully with a view to the role of the judge and the functions attributed to a judgment.

What are the pros and cons for allowing separate opinions? In favour of dissenting opinions are the role and the self-perception of the judges. An independent judge should express his/her view whenever s/he so wishes.[753] It is interesting to note that in all the Statutes discussed above, the ICJ, the ECtHR, as well as the German Constitutional Court, a judge has a right to issue a separate opinion. Furthermore dissenting opinions might help the development of a new area of law, as is the case with international criminal law. Finally, a separate opinion might assist the accused in that it presents arguments against the verdict, which might be useful on appeal.[754]

Several arguments can be brought against signed dissents. First, the confidentiality of the deliberations is breached as a dissenting opinion unfolds the discussions and arguments amongst the judges.[755] As the minority judge identifies himself, the majority judges are known as well. Secondly, the verdict is weakened by separate opinions. This indeed might damage the acceptability of the court altogether and the administration of justice in general might sustain a loss. This is true in particular for criminal verdicts and the decision on the facts of the case. If the threshold of proof 'beyond reasonable doubts' is overstepped if two judges agree and one judge disagrees, the latter judge obviously had doubts. Should these doubts be termed 'unreasonable', which they must be if one wishes to keep to the standard of proof beyond reasonable doubt-formula? Granted that this argument is rather syllogistic, it would still be necessary to explain to the convicted person that doubts of one judge out of three do not suffice. This becomes even worse if the dissenting judge explains in detail by way of delivering a signed dissenting opinion why s/he could not agree with the majority. In the present author's view, this would not be acceptable for the convicted person.

---

752 Eg, the US Supreme Court, and the English Supreme Court.

753 *See* Boas/Bischoff/Reid/Taylor, *ICL III*, 384.

754 Boas/Bischoff/Reid/Taylor, *ICL III*, 384 are in favour of admitting signed dissenting opinions.

755 *See* Cassese/Gaeta/Jones/*Terrier*, Vol II, 1314 *et subs.*

The balance is thus tipped against allowing signed dissenting opinions at the Trial Chamber level. At the appeals level this is different. There the question is not whether the accused is guilty or not. The standard of proof 'beyond reasonable doubt' does not apply as appeals judges only look into the conformity of the trial judgment with the law. Dissenting opinions concerning questions of law do not pose problems regarding the acceptability of the decision.

The Statute of the ICC tries a 'third way' as so often and attempts to combine the advantages of one solution with the advantages of the other. The wording of Art. 74 (3) ICCSt supposes that there are no signed dissenting views, but the judgment must identify the passages which were not voted on unanimously and it must clarify the reasons for this. Thus the image of one single judgment is sustained whereas the convicted person and the Prosecutor are given ideas of where the disagreements were amongst the judges and how the argument could be on appeal.

Of course 'third way' approaches are often charged with being neither fish nor fowl. Similarly here one could argue that the Statute weakens the verdict as any prudent observer would realize that unanimity could not be reached amongst the judges, while at the same time an open and fair discourse is being cut off because the minority remains anonymous.

Despite all these difficulties, what can be secured is the will of the ICCSt to avoid the identification of a judge as the minority.[756] In the Trial Chamber, in determining the guilt of the accused, the judges should strive hard for a unanimous judgment. This would indeed make the verdict more powerful and increase the chances of it being acceptable for the participating parties and the general public.

VI. Conclusion

The judgments at international courts or Tribunals serve one aim: to communicate with the accused and the public. The public censure contained in a guilty verdict must thus be explained both to the convicted person and to the global audience. Should the judgment lack convincing reasoning, the decision runs the danger of not being accepted, which would seriously harm the authority of the court and the legitimacy of the proceedings. As justice must not only be done but must be seen to be done, the judgment must be pronounced publicly and should leave no doubt as to the guilt of the defendant in the case of a conviction. If doubts cannot be silenced by reasonable arguments, the defendant is to be discharged, as the standard of proof of guilt beyond a reasonable doubt cannot be met. Under these premises, the admissibility of majority judgments seems somewhat unfortunate.

756 Triffterer/*Triffterer*, Art. 74 MN 35.

G. Victim's Participation

Victims are to be integrated into the proceedings at all stages where their personal interests are affected, Art. 68 (3) ICCSt.[757] Naturally, this participation stretches to the trial stage. The ICC provisions as we have seen before only establish a basic outline of the rights of participating victims. Instead of setting down a detailed procedure, the judges are granted extensive discretion when deciding the scope of victim participation (*see* Rule 89 RPE ICC). The few trials which have been conducted before ICC Trial Chambers to-date do not provide enough evidence of how, in general, victims' participation will work. It is up to the Chamber to decide which competences will be attributed to the victims. In order to allow the court to remain flexible throughout the course of the proceedings, Rule 91 (1) RPE ICC permits a chamber to modify a previous ruling regarding the extent of victim participation.[758] We can, however, draw some conclusions from the Pre-Trial Chambers' ruling on victims' rights during the confirmation hearings. The following rights will thus be available at the trial stage as well, but determined by the Chamber on a case-by-case basis.[759]

(1) The right for a participating victim to choose a legal representative according to Rule 90 (1) RPE ICC,[760] who has the same competence and legal qualification as defence counsel, as set down in Rule 22 (1) RPE ICC.[761]

(2) Where a great number of victims are admitted to participate, the court can limit the number of lawyers representing them, Rule 90 (2)-(4) RPE ICC.

(3) Those victims without the means to pay for a lawyer may be awarded legal aid.[762]

(4) The victim has the right to make an opening and a closing statement, which can be exercised through legal assistance.[763]

---

757 In greater detail *see* also C Safferling, 'The Role of the Victim in the Criminal Process: A Paradigm Shift in National German and International Law?', 11 *ICLR* (2011) 183, 202 *et subs.*

758 B Timm, 'The Legal Position of Victims in the Rules of Procedure and Evidence', in: H Fischer, C Kreß, and S R Lüder (eds), *International and National Prosecution of Crimes under International Law: Current Developments* (Spitz 2001) 289, 298.

759 *See* ICC *Prosecutor v Lubanga*, TC I, ICC-01/04-01/06-1119, 18 January 2008, Decision on Victim's Participation, para 105 *et subs.*; *see* also *Prosecutor v Lubanga*, TC I, ICC-01/04-01/06-1556, 15 December 2008, Decision on the Applications by Victims to Participate in the Proceedings, para 135.

760 *See* C Safferling, 'Das Opfer völkerrechtlicher Verbrechen', 115 *ZStW* (2003) 352, 376.

761 Ahlbrecht/*Kirsch*, MN 1452.

762 To date, 17 victims have been awarded legal aid; *see* Report of the ICC to the UN, 22.08.2008, UN Doc. A/63/323, p 7.

763 Pre-Trial Chamber I seems to regard this as an essential right of victims; *see* ICC *Prosecutor v Lubanga*, PTC I, ICC-01/04-01/06, 22 September 2006, Decision on the Arrangements for Participation of Victims a/0001/06, a/0002/06 and a/0003/06 at the Confirmation Hearing, p 6.

(5) The victim's representative may, within the limits set by the Chamber's ruling on the extent of participation, generally attend and participate in hearings and at status conferences (*see* Rule 90 (2) RPE), that is, s/he is entitled to make oral and written submissions and may file motions.[764]

(6) Upon leave granted by the Chamber the victim may introduce evidence and challenge the admissibility and relevance of the parties' evidence.[765]

(7) Moreover, the victim's representative may also be permitted to question witnesses and/or the accused him or herself. Nonetheless, it must be borne in mind that such examinations remain under the strict control of the Chamber. Indeed, the Chamber may require the questions to be submitted in writing prior to the relevant session. Furthermore, the Chamber may direct that the court, on behalf of the victim's representative, put the questions to the witness or accused (Rule 91 (3) RPE).

The increased involvement and influence of victims and their lawyers poses a serious threat to the structure of defendants' rights.[766] In a system that generally leaves the presentation of evidence to the parties, procedural fairness is likely to suffer due to imbalances between the parties. Clearly, where an additional party is permitted to join the proceedings on the side of the prosecution, the equality of arms is distorted in favour of the prosecution and to the disadvantage of the accused.[767] Art. 66 (2) ICCSt demonstrates that the accused is only confronted with the Prosecutor as his 'adversary', whose role is to disprove the presumption of innocence.[768] Furthermore, delays in the proceedings are inevitable in cases where victims participate, not only because of the possible need for extra translations,[769] but also because the court faces a vast amount of further input in the form of motions, objections, opinions, etc.[770]

---

764 S Bock, 'Das Opfer vor dem internationalen Strafgerichtshof', 119 *ZStW* (2007) 664.

765 ICC *Prosecutor v Lubanga*, AC, ICC-01/04-01/06-1432-OA9OA10, 11 July 2008, Judgment on the Appeals of the Prosecutor and the Defence against Trial Chamber I's Decision on Victims' Participation of 18 January 2008, para 93. Judge Pikis dissented in this regards, *see* ibid, Partly Dissenting Opinion of Judge Pikis, para 19.

766 Regarding the status of defence counsel at the ICTY generally *see* Ahlbrecht/*Kirsch*, MN 1333–45 and for the ICC *see* MN 1446.

767 *See* S Zappalá, 'The Rights of Victims *v* the Rights of the Accused', 8 *JICJ* (2010) 137, 150.

768 ICC *Prosecutor v Lubanga*, AC, ICC-01/04-01/06-1432-OA9OA10-Anx, 11 July 2008, Judgment on the Appeals of the Prosecutor and the Defence against Trial Chamber I's Decision on Victims' Participation of 18 January 2008, Partially dissenting Opinion of Judge Philippe Kirsch, para 24.

769 Cf J Karton, 'Lost in Translation: International Criminal Tribunals and the Legal Implications of Interpreted Testimony', 41 *Vand J Transnat'l L* (2008) 1, 53, who points out that interpreters in the Nuremberg proceedings at the IMT faced far less difficulties than interpreters at the *ad hoc* tribunals or at the ICC.

770 *See* S Johnson, 'Neither Victims nor Executioners: The Dilemma of Victim Participation and the Defendant's Right to a Fair Trial at the International Criminal Court', 16 *ILSA J Int'l & Comp L* (2010) 489, 490, 495.

An additional problem can be seen in the fact that victims who are present throughout the entire proceedings may be tempted to finetune their testimony in order to secure a conviction. It has thus been argued that the victim who participates actively in the proceedings is barred from giving testimony in court.[771] The victim has to decide at some point which role s/he wants to play at trial. There are two options: (1) exercising the participatory rights as described above, or (2) participating as a witness. Both options, as has been suggested, exclude one another. The Trial Chamber in *Katanga and Chui* has not drawn such a strict line and has admitted testimony of a victim who participated in the proceedings, as long as 'the testimony of the victim can make a genuine contribution to the ascertainment of the truth'.[772] If testimony of a participating victim is allowed, the burden rests on the judge to evaluate the truthfulness and reliability of such a witness. It would be more reasonable to exclude the witness who participates as a victim from the witness box altogether.

The immanent conflict between victim participation and defendants' rights is why the Trial Chamber has and must retain strict control over victims' rights in that it evaluates the request of the victim to participate and how the participation would be consistent with the rights of the accused to a fair and expeditious trial.[773] The question of guilt or innocence should indeed be decided without prominent participation of the victim.[774]

---

[771] S Zappalá, 'The Rights of Victims *v* the Rights of the Accused', 8 *JICJ* (2010) 137, 151, pointing at the situation at the STL.

[772] *See* ICC *Prosecutor v Katanga and Chui*, TC II, 20, ICC-01/04-01/07-1665, 20 November 2009, Direction for the Conduct of the Proceedings and Testimony in Accordance with Rule 140, by Presiding Judge Bruno Cotte, para 47.

[773] *See* also Boas/Bischoff/Reid/Taylor, *ICL III*, 326 *et subs.*

[774] S Johnson, 'Neither Victims nor Executioners: The Dilemma of Victim Participation and the Defendant's Right to a Fair Trial at the International Criminal Court', 16 *ILSA J Int'l & Comp L* (2010) 489, 490.

9

APPEAL AND REVISION (*ALENA HARTWIG*)

A. Appeal

The Prosecutor, as well as the accused or convicted person, is entitled to different legal remedies against decisions of the Pre-Trial or Trial Chambers.

First and foremost, Arts 81, 82 ICCSt provide for the possibility to appeal a decision of the Court. Whereas Art. 81 ICCSt, together with Rules 150–152 RPE ICC, deal with appeals against a final judgment on both the question of guilt and the amount of punishment, Art. 82 ICCSt shaped by Rules 154–158 RPE ICC allows the appeal against 'other decisions', which is why these appeals are called 'OA' as in 'other appeal'. Art. 83 ICCSt contains directives for the proceedings on appeal. Considering that final judgments have not been issued so far, the possibility to appeal other decisions has been proven to be of a greater practical importance in the current appellate jurisprudence.

The possibility to apply for the revision of the final judgment of conviction or sentence is provided for in Art. 84 ICCSt.

The Statutes and Rules of Procedure and Evidence of the *ad hoc* Tribunals foresee a similar appeals scheme. Here too, the accused or convicted person and the Prosecutor are entitled to file an appeal against either a judgment of the Trial Chamber[1] or against other decisions of the Tribunals.[2]

Since the concept of an appeal is not defined in the Rome Statute, the nature of an appeal needs to be clarified before elaborating on the current appeals procedure in the Statute.

---

[1] Appeal against conviction, acquittal, or sentence.

[2] Whereas Rule 117 (1) RPE ICTR restricts the possibility of interlocutory appeals mainly to jurisdictional matters and provisional release, Rule 116*bis* (1) RPE ICTY also provides for appeals in procedural matters. *See* M Drumbl and K Gallant, 'Appeals in the *ad hoc* International Criminal Tribunals: Structure, Procedure, and Recent Cases', 3 *J App Prac & Process* (2001) 589, 613 *et subs.*

Basically, the establishment of the Appeals Chamber may not be seen as the expression of an intention to retrial.[3] The system of the different chambers is indeed hierarchical and the Appeals Chamber holds a supervisory role,[4] so that its conception is not that of a second Trial Chamber. A trial *de novo* is not intended by the appeal.[5] Besides the concept of appeals prevailing in national law,[6] the appeal has a solely corrective nature. More than once, the ICC Appeals Chamber has refused to abandon the corrective scope of the appeal by ruling on questions in the abstract.[7] Instead, the focus of the Appeals Chamber is in principle restricted to the submissions of the parties on the respective matter.

Nevertheless, with respect to the determinations concerning questions of law, the Appeals Chamber has extensive powers in order to form its own opinion. These powers follow from the wording of Art. 83 ICCSt. Thus, the Appeals Chamber is vested with all the powers of a Trial Chamber by virtue of Art. 83 (1) ICCSt, and even has the possibility to re-examine the case by calling evidence, Art. 83 (2) ICCSt.

The scope of appeal at the *ad hoc* Tribunals is understood to be restricted in the same manner as the approach to the appeals scheme of the ICC.[8]

I. The right to appeal

According to Art. 81, 82 ICCSt, the parties to the proceedings are entitled to file an appeal. In case of an appeal against a final judgment, both the Prosecutor and the convicted person are explicitly mentioned as being allowed to file appeals. In appeals against other decisions, the Prosecutor as well as the defence counsel on behalf of the suspect or the accused has a right to appeal. Furthermore, Art. 82 (4)

---

[3] ILC 1994 Draft Statute, p 127.

[4] H Friman, 'Interlocutory Appeals in the Early Practice of the International Criminal Court', in: C Stahn and G Sluiter (eds), *The Emerging Practice of the International Criminal Court* (Martinus Nijhoff Publishers 2009) 553, 554.

[5] Triffterer/*Staker*, Art. 81 MN 20; yet considering the depths of the review applied by the Appeals Chambers of the respective international courts and tribunals one often is reminded of a trial *de novo* as opined by W Schabas, *ICC* (OUP 2010) 934.

[6] M Fleming, 'Appellate Review in the International Criminal Tribunals', 37 *Texas International Law Journal* (2002), 111, 114, referring to the goals of appellate proceedings as creating a consistency of verdicts, development of law and the pursuit of justice in the individual case. *See* also L O'Neill and G Sluiter, 'The Right to Appeal a Judgment of the Extraordinary Chambers in the Courts of Cambodia', 10 *Melb J Int'l L* (2009) 596, 602 *et subs.*

[7] ICC *Situation in Darfur*, AC, ICC-02/05-138, 18 June 2008, Decision on Victim Participation in the Appeal of the Office of Public Counsel for the Defence against Pre-Trial Chamber I's Decision of 3 December 2007 and in the Appeals of the Prosecutor and the Office of Public Counsel for the Defence against Pre-Trial Chamber I's Decision of 6 December 2007, para 18 *et subs.* Compare B Batros, 'The Judgment on the *Katanga* Admissibility Appeal: Judicial Restraint at the ICC', 23 *LJIL* (2010) 343, 349 with further references.

[8] ICTY *Prosecutor v Blaškić*, AC, IT-95-14-A, 29 July 2004, Judgment, para 13 *et subs.*, and X Tracol, 'The Appeals Chambers of the International Criminal Tribunals', 12 *CLF* (2001) 137, 143 *et subs.*

ICCSt refers to the legal representative of the victims, who may, amongst others, appeal against a reparation order issued pursuant to Art. 75 ICCSt. Additionally, Art. 82 (2) ICCSt provides that the States concerned also have a right to appeal a decision of the Pre-Trial Chamber under Art. 57 (3) (d) ICCSt.

The right to appeal, at least for the convicted person, is an internationally recognized human right. Art. 14 (5) ICCPR clearly gives this right to the convict. Whereas the ECHR as another major human rights convention does not guarantee an express right to appeal to a convicted person, it is nevertheless recognized that the guarantees of Art. 6 (1) ECHR are applicable if national law provides for such a right, depending upon the nature of the particular proceedings.[9] This principle can be transferred to international criminal procedure, which means that in particular, the 'reasonable time' requirement and that of an independent and impartial tribunal constitute fundamental guarantees for the appellant.

In international criminal proceedings, the right to appeal was first recognized in the Statutes and Rules of Procedure and Evidence of the *ad hoc* Tribunals, representing a departure of the previous practice of Nuremberg and Tokyo.[10] At the IMT in Nuremberg the judgment was not reviewable according to Art. 26 IMTSt. The Control Council for Germany was empowered to reduce the sentence pursuant to Art. 29 IMTSt. Apart from Kaltenbrunner, Speer, and von Schirach, all other convicted Nazi criminals filed for pardon under Art. 29 IMTSt, which however was not granted.[11] A similar rule was inserted in Art. 17 IMTFESt, giving the power to alleviate the sentences to the Supreme Commander of the Allied Forces. Otherwise the judgment of the IMTFE was final.

II. Constitution of the Appeals Chambers

The Appeals Chamber of the ICC is currently composed of five judges, Art. 39 (2) (b) (i) ICCSt. The so-called 'Appeals Division' consists of the President, serving as one of the five judges, and four other judges, Art. 39 (1) ICCSt. The judges shall only serve in that division, Art. 39 (4) ICCSt, for their entire term of office, Art. 39 (3) (b) ICCSt. An exception is made only in case of necessity; that is, if a member of the Appeals Chamber is disqualified, or is unavailable for a substantial reason by virtue of Regulation 12 RegC. In that case the Presidency shall attach a judge to the Appeals Chamber from either the Trial or the Pre-Trial Division on a temporary basis, but only if this judge did not participate in the case at a previous stage.[12]

---

9 C Safferling, *Towards an International Criminal Procedure* (OUP 2003) 336.

10 *See* J Manning, 'On Power, Participation and Authority: The International Criminal Court's Initial Appellate Jurisprudence' 38 *Geo J Int'l L* (2007) 803, 806 *et subs.*

11 *See* W Harris, *Tyranny on Trial* (Southern Methodist University Press 1999) 463 *et subs.*

12 W Schabas, *ICC* (OUP 2010) 557.

This composition reflects a certain permanence and stability. Having said this, it must be considered that the Appeals Chamber is understood to be of a higher nature only in the hierarchical sense. Structurally speaking, the Appeals Chamber is composed of a balance of judges with similar competences as their colleagues in the Pre-Trial and Trial Chambers. This is due to the requirements stipulated in Art. 36 ICCSt, regarding the qualification, nomination, and election of all judges.

According to a report of the Secretary-General, the establishment of the ICTR, with the ICTY already existing at that time, mandated a certain 'organizational and institutional link' to be established between the two Tribunals.[13] This policy aimed at ensuring a consistent legal approach as well as 'economy and efficiency of resources'. For these reasons, the ICTY and the ICTR formally have their own Appeals Chamber. However, given the fact that the Chambers consist of the same judges, practically only one Appeals Chamber exists for both Tribunals.[14] The Appeals Chamber is composed of five permanent judges of the ICTY and two permanent judges of the ICTR.[15] Appeals are decided by a bench of five judges.

III. The appeal against a decision of acquittal or conviction or against sentence

According to Art. 81 ICCSt, either the convicted person or the Prosecutor may seek to appeal a final decision of the Court to a higher instance. Lacking an external superior revision, the appeal is directed to the Appeals Chamber of the International Criminal Court, which serves as the highest instance in the court structure.

The final decision of a Trial Chamber[16] may be appealed on the grounds listed in Art. 81 (1) ICCSt. The Prosecutor may lodge an appeal on the grounds of a procedural error, an error of fact, or an error of law, Art. 81 (1) (a) ICCSt. The convicted person, on the other hand, may *additionally* make an appeal on 'any other ground that affects the fairness or reliability of the proceedings or decision', Art. 81 (1) (b) ICCSt. The Prosecutor may only file an appeal on this ground on behalf of the convicted person.[17]

[13] Report of the Secretary-General Pursuant to Paragraph 5 of Security Council Resolution 955 (1994), UN Doc. S/1995/134, 13 February 1995, para 9.

[14] Art. 13 (4) ICTRSt.

[15] Art. 14 (2), (3) ICTYSt, Art. 13 (3) ICTRSt.

[16] The final judgment convicting or acquitting the accused is referred to by that article, even though the wording refers merely to 'a decision under article 74', *see* Triffterer/*Staker*, Art. 81 MN 7.

[17] The possibility of the Prosecutor filing an appeal on the person's behalf follows from the understanding of his/her role as objective. This is illustrated by several provisions in the Rome Statute. Hence, the Prosecutor is also obliged to safeguard the rights of the accused and, herewith, entitled to appeal if the person was convicted on an erroneous basis.

1. Grounds for appeal

The Statutes of the *ad hoc* Tribunals[18] provide for two grounds of appeal in Art. 25 ICTYSt, Art. 24 ICTRSt. A decision of the Court may be appealed against on the ground of (1) an error on a question of law invalidating the decision, or (2) an error of fact which has occasioned a miscarriage of justice. As a third, unwritten ground of appeal, the Appeals Chambers of the ICTY and the ICTR have acknowledged 'the exceptional situation where a party has raised a legal issue that is of general significance to the Tribunal's jurisprudence'.[19]

a. Procedural error According to Art. 81 (1) (a) (i), (b) (i) ICCSt, a decision may be appealed on the ground of a 'procedural error', amongst others. This category is a novelty in international criminal law, first being established in the Statute of the SCSL, Art. 20 SCSLSt. Still, this error is referred to infrequently, mainly due to the 'considerable overlap'[20] with the 'error of law' as another ground for appeal.

A procedural error occurs when: (1) a Chamber does not comply with mandatory procedural requirements of the Statute and Rules of Procedure and Evidence, or (2) when a Chamber erroneously exercises its discretion.[21] This definition illustrates the difficulties already arising in distinction to an error of law, which can also involve procedural issues.

Errors within the first category of non-compliance with mandatory procedural requirements, such as a violation of the rights of the accused, do not necessarily lead to the invalidity of the decision.[22] The question is whether the appellant suffered from prejudice.[23] The appeal succeeds if the procedural error 'materially affected' the final decision Art. 83 (2) ICCSt, or in the words of the Appeals Chamber of the SCSL 'vitiates the proceedings'.[24]

It is furthermore suggested that the 'responsibility gap' regarding the searching for the truth, which was identified before,[25] is filled by accepting a procedural error in case the Trial Chamber did not properly comply with its obligation to request all the evidence necessary for establishing the truth. This is the case in particular if the Chamber did not meet the request of the defence to hear further evidence.

---

18 For the appeals scheme of the ECCC as a hybrid tribunal compare L O'Neill and G Sluiter, 'The Right to Appeal a Judgment of the Extraordinary Chambers in the Courts of Cambodia', 10 *Melb J Int'l L* (2009) 596, 609 *et subs.*

19 M Drumbl and K Gallant, 'Appeals in the Ad Hoc International Criminal Tribunals: Structure, Procedure, and Recent Cases', 3 *J App Prac & Process* (2001) 589, 618 *et subs.*; X Tracol, 'The Appeals Chambers of the International Criminal Tribunals' 12 *CLF* (2001), 137, 144 *et subs.*

20 Triffterer/*Staker*, Art. 81 MN 26.

21 Ibid Art. 81 MN 24 *et subs.*

22 *See* Boas/Bischoff/Reid/Taylor, *ICL III*, 446 *et subs.*

23 Triffterer/*Staker*, Art. 81 MN 24.

24 SCSL *CDF Case*, AC, SCSL-04-14-A, 28 May 2008, Judgment, para 35.

25 *See* Chapter 8, p 435.

If such a failure is found to have 'materially affected' the final decision, the appeal will succeed.

In relation to the second category of procedural errors—the exercise of discretion— the Appeals Chamber does not review whether the decision, that is, the outcome of the exercise of discretion, was correct. Rather, the issue is whether the deciding chamber exercised its discretion in a proper manner. The test applied to this determination has been expressed as examining whether (1) the exercise of discretion is based on an erroneous interpretation of the law, (2) the discretion is exercised on patently incorrect conclusion of fact, or (3) the decision is so unfair and unreasonable as to constitute an abuse of discretion.[26] Here too, the Appeals Chamber has held that it would not interfere with a decision of the Trial Chamber unless the error in question materially affected the decision.[27]

b. Error of fact An error of fact as a second ground of appeal occurs when a chamber errs in the factual findings that it makes on the evidence before it. As to the applicable standard of review, the appraisal of the relevant evidence lies with the Pre-Trial or Trial Chamber. That means the Appeals Chamber does not review the evidence anew, but rather determines whether a *reasonable* chamber could have been satisfied beyond reasonable doubt of the issue in question.[28] In cases of an error of fact, the Chamber's decision is characterized by unreasonableness as to the conclusions drawn from the facts and evidence presented before it.[29]

The Appeals Chamber may interfere if the respective Chamber does not appreciate the facts on which its decision is found, disregards relevant facts or takes into account facts extraneous to the *sub judice* issues.[30] Based on the circumstance that the Chamber of first instance appraises the evidence, the scope of an error of fact is to be extended to the situation when this Chamber misapprehends the evidence, draws unreasonable conclusion from such evidence or reaches factual conclusions from evidence that would not have been accepted by a reasonable Chamber.[31]

---

[26] ICC *Prosecutor v Kony et al.*, AC, ICC-02/04-01/05-408, 16 September 2009, Judgment on the Appeal of the Defence against the 'Decision on the Admissibility of the Case under Article 19 (1) of the Statute' of 10 March 2009, para 80. For further references compare Triffterer/*Staker*, Art. 81 MN 25.

[27] Ibid.

[28] SCSL *CDF Case*, AC, SCSL-04-14-A, 28 May 2008, Judgment, para 35; ICTY *Prosecutor v Dragomir Milošević*, AC, IT-98-29/1-A, 12 November 2009, Judgment, para 15; *see* also Triffterer/*Staker*, Art. 81 MN 29.

[29] *See* Boas/Bischoff/Reid/Taylor, *ICL III*, 444.

[30] ICC *Prosecutor v Bemba*, AC, ICC-01/05-01/08-962, 19 October 2010, Judgment on the Appeal of Mr Jean-Pierre Bemba Gombo against the Decision of Trial Chamber III of 24 June 2010 entitled 'Decision on the Admissibility and Abuse of Process Challenges', para 63 with further references.

[31] With regard to the jurisprudence of the *ad hoc* Tribunals, the standard to be applied is also that of 'reasonableness'. ICTY *Prosecutor v Blaškić*, AC, IT-95-14-A, 29 July 2004, Judgment, para 16.

c. Error of law As a third ground of appeal, Art. 81 (1) ICCSt lists the error of law. An error of law occurs when a Chamber's decision is based on an incorrect interpretation of the governing law. This includes the application of the wrong legal standard.[32] In questions of law, there is no discretion for the Trial Chamber involved; one could thus say that the Appeals Chamber reviews claims alleging an error of law *de novo*.[33] The Appeals Chamber will certainly overrule the Trial Chamber decision only if the error invalidates the decision.[34]

From this definition, the difficulty to differentiate the error of law from a procedural error becomes evident. An error of law could easily relate to a wrong interpretation of procedural law or, for example, to a misconception regarding the scope of the rights of the accused. In order not to make the category of the procedural error superfluous, the error of law may only be applied as long as formal violations of the Statute or the Rules of Procedure and Evidence are not concerned.[35]

d. Any other ground that affects the fairness or reliability of the proceedings or decision Additionally, the convicted person, or the Prosecutor on that person's behalf, is entitled to an appeal on 'any other ground that affects the fairness or reliability of the proceedings or decision', Art. 81 (1) (b) (iv) ICCSt. The wording of this ground of appeal is rather vague and unspecified. It is assumed that the intention pursued with the additional ground for appeal was to create 'a "catch-all" provision'[36] in order not to unduly limit the grounds for an appeal.[37]

Here, too, it is difficult to point out the difference in relation to procedural errors. *Roth* and *Henzelin* propose that procedural errors should refer to formal violations whilst the ground of appeal under Art. 81 (1) (b) (iv) ICCSt includes violations of a substantive nature.[38]

Considering that under Art. 81 (1) (b) ICCSt only the convicted person, or the Prosecutor on that person's behalf, may file the appeal, it becomes evident that this additional ground of appeal serves the purpose of a 'catch-all' provision in order to secure the right of the convicted person to appeal in almost any case.

32 ICC *Prosecutor v Al Bashir*, AC, ICC-02/05-01/09-73, 3 February 2010, Judgment on the Appeal of the Prosecutor against the 'Decision on the Prosecution's Application for a Warrant of Arrest against Omar Hassan Ahmad Al Bashir', paras 39, 41.

33 *See* Boas/Bischoff/Reid/Taylor, *ICL III*, 443.

34 This is the wording of Art. 25 (1) (a) ICTYSt. *See* also W Schabas, *ICC* (OUP 2010) 934, who rightly argues that this standard is to be applied by the ICC as well.

35 *See* Cassese/Gaeta/Jones/*Roth and Henzlin*, 1544.

36 Triffterer/*Staker*, Art. 81 MN 37.

37 Cassese/Gaeta/Jones/*Roth and Henzlin*, 1544.

38 Ibid.

2. Appeal against sentence or conviction only

Two scenarios must be kept apart as regards Art. 81 (2) ICCSt concerning the review of the sentence: Art. 81 (2) (c) ICCSt provides that the Appeals Chamber may extend the subject matter of the appeal at its own discretion under certain circumstances, distinguishing between decisions concerning the conviction (Art. 74 ICCSt) and the sentence (Art. 76 ICCSt).

Art. 81 (2) (a), (b) ICCSt refers to an *appeal against a sentence only*. As to the ground for appeal against sentence, Art. 81 (2) (a) ICCSt determines the disproportion between the crime and the sentence. 'Disproportionality' of the sentence as the parameter for reviewing the sentencing decision gives a rather wide trigger to either the Prosecutor or the convict. At the *ad hoc* Tribunals the standard was that of a 'discernible error' in exercising the discretion.[39] It remains to be seen whether the ICC Appeals judges will use this norm to develop its own concept of sentencing.[40]

According to Art. 81 (2) (b) ICCSt, the Appeals Chamber may invite the Prosecutor or the convicted person to submit grounds for appeal under Art. 81 (1) ICCSt if it is convinced that the appeal against the sentence might also have an impact on the conviction. This means that even if the Appeals Chamber is only called to rule on the possible disproportion between crime and sentence criticized by the appellant, it may decide *proprio motu* to extend the appeal to the conviction if this latter decision is considered to be affected in the course of the Appeals Chamber's findings. For the purpose of reviewing the decision on conviction, as a matter of discretion, the Appeals Chamber may invite the Prosecutor and the convicted person to additionally submit grounds for appeal under Art. 81 (1) ICCSt.

The same applies to the opposite case: if the Appeals Chamber, in an appeal *against conviction only*, considers that the decision concerning the sentence (Art. 76 ICCSt) might be affected by the determination of the Appeals Chamber, the Prosecutor and the convicted person are invited to submit observations on a possible disproportion between crime and sentence, Art. 81 (2) (c) ICCSt.

3. Procedure

The procedure for an appeal pursuant to Art. 81 ICCSt is governed by Art. 83 ICCSt and Rules 150–153 RPE ICC.

Rule 150 RPE ICC contains the formal requirements of an appeal against a final decision of the Trial Chamber. According to Rule 150 (1) RPE ICC, the appeal must be filed within thirty days from the date on which the party seeking to file

[39] *See* eg, ICTY *Prosecutor v Blaskic*, AC, IT-95-14-A, 29 July 2004, Judgment, para 680; *Prosecutor v Kristic*, AC, IT-98-33-A, 19 April 2004, Judgment, para 242; ICTR *Prosecutor v Serushago*, AC, ICTR-98-39-A, 4 April 2000, Decision, para 32.

[40] *See* also W Schabas, *ICC* (OUP 2010) 935.

the appeal is notified of the decision. Contrary to the wording of Art. 81 ICCSt, Rule 150 (1) RPE ICC also refers to appeals against reparation orders issued in accordance with Art. 75 ICCSt. The possibility to lodge an appeal against a reparation order is foreseen in Art. 82 (4) ICCSt. This being the exception, Rules 150–153 RPE ICC merely refer to appeals under Art. 81 ICCSt. Rule 150 (2) RPE ICC stipulates that the time period of thirty days may be extended by the Appeals Chamber upon the application of the party seeking appeal. The appeal must be filed with the Registrar, Rule 150 (3) RPE ICC. In the case of non-compliance with these formal conditions, the judgment of the Trial Chamber shall become final, Rule 150 (4) RPE ICC.

The content of the appeal document that Rule 150 RPE ICC refers to is further specified in Regulation 57 RegC. According to this provision, the so-called 'notice of appeal'—that is, the appeal referred to in Rule 150 RPE ICC—shall contain certain minimum information, namely the name and number of the case, the date of the final decision, the subject matter of the appeal and the relief sought.

Once the appeal is filed with the Registrar, s/he transmits the trial record to the Appeals Chamber according to Rule 151 (1) RPE ICC. The Registrar also notifies the other parties that an appeal has been filed, Rule 151 (2) RPE ICC.

After submitting the appeal within the time frame of Rule 150 RPE ICC, the appellant shall furthermore produce a 'document in support of the appeal'. The formal requirements this document must fulfil are laid down in Regulation 58 RegC. Whereas Regulation 58 (1) RegC provides the appellant with a time period of ninety days from the notification of the respective decision, Regulation 58 (2)–(4) RegC elaborate on the content and structure of the document in support of the appeal. Finally, Regulation 58 (5) RegC sets a page limit of 100 pages. Experience at the *ad hoc* Tribunals shows that the Appeals Chamber will become more aggressive as the judges grow busier and dismiss claims on the ground of deficient submission.[41]

According to Regulation 59 (1) RegC, the participants in the proceedings before the Trial Chamber are entitled to file a response. Whilst an appeal can only be filed by a 'party' of the proceedings—that is, the Prosecutor or the defence—the 'participants' in the proceedings have the possibility to respond to this appeal, including the legal representative of the victims. This response must be filed within sixty days from the notification of the document in support of the appeal. Specifications as to the content and structure are given in Regulation 59 (1) (a)–(c) RegC.

The appellant may file a reply to this response if the Appeals Chamber considers this to be necessary in the interests of justice, Regulation 60 RegC.

41 *See* Boas/Bischoff/Reid/Taylor, *ICL III*, 449.

Rule 152 RPE ICC provides for the possibility of discontinuance of the appeal proceeding. If no such notice of discontinuance has been filed with the Registrar, the Appeals Chamber renders a judgment in accordance with Art. 83 ICCSt.

As for the judgment of the Appeals Chamber, Art. 83 (2) ICCSt is of particular importance. Under certain prerequisites, the Appeals Chamber may either (1) reverse or amend the decision or sentence issued by the Trial Chamber, or (2) it may order a new trial before a different Trial Chamber.[42] As a condition, the Appeals Chamber must come to the conclusion that the proceedings were unfair in a way that affected the reliability of the decision or sentence, or the Appeals Chamber must find that the decision or sentence was materially affected by a specific error mentioned in Art. 81 (1) (a) ICCSt. According to the intention of the ILC, the error has to be a 'significant element' in the respective decision.[43]

Hence, the Appeals Chamber is empowered to overturn every final decision of the Trial Chamber under the given requirements.[44]

According to Art. 25 (2) ICTYSt, Art. 24 (2) ICTRSt, the Appeals Chamber of the Tribunals may also 'affirm, reverse, or revise' the decisions of the Trial Chambers. Additionally, the Rules of Procedure and Evidence provide the Appeals Chamber with the ability to remand for retrial after conviction or acquittal by a Trial Chamber.[45] For the purpose of retrial, evidence not presented at the initial proceedings before the Trial Chamber may be admitted. The Appeals Chamber may restrict the scope of a retrial, but must say so explicitly.[46]

In order to determine whether the proceedings suffer from an error and whether this error affected the decision or sentence, the Appeals Chamber may itself call evidence on this issue. For this purpose, Art. 83 (1) ICCSt provides the Appeals Chamber with the powers of the Trial Chamber. Rule 149 RPE ICC further specifies the applicability of trial provisions to proceedings before the Appeals Chamber. Art. 83 (2) ICCSt also clarifies that in case of an appeal filed by the convicted person, or by the Prosecutor on the convicted person's behalf, the decision of the

---

[42] *See* also W Schabas, *ICC* (OUP 2010) 952.

[43] ILC 1994 Draft Statute, p 61.

[44] In this point the Rome Statute goes beyond what was proposed by the ILC. Eg, the ILC 1994 Draft Statute did not provide the Appeals Chamber with the power to reverse a decision to acquit the accused. According to this proposal, the Appeals Chamber could only order for a retrial, *see* ILC 1994 Draft Statute, p 126.

[45] Rule 117 (C) RPE ICTY, Rule 118 (C) RPE ICTR. *See* also ICTR *Prosecutor v Muvunyi*, AC, ICTR-00-55, 29 August 2008, Judgment (prior conviction by Trial Chamber), and ICTY *Prosecutor v Haradinaj*, AC, IT-04-84*bis* AR73.1, 31 May 2011, Decision on Haradinaj's Appeal on Scope of Partial Retrial (prior acquittal by Trial Chamber).

[46] ICTY *Prosecutor v Haradinaj*, AC, IT-04-84*bis*-AR73.1, 31 May 2011, Decision on Haradinaj's Appeal on Scope of Partial Retrial, para 22.

Trial Chamber cannot be amended to that person's detriment, expressly declaring a prohibition of a *reformatio in peius*.[47]

In case of an appeal according to Art. 81 (2) (a) ICCSt, the Appeals Chamber may amend the sentence if it is convinced that the sentence is disproportionate to the crime, Art. 83 (3) ICCSt.

Pursuant to Art. 83 (4) ICCSt, the Appeals Chamber shall take its judgment by a majority of the judges. However, a judge may issue a separate or dissenting opinion on a question of law. The judgment must be delivered in open court, but as Art. 83 (5) ICCSt expressly states, it may do so in the absence of the convicted or acquitted person.

4. Detention pending trial

Art. 81 (3) ICCSt is directed at the question of custody of the convicted person in case of an appeal. As a general principle, Art. 81 (3) (a) ICCSt clarifies that a convicted person shall remain in custody pending appeal. As an exception to this, that person shall be released if the time spent in custody already exceeds the sentence of imprisonment imposed, Art. 81 (3) (b) ICCSt. On the other hand, if the Prosecutor has also filed an appeal and therefore the Trial Chamber's verdict can be amended to the detriment of the accused, the release of the person is subject to specific conditions.

These conditions are listed in Art. 81 (3) (c) (i) ICCSt. The criteria are similar to those essential for the determination of the justification of ongoing detention.[48] In principle, the Trial Chamber may maintain the detention of the person under exceptional circumstances, having regard to the risk of flight, the seriousness of the offence, and the probability of success of the appeal. This means the following: (1) the jurisdiction on this question rests with the Trial Chamber, (2) the Trial Chamber is entitled to discretion ('*may*'), and (3) the wording is evident as to the exceptional character of ongoing detention. The criteria that must be considered are especially linked to the successful enforcement of a sentence. Art. 81 (3) (c) (i) ICCSt is genuinely governing the situation of an acquittal of the accused. In this case he or she shall be released immediately, unless the Prosecutor requests the further detention and the Trial Chamber concurs in that the detention must be upheld for the reasons set out in Art. 81 (3) (c) (i) ICCSt. If the Trial Chamber orders the ongoing detention of the acquitted, s/he has a right to appeal this decision according to Art. 81 (3) (c) (ii) ICCSt. Rule 154 (1) RPE ICC provides for a time limit of five days beginning with the notification of the relevant decision. Apart from that, Rule 154 (3) RPE ICC refers to the principles laid down in Rule 150 RPE ICC.

[47] *See* C Safferling, *Towards an International Criminal Procedure* (OUP 2003) 334.

[48] *See* Chapter 6, p 300.

IV. Appeal against other decisions

Besides the possibility to file an appeal against final decisions of the Trial Chambers, Art. 82 ICCSt provides for an appeal against 'other decisions'. This possibility to place an 'interlocutory appeal' has been acknowledged by all international criminal tribunals, and has proven to be of great practical significance.[49]

The 'other decisions' Art. 82 ICCSt refers to, are decisions of an interim nature. Art. 82 ICCSt presents an exhaustive list of those decisions which may be appealed against. Interlocutory appeals—that is, appeals against decisions other than final decisions—with respect to jurisdiction, admissibility, detention, and the question of the Pre-Trial Chamber acting on its own initiative, do not require the leave of a Pre-Trial or Trial Chamber.[50] On the contrary, Rule 155 RPE ICC specifies the appeals that require the leave of the Court to the appealable decisions under Art. 82 (1) (d), (2) ICCSt. These are, namely, decisions against which an appeal would ensure the expeditious conduct of the trial, or an appeal against a decision of the Pre-Trial Chamber pursuant to Art. 57 (3) (d) ICCSt.

As to the errors on which the impugned decision may be appealed, it is recognized that the categories of errors listed in Art. 81 (1) (a) ICCSt apply within the scope of Art. 82 ICCSt.[51] This holds also true for the interpretation of the different types of errors.

The Statutes of the *ad hoc* Tribunals do not provide for the possibility of interlocutory appeals. Nonetheless, these are allowed for by the Rules of Procedure and Evidence of both Tribunals. Whilst Rule 72 RPE ICTY/ICTR is concerned with 'Preliminary Motions', Rule 73 RPE ICTY/ICTR includes regulations on ('Other') 'Motions'. The difference between the two provisions is indicated by the fact that Rule 72 RPE ICTY/ICTR is applicable to objections prior to trial ('Preliminary'), mainly with respect to jurisdiction or the form of the indictment. Hence, these are motions which need to be dealt with before the beginning of the proceedings.[52] Rule 72 (A) RPE ICTY/ICTR explicitly lists those challenges, which after a decision of the Trial Chamber may be subject to appeal. Basically, Rule 72 (B) RPE ICTY/ICTR stipulates that decisions on preliminary motions 'are without interlocutory appeal'. Thereafter, sub-paragraphs (i) and (ii) refer to

[49] *See* Boas/Bischoff/Reid/Taylor, *ICL III*, 435.

[50] Art. 82 (1) (a)–(c) ICCSt.

[51] ICC *Prosecutor v Lubanga*, AC, ICC-01/04-01/06-568 OA3, 13 October 2006, Judgment on the Prosecutor's Appeal against the Decision of Pre-Trial Chamber I entitled 'Decision Establishing General Principles Governing Applications to Restrict Disclosure Pursuant to Rule 81 (2) and (4) of the Rules of Procedure and Evidence', para 19; *Prosecutor v Bemba*, AC, ICC-01/05-01/08-962 OA3, 19 October 2010, Judgment on the Appeal of Mr Jean-Pierre Bemba Gombo against the Decision of Trial Chamber III of 24 June 2010 entitled 'Decision on the Admissibility and Abuse of Process Challenges', para 63.

[52] J Hocking, 'Interlocutory Appeals before the ICTY', in: R May *et al.* (eds), *Essays on ICTY Procedure and Evidence in Honour of Gabrielle Kirk McDonald* (Kluwer 2001) 459, 460.

the possibility of interlocutory appeals by way of exception. According to Rule 72 (B) (i) RPE ICTY/ICTR, a motion challenging jurisdiction may be appealed as of right.[53] In contrast, interlocutory appeals with respect to 'other cases' require the leave of the Trial Chamber. Here, the wording of Rule 72 (B) (ii) RPE ICTY/ICTR stipulates the same requirements for certification as Art. 82 (1) (d) ICCSt.

Rule 73 RPE ICTY/ICTR is directed at motions after the beginning of the trial.[54] After the Trial Chamber's decision on the motion of a party, that decision may only be subject to an interlocutory appeal with the leave of the Trial Chamber, Rule 73 (B) RPE ICTY/ICTR. Here too, the conditions for certification are the same as spelled out in Art. 82 (1) (d) ICCSt.[55]

In addition to Rule 72, 73 RPE ICTY/ICTR, separate possibilities of appeal are provided for in Rules 54*bis* (C), 65 (D), 77 (J), 108*bis* RPE ICTY, or respectively Rules 65 (D), 77 (J), 91 (I) RPE ICTR.

1. Grounds of appeal that do not require leave

a. Decisions with respect to jurisdiction or admissibility According to Art. 82 (1) (a) ICCSt, either party—that is, the Prosecutor and the Defence—may appeal a decision concerning questions of jurisdiction or admissibility. It is presumed that the reference to jurisdiction and admissibility encompasses decisions issued in accordance with Part 2 of the Rome Statute, including issues related to Art. 21 ICCSt.[56]

Primarily, the suspect or accused, the State concerned, or the Prosecutor[57] may appeal a decision that the Pre-Trial or Trial Chamber issued on the basis of a challenge to jurisdiction or admissibility under Art. 19 (6) ICCSt. In this particular case, the jurisdiction of the Appeals Chamber to rule on the issue is clear, as Art. 19 (6) ICCSt contains an explicit reference to Art. 82 ICCSt. The same holds true for Art. 18 (4) ICCSt, also referring explicitly to the possibility of an appeal. The appealable decision under Art. 18 ICCSt consists in the decision of the Pre-Trial Chamber to defer a situation to the requesting state. Art. 19 (6) ICCSt, on the contrary, elaborates on the right of the above-mentioned person or institution to seek a decision of the respective chamber, challenging the admissibility of a case or the jurisdiction of the Court.

---

[53] See Boas/Bischoff/Reid/Taylor, *ICL III*, 435 *et subs.*

[54] Rule 73 (A) RPE ICTR refers to the 'initial appearance of the accused', whilst Rule 73 (A) RPE ICTY speaks of the assignment of a case to a Trial Chamber.

[55] The Rules of both the ICTY and the ICTR on interlocutory appeals and their certification by the Trial Chamber have been amended and articulated similar to Art. 82 (1) (d) ICCSt in 2001 and 2003, respectively.

[56] Triffterer/*Staker*, Art. 82 MN 7.

[57] *See* Art. 19 (2), (3) ICCSt.

As to matters of jurisdiction on appeal, particular reference shall be made to a decision of the Appeals Chamber in *Lubanga*.[58] There, the Chamber elaborated upon the ambit of the concept of jurisdiction under the Rome Statute. First, it held that basically the concept of jurisdiction consisted of four different facets: *ratione materiae*, *ratione personae*, *ratione loci*, and *ratione temporis*.[59] Issues relating to one of these aspects can therefore clearly be considered as jurisdictional matters in the terms of Art. 82 (1) (a) ICCSt. But beyond that, the Appeals Chamber held that it acknowledged applications *sui generis* as atypical motions under certain circumstances. As was the case in *Lubanga*, the Defence challenged the jurisdiction of the Court on the basis of abuse of process and violation of the fundamental rights of the accused. Here, the Appeals Chamber clarified that in the terms of Art. 21 (3) ICCSt, the deprivation of fundamental fair trial guarantees may outweigh the interest of the world community in the conduct of the trial and thus may proceed to discontinue the proceedings.[60] Hence, besides the challenge to one of the basic facets of jurisdiction, the Appeals Chamber acknowledged that questions relating to Art. 21 (3) ICCSt may also affect the jurisdiction of the Court if the proceedings are not consistent with internationally recognized human rights.[61]

Here, the ICC adopted an approach similar to the one established in an early decision of the ICTY. In the case against *Duško Tadić*, the Appeals Chamber found that a challenge to the legality of the creation of the Tribunal related to the question of jurisdiction, hereby acknowledging an appeal as of right under Rule 72 (B) (i) ICTY-RPE. The Chamber held that a narrow concept of jurisdiction was not warranted in international criminal law due to the lack of centralized structures.[62] The challenge as to the invalidity of the constitution of the Tribunal was seen as going to the 'very essence of jurisdiction',[63] contradicting the view of the Prosecutor.

The Rules have since been amended, now including Rule 72 (D) RPE ICTY/ICTR. This sub-paragraph contains a clear restriction as to the meaning of jurisdiction for interlocutory appeals.

---

[58] ICC, *Prosecutor v Lubanga*, AC, ICC-01/04-01/06-772 (OA4), 14 December 2006, Judgment on the Appeal of Mr Thomas Lubanga Dyilo against the Decision on the Defence Challenge to the Jurisdiction of the Court Pursuant to Article 19 (2) (a) of the Statute of 3 October 2006.

[59] Ibid, para 21. *See* also Chapter 2.

[60] Ibid, para 36 *et subs*. This was not the case in *Lubanga*, though. The alleged violations of fundamental human rights were not confirmed on appeal.

[61] *See* also F Eckelmans, 'The First Jurisprudence of the Appeals Chamber of the ICC' in: C Stahn and G Sluiter (eds), *The Emerging Practice of the International Criminal Court* (Martinus Nijhoff Publishers 2009) 527, 533.

[62] ICTY *Prosecutor v Tadić*, AC, IT-94-1, 2 October 1995, Decision on the Defence Motion for Interlocutory Appeal on Jurisdiction, para 11.

[63] Ibid, para 12.

As regards appeals relating to the second ground of appeal under Art. 82 (1) (a) ICCSt, the purpose is 'to determine whether or not a case is *admissible*'.[64] This determination must be made on the basis of the factual situation of the proceedings at the time of the admissibility challenge.[65]

The Appeals Chamber in *Katanga and Ngudjolo Chui* held that, as a prerequisite, the error raised by the appellant must have materially affected the impugned decision.[66] By stating this, the Appeals Chamber adopts the standard of Art. 83 (2) ICCSt, contradicting a previous ruling[67] where it held that this provision could not be applied to 'other appeals' pursuant to Art. 82 ICCSt.

b. Decisions granting or denying release Under Art. 82 (1) (b) ICCSt, a decision denying or granting release of the suspect or accused can be subjected to an appeal by either the Prosecutor or the person concerned. The Appeals Chamber has dealt with questions relating to interim release on numerous occasions. The 'decision' referred to in Art. 82 (1) (b) ICCSt relates to decisions issued in accordance with Art. 60 ICCSt.

The Appeals Chamber has elaborated on important material and procedural issues concerning interim release throughout many judgments over the past few years. Problems arising in the context of Art. 60 ICCSt, such as the relationship between the different sub-paragraphs[68] or their requirements,[69] have been dealt

[64] ICC *Prosecutor v Katanga and Chui*, AC, ICC-01/04-01/07-1497 OA8, 25 September 2009, Judgment on the Appeal of Mr Germain Katanga against the Oral Decision of Trial Chamber II of 12 June 2009 on the Admissibility of the Case, para 56. On this first ruling on a challenge to admissibility *see* also B Batros, 'The Judgment on the *Katanga* Admissibility Appeal: Judicial Restraint at the ICC' 23 *LJIL* (2010) 343.

[65] ICC *Prosecutor v Katanga and Chui*, ibid, para 56.

[66] Ibid, para 37. *See* also ICC *Prosecutor v Lubanga*, AC, ICC-01/04-01/06-1487 OA12, 21 October 2008, Judgment on the Appeal of the Prosecutor against the Decision of Trial Chamber I entitled 'Decision on the Release of Thomas Lubanga Dyilo', para 44.

[67] ICC *Prosecutor v Lubanga*, AC, ICC-01/04-01/06-568 OA3, 13 October 2006, Judgment on the Prosecutor's Appeal against the Decision of Pre-Trial Chamber I entitled 'Decision Establishing General Principles Governing Applications to Restrict Disclosure Pursuant to Rule 81 (2) and (4) of the Rules of Procedure and Evidence', para 12 *et subs.*

[68] ICC *Prosecutor v Lubanga*, AC, ICC-01/04-01/06-824 OA7, 13 February 2007, Judgment on the Appeal of Mr Thomas Lubanga Dyilo against the Decision of Pre-Trial Chamber I entitled 'Décision sur la demande de mise en líberté provisoire de Thomas Lubanga Dyilo'; *Prosecutor v Katanga and Chui*, AC, ICC-01/04-01/07-572 OA4, 9 June 2008, Judgment in the Appeal by Mathieu Ngudjolo Chui of 27 March 2008 against the Decision of Pre-Trial Chamber I on the Application of the Appellant for Interim Release.

[69] ICC *Prosecutor v Bemba*, AC, ICC-01/05-01/08-323 OA1, 16 December 2008, Judgment on the Appeal of Mr Jean-Pierre Bemba Gombo against the Decision of Pre-Trial Chamber III entitled 'Decision on application for Interim Release'; AC, ICC-01/05-01/08-1019 OA4, Judgment on the Appeal of Mr Jean-Pierre Bemba Gombo against the Decision of Trial Chamber IIII of 28 July 2010 entitled 'Decision on the Review of the Detention of Mr Jean-Pierre Bemba Gombo Pursuant to Rule 118 (2) of the Rules of Procedure and Evidence'.

with in particular. Beyond these, the question of interim release as a possible consequence of a (conditional) stay of proceedings gained importance in the trial against *Lubanga*.[70] In relation to decisions of the Pre-Trial or Trial Chambers ordering the release of the accused, requests of the Prosecutor for suspensive effect have been made in accordance with Art. 82 (3) ICCSt and Rule 156 (5) RPE ICC.

At the *ad hoc* Tribunals, Rule 65 (D) RPE ICTY/ICTR provides a separate procedure for applications for provisional release. The following sub-paragraphs relate to further questions as to, for example, the possibility to request the stay of a decision to release an accused or the custody of convicted persons.

c. Decisions of the Pre-Trial Chamber pursuant to Art. 56 (3) ICCSt According to Art. 82 (1) (c) ICCSt, a decision of the Pre-Trial Chamber to act on its own initiative under Art. 56 (3) ICCSt may be subject to appeal. Strangely, the right to appeal this decision is provided for twice by the Rome Statute, since Art. 56 (3) (b) ICCSt also foresees the possibility of an appeal. Whilst the chapeau of Art. 82 (1) ICCSt refers to 'either party' as possible appellants, Art. 56 (3) (b) ICCSt only speaks of the Prosecutor. However, considering the purpose of this provision as providing the Pre-Trial Chamber with the power to preserve evidence 'that it deems would be essential for the defence at trial', the restriction to the Prosecutor as the institution entitled to appeal seems plausible.[71]

2. Grounds of appeal that require leave of the Court

Rule 155 RPE ICC refers to appeals against decisions under Art. 82 (1) (d), (2) ICCSt as requiring leave of the Court.

a. Appeals pursuant to Art. 82 (1) (d) ICCSt This last sub-paragraph of Art. 82 (1) ICCSt is designed as a 'catch-all' provision—however, subjected to certain conditions—for issues not included in the foregoing paragraphs. Whilst the ambit of the other possibilities to file interlocutory appeals is expressly mentioned, this provision is intended to apply to any type of interlocutory decision. Nonetheless,

[70] In the case of *Lubanga*, Trial Chamber I ordered the release of Thomas Lubanga due to a conditional stay of the proceedings. The Appeals Chamber reversed the decision, holding that the release of the accused was not the inevitable consequence of such a stay. ICC *Prosecutor v Lubanga*, AC, ICC-01/04-01/06-1487 OA12, 21 October 2008, Judgment on the Appeal of the Prosecutor against the Decision of Trial Chamber I entitled 'Decision on the Release of Thomas Lubanga Dyilo'.

[71] A different view is taken by W Schabas, *ICC* (OUP 2010) 694, who suggests that the defence should be given the same rights as the Prosecutor. This opinion however is based on the assumption that Art. 56 ICCSt aims also at the protection of defence rights. This in our opinion is not the case, *see* C Safferling, 'The Rights and Interests of the Defence in the Pre-Trial Phase', 9 *JICJ* (2011) 651, 660.

in order to restrict the scope of application, Art. 82 (1) (d) ICCSt stipulates that certain requirements must be fulfilled.

As a procedural prerequisite, appeals under Art. 82 (1) (d) ICCSt require leave of the chamber which rendered the impugned decision. Prior to elaborating on the aforementioned substantive requirements, attention must be drawn to an early decision of Pre-Trial Chamber II in the *Situation of Uganda*. Here, the Pre-Trial Chamber held that

> any determination of the Prosecutor's application for leave to appeal must be guided by three principles, namely: (i) the restrictive character of the remedy provided for in article 82, paragraph 1 (d), of the Statute; (ii) the need for the applicant to satisfy the Chamber as to the existence of the specific requirements stipulated by this provision; and (iii) the irrelevance of or non-necessity at this stage of the Chamber to address arguments relating to the merit or substance of the appeal.[72]

With the determination of these principles, Pre-Trial Chamber II provided guidance for subsequent decisions on this matter as to the interpretation of this provision. Accordingly, it considered Art. 82 (1) (d) ICCSt as designed to be accessible only under 'limited and very specific circumstances'.[73]

The Rules of Procedure and Evidence at the *ad hoc* Tribunals provide for the possibility of interlocutory appeals under the same requirements as the Rome Statute. However, the respective provision of Rule 73 (B) RPE ICTY/ICTR vests the Trial Chamber with discretion as to granting leave, even if the twofold requirement is met.[74]

Considering the restrictive character of Art. 82 (1) (d) ICCSt, the Appeals Chamber is only entitled to rule on the issue in question after the chamber of first instance granted leave to appeal. Neither has the party seeking leave a right to appeal every decision, nor has the Appeals Chamber the competence to review a decision not stating an appealable issue. Only the chamber of first instance has the power to certify the existence of an appealable decision.[75] This corresponds with the above-mentioned nature of an appeal. Hence, there is no possibility to appeal the very decision of a Pre-Trial or Trial Chamber to deny leave to appeal. This also applies to 'extraordinary reviews' not foreseen in the Statute or the Rules of Procedure and Evidence, or to the contention of a lacuna in the law.[76] The mere fact of a ruling of

---

72 ICC *Situation in Uganda*, PTC, ICC-02/04-01/05-20-US-Exp, 19 August 2005, Decision on Prosecutor's Application for Leave to Appeal in Part Pre-Trial Chamber II's Decision on the Prosecutor's Applications for Warrants of Arrest under Article 58, para 15.

73 Ibid, para 16.

74 *See* Boas/Bischoff/Reid/Taylor, *ICL III*, 436–8.

75 ICC *Situation in the Democratic Republic of the Congo*, AC, ICC-01/04-168 OA3, 13 July 2006, Judgment on the Prosecutor's Application for Extraordinary Review of Pre-Trial Chamber I's 31 March 2006 Decision Denying Leave to Appeal, para 20. This approach is strongly criticized by Jason Manning, 'On Power, Participation and Authority: The International Criminal Court's Initial Appellate Jurisprudence', 38 *Geo J Int'l L* (2007) 803, 817.

76 Ibid, para 33 *et subs.*

the Appeals Chamber being of general interest or importance for the present and future proceedings does not suffice as a justification for granting leave to appeal.

Sub-paragraph (d) nominates two requirements of a *substantive* nature which must be demonstrated by the party seeking leave. Fulfilling these requirements is considered as the 'sole factor of relevance',[77] whereas arguments on the merits or the substance of the appeal are of no importance at this stage.

As a first component, the decision of the Pre-Trial or Trial Chamber must involve 'an issue that would significantly affect the fair and expeditious conduct of the proceedings or the outcome of the trial'. Stating this, the Statute describes the prerequisites of an appealable issue. An 'issue' has been understood to be an 'identifiable subject or topic requiring a decision for its resolution, not merely a question over which there is disagreement or conflicting opinion'.[78] This term is further made conditional in that it must 'significantly affect' either the fair and expeditious conduct of the proceedings or the outcome of the trial. Here, it has been held that the issue in question must be likely to have an impact on either of the said aspects.[79] The term 'fair' is clearly related to the notion of a fair trial, a principle which also applies to the pre-trial and the investigation stage of either a case or a situation.[80] The reference to the expeditiousness also constitutes an attribute of fairness.[81] Thereby the risk of lengthy trials should be avoided in cases where the Appeals Chamber could have resolved the issue immediately.[82] In summary,

> [b]reach of or deviation from the rules of a fair trial at the pre-trial stage of the proceedings may have implications on the proceedings and may affect the outcome of the trial. Purging the pre-trial process of errors consequential in the above sense is designed as a safeguard for the integrity of the proceedings. This is at the core of article 82 (1) (d) of the Statute.[83]

[77] ICC *Situation in Uganda*, PTC, ICC-02/04-01/05-20-US-Exp, 19 August 2005, Decision on Prosecutor's Application for Leave to Appeal in Part Pre-Trial Chamber II's Decision on the Prosecutor's Applications for Warrants of Arrest under Article 58, para 22.

[78] ICC *Situation in the Democratic Republic of the Congo*, AC, ICC-01/04-168 OA3, 13 July 2006, Judgment on the Prosecutor's Application for Extraordinary Review of Pre-Trial Chamber I's 31 March 2006 Decision Denying Leave to Appeal, para 9.

[79] Ibid, para 10.

[80] ICC *Situation in the Democratic Republic of the Congo*, PTC, ICC-01/04-135, 31 March 2006, Decision on the Prosecution's Application for Leave to Appeal the Chamber's Decision of 17 January 2006 on the Applications for Participation in the Proceedings of VPRS 1, VPRS 2, VPRS 3, VPRS 4, VPRS 5, and VPRS 6, para 36.

[81] ICC *Situation in the Democratic Republic of the Congo*, AC, ICC-01/04-168 OA3, 13 July 2006, Judgment on the Prosecutor's Application for Extraordinary Review of Pre-Trial Chamber I's 31 March 2006 Decision Denying Leave to Appeal, para 11, *see* also Chapter 8, p 383.

[82] ICC *Situation in Uganda*, PTC, ICC-02/04-01/05-20-US-Exp, 19 August 2005, Decision on Prosecutor's Application for Leave to Appeal in Part Pre-Trial Chamber II's Decision on the Prosecutor's Applications for Warrants of Arrest under Article 58, para 36, pointing to the case-law of the *ad hoc* Tribunals.

[83] ICC *Situation in the Democratic Republic of the Congo*, AC, ICC-01/04-168 OA3, 13 July 2006, Judgment on the Prosecutor's Application for Extraordinary Review of Pre-Trial Chamber

According to the wording of Art. 82 (1) (d) ICCSt, this first component requires the issue to affect the notions of both fairness and expeditiousness cumulatively. Hence, the failure to demonstrate an influence on one of these principles exonerates the Chamber from assessing the other notion.[84]

This also applies in relation to elaborations on the second requirement of Art. 82 (1) (d) ICCSt, which need not be made if the first prerequisite was not sufficiently demonstrated.[85]

In relation to this second substantive requirement, sub-paragraph (d) stipulates that an immediate resolution of the issue by the Appeals Chamber may materially advance the proceedings. Here, the Pre-Trial Chamber held that it must be presumed that the Appeals Chamber might preserve the judicial process of possible mistakes with its ruling on the issue.[86] For this purpose, the term 'advance' is not understood as relating to the notion of expeditiousness, but rather means that the proceedings 'move forward' by ensuring that the right course is followed.[87] The phrasing 'immediate resolution' emphasizes the importance of resolving potential errors the earliest possible. 'Put in a nutshell, the object of paragraph (d) of article 82 (1) of the Statute is to pre-empt the repercussions of erroneous decisions on the fairness of the proceedings or the outcome of the trial.'[88]

Only under these circumstances is the chamber of first instance entitled to grant leave to appeal, so that the Appeals Chamber may resolve the matter for the benefit of the judicial process. When appealing the initial decision with leave of the respective chamber, the grounds of appeal listed in Art. 81 (1) (a) ICCSt are applicable to appeals brought under Art. 82 (1) (d) ICCSt as well.[89]

The restrictive approach of the early decisions of the Pre-Trial Chambers referred to above[90] must be put into perspective:

I's 31 March 2006 Decision Denying Leave to Appeal, para 11. Needless to say, this *ratio* is not restricted to the pre-trial phase of the proceedings.

84 *See* also W Schabas, *ICC* (OUP 2010) 945 *et subs.*

85 Triffterer/*Staker*, Art. 82 MN 11.

86 ICC *Situation in the Democratic Republic of the Congo*, AC, ICC-01/04-168 OA3, 13 July 2006, Judgment on the Prosecutor's Application for Extraordinary Review of Pre-Trial Chamber I's 31 March 2006 Decision Denying Leave to Appeal, para 14.

87 Ibid, para 15.

88 Ibid, para 19.

89 ICC *Prosecutor v Lubanga*, AC, ICC-01/04-01/06-568 OA3, 13 October 2006, Judgment on the Prosecutor's Appeal against the Decision of Pre-Trial Chamber I entitled 'Decision Establishing General Principles Governing Applications to Restrict Disclosure Pursuant to Rule 81 (2) and (4) of the Rules of Procedure and Evidence', para 19.

90 For a detailed analysis compare the report of the War Crimes Research Office, Interlocutory Appellate Review of Early Decisions by the International Criminal Court (Legal Analysis and Education Project, January 2008) p 23 *et subs.* According to R Blattmann and K Bowman, 'Achievements and Problems of the International Criminal Court—A View from Within', 6 *JICJ* (2008) 711, 726, this approach has meanwhile been widened.

> ...in striking the balance between the convenience of deciding certain issues at an early stage of the proceedings, and the need to avoid possible delays and disruptions caused by recourse to interlocutory appeals, the provisions enshrined...in the ICC Statute, favour as a principle the deferral of appellate proceedings until final judgment, and limit interlocutory appeals to a few, strictly defined, exceptions.[91]

On the one hand, this appraisal of the Pre-Trial Chamber in the *Situation of Uganda* seems correct insofar as interlocutory appeals are in principle likely to hamper the course of judicial proceedings when used excessively.[92] However, on the other hand, this concern must, under certain circumstances, be outweighed by the need to strike a proper balance as to cognition of the benefits of early appellate review. Interlocutory appeals are of great importance to the proceedings and the development of law, foremost the interpretation of the Rome Statute and respective provisions in the Rules of Procedure and Evidence. It shall not be proposed here that all applications seeking leave should have been granted, but the early review of the Appeals Chamber on certain questions[93] might generally contribute to avoid lengthy trials.[94] Moreover, the Appeals Chamber might help to ensure certainty and consistency in the application of the law.[95] Since the Appeal Chamber is only able to fulfil its important role if allowed to do so by the chambers of first instance, the tendencies developed in the meantime to broaden the approach all contribute to warranting the fairness, effectiveness, and efficiency of the Court's proceedings.

b. Appeals pursuant to Art. 82 (2) ICCSt Art. 82 (2) ICCSt provides for an appeal against a decision of the Pre-Trial Chamber under Art. 57 (3) (d) ICCSt; that is, the authorization of the Prosecutor to investigate within the territory of a State Party. As a condition for the ruling of the Appeals Chamber on this matter, Art. 82 (2) ICCSt expressly refers to leave of the respective Pre-Trial Chamber. The standard for certifying the appeal is not mentioned despite the fact that one cannot simply transpose the terms of Art. 82 (1) (d) ICCSt, which focuses on adversarial proceedings.[96] Only the Prosecutor and the State concerned are entitled to appeal. Remarkably, the second sentence of paragraph (2) stipulates that

---

[91] ICC *Situation in Uganda*, PTC, ICC-02/04-01/05-20-US-Exp, 19 August 2005, Decision on Prosecutor's Application for Leave to Appeal in Part Pre-Trial Chamber II's Decision on the Prosecutor's Applications for Warrants of Arrest under Article 58, para 19.

[92] For possible delays arising out of the interlocutory appellate process *see* the report of the War Crimes Research Office, Expediting Proceedings of the International Criminal Court (Legal Analysis and Education Project, June 2011) p 46 *et subs.*

[93] Foremost, one might think of issues relating to questions of disclosure of evidence and victim participation.

[94] Triffterer/*Staker*, Art. 82 MN 11.

[95] H Friman, 'Interlocutory Appeals in the Early Practice of the International Criminal Court', in: C Stahn and G Sluiter (eds), *The Emerging Practice of the International Criminal Court* (Martinus Nijhoff Publishers 2009) 553, 560; War Crimes Research Office, Interlocutory Appellate Review of Early Decisions by the International Criminal Court (Legal Analysis and Education Project, January 2008) p 12.

[96] *See* W Schabas, *ICC* (OUP 2010) 948.

the appeal shall be heard on an expedited basis. This duplication seems redundant and ambiguous when considering the wording of Rule 156 (4) RPE ICC.

3. Suspensive effect of the appeal

As expressed in Art. 82 (3) ICCSt and Rule 156 (5) RPE ICC, an appeal does not have suspensive effect of itself. Rather, the Appeals Chamber may order suspensive effect upon the request of the party filing the appeal.[97] This request can be considered as an 'annex' to the appeal.[98]

4. Procedure for interlocutory appeals

a. Procedure for appeals that do not require leave of the Court In the case of an appeal according to Art. 82 (1) (a)–(c) ICCSt, the procedural course follows from Rules 154, 156 RPE ICC. Appeals under Art. 82 (1) (a), (b) ICCSt must be filed within five days from the notification of the decision, Rule 154 (1) RPE ICC, whereas appeals under Art. 82 (1) (c) ICCSt are subjected to a time period of two days from the notification of the decision, Rule 154 (2) RPE ICC. According to Rule 154 (3) RPE ICC, referring to Rule 150 RPE ICC, the appeal must be filed with the Registrar. In case of non-compliance with the aforesaid procedural prerequisites, the decision shall become final. The content and form of the appeal is specified in Regulation 64 (1) RegC.

Rule 156 RPE ICC elaborates on the procedure for appeal. After it has been filed, the Registrar shall transmit the record of the proceedings subjected to appeal to the Appeals Chamber. Furthermore, s/he shall give notice of the appeal to all parties participating in the respective proceedings, Rule 156 (2) RPE ICC.

Additionally, the appellant shall file a document in support of the appeal within twenty-one days from the notification of the decision, Regulation 64 (2) RegC. This provision, together with sub-paragraph (3), also specifies the requirements of content for this document. A response may be filed by other participants pursuant to Regulation 64 (4) RegC.

Sub-paragraphs (5) and (6) shorten the time periods for certain appeals. Hence, for appeals under Art. 82 (1) (b) ICCSt, the document in support of the appeal shall be filed within only seven days, and the response hereto must be filed within five days, Regulation 64 (5) RegC. As to appeals under Art. 82 (1) (c) ICCSt, the appellant must file a document in support of the appeal within four days, whilst the participants have only two days to respond, Regulation 64 (6) RegC.

[97] The respective requests have been granted by the Appeals Chamber, *see* eg, ICC *Prosecutor v Lubanga*, AC, ICC-01/04-01/06-2536 OA17, 23 July 2010, Decision on the Prosecutor's Request to give Suspensive Effect to the Appeal against Trial Chamber I's Oral Decision to Release Mr Thomas Lubanga Dyilo.

[98] The documents are labelled with the same OA number as the judgment of the Appeals Chamber pending the determination of the appeal.

b. Procedure for appeals requiring leave of the Court Rule 155 RPE ICC refers to appeals against decisions which require leave of the Court. Here too, the party wishing to appeal must file the request for leave within five days from the notification of the impugned decision, Rule 155 (1) RPE ICC. This provision further specifies that the party requesting leave must set out the reasons. Hence, when seeking leave, the party does not need to elaborate on the grounds of appeal, but rather has to convince the chamber of first instance as to the necessity of the Appeals Chamber's ruling in that matter. The standard as to form and content of the request for leave is laid down in Regulation 65 (1) RegC. In case the applicant requests leave to appeal under Art. 82 (1) (d) ICCSt, s/he shall additionally specify the reasons warranting an immediate resolution of this matter by the Appeals Chamber, Regulation 65 (2) RegC.[99] When looking at the wording of Regulation 65 (3) RegC, it becomes evident that already at this point, the other participants must be notified of the application. Contrary to this, the Rules provide for notification only when the chamber renders its decision as to the request for leave. Pursuant to Rule 155 (2) RPE ICC, the chamber shall decide on the certification and notify the participants in the proceedings in question hereof. But as Regulation 65 (3) RegC clearly stipulates, the other participants are entitled to file a response as to the request for leave and must therefore receive notification at an earlier point.

As soon as the Chamber decides to grant leave, the Registrar shall transmit the record of the proceedings to the Appeals Chamber, Rule 156 (1) RPE ICC. A separate notification to the participants in the proceedings is not necessary, since the chamber of first instance already informed the participants of the decision granting (or denying) leave, Rule 156 (2) RPE ICC.

According to Regulation 65 (4) RegC, the appellant shall file a document in support of the appeal within ten days from notification of the decision granting leave. For this purpose, reference to Regulation 64 (2) RegC is made as to the requirements of this document. Again, the participants are entitled to file a response within ten days from notification of the document in support of the appeal, see Regulation 65 (5) RegC with reference to Regulation 64 (4) RegC.

c. Common provisions Rule 156 (3) RPE ICC stipulates that the appeal proceedings shall basically be in writing. However, the Appeals Chamber may also, in a discretionary manner,[100] decide to convene a hearing.

In order to avoid delays, Rule 156 (4) RPE ICC contains the directive that appeals shall be heard as expeditiously as possible. For some cases, this principle

[99] Interestingly, nothing is said as to the elaboration on the first substantive requirement of Art. 82 (1) (d) ICCSt.

[100] ICC *Prosecutor v Bemba*, AC, ICC-01/05-01/08-962 OA3, 19 October 2010, Judgment on the Appeal of Mr Jean-Pierre Bemba Gombo against the Decision of Trial Chamber III of 24 June 2010 entitled 'Decision on the Admissibility and Abuse of Process Challenges', para 25.

is additionally provided for in the Statute, Arts 18 (4), 56 (3), 82 (2) ICCSt. However, it remains unclear what the 'expedited basis' referred to in these provisions implies.

Rule 156 (5) RPE ICC relates to Art. 82 (3) ICCSt. Hence, the request for suspensive effect shall be made when filing the appeal.

Pursuant to Rule 157 RPE ICC, any party who has filed an appeal may withdraw it before the delivery of the Appeals Chamber's judgment. In order to do so, the appellant shall file a notice of discontinuance with the Registrar, who in turn shall inform the other parties thereof.

The Appeals Chamber renders its judgment by virtue of Rule 158 RPE ICC and may confirm, reverse or amend the decision of the Pre-Trial or Trial Chamber, Rule 158 (1) RPE ICC. Sub-paragraph (2) refers to Art. 83 (4) ICCSt, according to which the judgment shall be taken by a majority of the judges and shall be delivered in open court. Art. 83 (2) ICCSt has been held not to apply to interlocutory appeals. The Appeals Chamber in the case of *Lubanga* elaborated on the applicability of this provision to Art. 82 (1) (d) ICCSt in particular and answered a respective submission of the Defence in the negative.[101] In later judgments, the Appeals Chamber nonetheless adopted the standard of Art. 83 (2) ICCSt (whether the alleged error *materially affected* the impugned decision) for appeals under Art. 82 ICCSt.[102] However, the consequences of an appeal under Art. 82 ICCSt are clearly laid down in Rule 158 RPE ICC, so that this application *mutatis mutandis* does not relate to the powers of the Appeals Chamber of how to resolve the matter before it.

V. Admissibility of an appeal

Apart from the rather 'material' requirements referred to above, the mounting of an appeal or respectively the exercise of the right to appeal is subjected to certain formal conditions. The Appeals Chamber referred to this issue as the 'admissibility of an appeal'.[103] Accordingly, specific issues are not considered to be a matter of the merits of the appeal, but rather of its (formal) 'admissibility'. An appeal may be

[101] ICC *Prosecutor v Lubanga*, AC, ICC-01/04-01/06-568 OA3, 13 October 2006, Judgment on the Prosecutor's Appeal against the Decision of Pre-Trial Chamber I entitled 'Decision Establishing General Principles Governing Applications to Restrict Disclosure Pursuant to Rule 81 (2) and (4) of the Rules of Procedure and Evidence', para 12 *et subs.*

[102] ICC *Prosecutor v Katanga and Chui*, AC, ICC-01/04-01/07-1497 OA8, 25 September 2009, Judgment of Mr Germain Katanga against the Oral Decision of Trial Chamber II of 12 June 2009 on the Admissibility of the Case, para 37. *See* also *Prosecutor v Lubanga*, AC, ICC-01/04-01/06-1487 OA12, 21 October 2008, Judgment on the Appeal of the Prosecutor against the Decision of Trial Chamber I entitled 'Decision on the Release of Thomas Lubanga Dyilo', para 44.

[103] For a detailed analysis of the respective Appeals Chamber's jurisprudence *see* F Eckelmans, 'The First Jurisprudence of the Appeals Chamber of the ICC', in: C Stahn and G Sluiter (eds), *The Emerging Practice of the International Criminal Court* (Martinus Nijhoff Publishers 2009) 527, 538 *et subs.*

dismissed, for instance, in case of lack of jurisdiction of the Appeals Chamber[104] or lack of certification of the Pre-Trial or Trial Chamber as the chamber of first instance.[105] Furthermore, when mounting an appeal, one may presume that the appellant must comply with the prerequisites of the Rules of Procedure and Evidence as well as the Regulations of the Court, otherwise the Appeals Chamber might render the appeal inadmissible.[106]

VI. Additional evidence before the Appeals Chamber

The Rome Statute explicitly provides for the possibility to adduce new evidence on appeal.[107] Thus the Appeals Chamber is itself enabled to determine factual issues. Considering the nature of appeals as merely corrective, the Appeals Chamber may not be understood as a 'second chamber of first instance'. Hence, the possibilities for the parties to introduce new evidence on the appeals stage are limited. The same holds true for the *proprio motu* power of the Appeals Chamber to call evidence itself.

It is to be noted that presumably Regulation 62 RegC, as well as the respective sections in Art. 83 ICCSt, are only applicable to appeals against final decisions, and not to appeals under Art. 82 ICCSt.[108] Foremost, this is due to the wording of these provisions, as they refer to the 'Trial Chamber' only. In addition, Art. 83 (2) ICCSt lists the powers of the Appeals Chamber as to an appeal against a final decision of the Trial Chamber pursuant to Art. 81 ICCSt only, and stipulates that 'for these purposes' the Appeals Chamber may itself call evidence. Furthermore, Regulation 62 RegC is positioned systematically in the section of provisions related to appeals under Arts 81, 83 ICCSt. Finally, the remarkable power of the Appeals Chamber to take new evidence into consideration must teleologically be restricted to decisions of the Trial Chamber terminating the proceedings. Nevertheless, the possibility to present additional evidence in appeals under Art. 82 ICCSt has yet to be discussed in the jurisprudence of the Appeals Chamber.

According to Regulation 62 RegC, a participant seeking to present new evidence before the Appeals Chamber shall file an application. Thereupon the Appeals Chamber decides on the admissibility of the additional evidence. Regulation 62

104 ICC *Prosecutor v Lubanga*, AC, ICC-01/04-01/06-926 OA8, 13 June 2007, Decision on the Admissibility of the Appeal of Mr Thomas Lubanga Dyilo against the Decision of Pre-Trial Chamber I entitled 'Décision sur la confirmation des charges' of 29 January 2007.

105 ICC *Situation in the Democratic Republic of the Congo*, AC, ICC-01/04-168 OA3, 13 July 2006, Judgment on the Prosecutor's Application for Extraordinary Review of Pre-Trial Chamber I's 31 March 2006 Decision Denying Leave to Appeal, para 20.

106 This question has not yet been answered by the Appeals Chamber, compare F Eckelmans, 'The First Jurisprudence of the Appeals Chamber of the ICC', in: C Stahn and G Sluiter (eds), *The Emerging Practice of the International Criminal Court* (Martinus Nijhoff Publishers 2009) 527, 541.

107 Compare Art. 83 (1), (2) ICCSt.

108 *See* W Schabas, *ICC* (OUP 2010) 952.

(1) RegC defines the content of a respective application. The requirement under sub-paragraph (b) was specified as to requiring that the evidence was unavailable in the proceedings before the Trial Chamber.[109]

The *ad hoc* Tribunals have adopted a considerably strict approach as to the admission of additional evidence at the appeals stage.[110] The requirements are governed by Rule 115 RPE ICTY/ICTR.[111] Here, it has been held on various occasions that 'CONSIDERING that, to be admissible pursuant to Rule 115, evidence which was not available at trial and could not have been discovered through the exercise of due diligence must be relevant to a material issue and credible and such that it *could* have had an impact on the verdict.'[112]

As to the procedural stages at which additional evidence might be introduced on appeals, Rule 115 RPE ICTY/ICTR was held equally applicable to interlocutory appeals, such as to decisions denying provisional release.[113]

VII. Authority of previous judgments

With respect to the jurisprudence of the Appeals Chamber and its impact on other decisions of the Court, regard must be had to Art. 21 (2) ICCSt. This provision states that 'the Court may apply principles and rules of law as interpreted in its previous decisions'. Hence, the Court is not bound to follow previous rulings, using them as a source of law.[114] However, in practice the ICC Pre-Trial and Trial Chambers refer frequently to the Appeals Chamber's jurisprudence or to one another as persuasive precedent.

The Appeals Chamber of the *ad hoc* Tribunals has established a doctrine of precedent, binding the other chambers of the appellate jurisprudence for present and future cases.[115]

---

[109] ICC *Prosecutor v Bemba*, AC, ICC-01/05-01/08-962 OA3, 19 October 2010, Judgment on the Appeal of Mr Jean-Pierre Bemba Gombo against the Decision of Trial Chamber III of 24 June 2010 entitled 'Decision on the Admissibility and Abuse of Process Challenges', para 32, explicitly leaving open the question of the applicability of Reg 62 RegC to interlocutory appeals under Art. 82 ICCSt.

[110] ICTY *Prosecutor v Kupreškić, et al.*, AC, IT-95-16-A, 23 October 2001, Judgment, para 66.

[111] For a detailed analysis of the test provided for especially by Rule 115 (B) RPE ICTY/ICTR *see* L Bianchi and I Onsea, 'Additional Evidence on Appeal, Review Proceedings, and Reconsideration' in: K Khan, C Buisman, and C Gosnell (eds), *Principles of Evidence in International Criminal Justice* (OUP 2010) 723, 726 *et subs.*

[112] ICTY *Prosecutor v Krstić*, AC, IT-98-33, 5 August 2003, Decision on Applications for Admission of Additional Evidence on Appeal.

[113] ICTY *Prosecutor v Haradinaj et al.*, AC, IT-04-84-AR65.2, 3 March 2006, Decision on Lahi Brahimaj's Request to Present Additional Evidence under Rule 115, para 9.

[114] As to the jurisprudence of the *ad hoc* Tribunals being used as precedent *see* V Nerlich, 'The Status of ICTY and ICTR Precedent in Proceedings before the ICC', in: C Stahn and G Sluiter (eds), *The Emerging Practice of the International Criminal Court* (Martinus Nijhoff Publishers 2009) 305.

[115] ICTY *Prosecutor v Aleksovski*, AC, IT-95-14, 24 March 2004, Judgment, para 107 *et subs. See* also Boas/Bischoff/Reid/Taylor, *ICL III*, 430 *et subs.*

VIII. Victim participation in appeal proceedings

Victims have a broad range of opportunities to participate in proceedings before the ICC which also extend to the appeals stage. By virtue of Art. 68 (3) ICCSt, the Court shall permit the views and concerns of the victims to be presented at different stages of the proceedings when deemed appropriate. The Appeals Chamber has held on various occasions that, under certain circumstances, victims also have a right to participate in the appellate stage of the proceedings, establishing fundamental guidelines as to the requirements hereto.[116]

In its first judgment in this matter, the Appeals Chamber held that victims, in order to participate in an interlocutory appeal, must file an application seeking leave to participate.[117] This was determined in an appeal under Art. 82 (1) (b) ICCSt which, according to the statutory provisions, does not require leave, neither for the appellant nor for the participants filing a response.[118] Nevertheless, the requirement of victims filing an application seeking leave to participate applies irrespective of the kind of interlocutory appeal.[119]

Furthermore, the Appeals Chamber in the same judgment held that the leave of the Pre-Trial Chamber as to participation in pre-trial proceedings was not applicable to the appeals stage.[120] Thus, the mere fact that a victim was authorized to participate before the Pre-Trial Chamber cannot automatically bind the Appeals Chamber to its determination of whether a particular person is qualified to participate as a victim. This means that a victim wishing to participate in an appeal must file a (new) application, seeking leave to participate in proceedings before the Appeals Chamber and convince the Chamber that his or her personal interests are affected by this specific interlocutory appeal at issue.[121] However, it is not required to elaborate on the status as a victim according to Rule 85 (a) RPE ICC.[122]

---

[116] Since no final judgment has been issued so far, the current jurisprudence relates to interlocutory appeals exclusively.

[117] ICC *Prosecutor v Lubanga*, AC, ICC-01/04-01/06-824 OA7, 13 February 2007, Judgment on the Appeal of Mr Thomas Lubanga Dyilo against the Decision of Pre-Trial Chamber I entitled 'Décision sur la demande de mise en líberté provisoire de Thomas Lubanga Dyilo', para 38.

[118] Reg 64 (4) RegC.

[119] The Appeals Chamber drew this conclusion from the wording of Art. 68 (3) ICCSt, stating that this provision mandated a specific determination by the Appeals Chamber as to the appropriateness of victim participation, ICC *Prosecutor v Lubanga*, AC, ICC-01/04-01/06-824 OA7, 13 February 2007, Judgment on the Appeal of Mr Thomas Lubanga Dyilo against the Decision of Pre-Trial Chamber I entitled 'Décision sur la demande de mise en líberté provisoire de Thomas Lubanga Dyilo', para 40.

[120] Ibid, para 43.

[121] *See* Boas/Bischoff/Reid/Taylor, *ICL III*, 329.

[122] ICC *Situation in Darfur*, AC, ICC-02/05-138, 18 June 2008, Decision on Victim Participation in the Appeal of the Office of Public Counsel for the Defence Against Pre-Trial Chamber I's Decision of 3 December 2008 and in the Appeals of the Prosecutor and the Office of Public Counsel for the Defence Against Pre-Trial Chamber I's Decision of 6 December 2007, para 53.

As far as the procedure for the application is concerned, it has been held that the application shall be made 'as soon as possible after the appeal is filed'.[123] Pursuant to Rule 89 (1) RPE ICC, the Prosecutor and the Defence are entitled to file a reply. If the Appeals Chamber permits the victims to participate, both the Prosecutor and the Defence are allowed to reply to any subsequent filing of the victims.

The above-mentioned principles governing victim participation were upheld in subsequent judgments of the Appeals Chamber,[124] and were considered to apply to other grounds of interlocutory appeals pursuant to Art. 82 (1) ICCSt and to the situation phase of proceedings equally.[125]

Having established the procedural framework of the victim participation scheme on appeals proceedings, some remarks on substantial considerations of the Appeals Chamber shall be made. Whilst the jurisprudence of the Pre-Trial and Trial Chambers is based on a rather extensive approach as to the interpretation of the 'personal interests' requirement, the Appeals Chamber has followed a more restrictive path.[126] Thus, concurring with the chambers of first instance, the personal interests of the victims are seen to be generally affected by the proceedings at the ICC. This follows directly from the approval of the status as a victim pursuant to Rule 85 (a) RPE ICC.[127] The Appeals Chamber, however, examines the affect of personal interests on a case-by-case basis.[128] However, in most cases the Appeals Chamber has allowed

[123] ICC *Prosecutor v Lubanga*, AC, ICC-01/04-01/06-824 OA7, 13 February 2007, Judgment on the Appeal of Mr Thomas Lubanga Dyilo against the Decision of Pre-Trial Chamber I entitled 'Décision sur la demande de mise en líberté provisoire de Thomas Lubanga Dyilo', para 46. J Manning, 'On Power, Participation and Authority: The International Criminal Court's Initial Appellate Jurisprudence', 38 *Geo J Int'l L* (2007) 803, 821 points out that by this procedure, the intended expediency of interlocutory appeals is threatened.

[124] Compare ICC *Prosecutor v Lubanga*, AC, ICC-01/04-01/06-2555 OA17, 17 August 2010, Decision on the Participation of Victims in the Appeal against Trial Chamber I's Oral Decision of 15 July 2010 to Release Thomas Lubanga Dyilo, para 15 *et subs.* In another decision in the case of *Lubanga*, the Appeals Chamber held that these principles must even be followed with respect to preliminary issues determined in appeals proceedings. *See* ICC *Prosecutor v Lubanga*, AC, ICC-01/04-01/06-925 OA8, 13 June 2007, Decision of the Appeals Chamber on the Joint Application of Victims a/0001/06 to a/0003/06 and a/0105/06 Concerning the 'Directions and Decision of the Appeals Chamber' of 2 February 2007, para 24 *et subs.*

[125] ICC *Situation in Darfur*, AC, ICC-02/05-138, 18 June 2008, Decision on Victim Participation in the Appeal of the Office of Public Counsel for the Defence against Pre-Trial Chamber I's Decision of 3 December 2007 and in the Appeals of the Prosecutor and the Office of Public Counsel for the Defence against Pre-Trial Chamber I's Decision of 6 December 2007, para 24 with further references.

[126] Compare C Trumbull, 'The Victims of Victim Participation in International Criminal Proceedings', 29 *Mich J Int'l L* (2008) 777, 797 *et subs.* and M Cohen, 'Victims' Participation Rights within the International Criminal Court: A Critical Overview', 37 *Denv J Int'l L & Pol'y* (2009) 351, 368 *et subs.*

[127] ICC *Situation in Uganda*, PTC, ICC-02/04-101, 10 August 2007, Decision on Victims' Applications for Participation a/0010/06, a/0064/06 to a/0070/06, a/0081/06 to a/0104/06 and a/0111/06 to a/0127/06, para 9.

[128] ICC *Prosecutor v Lubanga*, AC, ICC-01/04-01/06-925 OA8, 13 June 2007, Decision of the Appeals Chamber on the Joint Application of Victims a/0001/06 to a/0003/06 and a/0105/06

the victims to participate, concurring with the intention of the drafters of the Rome Statute to provide extensive participatory rights to victims.

Whether or not the Appeals Chamber is willing to adjudicate in appeals from a conviction or acquittal in a similar manner, remains to be seen.[129] However, it seems odd to envisage a situation in which a victim, who has been recognized under Rule 85 RPE ICC is not affected in his or her 'personal interests' by the final decision of the Trial Chamber. This might be a reason to develop an automatic admissibility concept for victims participating in the appellate proceedings.

B. Revision

Revision is something other than appeal. It is not the Trial Chamber judgment that is at issue but rather 'new evidence' has appeared or one of the previous judges has misbehaved. It is only available to the convict and not to the Prosecutor in order to challenge an acquittal. This would fall within the scope of the double jeopardy provision (*ne bis in idem*).[130]

The Statutes of the *ad hoc* Tribunals speak of 'review proceedings' in this respect. Art. 26 ICTYSt and Art. 25 ICTRSt provide for the possibility of a review of the final judgment when a new fact is discovered that could have been a decisive factor in reaching the judgment.[131] These criteria have been further elaborated upon in the jurisprudence of the Tribunals.[132] Here too, the respective chamber decides by way of a preliminary examination whether to grant revision.

Art. 84 ICCSt provides for the possibility of revision of conviction or sentence. The ILC considered the option of revision necessary, providing a remedy where 'factual error relating to material not available to the accused and therefore not brought to the attention of the Court at the time of the initial trial or of any appeal'.[133] As guaranteed in Art. 14 (6) ICCPR as one of the major human rights instruments, the remedy of revision applies when new facts arise after the proceedings have terminated.[134]

---

concerning the 'Directions and Decision of the Appeals Chamber' of 2 February 2007, para 28; AC, ICC-01/04-01/06-1452 OA12, 6 August 2008, Decision on the Participation of Victims in the Appeal, para 10.

[129] Boas/Bischoff/Reid/Taylor, *ICL III*, 330 forecast that the Appeals Chamber would do so.

[130] W Schabas, *ICC* (OUP 2010) 960.

[131] *See* also Rules 119–22 RPE ICTY, Rules 120–3 RPE ICTR.

[132] ICTR *Prosecutor v Barayagwiza*, AC, ICTR-97-19-AR72, Decision (Prosecutor's Request for Review or Reconsideration), 31 January 2000, para 41 ('... [the Chamber] must be satisfied that four criteria have been met. There must be a new fact; this new fact must not have been known by the moving party at the time of the original proceedings; the lack of discovery of the new fact must not have been through the lack of due diligence on the part of the moving party; and it must be shown that the new fact could have been a decisive factor in reaching the original decision.')

[133] ILC 1994 Draft Statute, p 128.

[134] Boas/Bischoff/Reid/Taylor, *ICL III*, 452.

The provision of Art. 84 ICCSt refers only to the convicted person (or that person's representative after his or her death)[135] or the Prosecutor on that person's behalf as possible applicants. That means that the subject matter of revision is a conviction or a sentence, and, hence, that the revision cannot result detrimental to the person seeking remedy.[136]

The grounds for revision are laid down in Art. 84 (1) ICCSt. First, sub-paragraph (a) refers to the discovery of new evidence. As a limitation or condition, the applicant must demonstrate that this new evidence was not available at the time of trial (i), and the availability at trial would have led to a different verdict due to the importance of the evidence (ii).[137] As a second ground for revision, Art. 84 (1) (b) ICCSt stipulates that decisive evidence introduced at trial and upon which the conviction depends was 'false, forged or falsified'. Thirdly, revision may be sought if at least one of the judges participating in the confirmation of charges or the conviction committed 'an act of serious misconduct or serious breach of duty', Art. 84 (1) (c) ICCSt.

Applications for revision are to be addressed to the Appeals Chamber.[138] If the Chamber considers an application to be unfounded, it shall reject it by virtue of Art. 84 (2) ICCSt. On the other hand, if the application is considered to be meritorious by way of a preliminary assessment, the Appeals Chamber may either reconvene the original Trial Chamber, constitute a new Trial Chamber, or retain jurisdiction over the matter, Art. 84 (2) (a)–(c) ICCSt, and thus exercise a power which is ordinarily attributed to the Presidency.[139] In doing so, the Appeals Chamber shall aim at 'arriving at a determination on whether the judgment should be revised'. For the purpose of this determination, a hearing shall be held in accordance with the Rules of Procedure and Evidence. Here, Rules 160, 161 RPE ICC provide further guidance. Strikingly, these do not speak of the 'Appeals Chamber', but refer simply to the 'relevant Chamber'. From this it can be assumed that the determination on revision can also be taken by a Trial Chamber.[140] This may depend on the chamber that issued the final judgment.

Regard shall be taken to the purpose of revision, since it does not intend to conduct a retrial of the case. Rather, considerations shall be made on whether the judgment should be revised in light of the new circumstances.

---

[135] This might be relatives of the offender or any other person alive at the time of the accused's death who has been given express written instruction from the accused to bring such a claim, *see* W Schabas, *ICC* (OUP 2010) 960.

[136] Triffterer/*Staker*, Art. 84 MN 5.

[137] *See* Boas/Bischoff/Reid/Taylor, *ICL III*, 453 *et subs.* for further details.

[138] Rule 159 RPE ICC and Reg 66 RegC give further guidance on the requirements of an application for revision.

[139] *See* W Schabas, *ICC* (OUP 2010) 962.

[140] Triffterer/*Staker*, Art. 84 MN 25 *et subs.*

10

CONTEMPT OF COURT (*HILDE FARTHOFER*)

In every national legal system courts have the right to sanction contempt of court, in order to enforce their integrity as well as to ensure the smooth flow of court procedure. The differences between the regulations lie mainly in the legal classification of single conduct; this means in the 'gravity' of the offence.[1] The Rome Statute provides explicit regulations for cases where a party tampers with evidence, disobeys its orders, or disrupts a trial.

Neither the Statute of the ICTY nor of the ICTR provides any provision for the case when contempt of court will occur. This is largely due to the affinity of the *ad hoc* Tribunals to the common law concept of contempt of court.[2] This is based on the presumption that a court has the inherent right to shield itself from any behaviour that could have any negative impact on the course of proceedings or constitutes a threat to its integrity. The courts of record have the right to punish contempt with greater discretionary power than in civil law-based legal systems.[3] Rule 77 RPE ICTY/ICTR restricts judicial discretion. Over the years these particular provisions have been subject to several amendments.[4] Nevertheless, the SCSL does not view Rule 77 RPE SCSL as a limitation to its discretionally inherent power to punish contempt of court.[5]

According to Art. 15 ICTYSt and in identical words in Art. 14 ICTRSt, 'judges shall adopt rules of procedure and evidence for the conduct of the pre-trial phase

---

1 Triffterer/*Piragoff.*, Art. 71 MN 1 *et subs.*

2 ICTY *Prosecutor v Tadić*, AC, IT-94-1-A-R77, 31 January 2000, Judgment on Allegation of Contempt against Prior Counsel, Milan Vujin, para 15 *et subs.*

3 In the legal systems of common law countries, contempt of court offences are developed by the courts, according to the principle *malus, per se*, and are not based on actual legislation as, eg, in Germany, a civil law system country.

4 S. D'Ascoli, 'Sentencing Contempt of Court in International Criminal Justice', 5 *JICJ* (2007) 735 and Cassese/Gaeta/Jones/*Terrier*, 1432 *et subs.*

5 SCSL *Independent Counsel v Brima et al.*, TC I, SCSL-2005-02, 21 September 2005, Sentencing Judgment in Contempt Proceedings, para 12.

of the proceedings, trials and appeals...'. However, that does not allow them to include new offences by broadening the interpretation, 'but it does permit the judges to adopt rules of procedures of evidence for the conduct of matters falling within the inherent jurisdiction of the Tribunal as well as matters within its statutory jurisdiction.'[6]

Furthermore the Appeals Chamber observed that '[t]he inherent power of the Tribunal to deal with contempt has necessarily existed ever since its creation and the existence of that power does not depend upon a reference being made to it in the Rules of Procedure and Evidence.'[7]

It can be concluded that the fact that the Rome Statute comprises provisions which explicitly govern contempt of court offences, emphasizes that the ICC is more influenced by the civil law system on this issue. Problems encountered in the course of proceedings before the ICTY and ICTR regarding 'new offences' may thus be minimized.

In the Rome Statute, contempt of court offences are divided into two categories based on the 'gravity' of the breach of discipline and duty before the Court. Art. 70 ICCSt focuses on offences against the administration of justice whilst Art. 71 ICCSt deals with misconduct before the Court. The latter will fill in possible lacunae caused when undesired behaviour is not covered by the more specific provision of Art. 70 ICCSt.

The use of the word 'including' indicates that the list of offences in Rule 77 RPE ICTY/ICTR/SCSL is not exhaustive and, therefore, all behaviour which may lead to interference with the proceedings of a trial, may fall under the scope of the provision.

I. Offences against the administration of justice

In contrast, Art. 70 (1) ICCSt comprises an exhaustive list of six offences, over which the court has jurisdiction if the offences are committed intentionally.[8] Pursuant to Art. 30 (2) ICCSt, a person acts intentionally if he or she wishes to create a certain demeanour, or the acts committed are focused on achieving a desired effect.[9] There was no agreement on the proposed concept of recklessness or *dolus eventualis* during the negotiations for the establishment of an international criminal court.[10] Both

---

[6] ICTY *Prosecutor v Tadić*, AC, IT-94-1-A-R77, 31 January 2000, Judgment on Allegation of Contempt against Prior Counsel, Milan Vujin, para 24.

[7] Ibid, para 28.

[8] Cassese/Gaeta/Jones/*Terrier*, 1436.

[9] More detailed regarding the mental elements R Cryer, H Friman, D Robinson, and E Wilmshurst, *International Criminal Law and Procedure* (CUP 2008) 318 *et subs*.

[10] Eg, Report of the Preparatory Committee on the Establishment of an International Criminal Court, Volume II, (Compilation of Proposals), 92 *et subs*.

Contempt of court

Art. 70 ICCSt.
Offences against the administration of justice

- False testimony
- Presenting false evidence
- Interferences with witnesses and evidences
- Interferences with officials of the court
- Retaliating against an official of the court
- Soliciting or accepting a bribe as an official of the court

Sanctions:

- fine (not more than 50 per cent of the income) or
- (as last resort) term of maximum imprisonment of five years

Art. 71 ICCSt.
Misconduct before the court

- Disruption of proceedings
- Refusal to comply with a direction by the court

Sanctions (after prior warning)

- Exclusion of the courtroom (not more than 30 days)
- Fine of €2,000 per day

Figure 10.1 Contempt of court

forms of *mens rea* are not yet provided in the Statute or the Elements of Crimes and therefore, *dolus eventualis* does not suffice.[11]

It is not undisputed that the word 'intent' as defined in Art. 30 (2) ICCSt should apply to the *mens rea* requirement in Art. 70 (1) ICCSt. The main argument against the application of Art. 30 (2) ICCSt on offences such as those included in Art. 70 ICCSt, is based on the claim that offences against the administration of justice do not constitute core crimes as listed in Art. 5 (1) ICCSt.[12] However, Rule 163 (1) RPE ICC points out that 'the Statute and the Rules shall apply *mutatis mutandis* to ... offences defined in Article 70.' According to Rule 163 (2) and (3) RPE ICC, only the provisions of Parts 2 and 10 with some exceptions listed therein, should not be applied.

Another argument is based on the assumption that the wording '[u]nless otherwise provided' in Art. 30 (1) ICCSt excludes the application of Art. 30 (2) ICCSt to offences against the administration of justice because Art. 70 ICCSt constitutes a specific provision. This notion would only fit if either the Rules or the Rome Statute provide specific guidelines regarding the mental element required for contempt of court,[13] until then, 'intent and knowledge apply as long as the definition of the relevant crime does not expressly contain a different subjective element.'[14]

[11] Triffterer/id., Art. 71 MN 27.

[12] In favour of the application of Art. 30 ICCSt to this issue Triffterer/*Piragoff*, Art. 70 MN 5.

[13] Triffterer/id., Art. 71 MN 10.

[14] ICC *Prosecutor v Katanga and Chui*, PTC I, ICC-01/04-01/07-717, 30 September 2008, Decision on the Confirmation of Charges, para 532.

The jurisprudence of both the ICTY[15] and SCSL has established guidelines for the *mens rea* prerequisites within Rule 77 RPE ICTY/SCSL for contempt of court when conducted before an *ad hoc* Tribunal. Trial Chamber I of the SCSL held that 'the requirement of *mens rea* includes both actual knowledge or wilful blindness, but not mere negligence. This *mens rea* will apply not only to the general elements of contempt, but also to the specific intent to interfere with the administration…'.[16]

In other words, the offender must not only know that he or she is committing an offence which falls within the jurisdiction of the court, that is, by presenting false evidence, but must also be aware that his or her behaviour interferes with the administration of justice of the court.

Offences against the administration of justice pose a threat which should not be underestimated for both the truth-finding process and the rights of the accused and, therefore, to the conduct of due process. In the majority of the cases the perpetrator will commit the crime not directly in the courtroom but rather outside, that is, in another country where protected witnesses are housed. Art. 70 (4) (a) ICCSt therefore provides that each State Party should extend its national code of criminal procedure to ensure the punishment of offences against the administration of justice when pertaining to the ICC. When the crime has been committed within the borders of a state, the ICC has the opportunity to submit the case to the competent authorities of the State Party where the action in question took place. However, this decision remains solely in the hands of the Court, pursuant to Art. 70 (1) (b) ICCSt. Rule 162 (1) RPE ICC emphasizes that the Court 'may consult' the state concerned. This implies that the Court is not bound to do so.[17] In making a decision, the Court should take into consideration a request by a State Party to waive its power of jurisdiction. The period of limitation for exercising its jurisdiction over an offence against the administration of justice expires after five years.

1. *False testimony*

The Rome Statute, as well as all national codes of criminal procedure, contains the obligation of a witness to tell the truth when testifying before the Court, especially when under oath. According to Art. 69 (1) ICCSt, the Court must instruct a witness of this duty before commencement of testimony. If there are reasons to believe the assertion of a witness who is believed to have given perjured testimony, the prosecutor may initiate investigations into the offence of giving false testimony contained in Art. 70 (1) (a) ICCSt.

---

[15] ICTY *Prosecutor v Aleksovski*, AC, IT-95-14/1-AR77, 30 May 2001, Judgment on Appeal by Anto Nobilo against Finding on Contempt, para 39 *et subs.*

[16] SCSL *Prosecutor v Samura*, TC I, SCSL-2005-01, 26 October 2005, Judgment in Contempt Proceedings, para 27.

[17] Cassese/Gaeta/Jones/*Terrier*, 1310 *et subs.*

Under Rule 91 RPE ICTY, the Court should direct the Prosecutor to investigate a case of false testimony if there are reasonable grounds to believe an offence has been committed. The perpetrator must have acted knowingly and wilfully, according to Rule 77 RPE ICTY. An attempt to commit contempt of court also falls within the jurisdiction of the Court, pursuant to Rule 77 (B) RPE ICTY. Thus a witness who, for example, signs a false statement and agrees to testify in court, has already interfered with the administration of justice.[18]

Regarding false testimony, the SCSL has ruled that 'in all cases where accused persons are convicted of crimes, they would also be liable to be punished for perjury as well, in that they had lied in the defense because the jury, as the case may be, did not believe their story.'[19]

Judge Doherty substantiated his dissenting opinion on this count on the grounds that the person concerned had waived his right to remain silent during a meeting on the issue before Trial Chamber I, gave a false statement, and should be punished for it.[20]

2. *Presenting false evidence*

The Code of Conduct for Lawyers in the European Union states in Art. 4.4 that '[a] lawyer shall never knowingly give false or misleading information to the court'.[21] The Draft Code of Professional Conduct for Prosecutors of the International Criminal Court is formulated likewise.

Pursuant to Art. 70 (1) (b) ICCSt, the presentation of false or forged evidence by one of the parties during the course of proceedings amounts to an offence against the administration of justice. The party concerned must be aware of the falsification or forgery of the evidence.

The Appeals Chamber of the ICTY pointed out that this poses high demands on lawyers when dealing with evidence. The required standard for counsel as well as for the Prosecutor is the qualification that as an 'experienced lawyer' for whom the mere 'reasonable possibility' that the evidence is false or forged must suffice to prevent its presentation before the Court.[22]

3. *Interference with witnesses and evidence*

Art. 70 (1) (c) ICCSt lists various means by which witnesses might be influenced or the collection of evidence manipulated. Again, the perpetrator must act intentionally

[18] ICTY *Prosecutor v Tabaković*, TC II, IT-98-32/1-R77.1, 18 March 2010.

[19] SCSL *Code of Conduct Hearing against Williams and Yillah*, 10 November 2005, p 5 *et subs.*

[20] Ibid, p 6 *et subs.*

[21] Council of the Bars and Law Societies of the European Union, Code of Conduct for Lawyers in the European Union, 1988; last amendment on 6 December 2002, p 14.

[22] ICTY *Prosecutor v Tadić*, AC, IT-94-1-A-R77, 31 January 2000, Judgment on Allegation of Contempt against Prior Counsel, Milan Vujin, para 137.

when affecting the findings of the proceedings. This can be done through the undertaking or the surrender of a financial or other benefit to a potential witness, for the purpose of hindering witness testimony altogether, or to manipulate testimony in order to achieve the desired statement. The use of force, coercion, or any form of intimidation against a witness or any other person related to that witness are further methods by which influence might be sought. '"Intimidation" means any direct, indirect or potential threat to a witness, which may lead to interference his/her duty to give testimony free from influence of any kind whatsoever.'[23]

An offence against the administration of justice can also be committed by way of retaliation, after a witness has given testimony. To prevent this, Art. 68 ICCSt places both the Court as well as the Prosecutor under the obligation to guarantee that appropriate measures for the protection of witnesses are taken at all stages of the proceedings.

Regarding interference with witnesses, the majority of the cases the ICTY, and the ICTR to a lesser extent, have had to deal with were committed by staff members of defence counsel.[24] However, in the case of *Vojislav Šešelj* the behaviour of the Office of the Prosecutor came under scrutiny.[25]

The destruction or the manipulation of evidence is a further offence against the administration of justice. Such conduct may render finding the truth impossible. The same problem emerges from interfering with the collection of evidence. The Prosecutor of the ICC relies mostly on the support of the government of the state where the alleged atrocities occurred. This may lead to difficulties for the investigation team of the Office of the Prosecutor. For example, parts of the government in power might attempt to interfere with investigations by restricting access to evidence which might have a negative impact on their own political or personal positions.

4. Interference with officials of the Court

The term 'officials of the court' used in Art. 70 (1) d ICCSt is not defined in either the Rome Statute or in its Rules. This leads to the assumption that the notion

[23] Counsel of Europe, Committee of Ministers to Member States Concerning of Intimidation of Witnesses and the Rights of the Defence, 10 September 1997, Appendix to the Recommendations No. R (97) 13, I. Definitions; referred to in the ICTY judgment of *Prosecutor v Beqaj*, TC I, IT-03-66-T-R77, 27 May 2005, Judgment on Contempt Allegations, para 17.

[24] Eg, ICTY *Prosecutor v Haraqija and Morina*, TC I, IT-04-84-T-R77.4, 17 December 2008, Judgment on Allegation of Contempt; ICTY *Prosecutor v Tadić*, AC, IT-94-1-A-R77, 31 January 2000, Judgment on Allegation of Contempt against Prior Counsel, Milan Vujin; ICTY *Prosecutor v Rašić*, PTC, IT-98-32/1-R77.2; and ICTR *Prosecutor v Nshogoza*, TC III, ICTR-99-54A-T, 2 July 2009.

[25] ICTY Prosecutor v Šešelj, TC III, IT-03-67-T, 29 June 2010, Redacted Version of the 'Decision in Reconsideration of the Decision of 15 May 2007 on Vojislav Šešelj's motion for Contempt against Carla del Ponte, Hildegard Uertz-Retzlaff and Daniel Saxon'; the Court stated that there were reasonable grounds to believe that the crime in question had been committed and therefore, decided that the amicus curiae had to initiate investigations concerning the allegations.

'official' may be given a broader interpretation than its literal sense. The limitation to persons who work in a higher position at the Court, for example a judge or the Chief Prosecutor, or someone who personally presents the case during trial, would be pointless. Thus, the term 'official' comprises any directly, involved person who is in a position to bias the proceedings and thereby obstruct the truth-finding process.[26]

Pursuant to that provision, the promise, offering, or giving of a financial or any other benefit to an official, in order that the person concerned refrains from exercising or exercises improperly his or hers duties is an offence against the administration of justice. Equally, the offence is also carried out by impeding the work of the person concerned or by intimidating the official with the use of force, coercion, or any other means appropriate to achieve the desired outcome.

5. *Retaliating against an official of the Court*

As mentioned earlier, the term 'official' comprises any person who carries out his or her work in connection with a particular trial. Not only must a witness be protected against retaliation after his or her testimony but so too must an official who has participated at some stage of the proceedings. The reprisals have to be connected not to the performance of duties of the affected person, but to the work of an official of the Court.

6. *Soliciting or accepting a bribe as an official of the Court*

An official of the Court[27] commits an offence against the administration of justice by soliciting or accepting a bribe. The term 'bribe' is neither defined in the Rome Statute nor in any related document. However, the term may be interpreted in the meaning of its definition included in the OECD Anti-Bribery Convention. Accordingly, bribery is 'any undue pecuniary or other advantage'[28] offered, promised, or given to an official in relation to the performance of his or her duties.

7. *Sanctions for offences against the administration of justice*

As mentioned, it is a controversial issue whether the provisions provided for the core crimes in the Rome Statute, for example for the mental elements, are applicable to the offence of contempt of court. The wording of Rule 166 (2) RPE ICC implies this presumption by explicitly prohibiting the application of Art. 77 ICCSt with the exception of an order of forfeiture according to Art. 77 (2) (b) ICCSt. It would not make sense to exclude the application of some articles if others may not be applied equally.

---

[26] Triffterer/*Piragoff*, Art. 70 MN 10.

[27] See definition at 4, p 565.

[28] OECD, Convention on Combating Bribery of Foreign Public Officials in International Business Transactions, 21 November 1997.

The Court has the power to impose a fine, which must not exceed half the value of the convicted person's identifiable assets or income. Nevertheless, the offender must be given a reasonable period to fulfil his or her obligations, pursuant to Rule 166 (3) and (4) RPE ICC. Imprisonment may only be imposed as a last resort, pursuant to the formulation of Rule 166 (5) RPE ICC, which means only if the convicted person is not willing to pay the fine. Moreover, the term of imprisonment is limited to five years, under Art. 70 (3) ICCSt.

Pursuant to Rule 77 (G) RPE ICTY, the maximum punishment for contempt of court may not exceed seven years' imprisonment or a fine amounting to 100,000 Euros. In contrast, Rule 77 (G) RPE ICTR provides for contempt of court offences a term of five years' maximum imprisonment and a fine of up to 10,000 USD. It remains unclear which reasons lead to these considerable differences and why Rule 77 (G) RPE SCSL allows for a six-month maximum term of imprisonment, and alternatively or cumulatively, a maximum fine of two million Leones (equal to 400 Euros). An extended term of imprisonment is only provided if the Registrar of the Court or experienced independent counsel is appointed to investigate the offence because the Court is not itself able to deal with the issue summarily. Rule 77 (G) RPE SCSL allows for a seven-year maximum prison term.

As previously mentioned, the legal provisions in the Rules of Procedure and Evidence of the *ad hoc* Tribunals illustrate considerable disparities in punishing the same criminal behaviour.[29] The different standards provided in the Rules of the *ad hoc* Tribunals may cause a threat to the rights of the accused and may prejudice the truth-finding process. Criminal behaviour which is aimed at interference with the administration of justice ought to be punished, but there are no reasons for such considerably different sanctions. Common provisions regarding sanctioning of contempt of court would therefore be most welcome and are unlikely to impede the discretionary powers of the judges.

II. Misconduct before the Court

Every court has the inherent right to shield itself from any disturbance during trial, in other words they must have the power to take appropriate measures in order to prevent disruptive behaviour and to impose sanctions where such behaviour has occurred. The Appeals Chamber 'notes that article 71 of the Statute provides Trial Chambers with a specific tool to maintain control of proceedings and, thereby, to ensure a fair trial when faced with the deliberate refusal of a party to comply with its directions.'[30]

---

[29] Further arguments on this problem: S D'Ascoli, 'Sentencing Contempt of Court in International Criminal Justice', 5 *JICJ* (2007) 735–56. For interference with witnesses the ICTY imposes penalties between three and four months, the ICTR imposes penalties between nine and ten months, and the SCSL has not imposed any sanction thus far.

[30] ICC *Prosecutor v Lubanga*, AC, ICC-01/04-01/06-2582 OA 18, 8 October 2010, Judgment on the Appeal of the Prosecutor against the Decision of Trial Chamber I of 8 July 2010 entitled

It should be noted that Art. 71 (1) ICCSt only applies if the conduct in question is not covered under Art. 70 (1) ICCSt. According to Rule 172 RPE ICC, where both regulations can be applied, Art. 70 (1) ICCSt and Rules 162 to 169 RPE ICC take precedence.

Neither the Statute nor the Rules of Procedure and Evidence of the *ad hoc* Tribunals comprise a similar separation regarding contempt of court offences into offences against administration and misconduct before the Court, according to the 'gravity' of the crime.[31] Rule 77 (A) (i)–(v) RPE ICC contains a non-exhaustive list of several offences, such as disclosure of information in violation of a court order or intimidation of a witness. Rule 77 RPE ICC does not differentiate between offences against the administration of justice and misconduct before the Court.

Art. 71 (1) ICCSt refers to 'persons present before' the Court. This wording is ambiguous, regarding where and when the behaviour must occur. The formulation leads to the conclusion that it is limited geographically to the courtroom and limited temporally by the duration of the trial.[32] In the majority of cases, the offence of disobedience to an order of the Court will not be committed in the courtroom although the order will be issued there and, therefore, an excessively narrow interpretation cannot assist the procedure.

As mentioned above, the judges of the *ad hoc* Tribunals have greater discretionary power and, hence, there are no such limitations.

Furthermore, the Rome Statute provides in Arts 46 and 47 ICCSt specific regulations for certain groups of persons belonging to the organs of the Court; that is, the Prosecutor or a judge. If one of these persons commits misconduct before the Court, he or she shall be removed from office.[33] The Appeals Chamber clearly expressed that, '[e]ven if there is a conflict between the orders of a Chamber and the Prosecutor's perception of duties, the Prosecutor is obliged to comply with the orders of the Chamber.'[34]

Possible grounds for excluding criminal liability will be discussed below.

'Decision on the Prosecution's Urgent Request for Variation of the Time-Limit to Disclose the Identity of Intermediary 143 or Alternatively to Stay Proceedings Pending Further Consultations with the VWU', para 59.

[31] Triffterer/*Piragoff*, Art. 70 MN 4.

[32] In favour of a narrow interpretation: Triffterer/*Piragoff*, Art. 71 MN 10 *et subs*.

[33] The Secretariats of the International Association of Prosecutors and the Coalition for the International Criminal Court drafted a Code of Conduct for Prosecutors of the International Criminal Court wherein the offences and misconduct against the court are comprised in Art. 14.

[34] ICC *Prosecutor v Lubanga*, AC, ICC-01/04-01/06-2582 OA 18, 8 October 2010, Judgment on the Appeal of the Prosecutor against the Decision of Trial Chamber I of 8 July 2010 entitled 'Decision on the Prosecution's Urgent Request for Variation of the Time-Limit to Disclose the Identity of Intermediary 143 or Alternatively to Stay Proceedings Pending Further Consultations with the VWU', p 3.

The ICC has implemented a special code of professional conduct for counsel with the right to represent an accused or a victim before the court.[35] Pursuant to Art. 31 (a) Code of Conduct, counsel is responsible for disregarding the code of conduct or for violation of the Statute, the Rules of Procedure and Evidence, or the Regulations. The act which may constitute an offence of misconduct before the Court is not determined. Moreover, breaches of professional behaviour within the counsel–client relationship are also included within the regulations of the Code of Conduct.[36]

The *ad hoc* Tribunals have also adopted codes of professional conduct for defence and victims' counsel. Regarding Art. 31 ICC Code of Conduct, the phrasing of the other provisions is not identical. Art. 31 ICTY Code of Conduct is formulated likewise; however, Art. 20 ICTR Code of Conduct as well as Art. 27 SCSL Code of Conduct does not make any reference to its Statute or its Rules of Procedure and Evidence. Nevertheless, it is obvious that counsel when acting before a court have to respect all provisions regarding their function as representatives of an accused or a victim. In 2005 the SCSL held a Code of Conduct Hearing due to a breach committed by two members of defence counsel. One of the accused physically assaulted a staff member of the Court. In its decision the majority of the judges decided that the offender had infringed Art. 7 of the SCSL Code of Conduct, meaning that he committed a breach of his duty of professional courtesy.[37]

The offence of misconduct before the Court is twofold, according to Art. 71 (1) ICCSt. The first offence deals with disruption of the trial; that is, by registering disagreement during trial. The second behaviour which may have a negative impact on the trial is unwillingness of a person presented in Court to follow the orders of the Court. In contrast to Art. 70 ICCSt, the offences listed in Art. 71 ICCSt are not exhaustive. This implies the use of the word 'including'.

The lack of determination exists only on paper because the presiding judge first has to warn the alleged perpetrator before sanctioning him or her, according to Rule 170 (a) RPE ICC. If the person concerned does not follow the order and cease the behaviour in question, he or she commits another offence; that is, the offence of not following the directive of the Court.[38] Consequently the prior warning has two functions; on the one hand the offender is granted the possibility of discontinuing the undesired behaviour, and on the other hand, the 'prior warning' fills in the lacuna which can be caused when a certain type of misconduct is not provided for in the legal text.

[35] For the ICC, Code of Professional Conduct for Counsel, Res. ICC-ASP/4/Res.1 (hereinafter: Code of Conduct).

[36] Eg, the behaviour regarding the counsel–client relationship, according to Art. 9 Code of Conduct.

[37] SCSL, *Code of Conduct Hearing against Williams and Yillah*, 10 November 2005, p 4.

[38] Triffterer/*Piragoff*, Art. 71 MN 24 *et subs*.

During *Lubanga*, the Prosecutor repeatedly refused to comply with the order of the Court to disclose information about an intermediary, and hence the Court imposed an official warning against the Prosecutor and the Deputy Prosecutor.[39]

According to the jurisdiction of the ICTY, the Court has to advise and warn the person concerned before deciding to punish his or her behaviour. The same principle is followed for counsel, that is, Rule 46 (A) RPE ICTR expresses clearly that counsel has to be held liable if he or she, after being warned, maintains the adverse conduct before the Court. The majority of contempt of court cases before the ICTY deal with the disclosure of confidential information.[40]

Another important issue concerns the *mens rea* of the alleged perpetrator of the offence of misconduct before the Court. The wording of Art. 71 (1) ICCSt does not give any indication of the required mental element, with exception of the word 'deliberate' regarding a refusal to comply with a court order. Thus the perpetrator has to act with actual knowledge or wilful blindness when committing the offence of misconduct.[41] On the other hand, the refusal of the offender to comply with an order of the Court has been fully considered.

As mentioned, pursuant to the Statutes of the *ad hoc* Tribunals, the perpetrator has to act knowingly and wilfully regarding interference with the administration of justice. Specific conducts are defined in more detail in Rule 77 RPE of the *ad hoc* Tribunals but nevertheless, can be extended. The requirements of the mental elements remain the same for each contempt of court offence.

1. Disruption of proceedings

Disruption of proceedings can occur by a statement made by one of the parties when not given the floor as well as by members of the public. Such adverse behaviour includes, for example, shouts of disagreement or agreement, leaving the courtroom during the proceedings, or insulting a judge. Although not testifying in court, victims are under considerable strain which may provoke an outburst during trial. The presiding judge should take this into account when warning and subsequently convicting the concerned person.

During the trial against the former President of Liberia, Charles Taylor, before the SCSL, his defence counsel was warned by the presiding judge because of his behaviour; he refused to sit down during the speech of the Prosecutor. After being warned, defence counsel left the courtroom without

---

[39] ICC *Prosecutor v Lubanga*, Hearing before the Trial Chamber I, ICC-01/04-01/06-T-314-ENG, 15 July 2010, p 22, line 9 *et subs.*

[40] Of 21 contempt of court cases before the ICTY, 9 cases are related to the disclosure of confidential information.

[41] ICTY *Prosecutor v Aleksovski*, AC, IT-95-14/1-AR77, 30 May 2001, Judgment on Appeal by Anto Nobilo against Finding of Contempt, para 54.

permission.[42] This conduct was a clear breach of the duties of counsel before the Court and therefore constituted a punishable offence. According to Rule 46 RPE SCSL, the chamber may sanction counsel if 'his conduct remains offensive or abusive, obstructs the proceedings, or is otherwise contrary to the interests of justice'.

2. *Refusal to comply with a direction by the Court*

A court has the right to impose orders if it is necessary for the truth-finding process, the smooth course of trial, or to maintain the due process. Furthermore Trial Chamber I stated regarding the *Lubanga* Trial that '[n]o criminal court can operate on the basis that whenever it makes an order in particular area, it is for the Prosecutor to elect whether or not to implement it, depending on his interpretation of his obligations.'[43]

Such a direction can include the disclosure of documents, the duty of a witness to answer questions truthfully, as well as appearance before the Court. The Court has to take into account some exceptions resulting from procedural rights; that is, the right of the accused to remain silent, or the right of a witness not to testify against him or herself.

Rule 68*bis* RPE ICTY determines the sanction for a party to the trial who refuses to comply with a disclosure order of the Pre-Trial or the Trial Chamber. However, the Court has to deal *de facto* with the converse problem that one member of a party discloses information against an order of the Court. Florence Hartmann, a spokeswoman for the Prosecutor, wrote a book in which she disclosed confidential information against an Appeals Chamber order.[44] Another notorious case concerned the former editor of a Kosovo newspaper, who in his article revealed the identity of a protected witness against a court order.[45]

The mental prerequisites for the perpetrator are not clearly expressed in the legal text of Art. 71 (1) ICCSt, but as mentioned, the perpetrator has to act intentionally. The word 'deliberate' implies that the person concerned has carefully weighted his or her motivation for the denial and the ensuing consequences before refusing to fulfil the court ruling. Put another way, the act as well as its consequences are wilfully carried out by the offender.

[42] SCSL *Prosecutor v Charles Taylor*, TC II, Transcript of the Open Session of the 8 February 2011, time 9:22:38.

[43] ICC *Prosecutor v Lubanga*, TC I, ICC-01/04-01/06-2517-RED, 8 July 2010, Redacted Decision on the Prosecution's Urgent Request for Variation of the Time-Limit to Disclose the Identity of Intermediary 143 or Alternatively to Stay Proceedings Pending Further Consultations with the VWU, para 27.

[44] ICTY *Prosecutor v Florence Hartmann*, TC, IT-02-54-R77.5, 14 September 2009, *Amicus curiae*.

[45] ICTY *Prosecutor v Haxhiu*, TC, IT-04-84-R77.5, 24 July 2008, Judgment on Allegations of Contempt.

As mentioned earlier, the offender of contempt of court has to commit the act 'knowingly and wilfully', according to Rule 77 of the *ad hoc* Tribunals. The mental elements have to refer to all facts of the case but do not have to be verified by a statement of the person concerned.

The SCSL had to deal with a request by the Prosecutor over an alleged contempt of court offence. Defence counsel was believed to have disclosed the identities of seven protected witnesses to a third person, Professor Schabas of the Irish Centre of Human Rights, who posted the documents concerned on the internet. The Prosecutor pointed out that 'lead [the] Defence Counsel acted with, at minimum, reckless indifference to court orders, rules and directives'[46] whereupon defence counsel argued that the disclosure was an 'unintentional mistake'.[47] The majority of the Trial Chamber decided to postpone judgment of the alleged offence until the trial was completed.[48]

The Appeals Chamber of the ICTY decided regarding the finding of whether the mental element requirements are fulfilled that '[s]uch knowledge may be proven by evidence other than the accused's statement expressing a particular intent to disclose protected witness identities.'[49]

3. Sanctioning provided for misconduct before the Court

After warning the person concerned, the presiding judge can impose different sanctions to maintain control over the proceedings when misconduct before the Court occurs. According to Rule 170 (b) RPE ICC, the Court may interdict the offender from attending proceedings if they have disrupted the trial. If the person wilfully disobeys the order of the Court, Rule 171 RPE ICC provides different measures contingent on the gravity of the offence and the person who commits the offence.

Pursuant to Rule 171 (1) RPE ICC, the presiding judge might exclude the perpetrator from the courtroom 'for a period not exceeding 30 days'. However, if the offence is of a more serious nature, the Court can impose a fine not exceeding 2,000 Euros per every day of not complying with the direction of the Court. If the person concerned is an official of the Court, that is, the Prosecutor or counsel, the presiding judge might interdict him or her from exercising his or her functions. The period of interdiction may not exceed thirty days.

---

46 SCSL *Prosecutor v Charles Taylor*, TC II, SCSL-03-1-T, 24 March 2011, Decision on Confidential Annexes A-E Prosecution Motion for the Trial Chamber to Summarily Deal with Contempt of the Special Court for Sierra Leone and for Urgent Interim Measures, para 4.

47 Ibid, para 10.

48 Ibid, para 15.

49 ICTY Amicus curiae Prosecutor v *Šešelj*, AC, IT-03-67-R77.1-A, 19 May 2010, Judgment.

All these sanctions regarding a deliberate refusal to comply with an order of the Court can only be imposed if the offender had the possibility to justify his or her behaviour during an official hearing on the matter before the Court, pursuant to Rule 171 (5) RPE ICC. Hence, the principle of *audiatur et altera pars*,[50] that is, the right of the offender to challenge the allegations, will be respected.

III. Grounds for excluding criminal liability

As mentioned earlier, everyone without exception may be held liable for offences against the administration of justice or for misconduct before the Court. It does not suffice for excluding criminal liability that, for example, the Prosecutor prefers to fulfil his or her duties regarding a protected witness instead of obeying a direction of the Court. Only if the contemnor commits the crime in question under duress, ie in state of necessity, may he or she be justified, according Art. 31 (1) (d) ICCSt.[51]

If, for example, an official of the Court reveals the whereabouts of a protected witness to someone who has threatened his/her family, he or she will only be justified in having done so if the threat was imminent and serious, that is, if his or her family was under threat of death or serious bodily harm. Furthermore, the conduct must be necessary and reasonable to avoid the risk for his/her family and he or she may not have the intent of causing greater harm. The term 'reasonable' leads to a proportionality test between the lives of the officials' family and the life of the protected witness who lost his or her protection. Judge Cassese defined this balance in his dissenting opinion in the ICTY *Erdemovic* judgment as follows: 'In other words, in order not to be disproportionate, the crime committed under duress must be, on balance, the lesser of two evils.'[52]

If counsel of an accused is threatened with serious bodily harm in order to delay proceedings and therefore leaves the courtroom without permission from the chamber or files various pointless requests to block further proceedings, the threat can pose a ground for excluding criminal liability of the offence of misconduct before the Court. The disruption of legal proceedings is not disproportionate to the balance to the life and physical integrity of a person and, additionally, counsel certainly did not have the intent to cause greater harm.

---

[50] This principle has constitutional status, in most legal systems eg, in Germany, Art. 103 Basic Law for the Federal Republic of Germany (Deutsches Grundgesetz).

[51] More detailed Triffterer/*Eser*, Art. 31 MN 1 *et subs.*

[52] ICTY *Prosecutor v Erdemovic*, AC, IT-96-22-A, 7 October 1997, Separate and Dissenting Opinion of Judge Cassese, para 14.

BIBLIOGRAPHY

1. COMMENTARIES

Cassese, Antonio, Gaeta, Paola, and Jones, John (eds), *The Rome Statute of the International Criminal Court, A Commentary* (OUP 2002).

Frowein, Jochen, and Peukert, Wolfgang, *Europäische Menschenrechtskonvention* (3rd edn, Engel 2009).

Gaeta, Paola (ed), *The UN Genocide Convention. A Commentary* (OUP 2009).

Grabenwarter, Christoph, *Europäische Menschenrechtskonvention* (4th edn, CH Beck 2011).

Meyer-Gossner, Lutz, *Strafprozessordnung* (54th edn, CH Beck 2011).

Meyer-Ladewig, Jens, *Europäische Menschenrechtskonvention. Handkommentar* (2nd edn, Nomos 2006).

Nowak, Manfred, *UN Covenant on Civil and Political Rights: CCPR Commentary* (2nd edn, Engel 2005).

Stavros, Stephanos, *The Guarantees for Accused Persons under Article 6 of the European Convention on Human Rights* (Nijhoff 1993).

Triffterer, Otto (ed), *Commentary on the Rome Statute of the International Criminal Court* (2nd edn, CH Beck 2008).

2. BOOKS

Abernathy, M Glenn, and Perry, Barbara, *Civil Liberties under the Constitution* (6th edn, Univ. South Carolina Press 1993).

Abo Youssef, Omar, *Die Stellung des Opfers im Völkerstrafrecht* (Schulthess 2008).

Ahlbrecht, Heiko, *Geschichte des völkerrechtlichen Strafgerichtsbarkeit* (Nomos 1999).

Ambos, Kai, *Der Allgemeine Teil des Völkerstrafrechts: Ansätze einer Dogmatisierung* (Duncker & Humblot 2002).

—— *Internationales Strafrecht* (3rd edn, CH Beck 2011).

Bassiouni, Mahmoud Cherif, *International Criminal Law Vol 3: International Enforcement* (3rd edn, Martinus Nijhoff Publishers 2008).

Bassiouni, Mahmoud Cherif, and Manikas, Peter, *The Law of the International Criminal Tribunal for the Former Yugoslavia* (Transnational Publishers 1995).

Beck, Susanne, Burchard, Christoph, and Fateh-Moghadam, Bijan (eds), *Strafrechtsvergleichung als Problem und Lösung* (Nomos 2011).

Benzing, Markus, *Das Beweisrecht vor internationalen Gerichten und Schiedsgerichten in zwischenstaatlichen Streitigkeiten* (Springer 2010).

Boas, Gideon, *The Milošević Trial: Lessons for the Conduct of Complex International Criminal Proceedings* (CUP 2007).

Boas, Gideon, Bischoff, James, Reid, Natalie, and Taylor, B Don, *International Criminal Law Practitioner Library, Vol III—International Criminal Procedure* (CUP 2011).
Boister, Neil, and Cryer, Robert, *The Tokyo International Military Tribunal: A Reappraisal* (OUP 2008).
Brauneck, Anna-Eva, *Allgemeine Kriminologie* (Rowolth 1974).
Brownlie, Ian, *Principles of Public International Law* (5th edn, OUP 1998).
Buergenthal, Thomas, and Thürer, Daniel, *Menschenrechte. Ideale, Instrumente, Institutionen* (Nomos 2010).
Cassese, Antonio, *International Criminal Law* (2nd edn, OUP 2008).
—— (ed), *The Oxford Companion to International Criminal Justice* (OUP 2009).
Coester-Waltjen, Dagmar, *Internationales Beweisrecht* (CH Beck 1983).
Cryer, Robert, Frimann, Håkan, Robinson, Darryl, and Wilmshurst, Elizabeth, *International Criminal Law and Procedure* (CUP 2007).
—— —— —— —— *An Introduction to International Criminal Law and Procedure* (2nd edn, CUP 2010).
Dixon, Rodney, and Khan, Karim, *International Criminal Courts, Practice, Procedure and Evidence* (2nd edn, OUP 2005).
Drost, Peter, *The Crime of State, Vol II: Genocide* (AW Sythoff 1959).
Drumbl, Mark, *Atrocity, Punishment and International Law* (CUP 2007).
Dworkin, Ronald, *Taking Rights Seriously* (Duckworth 1996).
Esser, Robert, *Auf dem Weg zu einem europäischen Strafverfahrensrecht* (DeGruyter 2002).
Etcheson, Craig, *The Extraordinary Chambers* (Open Society Justice Initiative 2006).
Fastenrath, Ulrich, *Lücken im Völkerrecht* (Duncker & Humblot 1991).
Fawcett, James, Carruthers, Janeen, and North, Peter, *Private International Law* (14th edn, OUP 2008).
Fikentscher, Wolfgang, *Methoden des Rechts, Volume 2* (Mohr Siebeck 1975).
Gaede, Karsten, *Fairness als Teilhabe—Das Recht auf konkrete und wirksame Teilhabe durch Verteidigung gemäß Art. 6 EMRK* (Duncker & Humblot 2006).
Garner, Bryan (ed), *Black's Law Dictionary* (3rd edn, Thomson West 2006).
Gilbert, G, *Nuremberg Diary* (DaCaop Press 1995).
Göppinger, Hans, *Kriminologie* (6th edn, CH Beck 2008).
Hager, Günter, *Rechtsmethoden in Europa* (Mohr Siebeck 2009).
Hankel, Gerd, *Die Leipziger Prozesse* (Hamburger Edition HIS Verlag 2003).
Harris, David, O'Boyle, Michael, Bates, Ed, and Buckley, Carla, *The Law of the European Convention on Human Rights* (2nd edn, OUP 2009).
Harris, Whitney (ed), *Tyranny on Trial* (Southern Methodist University Press 1999).
—— *Murder by the Millions. Rudolf Hoess at Auschwitz* (Robert H Jackson Center 2005).
Hassemer, Winfried, *Einführung in die Grundlagen des Strafrechts* (CH Beck 1990).
Hatchard, John, Huber, Barbara, and Vogler, Richard, *Comparative Criminal Procedure* (BII CL 1996).
Hay, Peter, *US-Amerikanisches Recht* (CH Beck 2000).
Heldrich, Andreas, *Internationale Zuständigkeit und anwendbares Recht* (DeGruyter 1969).
Hirsch, Andrew von, and Ashworth, Andrew, *Principled Sentencing* (Northeastern University Press 1992).

Höffe, Otfried, *Gibt es ein interkulturelles Strafrecht?* (Suhrkamp 1999).
Holmes, Oliver Wendell, *The Common Law* (Belknap Press of Harvard University Press 2009).
Hühnerbein, Iris, *Die Straftatenkonkurrenz im Völkerstrafrecht* (Duncker & Humblot 2005).
Jaeckel, Fritz, *Die Reichweite der lex fori im internationalen Zivilprozessrecht* (Duncker and Humblot 1995).
Jäger, Herbert, *Makrokriminalität* (Suhrkamp 1989).
Jakobs, Francis, White, Robin, and Ovey, Clare, *The European Convention on Human Rights* (5th edn, OUP 2010).
Jescheck, Hans-Heinrich, *Die Verantwortlichkeit der Staatsorgane nach Völkerstrafrecht* (Röhrscheid 1952).
Jones, John, and Powles, Steven, *International Criminal Practice* (3rd edn, OUP 2003).
Kamardi, Christiane, *Die Ausformung einer Prozessordnung sui generis durch das ICTY unter Berücksichtigung des Fair-Trial-Prinzips* (Springer 2009).
Kastner, Klaus, *Von den Siegern zur Rechenschaft gezogen* (Hoffmann 2001).
Kempen, Bernhard, and Hillgruber, Christian, *Völkerrecht* (CH Beck 2007).
Khan, Karim, Buismann, Caroline, and Gosnell, Chris, *Principles of Evidence in International Criminal Justice* (OUP 2010).
—— and Dixon, Rodney (eds), *Archbold International Criminal Courts: Practice, Procedure and Evidence* (3rd edn, Sweet and Maxwell Ltd 2009).
Kirsch, Stefan, *Der Begehungszusammenhang der Verbrechen gegen die Menschlichkeit* (Peter Lang 2009).
Kiza, Ernesto, Rathgeber, Corene, and Rohne, Holger-C, *Victims of War: An Empirical Study on Victimization and Victims' Attitudes towards Addressing Atrocities* (Hamburger Edition HIS Verlag 2006).
Knoops, Geert-Jan, *Theory and Practice of International and Internationalized Criminal Proceedings* (Kluwer Law International 2007).
Kohlbacher, Ursula, *Verteidigung und Verteidigungsrechte unter dem Aspekt der 'Waffengleichheit'* (Schulthess 1979).
Kranzbühler, Otto, *Rückblick auf Nürnberg* (Zeit-Verlag 1949).
Krieger, Heike, *The Kosovo Conflict and International Law: an Analytic Documentation 1974–1999* (CUP 2001).
Kröber, Hans-Ludwig, Dölling, Dieter, Leygraf, Norbert, and Sass, Henning, *Handbuch der forensischen Psychiatrie*, Vol 4 (Springer 2009).
Krupna, Karsten, *Das Konzept der 'Hate Crimes' in Deutschland* (Peter Lang 2010).
Kudlich, Hans, *Strafprozess und allgemeines Missbrauchsverbot* (Duncker & Humblot 1998).
LaFave, Wayne, Israel, Jerold, King, Nancy, and Kerr, Orin, *Criminal Procedure* (3rd edn, Thomson/West 2007–2009).
Lafleur, Laurent, *Der Grundsatz der Komplementarität, Der Internationale Strafgerichtshof im Spannungsfeld zwischen Effektivität und Staatensouveränität* (Nomos 2011).
Leigh, L, *Police Powers in England and Wales* (2nd edn, Butterworth 1985).
Lippe, Viktor von der, *Nürnberger Tagebuchnotizen* (Knapp 1951).
Manske, Gisela, *Verbrechen gegen die Menschlichkeit als Verbrechen an der Menschheit* (Duncker & Humblot 2003).

Marrus, Michael, *The Nuremberg War Crimes Trial 1945–46. A Documentary History* (Bedford/St Martin's 1997).
Matthews, Paul, and Malek, Hodge, *Disclosure* (3rd edn, Sweet & Maxwell 2010).
McGoldrick, Dominic, *The Human Rights Committee: Its Role in the Development of the International Covenant on Civil and Political Rights* (2nd edn, OUP 1994).
Meißner, Jorg, *Die Zusammenarbeit mit dem Internationalen Strafgerichtshof nach dem Römischen Statut* (CH Beck 2003).
Melloh, Florian, *Einheitliche Strafzumessung in den Rechtsquellen des ICC-Statuts* (Duncker & Humblot 2010).
Möller, Christine, *Völkerstrafrecht und Internationaler Strafgerichtshof—kriminologische, straftheoretische und rechtspolitische Aspekte* (LIT 2003).
Morris, Virginia, and Scharf, Michael, *An Insider's Guide to the International Criminal Tribunal for the Former Yugoslavia, Vol. I* (Hotei Publishing 1995).
Nemitz, Volker, *Strafzumessung im Völkerstrafrecht* (Nomos 2002).
Neubacher, Frank, *Kriminologische Grundlagen einer internationalen Strafgerichtsbarkeit* (Mohr Siebeck 2005).
Osten, Philipp, *Der Tokioter Kriegsverbrecherprozess und die japanische Rechtswissenschaft* (Berliner Wissenschaftsverlag 2003).
Radbruch, Gustav, *Der Geist des Englischen Rechts* (Vadenhoeck & Ruprecht 1956).
Ragland, George, *Discovery before Trial* (Callaghan & Co 1932).
Roxin, Claus, *Strafrecht Allgemeiner Teil, Vol. 1* (4th edn, CH Beck 2006).
Rzepka, Dorothea, *Zur Fairness im deutschen Strafverfahren* (Klostermann 2000).
Sadat, Leila, *The International Criminal Court and the Transformation of International Law: Justice for the New Millenium* (Transnational Publishers 2002).
Safferling, Christoph, *Towards an International Criminal Procedure* (OUP 2003).
—— *Internationales Strafrecht* (Springer 2011).
Satzger, Helmut, *Internationales und Europäisches Strafrecht* (4th edn, Nomos 2010).
Savigny, Friedrich Carl von, *System des heutigen Römischen Rechts, Vol. 1* (1840).
Schabas, William, *The International Criminal Court* (OUP 2010).
—— *Introduction to the International Criminal Court* (4th edn, CUP 2011).
Schilling, Sandrine, *Gegen das Vergessen: Justiz, Wahrheitsfindung und Versöhnung nach dem Genozid in Rwanda durch Mechanismen transitionaler Justiz* (Peter Lang 2005).
Schneider, Hans, *Kriminologie der Gewalt* (Hirzel 1994).
Schulz, Sabine, *Transitional Justice und hybride Gerichte* (LIT 2009).
Sluiter, Göran, *International Criminal Adjudication and the Collection of Evidence: Obligations of States* (Intersentia 2002).
Smith, Bradley, *Reaching Judgment at Nuremberg* (Basic Books 1977).
Sprack, John, *Criminal Procedure* (OUP 2008).
Streng, Franz, *Jugendstrafrecht* (2nd edn, CF Muller 2008).
Taylor, Telford, *The Anatomy of the Nuremberg Trials* (Bloomsbury 1993).
Tochilovsky, Vladimir, *Jurisprudence of the International Criminal Courts* (Wolf Legal Publishers 2006).
—— *Jurisprudence of the International Criminal Courts and the European Court of Human Rights* (Martinus Nijhoff Publishers 2007).
Trechsel, Stefan, and Summers, Sarah, *Human Rights in Criminal Proceedings* (OUP 2006).

Van Dijk, Pieter *et al.*, *Theory and Practice of the European Convention on Human Rights* (4th edn, Intersentia 2006).
Verdross, Alfred, and Simma, Bruno, *Universelles Völkerrecht* (4th edn, Duncker & Humblot 1984).
Vormbaum, Thomas, *Einführung in die moderne Strafrechtsgeschichte* (Springer 2008).
Werle, Gerhard, *Völkerstrafrecht* (2nd edn, Mohr Siebeck 2007).
Wessells, Michael, *Child Soldiers: From Violence to Protection* (Harvard University Press 2007).
Wiggenhorn, Harald, *Verliererjustiz. Die Leipziger Kriegsverbrecherprozesse nach dem Ersten Weltkrieg* (Nomos 2005).
Wigmore, John Henry, *A Treatise on the Anglo-American System of Evidence in Trials at Common Law, Vol. 6* (3rd edn, Little, Brown 1940).
Wolf, Christian, *Die institutionelle Handelsschiedsgerichtsbarkeit* (CH Beck 1992).
Zahar, Alexander, and Sluiter, Göran, *International Criminal Law* (OUP 2007).
Zappalà, Salvatore, *Human Rights in International Criminal Proceedings* (OUP 2003).
Zeidy, Mohamed El, *The Principle of Complementarity in International Criminal Law: Origin, Development and Practice* (Martinus Nijhoff Publishers 2008).

3. ARTICLES AND CHAPTERS

Abas, Ademola, 'The International Criminal Court and Universal Jurisdiction', 6 *ICLR* (2006) 349.
Acquaviva, Guido, 'New Paths in International Criminal Justice? The Internal Rules of the Cambodian Extraordinary Chambers', 6 *JICJ* (2008) 129.
Affolder, Natasha, 'Tadić, the Anonymous Witness and the Sources of International Procedural Law', 19 *Mich Int'l L* (1998) 448.
Akande, Dapo, 'The Jurisdiction of the International Criminal Court over Nationals of Non-Parties: Legal Basis and Limits', 1 *JICJ* (2003) 618.
—— 'The Legal Nature of Security Council Referrals to the ICC and its Impact on Al Bashir's Immunities', 7 *JICJ* (2009) 333.
Aldana-Pindell, Raquel, 'An Emerging Universality of Justiciable Victims' Rights in the Criminal Process to Curtail Impunity for State-Sponsored Crimes', 26 *Human Rights Quarterly* (2004) 607.
Aldermann, Sidney, 'Negotiating on War Crimes Prosecution, 1945', in: Dennett, Raymond, and Johnson, Joseph (eds), *Negotiating with the Russians* (World Peace Foundation 1951) 52.
Alvarez, Jose, 'Nuremberg Revisited: The *Tadić* Case', 7 *EJIL* (1996) 245.
Ambos, Kai, 'Der EGMR und die Verfahrensrechte', 115 *ZStW* (2003) 583.
—— 'International Criminal Procedure: "Adversarial", "Inquisitorial" or "Mixed"?', 3 *ICLR* (2003) 1.
—— ' "Witness Proofing" before the International Criminal Court: A Reply to Karemaker, Taylor, and Pittman', 21 *LJIL* (2008) 911.
—— 'Confidential Investigations (Article 54(3)(e) ICC Statute) vs. Disclosure Obligations: The Lubanga Case and National Law', 12 *New Criminal Law Review* (2009) 543.
—— 'Critical Issues in the Bemba Confirmation Decision', 22 *LJIL* (2009) 715.

—— 'The Legal Framework of Transitional Justice: A Systematic Study with a Special Focus on the Role of the ICC', in: Ambos, Kai, Large, Judith, and Wierda, Marieke (eds), *Building a Future on Peace and Justice* (Springer 2009).

—— and Miller, Dennis, 'Structure and Function of the Confirmation Procedure before the ICC from a Comparative Perspective', 7 *ICLR* (2007) 335.

—— and Steiner, Christian,'Vom Sinn des Strafens auf innerstaatlicher und supranationaler Ebene', 41 *Juristische Schulung* (2001) 9.

Amoury Combs, Nancy, 'Copping a Plea to Genocide: The Plea Bargaining of International Crimes', 151 *U Pa L Rev* (2002) 1.

Aptel, Cécile, 'Some Innovations in the Statute of the Special Tribunal for Lebanon', 5 *JICJ* (2007) 1107.

Apuuli, Kasaija Phillip, 'The ICC Arrest Warrants for the Lord's Resistance Army Leaders and Peace Prospects for Northern Uganda', 4 *JICJ* (2006) 179.

—— 'The ICC's Possible Deferral of the LRA Case to Uganda', 6 *JICJ* (2008) 801.

Arbia, Silvana, 'The International Criminal Court: Witness and Victim Protection and Support, Legal Aid and Family Visits', 36 *Commonwealth Law Bulletin* (2010) 519.

Arsanjani, Mahnoush H, 'The Rome Statute of the International Criminal Court', 93 *AJIL* (1999) 22.

Aßmann, Jürgen, 'The Challenges of Genocide Trials: "The Cambodian Situation"', in: Safferling, Christoph, and Conze, Eckart (eds), *The Genocide Convention 60 Years after its Adoption* (TMC Asser Press 2010).

Aznar-Gómez, Mariano, 'A Decade of Human Rights Protection by the UN Security Council: A Sketch of Deregulation?', 13 *EJIL* (2002) 223.

Bank, Roland, 'Cooperation with the International Criminal Tribunal for the Former Yugoslavia in the Production of Evidence', 4 *Max Planck UNYB* (2000) 233.

Bassiouni, Mahmoud Cherif, 'World War I: "The War to End all Wars" and the Birth of a Handicapped International Criminal Justice System', 30 *Denver J Int'l Law & Pol'y* (2002) 244.

Batros, Ben, 'The Judgment on the *Katanga* Admissibility Appeal: Judicial Restraint at the ICC', 23 *LJIL* (2010) 343.

Bazyler, Michael, 'The Role of the Soviet Union in the International Military Tribunal at Nuremberg', in: Reginbogin, Herbert R, and Safferling, Christoph (eds), *The Nuremberg Trials: International Criminal Law since 1945* (Saur 2006) 42.

Beck, Susanne, 'Does Age Prevent Punishment? The Struggles of the German Juridical System with Alleged Nazi Criminals: Commentary on the Criminal Proceedings against John Demjanjuk and Heinrich Boere', 11 *GLJ* (2010) 347.

Bedermann, David, 'International Criminal Law—Mens Rea—Intent and Guilty Knowledge', 104 *AJIL* (2010) 241.

Bekou, Olympia, 'Prosecutor v Thomas Lubanga Dyilo—Decision on the Confirmation of Charges', 8 *HRLR* (2008) 343

—— and Cryer, Robert, 'The International Criminal Court and Universal Jurisdiction—A Close Encounter?', 56 *International & Comparative Law Quarterly* (2007) 48.

Benzing, Markus, 'The Complementarity Regime of the ICC', 7 *Max Planck UNYB* (2003) 591.

Bertodano, Sylvia de, 'Current Developments in Internationalized Courts', 2 *JICJ* (2004) 910.

—— 'What Price Defence? Resourcing the Defence at the ICTY', 2 *JICJ* (2004) 503.

—— 'Problems Arising from the Mixed Composition and Structure of the Cambodian Extraordinary Chambers', 4 *JICJ* (2006), 285.

Bhuta, Nehal, 'How Shall We Punish the Perpetrators? Human Rights, Alien Wrongs and the March of International Criminal Law', 27 *Melbourne University Law Review* (2003) 255.

Bianchi, Linda, and Onsea, Inneke, 'Additional Evidence on Appeal, Review Proceedings, and Reconsideration' in: Khan, Karim, Buisman, Caroline, and Gosnell, Christopher (eds), *Principles of Evidence in International Criminal Justice* (OUP 2010) 723.

Bisset, Alison, 'Rethinking the Powers of Truth Commissions in Light of the ICC Statute', 7 *JICJ* (2009) 963.

Bitti, Gilben, 'Two Bones of Contention Between Civil and Common Law: The Record of the Proceedings and the Treatment of a Concursus Delictorum', in: Fischer, Horst, Kreß, Claus, and Lüder, Sascha Rolf (eds), *International and National Prosecution of Crimes Under International Law* (Berlin Verlag 2001).

Blattmann, René, and Bowman, Kirsten, 'Achievements and Problems of the International Criminal Court—A View from Within', 6 *JICJ* (2008) 711.

Boas, Gideon, 'Creating Laws of Evidence for International Criminal Law: The ICTY and the Principle of Flexibility', 12 *CLF* (2001) 41.

—— 'Developments in the Law of Procedure and Evidence at the ICTY and the ICC', 12 *CLF* (2001) 167.

—— 'Self-Representation before the ICTY. A Case for Reform', 9 *JICJ* (2011) 53.

Bock, Stefanie, 'Das Opfer vor dem Internationalen Strafgerichtshof', 119 *ZStW* (2007) 664.

Bohlander, Michael, 'Plea-Bargaining before the ICTY', in: May, Richard *et al.* (eds), *Essays on ICTY Procedure and Evidence in Honour of Gabrielle Kirk McDonald* (Kluwer 2001).

—— 'The International Criminal Judiciary: Problems of Judicial Selection, Independence and Ethics', in: Bohlander, Michael (ed), *International Criminal Justice: A Critical Analysis of Institutions and Procedures* (Cameron May 2007) 325.

—— 'Pride and Prejudice or Sense and Sensibility? A Pragmatic Proposal for the Recruitment of Judges at the ICC and other International Criminal Courts', 12 *New Criminal Law Review* (2009) 529.

Bohlander, Michael, and Winter, Renate, 'Internationalisierte Strafgerichte auf nationaler Ebene—Kosovo, Kambodscha, Sierra Leone und Timor-Leste', in Kirsch, Stephan (ed), *Internationale Strafgerichtshöfe* (Nomos 2005) 261.

Bonomy, Iain, 'The Reality of Conducting a War Crimes Trial', 5 *JICJ* (2007) 348.

Bourgon, Stéphane, 'Judgments, Decisions and Other Relevant Materials Issued by International Courts and Other International Bodies on Human Rights', 1 *JICJ* (2003) 555.

—— 'Procedural Problems Hindering Expeditious and Fair Justice', 2 *JICJ* (2004) 526.

Brady, Helen, 'Disclosure of Evidence', in: Lee, Roy S (ed), *The International Criminal Court; Elements of Crimes and Rules of Procedure and Evidence* (Transnational Publishers 2001).

—— 'Setting the Record Straight: A Short Note on Disclosure and "the Record of the Proceedings"', in: Fischer, Horst, Kreß, Claus, and Lüder, Sascha Rolf (eds), *International and National Prosecution of Crimes Under International Law: Current Developments* (Berlin Verlag 2001).

Brennan, William J, 'The Criminal Prosecution: Sporting Event or the Quest for Truth?', 3 *Washington University Law Quarterly* (1963) 279.

—— 'The Criminal Prosecution: Sporting Event or the Quest for Truth? A Progress Report', 68 *Washington University Law Quarterly* (1990) 1.

Brensike Primus, Eve, 'Structural Reform in Criminal Defense: Relocating Ineffective Assistance of Counsel Claims', 92 *Cornell L Rev* (2006–2007) 679.

Brubacher, Matthew, 'Prosecutorial Discretion within the International Criminal Court', 2 *JICJ* (2004) 71.

Bull Kovera, Margaret, Park, Roger, and Penrod, Steven, 'Jurors' Perceptions of Eyewitnesses and Hearsay Evidence', 76 *Minnesota Law Review* (1991–1992) 703.

Burgess, Patrick, 'Justice and Reconciliation in East Timor: The Relationship between the Commission for Reception, Truth and Reconciliation and the Courts', 15 *CLF* (2004) 135.

Burghardt, Boris, and Geneuss, Julia, 'Der Präsident und sein Gericht: Die Entscheidung des Internationalen Strafgerichthofs über den Erlass eines Haftbefehls gegen Al Bashir', 4 *ZIS* (2009) 126.

Butler, A, 'Funke v. France and the Right against Self-Incrimination', 11 *CLF* (2000) 461.

Cerruti, Eugene, 'Self-Representation in the International Arena: Removing a False Right of Spectacle', 40 *Geo J Int'l L* (2009) 919.

Chaitidou, Eleni, 'Rechtsprechungsübersicht: Aktuelle Entwicklungen am Internationalen Strafgerichtshof', 5 *ZIS* (2010) 726.

Chang, Youg, 'The Thief of History—Cambodia and the Special Court', 1 *International Journal of Transitional Justice* (2007) 161.

Chaplin, Herman W, 'Reform in Criminal Procedure', 7 *HLR* (1895) 189.

Chardwick, Elizabeth, 'A Tale of Two Courts: The "Creation" of a Jurisdiction', 9 *J Conflict & Security Law* (2004) 71.

Chinkin, Christine, 'Due Process and Witness Anonymity', 91 *AJIL* (1997) 74.

Clark, Janine Natalya, 'Plea Bargaining at the ICTY: Guilty Pleas and Reconciliation', 20 *EJIL* (2009) 415.

Cohen, Miriam, 'Victims' Participation Rights Within the International Criminal Court: A Critical Overview', 37 *Denv J Int'l L & Pol'y* (2009) 351.

Combs, Nancy, 'International Criminal Jurisprudence Comes of Age: The Substance and Procedure of Emerging Discipline (Book Review)', 42 *Harv Int'l L J* (2001) 555.

Conway, Gerard, 'Ne bis in idem and the International Criminal Tribunals', 14 *CLF* (2003) 351.

Côté, Luc, 'Reflections on the Exercise of Prosecutorial Discretion in International Criminal Law', 3 *JICJ* (2005) 162.

Crawford, James, 'The ILC Adopts a Statute for an International Criminal Court', 89 *AJIL* (1995) 404.

Creta, Vincent, 'The Search for Justice in the Former Yugoslavia and Beyond: Analyzing the Rights of the Accused Under the Statute and RPE of the ICTY', 20 *Houst J Int'l L* (1998) 381.

Croquet, Nicolas, 'The International Criminal Court and the Treatment of Defence Rights: A Mirror of the European Court of Human Rights' Jurisprudence?', 11 *HRLR* (2011) 91.

Cross, Matthew, and Williams, Sarah, 'Recent Developments at the ICC: Prosecutor v Germain Katanga and Mathieu Ngudjolo Chui. A Boost for "Co-operative Complementarity?"', 10 *HRLR* (2009) 336.

D'Ascoli, Silvia, 'Sentencing Contempt of Court in International Criminal Justice', 5 *JICJ* (2007) 735.

Damaska, Mirjan, 'Structures of Authority and Comparative Criminal Procedure', 84 *Yale Law Journal* (1975) 480.

—— 'Negotiated Justice in International Criminal Courts', 2 *JICJ* (2007) 1018.

—— 'What is the Point of International Criminal Justice?', 83 *Chi-Kent L Rev* (2008) 329.

—— 'Problematic Features of International Criminal Procedure', in: Cassese, Antonio (ed), *The Oxford Companion to International Criminal Justice* (OUP 2009) 175.

Danner, Allison, 'Enhancing the Legitimacy and Accountability of Prosecutorial Discretion at the International Criminal Court', 97 *AJIL* (2003) 510.

DeFrank, Matthew, 'ICTY Provisional Release: Current Practice, a Dissenting Voice, and the Case for a Rule Change', 80 *Texas Law Review* (2002) 1429.

Delmas-Marty, Mireille, 'Interactions between National and International Criminal Law in the Preliminary Phase of Trial at the ICC', 4 *JICJ* (2006) 2.

De Smet, Simon, 'A Structural Analysis of the Role of the Pre-Trial Chamber in the Fact-Finding Process of the ICC', in: Stahn, Carsten, and Sluiter, Göran (eds), *The Emerging Practice of the International Criminal Court* (Martinus Nijhoff Publishers 2009) 405.

Dieckmann, Jens, and Kerll, Christina, 'Representing the "General Interests of the Defence": Boon or Bane?—A Stocktaking of the System of *ad hoc* Counsel at the ICC', 11 *ICLR* (2011) 105.

DiPardo, Elizabeth M, 'Caught in a Web of Lies: Use of Prior Inconsistent Statements to Impeach Witnesses before the ICTY', 31 *Boston College International and Comparative Law Review* (2008) 277.

Dölling, Dieter, 'Generalprävention durch Strafrecht: Realität oder Illusion', 102 *ZStW* (1990) 1.

Dölling, D, 'Zur Stellung des Verletzten im Strafverfahren', in Müller-Dietz, H *et al.* (eds), *Festschrift fur Jung* (Nomos 2007) 77.

Douglas, Lawrence, 'History and Memory in the Courtroom: Reflections on Perpetrator Trials', in: Reginbogin, Herbert, and Safferling, Christoph (eds), *The Nuremberg Trial: International Criminal Law Since 1945* (Saur 2006) 89.

Drumbl, Mark, and Gallant, Kenneth, 'Appeals in the Ad Hoc International Criminal Tribunals: Structure, Procedure, and Recent Cases', 3 *J App Prac & Process* (2001) 589.

Easterday, Jennifer, 'Deciding the Fate of Complementarity: A Columbian Case Study', 26 *Arizona Journal of International & Comparative Law* (2009) 50.

Easterday, Jennifer, 'The Trial of Charles Taylor Part I: Prosecuting Persons who bear the Greatest Responsibility', *UC Berkeley War Crimes Studies Center* (2010) 7.

Eckelmans, Franziska,'The First Jurisprudence of the Appeals Chamber of the ICC', in: Stahn, Carsten, and Sluiter, Göran (eds), *The Emerging Practice of the International Criminal Court* (Martinus Nijhoff Publishers 2009) 527.

Ellis, Mark, 'The Evolution of Defence Counsel Appearing before the International Criminal Tribunal for the Former Yugoslavia', 37 *New Engl L Rev* (2003) 949.

Eser, Albin, 'Verteidigung in der internationalen Strafgerichtsbarkeit—Eine rechtsvergleichende Analyse', in Schöch, Heinz *et al.* (eds), *Strafverteidigung, Revision und die gesamten Strafrechtswissenschaften* (Carl Heymanns Verlag 2008) 147.

Eser, Albin, 'Procedural Structure and Feature of International Criminal Justice: Lessons from the ICTY', in: Swart, Bert, Zahar, Alexander, and Sluiter, Göran (eds), *The Legacy of the International Criminal Tribunals for the Former Yugoslavia* (OUP 2011) 108.

Fabian, Kellye, 'Proof and Consequences: An Analysis of the Tadić and Akayesu Trials', 49 *DePaul Law Review* (2000) 981.

Falvey, Joseph, 'United Nations Justice or Military Justice: Which is the Oxymoron?', 19 *Fordham Int'l L J* (1995) 475, 492.

Fassbender, Bardo, 'Reflections on the International Legality of the Special Tribunal for Lebanon', 5 *JICJ* (2007) 1091.

Fichtelberg, Aaron, 'Fair Trials and International Courts: A Critical Evaluation of the Nuremberg Legacy', 28 *Criminal Justice Ethics* (2009) 5.

Fleming, Mark, 'Appellate Review in the International Criminal Tribunals', 37 *Texas International Law Journal* (2002), 111.

Form, Wolfgang, 'Justizpolitische Aspekte west-allierter Kriegsverbrecherprozesse 1942–1950', in: Eiber, Ludwig von, and Sigel, Robert (eds), *Dachauer Prozesse—NS-Verbrechen vor amerikanischen Militärgerichten in Dachau 1945–1948* (Wallstein 2007).

Francis, Leslie, and Francis, John, 'International Criminal Courts, the Rule of Law, and Prevention of Harm', in: May, Larry, and Hoskins, Zachary (eds), *International Criminal Law and Philosophy* (CUP 2010).

Friman, Håkan, 'Investigation and Prosecution', in: Lee, Roy (ed), *The International Criminal Court—Elements of Crimes and Rules of Procedure and Evidence* (Transnational Publishers 2001) 493.

Friman, Håkan 'Interlocutory Appeals in the Early Practice of the International Criminal Court', in: Stahn, Carsten, and Sluiter, Göran (eds), *The Emerging Practice of the International Criminal Court* (Martinus Nijhoff Publishers 2009) 553.

Fuller, L, 'Reason and Fiat in Case Law', 59 *HLR* (1946) 376.

Gaeta, Paola, 'Is the Practice of "Self-Referrals" a Sound Start for the ICC?', 2 *JICJ* (2004) 949.

Gallant, Kenneth, 'Securing the Presence of Defendants before the ICTY: Breaking with Extradition', 5 *CLF* (1994) 557.

Gallavin, Chris, 'Prosecutorial Discretion within the ICC: Under Pressure of Justice', 17 *CLF* (2006) 43.

Gallmetzer, Reinhold, 'The Trial Chamber's Discretionary Power to Devise the Proceedings Before it and its Exercise in the Trial of Thomas Lubanga Dyilo', in: Stahn, Carsten, and Sluiter, Göran (eds), *The Emerging Practice of the International Criminal Court* (Martinus Nijhoff Publishers 2009) 501.

Gardner, Maggie, 'Reconsidering Trials in Absentia at the Special Tribunal for Lebanon: An Application of the Tribunals Early Jurisprudence', 43 *George Washington International Law Review* (2011) 91.

Garkawe, Sam, 'Victims and the ICC: Three Major Issues', 3 *ICLR* (2003) 345.

Geneuss, Julia, 'Fostering a Better Understanding of Universal Jurisdiction', 7 *JICJ* (2009) 945.

Giannelli, Paul, 'The Abuse of Scientific Evidence in Criminal Cases: The Need for Independent Crime Laboratories', 4 *Virginia Journal of Social Policy & the Law* (1996–1997) 439.

Gibson, Kate and Rudy, Daniella, 'A New Model of International Criminal Procedure? The Progress of the Duch Trial at the ECCC', 7 *JICJ* (2009) 1005.

—— and Lusiaá-Berdou, Cainnech, 'Disclosure', in: Khan, Karim, Buisman, Caroline, and Gosnell, Christopher (eds), *Principles of Evidence in International Criminal Justice* (OUP 2010) 306.

Gillett, Matthew, and Schuster, Matthias, 'Fast Track Justice. The Special Tribunal for Lebanon Defines Terrorism', 9 *JICJ* (2011) 989.

—— 'The Special Tribunal for Lebanon Swiftly Adopts its Rules for Procedure and Evidence', 7 *JICJ* (2009) 885.

Golash, Deirdre, 'The Justification of Punishment in the International Context', in: May, Larry, and Hoskins, Zachary (eds), *International Criminal Law and Philosophy* (CUP 2010) 201.

Gordon, Gregory, 'Toward an International Criminal, Procedure: Due Process Aspirations and Limitations', 45 *Colum J Transnat' l* (2007) 635.

Guariglia, Fabricio, 'The Selection of Cases by the Office of the Prosecutor of the International Criminal Court', in: Stahn, Carsten, and Sluiter, Göran (eds), *The Emerging Practice of the International Criminal Court* (Martinus Nijhoff Publishers 2009) 209.

Guhr, Alexandra Hilal, 'Aktuelle Entwicklungen zur Beteiligung von Opfern im Strafverfahren vor dem ICC', 3 *ZIS* (2008) 367.

Gurmendi, Silvia de, and Friman, Håkan, 'The Rules of Procedure and Evidence of the ICC', 3 *YB Int'l Hum L* (2000) 112.

Haensel, Carl, 'The Nuremberg Trial Revisited', 13 *DePaul Law Review* (1963–1964) 248.

Hanlon, Kimberly, 'Peace or Justice: Now that Peace Is Being Negotiated in Uganda, Will the ICC Still Pursue Justice?', 14 *Tulsa J Comp & Int'l L* (2007) 295.

Harmon, Marc, 'The Pre-Trial Process at the ICTY as a Means of Ensuring Expeditious Trials', 5 *JICJ* (2007) 377.

—— and Gaynor, Fergal, 'Prosecuting Massive Crimes with Primitive Tools: Three Difficulties Encountered by Prosecutors in International Criminal Proceedings', 2 *JICJ* (2004) 403.

Harris, David, 'The Right to a Fair Trial in Criminal Proceedings as a Human Right', 16 *International & Comparative Law Quarterly* (1967) 355.

Harris, Whitney, 'Tyranny on Trial', in Reginbogin, Herbert, and Safferling, Christoph (eds), *The Nuremberg Trials: International Criminal Law since 1945* (Saur 2006) 100.

Heeger, Anastasia, 'Securing a Journalist's Testimonial Privilege in the International Criminal Court', 6 *San Diego Int'l L J* (2005) 295.

Heinsch, Robert, 'How to Achieve Fair and Expeditious Trial Proceedings before the ICC: Is it Time for a more Judge-Dominated Approach?', in Stahn, Carsten, and Sluiter, Göran (eds), *The Emerging Practice of the International Criminal Court* (Martinus Nijhoff Publishers 2009) 479.

Heller, Kevin, 'The Shadow Side of Complementarity: The Effect of Article 17 of the Rome Statute on National Due Process', 10 *CLF* (2006) 255.

Hemptinne, Jérôme de, 'The Creation of Investigation Chambers at the International Criminal Court: An Option Worth Pursuing?', 5 *JICJ* (2007) 402.

—— and Rindi, Francesco, 'ICC Pre-Trial Chamber Allows Victims to Participate in the Investigation Phase of Proceedings', 4 *JICJ* (2006) 342.

Henderson, Marcus Procter, 'Truly Ineffective Assistance: A Comparison of Ineffective Assistance of Counsel in the United States of America and the United Kingdom', 13 *Ind Int'l & Comp L Rev* (2002–2003) 317.

Henham, Ralph, 'Plea Bargaining and the Legitimacy of International Trial Justice: Some Observations on the Dragan Nikolic Sentencing Judgment of the ICTY', 5 *ICLR* (2005) 601.

—— and Drumbl, Mark, 'Plea Bargaining at the International Criminal Tribunal for the Former Yugoslavia', 16 *CLF* (2005) 53.

Higgins, Gillian, 'Fair and Expeditious Pre-trial Proceedings: The Future of International Criminal Trials', 5 *JICJ* (2007) 394.

Hirsch, Francine, 'The Soviets at Nuremberg: International Law, Propaganda, and the Making of the Postwar Order', 113 *American Historical Review* (2008) 701.

Hocking, John, 'Interlocutory Appeals before the ICTY', in: May, Richard *et al.* (eds), *Essays on ICTY Procedure and Evidence in Honour of Gabrielle Kirk McDonald* (Kluwer 2001) 459.

Hodžić, Refik, 'Living the Legacy of Mass Atrocities: Victims' Perspectives on War Crimes Trials', 8 *JICJ* (2010) 113.

Hoffmeister, Frank, and Knoke, Sebastian, 'Das Vorermittlungsverfahren vor dem Internationalen Strafgerichtshof—Prüfstein für die Effektivität der neuen Gerichtsbarkeit im Völkerstrafrecht', 59 *ZaöRV* (1999) 785.

Holmes, John, 'The Principle of Complementarity', in: Lee, Roy, *The International Criminal Court: The Making of the Rome Statute* (Kluwer Law International 1999) 41.

Holthuis, Hans, 'Operational Aspects of Setting up the International Criminal Court: Building on the Experience of the ICTY', 27 *Int'l Legal Prac* (2002) 41.

Hoven, Elisa, 'Opfer im Völkerstrafrecht—Probleme der Nebenklägerbeteiligung am Rote-Khmer-Tribunal, 122 *ZStW* (2010) 706.

Hunt, David, 'The International Criminal Court—High Hopes, "Creative Ambiguity" and an Unfortunate Mistrust in International Judges', 2 *JICJ* (2004) 56.

Jackson, John, 'Finding the Best Epistemic Fit for International Criminal Tribunals: Beyond the Adversarial Inquisitorial Dichotomy', 7 *JICJ* (2009) 17.

Jackson, Robert H, 'The Rule of Law amongst Nations', 19 *Temple Law Quarterly* (1945–46) 135.

—— 'Introduction', in: Harris, Whitney (ed), *Tyranny on Trial* (3rd edn, Southern Methodist University Press 1999) xxxii.

Jeannet, Stéphane, 'Recognition of the ICRC's Long-standing Rule of Confidentiality', 838 *IRRC* (2000) 403.

Jerouschek, Günter, and Kölbel, Ralf, 'Folter von Staats wegen?', 12 *JZ* (2003) 613.

Johnson, Scott, 'Neither Victims nor Executioners: The Dilemma of Victim Participation and the Defendant's Right to a Fair Trial at the International Criminal Court', 16 *ILSA J Int'l & Comp L* (2010) 489.

Jones, John, 'The Gamekeeper turned Poacher's Tale', 2 *JICJ* (2004) 486.

—— Carlton-Hanciles, Clare, Kah-Jallow, Haddijatou, Scratch, Sam, and Yillah, Inriham, 'Notes and Comments—The Special Court for Sierra Leone: A Defence Perspective', 2 *JICJ* (2004) 211.

Jordash, Wayne, 'The Practice of "Witness Proofing" in International Criminal Tribunals: Why the International Criminal Court Should Prohibit the Practice', 22 *LJIL* (2009) 501.

Jørgensen, Nina, 'The Genocide Acquittal in the Sikirica Case Before the International Criminal Tribunal for the Former Yugoslavia and the Coming of Age of the Guilty Plea', 15 *LJIL* (2002) 407.

Karemaker, Ruben, Taylor, B Don, and Pittman, Thomas Wayde, 'Witness Proofing in International Criminal Tribunals: Response to Ambos', 21 *LJIL* (2008) 917.

—— 'Witness Proofing in International Criminal Tribunals: A Critical Analysis of Widening Procedural Divergence', 21 *LJIL* (2008) 683.

Karnavas, Michael G, 'Gathering Evidence in International Criminal Trials—The View of the Defence Lawyer', in: Bohlander, Michael (ed), *International Criminal Justice: A Critical Analysis of Institutions and Procedures* (Cameron May 2007) 75.

Karton, Joshua, 'Lost in Translation: International Criminal Tribunals and the Legal Implications of Interpreted Testimony', 41 *Vand J Transnat'l L* (2008) 30.

Kastner, Klaus, 'Nazi Party, the Rallies and the Racial Laws', in: Reginbogin, Herbert, and Safferling, Christoph (eds), *The Nuremberg Trials: International Criminal Law since 1945* (Saur 2006) 114.

Katzman, Rachel, 'The Non-Disclosure of Confidential Exculpatory Evidence in the Lubanga Proceedings: How the ICC Defence Sytem Affects the Accused's Right to a Fair Trial', 8 *Northwestern JIHR* (2009) 77.

Kaul, Hans-Peter, 'Der Internationale Strafgerichtshof: Das Ringen um seine Zuständigkeit und Reichweite', 11 *Humanitäres Völkerrecht* (1998) 138.

—— 'Begegnungen mit Whitney Harris', in: Harris, Whitney, *Tyrannen vor Gericht* (BWV 2009) V.

Kay, Steven, 'The Move from Oral Evidence to Written Evidence', 2 *JICJ* (2004) 495.

Keller, Linda M, 'Achieving Peace with Justice: The International Criminal Court and Ugandan Alternative Justice Mechanisms', 23 *Conn J Int'l L* (2008) 209.

Kirsch, Philippe, 'Applying the Principles of Nuremberg in the International Criminal Court', 6 *Wash U Global Studies L Rev* (2007) 501.

—— and Oosterveld, Valerie, 'Negotiating an Institution for the Twenty-First Century: Multilateral Diplomacy and the International Criminal Court', 46 *McGill L J* (2001) 1141.

Kirsch, Stefan, 'The Trial Proceedings before the ICC', 6 *ICLR* (2006) 275.

—— and Oehmichen, Anna, 'Judges Gone Astray: The Fabrication of Terrorism as an International Crime by the Special Tribunal for Lebanon', 1 *Durham Law Review* (2011) 32.

Kleffner, Jann, 'The Impact of Complementarity on National Implementation of Substantive International Criminal Law', 1 *JICJ* (2003) 86.

Klinker, Melanie, 'Proving Genocide, Forensic Expertise and the ICTY', 6 *JICJ* (2008) 447.

Klinker, Melanie, 'Forensic Science Expertise for International Criminal Proceedings: An Old Problem, a New Context and a Pragmatic Resolution', 13 *The International Journal of Evidence & Proof* (2009) 102.

Kranzbühler, Otto, 'Nuremberg Eighteen Years Afterwards', 14 *DePaul Law Review* (1964–1965) 333.

Kreß, Claus, 'Vorbemerkungen Vor III 26 ("Internationaler Strafgerichtshof")', in: Grützner, Heinrich, Pötz, Paul-Günter, and Kreß, Claus (eds), *Internationaler Rechtshilfeverkehr in Strafsachen* (CF Muller 2002) MN 136.

—— 'The Procedural Law of the International Criminal Court in Outline: Anatomy of a Unique Compromise', 1 *JICJ* (2003) 603.

—— '"Self-Referrals" and "Waivers of Complementarity": Some Considerations in Law and Policy', 2 *JICJ* (2004) 944.

—— 'Universal Jurisdiction over International Crimes and the Institut De Droit International', 4 *JICJ* (2006) 561.
—— 'Grundlagen des Völkerstrafprozessrechts' in Radtke, Henning, Rössner, Dieter, Schiller, Theo, and Form, Wolfgang (eds), *Historische Dimensionen von Kriegsverbrecherprozessen nach dem Zweiten Weltkrieg* (Nomos 2007) 37.
—— 'The Procedural Texts of the International Criminal Court', 5 *JICJ* (2007) 537.
—— and Holtzendorff, Leonie von, 'The Kampala Compromise on the Crime of Aggression', 8 *JICJ* (2010) 1179.
Kroker, Patrick, 'Auf gutem Weg: Die Verfahren vor dem Rote-Khmer-Tribunal in Kamodscha', 122 *ZStW* (2010) 685.
Kuschnik, Bernhard, 'International Criminal Due Process in the Making: New Tendencies in the Law on Non-Disclosure in the Proceedings of the ICC', 9 *ICLR* (2009) 157.
Kwon, O-Gon, 'The Challenge of an International Criminal Trial as Seen from the Bench', 5 *JICJ* (2007) 360.
Lagodny, Otto, 'Legitimation und Bedeutung des ständigen Internationalen Strafgerichtshofes', 113 *ZStW* (2001) 800.
Landau, Herbert, 'Die Pflicht des Staates am Erhalt einer funktionstüchtigen Strafrechtspflege', 27 *NStZ* (2007) 121.
Langenbucher, Katja, 'Argument by Analogy in European Law', 57 *CLJ* (1998) 481.
Laternser, Hans, 'Looking Back at the Nuremberg Trials with Special Consideration of the Processes against Military Leaders', 8 *Whittier Law Review* (1986–1987) 557.
Leigh, L, 'The Protection of the Rights of the Accused in Pre-Trial Procedure: England and Wales', in: Andrews, John, *Human Rights in Criminal Procedure—A Comparative Study* (Martinus Nijhoff Publishers 1982) 37.
Leigh, Monroe, 'The Yugoslav Tribunal: Use of Unnamed Witnesses against Accused', 90 *AJIL* (1996) 216.
—— 'Witness Anonymity is Inconsistent with Due Process', 91 *AJIL* (1997) 80.
Lewis, Peter, 'The Rules of Procedure and Evidence of the International Criminal Court: Confirmation Hearing to Trial', in: Fischer, Horst, Kreß, Claus, and Lüder, Sascha Rolf (eds), *International and National Prosecution of Crimes under International Law: Current Developments* (Berlin Verlag 2001) 219.
Lindenmann, Jürg, 'The Rules of Procedure and Evidence on Jurisdiction and Admissibility, in Fischer, Horst, Kreß, Claus, and Lüder, Sascha Rolf (eds), *International and National Prosecution of Crimes under International Law* (Berlin Verlag 2001) 173.
Liszt, Franz von, 'Der Zweckgedanke im Strafrecht', 3 *ZStW* (1883) 1.
Loucaides, Loukis, 'Personality and Privacy under the European Convention of Human Rights', 61 *BYIL* (1990) 175.
Luban, David, 'Fairness to Rightness: Jurisdiction, Legality, and the Legitimacy of International Criminal Law', Georgetown Law Faculty Working Papers 2008.
Luzzati, Sara, 'On the Admissibility of Statements Made by the Defendant Prior to Trial', 8 *JICJ* (2010) 221.
Lynch, Michael E, 'Closure and Disclosure in Pre-Trial Argument', 5 *Human Studies* (1982), 285.
Maged, Adel, 'Withdrawal of Referrals—A Serious Challenge to the Function of the ICC', 6 *ICLR* (2006) 419.

Mahoney, P, 'The Right to a Fair Trial in Criminal Matters under Article 6 ECHR', 4 *Jud Stud Inst J* (2004) 107.

Mamiya, Ralph, 'Taking Judicial Notice of Genocide? The Problematic Law and Policy of the Karemera Decision', 25 *Wisconsin International Law Journal* (2007) 1.

Manning, Jason, 'On Power, Participation and Authority: The International Criminal Court's Initial Appellate Jurisprudence' 38 *Geo J Int' l L* (2007) 803.

Marston Danner, Allison, and Martinez, Jenny S, 'Guilty Associations: Joint Criminal Enterprise, Command Responsibility, and the Development of International Criminal Law', 93 *California Law Review* (2005) 75.

May, Richard, and Wierda, Marieke, 'Trends in International Criminal Evidence: Nuremberg, Tokyo, The Hague, and Arusha', 37 *Colum J Transnat'l L* (1998–1999) 725.

McIntyre, Gabrielle, 'Defining Human Rights in the Arena of International Humanitarian Law: Human Rights in the Jurisprudence of the ICTY', in: Boas, Gideon, and Schabas, William (eds), *International Criminal Law Developments in the Case Law of the ICTY* (Kluwer Law International 2003) 193.

—— 'Equality of Arms—Defining Human Rights in the Jurisprudence of the International Criminal Tribunal for the Former Yugoslavia', 16 *LJIL* (2003) 269.

McKeever, David, 'Evidence Obtained through Torture before the Khmer Rouge Tribunal, Unlawful Pragmatism?', *8 JICJ* (2010) 615.

McMunigal, Kevin C, 'Disclosure and Accuracy in the Guilty Plea Process', 40 *Hastings Law Journal* (1989) 957.

Mégret, Frédéric, 'In Defence of Hybridity: Towards a Representational Theory of International Criminal Justice', 38 *Cornell International Law Journal* (2005) 725.

Meijer, Ernestine E, 'The Extraordinary Chambers in the Courts of Cambodia for Prosecuting Crimes Committed by the Khmer Rouge: Jurisdiction, Organisation, and Procedure of an Internationalized National Tribunal', in: Romano, Cesare P R, Nollkaemper, André, and Kleffner, Jann (eds), *Internationalized Criminal Courts* (OUP 2004) 204.

Miraglia, Michela, 'The First Decision of the ICC Pre-Trial Chamber', 4 *JICJ* (2006) 188.

—— 'Admissibility of Evidence, Standard of Proof, and Nature of the Decision in the ICC Confirmation of Charges in *Lubanga*', 6 *JICJ* (2008) 489.

Mohan, Mahdev, 'The Paradox of Victim-Centrism: Victim Participation at the Khmer Rouge Tribunal', 9 *ICLR* (2009) 733.

Möller, Christina, 'Das Vorverfahren im Strafprozess vor dem Internationalen Straftribunal für das ehemalige Jugoslawien ("Pre-Trial and Preliminary Proceedings")', in Kirsch, Stefan (ed), *Internationale Strafgerichtshöfe* (Nomos 2005) 19.

Moreno-Ocampo, Luis, 'Keynote Address: Integration the Work of the ICC into Local Justice Initiatives', 21 *American University International Law Review* (2005) 497.

Müller, A Clemens, 'The Law of Interim Release in the Jurisprudence of the International Criminal Tribunals', 8 *ICLR* (2008) 589.

Müller, Andreas, and Stegmiller, Ignaz, 'Self-Referrals on Trial, From Panacea to Patient', 8 *JICJ* (2010) 1267.

Mundis, Daryl, 'Improving the Operation and Functioning of the International Criminal Tribunals,' 94 *AJIL* (2000) 759.

Murphy, Coleen, 'Political Reconciliation and International Criminal Trials', in May, Larry, and Hoskins, Zachary (eds), *International Criminal Law and Philosophy* (CUP 2010).

Murray, Juliana, 'Assessing Allegations: Judicial Evaluation of Testimonial Evidence in International Tribunals', 10 *Chi J Int'l L* (2010) 769.

Negri, Stefania, 'The Principle of Equality of Arms and the Evolving Law', 5 *ICLR* (2005) 513.

Nemitz, Jan, 'Sentencing in the Jurisprudence of the International Criminal Tribunals for the Former Yugoslavia and Rwanda', in: Fischer, Horst, Kreß, Claus, and Lüder, Sascha Rolf (eds), *International and National Prosecution of Crimes Under International Law* (Berlin Verlag 2001) 605.

—— 'Die Hauptverhandlug unter besonderer Berücksichtigung des Beweisrechts', in Kirsch, Stefan (ed), *Internationale Strafgerichtshöfe* (Nomos 2005) 53.

Nerlich, Volker, 'The Status of ICTY and ICTR Precedent in Proceedings before the ICC', in: Stahn, Carsten, and Sluiter, Göran (eds), *The Emerging Practice of the International Criminal Court* (Martinus Nijhoff Publishers 2009) 305.

Nestler, Cornelius, 'European Defence in Trans-National Criminal Proceedings', in: Schünemann, Bernd (ed), *A Programme for European Criminal Justice* (Carl Heymanns 2006) 415.

Newton, Michael, 'Comparative Complementarity: Domestic Jurisdiction consistent with the Rome Statute of the International Criminal Court', 167 *Military Law Review* (2001) 20.

Oeter, Stefan, 'Völkerrechtliche Rahmenbedingungen und die Staatengemeinschaft', in: Melcic, Dunja (ed), *Der Jugoslawienkrieg* (2nd edn, VS 2007) 485.

Ohlin, Jens, 'Peace, Security, and Prosecutorial Discretion', in Stahn, Carsten, and Sluiter, Göran (eds), *The Emerging Practice of the International Criminal Court* (Martinus Nijhoff Publishers 2009) 185.

Olásolo, Héctor, 'The Prosecutor of the ICC before the Initiation of Investigations: A Quasi-Judicial or a Political Body?', 3 *ICLR* (2003) 87.

—— 'Reflections on the ICC's Jurisdictional Reach', 16 *CLF* (2005) 279.

—— 'The Triggering Procedure of the International Criminal Court, Procedural Treatment of the Principle of Complementarity and the Role of Office of the Prosecutor', 5 *ICLR* (2005) 121.

O'Neill, Lily, and Sluiter, Goran, 'The Right to Appeal a Judgment of the Extraordinary Chambers in the Courts of Cambodia', 10 *Melb J Int'l L* (2009) 596.

Osakwe, Christopher, 'The Bill of Rights for the Criminal Defendant in American Law', in: Andrews, John, *Human Rights in Criminal Procedure—A Comparative Study* (Martinus Nijhoff Publishers 1982) 259.

O'Sullivan, Eugene, and Montgomery, Deirdre, 'The Erosion of the Right to Confrontation under the Cloak of Fairness at the ICTY', 8 *JICJ* (2010) 511.

Othman, Mohamed, 'East Timor: A Critique of the Model of Accountability for Serious Human Rights and International Humanitarian Law Violations', 72 *Nordic Journal of International Law* (2003) 449.

Overy, R, 'The Nuremberg Trials: International Law in the Making', in: Sands, Philippe (ed), *From Nuremberg to The Hague* (CUP 2003) 1.

Pati, Roza, 'The ICC and the Case of Sudan's Omar Al Bashir: Is Plea-Bargaining a Valid Option?', 15 *UC Davis J Int'l L & Pol'y* (2009) 265.

Paulus, Andreas L, 'Legalist Groundwork for the International Criminal Court: Commentaries on the Statute of the International Criminal Court', 14 *EJIL* (2003) 843.
Pearson, Zoe, 'Non-Governmental Organizations and the International Criminal Court: Changing Landscapes of international Law', 39 *Cornell Int'l L J* (2006) 243.
Pella, Vespasian, 'Towards an International Criminal Court', 44 *AJIL* (1950) 37.
Petrig, Anna, 'Negotiated Justice and the Goals of International Criminal Tribunals with a Focus on the Plea-Bargaining Practice of the ICTY and the Legal Framework of the ICC', 8 *Chi-Kent J Int'l & Comp L* (2008) 1.
Philips, Ruth, 'The International Criminal Court Statute: Jurisdiction and Admissibility', 10 *CLF* (1999) 61.
Rastan, Rod, 'Testing Co-Operation: The International Criminal Court and National Authorities', 21 *LJIL* (2008) 431.
——'Review of the ICC Jurisprudence 2008', 7 *Northwestern JIHR* (2009) 261.
Rearick, Daniel, 'Innocent until Alleged Guilty: Provisional Release at the ICTR', 44 *Harv Int'l L J* (2003) 577.
Redmayne, Mike, 'Rethinking the Privilege Against Self-Incrimination', 27 *Oxford Journal of Legal Studies* (2007) 209.
Reinisch, August, 'Das Jugoslawientribunal der Vereinten Nationen und die Verfahrensgarantien des II. VN-Menschenrechtspaktes: Ein Beitrag zur Frage der Bindung der Vereinten Nationen an nicht ratifiziertes Vertragsrecht', 47 *Austrian JPIL* (1995) 173.
Renzikowski, Joachim, '"Fair Trial" im Strafprozess', in: Dölling, Dieter *et al.* (eds), *Jus humanum: Grundlagen des Rechts und Strafrecht—Festschrift für E-J Lampe* (De Gruyter 2003) 791.
Röben, Volker, 'The Procedure of the ICC: Status and Function of the Prosecutor', 7 *Max Planck UNYB* (2003) 513.
Robinson, Patrick, 'Ensuring Fair and Expeditious Trials at the ICTY', 11 *EJIL* (2000) 569.
—— 'Rough Edges in the Alignment of Legal Systems in the Proceedings at the ICTY', 3 *JICJ* (2005) 1037.
Roht-Arriaza, Naomi, 'Impunity and Human Rights', in: Roht-Arriaza, Naomi (ed), *Impunity and Human Rights in International Law and Practice* (OUP 1995) 21.
Rose, Cecily, 'Troubled Indictments at the Special Court for Sierra Leone', 7 *JICJ* (2009) 353.
Roxin, Claus, 'Zum Hörfallen-Beschluss des Großen Senats für Strafsachen', 17 *NStZ* (1997) 18.
SáCouto, Susana, and Clearly, Katherine, 'The Gravity Threshold of the International Criminal Court', 23 *American University International Law Review* (2008) 807.
Safferling, Christoph, 'The Justification of Punishment in International Criminal Law', 4 *ARIEL* (1999) 126
—— 'International Criminal Procedure and its Participants: An Examination of Judges, Prosecutor and Defence at the Yugoslav Tribunal', 5 *YB Int'l Hum L* (2002) 219.
—— 'Das Opfer völkerrechtlicher Verbrechen', 115 *ZStW* (2003) 352.
—— 'Audiatur et al tera pars—die prozessuale Waffengleichheit als Prozessprinzip?', 24 *NStZ* (2004) 181.

—— 'Die EMRK und das Völkerstrafprozessrecht', in: Renzikowski, Joachim (ed), *Die EMRK im Zivil-, Straf- und Öffentlichen Recht—Grundlagen einer Europäischen Rechtskultur* (Schulthess 2004) 137.

—— 'Verdeckte Ermittler im Strafverfahren, deutsche und europäische Rechtssprechung im Konflikt?', 26 *NStZ* (2006) 75.

—— 'German Participation in the Nuremberg Trials and its Implications for Today', in: Griech-Polelle, Beth A (ed), *The Nuremberg War Crimes Trial and Its Policy Consequences for Today* (Nomos 2009) 33.

—— 'BVerfG 2 BvR 547/08 Entscheidung der 2. Kammer des 2. Senats vom 8.10.2009', 7 *StV* (2010) 337.

—— 'The Special Intent Requirement in the Crime of Genocide', in: Safferling, Christoph and Conze, Eckart (eds), *The Genocide Convention Sixty Years After Its Adoption* (TCM Asser 2010) 163.

—— 'The Rights and Interests of the Defence in the Pre-Trial Phase', 9 *JICJ* (2011) 651.

—— 'The Role of the Victim in the Criminal Process: A Paradigm Shift in National German and International Law?', 11 *ICLR* (2011) 183.

—— and Graebke, Philipp, 'Strafverteidigung im Nürnberger Hauptkriegsverbrecherprozess: Strategien und Wirkungen', 123 *ZStW* (2011) 47.

—— —— Hansen, Florian, and Hörmann, Sascha, 'Das Monitoring-Projekt des Forschungs- und Dokumentationszentrums für Kriegsverbrecherprozesse (ICWC), Marburg', 7 *ZIS* (2011) 564.

Schabas, William, 'The Jelisic Case and the Mens Rea of the Crime of Genocide' 14 *LJIL* (2001) 125.

—— 'United States Hostility to the International Criminal Court: t's All About the Security Council', 15 *EJIL* (2004) 701.

—— 'Prosecutorial Discretion v. Judicial Activism at the International Criminal Court', 6 *JICJ* (2008) 731.

—— 'The Special Tribunal for Lebanon: Is a "Tribunal of an International Character" Equivalent to an "International Criminal Court"?', 21 *LJIL* (2008) 513.

Schäfer, Helmut, 'Die Grenzen des Rechts auf Akteneinsicht durch den Verteidiger', 4 *NStZ* (1984) 204.

Scharf, Michael, 'Trading Justice for Efficiency: Plea-Bargaining and International Tribunals', 2 *JICJ* (2004) 1070.

—— 'Self-Representation versus Assignment of Defence Counsel before International Criminal Tribunals', 4 *JICJ* (2006) 31.

—— 'Tainted Provenance: When, If Ever, Should Torture Evidence Be Admissible?', 65 *Washington & Lee Law Review* (2008) 129.

—— and Dowd, Patrick, 'No Way Out? The Question of Unilateral Withdrawals or Referrals to the ICC and Other Human Rights Courts', 9 *Chi J Int'l L* (2009) 573.

Scheffer, David, 'The United States and the International Criminal Court', 93 *AJIL* (1999) 12.

Schmalenbach, Kirsten, 'Das Verbrechen der Aggression vor dem Internationalen Strafgerichtshof: Ein politischer Erfolg mit rechtlichen Untiefen', 65 *JZ* (2010) 745.

Schöch, Heinz, and Schreiber, Hans-Ludwig, 'Ist die Zweiteilung der Hauptverhandlung praktikabel?', 11 *Zeitschrift für Rechtspolitik* (1978) 457.

Schomburg, Wolfgang, 'Wahrheitsfindung im Internationalen Gerichtssaal', *Vereinte Nationen* (2009) 3.

Seibert-Fohr, Anja, 'Das Verbrechen der Aggression im Rom-Statut: Fragen der Vertragsänderung und Jurisdiktion', 3 *ZIS* (2008) 361.

Selbmann, Frank, and Wesemann, Dorette, 'Der Pol Pot-Ieng Sary-Prozess Revisited—Anmerkung zum Prozess gegen führende Rote Khmer im Jahr 1979', 2 *ZIS* (2010) 116.

Sharp, Walter, 'International Obligations to Search for and Arrest War Criminals: Government Failure in the Former Yugoslavia?', 7 *Duke Journal of Comparative and International Law* (1997) 411.

Simma, Bruno, 'Nato, the UN, and the Use of Force: Legal Aspects', 10 *EJIL* (1999) 1.

Skilbeck, Rupert, 'Building the Fourth Pillar: Defence Rights at the Special Court for Sierra Leone', 1 *Essex Human Rights Review* (2004) 66.

—— 'Frankenstein's Monster: Creating a New International Procedure', 8 *JICJ* (2010) 451.

Sluiter, Göran, 'Due Process and Criminal Procedure in the Cambodian Extraordinary Chambers', 4 *JICJ* (2006) 314.

—— 'Karadžić on Trial—Two Procedural Problems', 6 *JICJ* (2008) 617.

—— '"I Beg You, Please Come Testify"—The Problematic Absence of Subpoena Powers at the ICC', 12 *New Criminal Law Review* (2009) 590.

Solera, Oscar, 'Complementary Jurisdiction and International Criminal Justice', 84 *IRRC* (2002) 145.

Sorokina, Marina,'On the Way to Nuremberg: The Soviet Commission for the Investigation of Nazi War Crimes', in: Griech-Polelle, Beth A (ed), *The Nuremberg War Crimes Trial and its Policy Consequences Today* (Nomos 2009) 21.

Spiga, Valentina, 'Indirect Victims' Participation in the *Lubanga* Trial', 8 *JICJ* (2010) 183.

Stahn, Carsten, 'Complementarity, Amnesties and Alternative Forms of Justice: Some Interpretative Guidelines for the International Criminal Court', 3 *JICJ* (2005) 695.

—— 'Why Some Doors May be Closed Already: Second Thoughts on a 'Case-by-Case' Treatment of Article 12 (3) Declarations', 75 *Nordic Journal of International Law* (2006) 243.

—— Olásolo, Héctor, and Gibson, Kate, 'Participation of Victims in Pre-Trial Proceedings of the ICC', 4 *JICJ* (2006) 217.

Starygin, Stan, 'Internal Rules of the Extraordinary Chambers in the Courts of Cambodia (ECCC): Setting an Example of the Rule of Law by Breaking the Law?', 3 *Journal of Law and Conflict Resolution* (2011) 20.

Stimson, Henry, 'Nuremberg: Landmark in Law', 25 *Foreign Affairs* (1947) 187.

Streng, Franz, 'Schuld ohne Freiheit', 101 *ZStW* (1989) 273.

—— 'Sentencing in Germany—Basic Questions and New Developments', 8 *GLJ* (2007) 153.

Stroh, Dagmar, 'State Cooperation with the International Criminal Tribunals for the Former Yugoslavia and for Rwanda', 5 *Max Planck UNYB* (2001) 249.

Studzinsky, Silke, 'Nebenklage vor den Extraordinary Chambers of Cambodia (ECCC)—Herausforderung und Chance oder mission impossible?', 4 *ZIS* (2009) 43.

Swoboda, Sabine, 'The ICC Disclosure Regime', 19 *CLF* (2008) 449.

Thienel, Tobias, 'The Admissibility of Evidence Obtained by Torture under International Law', 17 *EJIL* (2006) 349.

Timm, Birte, 'The Legal Position of Victims in the Rules of Procedure and Evidence', in: Fischer, Kreß, and Lüder (eds), *International and National Prosecution of Crimes Under International Law: Current Developments* (Spitz 2001) 289.

Tracol, X, 'The Appeals Chambers of the International Criminal Tribunals', 12 *CLF* (2001) 137.

Trumbull, Charles, 'The Victims of Victim Participation in International Criminal Proceedings', 29 *Mich J Int'l L* (2008) 777.

Tuinstra, Jarinde, 'Defending the Defenders—The Role of Defence Counsel in International Criminal Trials', 8 *JICJ* (2010) 463.

Tumber, Howard, 'Journalists, War Crimes and International Justice', 1 *Media War & Conflict* (2008) 261.

Turner, Jenia, 'Defense Perspectives on Law and Politics in International Criminal Trials', 48 *Va J Int'l L* (2008) 529.

Volk, Klaus, 'Napoleon und das deutsche Strafrecht', 31 *Juristische Schulung* (1991) 281.

Wald, Patricia, 'The International Criminal Tribunal for the Former Yugoslavia Comes of Age: Some Observations on Day-To-Day Dilemmas of an International Court', 5 *Washington University Journal of Law & Policy* (2001) 87.

—— 'To Establish Incredible Events by Credible Evidence: The Use of Affidavit Testimony in Yugoslavia War Crimes Tribunal Proceedings', 42 *Harv Int'l L J* (2001) 535.

Walsh, Martha, 'The International Bar Association Proposal for a Code of Professional Conduct for Counsel before the ICC', 1 *JICJ* (2003) 490.

Weigend, Thomas, 'Anmerkung zu LG Frankfurt/M., 9 April 2003 ñ 5/22 Ks 3490 Js 230118/02', 8 *StV* (2003) 436.

——'Intent, Mistake of Law and Co-Perpetration in the Lubanga Decision on the Confirmation of the Charges', 6 *JICJ* (2008) 471.

——'Perpetration through an Organization: The Unexpected Career of a German Legal Concept', 9 *JICJ* (2011) 91.

—— 'Should We Search for the Truth, and Who Should Do it?' 36 *North Carolina Journal of International Law and Commercial Regulation* (2011) 389.

Whiting, Alex, 'In International Criminal Prosecutions, Justice Delayed Can Be Justice Delivered', 50 *Harv Int'l L J* (2009) 323.

—— 'Lead Evidence and Discovery before the International Criminal Court: The *Lubanga* Case', 14 *UCLA Journal of International Law and Foreign Affairs* (2009) 207.

Wilson, Richard, 'Assigned Defence Counsel in Domestic and International War Crimes Tribunals: The Need for a Structural Approach', 2 *ICLR* (2002) 145.

Wladimiroff, Michaïl, 'The Assignment of Defence Counsel before the International Criminal Tribunal for Rwanda', 12 *LJIL* (1999) 957.

Zappalà, Salvatore, 'The Rights of the Accused', in: Cassese, Antonio, Gaeta, Paula, and Jones, John (eds), *The Rome Statute of the International Criminal Court: A Commentary* (OUP 2002).

—— 'International Criminal Jurisdiction over Genocide', in Gaeta, Paola (ed), *The Genocide Convention* (OUP 2009) 259.

—— 'The Rights of Victims *v.* the Rights of the Accused', 8 *JICJ* (2010) 137.

Zeidy, Mohamed El, 'The Ugandan Government Triggers the Complimentary Principle', 5 *ICLR* (2005) 83.

——'Critical Thoughts on Art. 59 (2) of the ICC Statute', 4 *JICJ* (2006) 448.
—— 'The Legitimacy of Withdrawing State Party Referrals and ad hoc Declarations under the Statute of the International Criminal Court', in: Stahn, Carsten, and Sluiter, Göran (eds), *The Emerging Practice of the International Criminal Court* (Brill 2009) 55.
Zimmermann, Andreas, 'Die Schaffung eines ständigen Internationalen Strafgerichtshofes. Perspektiven und Probleme vor der Staatenkonferenz in Rom', 58 *ZaöRV* (1998) 45.
—— 'Das juristische Erbe von Nürnberg', in: Reginbogin, Herbert, and Safferling, Christoph (eds), *The Nuremberg Trials: International Criminal Law since 1945* (Saur 2006) 247.
Zimmermann, Reinhard, 'Statuta sunt stricte interpretanda?', 56 *CLJ* (1997) 315.

4. REPORTS

Report of Robert H Jackson United States Representative to the International Conference on Military Trials, London 1945 (Department of State 1949).
Situation of Human Rights in Timor-Leste—Report of the United Nations High Commissioner for Human Rights, E/CN.4/2003/37, 4 March 2003.
Report of the International Criminal Court to the UN General Assembly for 2009/2010, 19 August 2010, UN Doc. A/65/313.
UN Secretary-General, *The Rule of Law and Transitional Justice in Conflict and Post-conflict Societies*, 23 August 2004, UN Doc. S/2004/616.
UN Secretary-General, 'Historical Survey of the Question of International Criminal Jurisdiction', UN Doc. A/CN.4/7/Rev. 1 (1949).
Report of the Secretary-General pursuant to Security Council Resolution 1559 (2004), S/2004/777, 1 October 2004.
UNHCR, Survey Report on the Situation of non-ID Palestinian Refugees in Lebanon, (Beirut, September 2007).
Report of the International Independent Investigation Commission established pursuant to Security Council Resolution 1595 (2005).

5. OTHERS

Buckley-Zistel, Susanne, *Transitional Justice als Weg zu Frieden und Sicherheit* (SFB-Governance Working Paper Series, No 15, July 2008).
Digest of the Jurisprudence of the Special Panels for Serious Crimes, Judicial System Monitoring Programme, Dili, Timor-Leste, April 2007.
Hirst, Megan, and Varney, Howard, 'Justice Abandoned? An Assessment of the Serious Crimes Process in East Timor', International Centre for Transitional Justice (June 2005).
Human Rights Center, University of California (Publ.), *So We Will Never Forget* (2009).
ICTY Manual on Developed Practices (2009).
International Law Middle East and North Africa Programmes, 'The Special Tribunal for Lebanon and the Quest for Truth Justice and Stability' (London, Meeting Report December 2010).
Mole, Nuala, and Harby, Cateherina, 'The Right to a Fair Trial, A Guide to the Implementation of Article 6 of the European Convention on Human Rights' (2nd edn, Council of Europe 2006).

Natanda Nsereko, Daniel, 'Prosecutorial Discretion before National Courts and International Tribunals', Guest Lectures Series of the Office of the Prosecutor (2004).

Richter, Harald, *Opfer krimineller Gewalttaten. Individuelle Folgen und ihre Verarbeitung; Ergebnisse einer Untersuchung* (Weisser Ring 1997).

SCSL *Code of Conduct Hearing against Williams and Yillah*, 10 November 2005.

Shehadi, Nadim, and Wilmshurst, Elizabeth, 'The Special Tribunal for Lebanon: The UN on Trial?', Middle East/International Law Briefing Paper (Chatham House 2007).

Staggs Kelsall, Michelle *et al.*, *Lessons Learned from the 'Duch' Trial, A Comprehensive Review of the First Case before the Extraordinary Chambers in the Courts of Cambodia*, A Report Produced by the Asian International Justice Initiative's KRT Trial Monitoring Group, 2009.

INDEX